ORAL
AND
MAXILLOFACIAL
TRAUMA

ORAL AND MAXILLOFACIAL TRAUMA

Edited by

RAYMOND J. FONSECA, DMD

Dean, University of Pennsylvania School of Dental Medicine,
Philadelphia, Pennsylvania

ROBERT V. WALKER, DDS, FACD

Professor,
Division of Oral and Maxillofacial Surgery,
University of Texas Southwestern Medical Center,
Dallas, Texas

Volume 2

1991

W.B. SAUNDERS COMPANY

Harcourt Brace Jovanovich, Inc.

Philadelphia, London, Toronto, Montreal, Sydney, Tokyo

W.B. SAUNDERS COMPANY
Harcourt Brace Jovanovich, Inc.

The Curtis Center
Independence Square West
Philadelphia, PA 19106

Library of Congress Cataloging-in-Publication Data

Oral and maxillofacial trauma / edited by Raymond J. Fonseca, Robert V. Walker.
    p.   cm.
    ISBN 0-7216-2568-1 (set). — ISBN 0-7216-2566-5 (v. 1). — ISBN 0-7216-2567-3 (v. 2)
    1. Face — Wounds and injuries. 2. Mouth — Wounds and injuries. 3. Maxilla — Wounds and injuries. I. Fonseca, Raymond J. II. Walker, Robert V.
    [DNLM: 1. Maxillofacial Injuries. 2. Wounds and Injuries — therapy. WU 610 0628]
RD523.067   1991
616.5′2044 — dc20
DNLM/DLC   90-8193

Acquisition Editor: Darlene Pedersen
Editor: John Dyson
Developmental Editor: David Kilmer
Manuscript Editor: Bonnie Boehme
Designer: Lorraine B. Kilmer
Production Manager: Frank Polizzano
Illustration Coordinator: Joan Sinclair
Indexer: Angela Holt

Set ISBN 0-7216-2568-1
Vol. 1 ISBN 0-7216-2566-5
Vol. 2 ISBN 0-7216-2567-3

ORAL AND MAXILLOFACIAL TRAUMA

Last digit is the print number: 9   8   7   6   5   4   3   2   1

To Marilyn, Tiffany and Gabe—
the inspirations in my life.

R. J. Fonseca

To Emily—
who has endured a lot and allowed
great things to happen.

R. V. Walker

CONTRIBUTORS

ISAM AL-QURAINY, M.B., CH.B., M.C.Ophth., D.O.

Research Fellow, Tennent Institute of Ophthalmology, University of Glasgow, Glasgow, Scotland.

Ophthalmic Consequences of Maxillofacial Injuries

ROBERT H. BARTLETT, M.D.

Professor of Surgery, University of Michigan Medical School; Attending Staff, University of Michigan Medical Center, Ann Arbor, Michigan

The Metabolic Response to Trauma

ROBERT A. BAYS, D.D.S.

Associate Professor and Chairman and Graduate Program Director, Department of Oral and Maxillofacial Surgery, Emory University School of Postgraduate Dentistry; Chief of Oral and Maxillofacial Surgery at Emory University Hospital, Crawford W. Long Hospital, Grady Memorial Hospital, and Henrietta Egleston Hospital for Children; Consultant, Atlanta Veterans Administration Center and Scottish Rite Hospital, Atlanta, Georgia

Pathophysiology and Management of Gunshot Wounds to the Face

JAMES E. BERTZ, D.D.S., M.D.

Clinical Professor of Oral/Maxillofacial Surgery, Northwestern University; Attending Staff, Scottsdale Memorial Hospital — North and South, Humana Hospital, and Good Samaritan Hospital, Phoenix, Arizona

Management of Soft Tissue Injuries

GEORGE E. BONN, D.D.S.

Attending Staff, Veterans Administration Medical Center, and Associate Staff, Long Beach Memorial Medical Center, Long Beach, California

Shock

ROBERT BRUCE, D.D.S., M.S.

Clinical Professor of Oral and Maxillofacial Surgery, University of Michigan School of Dentistry; Attending Staff, E.L. Bixby Hospital, Ann Arbor, Michigan

Mandibular Fractures

MICHAEL N. BUCCI, M.D.

Attending Neurosurgeon, Anderson Memorial Hospital, Anderson, South Carolina

Neurologic Evaluation and Management

ROBERT M. BUMSTED, M.D.

Professor and Vice Chairman, Otolaryngology-Head and Neck Surgery, University of Chicago; Attending Staff, University of Chicago Hospitals, Chicago, Good Samaritan Hospital, Downer's Grove, and Ingalls Memorial Hospital, Harvey, Illinois

Nasal Fractures

RICHARD E. BURNEY, M.D., F.A.C.S.

Associate Professor of Surgery, University of Michigan Medical School; Attending Surgeon, Trauma Service and Chief, Division of Emergency Services, University of Michigan Hospitals, Ann Arbor, Michigan

Abdominal Evaluation and Management

ROBERT L. CAMPBELL, D.D.S.

Professor of Oral and Maxillofacial Surgery and Professor of Anesthesiology, Medical College of Virginia; Attending Staff, Medical College of Virginia, Richmond, Virginia

Anesthetic Management of Maxillofacial Trauma

MICHAEL CHANCELLOR, M.D.

College of Physicians and Surgeons of Columbia University, New York, New York

Urologic Injuries

DAVID W. COOK, M.D.

Chief Surgical Resident, Oregon Health Sciences University, Portland, Oregon

Emergency and Intensive Care of the Trauma Patient

CHRISTOPHER L. DAVIS, D.D.S., M.D.

Clinical Instructor, Department of Oral and Maxillofacial Surgery, University of Southern California, Los Angeles; Attending Physician, Memorial Hospital Medical Center of Long Beach and Downey Community Hospital, Los Angeles, California

Shock

GORDON N. DUTTON, M.D., F.R.C.S.

Consultant Senior Lecturer in Ophthalmology, Tennent Institute of Ophthalmology, University of Glasgow, Glasgow, Scotland

Ophthalmic Consequences of Maxillofacial Injuries

EDWARD ELLIS III, D.D.S., M.S.

Associate Professor, Division of Oral and Maxillofacial Surgery, University of Texas Southwestern Medical School; Attending Staff, Parkland Memorial Hospital, Dallas, Texas

Fractures of the Zygomatic Complex and Arch

STEPHEN E. FEINBERG, D.D.S., M.S., Ph.D.

Associate Professor and Chairman, Department of Oral Medicine/Oral Pathology and Oral and Maxillofacial Surgery, University of Michigan School of Dentistry and University Hospital, Ann Arbor, Michigan

Healing of Traumatic Injuries

RAYMOND J. FONSECA, D.M.D.

Dean, University of Pennsylvania School of Dental Medicine; Attending Staff, Hospital of the University of Pennsylvania and Children's Hospital of Philadelphia, Philadelphia, Pennsylvania

Mandibular Fractures; Management of Soft Tissue Injuries

DAVID E. FROST, D.D.S., M.S.

Clinical Assistant Professor for Research, Department of Oral and Maxillofacial Surgery; Part-time Faculty, University of North Carolina at Chapel Hill; Attending Staff, Durham County General Hospital, Durham, North Carolina

Applied Surgical Anatomy of the Head and Neck

BEAT HAMMER, M.D., D.D.S.

Clinic for Maxillofacial, Plastic and Reconstructive Surgery, Department of Surgery, University Clinic of Basel, Basel, Switzerland

Rigid Fixation of Facial Fractures

JOHN F. HELFRICK, D.D.S., M.S.

Professor and Chairman, Department of Oral and Maxillofacial Surgery, University of Texas Health Science Center, Houston, Texas

Early Assessment and Treatment Planning of the Maxillofacial Trauma Patient

JULIAN T. HOFF, M.D.

Professor, Department of Surgery, and Section Head, Neurosurgery, University of Michigan Medical School; Attending Staff, University of Michigan Hospitals, Ann Arbor, Michigan

Neurologic Evaluation and Management

HENRY T. HOFFMAN, M.D.

Assistant Adjunct Professor, Division of Otolaryngology, University of California, San Diego, San Diego, California

Traumatic Injuries to the Frontal Sinus

RICHARD E. JONES, M.D.

Associate Professor of Orthopedics, University of Texas Southwestern Medical School; Chief of Orthopedic Surgery, Veterans Administration Hospital, Dallas, Texas

Initial Assessment and Management of the Polytrauma Patient with Orthopedic Injuries

NESTOR D. KARAS, D.D.S.

Resident in Oral and Maxillofacial Surgery, Division of Oral and Maxillofacial Surgery, University of Texas Southwestern Medical Center, Parkland Memorial Hospital, Dallas, Texas

Radiographic Evaluation of Facial Injuries

BARRY D. KENDELL, D.M.D., M.S.

Part-time Clinical Assistant Professor, Faculty of Oral and Maxillofacial Surgery, University of North Carolina School of Dentistry at Chapel Hill; Attending Surgical Staff, Durham County General Hospital, Durham, North Carolina

Applied Surgical Anatomy of the Head and Neck; Management of Facial Fractures in the Growing Patient

JOHN N. KENT, B.A., D.D.S., F.A.C.D., F.I.C.D.

Boyd Professor and Head, Department of Oral and Maxillofacial Surgery, Louisiana State University Medical Center School of Dentistry; Chief of Oral and Maxillofacial Surgery, Charity Hospital; Chairman of EENT, Hotel Dieu Hospital; Consultant, Ochsner, Children's, Doctors, Veterans Administration, East Jefferson Hospitals, New Orleans, Louisiana,

Biomaterials for Cranial, Facial, Mandibular and TMJ Reconstruction

MARVIN M. KIRSH, M.D.

Professor of Surgery, Section of Thoracic Surgery, University of Michigan Medical School; Attending Staff, University of Michigan Medical Center, Ann Arbor, Michigan

Management of Nonpenetrating Chest Trauma

CHARLES J. KRAUSE, M.D.

Professor and Chairman of Otolaryngology Head and Neck Surgery, University of Michigan Medical School, Professor and Chairman, Department of Otolaryngology, Head and Neck Surgery, University of Michigan Medical Center, Ann Arbor, Michigan

Traumatic Injuries to the Frontal Sinus

TIMOTHY F. KRESOWIK, M.D.

Assistant Professor of Surgery, University of Iowa College of Medicine; Attending Surgeon, University of Iowa Hospitals and Clinics, Iowa City, Iowa

Nutritional Considerations Following Trauma

PETER E. LARSEN, D.D.S.

Assistant Professor, Department of Oral and Maxillofacial Surgery, Ohio State University College of Dentistry; Attending Staff, Ohio State University Hospital and Columbus Children's Hospital, Columbus, Ohio

Healing of Traumatic Injuries

DENIS C. LEE, B.S., M.C.

Professor of Art and Professor of Postgraduate Medicine, Director, Graduate Program; Medical and Biological Illustration, University of Michigan Medical School; Assistant Professor of Plastic Surgery and Director of Medical Sculpture, University of Michigan Hospitals, Ann Arbor, Michigan

Maxillofacial Prosthetics for the Trauma Patient

DANIEL LEW, D.D.S.

Associate Professor and Chief, Oral and Maxillofacial Surgery, Louisiana State University Medical Center School of Dentistry; Attending Staff, Louisiana State University Medical Center, Veterans Administration Medical Center, Shriners Hospital, and Doctors' Hospital, Shreveport, Louisiana

Diagnosis and Treatment of Midface Injuries

STUART E. LIEBLICH, D.M.D.

Assistant Professor, Oral and Maxillofacial Surgery, University of Connecticut School of Dental Medicine; Attending Staff, Hartford Hospital and Newington Children's Hospital, Avon, Connecticut

Infection in the Patient with Maxillofacial Trauma

KENNETH A. MacAFEE II, D.M.D.

Assistant Professor and Clinic Director, Department of Oral and Maxillofacial Surgery, University of Pennsylvania School of Dental Medicine; Clinical Instructor and Lecturer, University of Pennsylvania Oral and Maxillofacial Surgery; Residency Training Program, Staff Surgeon, University of Pennsylvania Medical Center, Philadelphia, Pennsylvania

Burns of the Head and Neck

ROBERT E. MARX, D.D.S.

Associate Professor of Surgery and Director of Graduate Training and Research, University of Miami School of Medicine, Jackson Memorial Medical Center; Director, Center for Maxillofacial Reconstruction at Jackson Memorial Medical Center, Doctors Hospital of Coral Gables, Miami Veterans Administration Medical Center, Miami, Florida

Reconstruction of Avulsive Maxillofacial Injuries

JAMES R. MAULT, M.D.

Department of Surgery, Duke University Medical Center, Durham, North Carolina

The Metabolic Response to Trauma

BARBARA B. MAXSON, D.D.S., M.S.

Assistant Professor of Dentistry, University of Michigan School of Medicine; Staff Prosthodontist, University of Michigan Hospitals, Ann Arbor, Michigan

Maxillofacial Prosthetics for the Trauma Patient

KATHLEEN HOGAN MAYO, D.D.S.

Clinical Associate Professor, University of Michigan School of Dentistry, Ann Arbor; Attending Staff, St. Joseph's Hospital, Pontiac, Michigan

Burns of the Head and Neck

EDWARD J. McGUIRE, M.D.

Chairman, Section of Urology, Department of Surgery, University of Michigan Medical School, Ann Arbor, Michigan

Urologic Injuries

DALE J. MISIEK, B.A., D.M.D.

Associate Professor of Oral and Maxillofacial Surgery, Louisiana State University Medical Center School of Dentistry, New Orleans; Director of Residency Training, Oral and Dental Surgery, Charity Hospital; Active Staff, Hotel Dieu Hospital, New Orleans, East Jefferson General Hospital, Metairie; Courtesy or Consultant Staff, Eye, Ear, Nose and Throat Hospital, Tulane Medical Center, Veterans Administration Medical Center, Touro Infirmary, Southern Baptist Hospital, Mercy Hospital, Children's Hospital, New Orleans; Doctors' Hospital, East Jefferson General Hospital, Metairie; St. Jude Medical Center, Kenner, Our Lady of the Lake Regional Medical Center, Baton Rouge, Louisiana

Biomaterials for Cranial, Facial, Mandibular, and TMJ Reconstruction

THOMAS E. OSBORNE, D.D.S.

Assistant Professor of Oral and Maxillofacial Surgery, Emory University School of Postgraduate Dentistry; Assistant Chief of Oral and Maxillofacial Surgery, Grady Memorial Hospital; Attending Staff, Crawford W. Long Hospital and Henrietta Egleston Hospital for Children; Consultant, Atlanta Veterans Administration Hospital, Atlanta, Georgia

Pathophysiology and Management of Gunshot Wounds to the Face

JAMES K. PITCOCK, M.D.

Assistant Professor of Surgery, Otolaryngology-Head and Neck Surgery, University of California, Irvine; Director; Head and Neck Surgical Oncology, University of California, Irvine Medical Center and Long Beach Veterans Administration Medical Center, Orange, California

Nasal Fractures

MICHAEL P. POWERS, D.D.S., M.S.

Assistant Professor, Department of Oral and Maxillofacial Surgery, and Assistant Professor, Department of Surgery, Case Western Reserve University School of Medicine; Attending Staff, University Hospitals of Cleveland; Active Staff, Meridian Euclid Hospital, Euclid, Lakewood Hospital, Lakewood, and Consultant, Veterans Administration Medical Center of Cleveland, Cleveland, Ohio

Diagnosis and Management of Dentoalveolar Injuries; Management of Soft Tissue Injuries

JOACHIM PREIN, M.D., D.D.S.

Head, Clinic for Maxillofacial, Plastic and Reconstructive Surgery, Department of Surgery, University Clinic of Basel, Basel, Switzerland

Rigid Fixation of Facial Fractures

JEFFREY L. RAJCHEL, D.D.S., M.S.

Attending Staff, St. Joseph's Hospital and Memorial Mission Hospital, Asheville, North Carolina

Emergency Airway Management in the Traumatized Patient

JURGEN REUTHER, M.D., D.M.D.

Professor and Head, Department of Oral and Maxillofacial Surgery, University of Würzberg, Würzberg, Federal Republic of Germany

Rigid Fixation of Facial Fractures

WILFRIED SCHILLI, M.D., D.M.D.

Professor and Head, Department of Oral and Maxillofacial Surgery, University of Freiburg, Freiburg, Federal Republic of Germany

Rigid Fixation of Facial Fractures

RICHARD F. SCOTT, D.D.S., M.S.

Assistant Professor, Department of Oral and Maxillofacial Surgery, University of Michigan School of Dentistry, Ann Arbor, Michigan

Oral and Maxillofacial Trauma in the Geriatric Patient

J. ROBERT SCULLY, D.D.S., M.S.

Attending Staff, St. Joseph's Hospital and Memorial Mission Hospital, Asheville, North Carolina

Emergency Airway Management in the Traumatized Patient

STEEN SINDET-PEDERSEN, D.D.S.

Staff Member, Department of Oral and Maxillofacial Surgery, Aarhus University Hospital, Aarhus, Denmark

Rigid Fixation of Facial Fractures

DOUGLAS P. SINN, D.D.S.

Professor and Chairman, Division of Oral and Maxillofacial Surgery, University of Texas Southwestern Medical Center; Director, Division of Oral and Maxillofacial Surgery, Parkland Hospital, St. Paul Hospital, University Medical Center, and Children's Medical Center, Dallas, Texas

Radiographic Evaluation of Facial Injuries; Diagnosis and Treatment of Midface Fractures

MARK R. STEVENS, D.D.S.

Assistant Professor of Surgery, Division of Oral and Maxillofacial Surgery, University of Miami School of Medicine, Jackson Memorial Medical Center; Director, Center for Dento-facial Deformities and Director, Center for Temporomandibular Joint Disorders, Jackson Memorial Medical Center, Doctors' Hospital of Coral Gables, Miami Veterans Administration Medical Center, Miami, Florida

Reconstruction of Avulsive Maxillofacial Injuries

RICHARD G. TOPAZIAN, D.D.S.

Professor and Chairman, Department of Oral and Maxillofacial Surgery, University of Connecticut School of Dental Medicine; Professor of Surgery, University of Connecticut School of Medicine; Clinical Chief, Department of Dentistry, University of Connecticut John N. Dempsey Hospital, Farmington, Connecticut

Infection in the Patient with Maxillofacial Trauma

DONALD D. TRUNKEY, M.D.

Professor and Chairman, Department of Surgery, Oregon Health Sciences University, Portland, Oregon

Emergency and Intensive Care of the Trauma Patient

TIMOTHY A. TURVEY, D.D.S.

Professor, Department of Oral and Maxillofacial Surgery, University of North Carolina School of Dentistry; Attending Staff, University of North Carolina Hospitals, Chapel Hill, North Carolina

Management of Facial Fractures in the Growing Patient

L. GEORGE UPTON, D.D.S., M.S.

Professor and Interim Chairman, Department of Oral Medicine, Pathology and Surgery, University of Michigan School of Dentistry and Associate Professor, University of Michigan Medical School; Attending Staff, University of Michigan Hospitals; Co-director, University of Michigan Cleft Palate Team, Ann Arbor, Michigan

Management of Injuries to the Temporomandibular Joint Region

ROBERT G. VIERE, M.D.

Spine Fellow, Case Western Reserve University School of Medicine; Spinal Cord Injury Fellow, Cleveland Wade Park Veterans Hospital, Cleveland, Ohio

Initial Assessment and Management of the Polytrauma Patient with Orthopedic Injuries

GEORGE A. ZARB, B.CH.D (MALTA); M.S., D.D.S. (MICH.); M.S. (OHIO), FRCD(O), DR. ODONT (H.C.)

Professor and Chairman of Prosthodontics, Faculty of Dentistry, University of Toronto; Consultant, Hospital for Sick Children and New Mount Sinai Hospital, Toronto, Ontario, Canada

Maxillofacial Prosthetics for the Trauma Patient

DEBORAH L. ZEITLER, D.D.S., M.S.

Associate Professor and Director of Graduate Studies, University of Iowa; Attending Staff, University of Iowa Hospital and Clinic, Veterans Administration Medical Center, City of Iowa, Iowa City, Iowa

Burns of the Head and Neck

ACKNOWLEDGMENTS

Oral and Maxillofacial Trauma represents the culmination of four years of a labor of love. Our gratitude to the numerous expert contributors cannot be expressed completely in words. These persons provided us with comprehensive authoritative treatises in their respective areas. This book exemplifies the interdependence of man and the higher level of achievement that can be reached through cooperative efforts.

We would also like to extend our thanks and appreciation to all the residents we have worked with, many of whom are contributors to this text. They have provided the intellectual stimulation, inspiration, and friendship without which this book would not have been written. We would also like to thank Bonnie Andrews and Natalie Giuliano for their assistance in the preparation of this manuscript.

Personal thanks are also due to the editors and staff of the W.B. Saunders Company for their constant support and patient collaboration.

PREFACE

Approximately four years ago the seed of a thought was planted. At that time we envisioned a text that would represent the most definitive reference source for the practitioner treating the oral and maxillofacial injured patient. It was first our desire, and then ultimately our goal, to assemble a multiauthored text on the subject, bringing together the authorities in the field of oral and maxillofacial trauma. As might be anticipated, this original seed grew into a flower beyond our expectations.

Oral and Maxillofacial Trauma is an amitious endeavor consisting of four sections and 33 chapters. We have divided the book into four sections on the basis of the four distinct areas presented.

Section One covers the basic principles in the management of the trauma patient. Included in this section are chapters discussing the metabolic response to trauma, the healing of traumatic injuries, nutritional considerations following trauma, and the pathophysiology and management of shock.

Section Two is divided into seven chapters that deal with the recognition and management of concomitant injuries in the patient with maxillofacial trauma. Each chapter in this section could be the subject of an entire text; therefore, we have attempted to present the subject matter with emphasis on diagnosis and initial management of these injuries. We were fortunate to recruit some of the most widely respected experts in their fields to contribute chapters in this section.

Section Three begins with one of the most comprehensive and well-illustrated chapters in existence on applied surgical anatomy of the head and neck that is not in an atlas. The remainder of the chapters in this section discuss oral and maxillofacial injuries. Each chapter represents the diagnosis and management of a specific anatomic structure, area, or tissue.

Section Four deals with special considerations in the area of maxillofacial injuries. Chapters discussing the management of geriatric and pediatric patients are presented. The pathophysiology and management of gunshot wounds, burns, and infections are discussed in separate chapters. Treatment of patients with extensive facial injuries requiring secondary reconstruction, use of alloplastic materials, and prosthetic rehabilitation are presented comprehensively. An excellent discussion of anesthetic management of the traumatized patient is also presented. Finally, a detailed multiauthored chapter on rigid fixation of facial fractures is presented.

Our goal was to assemble a comprehensive text that would encompass as broad a perspective as possible within two volumes. We apologize for the areas that we inadvertently missed or did not cover as thoroughly as our readers would have liked. Nevertheless, we are extremely proud of *Oral and Maxillofacial Trauma* and offer it as the most comprehensive text on the subject.

RAYMOND J. FONSECA
ROBERT V. WALKER

CONTENTS

II SYSTEMATIC EVALUATION OF THE TRAUMATIZED PATIENT

CHAPTER 18

CHAPTER 19

CHAPTER 20

CHAPTER 21

VOLUME 2

IV SPECIAL CONSIDERATIONS IN THE MANAGEMENT OF TRAUMATIC INJURIES

IV

SPECIAL CONSIDERATIONS in the MANAGEMENT of TRAUMATIC INJURIES

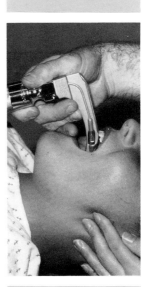

CHAPTER 24

ANESTHETIC MANAGEMENT OF MAXILLOFACIAL TRAUMA

ROBERT L. CAMPBELL, D.D.S.

Trauma to the oral and maxillofacial region can result in any combination of dental, bone, or soft tissue injury. An extension of these injuries may also include the orbit, laryngotracheal, or cerebrospinal structures. Depending upon the force of contact and whether or not the injury was caused by a high-speed motor vehicle accident, trauma may be obvious and extensive or may be an insidious injury to the long bones, abdomen, and chest that may require several hours for overt clinical signs to develop. These general considerations are discussed chronologically, leading up to the induction of anesthesia in the trauma patient.

EMERGENCY ROOM TREATMENT

Injury that appears to be limited to the head and neck may present a serious airway compromise. If emergency airway maintenance is necessary, a quick examination of the mouth for the presence of blood, broken teeth, bone fragments, or other foreign material should precede attempts at ventilation. Placement of a full face mask and an oral or nasal airway may be necessary to establish immediate ventilation before tracheal intubation is tried. If the tongue is swollen secondary to edema or hematoma, or if the motion of the mandible is uncontrollable or restricted, conventional mask-bag ventilation may be very difficult and occasionally not possible. Therefore, an alternative to the mask-bag technique for airway management must be considered. The role of tracheal intubation, cricothyroidotomy, and tracheostomy is discussed later in this chapter.

Control of regional bleeding and overall blood loss is an additional concern. Aspiration of blood may complicate the management of the airway by decreasing the visibility of the pharynx, making visualization of the trachea and intubation extremely difficult regardless of the level of consciousness or cooperation of the patient. Significant amounts of blood loss can occur from intraoral or extraoral lacerations, resulting in hypovolemia, hypotension, and, in the most severe form, cardiovascular collapse. Therefore, in cases in which the level of consciousness is decreased, even with no other overt evidence of open-head, abdominal, or chest trauma, establishment of multiple intravenous access is mandatory. Fluid resuscitation may be administered until control of bleeding is established; appropriate laboratory tests are done and monitors are placed to titrate further the quantity and type of fluids needed to stabilize the patient's condition prior to a careful, systematic preoperative evaluation.

PREOPERATIVE PERIOD

In general, a patient suffering major organ system trauma does not ordinarily require immediate emergency room treatment for most facial fractures; such treatment can often be delayed several hours or even for 1 to 3 days. However, it may be important to involve the anesthesiologist early in the evaluation of patients with facial trauma, even when the patient is not going to have definitive treatment within the next few hours. This practice allows the anesthesiologist to plan properly for complications that can occur during the critical airway establishment period and to suggest, early on, preoperative studies that might otherwise delay the operation.

After the "resuscitation period" in the emergency room has passed, preoperative assessment for the operating room begins. Injury to the cervical spine should be evaluated on the basis of clinical and radiographic signs. Although voluntary flexion and extension are encouraging findings, many patients have acute muscle spasm from neck sprain and are unable to demonstrate good range of motion for several days. Assessment of paresthesia in the hands in response to neck movement is not always possible or safe until appropriate x-ray films have been taken. Therefore, verification of normal odontoid position as well as assessment for traumatic subluxation of cervical vertebrae can be done by lateral and anteroposterior neck radiographs. To be an adequate screen for acute subluxation injuries, the film should show the complete cervical anatomy down to the first thoracic vertebra. An alternative method of assessment would be the use of computerized tomography (CT), which may allow less movement of the head and neck and may be performed in conjunction with scanning for other injuries at the same time.

If a patient must be operated on soon after the trauma (i.e., within hours), yet a full neurologic examination has not been completed, special care of the neck should be considered. To perform laryngoscopy safely, the neck should be stabilized by pulling gently in a rostral direction, gripping the head with two hands in back of the mastoid area (Fig. 24–1). This maneuver should not be a substitute for cervical radiographs but is most helpful if films cannot be taken and cranial subluxation has not been ruled out.

HISTORY, PHYSICAL EXAMINATION, AND LABORATORY EVALUATION

The circumstances associated with maxillofacial trauma may influence the timing of the definitive treatment of facial injuries. Blunt trauma to the abdomen (e.g., fight, automobile accident, or sports trauma) may result in insidious spleen damage or other intraperitoneal or retroperitoneal bleeding. A patient may not complain of pain secondary to a hematoma, contusions, or abdominal injury if facial pain is severe enough to distract the victim and the clinician. An intravenous hemoglobin measure may or may not be a helpful diagnostic test, depending on the amount of blood loss from the facial injuries. A baseline value compared with subsequent serial measures, especially in the immediate postoperative period, may be very important. Extravasation of blood and third space fluid shift are not seen with isolated facial trauma, as they are in trauma to the abdomen or chest. Therefore, in facial trauma, hemoglobin measures will bear a direct relationship to actual blood loss. Chest trauma can occur even in patients restrained by motor vehicle seat belts. Pneumothorax, hemothorax,

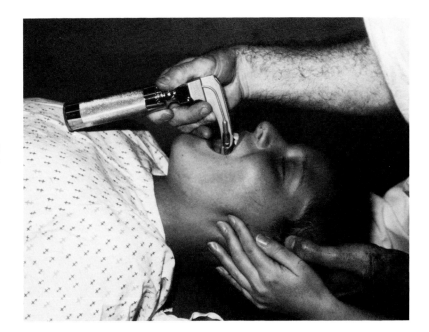

FIGURE 24–1. Traction on the neck during direct laryngoscopy in the patient with potentially unstable cervical vertebra.

or cardiac damage can often be ruled out by chest radiograph and by electrocardiographic and physical examination. Arterial blood gases may also be helpful in determining whether pulmonary artery contusion or an embolic phenomenon is present. Normal carbon dioxide levels, with a decrease in arterial oxygenation, may signal pulmonary vasoconstriction and decreased perfusion to the lung (e.g., pulmonary contusion).[1] A similar pattern may be seen with pulmonary restrictive disease or aspiration, although with pulmonary aspiration, other physical and radiographic findings are often present.

If a patient has lost consciousness as the result of trauma, even though serious closed-head injury has been ruled out, pulmonary aspiration may have already occurred. Aspiration of blood and saliva or small amounts of gastric fluid may not produce a fulminant aspiration syndrome but, rather, only moderate changes in lung function, which may be reflected in subtle arterial blood gas changes.[2]

Patients who have been drinking alcohol prior to trauma may present with several problems related to anesthesia use, not the least of which is cooperation for awake intubation techniques. Alcohol also delays gastric emptying and may increase gastric acid secretion, leading to a greater incidence of aspiration and pulmonary sequelae.[3] Chronic alcohol abuse may cause relative dehydration and acutely elevated liver enzyme function, which may in turn lead to decreased levels of narcosis from a "standard" amount of sedation drugs (i.e., tolerance). Hypocalcemia and hypomagnesemia in chronic alcoholics may cause decreased cardiac function and increased myocardial irritability during anesthesia. If sedatives or narcotics are used when measurable levels of alcohol are present, respiratory depressant effects may occur, resulting in levels of sedation deeper than anticipated. This condition could lead to unexpected somnolence and inadequate cooperation for an awake intubation.

Patients who have a history of intravenous drug abuse may also present with cardiac and pulmonary problems.[4] Talcum powder is occasionally used to dilute powder drugs and may cause pulmonary fibrosis from the contaminants being filtered out in the lung. If large amounts of sodium bicarbonate are used as a powder diluent, a metabolic alkalosis may result. Acute cocaine intoxication could produce an increase in sympathetic tone or cardiac arrhythmias or both. Chronic use may result in unsuspected cardiomyopathy secondary to chronic myocardial ischemia and subsequent scarring. All those patients who are at high risk for hepatitis and human immunodeficiency virus (HIV) antigen should be treated with the currently accepted body fluid precautions during vulnerable times throughout the perianesthesia period and especially during intubation.

THE MEDICALLY COMPROMISED PATIENT

When a patient has significant debilitating or incapacitating systemic disease, serious enough to warrant an A.S.A. (American Society of Anesthesiology) Classification III or IV, further preanesthesia evaluation should be done if possible. If surgery cannot be delayed for 24 to 48 hours, the patient may require placement of invasive monitors, including an arterial line or a Swan-Ganz pulmonary catheter or both. The arterial monitor is the simpler of the two to place and is most helpful prior to induction and during maintenance of anesthesia in patients with cardiac disease. At a very minimum in these patients, an arterial access allows continuous monitoring of arterial blood pressure during induction and arterial blood gas analysis postoperatively. The pulmonary artery catheter can measure cardiac function, including ventricular filling pressures, cardiac output, and systemic fluid status. The indications for this monitor include any clinical situations in which adrenergic inotropes or vasodilators may be needed to improve cardiac function and when fluid replacement becomes critical.[5] For example, a patient with a history of serious cardiac dysfunction, who may need large amounts of fluid replacement from the surgical standpoint or significant fluid restrictions because of heart disease, may become hypotensive from either blood loss from facial trauma or primary cardiac depression during anesthesia. Pulmonary artery catheter monitoring would probably decrease the mortality associated with the trauma surgery but should not be a substitute for good presurgical clinical evaluation and conventional intraoperative monitoring.

AIRWAY MANAGEMENT

When time allows, the trauma findings should be systematically reviewed. The extent of the facial fractures and the surgical plan should be discussed with the surgeon to avoid "surprises." The need for nasal intubation, intermaxillary fixation, and intranasal packing should be known as early as possible prior to intubation for general anesthesia. The status of the most recent food intake should be considered when deciding whether rapid-sequence induction and intubation are feasible or necessary. A nasal intubation should *never* be attempted after a rapid-sequence delivery of anesthetic drugs. In contrast to the oral route, nasal intubation, which by its very nature involves "slower technical" maneuvers, should not be considered as a rapid sequence technique. When midface fractures are present, meticulous cleaning of the nasal airway and assessment of patency are necessary, which contraindicates the use of the nasal route for achieving intubation with a rapid-sequence delivery of drugs.

A patient with isolated mandibular trauma who has not taken solid or liquid foods for the previous 8 hours can usually be managed by routine anesthesia induction and nasal intubation. If the status regarding intake of solids and liquids is in doubt, one of four possible techniques for airway management can be employed:

1. Rapid-sequence oral intubation
2. Blind awake (or partial sedation) nasal intubation
3. Awake (or partial sedation) fiberoptic nasal intubation
4. Routine mask intubation (for pediatric patient)

Rapid-Sequence Techniques

To decrease the chances of aspirating gastric contents, a rapid-sequence induction and tracheal intubation should be considered.[6] However, several clinical observations of the patient's condition are necessary before drugs are delivered in rapid sequence. For example, if intravascular volume is depleted from bleeding or loss of plasma volume, a rapid delivery of anesthetic agents may cause significant "induction hypotension." Although adequate volume replacement should be complete prior to induction, the administration of blood, plasma expanders, or lactated Ringer's solution does not guarantee that cardiovascular collapse with rapid-sequence induction will not occur. Patients with cardiovascular disease, especially those taking cardiac depressants, antihypertensives, or diuretics (particularly the potassium-depleting agents), may become hypotensive after the rapid infusion of a barbiturate anesthetic agent.[7,8] Such patients may be best managed by an alternative technique.

During rapid-sequence induction, the patient is usually given 100 per cent oxygen for at least 3 minutes for complete pulmonary alveolar denitrogenation, so that a high partial pressure of oxygen in the lungs may be achieved. An alternative method would employ four successive "vital capacity"–type breaths with 100 per cent oxygen.[9] This method allows most patients to become apneic for about 1 minute, so that laryngoscopy may be accomplished without the patient's becoming hypoxemic. Gentle but continuous pressure applied over the cricoid cartilage (the Sellick maneuver) closes the esophagus and decreases the chance of regurgitation of stomach fluids into the pharynx. The patient is not ventilated after the administration of the induction agent and muscle relaxant to eliminate the possibility of inflating the stomach with air, which could result in increased intragastric pressure and opening of the gastroesophageal ring, with subsequent regurgitation. Laryngoscopy and intubation are then performed after adequate relaxation of the masseter, medial pterygoid, and temporalis muscles.

If the anatomy of the upper airway appears to be difficult to manage by preoperative examination, an alternate method to rapid sequence should be considered. Mandibular retrognathia and severe Class II malocclusion may make visualization of the larynx difficult. Palpation of the hyoid bone may be helpful in assessing the difficulty of intubation,[10] but even if the hyoid is palpable, this is not always a guarantee of a normal laryngeal position. Examination of a lateral neck soft tissue film or the cervical film series used to evaluate the intactness of the cervical vertebrae will also aid the anesthesiologist in determining the normality of upper airway anatomy (Fig. 24–2). If the patient is in a sitting position with the mouth wide open and the posterior pharyngeal wall is visible, the likelihood of successful intubation increases.[11] However, in a patient with mandibular fractures, this clinical test may not be useful owing to a decrease in jaw mobility from pain. If intubation fails on the first attempt,

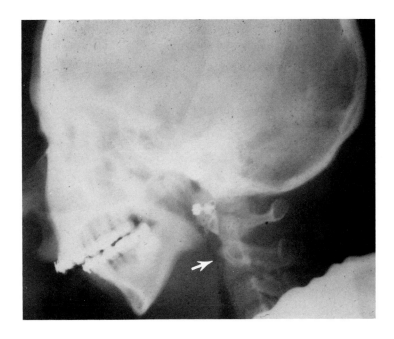

FIGURE 24–2. Airway closure in the pharynx *(arrow)* caused by a retropositioned, fractured mandible.

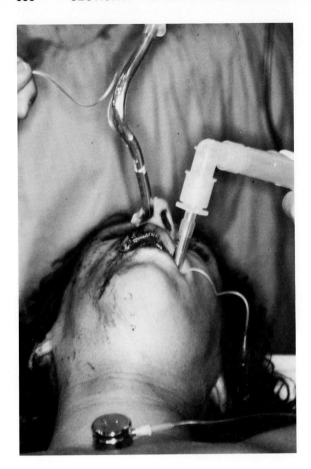

FIGURE 24–3. Changing the oral endotracheal tube to a nasal tube under direct vision after induction and controlled ventilation.

ventilation should be performed, with continuous application of pressure on the cricoid cartilage. A second attempt at laryngoscopy should be made before the muscle relaxant is redistributed or metabolized. Four tidal volume–type breaths with 100 per cent oxygen should allow another 1-minute period of apnea and laryngoscopy without hypoxemia.

If oral intubation is successful, a transfer from the oral tube to a nasal endotracheal tube is usually necessary before surgery can be undertaken. With the airway secured, the surgeon or anesthesiologist can clear the nasal passages and carefully place an endotracheal tube into the pharynx (Fig. 24–3). After reaching an adequate surgical plane of anesthesia and complete muscle relaxation, preferably with nondepolarizing muscle relaxants, a tube transfer can be done. Under direct laryngoscopic visualization and with good suctioning of the pharynx, the oral tube can be shifted to the left side of the patient's mouth. An anesthesia assistant can remove the previously placed oral tube, and the nasal tube can usually be passed without any difficulty, with or without the aid of a Magill forceps.

Blind Awake Intubation

Successful control of the airway prior to induction can be accomplished in the awake patient. Cooperation by the patient often depends upon a good explanation of the technique and the technical skills of the anesthesiologist. Direct visualization of the larynx by a transoral approach in the trauma patient is all but impossible except in an obtunded patient. Generally, the judicious utilization of a local anesthetic agent sprayed or nebulized into the nasal passages or given in the form of nerve blocks can be helpful. Placement of bilateral superior laryngeal block and transtracheal topical anesthetic can decrease pain during intubation. The internal branch of the superior laryngeal nerve supplies sensation to the vallecula, the mucosa above the vocal cords, and the lateral wall of the laryngeal pharynx.[12] This block can be done by infiltrating 2 ml of 2 per cent lidocaine (Xylocaine) from the lateral neck, via a percutaneous approach, into the thyrohyoid membrane anterior to the sternocleidomastoid muscle bilaterally. Transtracheal injection of 2 ml of 2 to 4 per cent lidocaine (Xylocaine) given through the cricothyroid space can give additional topical anesthesia in the tracheal mucosa.[13]

An effective alternative to the injection of local anesthesia into the neck would be the use of a mask and nebulizer with lidocaine (Xylocaine). Approximately 8 to 10 ml of 2 per cent lidocaine (Xylocaine) can be administered by face tent or mask for 10 to 15 minutes prior to laryngoscopy or blind attempts at intubation. Diazepam (0.07 to 0.1 mg/kg), midazolam (0.03 to 0.07 mg/kg), and droperidol and fentanyl citrate (Innovar) (2 to 4 ml) are popular agents.

Although there are no substantial research studies in humans, it is thought that the use of deep sedation or local anesthesia at least partially blunts the protective laryngeal reflex against pulmonary aspiration. In a previously completed study, it was shown in six cases that after deep sedation was accomplished with narcotics, prior to blind nasal intubation, mild-to-moderate hypoxia occurs.[13] The deeper the level of sedation, or the less responsive the patient is to oral or nasal sensory stimulation, the greater the degree of arterial desaturation (Fig. 24–4). Carbon dioxide levels and pH measures were physiologically acceptable. On the basis of these limited results, administration of oxygen during this process is recommended, especially in patients with suspected cardiac or pulmonary disease. To obtain satisfactory conditions for blind intubation, the anesthesiologist must weigh the benefits of using intravenous agents or local anesthetics against the risks previously mentioned.[14]

After careful preparation with local anesthesia and sedation, the nasal endotracheal tube can be softened by placement into a sterile bottle of warm saline. At this time, the cuff can also be inflated and tested for air leaks. It should then be placed through the nostril and into the pharynx and advanced while the anesthesiologist listens to breath sounds. An esophageal stethoscope can be placed inside the lumen of the endotracheal tube and attached to a monaural ear piece (Fig. 24–5). This practice allows the anesthesiologist to listen to breath sounds and simultaneously to observe directly the movement of the soft tissue on the side of the neck and the thyroid cartilage as the tube is advanced. Thus, the position of the laryngeal opening can be controlled by flexion, extension, or rotation of the neck without the anesthesiologist's having to turn his or her ear to the side to listen to the breath sounds. If the endotracheal tube is repeatedly introduced into the esophagus, flexion of the neck or displacement of the larynx by applying manual pressure to the thyroid cartilage can be done. If these maneuvers fail within a short period, persistent attempts are likely to

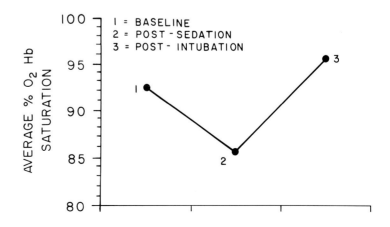

FIGURE 24–4. Arterial desaturation after deep sedation with droperidol and fentanyl citrate (Innovar) prior to nasotracheal intubation.

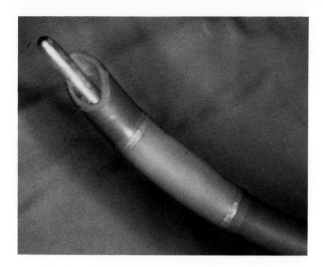

Figure 24–5. Esophageal stethoscope protruding beyond the endotracheal tube to evaluate breath sounds during blind awake intubation.

increase nasal bleeding, and the patient will become adversely stimulated as the local anesthesia and sedatives become less effective. Before this technique is discontinued, one last attempt can be made by rotating the endotracheal tube 180 degrees from its original introduction position. Persisting in blind attempts after a reasonable time is very often self-defeating and potentially dangerous.

Fiberoptic Intubation

An endotracheal tube of appropriate size should be passed over the endoscope prior to attempting intubation. Usually, a pediatric size fiberoptic bronchoscope is necessary to fit into endotracheal tubes that have an inside diameter smaller than 7.0 mm after the scope is placed into the nose and introduced into the pharynx. To decrease the examination time, the overhead operating room lights can be turned out, and the scope light position is visualized as the light is transilluminated through the anterior neck and paralaryngeal area. When the lights of the operating room are turned out, a second assistant should be continually monitoring breathing, oxygen saturation, and vital signs. The tip of the scope is readily located, after which anatomic structures can be observed directly through the scope. The use of the side arm suction and irrigation system is usually helpful in clearing any blood that may obscure the field. The endotracheal tube can then be easily passed over the scope, as it now functions as a stylet in the trachea.

The successful use of the fiberoptic bronchoscope depends on the skills developed from frequent use.[15] The functions of the scope that indicate the directional movement of the fiberoptic tip should be practiced frequently prior to the placement of the scope over the endotracheal tube. Practice by viewing some typed or written words will allow the anesthesiologist to gauge the focal or working distance of the scope.

Mask Induction

Maxillofacial trauma in a pediatric patient presents some unique additional problems. It may be very difficult to use awake or sedation-intubation techniques even in the older adolescent. In contradistinction to the elective surgery situation, in a pediatric trauma patient, intravenous access should be attempted prior to induction even if physical restraint is necessary. The placement of a full face mask may be difficult in severe trauma, and pain may occur when a tight fit is attempted. If intravenous access is not possible, the pediatric patient can be induced with halothane while in the 30-degree head-up position with the use of gentle pressure on the cricoid. The head elevation will allow gravity to pool gastric contents and decrease the likelihood of regurgitation and will slightly improve spontaneous ventilation during induction. Other positions, including the head-down and lateral decubitus positions, will increase the chance of airway obstruction and the possibility of regurgitation of stomach contents. Some advocates of the head-down position argue that aspiration is less likely, which theoretically is true. However, smooth induction is also considerably less likely with this body position.

The technique of mask induction is admittedly risky. Careful review of the literature shows that even inpatients and outpatients who have had no oral intake of food or liquid have significant volumes of residual gastric contents (i.e., greater than 0.3 ml/kg).[16] However, clinical signs of aspiration are rare in these patients (2 to 5 per cent).[17,18] Therefore, every effort should be made to ensure a smooth induction with minimal airway obstruction during this critical period, and the head-up position is warranted in this situation. During any induction of the trauma patient, but particularly in an attempted mask induction, two large-bore tonsil suctions should be ready at all times. Emergency tracheostomy or cricothyroidotomy equipment should also be available in the event of complete laryngospasm secondary to aspiration of semisolid foreign material.[19]

Preoxygenation for 3 to 5 minutes prior to induction plays a dual role. Denitrogenization before the administration of nitrous oxide and halothane will allow a quicker induction owing to the principles of the concentration and the second gas effects.[9] In addition, if effective respiration is interrupted during induction (e.g., laryngospasm), it will take longer for arterial oxygen desaturation to occur, as previously mentioned.[20] Halothane concentration should be increased in 0.5 per cent increments every 8 to 10 breaths. More rapid changes may result in vapor irritation in the tracheobronchial tree and subsequent laryngospasm or, more commonly, breath holding. If either occurs, a choice must be made whether to assist ventilation to hasten induction or administer a muscle relaxant. At least one successful inflation of the lungs with oxygen is necessary prior to administration of muscle relaxant. It is crucial that the ability to maintain ventilation be verified before muscle relaxants are used. The utilization of "overpressure" to speed up the induction should be discouraged. The overpressure principle involves the use of 3 to 4 per cent enflurane or halothane or 5 per cent isoflurane to increase the alveolar partial pressure immediately, with the aim of decreasing the induction time.[21] The potential hazards, including laryngospasm and hypotension, in the hypovolemic patient probably contraindicate the routine use of the technique in the pediatric trauma patient.

Mask induction is much slower in adult patients than in children, primarily because of a lower ratio of functional residual lung volume and alveolar ventilation.[9] For this reason, mask induction in an adult with maxillofacial trauma who may possibly have a full stomach should be a last resort or perhaps even not considered at all. If it is attempted, halothane remains the best choice over other potent, volatile agents.

Urgent Surgical Airway Access

Several invasive techniques are available to establish an airway prior to induction. A transcricothyroid needle can be placed with the patient under local anesthesia. A 14-gauge, straight intravenous catheter or a 13-gauge, preformed, curved needle (Fig. 24–6) and catheter can be used as a temporary airway. Oxygenation can be accomplished, but adequate ventilation, even with a manual Saunders ventilator attachment, is more difficult and occasionally impossible in a nonparalyzed, spontaneously breathing patient. However, the catheter can be attached to a high-frequency jet ventilator with excellent oxygenation and ventilation guaranteed before induction.[22] From the technical standpoint, for ease of placement, the patient should be adequately sedated to minimize the swallowing reflex that is often stimulated when

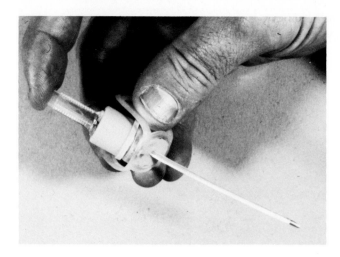

FIGURE 24–6.   Proper finger position over the preformed, curved needle and catheter to prevent needle displacement during transcutaneous entry.

working around the larynx. The major disadvantage of a straight catheter over a curved one is kinking of the catheter as it enters the lumen of the trachea. Oxygenation is still possible under these circumstances, but adequate ventilation (i.e., carbon dioxide removal) is unlikely.

If a large, 8-gauge cricothyroidotomy cannula is considered, a surgical incision is required, and the instruments necessary to tamponade the bleeding that will occur must be readily available.[19] If cricothyroidotomy is used to establish ventilation, within 24 hours, this airway should be removed, and either an endotracheal tube or a tracheostomy tube should be substituted. There is a high incidence of tracheal stenosis at the vocal cord level because of the displacement of the cricoid cartilage and the development of chronic inflammatory tissue in the area immediately below the cords. Tracheostomy is usually the last resort to maintaining a controlled airway and is used only if conventional endotracheal techniques have failed. An unhurried, planned procedure is less dangerous and should be considered long before a patient is involved in an emergent, life-threatening situation. However, if there is the need for prolonged postoperative ventilation control or history of acute blunt laryngeal-tracheal trauma, this alternative may be the best rather than attempting endotracheal intubation. A more detailed description of cricothyroidotomy and tracheostomy techniques is presented in Chapter 6.

Delayed Surgery

A delay in surgery may result in increased facial tissue edema, and swelling will usually peak in 48 hours. If a delay in surgical treatment is necessary, adrenocortical steroids may be useful in limiting edema. From the standpoint of airway management, swelling in the floor of the mouth and in the submandibular space may theoretically cause more difficulty during induction. However, to date, there are no objective studies to support the use of steroid prophylaxis in this situation, and it is not generally a clinical problem in this author's opinion.

When definitive surgery is postponed for as long as 5 to 7 days, the possibility of acute fascial space infection increases. This is especially the case with mandibular fractures that are compound through the periodontal support of erupted teeth. If the patient presents to the operating room at this stage, with large amounts of pus draining intraorally, awake intubation techniques should be considered regardless of whether the patient has had no oral intake of food or liquid. If a face mask is placed on the patient and the anesthesiologist applies pressure to the mandible to support the airway, large amounts of pus can flow unnoticed into the pharynx, resulting in laryngospasm or aspiration. An alternative would be rapid-sequence induction and oral intubation if other airway conditions are optimal. These patients are generally receiving antibiotic therapy for the fractures, so further alteration of existing antibiotic regimens are necessary only if pulmonary aspiration occurs. From the prophylactic standpoint, a postoperative chest radiograph should be considered if any airway problems develop during the induction of anesthesia.

High-Frequency Jet Ventilation (HFJV)

If the airway was established by the use of the cricothyroid needle, the induction can be completed by intravenous agents, and the patient can be paralyzed with a nondepolarizing muscle relaxant. The HFJV apparatus is then attached to the catheter. In the adult, preliminary settings would include the following: 100 breaths per minute (BPM), 30 to 45 psi drive pressure (0.5 psi/kg), and a 20 per cent or greater ratio of inspiratory/expiratory time.[23] When these settings are utilized, adequate ventilation is predictable as long as the catheter is not kinked in the neck tissue or the tracheal lumen. A formula is used to calculate the total inspiratory time per breath. When the time averages 0.14 second (range of 0.12 to 0.16 second), adequate carbon dioxide is eliminated from the alveoli (Table 24 – 1). Normal levels of arterial carbon dioxide should be verified with either an end-tidal carbon dioxide monitor or direct measurement of arterial blood gases for patients undergoing prolonged ventilation by the transtracheal route. When HFJV is used mainly for establishment of an airway and induction of anesthesia, measures of carbon dioxide are not necessary. Even if a catheter is kinked, leading to decreased inspired airflow, elevation of carbon dioxide is a slow process, and unacceptable levels above 55 to 60 mm Hg are not reached until a minimum of 30 minutes of HFJV. In a recent study, adequate ventilation at the

TABLE 24 – 1. INSPIRATORY TIME CHART*

CPM (rate)	Per Cent Inspiratory Time								
	1%	5%	10%	15%	20%	25%	30%	40%	50%
1	0.60	3.00	—	—	—	—	—	—	—
10	0.06	0.30	0.60	0.90	1.20	1.50	1.80	2.40	3.00
20	0.03	0.15	0.30	0.45	0.60	0.75	0.90	1.20	1.50
30	0.02	0.10	0.20	0.30	0.40	0.50	0.60	0.80	1.00
40	0.02	0.08	0.15	0.23	0.30	0.38	0.45	0.60	0.75
45	0.01	0.07	0.13	0.20	0.27	0.33	0.40	0.53	0.67
50	0.01	0.06	0.12	0.18	0.24	0.30	0.36	0.48	0.60
55	0.01	0.06	0.11	0.16	0.22	0.27	0.33	0.44	0.55
60	0.01	0.05	0.10	0.15	0.20	0.25	0.30	0.40	0.50
65	—	0.05	0.09	0.14	0.19	0.23	0.28	0.37	0.46
70	—	0.04	0.09	0.13	0.17	0.21	0.26	0.34	0.43
75	—	0.04	0.08	0.12	0.16	0.20	0.24	0.32	0.40
80	—	0.04	0.08	0.11	0.15	0.19	0.23	0.30	0.38
85	—	0.04	0.08	0.11	0.14	0.18	0.21	0.28	0.35
90	—	0.03	0.07	0.10	0.13	0.17	0.20	0.27	0.33
95	—	0.03	0.06	0.10	0.13	0.16	0.19	0.25	0.32
100	—	0.03	0.06	0.09	0.12	0.15	0.18	0.24	0.30
105	—	0.03	0.06	0.09	0.11	0.14	0.17	0.23	0.29
110	—	0.03	0.06	0.08	0.11	0.14	0.16	0.22	0.27
115	—	0.03	0.05	0.08	0.10	0.13	0.16	0.21	0.26
120	—	0.03	0.05	0.08	0.10	0.13	0.15	0.20	0.25
125	—	0.02	0.05	0.07	0.10	0.12	0.14	0.19	0.24
130	—	0.02	0.05	0.07	0.09	0.12	0.14	0.19	0.23
135	—	0.02	0.04	0.07	0.09	0.11	0.13	0.18	0.22
140	—	0.02	0.04	0.06	0.09	0.11	0.13	0.17	0.21
145	—	0.02	0.04	0.06	0.08	0.10	0.12	0.17	0.21
150	—	0.02	0.04	0.06	0.08	0.10	0.12	0.16	0.20

* Inspiratory time is calculated as follows: T_1 in seconds = $(60/\text{rate}) \times (\%T_1/100)$.

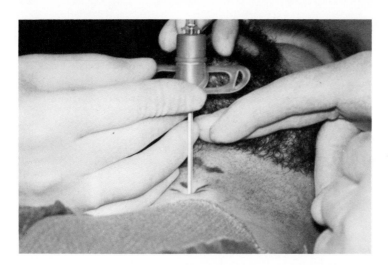

FIGURE 24-7. Placement of a transcricothyroid, 13-gauge catheter under local anesthesia in the sedated patient.

above settings was observed, with serial arterial blood gas samples taken every 15 minutes in 10 patients (R.L. Campbell, unpublished data). The HFJV technique was maintained 1 to 3 hours in several patients with acceptable oxygen and carbon dioxide levels.

High-frequency jet ventilation has been used on more than 30 patients with various airway problems in maxillofacial surgery at the Medical College of Virginia. This technique should be carefully planned preoperatively rather than used for the establishment of emergency airway by inexperienced personnel. Anatomic landmarks in the neck, including the thyroid notch and cricothyroid space, should be palpable and identified with a skin-marking pencil (Fig. 24-7). Local anesthesia infiltration with 2 per cent lidocaine (Xylocaine) with 1:100,000 epinephrine dilution is placed on the skin over the cricothyroid membrane. A syringe filled with local anesthetic and a 25-gauge long needle are advanced into the trachea. Aspiration of air verifies the accuracy of needle placement. The needle is then disconnected and left in the trachea temporarily. Immediately before the introduction of the catheter, the 25-gauge needle is removed, and the depth of needle placement from skin to the needle tip can be measured. This practice allows a better estimate of the proper depth at which to place the 13-gauge needle and catheter. A small skin incision is very helpful in easing the placement of the catheter through the skin and into the subcutaneous tissues.

COMPLICATIONS

When free airflow is verified, one or two jet blasts are administered. The most common complication to date, seen in 2 of 30 patients, is air emphysema in the lateral neck from inaccurate placement. This condition is readily identifiable within seconds and is generally of no consequence. If subcutaneous emphysema does occur, nitrous oxide should probably not be used. If airflow out of the mouth is present, catheter patency and proper placement are assured. A theoretical complication would be accidental placement into the esophagus if the catheter is inserted too deeply.

The exhalation of gas flow through the mouth must remain unobstructed. If throat packs are placed and exhalation impeded, a dangerous build-up of intra-alveolar pressure can cause barotrauma and possible tension pneumothorax if not recognized early. For this reason, the temporary placement of a nasal pharyngeal tube is recommended until an endotracheal tube is passed.

Aspiration of gastric contents and pharyngeal secretions will not occur, providing a minimal drive pressure of 20 psi, an inhalation-exhalation ratio of 20 per cent, and a respiration rate of 100 cpm are maintained uninterrupted. The lack of radiographic evidence of aspiration of radiocontrast material that has been placed into the pharynx after HFJV has been established tends to support this claim. However, aspiration can occur if the patient begins spontaneous respiration, which may counteract the continuous positive pressures generated in the trachea with the high flow rate. For this reason, adequate muscle relaxation is necessary to control ventilation until other airway protection techniques are used (e.g., tracheostomy or endotracheal tube).

The judicious use of narcotics and sedatives prior to the catheter placement can be very helpful. The typical response of the patient to manipulation of the neck either by palpation or by penetration with a needle is reflex swallowing or coughing. This protective function can distort the larynx during the needle-catheter entry into the trachea. This complication has been encountered but only makes needle placement more difficult. Adequate sedation will decrease the frequency of swallowing and laryngeal movement without any greater loss in tracheal protection than that associated with the sedation technique used for nasal endotracheal tube placement.

Monitors

As previously mentioned, the placement of a direct arterial monitor is helpful whenever a labile blood pressure is likely to occur or when frequent arterial blood gas analysis is necessary. If a patient requires a tracheostomy prior to induction because of airway problems, the status of the ventilation can be evaluated more readily by using an arterial line. In addition, patients who have chest injuries that may impair postoperative ventilation are also candidates for intraoperative arterial monitoring. The radial artery is the most reasonable site for catheterization in the absence of upper extremity injury. To estimate the competence of radial and ulnar blood flow, an Allen test may be done in an elective surgical situation (e.g., prior to hypotensive anesthesia for maxillary osteotomies) but is seldom applied in situations (e.g., trauma) in which the benefit of arterial monitoring is obvious. Irreversible thrombosis is exceedingly rare, and local site infection is also an infrequent complication.[24] When a catheter is placed, a small, 20-gauge type should be used to decrease the chances of thrombosis peripheral to the entrance site. The surgeon or anesthesiologist may place the arterial monitor prior to the patient's induction under local anesthesia, while the pulse is strong and easily palpable. If the pulse is barely palpable owing to low blood pressure, a Doppler sound device may aid in the placement of the catheter into the radial artery.

When there is a significant chance that the administration of large amounts of fluid or vasopressor agents may be needed, a pulmonary artery catheter should be placed, as previously described. The need for this monitor is rare in patients with isolated maxillofacial trauma, except perhaps in those with a history of severe coronary artery disease or of congestive heart failure, in which the risk of fluid overload is present.

SURGICAL PERIOD

Premedication

Narcotics that are usually routinely prescribed prior to the patient's arrival in the operating room should be omitted. Although a trauma patient is evaluated for neurologic damage, particularly for signs of increasing intracranial pressure, an occasional patient may have subclinical symptoms that are not detected. For example, trauma to the neck may result in carotid artery contusion, intimal wall tear, and cerebrovascular thrombosis within 48 hours.[25] Routine imaging studies may not be indicated clinically in certain cases, but major complications may occur immediately prior to induction of anesthesia. In this situation, narcotics may obtund the level of consciousness and mask an impending change in neurologic status.

Generally, even in severe cases of facial fractures, there is not a great deal of acute pain unless the fractures are manipulated. In most cases, the nerves that supply the bones and soft tissues of the face course through canals prior to their exit onto the face, so a state of "localized neurogenic shock" may explain why there is a low level of pain in most patients with facial trauma. Therefore, narcotic premedication is usually not needed for pain preoperatively. Sedatives and anticholinergic drugs can be administered in the operating room holding area just before the induction of anesthesia. Benzodiazepam, 0.05 to 0.15 mg/kg given intravenously, produces a slower onset and a more predictable Verrill sign (ptosis of the upper eyelid over one half of the pupil) than midazolam. Midazolam, which has lower fat solubility, appears to have a more intense therapeutic effect after injection. There have been multiple reports of apnea or inadvertent airway obstruction, especially in the elderly.[26] With midazolam, doses should be limited to 0.04 to 0.07 mg/kg) in patients under 60 and 0.02 to 0.05 mg/kg in those older than 60 years of age.[27]

Droperidol, in doses of 2.5 to 5.0 mg for adult patients given intravenously, will produce adequate sedation for up to 12 hours, with little or no respiratory depression when used alone.[28] It is a strong antiemetic, which may be useful if patients are nauseated preoperatively because they have swallowed blood, a frequent occurrence with intraoral compound fractures or lacerations. Droperidol must be used carefully in hypovolemic patients because of its alpha-adrenergic blocking function and potential for hypotension. Other sedative agents can be used, depending upon the individual preference and experience of the anesthesiologist. However, the most important objective in selecting premedication is to avoid respiratory depression or airway obstruction. A state of conscious sedation rather than deep sedation is preferable.

An anticholinergic agent (e.g., atropine or glycopyrrolate) can be given intravenously immediately prior to induction. Its effectiveness as an antisialagogue when it is given intravenously before induction is certainly less than if it is given intramuscularly 30 to 45 minutes before induction, but the partial vagal blockage of motor activity is more reliable.[29] During laryngoscopy, direct stimulation of the vagal nerves, as well as pain from the manipulation of mandibular bone fractures that produces either a trigeminal-sympathetic or a trigeminal-vagal reflex response, results in a change in cardiac rate. Therefore, intravenous anticholinergic agents may be useful in decreasing the incidence of laryngospasm and preventing bradycardia, especially in pediatric patients who receive succinylcholine prior to intubation. Anticholinergics will decrease lower esophageal muscle tone and could, theoretically, increase the likelihood of regurgitation. However, since there are several other pharmacologic techniques that can alter gastric acidity and volume, the use of intravenous anticholinergics should not be withheld for this reason.

All trauma patients are probably at greater risk of aspirating gastric contents[30] than those inpatients or outpatients who have had an 8-hour fasting period. Although gastric emptying is usually delayed after trauma, there are no documented studies to indicate an increased incidence of pulmonary aspiration in patients with isolated facial trauma. The use of histamine$_2$ receptor blocking agents (e.g., cimetidine and ranitidine) and gastrokinetics (e.g., metoclopramide) has not been considered routine in patients with facial trauma.[31] Although the use of these drugs has not been shown to be cost effective for fasting patients about to undergo routine elective or scheduled nonelective surgery, there may be a theoretical advantage to their use prior to induction for those at increased risk of airway difficulty or vomiting. The intravenous administration of metoclopramide at a dose of 0.15 mg/kg in the adult will improve gastric emptying within 20 to 30 minutes and will increase gastric fluid pH slightly.[32, 33] The use of a histamine$_2$ receptor blocking agent given orally will increase pH, but the gastric volume remains essentially unchanged. This route of administration may not be a good choice in some patients with displaced facial fractures or with intraoral lacerations because of the difficulty in swallowing oral medication. The use of both types of drugs would be the most reliable way of increasing pH and decreasing stomach volume.[31]

Induction Agents

Ultrashort-acting barbiturates are used in a manner similar to other types of surgical cases. Patients who have been sedated with medication, who are relatively hypovolemic from blood loss, or who are generally lethargic from the lack of sleep may need lower doses. If surgery is immediately necessary and, for some reason, crystalloid fluid loading has not been done prior to induction, ketamine (1 to 2 mg/kg given intravenously) has been advocated[34] as a good induction agent to depress memory recall prior to the administration of a muscle relaxant.[35] Advocates of this technique argue that barbiturate induction may cause a serious risk of hypotension in the trauma patient with inadequate blood or fluid replacement. Facial lacerations, particularly in the scalp or across major facial arteries, can cause high-volume blood loss. The merits of a ketamine induction technique are based on the ability of the drug to promote increases in circulating catecholamine levels and maintain blood pressure and cardiac output.[35] Etomidate, at a dose of 0.3 to 0.5 mg/kg, would also be useful for induction in a situation in which the maintenance of cardiac output is questionable.[36]

Inhalation Anesthetics

Nitrous oxide has traditionally been the foundation of general anesthesia for decades. Several basic properties continue to make it desirable as an adjunct to either narcotic-balanced anesthesia or more potent volatile agents. Its reduced solubility in the plasma (a blood gas coefficient of 0.47) allows for rapid uptake and equilibration and emergence from anesthesia.[37] Although the potency is low (i.e., a minimal alveolar concentration [MAC] of more than 100 per cent), there is a significant decrease in the anesthetic requirements for other agents when nitrous oxide is used.[9] Without it, higher doses of narcotics, muscle relaxants, and inhalation agents are often necessary, which can also be associated with more physiologically disturbing side effects. For example, if higher doses of narcotics are needed, the likelihood of a patient's being able to maintain spontaneous breathing and being able to be extubated at the completion of the surgery is decreased. Similarly, if higher doses of isoflurane are necessary in the absence of nitrous oxide, greater decreases in blood pressure may occur. The MAC for isoflurane in 100 per cent oxygen is approximately 1.15, but with 70 per cent nitrous oxide, the MAC is decreased to 0.6.

Another advantage of using nitrous oxide is the second gas effect, which allows a more rapid diffusion of an added second gas (e.g., halothane) across the alveolar capillary membrane, leading to more rapid induction of a surgical plane of anesthesia.[9] The second gas effect occurs because the rapid diffusion of nitrous oxide across the alveolar capillary membrane essentially allows high concentration of the second gas in the alveoli and a more rapid flow of the second gas into the capillary blood.[21]

Several disadvantages of using nitrous oxide have been noted. It appears that despite being a weak, rather inert drug undergoing little or no metabolic breakdown, a significantly higher incidence of birth defects, spontaneous abortion, and organ system disorders has been reported in exposed health care workers.[38] Scavenging exhaust gases may reduce the risk considerably, as demonstrated by animal and retrospective epidemiologic studies. Although potency is low, nitrous oxide can rapidly displace nitrogen in air-space cavities in the body. For example, the eustachian tube may be closed by infection or edema of the tubaris opening in the lateral pharynx. This phenomenon is possible soon after extensive midface maxillary trauma or maxillary sinusitis. Pressure build-up in the middle ear canal from nitrous oxide diffusion may produce ear pain during early recovery.[39]

Several investigators have reported an increased incidence of nausea and vomiting after nitrous oxide anesthesia, while others have not.[40] If patients are in intermaxillary fixation after fracture reduction, a theoretical danger of regurgitation and aspiration may exist in the postoperative period. However, measures to evacuate the gastric contents prior to emergence from anesthesia would allow the anesthesiologist to take full advantage of the benefits of using nitrous oxide with less concern for vomiting in the immediate postoperative period.

Isoflurane

Isoflurane has been used clinically since early 1980. With a MAC of 1.15, this agent is more potent than enflurane (MAC of 1.68) and less potent than halothane (MAC of 0.75). It ranks as the least metabolized drug (less than 1 per cent) of the potent volatile agents. Its low blood gas coefficient (1.4), compared with that of halothane (2.4) and enflurane (1.9), indicates rapid diffusion across the alveolocapillary membrane and plasma equilibration. This property allows for a clinically more rapid emergence from anesthesia. Therefore, patients in intermaxillary fixation may theoretically be extubated earlier after isoflurane anesthesia than with other inhalation agents. Isoflurane can produce better muscle relaxation than either halothane or enflurane. However, the muscle relaxation from inhalation anesthetics alone is often inadequate for the reduction and stabilization of fractures at the angle of the mandible even during open reduction. Reduced doses of nondepolarizing agents will potentiate the isoflurane and allow for easier approximation of fracture segments. Isoflurane depresses the myocardium less than halothane, and the resultant increased heart rates will generally allow nearly normal cardiac output in steady-state conditions.[41] Isoflurane does not seem to sensitize the myocardium to epinephrine-induced arrhythmias, as does halothane. Up to 10 μg of epinephrine per kilogram (0.30 ml/kg of 1:100,000) can be safely used during isoflurane anesthesia.

Upper airway secretions can be increased with the use of isoflurane, probably because of its ether molecular configuration and pungent odor. Although of little consequence during maintenance of anesthesia, after extubation the patient will still be exhaling the vapors. This situation may also stimulate secretions and require the recovery room staff to pay more strict attention to the airway, particularly in the presence of intermaxillary fixation.

Surgical Position

The position of the surgeons around the head of the table is more easily accomplished with the operating room table turned away from the anesthesia team. This usually means that access to the endotracheal tube and airway is "surrendered" after induction, which makes accidental extubation possible. Stabilization of the endotracheal tube and connections must be guaranteed prior to movement of the table.

The use of an RAE endotracheal tube with a curvature that allows adequate stabilization over the nose with fewer connectors is helpful. Additional aids, including alcohol, benzoin, or tape applied to plastic or metal adapters, can decrease the likelihood of accidental disconnection. A tonsil-type suction should always be readily available to suction the mouth quickly in case of accidental extubation, laceration of the endotracheal tube, or pilot tube and cuff failure. Suction is especially important for the accumulation of blood in the intraoral surgical site. Adequate eye protection, including taping the eyes closed *before* placing eye pads, is most helpful, since the surgeon often puts pressure over this part of the face. If eye pads are used alone without prior taping of the eyelids, corneal abrasion can still occur. Placement of an esophageal stethoscope through the mouth will interfere with the surgical field, and often the nose is obstructed because of the type of trauma to the maxilla and nose in this case. A suprasternal stethoscope is adequate in this situation to monitor breath sounds.

After the surgical table is rotated, there must be an adequate length of corrugated gas delivery tubing to extend to the gas machine. The utilization of a semiclosed system with a soda line cannister will require a double hose extending to the endotracheal tube. Since there is very little humidification delivered to the patient with this system, a disposable "artificial nose" can be attached between the endotracheal tube and the Y-connector. This device will trap moisture and, at least in part, prevent delivery of a completely dry fresh gas to the patient. In the circle system, the minimal flow of oxygen that is physiologically acceptable should be 1 L/min, along with 1 L or more of nitrous oxide. The 1 L of oxygen is not arbitrarily chosen; rather, it is based on the normal oxygen availability when considering physiologic variables, including cardiac output, normal hemoglobin concentration, and normal hemoglobin saturation (the Barcroft equation).[1]

$$\frac{\text{Cardiac}}{\text{output}} \times \frac{\text{arterial O}_2}{\text{saturation}} \times \frac{\text{hemoglobin}}{\text{concentration}} \times 1.39 = \frac{\text{oxygen}}{\text{availability}}$$

$$5000 \text{ ml} \times \frac{95}{100} \times \frac{15}{100} \times 1.39 = 1000 \text{ ml/min}$$
$$\underset{\text{(min)}}{} \qquad \qquad \underset{\text{g/ml}}{}$$

A Mapleson D partial rebreathing circuit can be used in lieu of the semiclosed circle absorption system. The fresh gas flow, including any volatile anesthetic agents, is delivered through small-diameter tubing close to the endotracheal tube connector. Exhalation is gathered into a larger bore corrugated tube moving toward the gas machine. Since there are no directional valves to separate inhaled from exhaled gas, carbon dioxide and anesthetic agents can be rebreathed. Therefore, the minimal total fresh gas flow to prevent carbon dioxide build-up in the reinhaled gas should be based on the size of the patient and whether the ventilation is controlled or assisted.[42] The potential dead space or rebreathed air is 500 to 700 ml, depending upon the type of Mapleson D tubing used. A minimal fresh gas flow setting should not be expected to prevent carbon dioxide rebreathing in a patient who is spontaneously breathing without occasional assistance. Tachypnea and apnea both can result in dangerous elevation of arterial carbon dioxide levels. The tachypneic patient may retain carbon dioxide because of inadequate fresh gas to evacuate the exhalation tube, whereas the apneic patient will become hypercarbic by not being able to eliminate the carbon dioxide accumulating in the alveoli. In both of these clinical situations, hypercarbia can occur. In a spontaneously breathing adult and pediatric patient, 100 ml/kg/min and 200 ml/kg/min of fresh gas flow, respectively, should be used. In a controlled ventilation mode, 70 ml/kg/min and 150 ml/kg/min should be used, respectively.

The physiologic consequence of excessive carbon dioxide accumulation has both anesthetic and surgical implications. Elevation of carbon dioxide levels may stimulate catecholamine release and result in hypertension, vascular dilation, and increased bleeding. If the systemic effects are blunted by using higher doses of inhalation anesthesia, local vascular dilation will still occur from venous bleeding at the surgical site. Although there may be a transient benefit of carbon dioxide accumulation and resultant sympathetic stimulation during induction, especially if there has been a significant decrease in fluid volume, this is a very fleeting effect. Sympathetic stimulation may be well tolerated in the young trauma patient with marginal cardiac reserve. However, if the plasma pH goes below 7.2, even in the healthy patient direct myocardial depression and increased irritability may occur.[1] The utilization of controlled ventilation with or without peripheral muscle relaxant drugs, as well as the use of a circle system, may be a more predictable way of establishing a normocarbic state.

CONCLUSION

The evaluation of the patient with maxillofacial trauma with regard to anesthesia begins in the emergency room. The airway and the status of blood volume, concerns in the acute phase of treatment, will eventually play an important role in the induction and maintenance of anesthesia. The timing of definitive surgery to correct the facial deformities depends upon whether other injuries are present and which organ systems are also affected by trauma.

Assuming that there are no significant contraindications to immediate surgical treatment, there are several factors that will have impact on the choice of anesthetic technique, including the stability of the airway after induction, the presence of gastric contents, the need for crystalloid volume expansion, and the cooperation of the patient. The selection of the anesthetic agent is less important, but considerations include the need to maintain postoperative airway support by endotracheal tube or tracheostomy, the length of surgery, and the experience of the anesthesiologist.

By involving the anesthesiologist in the preoperative evaluation of the trauma patient, the intervening time between the injury and surgical treatment will allow for thoughtful planning of the anesthetic care. A "no surprises" approach enables the anesthesiologist and surgeon to deliver quality intraoperative and postoperative treatment.

REFERENCES

1. Nunn JF: Applied Respiratory Physiology, 2nd ed. Boston, Butterworths, 1981, pp 301–309.
2. Goudsouzian N: Aspiration in children: Practical implications. Anesth Rev 11:6–16, 1984.
3. Casson WR, Jones RM: Alcohol and the anesthesiologist. Anesth Rev 13:59–65, 1986.
4. Thiagarajah S, Frost EA: Heroin addiction and anesthesia. Anesth Rev 10:12–18, 1983.
5. Parker EO: Invasive monitoring in the community hospital. Anesth Rev 11:22–28, 1984.
6. Gordon RA: Anesthetic management of the patient with airway problems. Int Anesth Clin 10:37–59, 1972.
7. Kirby RR, Brown DL: International Anesthesiology Clinics: Anesthesia for Trauma, Vol 25. Boston, Little, Brown, and Company, 1987, pp 37–60.
8. Chein S: Role of the sympathetic nervous system in hemorrhage. Physiol Rev 47:214–288, 1967.
9. Eger EI II: Effect of inspired anesthetic concentration on the rate of rise of alveolar concentration. Anesthesiology 24:153–157, 1963.
10. Norton ML, Wilton N, Brown AC: The difficult airway clinic. Anesth Rev 15:25–28, 1988.
11. Block C, Brechner VL: Unusual problems in airway management. II. The influence of the temporomandibular joint, the mandible and associated structures on endotracheal intubation. Anesth Analg 50:114–123, 1971.
12. Gotta AW, Sullivan CA: Superior laryngeal nerve block: An aid to intubating the patient with fractured mandible. J Trauma 24:83–85, 1984.
13. Gotta AW, Sullivan CA: Anesthesia of the upper airway using topical anesthetic and superior laryngeal nerve block. Br J Anaesth 53:1055–1058, 1981.
14. Kopman AF, Wollman SB, Ross K, Surks SN: Awake endotracheal intubation: A review of 267 cases. Anesth Analg 54:323–330, 1975.
15. Mulder DS, Wallace DH, Woolhouse FM: The use of fiberoptic bronchoscope to facilitate endotracheal intubation following head and neck trauma. J Trauma 15:638–640, 1975.
16. Ong BY, Palahniuk RJ, Comming M: Gastric volume in out-patients. Can Anaesth Soc J 25:36–39, 1978.
17. Manchikanti L, Colliver JA, Marrereo TC, et al: Ranitidine and metoclopramide for prophylaxis of aspiration pneumonitis in elective surgery. Anesth Analg 63:903–910, 1984.
18. Cote CJ, Goudsouzian NG, Liu LMP, et al: Assessment of risk factors related to the acid aspiration syndrome in pediatric patients: Gastric pH and residual volume. Anesthesiology 56:70–72, 1982.
19. Brantigan CO, Grow JB: Cricothyroidotomy: Elective use in problems requiring tracheostomy. J Thorac Cardiovasc Surg 71:72–81, 1976.
20. Sheffer L, Steffenson JL, Birch AA: Nitrous oxide–induced diffusion hypoxia in patients breathing spontaneously. Anesthesiology 37:436–439, 1972.
21. Wetchler V: Problems in Anesthesia—Outpatient Anesthesia. Vol 2. Philadelphia, JB Lippincott, 1988.
22. Miller J, Iovino W, Fine J, Klain M: High frequency jet ventilation in oral and maxillofacial surgery. J Oral Maxillofac Surg 40:790–793, 1982.
23. Carlon GC, Kahn RC, Howland WS, et al: Clinical experience with high frequency jet ventilation. Crit Care Med 9:47–50, 1981.
24. Kaplan JA: Cardiac Anesthesia. New York, Grune and Stratton, 1979, pp 71–115.
25. Sahni SK, Campbell RL, Rosner MJ, Goyne BW: Internal carotid arterial occlusion following mandibular osteotomy. J Oral Maxillofac Surg 42:394–399, 1984.
26. White PF: The role of midazolam in outpatient anesthesia. Anesthesiol Rev 12:55–60, 1985.
27. Dundee JW, Collier PS, Carlisle RJT, Harper KW: Prolonged midazolam elimination half-life. Br J Clin Pharmacol 21:425–429, 1986.
28. Rita L, Goodarzi M, Seleny F: Effect of low dose droperidol on post-operative vomiting in children. Can Anaesth Soc J 28:259–262, 1981.
29. Clark JM, Seager SJ: Gastric emptying follow-

ing premedication with glycopyrrolate or atropine. Br J Anaesth 55:1195–1199, 1983.

30. Todd JG, Nimmo WS: Effect of premedication on drug absorption and gastric emptying. Br J Anaesth 55:1189–1193, 1983.

31. Rao TLK, Madhavareddy S, Chinthagada M, El-Etr AA: Metoclopramide and cimetidine to reduce gastric fluid pH and volume. Anesth Analg 63:1014–1016, 1984.

32. Doze VA, Shafer A, White PF: Nausea and vomiting after outpatient anesthesia: Effectiveness of droperidol alone and in combination with metoclopramide. Anesth Analg 66:5–41, 1987.

33. Korttila K, Kauste A, Auvinen J: Comparison of domperidone, droperidol, and metoclopramide in the prevention and treatment of nausea and vomiting after balanced general anesthesia. Anesth Analg 58:396–400, 1979.

34. Waxman K, Shoemaker WC, Lippman M: Cardiovascular effects on anesthetic induction with ketamine. Anesth Analg 59:355–358, 1980.

35. White PF, Way WL, Trevor AJ: Ketamine: Its pharmacology and therapeutic uses. Anesthesiology 56:119–136, 1982.

36. Craido A, Maseda J, Novarro E, et al: Induction of anesthesia with etomidate: Haemodynamic study of 36 patients. Br J Anaesth 52:803–805, 1980.

37. Eger EI II, Gaskey NJ: A review of the present status of nitrous oxide. Am Assoc Nurse Anesth 54:1, 1986.

38. Hannifan MA, Reist PC, Campbell RL: Anesthetic waste gas exposure in dental surgery. Am Ind Hyg Assoc J 39:69–73, 1978.

39. Ravindran RS, Cummins DF: Spontaneous rupture of tympanic membrane following nitrous oxide anesthesia. Anesth Analg 10:24–26, 1983.

40. Korttila K, Hovorka J, Erkola O: Omission of nitrous oxide does not decrease the incidence or severity of emetic symptoms after isoflurane anesthesia. Anesth Analg 66:S98, 1987.

41. Dolan WM, Stevens WC, Eger EI II: The cardiovascular and respiratory effects of isoflurane–nitrous oxide anesthesia. Can Anaesth Soc J 21:557–568, 1974.

42. Spoerel WE, Aitken RR, Bain JA: Spontaneous respiration with the Bain Rebreathing Circuit. Can Anaesth Soc J 35:30–38, 1978.

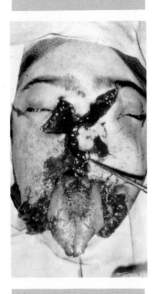

CHAPTER 25

PATHOPHYSIOLOGY AND MANAGEMENT OF GUNSHOT WOUNDS TO THE FACE

THOMAS E. OSBORNE, D.D.S.,
and ROBERT A. BAYS, D.D.S.

INCIDENCE OF FIREARM MORBIDITY AND MORTALITY IN THE UNITED STATES

Firearms are a leading public health problem in the United States today. During the past half century, there were over one million firearm-related deaths recorded. In this group 49 per cent were suicides, 38 per cent were homicides, and 12 per cent were unintentional. Approximately 84 per cent of the victims were male. In 1982, firearm-caused deaths exceeded 32,000 and closely approached the totals reported for cancer of the breast and diabetes mellitus.[1] This number was also more than half the number of U.S. fatalities in the 12 years of the Vietnam War (57,000 between 1961 and 1973) and more than half the number of fatalities each year in the United States from motor vehicle accidents (50,000).[2] Firearms now rank as the nation's eighth leading cause of death. As a category of trauma (the nation's leading cause of death between ages 1 and 38 years), firearm-associated mortality is second only to mortality from motor vehicle accidents.[3]

In 1982, the age-adjusted firearm mortality rate for the United States was 13.5 per 100,000 population. This is the highest rate since 1934, and more firearm deaths occurred in 1981 than in any other single year (33,066). Firearms now account for 65 per cent of all homicides and 57 per cent of all suicides in the United States.[3] Handguns are the most frequently utilized weapon and are the cause of 86 per cent of all homicides.[4] Shotguns are involved in 8 per cent and rifles in 5 per cent of the remaining homicides.[5] Firearms have been implicated in 58 per cent of suicides in men and 37 per cent of suicides in women.[1]

These mortality rates are compounded by the even greater morbidity caused by firearms. According to the National Center for Health, nonfatal firearm injuries are three to five times more frequent than fatal injuries.[5,6] It is interesting that rates for firearm-related homicide and suicide are inversely proportional to economic conditions, with peaks during depression years. In addition, there is a longitudinal association between firearm suicide and homicide and the availability of obtaining weapons. The number of new firearms available for sale in the United States and the rates of firearm-related homicide and suicide began to rise together beginning in the late

1950s. Since the 1970s, yearly changes in firearm availability and homicide and suicide incidence have occurred in parallel.[1]

Firearm violence is often thought to be a problem of the young. Among men, the emergence of teenagers and young adults into high-risk categories has actually occurred only recently. Prior to 1960, these groups were at relatively low risk, with men age 65 and over at greatest risk. Today, males between 25 and 34 are at highest risk, with teenagers and persons 65 and older close behind. The middle-aged man is least likely to be injured or killed by a firearm. As a group, women are less likely to be involved in altercations involving firearms; the homicide and suicide rate is one-fourth the male rate.[3] Among women, teenagers and young adults have always historically been at relatively high risk. This risk has continued to climb recently, so that among women, those 25 to 44 years of age are most likely to experience firearm violence. Older women have consistently been at lowest risk.[1]

HISTORICAL PERSPECTIVE

Firearms were introduced in Europe during the fourteenth century and presented surgeons with a new and challenging form of injury, the gunshot wound. Unlike most earlier forms of penetrating injuries, which were relatively clean and had obvious paths of penetration, these new wounds were considerably more contaminated and had penetration pathways that were unpredictable. There was also much greater inflammation and suppuration that developed after the injury occurred. Infection, rather than direct trauma by the bullet, was most frequently the prime cause of death.[2]

During the fifteenth and sixteenth centuries, it was believed that the bullets and gunpowder not only cut and burned the tissue but also poisoned the wound. Considerable effort was directed to locating and removing all bullets in the belief that by extracting the source of poison the wound would heal. Specialized instruments were specifically developed to facilitate this effort. The wound was often dilated mechanically, and, if needed, releasing incisions were used to facilitate the location and removal of the bullet. Horse hair was often drawn through the wound, and hot (occasionally boiling) oil was poured into it to extract or at least neutralize the poison. The development of suppuration was considered to be a favorable response, an indication that the body was mounting an effort to remove the poison. Indeed, many of the treatment modalities of the time were directed to induce suppuration. Commonly used agents that were introduced into the wound included turpentine, camphor, rose oil, or theriac ointment. For wounds that had become infected, amputation was advocated. The amputation was usually done through gangrenous rather than healthy tissue owing to fear of uncontrollable hemorrhage. For extensive wounds of the extremities, early amputation was recommended, with hemostasis achieved by hot irons or boiling oil.[7]

By the midsixteenth century, surgeons believed that the tissue was not poisoned by the bullet but, rather, that destruction was solely by the mechanical disruption of the tissues. The philosophy of promoting suppuration was abandoned. It was believed that the body had a great capacity for healing, and providing hemostasis could be achieved, primary closure was advocated. During this period, even the most extensive extremity injuries were treated in this manner, and amputation was reserved for use only in the face of progressive gangrene, when an otherwise fatal outcome was evident. Considering the absence of antibiotics, the practice of primary closure in this era was characterized by very high infection rates.[7]

The development of the rifled gun and smokeless gunpowder in the late nineteenth century introduced a new phenomenon, a higher velocity injury. The power and destructiveness of these weapons were much greater than had been seen before. The resulting wounds required different and more extensive management and shared many of the pathophysiologic parameters of other extensive soft and hard tissue injuries. The philosophy of treatment that evolved was also similar: managing the systemic problems required for survival; irrigation and debridement; immediate reconstruction, if possible; secondary reconstruction, if needed; and finally rehabilitation.[2]

In spite of the newly encountered destructiveness of the high-velocity weapon, the discovery of penicillin and subsequent development of antibiotic therapy, as well as advances in surgery (especially vascular and microvascular), have allowed great progress in the management of these injuries. For example, until the midnineteenth century, the treatment of gunshot wounds was limited to the extremities and to superficial wounds of the trunk, head, and neck. Wounds involving the body cavities were regarded as inevitably fatal. However, following the recognition that wounds were infected by microorganisms and with the subsequent development of antiseptic surgery and antibiotics, success was achieved in the treatment of intra-abdominal and intrathoracic gunshot wounds.

Tremendous advances in the management of gunshot injuries occurred during World War II. At the start of the war, extremity injuries were treated exclusively by ligation and amputation, as advocated by Ambroise Paré in the sixteenth century. By the end of the war, however, similar injuries were treated with major arterial reconstruction in an attempt to save the limb. During the Korean War, the use of the autologous saphenous vein interpositional graft was introduced for greater adaptability in major arterial reconstruction. Finally, during the Vietnam War, the need to repair associated major veins as well as arteries for successful reconstruction was recognized.[2] As a result, many limbs were salvaged that just two to three decades before would have inevitably been amputated.

CLASSIFICATION OF BULLETS AND FIREARMS

The "caliber" of a weapon refers to the diameter of its muzzle bore. The term may be used interchangeably with cartridge designation. The wounding power or lethal power of hand-held weapons is generally proportional to the size of the caliber, although any caliber rifle or handgun is capable of producing a lethal injury.[8]

Weapons responsible for most civilian injuries are hand held, such as a handgun or rifle. The handgun or pistol evolved primarily for the purpose of self-defense and ranges from .22 to .45 caliber, with a muzzle velocity ranging from 700 to 1000 ft/sec. The kinetic energy delivered from bullets fired from these weapons ranges from as little as 100 ft/lb of energy with the .22 caliber to as high as 1000 ft/lb of energy with the .44 magnum. Magnum handguns can deliver as much as 20 to 60 per cent more energy than their standard handgun equivalent because of the higher velocity attained from increasing the powder charge. They do not, however, match the power of a rifle having the same caliber.[8]

The rifle is a shoulder-braced firearm developed to produce maximal energy while maintaining the versatility of a hand-held weapon. Compared with the pistol of the same caliber, the rifle is capable of much greater energy. Calibers range from .17 to .460, with kinetic energy delivered up to 3000 ft/lb.[8] These weapons are called rifles because of the spiral shape or "rifling grooves" cut into the barrel. The spiral grooves cause the bullet to spin, giving it greater stability in flight, increasing its range, and improving its accuracy.[8–10]

Shotguns are smooth-bore, long-barreled guns designed primarily for killing fast-moving game, such as birds or small animals. In contrast to high-powered rifles, chamber pressures and muzzle velocities are low, and effective range is short.[11] The muzzle velocity of the shotgun is about 1000 ft/sec and falls off more rapidly than does a pistol or rifle.[12] Most shotgun barrels are 26 to 30 inches in length; however, the "sawed-off" shotgun has a barrel length of 20 inches. The "sawed-off" variety is the one most often used by law enforcement officers as well as by criminals.[11] A shot charge consists of a large number of small spheres that form a pattern when fired, thus overcoming the need for precision. The gauge of a shotgun depends on the size of a single solid shot just able to enter the gun muzzle. The number of these shots required to make a pound is the gauge.[11,12]

Firearm projectiles are referred to as bullets. The modern bullet is usually a lead projectile partially or wholly encased in a copper jacket. A fully jacketed bullet travels longer distances and with more accuracy, owing to less drag and minimal change in its aerodynamic shape. The copper jacket also prevents the deformation of the bullet on impact with tissue, minimizing the resulting tissue damage.[2,9] These are the only bullets that are approved by the Hague Convention (1908) for military use.[2,8,13] Expanding bullets, also known as hollow-point, soft-nose, or dum-dum bullets, are designed to deform in a predictable manner, thus increasing the effective diameter when entering tissue and causing much greater damage. The greatest degree of expansion is achieved by the soft-tipped bullet that expands its diameter two-fold to three-fold. This expansion at least quadruples the area of contact and causes much greater release of energy to the tissues. It also creates a larger wound cavity, is less likely to exit the body, and may fragment, causing significant damage far from the bullet's primary pathway.[8,14,15] These types of bullets have been strictly avoided for combat purposes around the world (as dictated by the Hague Convention); however, there are no restraints imposed upon private citizens or law enforcement officers. Many of these bullets are easily available for hunting purposes, and thus occasionally wounds inflicted in civilian life may be more severe and life threatening than those sustained in military combat.

The amount of injury a bullet can cause is primarily dependent upon its velocity. A low-velocity bullet is one that travels less than 2000 ft/sec and characteristically creates a small entrance-and-exit wound.[5,8,16] Such missiles cause damage by lacerating and crushing tissue. The injury is usually not serious unless vital organs or major blood vessels are injured directly. Only the tissues that are in immediate contact with the missile are damaged, and no significant injury is transmitted to tissue distant from the bullet track. High-speed photography of low-velocity bullets fired through gelatin blocks that simulate soft tissue show that the bullet simply cores out a track, with minimal displacement of gelatin.[9]

A high-velocity bullet is one that travels at speeds greater than 2000 ft/sec and causes considerably more destruction than the low-velocity type.[5,8,16] In addition to causing injury by laceration and crushing, the high-velocity projectile creates considerable damage by the production of shock waves and temporary cavitation.[5,8,16,17] The wound produced may have an entrance similar to that seen in wounds produced by low-velocity weapons, but the exit may vary from small to massive, depending on the types of tissues encountered, the thickness of the target, the impact velocity of the bullet, and the various movements of the bullet as it passes through the target.[2,18] The complexity of the high-velocity wound is considerable, and one must understand the basics of ballistics physics to appreciate the pathophysiology of the wounding process. The mechanisms of this injury are discussed further on in more detail.

Missiles traveling in excess of 4500 ft/sec are considered ultrahigh velocity.[2,5] They are currently under development for military purposes but in the future may be utilized by civilians and law enforcement personnel. These bullets disintegrate upon impact, cause explosive and extensive destruction up to several centimeters in all directions, and usually produce no exit wound.

WOUND BALLISTICS

Ballistics is the study of the motion a projectile acquires during its travel through the barrel of a firearm, its trajectory through the air, and after striking the target.[2] An understanding of basic ballistics physics is important to gain an understanding and appreciation of the nature of the wounding agents and to develop appropriate acumen in the evaluation and treatment of gunshot injuries.

The motion of the bullet in flight and within the tissues after impact depends on several variables. These include the size, shape, composition, and, most important, velocity and stability of the bullet.[17] Elasticity and density are the most important characteristics of tissue that influence the retardation and subsequent energy release of the bullet.[9] The impact velocity is the velocity of the missile when it hits the target. It is the most important ballistic parameter in determining the extent of injury. An impact to velocity of 50 m/sec is required to penetrate skin, and 65 m/sec is required to fracture bone.[8] However, any bullet, regardless of its velocity, is capable of inflicting serious or lethal injury if a vital structure, such as the eye, heart, or brain, is involved. Any wounding agent that can deliver an impact force of 58 pounds is capable of producing significant injury.[19] Compared with ballistics standards, these forces are minimal.

THE PHYSICS OF BALLISTICS

Three physical parameters have been used to explain and predict the damage caused by a bullet upon impact: kinetic energy, power, and momentum. Prior to World War II, the emphasis in the development of small weapons was on the mass of the bullet. Emphasis was placed on the ability of a bullet to knock down and injure, but not kill, the victim. The greater the mass of the bullet, the more likely this goal was achieved. However, more recently, the focus has been on the development of progressively smaller projectiles with increasingly higher and more lethal velocities.[2]

The most commonly utilized physical relationship in the design of modern weaponry is that of the kinetic energy and power of the bullet relative to its velocity. Kinetic energy (KE) is equal to the product of the mass (M) and velocity (V) squared, as in the following equation:

$$KE = \tfrac{1}{2} MV^2$$

Thus, by doubling the mass of the bullet, its kinetic energy is also doubled, but by doubling the velocity, the kinetic energy is quadrupled.[5,9,14]

The power of the bullet is proportional to the dissipation rate of kinetic energy as it passes through the tissue. More practically, it is related directly to the conversion of its kinetic energy into mechanical disruption and, thus, tissue damage. For low-velocity missiles, this relationship is described as follows:

$$P = M(V_{impact} - V_{exit})^2$$

However, as a projectile approaches or exceeds the speed of sound (1100 ft/sec), the rate of dissipation of the kinetic energy becomes proportional to the velocity cubed or to even higher powers.[2] Thus, the damage to tissue in a gunshot wound is much more a function of the velocity of the bullet than of its mass. These relationships have proved invaluable in the development of military weaponry. They have allowed for the creation of firearms that are exponentially more destructive without having to increase the size of the weapon or the bullet. In addition, smaller bullets have greater accuracy and have permitted easier mass transportation of ammunition to remote areas.

If maximal penetration is desired, the physical relationship of momentum can be utilized in the design of the weapon. Since momentum is directly related to mass and velocity equally (Mo = mass × velocity), the development of heavy, fully jacketed bullets that do not deform in tissue and maintain their kinetic energy longer can be utilized. These weapons are most often designed for large game hunting, in which penetration through thick skin, fat, and muscle is necessary to reach a vital organ for "a kill."[14]

Since the most important aspect of the wounding capability is the energy imparted at impact, gunshot wounds should be divided, as previously mentioned, into high-velocity, low-velocity, and shotgun types. With few exceptions, all pistols are low velocity, with kinetic energy of less than 400 ft/lb delivered at the muzzle. The .38-caliber Supervel high-power handgun and the .44 magnum pistol have initial velocities that approach high-caliber status.[2] In contrast, rifle bullets commonly strike with energies approaching 3000 ft/lb and, even at 300 yards, deliver energies of more than 1000 ft/lb. Almost all military firearms have bullets between 140 and 200 grains, with velocities ranging between 2300 ft/sec and 2900 ft/sec at the muzzle.[2,19] The shotgun injury is, in many ways, unique, and its pathophysiology is discussed separately.

Several variables influence the severity of wounds inflicted by similar weapons. For example, the distance between the muzzle and victim is an important factor. When rifle bullet wounds are inflicted at 100 yards or less, wound estimates on the basis of muzzle velocity are an adequate approximation of impact velocity. However, at ranges of 400 to 1000 yards, the impact velocity and wounding capability are reduced remarkably, often approaching those of a low-velocity weapon. Similarly, the wounding capacity of low-velocity weapons is greatly attenuated by target distance.[19]

The shape of a missile is equally important as a factor in wounding capacity.[20] In a bullet, the center of resistance to flight is at the nose, whereas the center of gravity lies well behind the nose. Such a situation is inherently unstable, and when a bullet approaches high velocity, it tends to oscillate around its long axis. This phenomenon is called "yaw." The spin imparted by the rifling of the bore greatly stabilizes the bullet in flight and induces other variations of motion, such as precession and nutation.[9] Precession is a circular form of yawing around the center of gravity that takes the shape of a decreasing spiral. Nutation is a rotational movement in small circles that forms a rosette pattern like a spinning top.[2,5,8,9,16,17]

These complicated movements also help stabilize the bullet in flight. Although they are inadequate for stabilization in media denser than air. Thus, when the bullet hits a target, it immediately becomes unstable as it passes through the target. Also, when the bullet in flight has lost much of its velocity, so that the gyroscopic properties given to it are no longer operative, it may tumble.[9] Tumbling is defined as the action of forward rotation around the center of mass[2,5,8,9,16,17] (Fig. 25–1).

These aerodynamic properties play a critical role in wounding capability because they act to increase the area of tissue the missile strikes as it hits the target. Upon

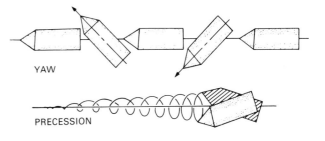

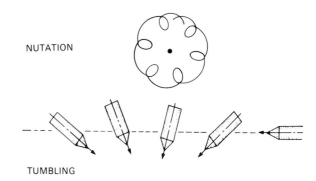

FIGURE 25–1. Variations in the motion of bullets. (Adapted from Swan KG, Swan RG: Gunshot Wounds: Pathophysiology and Management. Littleton, MA, PSG Publishing Company, 1980, p 9.)

impact, there is an increase in the magnitude of these movements as the bullet becomes more unstable. As a result, there is an increase in the retarding force that the tissue places upon the bullet and a corresponding increase in the dissipation of energy from the bullet to the tissues. The tissue damage is proportional to the amount of dissipation of kinetic energy, or the amount of mechanical disruption of tissue along the bullet track. If yaw is minimal and the bullet strikes head on, the bullet will likely traverse the tissues quickly, dissipating its energy over a greater distance with less retardation. It may even completely pass through the target, retaining most of its kinetic energy and causing little damage unless a vital organ is hit. However, a bullet hitting the target with a greater amount of yaw will have a larger surface area of presentation as it strikes, resulting in greater retardation and expenditure of its kinetic energy over a shorter distance. Such a bullet is likely to become even more unstable as it passes from air to tissue and starts to tumble or fragment, increasing its destructive capacity.[9,10,15,19]

The varying degree of tissue injury imparted by identical missiles with the same impact energy can often be explained by the angle at which the bullet strikes the tissue. A nontumbling bullet hitting at right angles to the target will have less contact with the tissues than one striking at an oblique angle. It is also more likely to remain stable as it passes through the target, and upon exit, it will have imparted less kinetic energy. However, a bullet that strikes at an oblique angle is much more likely to become unstable and tumble, thus releasing more of its kinetic energy and causing greater destruction.[12]

CLINICAL CLASSIFICATION OF GUNSHOT INJURIES

A simple way to classify gunshot injuries clinically is to categorize them according to their presentation[16,21]:

1. Penetrating
2. Perforating
3. Avulsive

In the penetrating wound, the missile is retained within the injured tissue. This retention indicates that the tissues have absorbed and dissipated all the kinetic energy of the bullet. This category can be further divided into superficial and deep penetrating injuries. The perforating wound is one in which the missile passes completely through the target. By definition, there is always an entrance and an exit wound. In this type of injury, the tissues absorb only a portion of the kinetic energy of the bullet. The avulsive wound is one in which large segments of hard or soft tissue, or both, are "blown out" of the wound. Usually, there is a small entrance wound and a large, gaping exit wound. These gunshot injuries have the greatest amount of tissue damage.

The penetrating wound is usually caused by low-velocity missiles. The entrance wound is typically small and ragged.[16] As the missile penetrates, the tissues are crushed and forced apart. Usually, only the tissues immediately in contact with the missile are damaged. However, when hard tissues are struck, fracture and comminution with possible displacement may occur. In this way, injury to nearby blood vessels, nerves, and other structures can occur without a direct strike by the bullet.[5,9]

The perforating wound is usually produced by missiles with higher velocities.[16,22] The entry wound is comparable with the size of the missile; however, the exit wound is often considerably larger. If the missile strikes bone or teeth during its course through tissue, secondary missiles may be created that cause more widespread tissue destruction and a larger exit wound.

The avulsive wound is usually caused by high-velocity missiles or rapidly moving artillery or mortar fragments. Those caused by conventional high-velocity bullets have a small entrance compatible with the missile size, whereas the exit wound is

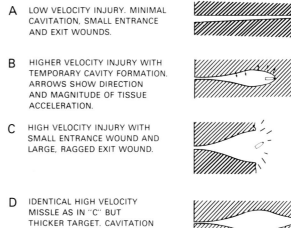

A   LOW VELOCITY INJURY. MINIMAL CAVITATION, SMALL ENTRANCE AND EXIT WOUNDS.

B   HIGHER VELOCITY INJURY WITH TEMPORARY CAVITY FORMATION. ARROWS SHOW DIRECTION AND MAGNITUDE OF TISSUE ACCELERATION.

C   HIGH VELOCITY INJURY WITH SMALL ENTRANCE WOUND AND LARGE, RAGGED EXIT WOUND.

FIGURE 25–2. Missile velocities and the types of wounds they produce. (Adapted from Owen-Smith MS: High Velocity Missile Wounds. London, Edward Arnold, Publisher, 1981, p 18.)

D   IDENTICAL HIGH VELOCITY MISSLE AS IN "C" BUT THICKER TARGET. CAVITATION OCCURS DEEP INSIDE TISSUE; BOTH ENTRANCE AND EXIT WOUNDS ARE SMALL.

E   WOUND PRODUCED BY ULTRAHIGH-VELOCITY PROJECTILE: FRAGMENTATION OF BULLET WITH AVUISION OF TISSUE AND NO EXIT WOUND.

usually a gaping, devastated area with the loss of large amounts of tissue.[16,21] The avulsive wound caused by the new ultrahigh-velocity missiles is, however, different. These missiles are traveling at such high velocity that they disintegrate, upon hitting the target, in an explosive manner. The type of avulsive wound they create is one of extensive damage several centimeters from the point of impact, but there is usually no exit wound[2,5] (Fig. 25–2).

Pathophysiology of the High-Velocity Gunshot Wound

As mentioned previously, the principal mechanism of injury from the low-velocity bullet is laceration and crushing of tissue as the missile traverses the target. The high-velocity missile has two additional very important means of causing extensive soft tissue damage: cavitation and production of pressure and shock waves.[2,5,8,9,16,17]

Cavitation develops during the passage of high-velocity bullets through tissue. When penetration occurs, there is rapid energy release. As energy is absorbed, the tissue starts to flow forward with the projectile. Along the curved surface of the bullet, the flow of the tissue separates from it and continues to flow forward and outward owing to its inertia. Thus, a large cavity is formed that reaches its maximal size in only a few milliseconds and may be 30 to 40 times the diameter of the bullet. The cavity that is produced is vapor filled, with a subatmospheric pressure, and is pulsatile in nature, expanding and collapsing repeatedly with diminishing amplitude. The target tissue eventually comes to rest, leaving a permanent cavity[2,8,9] (Fig. 25–3).

During cavitation, the pressure in the temporary cavity is lower than the ambient air pressure, causing contaminants to be sucked into the wound from both the exit and the entrance sites.[2,8,9] Experiments have shown that when barium sulfate is placed on the skin near the entrance where a high-velocity bullet is to be subsequently fired, there is radiographic evidence of the opaque substance deep within the wound.[23]

Bullets that fragment create much larger permanent cavities and cause extensive damage because of the production of secondary missiles. The secondary missile fragments traverse the tissue prior to the development of the temporary cavity.

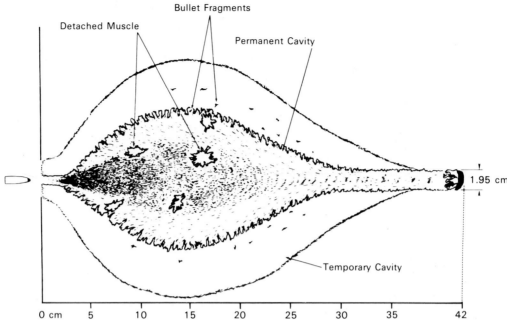

FIGURE 25–3.   Graph shows characteristic wound profile of a high-velocity soft-point bullet in tissue. Note characteristic large temporary and permanent cavities with massive tissue disruption. The wound profile of conventional copper-jacketed high-velocity bullet would reveal a smaller permanent cavity with less tissue destruction but a similar temporary cavity. (From Fackler MI, Bellamy RF, Malinowski JA: The wound profile: Illustration of the missile-tissue interaction. J Trauma [Suppl] 28:21–29, 1988; with permission. Copyright by The Williams and Wilkins Company.)

They macerate and weaken the tissue, so that during cavitation the immediately surrounding tissues are often easily split apart. Exploration of such wounds frequently reveals extensive necrotic, unattached muscle and connective tissue fragments[18,24] (Fig. 25–4).

Gunshot injuries usually involve multiple types of tissue that vary in susceptibility to injury. An important variable is the tensile strength of the involved tissue. Some organs, such as the lung or bowel, are composed of tissues that have predominantly low tensile strength. Therefore, they are more elastic in nature, a characteristic that minimizes damage in spite of allowing for large temporary cavitation. Other organs are composed of tissues with higher tensile strength, such as muscle, skin, and liver. These organs offer more resistance to cavitation but are much more severely damaged by absorption of the bullet's kinetic energy. For example, bone is the least elastic organ in the body and the most resistant to cavitation. It is also the most severely damaged organ when struck by a high-velocity missile.[9,25]

The clinical presentation of the high-velocity injury may vary considerably from the stereotypical small entrance, large exit wound. This variation may often be due to the nature of the target.[2] For example, if the target is thick, the maximal absorption of kinetic energy and temporary cavitation may occur deep within the tissues. On exiting the target, the bullet's velocity may have been diminished to that of a low-velocity weapon. This wound would look deceptively innocuous and resemble a low-velocity injury with a small entrance-and-exit wound. However, it is still a high-velocity injury, with the characteristic severe destruction hidden deep within the target. If the bullet breaks up in the wound, it may transfer all of its kinetic energy to the tissue and not exit the target. This wound may also look benign, but it is, in reality, severe, with massive internal injuries from extensive cavitation and secondary missiles (Fig. 25–2).

Exploration of high-velocity wounds may not reveal as large a permanent cavity or as much grossly displaced bony tissues as one might expect. Because of the elasticity

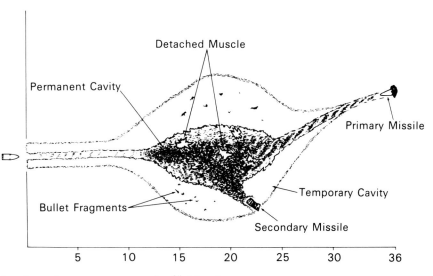

FIGURE 25–4. Graph shows characteristic wound profile of a high-velocity bullet that fragments in tissue. Note the massive amount of tissue destruction, detached muscle, and penetrating bullet fragments in addition to the large permanent and temporary cavities. (From Fackler MI, Bellamy RF, Malinowski JA: The wound profile: Illustration of the missile-tissue interaction. J Trauma [Suppl] 28:21–29, 1988; with permission. Copyright by The Williams and Wilkins Company.)

of tissue, the final wound is much smaller than the temporary cavity.[25] Also, because of connective tissue attachment, many of the bone fragments that become grossly displaced and act like secondary missiles during cavitation are drawn back close to their original position after passage of the bullet.[8,22]

The final mechanism of tissue injury from high-velocity missiles is by the production of shock and pressure waves.[2,8,9,16,17] As the missile is forcing a track through the tissue, it compresses the medium in front of it, causing compression waves that advance ahead of the projectile. Strong shock waves occur if the projectile has sufficient velocity to set tissue in motion at a speed equal to or higher than its sonic velocity.[9] The intensity of the shock wave that is produced is very high but lasts only for microseconds and causes comparatively little damage.[9,18] Nonetheless, it has been demonstrated that these waves can cause rupture of cell membranes, indirect bone fractures, coagulation of proteins, and distortion of peripheral and central nerve axoplasm in areas remote from the immediate wound.[23,26,27,28] Low-intensity pressure waves are also produced and are connected with the movements of the temporary cavity. They are measured in milliseconds.[18] Harvey and colleagues[29] demonstrated pulses as high as 200 atm during the impact of a high-velocity missile when recording devices were placed on the bodies of experimental animals. These positive forces were followed by a negative phase in which all measured areas were under tension. Blood vessels, nerves, and viscera have been shown to be damaged and even bones have been fractured by the compressive forces in areas distant from the bullet track or temporary cavity.[25,26,30] It has been hypothesized that fascial planes may act as conduits for the widespread dissipation of this energy.[18]

Biologic Response to Gunshot Wounds

The transfer of kinetic energy from a projectile to tissue is a direct cause of tissue damage. In addition to the local physical damage that is produced, there are the effects of altered tissue physiology distant from the immediately damaged area that play an important role in the overall morbidity of the injury. These include changes in microcirculation, regional circulation, electrolyte composition, water content, and metabolism. The sum of these changes has been shown to cause delayed tissue necrosis and enhanced wound infection. Holmstrom and colleagues[31] found that there were marked changes in sodium, potassium, magnesium, and chloride composition in tissue that appeared discolored after sustaining injury from a high-velocity bullet. The degree of electrolyte imbalance increased in severity when measured at 1, 5, and 10 hours. The changes in electrolyte composition corresponded proportionally to the changes in color. In discolored tissue, there was a marked increase in extracellular sodium and chloride and a decrease in potassium and magnesium suggestive of nonviability. These investigations demonstrate that although the criteria used to determine tissue viability in gunshot wounds, such as color, capillary bleeding, and contractility, may seem crude, they are nonetheless accurate according to histologic and biochemical analysis.

Almskog and associates[32] measured local metabolic changes in skeletal muscle following high-velocity missile injury by taking biopsies at 1, 2, 4, and 5 hours after injury from areas 8 mm, 16 mm, 24 mm, and 32 mm from the bullet track. Biopsies taken at 8 mm showed significantly decreased levels of adenosine triphosphate (ATP), creatine phosphate (CP), and glucose-6-phosphate (G-6-P) throughout the study. There were also persistent increased levels of glucose and lactate. These results indicate that a hypoxic state with metabolic changes consistent with irreversible cell damage occurs within 8 mm of the bullet path. The remaining biopsied areas had comparatively minimal metabolic and histologic changes. A similar study by Larsson and colleagues[33] compared metabolic changes in skeletal muscle injuries by low-velocity versus high-velocity projectiles. Their results were similar with respect to the high-velocity injury but showed only minimal metabolic changes in even the most immediate tissue around the wound channel produced by the low-velocity bullet. A similar study demonstrated that regardless of the missile shape the amount of necrotic tissue debrided from the hind legs of dogs was directly dependent on the impact velocity. Wounds produced by missiles having an impact velocity of 1400 m/sec required three to five times the amount of tissue extirpation required by those produced by missiles with impact velocities of 700 m/sec.

It has been demonstrated that early surgical debridement plays an important role in minimizing the ultimate loss of tissue. A highly significant increase in the amount of devitalized tissue was found when debridement was delayed from 6 to 12 hours, according to a study by Dahlgren and coworkers.[34] This investigation compared the amount of debrided muscle deemed nonviable by impaired contractility, discoloration, and lack of capillary bleeding at 1, 6, and 12 hours. Compared with the first hour, the amount of tissue that needed to be debrided was greater at 6 hours and even greater after 12 hours. Re-exploration of wounds debrided at 1 hour was done 12 hours later and showed that no further debridement was necessary.

It is thought that changes in metabolism as well as in microcirculation and macrocirculation occur along the wound track, leading to a zone of irreversible nonviability. The devitalized tissue (especially muscle) is an ideal medium for bacterial growth and, if not removed, will promote local infection. The establishment of infection compromises injured tissue even more, resulting in further devitalization. Huiming and colleagues[35] showed, in dogs, that for bullets with impact velocities between 730 and 1570 m/sec wounds are initially contaminated with 10^2 bacteria per gram of tissue. The number of aerobic bacteria in devitalized muscle tissue measured 10^3 to 10^4/gm at 6 hours and 10^5 at 12 and 24 hours. The number of anaerobes at 6 hours was 10^4. Considering that the critical level of bacteria needed per gram of tissue to cause infection is 10^5 to 10^6, the necessity of early debridement is obvious. In addition, since the patient's resistance is likely to be reduced from the systemic manifestations of the injury, an even smaller population of bacteria may be able to cause infection. Dahlgren and colleagues[36] later demonstrated that the use of penicillin retards devitalization for up to 12 hours. Wounds in animals treated with penicillin and debrided 12 hours after injury resembled those of animals debrided at 6 hours but not covered by antibiotics.[37]

Regardless of velocity, gunshot wounds are always contaminated, since they are primarily soiled with infectious agents.[22,35,38] In 1892, Lager first demonstrated that a bullet is not sterilized by being fired from a gun when he was able to transmit anthrax to animals by shooting them with bullets that had been contaminated with the blood of animals dying of the disease. The later work of Thoresby[23] and others confirmed that high-velocity bullets also are not sterilized by the act of firing. Bullets inoculated with a heat-labile vegetative organism fired through sterile nutrient-enriched gelatin will produce bacterial growth along the whole length of the bullet track.[24] The contamination of the gunshot wound is exponentially enhanced by debris that is sucked into the wound secondary to cavitation. Dziemian and Herget[38] have shown that barium sulfate powder and various dye stuffs could be drawn into the entrance and exit wounds by cavitation in both animal and gelatin block tissue models.

TREATMENT OF GUNSHOT INJURIES

The management of facial gunshot wounds can be divided into the following three phases[16,39]:

1. Primary
2. Intermediate
3. Reconstructive

The primary phase (Fig. 25–5) includes the resuscitative efforts that are required to stabilize the patient. Especially important is the establishment of an airway and restoration of hemodynamics. The airway must be guaranteed. Cleaning the oropharynx of blood, teeth or bone fragments, and displaced soft tissue must be attended to promptly. Patients with significant orofacial gunshot injuries should be intubated as soon as possible owing to impending edema and airway obstruction.[5,21] An immediate

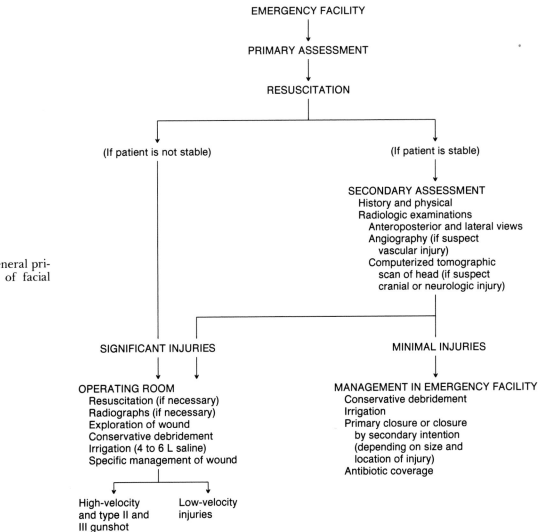

FIGURE 25–5. General primary management of facial gunshot injuries.

tracheostomy or cricothyroidotomy may be necessary, but if possible, this is best managed in the operating room with a patient who has been previously intubated orally. The control of bleeding is also very important. In addition to the potential development of hemodynamic instability and shock, excessive bleeding in an unintubated patient may severely compromise the ability to breathe. The aspiration of large blood clots may even obstruct the upper airway. Blindly clamping and cauterizing tissue in an attempt to stop bleeding should be avoided, since permanent damage can be rendered to the facial nerve or the salivary gland ducts. In most cases, a pressure pack over the bleeding area will slow the hemorrhage adequately until the patient can be brought to the operating room and selective ligation can be accomplished under more controlled conditions.

If packing and selective ligation fail to bring severe hemorrhage under control, consideration must be given to either unilateral or, occasionally, bilateral external carotid artery ligation. It must be appreciated that because of many vascular anastomoses severe bleeding may still occur, especially from the ophthalmic and ethmoidal arteries (branches of the internal carotid artery), the vertebral arteries via the circle of Willis, and the numerous veins that are present.[5] Another alternative is to pack the wound, locate the lacerated arterial vessels angiographically, and embolize them proximal to the laceration. In addition, neurosurgical and ophthalmologic injuries should be suspected and, if discovered, treated by the appropriate specialty.[40]

Also included in the primary phase of treatment is the early, definitive management of the facial injuries. Although wounds in other regions of the body require generous debridement and delayed primary closure, immediate primary closure with minimal debridement is more appropriate for wounds of the head and neck and results in lower morbidity.[16] The surgical treatment plan should always be approached in an orderly and systematic manner. Treatment objectives should include the following[5,16,21,40,41]:

1.   Repairing injuries to the eye and cranial nerves as well as protecting them from possible iatrogenic injury during surgery
2.   Preserving as much bony and soft tissue as possible
3.   Debriding only obviously nonviable tissue and removing accessible portions of bullets, wadding, or cartridge packing
4.   Stabilizing the bony framework by the simplest and most direct method feasible
5.   Closing the soft tissue primarily if possible
6.   Placing the patient on antibiotic therapy

If the patient is hemodynamically stable and control of the upper airway is established, then radiographs, including lateral and plain films, should be taken prior to surgery to help determine the location and extent of injury as well as the potential location of the bullet or its fragments. Computerized tomography (CT) is especially useful, since visualization of the cranial contents, the orbital and periorbital anatomy, and the major vessels is possible.[40] High-frequency ultrasonography has also been used to help localize bullets.[42] This technique is potentially very useful, since it is relatively easy to do either at the bedside or in the operating room during surgery (Fig. 25–6A and B).

Any evidence of injury near major arterial vessels of the maxillofacial area or penetration of the bullet into the neck should be investigated by carotid angiography.[43–46] Since the maxillofacial complex is one of the most vascular areas of the body, concomitant vascular injury is frequently seen. In addition to the obvious major bleeding encountered acutely by damage to a major vessel, delayed complications can be just as serious and deadly. These include arterial thrombosis, arteriovenous fistula formation, bullet embolus, and pseudoaneurysm.[43] The mortality in patients with penetrating wounds to the neck is between 3 and 6 per cent. The mortality is even higher if the penetrating wounds are limited to gunshot injuries.[44] In low-velocity injuries, damage to the vascular structures usually occurs only if the

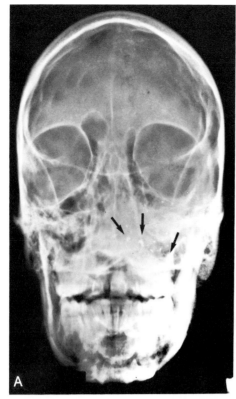
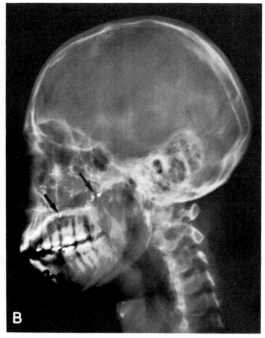

FIGURE 25–6. *A,* Anteroposterior radiograph of a patient who sustained a perforating low-velocity missile injury to the face. Arrows show distribution of bullet fragments along the missile path. Note that the fragments can be visualized only in a mediolateral direction with this view. *B,* Lateral radiograph of the same patient. Arrows show the location of bullet fragments along the missile path in an anteroposterior direction. By combining information in both radiographs and noting the relative sizes of the bullet fragments and their positions, the path of the bullet can be estimated. This patient was shot in the anterior left cheek, and the bullet traversed medially and posteriorly, exiting near the midline in the nasopharynx. Additional abdominal radiographs demonstrated that the remainder of the bullet had been swallowed.

vessel is hit. The missile deforms the vessel as it tears through its walls. The unpredictability of injury in this case is due to the course of the bullet and the chance of its hitting a major vessel.[47,48] In high-velocity injuries, damage to major vessels can occur even if they are not directly struck. The formation of the temporary cavity causes vascular damage by the production of severe stretching and tearing of the arterial tissue distant to the bullet.[30,47,48] If vascular injury is demonstrated arteriographically, surgical exploration and treatment can be more accurately planned and executed[43] (Figs. 25–7A and B and 25–8).

The wound should be thoroughly inspected while the patient is under general anesthesia, with careful unfolding and exploration. Many wounds that initially appear avulsive in nature may actually have little or no tissue loss and can easily be reconstructed and closed primarily.[40] After the wound is fully examined and the extent of the injury is known, conservative debridement and copious irrigation with as much as 4 to 6 L of saline should be performed.[49] This step is one of the most important in the primary management of the wound, since, by definition, gunshot wounds are both dirty and contaminated. In addition to lavage, all dirt and debris must be mechanically removed from the wound to prevent a tattoo scar as well as to minimize the chance of infection.[50] The tissues may need to be scrubbed with surgical soap.[49,51] Failure to adequately cleanse the wound creates an environment optimal for bacterial growth and subsequent severe infection. The use of antibiotics and anti-infective agents suspended in the irrigation medium remains controversial.[21]

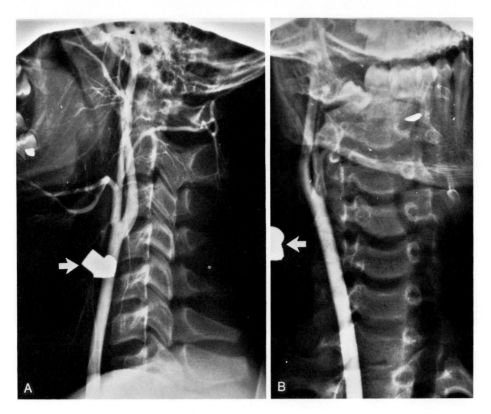

FIGURE 25–7. *A,* Lateral view of the neck during angiography. Radiograph reveals no damage to the common carotid artery in spite of the apparent close proximity of the bullet *(arrow). B,* Anteroposterior view of same patient during angiography. This radiograph reveals the true distance of the remaining bullet from the common carotid artery *(arrow).*

The use of pulsating jet lavage systems is an excellent way to clean a contaminated wound. The initial 50 to 70 psi compressive force, followed by the decompression interpulse phase, helps loosen the foreign debris, which is then washed out by the lavage. The cycle is repeated up to 800 pulsations per minute and has been shown to be three times more effective than bulb syringe lavage and seven times more effective than lavage by a conventional irrigation syringe.[52]

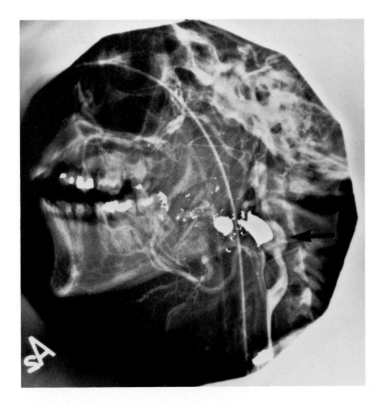

FIGURE 25–8. Angiography of patient sustaining gunshot wound to posterior mandible. Arrows show development of pseudoaneurysm in the internal carotid artery secondary to trauma inflicted by bullet.

If the bullet or its fragments are encountered during the exploration or debridement of the wound, they should be removed. However, without proper localization, the dissection and retrieval of a bullet is fraught with potential hazards, such as massive bleeding. Therefore, unless these objects have been documented to be close to vital structures, they are best left undisturbed.[40]

Since the tissues of the face have an excellent blood supply, they are more resistant to infection than are other areas of the body. Therefore, as conservative a debridement as possible should be done. Only obviously nonviable tissue should be removed, along with debris found within the wound. No bone that has an appreciable soft tissue attachment should be removed.[5,16,21,39,49] Teeth that are fractured with pulp exposure and are of no use in the immobilization of the fractures may be taken out, provided that by doing so there is no significant loss of alveolar bone. If this situation exists, the teeth should be retained, and either endodontic therapy is started or extractions are planned 4 to 6 weeks after bone consolidation.[5]

The basic principles in the immediate reconstruction of the gunshot wound are similar to those employed for other types of hard and soft tissue facial trauma: The deepest part of the soft tissue is closed first, and progress is made from the inside outward, so that skin is closed last.[51] The repair of skeletal fractures should start at the mandible and work upward to the most superior extent of bone injury. The continuity of the mandible must be established first to create a stable base for further reconstruction and to restore occlusion. Next, the remaining facial bones are repaired, working upward from the stabilized mandible. Bone repair should ideally be accomplished so that the contour attained is as close to normal as possible.[21,49]

For high-velocity injuries, the simplest and most direct method of fracture stabilization should be employed. Usually, maxillomandibular fixation is preferred; however, interosseous wiring and occasionally miniplates may be used if necessary.[5,16,21] Simplicity in treatment is recommended, since in these severely comminuted and contaminated wounds, the additional trauma of an open procedure in an already compromised area may exceed the physiologic ability of the bone to undergo repair. This extra burden would likely lead to devitalization of the bone fragments and loss of bony substance. The necessary additional stripping of mucoperiosteal attachment to bone fragments that is required in the adaptation and fixation of bone plates should preclude their use in severe injuries. Instead, such wounds should be treated in a closed fashion to ensure primary healing and early opportunity for bone grafting.[16] The use of the biphasic external pin fixation device to prevent collapse of the mandibular arch as well as to provide stability is often invaluable in these types of cases[5] (Fig. 25–9A and B).

The amount of injury produced from low-velocity weapons is usually considerably less than that produced by high-velocity weapons. This difference plays an important role in the management of these injuries (Figs. 25–10 and 25–11). Following conservative debridement, definitive primary reconstruction is more likely to be successful in the low-velocity injury. Techniques that include the use of alloplastic implant materials, such as stainless steel, cobalt-chromium alloy (Vitallium), or titanium, can be more predictably used. These include miniplates and meshed cribs to support autogenous bone grafts for the mandible. Similarly, miniplates may be utilized in the midface along the onlay calvarial, rib, or iliac bone grafts to repair discontinuity defects and restore facial form and function. They also provide a framework that resists soft tissue contracture, which is so difficult to correct secondarily. If successful, these efforts often expedite recovery, minimize the resulting defect, and prove more comfortable for the patient. However, they should be attempted only if there is adequate soft tissue coverage for both an intraoral and an extraoral closure, if the wound is treated early (preferably within 24 hours), and if the patient is in otherwise good health and can withstand the greater blood loss and operative time in the acute setting. Immediate reconstruction should not be attempted in massive or grossly contaminated injuries[40] (Fig. 25–12A to D).

Soft tissue associated with gunshot injuries of the face is often ragged, involves

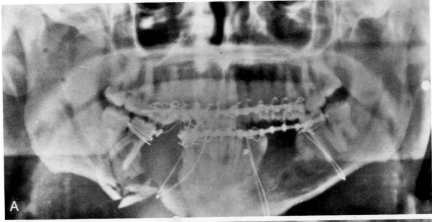
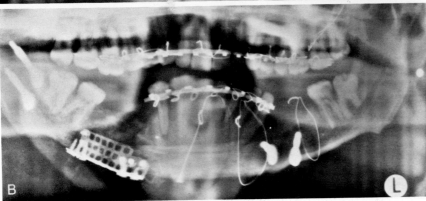

FIGURE 25–9. *A*, Radiograph shows closed reduction of an avulsive gunshot injury to the mandible utilizing arch bars, circum-mandibular skeletal wire, and maxillomandibular fixation. This patient was initially treated in a conservative manner owing to the severity of the soft tissue injury and the magnitude of bony comminution. *B*, Radiograph shows reconstruction of same patient using iliac corticocancellous bone graft, titanium mesh tray, and external biphasic pin fixation. Although a nonunion developed after initial conservative treatment, most of the comminuted segments survived and consolidated. This factor facilitated the final reconstruction by minimizing the amount of required bone graft and decreasing the amount of surgical exposure.

the mouth, and may include special structures, such as nerves and salivary ducts. Closure must start intraorally for injuries that involve the mouth, thus converting a through-and-through defect to an extraoral wound. After this conversion is attained, the injury should be irrigated again, reprepared and draped, and closed from the inside out. Injured parotid or submandibular ducts should be cannulated, and the

ASSESSMENT

↓

RESUSCITATION

↓

GENERAL PRIMARY MANAGEMENT

↓

SPECIFIC PRIMARY MANAGEMENT
  Skeletal wire fixation
  Intermaxillary fixation
  External biphasic pin fixation (if necessary)
  Attempted primary closure (If not possible, close skin to mucosa or pack wound and consider delayed primary closure or skin graft in 5 to 10 days)
  Drainage of submandibular and submental spaces if extensively involved
  Antibiotic coverage

(3 to 6 months)

↓

DEFINITIVE SECONDARY RECONSTRUCTION

FIGURE 25–10. Management of high-velocity injuries and types II and III shotgun injuries.

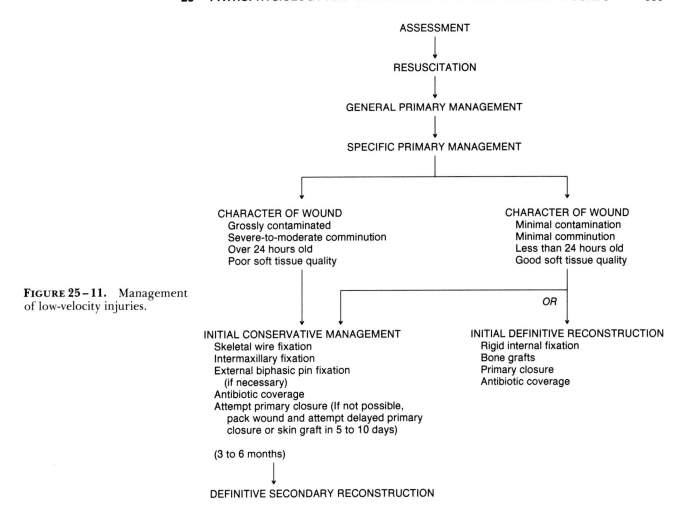

FIGURE 25–11. Management of low-velocity injuries.

cannula should be sewn into place to permit the drainage of saliva to prevent salivary fistula formation. The cannula should be allowed to remain in place as long as possible until the sutures are resorbed and it is expelled. This is generally a period of 3 to 4 weeks. If the submaxillary gland or duct is significantly damaged, it is best to remove the gland. Branches of the facial nerve that are encountered should be repaired primarily. If this is not possible, they should be marked with a nonresorbable suture for possible future repair.[5,21]

Wounds treated in the first 24 hours can usually be closed primarily without the use of a drain. Wounds seen after this period should be treated by delayed primary closure and drained. For more extensive wounds that involve the mandible, with loss of osseous structure and involvement of the oral cavity, a drain should be placed. In addition, wounds that involve the submandibular space should be drained.

Wound edges should be minimally excised by no more than 1 to 2 mm to create a nonbeveled margin. If necessary, skin can be mobilized by undermining the edges and can be closed primarily. Such undermining should not exceed 5 cm and, if possible, should be supported by subcutaneous sutures to minimize skin tension. If necessary, rotational flaps can be utilized to close larger avulsed areas. Careful consideration must be given to designing these flaps. First, they must not exaggerate the deformity, and second, they must come from donor tissue that is healthy. Areas that cannot be closed by flaps may be packed with fine mesh gauze that is changed frequently to allow secondary epithelialization. In 3 to 5 days, when healthy granulation tissue covers the wound, a full- or split-thickness skin graft can be used to help prevent wound contracture. Another alternative is to cover the wound with a split-thickness skin graft initially. Even if the graft does not take, it acts as a good temporary biologic

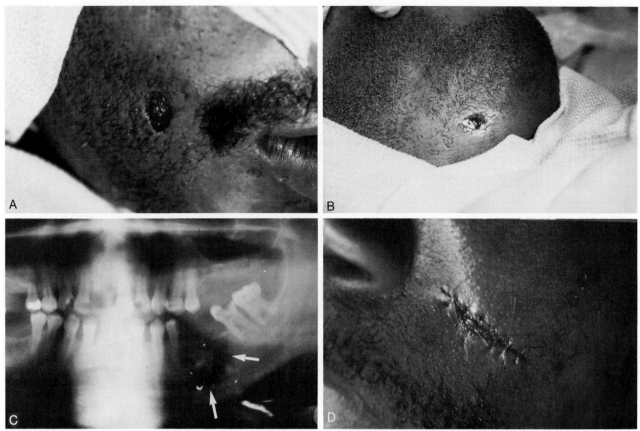

FIGURE 25–12. *A,* Example of low-velocity entrance wound in the cheek. Note the small, ragged, spherical nature of the wound. *B,* Example of low-velocity exit wound in opposite submandibular area of same patient. Note similar size and character of wound. *C,* Radiograph of same patient. Arrows show avulsive bony defect of mandible with multiple small bullet fragments. Note remaining continuity of the mandible at the inferior border. This patient was treated by conservative debridement, irrigation, and primary closure of all wounds. *D,* Example of low-velocity wound closed primarily after minimal debridement, irrigation, and excision of ragged margins.

dressing.[21,41] If the soft tissue deficit is through and through, involving the mouth, and is too large for primary closure, the postoperative wound contracture and scarring can be minimized by suturing the mucosal edges to the skin edges on the outside of the wound[16] (Fig. 25–13*A* to *F*).

FIGURE 25–13. *A,* Example of self-inflicted high-velocity gunshot wound to the lower face. Note the severity of soft tissue damage and the apparent avulsive character of the wound. *B,* Same patient with wound fully exposed prior to debridement and irrigation. Note the massive extent of soft tissue injury as well as the avulsive injury to the anterior maxilla and mandible. Also note the uneven, scalloped margins of the soft tissue wound. *C,* Postoperative radiograph revealing the extent of bony defect in the maxilla and mandible. Considerable debridement of bone was necessary because of severe comminution, lack of periosteal attachment, and contamination. *D,* Beginning of soft tissue closure. Note how margins of the wound can be "keyed" into place in spite of their seemingly random, scalloped appearance. Initial reapproximation of critical aesthetic and functional areas, such as the eyebrows, eyelids, ala of nose, and margins of the lips, should be accomplished first. This measure facilitates proper reorientation of the remaining soft tissue. *E,* Final primary closure of wound as viewed by orientation similar to that in *A.* In spite of the initial disoriented, avulsive-appearing character of the wound, little soft tissue was lost. Thus, by careful exploration, minimal debridement, and proper reorientation of margins, many gunshot wounds can be adequately closed primarily. *F,* Radiograph of secondary reconstruction of mandibular defect using block iliac bone graft.

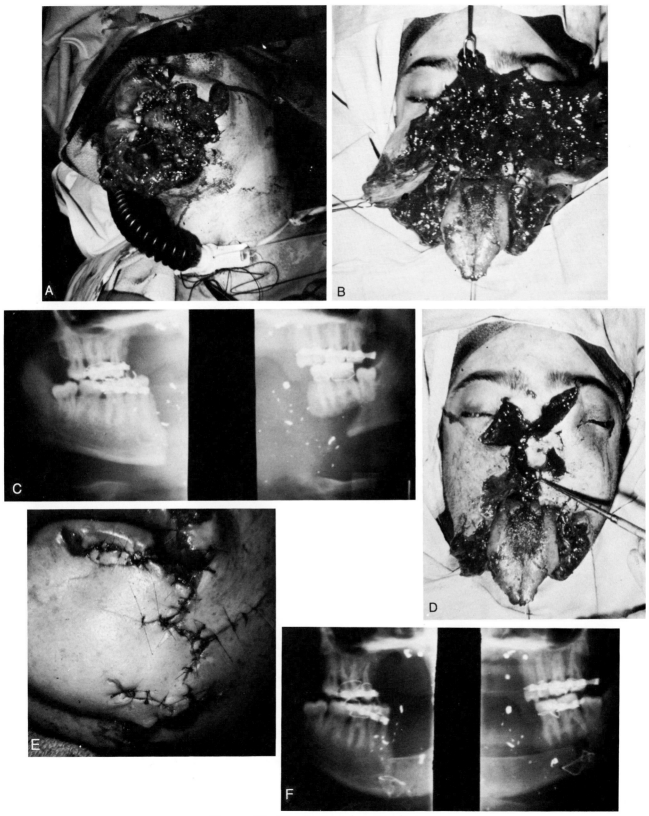

FIGURE 25–13. *See legend on opposite page.*

Intermediate Care

The intermediate phase includes supportive care and the prevention and treatment of complications, such as hemorrhage, infection, and sequestration.[16,39] During this phase, treatment rendered earlier should be reviewed and evaluated. Potential complications must be anticipated so that efforts can be directed to prevent their occurrence.

Proper wound care during this phase is mandatory. Soft tissue injuries can be guarded from infection by removal of crusts and nonviable tissue from the surface of the wound and by proper utilization of systemic antibiotics. The dressing should be changed regularly, and drains and sutures should be removed at the appropriate time. Long-term application of topical antibiotics is ineffective in preventing wound infection and may even select for resistant organisms. Wounds in the lower facial region are often bathed in saliva and thus are contaminated by oral flora from the mouth. The selection of antibiotics should, therefore, be directed toward a mixed gram-positive and gram-negative population and should be preferably bactericidal. In orofacial wounds, penicillin is the initial drug of choice, but any purulent material should be cultured and antibiotic sensitivity established. If infection is suspected, a thorough inspection of the injury, with re-evaluation of the therapy, should be carried out. It may be necessary to change antibiotics, remove fractured teeth, debride necrotic bone of soft tissue, and perform an incision and drainage.[40]

The general supportive care of the patient during this phase of recovery is also very important. The patient's fluid, electrolyte, and nutritional status should be closely evaluated.[21,39] Initially, the patient may be supported by intravenous fluids alone, but an effort should be made to feed the patient as soon as possible. Early placement of a nasogastric tube is helpful. This tube may function at first to decompress the stomach, evacuate swallowed blood, and reduce the incidence of nausea and vomiting. Later it can be used for feeding purposes. A well-balanced, high-calorie liquid diet is essential.[40,41]

Finally, attention must be directed to helping the patient from a psychosocial standpoint. These individuals are often victims of either an assault or a suicide attempt and suffer psychologically as much as physically. Early consultation with a psychiatrist, social service worker, and occupational therapist may be invaluable in helping this type of patient.

Reconstructive Phase

The reconstructive phase of treatment involves those patients who have some sort of residual defect.[39] It is usually directed toward the repair of scars and soft tissue deformities, closure of fistulae, obliteration of bone defects, and restoration of dental occlusion.[50] Severe gunshot wounds to the face differ often from other forms of mutilating facial trauma in that tissue loss is real, not just apparent, and the wounds are both superficial and deep. In many cases, both hard and soft tissue has been lost. Most often, the kinds of deformity encountered at the reconstructive stage include the following:

1. Deficient soft tissue
2. Deficient bony tissue
3. Microstomia
4. Fibrous union of bone segments
5. Fibrotic ankylosis of the temporomandibular joint (with restriction of mandibular function)
6. Lack of satisfactory foundation for a prosthesis[16,41]

General goals to be attained by reconstruction include the following:

1. Rebuilding facial features for functional as well as aesthetic reasons

2. Restoring function of the eyes, nose, and mouth
3. Closing the tracheostomy, if necessary
4. Integrating the patient back into society

The ultimate final treatment plan will depend on many variables, but the following conditions are most likely and should be treated if present:

1. Release of wound cicatrization
2. Restoration of the nasolacrimal system
3. Repair of motor and sensory nerves
4. Reconstruction of soft tissue continuity
5. Development of an adequate soft tissue bed for subsequent bone grafting if necessary
6. Reduction and fixation of bone segments using bone grafts if needed[39,40]

Since reconstruction involves both soft and hard tissue management, if a discontinuity defect exists, preparation should be made for bone grafting at the earliest practical time.[39] It is necessary to ensure that soft tissue coverage for the osseous grafts is sufficient and that no residual infection is present. Because of the risks of avascular necrosis, infection, and bone dehiscence, definite tissue replacement is best done when the wounds are completely epithelialized with mature, softened scars. This epithelialization is unlikely to occur before 3 to 6 months after injury.

Although every effort is made to attain good soft tissue closure during the initial treatment phases, it is likely in more severe injuries that secondary procedures will be needed. Small defects can be closed by undermining the wound margins or by rotating tissue with the use of local flaps.[16] Larger defects may require more significant flap design, ranging from localized areas of the face and neck, such as lateral and central forehead flaps, neck flap, and scalp flaps, to more distant areas, such as the pectoralis major myocutaneous flap, latissimus dorsi flaps, or free microvascular composite grafts. Myocutaneous and free microvascular grafts should be reserved for only the most extensive defects. Smaller fistulae can usually be closed by excising the edges and suturing the margins. Larger fistulae ordinarily require closure in two layers. The margins of the fistula should be excised, turned in, and sutured to repair the mucosal side. The cutaneous aspect is closed by utilizing a local transpositional flap.[41]

After primary treatment, one can almost always anticipate the need for minor cosmetic soft tissue procedures, usually as a result of scar contracture. The most frequently affected areas are the external canthus of the eye, the alar base of the nose, and the commissures of the mouth. The symmetry of these areas is essential from an aesthetic and functional standpoint. Other areas often in need of reconstruction are the vermilion border of the lip, position of the hairline, and remaining residual scars.[40,41]

Bone replacement can be provided by grafts from the cranium, iliac crest, or ribs or from allogeneic sources.[16,29] In addition, bone can be obtained as part of a vascularized composite-free graft from the ilium, the radius, or the rib.[40] Regardless of the choice, all grafts serve to restore normal continuity and function as well as improve facial appearance.[39] Autogenous bone has been used most extensively and successfully in both solid and particulate form.[50] If used in particulate form, a framework is needed to contain the graft, usually titanium or cobalt-chromium alloy (Vitallium) mesh or allogeneic bone crib.[39]

In planning the bone reconstruction, the following principles must be considered. The patient should otherwise be in good health, and the graft bed must consist of healthy tissue free from infection or significant scar tissue and must have good vascularity. Strict attention must be given to performing the operation using aseptic techniques, and the graft must be handled carefully to prevent contamination. There must be absolute fixation and immobilization of the graft to the host bone, and the wound should be closed in layers without tension. Hematoma formation must be prevented, and the patient should be placed on a regimen of appropriate antibiotics.[39]

After reconstruction, a prolonged period of rehabilitation can be expected.

Scarring and fibrosis, which restrict mandibular movement, often occur as a result of facial and masticatory muscle injury. Restriction is also common following prolonged maxillomandibular fixation. It may also occur secondary to contraction of facial scars or scalp wounds, especially when the temporalis muscle has been injured. During this period after the consolidation of bone grafts, vigorous stretching and masticatory exercises should be started. If done conscientiously, there will usually be a marked improvement in mandibular function. Occasionally, cases that do not progress may require surgical intervention.[16]

The watertight closure of the oral mucosa that is needed during primary treatment will often leave the patient with little or no vestibular depth. This condition prevents normal masticatory function and may preclude the fabrication of a denture. The releasing of scars and the use of the split-thickness vestibuloplasty can usually correct this situation.[16,39] In some cases, complete rehabilitation may include restoration of the appearance with a maxillofacial prosthesis in addition to a well-designed dental prosthesis. The inclusion of a maxillofacial prosthodontist early in the dental rehabilitation of such patients is indicated.[16]

Considering the magnitude of many of these gunshot injuries, the cosmetic result is often less than what was anticipated by the patient. Early in the reconstruction effort, the patient should be realistically informed of the limitations imposed by the injury. Similarly, the patient should be told to anticipate multiple minor procedures, such as scar revisions, to complete the reconstruction. It is important that mental health be considered throughout the lengthy physical restoration process in victims of gunshot injuries. Psychiatrists and social service workers should be actively involved throughout the surgical sequences of care and thereafter. All too frequently, the realization that no additional improvement is possible can cause extreme depression and possibly result in suicide.

SHOTGUN WOUNDS TO THE HEAD AND NECK

Shotguns deserve special consideration, since the design of the weapon and the types of injuries they produce are in many ways unique. For example, the amount of tissue destruction produced by identical shotguns is highly variable. At one extreme, they may produce injuries consisting of only a few scattered and insignificant pellet wounds. On the other hand, they may cause devastating wounds, similar to those caused by close-range high-velocity weapons.[53]

The severity of injury produced by a shotgun is most dependent on the distance of the victims from the muzzle of the gun.[53] Other contributing factors include the shotgun gauge, cartridge size, pellet load, powder charge, and angle of the shot.[11] The importance of these factors is explained by the characteristics of the shotgun and its ammunition. As stated earlier, the shotgun has a muzzle velocity of about 1000 ft/sec. This velocity is higher than that of most handguns but lower than that of most rifles. The velocity falls rapidly, however, and the maximal range is usually only about 100 yards. The shotgun shell consists of a paper or plastic tube and a brass base that encloses the gunpowder, wadding, primer, and pellets. After being fired, the shell and wadding fall away at approximately 6.09 m. The resulting spray of pellets then spreads out about 2.5 cm for each meter traveled. Thus, at 10 yards the shot forms a 7-inch circle, while at 40 yards it forms a 36-inch circle.[54] Considering the initial velocity and compact nature of gunshot ammunition, the devastating nature of close-range shotgun injuries is easily understood. Similarly, because of the rapid dispersal and dimunition velocity of the pellets, the marked decrease in injury with distance is explained (Figs. 25–14 and 25–15).

Shotgun wounds have often been described as self-inflicted, close range, or long range in nature.[40] Although seemingly descriptive, this classification system is some-

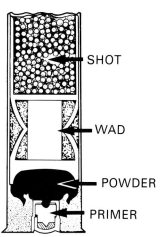

FIGURE 25-14. Diagram of cross-section of a shotgun shell. (From DeMuth WE: The mechanism of shotgun wounds. J Trauma 11:219–229, 1971; with permission. Copyright by The Williams and Wilkins Company.)

what ambiguous and does little to characterize the relationship of injury to the observed physical characteristics of the weapon and ammunition. Sherman and Parrish[55] improved the classification by correlating the distance traveled by the shot with the type of injury produced. These injuries were classified as types I, II, and III. Type I injuries include those inflicted from a relatively long range, over 7 m. In this type of wound, penetration of the pellets is usually restricted to subcutaneous tissue or deep fascia. The farther the victim is from the gun, the fewer the number of pellets are likely to strike, and their penetration will be less. Except for possible injury to specialized structures such as the eyes or ears, these types of injuries cause little significant morbidity. Type II injuries are produced at a range of 3 to 7 yards. They are perforating in nature and capable of entering body cavities. Although the charge is still compact, it has started to disperse. The wound is usually 5 to 12 cm in diameter and is intermediate in severity. Type III injuries occur when the victim is less than 3 yards from the gun muzzle. They are the most destructive of the shotgun injuries and are characterized by massive soft and hard tissue destruction and virtually a 100 per cent infection rate. With this type of injury, the entire charge, including shell fragments, wadding, pellets, and unburned gunpowder, implodes into the tissue.[12] In addition, hair and clothing are carried into the wound.[33] In contrast to the gunshot wound, in which tissue loss is usually more apparent than real, the shotgun wound at close range is often truly avulsive. The wound may be gaping in nature, with multiple comminuted bone fractures and extensively contused, lacerated, and contaminated soft tissue. In almost all cases, these injuries involve the oral, nasal, and pharyngeal cavities.[12]

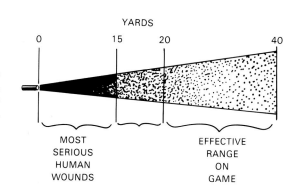

FIGURE 25-15. Side view diagram of shot pattern from fired shotgun. Note the distance from the muzzle that most commonly causes some form of significant human injury. (From DeMuth WE: The mechanism of shotgun wounds. J Trauma 11:219–229, 1971; with permission. Copyright by The Williams and Wilkins Company.)

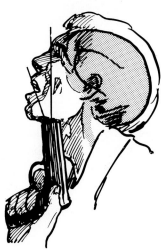

FIGURE 25–16. Gunshot wounds directed from a submental orientation may cause extensive facial injury but are usually nonlethal. (From Stump TE: Maxillofacial injuries from high velocity missiles: Mechanism, wounding action, and classification of gunshot wounds. *In* Jacobs JR [ed]: Maxillofacial Trauma: An International Perspective. New York, Praeger Publishers, 1983, p 48; with permission. Copyright 1983 by Praeger Publishers.)

Although appearing premoribund, if the shotgun victim arrives in the emergency room alive without significant intracranial injury, there is good prognosis for survival, providing the airway can be secured and hemorrhage controlled. For example, people who attempt suicide by placing the muzzle of the shotgun (or rifle) under the chin will often reflexively extend their head when firing the weapon. This maneuver creates a severe avulsive injury to the mandible and maxillofacial complex but frequently spares the central nervous system. Such wounds are grotesque but survivable (Fig. 25–16). Once emergency resuscitation is accomplished, lateral and posteroanterior radiographs should be obtained to determine the depth and position of the pellets. These may help determine if deeper structures, such as the brain, carotid sheath, or spinal cord, have been involved.[40,54]

Definitive management and exploration of shotgun injuries should be done only in the operating room (Figs. 25–10 and 25–17). The wide, gaping nature of the type III injury allows for easy and direct exploration of most deep structures.[54] All cartridge packing and wadding should be removed, and the powder marks should be debrided to avoid tattooing. Any pellets exposed during exploration and those in close proximity to skin should be removed. However, pellets that are deeply embedded should be left in place. Debridement is more liberal than that done with gunshot

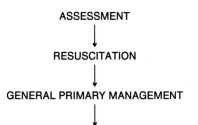

ASSESSMENT
↓
RESUSCITATION
↓
GENERAL PRIMARY MANAGEMENT
↓
SPECIFIC PRIMARY MANAGEMENT
   Exploration of wound
   Removal of easily accessible
     pellets from cutaneous wounds
   Irrigation
   Consultation if special areas
     involved (such as the eye)
   Antibiotic coverage
   Healing of pellet wounds by
     secondary intention

FIGURE 25–17. Management of type I shotgun injuries.

wounds, and all questionably viable tissue should be taken out (including bone fragments that are devoid of periosteal attachment) and the wound copiously irrigated with normal saline. The skeletal structures should be stabilized as simply as possible. For mandibular and maxillary fractures, maxillomandibular fixation is preferable. Bone fragments can be approximated either with 24- or 28-gauge wire or even with chromic sutures for smaller fragments. Absolute rigidity is not essential, but gross alignment to reduce the resulting defect should be attempted. If significant mandibular bone loss has occurred, the external biphasic pin fixation device should be considered to prevent collapse of the arch and anterosuperior rotation of the ramus. If extensive avulsion of soft tissue has occurred, the external aspect of the wound should not be closed primarily. Instead, the oral mucosa should be closed and the wound packed with a moist gauze. If the mucosa cannot be closed, it should be sutured to the skin, and the wound should be packed. Primary closure should be considered only if, after adequate debridement, the wound can be closed without tension and without having to use local flaps. In most cases, immediate primary closure is not possible and should be avoided owing to the resulting high rate of infection and soft tissue breakdown.[12,54]

Specialized areas, such as the eye, ear, and cranial nerves, are often injured in shotgun wounds and may require attention from specialists. In general, there is rarely an urgent need to remove an eye, since sympathetic ophthalmia does not occur until at least 10 days and often as long as 21 days after the injury. This period should allow for sufficient time to evaluate thoroughly and, if possible, treat the eye to save vision. For ear injuries, chondritis and the possible sequela of external cartilage destruction are disastrous complications. The ear should be carefully debrided, with an attempt to preserve all attached cartilage fragments. Early primary closure is advocated, with the use of split-thickness skin grafts, if necessary, to cover the areas of exposed cartilage. A bulky, moist compression dressing is also beneficial.[43] Nerve repair is not usually done at the time of initial debridement. Instead, if nerve ends are found, they should be tagged with suture and repaired, if necessary, in 1 month.[43,54] A high index of suspicion for intracranial injury is prudent, since the unrecognized development of intracerebral or extracerebral hematoma is life threatening. Neurosurgical consultation is mandatory for these significant facial injuries. Antibiotic and tetanus prophylaxis is indicated in all cases, with the use of broad-spectrum antibiotics in combination with penicillin being most efficacious.[12,53]

During the intermediate phase of care, the patient should be carefully evaluated for infection. If purulent loculations develop in wounds that were closed primarily, they should be opened, debrided, and drained. Consideration should also be given to placing drains that allow for irrigation into the wound. Similarly, sequestrations of small bone fragments are common and should be removed. Wounds that were packed open should have dressing changes done at least daily, with debridement of nonviable tissue. When the wound is clean, a delayed primary closure may be attempted for smaller defects. For larger wounds, a split-thickness skin graft may be attempted. This procedure is usually done 5 to 10 days after injury.[12]

The principles of reconstruction for shotgun injuries are similar to those for gunshot injuries, except for the following considerations. As previously mentioned, tissue loss in shotgun injuries (type II and especially type III) are much more severe than most gunshot wounds and result in greater defects as well as more severe superficial and deep scarring. As a consequence, the scarring that characteristically occurs takes longer to soften and mature. At least 3 months should be allowed to elapse between the initial therapy and reconstruction.[12] Secondary debridements are frequently necessary, and often additional pellets and wadding are removed. Should such procedures occur, reconstruction should be delayed owing to the increased likelihood of infection and the possibility of jeopardizing potential donor tissue.[40] If the reconstruction becomes infected, a second reconstructive effort should not be attempted for 6 to 12 months.[12] Finally, it is likely that many additional minor soft tissue procedures may be required to complete the soft tissue reconstruction.[12,40]

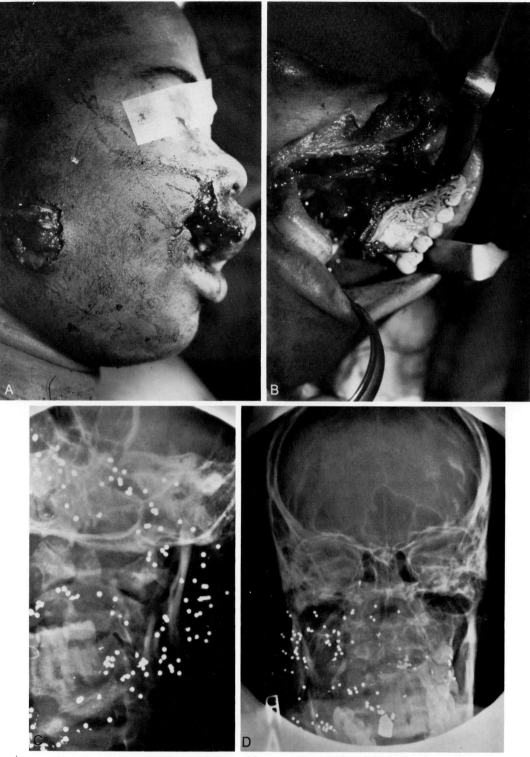

FIGURE 25–18. *A,* Type III shotgun injury with entrance wound at right angle of mandible and exit wound at right commissure of mouth, upper lip and ala of nose. Note ragged avulsed character of entrance site (corresponding to the circumference of penetrating shot pellets), and the stellate avulsive–appearing perioral exit wound. Although the cutaneous entrance wound was truly avulsive, the exit wound was not. *B,* The extensive avulsive character of this shotgun wound intraorally is shown. Note the complete avulsion of the right hemimaxilla, vomer, floor of nose, and comminution of zygomatic buttress and medial orbital rim. Also observe the degloving laceration of soft palate from remaining maxilla (leaving only a buccal pedical blood supply), and the extensive laceration of the right lateral lip and commissure of the mouth. *C* and *D,* Lateral and anteroposterior radiographs showing distribution of shot pellets. Also note avulsive and comminuted fracture at the right mandibular angle.

Illustration continued on opposite page

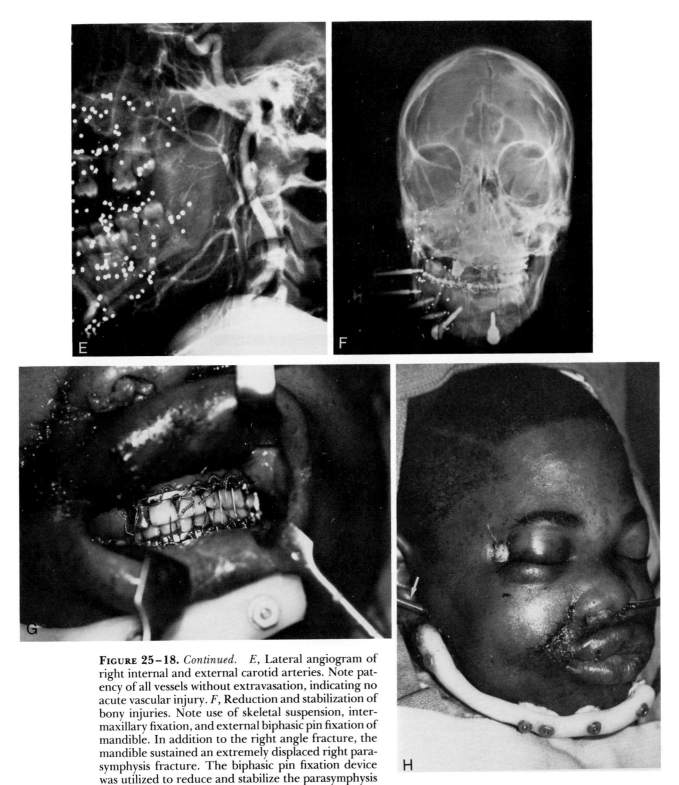

FIGURE 25–18. *Continued.   E,* Lateral angiogram of right internal and external carotid arteries. Note patency of all vessels without extravasation, indicating no acute vascular injury. *F,* Reduction and stabilization of bony injuries. Note use of skeletal suspension, intermaxillary fixation, and external biphasic pin fixation of mandible. In addition to the right angle fracture, the mandible sustained an extremely displaced right parasymphysis fracture. The biphasic pin fixation device was utilized to reduce and stabilize the parasymphysis fracture and to stabilize the avulsive right angle fracture from delayed scar contracture to facilitate placement of a future bone graft if needed. *G,* Remaining hemimaxilla in intermaxillary fixation. Note primary closure of perioral wounds. Maxillary gingiva maintained good vascular perfusion through the remaining buccal pedicle. *H,* Completion of initial surgery. Note primary closure of entrance and exit wounds, and placement of through and through fenestrated drain in the right submandibular space from posterior to anterior *(arrow).* When the cutaneous aspect of the entrance wound broke down, wet to dry dressings were used, and the defect was successfully closed with a skin graft.

REFERENCES

1. Wintemute GJ: Firearms as a cause of death in the United States 1970–1982. J Trauma 27:532–536, 1987.
2. Swan KG, Swan RG: Gunshot Wounds: Pathophysiology and Management. Littleton, MA, PSG Publishing Company, 1980.
3. Baker SP, O'Neill B, Korpf RS: The Injury Fact Book. Lexington, MA, Lexington Books, 1984.
4. Baker SP: 28,000 Gun deaths a year: What is our role? J Trauma 16:510–511, 1976.
5. Shelton DW: Gunshot Wounds of the Face: Pathophysiology and Management. Department of Oral and Maxillofacial Surgery, Medical College of Georgia, Augusta, Georgia, undated.
6. National Center for Health Statistics: Persons Injured and Disability Days by Delayed Type and Class of Accident, United States 1971–1972. Rockville, MD, 1976.
7. Billroth CAT: Historical studies on the nature and treatment of gunshot wounds from the fifteenth century to the present time. Yale J Biol Med 4:16–36, 119–148, 225–257, 1931–1932.
8. Jacobs JR: Maxillofacial Trauma: An International Perspective. New York, Praeger Publishers, 1981.
9. Owen-Smith MS: High Velocity Missile Wounds. London, Edward Arnold, Publishers, 1981.
10. Screpanovic D, Albret M, Erdelgan D, et al: Evaluation of the new type of military bullet and rifle. J Trauma 28:58–72, 1988.
11. DeMuth WE: The mechanism of shotgun wounds. J Trauma 11:219–229, 1971.
12. Spra LM, Hardy SB, Biggs TE, Gerow MD: Shotgun injuries of the face. Plast Reconstr Surg 39:449–458, 1967.
13. Ezz EM: Medical knowledge: An important factor in disarmament negotiations and increased international cooperation. J Trauma 28 [Suppl 1]:1–4, 1988.
14. DeMuth WE: Bullet velocity and design as determinants of wounding capability: An experimental study. J Trauma 6:222–232, 1966.
15. Berlin RH, Bo J, Ewa L, Gunnel N, et al: Terminal behavior of deforming bullets. J Trauma 28 [Suppl 1]:58–62, 1988.
16. Berlin R, Gerlin LE, Jenzon B, et al: Local effects of assault rifle bullets in live tissues. Acta Chir Scand [Suppl] 459:5–47, 1976.
17. Hopkinson DAW, Marshall TK: Firearm injuries. Br J Surg 54:344–353, 1967.
18. Tikka S, Cederberg A, Rokkanen P: Remote effects of pressure waves in missile trauma. The intra-abdominal pressure changes in anesthetized pigs wounded in one thigh. Acta Chir Scand [Suppl] 508:167–173, 1982.
19. DeMuth WE, Smith MD: High velocity missile wounds of muscle and bone: The basis of rational early treatment. J Trauma 6:744–755, 1966.
20. Yingqiu L, Xueming C, Weikung L, et al: Experimental study of treatment of high velocity projectile wounds with bacterial neutral protease. J Trauma 28 [Suppl 1]:227–229, 1988.
21. Kelly JF: Management of War Injuries to the Jaw and Related Structures. Washington, DC, US Government Printing Office, 1977.
22. Khalil AF: Civilian gunshot injuries to the face and jaws. Br J Oral Surg 18:205–211, 1980.
23. Thoresby FP, Darlow HM: The mechanisms of primary infections of bullet wounds. Br J Surg 54:359–361, 1967.
24. Zhengguo W, Chenggong T, Sveyun L, Tongzhov S: Early pathomorphologic characteristics of the wound track caused by fragments. J Trauma 28 [Suppl 1]:89–94, 1988.
25. Amoto JJ, Billy LJ, Lawson NS, Rich NM: High velocity missile injury: An experimental study of the retentive forces of tissue. Am J Surg 127:454–459, 1974.
26. Suneson A, Hanson HA, Seeman T: Central and peripheral nervous damage following high-energy missile wounds in the thigh. J Trauma 28 [Suppl 1]:197–203, 1988.
27. Ming L, Ma YY, Fu RX, Feng TS: The characteristics of the pressure waves generated in the soft target by impact and its contribution to indirect bone fractures. J Trauma 28 [Suppl 1]:104–109, 1988.
28. Jansson AM, Inguar DH, Kutyna F: Remote cerebral effects on EEG in high-energy missile trauma. J Trauma 28:204, 1988.
29. Harvey EN, Whiteley AH, Grundles H, McMillen JH: Piezoelectric crystal measurements of pressure changes in the abdomen of deeply anaesthetized animals during passage of a high velocity missile. Milit Surg 98:509–579, 1946.
30. Amoto JJ, Rich NM: Temporary cavity effects in blood vessel injury by high velocity missiles. J Cardiovasc Surg 13:147–155, 1972.
31. Holmstrom A, Larsson J, Liljedahl SO, Lewis DH: Effect of bullet wounding on pig skeletal muscle electrolytes and water content. Acta Chir Scand [Suppl] 489:173–178, 1979.
32. Almskog BA, Halgamae H, Hasselgren PO, et al: Local metabolic changes in skeletal muscle following high-energy missile injury. J Trauma 22:382–387, 1982.
33. Larsson J, Holmstrom A, Liljedahl SO, Lewis DH: Effect of bullet wounding on pig skeletal muscle metabolism. Acta Chir Scand [Suppl] 489:179–184, 1979.
34. Dahlgren B, Berlin R, Janzon B, et al: The extent of muscle tissue damage following missile trauma one, six and 12 hours after the infliction of trauma. Studied by current method of debridement. Acta Chir Scand [Suppl] 489:137–144, 1979.
35. Huiming T, Guanggui D, Mingjing H, et al: Quantitative bacteriological study of the wound track. J Trauma 28 [Suppl 1]:215–227, 1988.
36. Dahlgren B, Almskog B, Berlin R, et al: Local effects of antibacterial therapy (benzyl-penicillin) on missile wound infection rate and tissue devitalization when debridement is delayed for 12 hours. Acta Chir Scand [Suppl] 508:271–279, 1982.
37. Yinqiu L, Zueyun L, Shuguong LXC, et al: Wounding effects of small fragments of different shapes at different velocities on soft tissues of dogs. J Trauma 28 [Suppl 1]:95–98, 1988.
38. Dziemian AJ, Herget CM: Physical aspects of primary contamination of bullet wounds. Milit Surg 106:294, 1950.
39. Osbon DB: Intermediate and reconstructive care of maxillofacial missile wounds. J Oral Surg 31:429–437, 1973.
40. Schultz RC: Facial Injuries. Chicago, Year Book Medical Publishers, 1988.
41. Rowe NL, Williams JL: Maxillofacial Injuries.

Vol 2. Edinburgh, Churchill-Livingstone, 1985.

42. Yiengpruksowan A, Mariadason J, Ganepola GAP, Freeman HP: Localization and retrieval of bullets under ultrasound guidance. Arch Surg 122:1082–1084, 1987.

43. Kreutz RW, Bear SH: Selective emergency arteriography in cases of penetrating maxillofacial trauma. Oral Surg Oral Med Oral Pathol 60:18–22, 1985.

44. Sankaran S, Wah AJ: Penetrating wounds of the neck: Principles and some controversies. Surg Clin North Am 57:139–151, 1977.

45. Williams JW, Sherman RT: Penetrating wounds of the neck: Surgical management. J Trauma 13:435–442, 1973.

46. Ordog GJ: Penetrating neck trauma. J Trauma 27:543–554, 1987.

47. Amoto JJ, Billy LJ, Gruber RP, et al: Vascular injuries: An experimental study of high and low velocity missile wounds. Arch Surg 101:167–173, 1970.

48. Amoto JJ, Rich NM, Billy LJ, et al: High velocity arterial injury: A study of the mechanism of injury. J Trauma 11:412–416, 1971.

49. Joy ED: Early care of maxillofacial missile wounds. J Oral Surg 31:475–478, 1973.

50. Zamboni WA, Eriksson E, Zook EG: Management of acute facial powder burns. Ann Plast Surg 19:158–161, 1987.

51. Osbon DB: Early treatment of soft tissue injuries of the face. J Oral Surg 27:480–487, 1969.

52. Bhaskar SN, Cutright DE, Hunsuck EE, Gross A: Pulsating water jet devices in debridement of combat wounds. Milit Med 136:764–766, 1971.

53. Bell MJ: The management of shotgun wounds. J Trauma 11:522–527, 1971.

54. May M, West JW, Heeneman H, et al: Shotgun wounds to the head and neck. Arch Otolaryngol 98:373–376, 1973.

55. Sherman RT, Parrish RT: Management of shotgun injuries: A review of 152 cases. J Trauma 3:76, 1963.

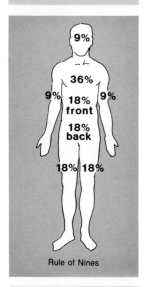

CHAPTER 26

9%

36%

9% | 18%
front | 9%

18%
back

18% | 18%

Rule of Nines

BURNS OF THE HEAD AND NECK

KENNETH A. MacAFEE, II, D.M.D.,
DEBORAH L. ZEITLER, D.D.S.,
and KATHLEEN MAYO, D.D.S.

The region of the head and neck is the most frequent site of thermal injury. The healing process from burns produces scar formation and contractures, which may result in severe cosmetic problems and functional disabilities. Patients with these injuries not only suffer physical damage but can also suffer adverse psychologic effects because of the sometimes horrifying facial appearance that results. In a study of 1444 patients with burn injuries in the Commonwealth of Virginia, 51.5 per cent had head and neck burns.[1] In a similar study done on 939 patients admitted to the Regional Burn Treatment Center of San Diego and Imperial Counties, 52 per cent had head and neck burns.[2] Another report reviewed a large burn unit and concluded that almost 60 per cent of all patients admitted to the burn unit had facial burns.[3] These burns not only result in obvious destruction of the facial structures but may also involve less obvious injury to the respiratory tract.

Prior to the early 1950s, the inordinate mortality from burn injury was directly related to infection of the wounds. Since 1964, with the advent of more organism-specific antibiotics and advances in local wound care, the prolongation of life has been greatly enhanced. Awareness on the part of the emergency physician and other medical personnel involved in the prehospital treatment phase plays a major role in minimizing morbidity and mortality in the patient with burn injuries.

EPIDEMIOLOGY

More than two million people suffer thermal burns annually in the United States. Although the great majority of these burns are minor, the National Consumer Safety Commission estimates that 3 to 5 per cent of all burns are life threatening. The most recent report of the National Commission on Fire Prevention and Control estimates that 20,000 Americans die each year as a direct result of the burn injury itself or its subsequent complications. House fires account for about 5000 deaths per year.[4]

Thermal burns include those caused by contact with direct flames, superheated gases, steam, hot water, electrical processes, and other agents.[5] The individuals most vulnerable to burn injury are the very young, the elderly, and the physically handicapped. In fact, burn injury is the second leading cause of death among children from birth to 12 years.[6] The most frequent cause of burns in children is hot tap water. Half of these victims are under 5 years old, and almost 10 per cent are over 65 years of age.[5] Almost all of these hot water burns could have been prevented by lowering the temperature of the water heater to below 54.4°C (130°F).[7]

Flame burns are the second most prevalent thermal burn, after hot water injury, especially those involving clothing ignition. Approximately 200,000 burn cases are associated with concomitant clothing fire, and approximately 100,000 of these victims require hospital care.[6] In 1975, Feller (personal communication to DL Larson, 1975) cited 4596 cases of flame burns; 3946 of these involved clothing ignition, and in 650 cases, clothing was not ignited. The victims whose clothing ignited experienced increased severity and extent of injury, including a mortality four times greater than that for victims whose clothing was not ignited. This report also revealed that the total burn area was nearly 100 per cent greater, the percentage of full-thickness injury was six times greater, and the number of hospital days was 60 per cent greater for victims whose clothing ignited.

Flammable liquids, such as gasoline, kerosene, and paint thinner, are also responsible for burn injuries, as these agents are frequently used for household purposes and are carelessly stored. Matches, lighters, cigarette butts, a spark from a metal object, and the pilot light of a hot water heater are commonly the cause of ignition of vapors. The resultant burn injuries often involve the facial region and are generally quite severe.

Facial and hand burns prevail in industrial accidents involving acid, chemicals, or molten metals.[8] These flash burns result in the subjection of exposed skin to intense heat. Effective protection is surprisingly provided by ordinary clothing in flash burn accidents. Rarely does clothing ignite in these situations. The opposite scenario occurs in automobile accidents in which the gas tank ruptures and the fuel explodes. Facial and hand burns invariably result when a great percentage of the passenger's clothing ignites.

PATHOPHYSIOLOGY OF BURN INJURY

The skin is the largest organ of the body, with a surface area of approximately 1.75 m² in adults and constituting about 15 per cent of the body weight. Its thickness varies from 1 to 3 mm, the thicker skin being located on dorsal and extensor surfaces of the body. The skin is a vapor barrier for the retention of water in the body, regulates heat losses, supplies the major barrier of the body against infection,[6] and is an important sensory organ for touch, pain, temperature, and pressure.[4]

The skin is composed of several layers, the two primary layers being the epidermis and underlying dermis (Fig. 26–1). The epidermis is the layer exposed to the environment, is mostly nonviable, and consists of five sublayers. From superficial to deep, these layers include (1) the stratum corneum, (2) the stratum lucidum (present only in thick areas, such as the palms of the hands and soles of the feet), (3) the stratum granulosum, (4) the stratum spinosum, and (5) the stratum germinativum.[5] The stratum corneum forms the vapor barrier of the body because of the presence of the lipid ethyl linoleate, demonstrated to be the agent principally responsible for passive water-holding function.[9] Damage to this layer may result in extensive fluid loss — up to 19 times the normal passive evaporative loss from the skin surface 18 hours subsequent to injury. Because of surface rehydration, evaporative water loss is decreased, and at the end of 18 hours, evaporative water loss is reduced to only four times normal.[10] Extensive water evaporation may result in hypothermia owing to the considerable loss of body heat. To maintain the body's core temperature, metabolic and caloric demands are increased.[11]

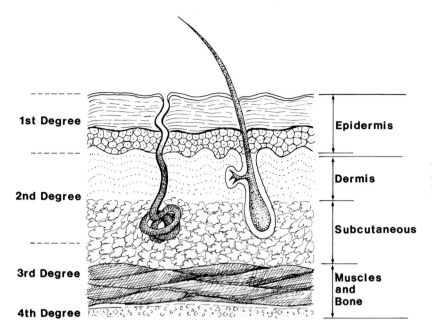

FIGURE 26–1. Cross-section of skin correlating the microanatomy to the classification of burn wound depth. (Adapted from Zuidema GD, Rutherford RB, Ballinger WF: The Management of Trauma. Philadelphia, WB Saunders Company, 1985, p 720.)

The stratum germinativum is the layer from which new epidermal cells are produced. Portions of the stratum germinativum are also found around some of the epidermal appendages that lie in the dermis, such as hair follicles, sebaceous glands, and sweat glands.[5] If a burn injury results in destruction of the entire epidermis, but the epidermal appendages within the dermis remain intact, a new epidermis may be regenerated by the stratum germinativum surrounding these appendages. Burns that transcend the so-called malpighian layer, the layer where pigment is stored, increase the prospect for alteration in skin pigmentation.[6] This layer is located immediately superficial to the stratum germinativum.

The dermis lies immediately below the epidermis and contains blood vessels and fibrous connective tissue, which support the epidermis and supply it with nutrients. The dermis also contains sweat glands, hair follicles, sebaceous glands, peripheral nerve fibers, and pressure and pain sense organs. Pain-transmitting nerve fibers lie deep in the dermis, and when they are irritated in superficial burn injuries, rather than destroyed in deeper burn injuries, increased pain results. Any injury that is deep enough to transcend the dermis may be associated with scarring and the probable need for replacement of skin through skin grafting or ingrowth of tissue from the edges of the wound.[12] The deeper the injury, the more scarring occurs owing to thinner epithelial regeneration.

Subcutaneous tissue lies beneath the dermis, which contains areolar and adipose tissue as well as collagen fibers that bind and support the more superficial layers.

Fairly high temperatures can be sustained by the skin because of its substantial water content. As long as the water content is not totally eliminated by the heat in thermal injury, the temperature of the skin will not exceed 82°C. Areas of increased vascularity allow heat to be transferred from the burn site because of high blood flow. This heat dissipation may decrease the depth of burn in such areas.[5]

Following a burn to the skin, the possibility of localized and subsequent systemic infection is increased. The skin undergoes coagulation necrosis, especially in deeper burns, thus producing a medium conducive to bacterial colonization. The vascular system is responsible for the transport of the majority of bacteria to the site of injury. The bacteria propagate owing to a decrease in the body's natural defense mechanisms. Vessel damage and alteration of white blood cell migration to the site of injury result in an increased risk of infection. The immune response of the host decreases in proportion to the extent and depth of the burn.[12]

Immediately after thermal injury, the vascularity of the skin in the involved area changes. Histamine is released in the local area of the burn, causing vasoconstriction. Within a few hours, vasodilation occurs, causing increased capillary permeability, which permits whole plasma to be extravasated into the burn wound. Within 24 hours after burn injury, thrombosis is produced by the abnormal aggregation of platelets and leukocytes adhering to vessel walls. This condition results in progressive vascular obstruction, which may produce an area of ischemia three to seven times greater in depth than the initial cellular damage caused by the heat.[13] The edema impairs the transport of oxygen and nutrients to damaged cells, thereby producing additional cellular damage. This phenomenon is present for a minimum of 5 days.

Three zones of vascular change are identified on the skin's surface at the site of injury. The area of greatest destruction is the *zone of coagulation,* which is located at the center of the injury and is seen particularly in deeper burns.[14] Thermal coagulation and cellular death occur within this area as all blood vessels and capillaries become occluded. This zone of coagulation extends more deeply into the skin as the intensity of the heat or length of exposure increases, thus producing a full-thickness destruction.[15]

Surrounding the zone of coagulation is the *zone of stasis.* This zone involves the vasculature of the dermis and initially appears red and blanches on pressure. Thrombosis occurs within minutes owing to the abnormal aggregation of formed blood elements. Blood flow is further decreased to the burn site by vasoconstriction. Appropriate early treatment can restore circulation to this zone because some blood vessels in the area remain patent. Improper treatment of the wound may cause irreversible damage to this zone, converting it to a zone of coagulation. Subsequent necrosis could result in a full-thickness injury.

The *zone of hyperemia* surrounds the zone of stasis and is the area least affected by the burn. This zone is bright red and blanches on pressure. Cellular death is minimal because of the maintenance of vascular integrity; thus, this zone serves as a partial protective barrier from microorganism invasion to the remainder of the body.

SEVERITY OF BURN INJURY

Assessing the severity of a burn injury requires accurate clinical staging, which will permit appropriate therapy to be initiated in the proper medical facility. It is important to determine the source and circumstances of the injury, the probable depth of cutaneous destruction, and the extent of the body surface involved.[4]

The common sources of cutaneous burns, as reported by Monafo and Crabtree,[4] are generally categorized as thermal, clinical, or electrical. In thermal burns, the extent and depth of injury are proportional to the intensity of the heat and the duration of exposure. In chemical accidents, the amount of tissue damage is proportional to the concentration of the agent and the duration of exposure. The extent of damage in electrical injuries is influenced by the voltage, the resistance offered by the tissues to current flow, the pathway of the current through the body, and the duration of the contact. Contact with sources exceeding 1000 V typically results in severe soft tissue destruction.[4]

Burn depth is classified as first-, second-, third-, or fourth-degree (Fig. 26–1). First-degree burns involve the superficial layers of the epidermis and are characterized by simple erythema, mild-to-moderate pain, and minimal tissue destruction. The skin may be slightly edematous and will blanch with pressure. This type of burn is typically seen in cases of acute overexposure to the sun, commonly known as sunburn.

Second-degree burns are associated with more tissue destruction of the epidermis and may involve the superficial areas of the dermis. Some epithelial elements in the hair follicles, sweat glands, and stratum germinativum remain viable. Regeneration of skin can result from the adnexal structures if no infection or further trauma occurs. Second-degree burns are described as partial-thickness burns because of this capability for epithelial regeneration. The nerve endings in partial-thickness second-degree burns have been damaged but not destroyed. This is the reason that severe pain is associated with this depth of burn. As second-degree burns heal, the nerve endings are regenerated and the pain is significantly decreased. The hallmark of second-degree burns is blister formation.

By definition, third-degree burns are characterized by total, irreversible destruction of all the skin, including the dermal appendages. This injury is a full-thickness burn, which precludes epithelial regeneration. Since all layers of the skin are coagulated and destroyed, pain is not perceived because the nerve endings have also been destroyed. The more telling criterion for full-thickness burning is the observation of thrombosed blood vessels in a firm, translucent surface.[6]

Burning to the depth of muscle, fascia, or bone is classified as a fourth-degree burn. Charring of the skin and subcutaneous structures is readily observed. Third- and fourth-degree burns can be severely debilitating, especially if damage to the body surface area is extensive.

The extent of a burn injury is expressed as the percentage of the total surface area involved with partial- and full-thickness wounds.[4] Facial burns are easily assessed owing to the exposure of the head and neck. However, further examination should be completed in the emergency department with all of the patient's clothing removed. There are a variety of ways to determine the extent of a burn. The "rule of palms" suggests that the palm size of the victim is approximately 1 per cent of the body surface area, and an equivalent number of "palms" of the victim that are burned will approximate the percentage of body surface involved.[6] Another method for determining the extent of burns involves the "rule of nines" (Fig. 26–2), in which the body is divided into 11 areas of 9 per cent, with the perineum giving the additional 1 per cent of body surface area.[6] The drawback with the rule of nines is that it does not accurately depict the percentages of body surface area in infants and small children; for instance, the head of an adult is approximately 9 per cent total body surface, whereas the head of a newborn is approximately 18 per cent. The Lund and Browder chart permits a more precise method for determining the percentage of body surface area involved, as it provides adjustments for the patient's age[16] (Fig. 26–3). In

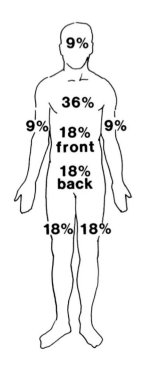

Rule of Nines

FIGURE 26–2.   Percentages used in determining the extent of burn by the "rule of nines."

Lund and Browder Chart

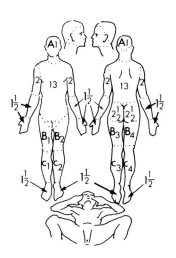

	ANT.	POST.
Head	A1	A2
Neck		
Rt. Arm		
Rt. Forearm		
Rt. Hand		
Lt. Arm		
Lt. Forearm		
Lt. Hand		
Trunk		
Buttock	(L)	(R)
Perineum		
Rt. Thigh	B1	B4
Rt. Leg	C1	C4
Rt. Foot		
Lt. Thigh	B2	B3
Lt. Leg	C2	C3
Lt. Foot		

Percentage of Areas Affected by Growth

Age	A = ½ Head	B = ½ One Thigh	C = ½ One Leg
0	9½	2¾	2½
1	8½	3¼	2½
5	6½	4	2¾
10	5½	4¼	3
15	4½	4½	3¼
Adult	3½	4¾	3½

Partial Thickness _____

Full Thickness _____

Total _____

FIGURE 26–3. The Lund and Browder chart is the most accurate method for assessment of the extent of body surface area burned by allowing for adjustments in the patient's age. (From Zuidema GD, Rutherford RB, Ballinger WF: The Management of Trauma. Philadelphia, WB Saunders Company, 1985; with permission.)

patients with extensive injuries, the unburned area can be more readily summed. An accurate assessment of total body surface area burned is essential, since this estimation will form the basis for most calculations of fluid resuscitation needs.[6]

TREATMENT OF BURN INJURY

Initial Assessment

The initial evaluation of the burned patient's condition must include assessment of the airway, breathing, and circulation. Along with evaluating the severity of the burn injury itself, it is important to obtain a careful history of the events of the accident and to determine if other injuries may have occurred. For instance, a victim involved in an explosion accident may readily sustain concomitant chest and head injuries. A brief past medical history not only will provide baseline data regarding the patient's general health status but also may explain what precipitated the accident (e.g., drug intoxication, seizure, or cerebrovascular injury).

Criteria for Hospital Admission

The initial problem in the management of a patient with thermal injury is to determine whether it is advantageous to admit that patient to a hospital or whether he or she can safely be treated as an outpatient. According to Hartford, the following patients with burns are usually considered for admission:

1. Most infants
2. Those in whom child abuse is suspected
3. Young children with burns in excess of 10 per cent of the body surface

4. Older children and adults with burns in excess of 15 per cent of the body surface area

5. Most aged patients

6. Those with chemical injury beyond obviously superficial or limited extent

7. Those with burns to parts of the body that render the patient incapacitated, such as burns of the face with swelling of the eyelids, resulting in obstruction of vision, burns of both hands, burns of the perineum, or burns of both feet

8. Those with high-voltage electrical injury

9. Those in whom upper respiratory tract complications (smoke inhalation syndrome, upper airway obstruction from edema, or carbon monoxide poisoning) are a possibility, such as when a patient is injured by a flame in a closed space

10. Those in whom an intercurrent injury, illness, or pre-existing medical condition might enhance morbidity or mortality

Resuscitation

Fluid resuscitation is among the most urgent treatment priorities and begins with the placement of a large-bore intravenous catheter in an upper extremity. Veins in the arm underlying nonburned skin are preferred; however, burned skin is not a deterrent to catheter placement. The saphenous, femoral, and internal jugular veins are alternative intravenous sites when the arm cannot be used. A central venous catheter is not warranted during the initial phase of treatment. Venous blood samples are obtained when the intravenous line is started, and the samples are sent for laboratory analysis and cross-matching. Arterial blood gas measurements are obtained to assess ventilation and oxygenation, especially if inhalation injury is suspected. An indwelling urinary catheter is inserted, and the adequacy of fluid resuscitation is monitored by maintaining a urine output volume of 50 ml/h.[17] To decrease the risk of vomiting and aspiration that can occur secondary to a traumatically induced ileus, a nasogastric tube is inserted and gastric contents are removed.

Fluid Regimens

Many formulae can be used to calculate the fluid necessary for the resuscitation of burn victims. Each provides an estimate of the fluid volumes needed and of the rate of administration. Edema formation is most rapid during the first 8 to 12 hours; therefore, approximately half the total 24-hour requirement is given during the first 8 hours. Harkin's formula (1942) and the Cope and Moore (1947) formula use a plasma and salt solution. The Evans formula,[18] proposed in 1952, was later modified by Brooke in 1953.[19] In these regimens, the fluid recommended for each of the first two 24-hour postburn periods is calculated from the body weight and the percentage of surface area of burn. A percentage of this fluid is given as crystalloid and a percentage as colloid.

Colloids.   The use of colloids has been advocated because the inherent oncotic pressure of these fluids tends to keep them in the intravascular space. However, it is possible that administered colloid may leak into the wound and increase interstitial pressure. More recently, the use of colloids during the initial resuscitative phase has come under scrutiny. Increased interstitial pressure may prolong the duration of wound edema and adversely affect pulmonary function if an inhalation injury exists. In addition, colloids are expensive, nearly 50 times as costly as crystalloid. Colloid preparations such as albumin are prepared from human blood and carry the same hazards as transfusions, that is, viral disease transmission and anaphylaxis.

Lactated Ringer's Formula.   The lactated Ringer's formula recommended by Baxter[20] is currently most popular. According to this regimen, the only intravenous fluid given during the first 24 hours is lactated Ringer's formula. The basic formula is as follows:

Percentage of body surface area burned $\times$ kilograms of body weight
$$\times 4 \text{ ml} = \text{amount for the first 24 hours}$$

One half of this total is given in the first 8 hours following the burn, and one quarter of the total is given in the subsequent two 8-hour periods. The first 8-hour period begins with the time of the burn, not the time the patient arrives in the emergency room. According to this formula, an 80-kg man with burns affecting 50 per cent of the body surface area would require 16 L of fluid during the first 24 hours: 8 L during the first 8 hours, 4 L from the ninth through sixteenth hours, and 4 L from the seventeenth through the twenty-fourth hours.[5] The adequacy of fluid resuscitation is assessed by hourly measurements of pH, specific gravity, output of urine, blood pressure, pulse, respirations, and level of consciousness. Satisfactory resuscitation usually requires between 18 and 30 hours. Shock persisting beyond this period is usually not the result of the burn injury, and other sources should be sought.

Most young, healthy adults with burns on less than two thirds of the body surface area can be successfully resuscitated by a variety of regimens. Infants and young children with burns covering more than 10 per cent of the body surface area and older children and adults with burns covering more than 15 per cent of the body surface should receive intravenous fluids to prevent burn shock.

TREATMENT OF HEMOGLOBINURIA

Grossly visible pigmenturia occurs as a result of extensive hemolysis or muscle injury or both and may lead to acute renal failure. Hemoglobinuria most commonly occurs in high-voltage electrical injuries. The combination of rapid fluid administration and osmotic diuretics to increase urine output to 75 to 150 ml/hr is recommended to clear the pigment from the kidney and prevent hemoglobin from depositing in the renal tubules.[5]

TREATMENT OF BURN SHOCK

Burn injury causes abnormal capillary permeability and allows a shift of intravascular fluids out of the blood vessels.[21] The loss of fluid from the intravascular space progressively decreases blood volume, cardiac output, and tissue perfusion. If the burn is large enough and intravascular hypovolemia is not treated, burn shock or circulatory failure occurs. Acute renal failure and cardiac arrest ensue if adequate and early treatment is not administered. The most common error is to give inadequate fluids, especially in the geriatric patient, because of concern about inducing congestive heart failure. However, acute congestive heart failure is a rare event in the initial resuscitative period. It is usually not until the third to seventh day after injury that any of the administered fluids are spontaneously mobilized into the circulation.

The timely administration of fluids to patients with large surface area burns prevents death from burn shock. These fluids must contain sodium,[22] but whether colloids are needed or even desirable is controversial. Until capillary leaks stop, intravenous fluid therapy is necessary to maintain the circulation and perfusion of tissues.

Drug Administration

Tetanus Prophylaxis. According to Braen (1987) and others, all burn patients should have up-to-date tetanus prophylaxis.[5] In the previously immunized patient, 250 units of human immunoglobulin should be given intramuscularly in one extremity, and 0.5 ml of tetanus toxoid should be given in another extremity. The patient who has been adequately immunized previously should still receive 0.5 ml of tetanus toxoid intramuscularly.

Anti-inflammatory Agents. Some anti-inflammatory drugs have been known to stimulate host defense mechanisms. These drugs act as immunomodulators and, experimentally, have shown promise in increasing host resistance to infections if begun shortly after injury.[23]

Antibiotic Therapy

Infection with systemic sepsis remains the major cause of death in burn patients.[24] Fifty-four per cent of the 75 deaths reported in 937 consecutive admissions to the New York Hospital Burn Center over a 4-year period were attributed to infection.[25] Reports from other burn centers cite similar findings. Since the introduction of penicillin in the 1940s, large quantities have been administered to burn patients topically, orally, and systemically. Paralleling the development of antibiotic agents, major advances have occurred in resuscitation, nutritional support, and wound care.

However impressive the results of antibiotic therapy may seem to be, the use of antibiotics is not itself considered definitive treatment. Meticulous wound care is the primary line of defense in preventing local septic complications. Since most burns are initially sterile, excessive cleansing with antiseptic soaks is unwarranted upon admission except when gross contamination has occurred.

Wound Flora. The wound microbial flora varies with the time after the injury, with the indigenous environmental flora, and to some extent with the topical agents and systemic antibiotics that are employed.[4] Therefore, a major principle in considering systemic antibiotic use in burn patients is that each individual burn unit varies in its baseline population of organisms over time and that generalizations drawn from one unit may have little applicability to others.[26]

During the first week, the wound is usually colonized by group D and group A beta-hemolytic streptococci. Eventually, *Staphylococcus aureus* and the aerobic gram-negative enteric flora colonize the wound. *Pseudomonas aeruginosa*, normally present in the stools of about 15 per cent of the population and commonly recovered from such sources as plants, vegetables, stagnant water, and faucet drains, is also a potential wound inhabitant.[4] Deep injuries that involve large volumes of skeletal muscle seem especially prone to clostridial or mixed anaerobic infections.[27]

Antibiotic Prophylaxis. In the past, systemic penicillin G was prophylactically administered for the first week in an effort to prevent streptococcal infections; however, this is no longer recommended.[28] Recent studies have demonstrated that prophylactic penicillin administration is of no benefit and may be dangerous. In a study performed at the University of Washington Burn Center, Durtschi and coworkers[29] found that routine administration of penicillin failed to lower the incidence of early gram-positive cellulitis. Other reports reveal severe *Pseudomonas* sepsis following antibiotic prophylaxis.[30] In 1970, Wickman[31] noted that a rapid emergence of resistant gram-negative organisms followed prophylactic administration of penicillin. Therefore, systemic antibiotic prophylaxis in the early management of burn patients is a practice that, although once common, should now be abandoned.[28]

According to Dasco and coworkers,[28] there are three clinical situations in which the prophylactic administration of systemic antibiotics still may be indicated:

1.   In burn-wound excision. Burn-wound manipulation at the time of burn-wound cleansing and debridement is associated with systemic bacteremia.[32] Therefore, a short course of preoperative systemic antibiotics seems advisable.

2.   In autografting. Autografting necessitates closed wound dressings for a number of days. The closed dressing creates a risk that infection with a gram-positive organism may proceed unobserved. Therefore, it has become common practice to

administer gram-positive antibiotic coverage from the preoperative period until the first dressing change.

3. In the immediate postburn period in children. Despite the proven lack of efficacy and potential harm in the adult population, it is still common practice to administer prophylactic penicillin in the early postburn period in children.[33]

Systemic Antibiotic Dosages for Burn Patients. According to Sawchuk and Rector,[34] burn injuries and their subsequent treatment create a dynamic pathophysiologic condition that may alter the pharmacokinetic characteristics and subsequent effectiveness of systemic antibiotics. After administration of systemic antibiotics, the serum levels in burn patients often have been low, even subtherapeutic.[35-37] These studies indicate that it is impossible to predict which patients would be likely to require increased antibiotic dosages. Frequent serum assays are necessary so that dosages can be adjusted to ensure therapeutic antibiotic levels.

Choice of Antibiotic in Burn Patients. The choice of agent must be based on considerations of the infecting organism, its pattern of sensitivity, status of the patient, impact on the endogenous flora of the unit, and availability of assay for serum determinations.[28] The various classes of antibiotics have their own characteristic therapeutic properties, side effects, and toxicities. With these considerations in mind, the clinician must constantly monitor the presence of organisms and their resistance and correlate these findings with the clinical progress of the patient.

Systemic Antibiotics. In 1987, Dasco and colleagues[28] proposed seven general rules for systemic antibiotic use in burn patients:

1. The burn patient will be exposed to microorganisms no matter how germ free the environment. Therefore, management will usually require antibiotic use in some form during the burn patient's course.

2. There is no single antibiotic or combination of agents that will destroy all microorganisms to which the burn patient is exposed. Prophylactic or therapeutic administration of antimicrobials in an attempt to eliminate all potential pathogens is unachievable and inevitably will result in the selection of resistant strains of microorganisms.[30,31,38,39]

3. Prior to selecting an antimicrobial agent, the organism and its pathogenic role must be determined (first the "bug," then the "drug"). "Shotgun therapy"— that is, the injudicious administration of a wide range of agents—in an attempt to eliminate all pathogens is to be condemned. Routine culturing of a patient, as well as longitudinal monitoring of changes in the microflora of the unit, will allow ample time to select appropriate narrow-spectrum agents to decrease the rate of growth or eliminate potentially troublesome organisms.[26]

4. If more than one agent is required, only tested combinations of agents should be used. An untested combination of agents may result in in vivo antagonism or a pharmacologic reaction that is unexpected.

5. The more agents used simultaneously, the greater the chance of fungal or highly resistant bacterial strain overgrowth. As the number of agents being administered simultaneously increases, so does the potential for superinfection by bacteria, yeast, or fungi that are resistant to multiple drugs.[39,40]

6. When any antibiotic is being used, it should not be stopped too soon or continued too long. If an agent has been selected to attack a specific microorganism believed to be causing clinical sepsis, then, at a minimum, it should be administered until adequate time has elapsed to achieve a clinical response (usually 5 to 7 days). Once the clinical response is achieved and there is confirmation that the organism has been eradicated (usually 10 to 14 days), then the agent should be discontinued.

7. When serum assays for a specific agent are available, the dose should be chosen on the basis of the serum concentration. It is becoming more evident that the dose of any systemic antibiotic agent required to achieve adequate serum levels may vary from patient to patient and in any patient at different stages of injury. The serum assay values, in conjunction with clinical response, serve as the mainstay of any systemic antimicrobial clinical protocol.

Topical Therapy. It has become clear during the past 20 years that topical antibacterial agents can provide significant, if imperfect, wound antisepsis.[4] Prior to the introduction of effective topical antimicrobial agents, up to 60 per cent of deaths in specialized burn treatment facilities were caused by burn wound sepsis.[41] Only a few topical antiseptic agents have proved to be effective and safe. About 10 years ago, silver sulfadiazine was introduced and has become the most popular agent currently in use. One per cent silver sulfadiazine is available in a white water-soluble propylene glycol cream. The mechanism of action is primarily topical and is probably due to the ionic silver rather than the sulfadiazine. Silver sulfadiazine does not stain and causes relatively little pain upon application. The primary disadvantages of silver sulfadiazine are its lack of eschar penetration and the development of gram-negative bacterial resistance.[42,43] The mode of resistance in some facilities is transferable, multiple antibiotic–resistant plasmid with selective sulfonamide resistance.[44] The concern is that the use of silver sulfadiazine in these situations can lead to the selection of organisms that are resistant to all clinically available antibiotics.

Inhalation Injury and Airway Management

Resuscitation of the patient with burns of the head and neck region requires immediate evaluation for possible injury to the respiratory tract and treatment of respiratory insufficiency. Continual observation and assessment of the airway are important throughout the first few days of a burn patient's care, since some respiratory injuries will not be evident in the initial presentation.

Initial airway management begins with the administration of 100 per cent oxygen as soon as possible following the burn injury. This measure treats both hypoxia and carbon monoxide intoxication. Identification of upper airway obstruction is a clear indication for immediate endotracheal intubation.[45] Direct damage from inhaled hot air may result in severe edema of the upper airway. This effect is normally encountered within 8 to 24 hours after the burn. The peak edema usually occurs in 48 hours and then begins to resolve.[45] When this problem becomes apparent, endotracheal intubation should be performed to maintain an airway. Many practitioners believe that nasoendotracheal intubation is best for patients with facial burns.[1] When a nasotracheal tube is used, care must be taken in gently securing the tube with cloth tapes tied loosely around the head. Adhesive tape is not recommended, since it may encourage infection in the burned skin.[1] When oral intubation is chosen for the patient with facial burns, stability of the endotracheal tube may be established by utilizing a dental bite block that is wired to the teeth and to which the tube is secured.

When edema of the respiratory tract goes unrecognized, tracheostomy may be necessary owing to the inability to place an endotracheal tube.[1] Although tracheostomy may be an effective means of airway management, the incidence of pulmonary infection and mortality is considerably higher with tracheostomy. In one study, the incidence of pulmonary infections in patients with tracheostomies was 78 per cent, compared with 12.5 per cent in burn patients without tracheostomies.[46] When the need for prolonged endotracheal intubation can be predicted early in burn treatment, consideration should be given to early debridement of the anterior neck and placement of skin grafts as soon as possible.[45] In that way, after healing, a tracheostomy may be placed through the healed, grafted skin. This measure may reduce the morbidity of tracheostomies in the burn patient. The effect of tight neck or chest eschar may also cause respiratory embarrassment. This effect, when recognized, can be treated by escharotomy.[47]

Inhalation injury may also be due to inhaled toxic gases. Classic indicators of possible inhalation injury include a flame burn sustained in a closed space and involving the face; singed nasal hair; soot in the airway; hoarseness; and rales, rhonchi, or wheezing.[1] Diagnostic confirmation can be made by the use of lung scans or fiberoptic bronchoscopy.[48] Again, the importance of constantly assessing the patient is emphasized, since inhalation injury may have a latent period of 6 to 48 hours before signs of respiratory distress appear.[1] Respiratory failure from other causes in the severely burned patient may be delayed in its development. Between the third and fifth days after the burn, such factors as atelectasis, disseminated intravascular coagulation, and metabolic acidemia may contribute to the development of respiratory insufficiency.[49]

Early Care of the Burn Wound

Treatment of thermal burns to the head and neck begins with a thorough cleansing of all burned areas. Special attention is paid to areas such as eyelashes, which may accumulate debris and coagulum. Care must also be taken in treating the patient with burns or injuries around the eye. Thorough evaluation for corneal injury must be performed. The burn wound is normally dressed with moist dressings that are changed frequently to prevent crust formation.[1] Frequent debridement of necrotic tissue is important to prevent deep-seated infection[50] (Fig. 26–4). Fortunately, the rich vascularity of the region of the head and neck contributes to relatively rapid healing of minor burns, with minimal secondary infection.

Although aggressive early excisional surgery and immediate skin grafting are increasingly used for burns of other parts of the body, this management has not been as popular for burns of the head and neck.[51] Traditional treatment of the facial burn has been to allow partial-thickness wounds to heal primarily and full-thickness burns to form granulation tissue before grafting. Two recent studies have challenged this practice and have evaluated early excisional therapy for deep partial-thickness and full-thickness burns of the head and neck. Both studies found promising results from early excision and autografting. Warden and coworkers[51] used closed mesh skin grafting, while Hunt and colleagues[52] used split-thickness skin grafting. Both studies indicated the need to control bleeding following the excisional procedure. Some of

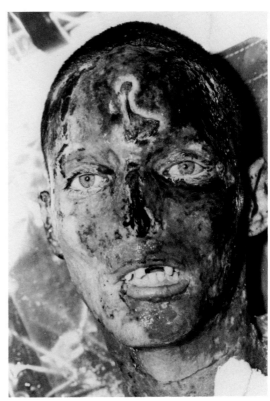

Figure 26–4. Frequent debridement of necrotic tissue is necessary for early burn care.

the advantages of this technique include earlier healing of the burn wound, shorter hospitalization, and improved cosmetic results.

Late Care of the Burn Wound

After initial cleansing and debridement of the burn wound, granulation will gradually form a bed acceptable for skin grafting. In the head and neck, relatively thick (0.014 to 0.018 inch) split-thickness grafts are recommended.[1] These thick skin grafts provide better quality grafts that appear to undergo less contraction. Mesh grafts are generally not recommended.[2] However, one recent article[51] advocated closed mesh skin grafting in which a mesh graft is placed with the cuts in the direction of the natural skin lines of the face. These mesh cuts, however, are meticulously closed during graft placement. The judgment of this group of investigators was that this type of graft resulted in an improved cosmetic appearance with a marked decrease in hypertrophic scarring and contracture formation.

The basic principles of grafting procedures done on the head and neck must include the importance of aesthetic facial units. When grafting is undertaken, replacing an entire aesthetic unit is indicated, rather than applying grafts in patches. Facial units generally include the forehead, the eyebrows, the upper eyelid area, the lower eyelid area, the cheek, the upper lip, and the lower lip with the chin included[53] (Fig. 26–5). Two areas that require special attention include the philtrum and the chin. In these areas, previous scars may be excised only superficially, leaving the depth of the scar to provide the prominence of these normally contoured regions of the face. Donor sites such as the scalp, the posterior auricular region, and the supraclavicular region then can provide excellent color match with intact facial skin.[54] The grafts may be stabilized by bolster stent or pressure dressing. The importance of immobilizing the graft cannot be overemphasized in the early healing period. To maintain immobilization, nasogastric feeding and discouraging the patient from talking may be necessary.[1]

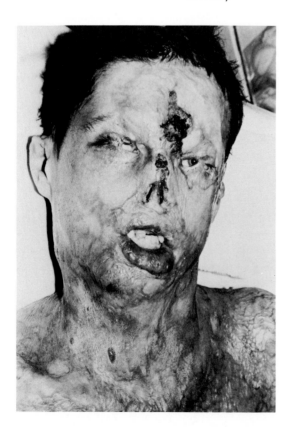

FIGURE 26–5.   Burns of the eyes, chin, and neck may result in severe wound contracture.

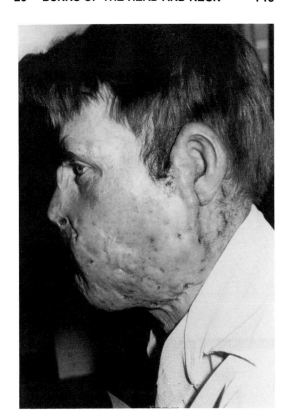

FIGURE 26-6. Hypertrophic scarring can be minimized by the use of pressure masks.

In conjunction with skin grafting, pressure therapy is generally accepted as the best noninvasive means of managing hypertrophic scarring after burn injury.[55] This type of scarring may result in significant cosmetic problems and functional disability (Fig. 26-6). Pressure therapy for scars of the head and neck may include the use of rigid neck braces, elastic face masks and chin straps, or transparent plastic masks molded individually for each patient.[1,56] The maintenance of pressure must begin as soon as possible after skin grafting and should be discontinued only for necessary activities, such as eating and bathing. Pressure is used until the skin graft has matured and softened, which may be 6 to 18 months after the burn.[1] In addition, positioning of the patient with the neck in extension will assist in preventing scar contracture. Range-of-motion exercises are also indicated.

Specific areas of the head and neck require special considerations in treatment. Each of these anatomic regions will be discussed, with emphasis on early care to prevent deformity and later reconstruction when necessary.

Burns of the Scalp

Because of the thickened nature of the skin of the scalp and the deep penetration of the hair follicles, burn injuries of the scalp tend to be partial thickness. The excellent blood supply of the scalp also contributes to the usual occurrence of spontaneous healing. Shaving of the hair is generally necessary for adequate cleansing.[50] Necrotic areas of skin will require debridement. Full-thickness injuries can be treated with rotational flaps or split-thickness skin grafting.[1]

More complicated burns that involve the underlying bone may require more complex treatment. These burns typically occur secondary to electrical injuries. The classic method of dealing with dead bone secondary to a burn injury is to allow sequestration or to fenestrate the bone to facilitate granulation from underneath.[57] In either case, a prolonged period of healing is typical. Secondary grafting must wait until sequestration is complete and granulation occurs. More recently, patients with deep burns of the scalp involving the bone of the skull have been treated with early rotation of a scalp flap to cover the dead bone. Ideally, this procedure is done as soon as possible following the burn to provide complete coverage of the damaged bone before bacterial colonization is present. Technetium bone scans assist in the evaluation of the success of this technique by demonstrating the extent of bone injury before, during, and after treatment.

Burns of the Ear

In contrast to the scalp, the ears have an extremely thin skin covering over a poorly vascularized cartilaginous structure. These facts, combined with the anatomic position of the ears, contribute to frequent and serious burn injuries. More than 90 per cent of burns to the head and neck have associated burns of the ears.[3] When burns of the ears occur, they often are very serious and may commonly result in ear loss. In a recent study by Goel and coworkers,[58] loss of the external ear occurred in 15 patients (22 ears) of 100 patients with ear burns. These authors recommend avoidance of pressure on the ears, local cleansing, and application of topical antibiotics. When complete debridement or separation has taken place, split-thickness grafts are applied if needed.

Close observation of the ear is also necessary to detect chondritis[58] (Fig. 26–7). This is a serious infection that may commonly lead to loss of the ear even when recognized early and treated aggressively. Important factors in the prevention of chondritis appear to be meticulous local care and prompt debridement and grafting. Should exposure of cartilage occur during debridement, excision of the exposed portion, with skin grafting to the perichondrium, may be indicated.[1] This measure is necessary because exposed cartilage commonly becomes infected even if dressed with antibiotics or homologous graft. Exposure of a large amount of cartilaginous framework may be treated by covering the ear with a local flap from postauricular skin or by burying the cartilage in a postauricular pocket.[1] In Goel's article,[58] when suppurative chondritis developed, it was generally several weeks after the burn. Of nine ears in which chondritis developed, severe destruction of the ear took place in eight.

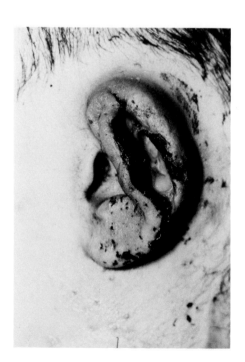

FIGURE 26–7. Chondritis may result in loss of the ear.

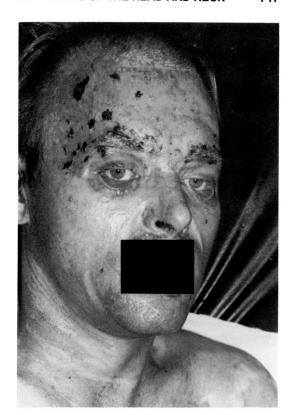

FIGURE 26–8. Burns of the eyelids that result in ectropion may require early grafting.

Burns of the Eye

Chemical burns of the eye constitute ocular emergencies. Acid burns of the eye are much better tolerated than alkali burns, which may result in injury ranging from mild corneal erosions to severe and generalized eye burn manifesting as blurring of the pupil and blanching of the conjunctiva and sclera.[59] The initial treatment is copious irrigation as soon as possible. This irrigation should be delivered in a continuous manner using intravenous tubing and normal saline.[1,59] Local anesthesia and retraction of the lids will assist in thorough irrigation.[1,59] After this procedure, staining of the eyes with fluorescein is done to detect corneal injury.[1] Intraocular pressure must be closely followed.[59] Pupils are dilated, and if corneal abrasion is present, a topical antibiotic is prescribed. The main complications of chemical burns of the eye are symblepharon and corneal ulceration.[59] Corneal ulceration manifests as clouding of the cornea. Prevention of corneal exposure and infection is important for treatment of corneal ulceration. Antibiotic therapy should be chosen on the basis of sensitivity to tests. Corneal ulcerations may progress to perforation and loss of the eye.[1]

Thermal burns are generally restricted to the eyelids.[59] It is important to examine for the presence of foreign bodies and to provide meticulous hygiene of the lashes for prevention of corneal abrasion. Most burns of the eyelids are partial-thickness burns and often heal spontaneously without skin grafting. However, deep partial-thickness or full-thickness burns involving skin loss of the lids will require skin grafting[1] (Fig. 26–8). When early skin grafting is necessary to protect the globe, it should be undertaken with the knowledge that later scar releases may become necessary. Split-thickness skin grafts from an area of good color match are indicated for upper eyelid grafting. For the lower lid, a full-thickness skin graft is preferred to provide rigidity and help maintain the position of the lower lid.[1] To immobilize the eyelids after skin grafting, a Frost stitch is used to fasten the margin of the lids together temporarily. Patching of both eyes is also indicated.[1]

Burns of the Nose

Burns of the nose occur in 70 per cent of patients with facial burns.[60] The thick skin on the lower portion of the nose can provide some protection to this area, but the skin across the lateral aspect and bridge of the nose is thin.[59] Generally, the nose is allowed to heal by spontaneous epithelialization. However, this process often leads to a deformity that gives a skeletonized appearance to the nose[61] (Fig. 26–9). Severe burn injury may lead to total loss of skin and nasal cartilage (Fig. 26–10). In addition, scarring of the face around the nose may distort the nasal structures. Surgical reconstruction of the nose may range from simple de-epithelialization with skin grafting to complete reconstruction of the nose with flap surgery. When scarring around the nose has led to the deformity, rather than nasal injury itself, reconstruction of the upper lip and cheek regions can provide restoration of appropriate nasal contour.[53] Composite tissue grafts from the ear can be used to reconstruct lost cartilage of the ala or columella region.[53,62]

Electrical Burns of the Mouth

Electrical burns of the mouth predominate in those in the 1- to 2-year age range and generally result from either putting the socket terminal of an extension cord into the mouth or sucking on the wall socket.[63] The tongue, lower and upper lips, and commissures may all be affected.[64] The initial electrical burn injury will generally show a firm area of tissue necrosis. The central area will be white and depressed and surrounded by a zone of erythematous tissue. Within a few hours, intense swelling will appear in the surrounding tissues. This edema generally takes from 5 to 12 days to resolve.[1]

It must be recognized in the initial assessment of the patient that the burn injury will eventually be larger than it appears in the initial presentation.[63] Many authors

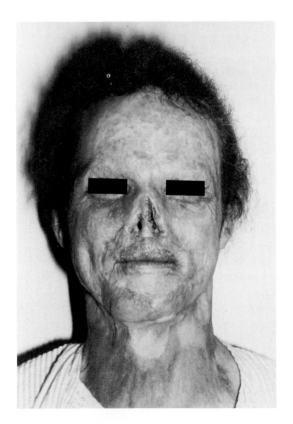

FIGURE 26–9. Healing by spontaneous epithelialization may lead to a skeletonized appearance of the nose.

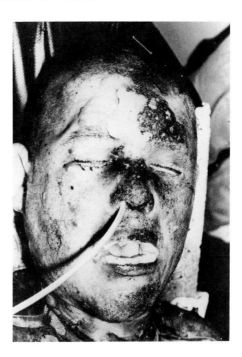

FIGURE 26–10. Severe facial burns may lead to loss of skin and nasal cartilage.

advocate a conservative approach of cleansing the area, keeping it moist, and allowing the eschar to separate.[65] Healing then takes place by secondary intention. This regimen attempts to maximize the preservation of uninjured tissue.[63] However, others advise early excision of the wound and primary closure. When surgical treatment is undertaken in the first week after injury, the healing time and length of hospital stay can be minimzed.[64] However, it is difficult to judge the true extent of the injury at this early time in treatment. This difficulty may result in an increased number of complications associated with the surgical procedure, such as wound dehiscence.[64] An alternative is to perform surgical reconstruction of the wound following 10 to 14 days of conservative care to allow full demarcation of the injured region to occur.[63] After any burn wound to the lips, especially to the commissures (Fig. 26–11), the use of a microstomia prevention appliance is extremely important in managing or preventing contracture. The use of such an appliance has been associated with the decreased need for surgical intervention in revising microstomia.[66] When conservative management of an electrical burn of the mouth is undertaken, special attention must be given to the fact that as eschar separates from the wound, significant bleeding from labial blood vessels may occur, especially when electrical burns of the lip are managed on an

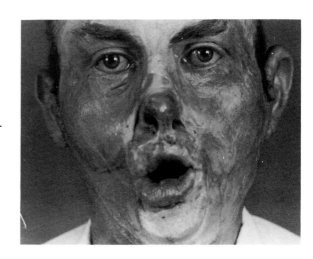

FIGURE 26–11. Perioral scar contracture may result in microstomia and limitation of jaw mobility.

outpatient basis.[65] Parents and other care takers must be educated in the high incidence of significant bleeding from the burn wound as healing occurs and the management of that bleeding. Ligation of the vessels is occasionally required for controlled bleeding.

Although many advances in initial treatment and reconstructive procedures for facial burns have been made, these injuries still may result in devastating effects on appearance, function, social acceptance, and self-image. Although studies are not conclusive that facial burns have a greater psychologic effect than burns elsewhere on the body, it is true that burn injuries of the face are more difficult to camouflage. Long-term support and emotional care will need to be provided to many patients.[67] In addition, because of scarring, even routine dental and medical care may require innovative techniques.[68] Continued research in wound healing and prevention of the effects of wound contracture may benefit burn patients in the future.

REFERENCES

1. Morgan RF, Nichter LS, Haines PC, et al: Management of head and neck burns. J Burn Care Rehabil 6:20, 1985.
2. Wachtel TL: Epidemiology and general considerations of burns of the head and neck. In Wachtel TL, Frank DH (eds): Burns of the Head and Neck. Philadelphia, WB Saunders Company, 1984, pp 1–3.
3. Dowling JA, Foley FD, Moncrief JA: Chondritis in the burned ear. Plast Reconstr Surg 42:115, 1968.
4. Monafo WW, Crabtree JH: Burns and electrical injuries. In Zuidema GD, Rutherford RB, Ballinger WF: The Management of Trauma. Philadelphia, WB Saunders Company, 1985, pp 719–746.
5. Braen RG: Burns. In Kravis TC, Warner CG (eds): Emergency Medicine—A Comprehensive Review. Rockville, MD, Aspen Publishers, 1987, pp 391–398.
6. Braen RG: Thermal injury (burns). In Rosen P (ed): Emergency Medicine: Concepts and Clinical Practice. St Louis, CV Mosby, 1988, pp 573–583.
7. Katcher M: Scald burns from hot tap water. JAMA 246:1219, 1981.
8. Converse JM, McCarthy JG, Dobrkovsky M, Larson DL: Facial burns. In Converse JM, McCarthy JG, Littler, WJ (eds): Reconstructive Plastic Surgery. Vol 3. Philadelphia, WB Saunders Company, 1977, p 1595.
9. Jelenko C III, Wheeler ML, Anderson AP et al: Studies in burns XIII. Effects of topical lipid on burned subjects and their wounds. Am Surg 41:466, 1975.
10. Jelenko C, III, Williams JB, Wheeler ML et al: Studies in shock and resuscitation. I. Use of a hypertonic albumin-containing fluid demand regimen (HALFD) in resuscitation. Crit Care Med 7:157, 1979.
11. Artz CP: What's new in burns. Med Times 104:128, 1976.
12. Baxter CR: Pathophysiology and treatment of burns and cold injury. In Hardy JD (ed): Rhoads Textbook of Surgery: Principles and Practice. 5th ed. Philadelphia, JB Lippincott, 1977.
13. Dimick AR: Pathophysiology of Burns. In Fisher SV, Helm PA (eds): Comprehensive Rehabilitation of Burns. Baltimore, Williams and Wilkins, 1984. pp 16–27.
14. Noble HG, Robson MC, Krizek TJ: Dermal

15. ischemia on the burn wound. J Surg Res 23:117, 1977.
15. Zawacki BE: Reversal of capillary stasis and prevention of necrosis in burns. Ann Surg 180:98, 1974.
16. Lund CC, Browder ND: The estimation of areas of burns. Surg Gynecol Obstet 79:352, 1944.
17. Baxter CR: Guidelines for fluid resuscitation. J Trauma 21 [Suppl 8]:687, 1981.
18. Evans EL, Purnell OJ, Robinett PW, et al: Fluid and electrolyte requirements in severe burns. Ann Surg 135:804, 1952.
19. Reiss E, Stirman JA, Artz CP, et al: Fluid and electrolyte balance in burns. JAMA 152:1309, 1953.
20. Baxter CR: Crystalloid resuscitation of burn shock. In Polk HC Jr, Stone HH: Contemporary burn management. Boston, Little, Brown, 1971, p 7.
21. Cotran RS, Remensnyder JP: the structural basis of increased vascular permeability after graded thermal injury: Light and electron microscopic studies. Ann NY Acad Sci 150:495, 1968.
22. Moyer CA, Margraf HW, Monafo WW: Burn shock and extravascular sodium deficiency—treatment with Ringer's solution with lactate. Arch Surg 90:799, 1965.
23. Ehrlich HP: Anti-inflammatory drugs in the vascular response to burn injury. Ann Surg 198:53, 1983.
24. Alexander JW: The body's response to infection. In Artz CP, Moncrief JA, Pruitt BA Jr: Burns: A team approach. Philadelphia, WB Saunders Company, 1979, p 107.
25. Curreri PW, Luterman A, Braun DW, Shires GT: Burn injury: Analysis of survival and hospitalization time for 937 patients. Ann Surg 192:472, 1980.
26. Wilkins TJ, Bennett JE: The selective use of systemic antibiotics in the treatment of burns. Surg Gynecol Obstet 151:404, 1980.
27. Monafo WW, Brentano L, Gravens DL, et al: Gas gangrene and mixed clostridial infections of muscle complicating deep thermal burns. Arch Surg 92:212, 1966.
28. Dasco CC, Luterman A, Curreri PW: Systemic antibiotic treatment in burned patients. Surg Clin North Am 67:57, 1987.
29. Durtschi MB, Orgain C, Counts GW, et al: A prospective study of prophylactic penicillin

in acutely burned hospitalized patients. J Trauma 22:11, 1982.

30. Stone HH: Review of pseudomonas sepsis in thermal burns. Ann Surg 163:297, 1966.

31. Wickman K: Studies on burns XIV, bacteriology II. Acta Chir Scand [Suppl]:408(8):1–34, 1970.

32. Lasaki TM, Welcjh GW, Jerrdon DN: Burn wound manipulation induced bacteremia. Presented at the Ninth Annual Meeting of the American Burn Association, April 1977.

33. Burke JF, Quinby WC, Bondoc CC, et al: The contribution of a bacterially isolated environment to the prevention of infection in seriously burned patients. Ann Surg 186:377, 1977.

34. Sawchuk RJ, Rector TS: Drug kinetics in burn patients. Clin Pharmacokinet 5:548, 1980.

35. Glew RH, Moellering RC, Burke JF: Gentamicin dosage in children with extensive burns. J Trauma 16:819, 1976.

36. Loirat P, Rohan J, Baullat A, et al: Increased glomerular filtration rate in patients with major burns and its effects on the pharmacokinetics of tobramycin. N Engl J Med 299:915, 1978.

37. Sawchuk RJ, Zaske DE: Pharmacokinetics of dosing regimens which utilize multiple intravenous infusion: Gentamicin in burn patients. J Pharmacokinet Biopharm 4:183, 1976.

38. Klainer AS, Beisel WR: Opportunistic infections: A review. Am J Med Sci 258:431, 1969.

39. Nathan P, Holder IA, MacMillan BG: Burn wounds: Microbiology, local host defenses and current therapy. CRC Crit Rev Clin Lab Sci 4: 61, 1973.

40. Nash G, Foley FD, Godwin MN, et al: Fungal burn wound infection. JAMA 215:1664, 1971.

41. Pruitt BA, O'Neill JA, Moncrief JA, et al: Successful control of burn wound sepsis. JAMA 203:1054, 1968.

42. Bridges K, Lowbury EJL: Drug resistance in relation to use of silver sulfadiazine cream in a burns unit. J Clin Pathol 30:160, 1977.

43. Lowbury EJL, Babb JR, Bridges K, et al: Topical chemoprophylaxis with silver sulfadiazine, silver nitrate, and chlorhexidine creams: Emergence of sulfonamide-resistant gram negative bacilli. Br Med J 1:493, 1976.

44. McManus AT, Denton CL, Mason AD Jr: Mechanism of in vitro sensitivity to sulfadiazine silver. Arch Surg 118:161, 1983.

45. Wachtel TL, Long WB, Frank HA: Thermal injuries of the upper respiratory tract. In Wachtel TL, Frank DH (eds): Burns of the Head and Neck. Philadelphia, WB Saunders Company, 1984, pp 7–14.

46. Eckhauser FE, Billote J, Burke JF, et al: Tracheostomy complicating massive burn injury. A plea for conservatism. Am J Surg 127:418, 1974.

47. Edlich RF, Haynes BW, Larkham N, et al: Emergency department treatment, triage, and transfer protocols for the burn patient. J Am Coll Emerg Phys 7:152, 1978.

48. Hunt JL, Agee RN, Pruitt BA Jr: Fiberoptic bronchoscopy in acute inhalation injury. J Trauma 15:641, 1975.

49. German JL, Allyn PA, Bartlett RH: Pulmo-nary artery pressure monitoring in acute burn management. Arch Surg 106:788, 1973.

50. Neale HW: Problem burns and their treatment. In Hummel RP (ed): Clinical Burn Therapy: A Management and Prevention Guide. London, John Wright–PSG, 1982, pp 239–278.

51. Warden GD, Saffle JR, Schnebly A, Kravitz M: Excisional therapy of facial burns. J Burn Care Rehabil 7:24, 1986.

52. Hunt JL, Purdue GF, Spicer T: Face burn reconstruction—does early excision and autografting improve aesthetic appearance? Burns 13:39, 1987.

53. Frank DH: Reconstruction of head and neck burn injury. In Wachtel TL, Frank DH (eds): Burns of the Head and Neck. Philadelphia, WB Saunders Company, 1984, pp 153–186.

54. Edgerton MT, Hansen FC: Matching facial color with split-thickness skin grafts from adjacent areas. Plast Reconstr Surg 25:455, 1960.

55. Cheng JCY, Evans JH, Leung KS, et al: Pressure therapy in the treatment of post-burn hypertrophic scar—a critical look into its usefulness and fallacies by pressure monitoring. Burns 10:154, 1984.

56. Law EJ: Minimizing burn scar and contracture. In Hummel RP (ed): Clinical Burn Therapy: A Management and Prevention Guide. London, John Wright–PSG, 1982, pp 301–320.

57. Pegg SP, Jenkins AM: Deep electrical burns to the scalp. Burns 13:62, 1987.

58. Goel TK, Law EJ, MacMillan BG: Management of the acutely burned ear. Burns 9:218, 1983.

59. Sevel D: Burns of the eye and adnexa. In Wachtel TL, Frank DH (eds): Burns of the Head and Neck. Philadelphia, WB Saunders Company, 1984, pp 7–14.

60. Boswick JA Jr: Burns of the head and neck. Surg Clin North Am 53:97, 1973.

61. Vecchione TR: The management of the "skeletonized" nose. Br J Plast Surg 33:224, 1980.

62. Brown JB, Cannon B: Composite free grafts of skin and cartilage from the ear. Surg Gynecol Obstet 82:253, 1946.

63. Orgel M: Electrical burns to the mouth. In Wachtel TL, Frank DH (eds): Burns of the Head and Neck. Philadelphia, WB Saunders Company, 1984, pp 89–93.

64. De la Plaza R, Questgas A, Rodriquez E: Treatment of electrical burns of the mouth. Burns 10:49, 1983.

65. D'Italia JG, Hulnick SJ: Outpatient management of electrical burns of the lip. J Burns Care Rehabil 6:465, 1984.

66. Heinle JA, Kealey GP, Cram AE, Hartford CE: The microstomia prevention appliance: 14 years of clinical experience. J Burn Care Rehabil 9:90, 1988.

67. Rest SM: Coping with facial burns. In Wachtel TL, Frank DH (eds): Burns of the Head and Neck. Philadelphia, WB Saunders Company, 1984, pp 195–208.

68. Dahlberg RC, Moline DO: Oral rehabilitation of the burn patient with severe microstomia: A report of a case. Special Care Dentistry 7:171–174, 1987.

CHAPTER 27

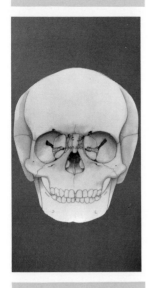

MANAGEMENT OF FACIAL FRACTURES IN THE GROWING PATIENT

TIMOTHY A. TURVEY, D.D.S., and
BARRY KENDELL, D.M.D., M.S.

GENERAL CONSIDERATIONS

The growing patient who sustains a facial fracture presents the clinician with a series of complex and thought-provoking circumstances. The general principles of fracture management (recognition, early reduction, stabilization, immobilization, and so on) must be applied while considering the effect of the injury and of the treatment upon future growth and development. Occasionally, a dilemma arises when deciding the most efficacious therapy for facial fractures occurring in the growing patient. The role of jaw function as a modulator of mandibular growth is indisputable.[1-6] The bone healing and remodeling potential of children is greater than that of adults, and this minimizes the amount of time necessary for immobilization.[7-15] Although intermaxillary fixation precludes the stimulation that function exerts on growing facial bones, this effect appears to be reversible, especially when it is applied for brief periods. In many circumstances, open reduction is tempting, particularly when intermaxillary fixation may be reduced or eliminated.[16-19] The benefits of open reduction must be carefully assessed in consideration of the possible untoward effects upon future growth that the additional disruption of the periosteum and soft tissue may provoke.

Peculiar to the jaw bones of growing patients is the consideration of dental development and the adversities that arise from surgical manipulation in the region of developing teeth. As a general rule, conservative therapy should be favored when treating facial fractures during childhood, especially in tooth-bearing regions.

When fractures occur in the facial skeleton of a growing patient, they generally present as "greenstick fractures" because the thin cortices and increased medullary bone encourage the bone to bend upon impact rather than fracture completely. Generally, when these fractures are reduced, they are self-retentive. The consistency of the growing patient's bone (greater cancellous and less cortical) is not conducive to utilizing screw fixation to fixate fractures internally, and wire may easily pull through the bone as well. For these reasons, closed reduction is an attractive and simple solution in most cases of facial fractures occurring in the growing patient.

The osteogenic and bone remodeling potential of the child exceeds that of the adult. Fractures of both the maxilla and the mandible that are not reduced within days of the injury often are unable to be adequately reduced because of the rapid bone healing that occurs. The authors have never observed nonunion of a facial fracture in a growing patient. Consequently, facial fractures that occur in growing children require timely attention unless life-threatening circumstances prevail. Another consequence of this rapid bone healing and remodeling potential is that small bone discrepancies, which may occur with nonanatomic alignment by closed reduction of facial bones in growing patients, are usually of no consequence by maturation.

The heights of contour of the crowns of deciduous teeth are below the gingival level, and this does not lend itself well to circumdental wiring when arch bars are required to stabilize fractures during childhood. In addition, resorption of roots and attrition of deciduous teeth make these teeth less helpful in maintaining arch bars in place. Often, it is necessary to supplement circumdental wiring with skeletal wiring (piriform aperture, circumzygomatic, or circum-mandibular) to maintain adequate fixation of arch bars or splints when relying upon the deciduous or mixed dentitions.[7, 20, 21] Care must be taken when placing these skeletal wires not to pull them through the child's soft bone.

FLUIDS AND ELECTROLYTES

The infant and, to a lesser extent, the child are more susceptible than adults to disorders of dehydration or acid-base imbalance, or both.[22-25] Because the pediatric trauma patient has a turnover rate of water, electrolytes, and acid and base that is approximately three times faster than that of an adult,[26] it is mandatory that the surgeon attempt to restore normal oral intake of food and fluid or provide an alternative during the early postoperative period. Careful monitoring of fluid and electrolytes and compiling a detailed intake and output diary are critical. Vomiting, diarrhea, insensible water loss, and blood loss will quickly deplete body stores of water, electrolytes, proteins, and glycogen much faster than in an adult. Unless the physician is faced with fatal hemorrhage, requiring immediate treatment, time must be taken to restore optimal cardiopulmonary and fluid balance status prior to surgery.

From shortly after birth until puberty, 65 per cent of a child's body weight is total body water (TBW). This amount decreases to 60 per cent at puberty and further decreases to 55 per cent by adulthood. The decrease is due to the anabolic addition of muscle and fat. The TBW is traditionally subdivided into that portion of water present within cell membranes (intracellular fluid, or ICF) and all of the water outside the cells (extracellular fluid, or ECF). The ECF can be further divided into plasma volume and interstitial fluid. The proportion of ICF increases with age, whereas the relative amount of ECF distribution decreases, similar to that of TBW.

Various shifts between spaces will occur, depending upon the amount and origin of loss and the influence of such factors as the release of antidiuretic hormone to conserve water and the renin-angiotensin-aldosterone system. Presurgical studies, such as an intravenous pyelogram and arteriograms, may involve the use of osmotic dyes, which also affect fluid balance.[27] The surgeon must be alert to these factors and take them into account in subsequent therapy. If fluid translocation has occurred, then clinical signs of interstitial fluid loss will appear, such as loss of skin turgor, sunken fontanelles, and sunken ocular globes.

Fluid Therapy

The child's fluid needs can be divided into maintenance requirements and replacement requirements. Usually, the maintenance component consists of compensating for losses via the insensible route (sweat, urine, and stool). There may be some abnormal requirements, such as losses during febrile states, the presence of open wounds, vomiting, or diarrhea. A healthy 70-kg adult has a water requirement of approximately 35 ml/kg/day, whereas an infant requires at least four times that amount, or 150 ml/kg/day based on weight alone.[25] Some prefer to base calculations on body surface area, while others use the caloric expenditure.[26] Charts are necessary to determine the body surface areas from known weight. Fever increases fluid losses approximately 12 per cent per degree Celsius rise in body temperature.

To satisfy maintenance requirements, solutions used for parenteral replacement therapy should be hypotonic with respect to sodium and potassium but should contain 5 per cent or more glucose (e.g., 5 per cent dextrose [D5] with ¼ normal saline [NS] or D5 with ½NS or D5 with lactated Ringer's solution). Major fluid losses, such as those seen in gastrointestinal tract losses and those secondary to major body trauma, require full-strength balanced salt solutions, such as lactated Ringer's solution.[16] Because the healthy kidney can tolerate overloads of sodium, there is little risk in using these types of replacement solutions if in doubt. The child is much more sensitive to hypoglycemia than the adult, and potentially this can result in central nervous system disorders. Hyperglycemia is not usually a concern unless hyperalimentation is used, and the consequence is hyperosmolar coma. If moderate dehydration or fluid loss is suspected, initial maintenance therapy would consist of 5 ml/kg/hr for the first 2 hours and then adjustment to a level of 1.5 to 2.0 ml/kg/hr. If the child has suffered major trauma and has endured prolonged general anesthesia, an additional 2 to 6 ml/kg/hr[22, 27, 28] is necessary. The desired urine output during surgery is 1 to 2 ml/kg/hr, which is higher than the normal 0.5 to 1.0 ml/kg/hr[29] in the adult.

During the postoperative period, especially if the patient has been treated with intermaxillary fixation or is compromised in other ways (such as being comatose, on a respirator, or unable to receive nutrition because of massive edema), nasogastric tube feeding or, in extremely complex situations, centrally placed total parenteral nutritional support may be necessary.

Blood Loss and Replacement

The blood volume is relatively high at birth; however, owing to the smaller total body mass of the patient, small amounts of blood loss may lead to hypovolemic shock subtly. Careful initial assessment of the patient and accurate measurement of intraoperative and postoperative blood loss can prevent serious problems. It also follows that overhydration and overtransfusion are possible when dealing with the smaller calculations.[29]

Obtaining a history from observers and relatives can be of value, but quite often, blood loss can be exaggerated by these sources. For this reason, clinical signs of significant blood loss need to be carefully noted; these include tachycardia, pallor, poor filling of terminal capillaries, and prerenal azotemia.[23] If the child has signs of multisystem trauma, such as abdominal distention, pelvic ecchymosis, or limb fractures, further sources of blood loss can be assumed.

Volume for volume, blood is the most efficient agent for filling the circulation, since the volume distribution of the erythrocytes is the blood volume itself.[25, 29] Whole blood is a logical choice for the patient who has sustained significant blood loss. The surgeon must be aware of some of the potential pitfalls of banked whole-blood therapy, especially in the pediatric trauma patient. The anticoagulant often used is an acid solution containing dextrose and citric acid – sodium citrate buffered at an acid pH. This solution can provide an acid load that will affect acid-base balance. Banked blood contains altered electrolytes, which, with time, increase the plasma concentration of potassium. A level of up to 25 mEq/L can result in blood stored longer than a week. Banked blood contains low levels of electrolytes and 23-diphosphoglycerate (DPG), shifting the oxygen saturation curve to the left. Therefore, it is preferable to use fresh whole blood, especially if relatively significant amounts of blood replacement are necessary.

Table 27 – 1 is provided for the calculation of blood volume based on 70 ml/kg of

TABLE 27-1. CALCULATION OF BLOOD VOLUME

Age (Years)	Average Weight (kg)/(lbs)	Blood Volume (ml)
2	12/26.4	840
3	15/33.0	1050
5	20/44.0	1400
7	23/50.6	1610
9	28/61.6	1960
12	35/77.0	2450

body weight.[14] General principles of replacing blood loss are otherwise similar to those in the adult; that is, use of blood products is to be considered if the estimated blood loss approaches 20 per cent of the patient's total blood volume or before if clinical signs dictate. Three to 4 ml of balanced salt solution should be administered for every 1 ml of blood loss because of the equilibrium effect of fluids; the red blood cells, in contrast, stay in the blood volume.

INCIDENCE OF FACIAL FRACTURES IN GROWING PATIENTS

An infant's facial mass and proportion are small relative to those of a child, and tremendous facial growth occurs during the first several years of life. By the sixth year, facial proportion is established and remains relatively constant throughout life unless growth is disturbed or manipulated with orthodontic-orthopedic forces.[30] The nose is the sole exception to this generalization, and it continues growing with increasing proportion into adulthood.[2]

Fractures of the facial skeleton are reported to occur very infrequently (<2 per cent) prior to the fifth year of life. Although the young child may be more prone to falls, the shorter distance and the decreased body mass do not generate significant force, and consequently, most often facial fractures do not result. The child's sheltered atmosphere, the soft consistency of his bone, and decreased facial mass and proportion all contribute to this minimal incidence of fracture. Unfortunately, the incidence of head injury in this population is high because of the relatively thin frontal bone and the greater projection of the frontal lobes.

Once the child begins school, initiates participation in sports, and becomes more extroverted, his risk of sustaining facial fractures also increases. The greater proportion of cancellous bone, which is pliable, the thin buccal and lingual cortical plates, and the taut periosteum are protective mechanisms against fracture and displacement in this age group. The piriform region and zygomaticomaxillary buttress regions are thickened with cancellous bone and tooth buds. Consequently, the child's maxilla is more resistant to fracture.[12, 15, 21, 31] In the growing child, the cartilaginous skull base (sphenoid) is less likely to fracture and encourages the midface to displace upon impact. Similarly, the mandibular condyle is capped with cartilage, which cushions the temporal fossa from mandibular trauma.

The second decade of life is accompanied by a higher incidence of facial fracture than the first. Bone in this population, relative to younger patients, has a thicker cortical and less cancellous consistency in the mandible and increased pneumatization of the sinuses of the midface, which weakens the midfacial structure. Greater socialization and the change in bone consistency account for the increased incidence of facial fixation.

CLINICAL EXAMINATION

Examination of the child who has sustained a facial injury is no different from that of an adult. Lack of cooperation sometimes precludes adequate examination, and

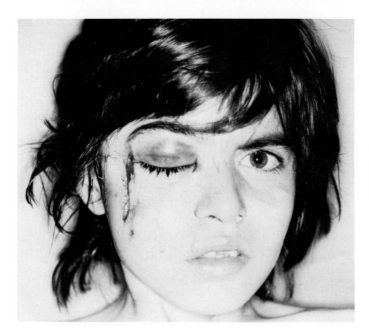

FIGURE 27–1. The periorbital ecchymosis and edema demonstrated by this 9-year-old boy, who sustained these injuries in an automobile accident, are highly suggestive of a zygomatic complex injury.

additional assistance or restraints are occasionally necessary. Sedation during the immediate postinjury stage is sometimes tempting but should be avoided, since it masks neurologic changes. A frightened, uncooperative child will usually become helpful once an explanation for the examination has been given and gentleness during the examination is demonstrated.

Swelling can mask or bring attention to an underlying facial fracture. Facial edema, periorbital ecchymosis, subconjunctival ecchymosis, subcutaneous emphysema, nasal bleeding, and identification of intraoral ecchymosis, especially in the mucobuccal folds or sublingual area, should alert the examiner to the possibilities of facial fractures (Figs. 27–1 to 27–4). The presence of postauricular ecchymosis (Battle's sign) or hemotympanum is suggestive of a basal skull fracture, and these findings should always raise the suspicion of an accompanying facial fracture.

The periorbital and nasal regions should be palpated in an attempt to appreciate areas of bone deformation, subcutaneous emphysema, and crepitation, which, if

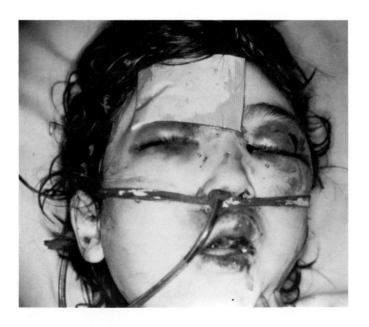

FIGURE 27–2. This photograph of a 6-year-old child demonstrates more significant and bilateral facial edema, suggestive of complete disruption of the bones of the middle face.

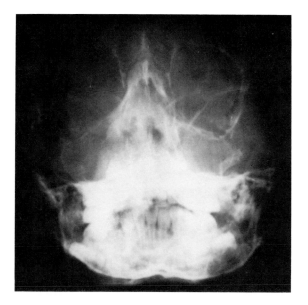

FIGURE 27-3. A Waters view radiograph of the patient in Figure 27-2 indicates severe bilateral disruption of the middle face, confirming the clinical examination.

present, indicate an underlying facial fracture. Especially when orbital fractures are suspected, a vision screening examination, checking for diplopia and range of movement of the globes, should be done. The presence of a malocclusion or loose teeth should alert the practitioner to the possibilities of underlying jaw fracture. Deviation upon opening the mouth or limited ability of the mandible to protrude or perform lateral excursion is noteworthy and suggests a mandibular condylar fracture. In addition, lacerations or contusions, especially in the submental regions, should alert the examiner to the possibility of a condylar fracture. A neurosurgical consultation is mandatory if there is loss of consciousness, altered behavior, postauricular ecchymosis, cerebrospinal fluid rhinorrhea, facial nerve changes, or hemotympanum.

An accurate history by a reliable witness of the event that led to the child's presentation is indispensable. The height of a fall, the magnitude of the impact of the blow, the loss of consciousness after the event, the behavior following the accident, and so on are all important facts that permit accurate assessment of the child's injury. Children are prone to develop epidural hematomas, and it is critical to observe their

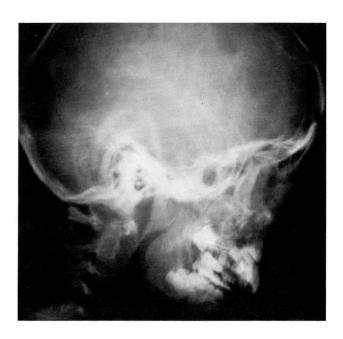

FIGURE 27-4. A lateral skull radiograph demonstrates severe disruption of the facial skeleton and a depressed frontal fracture in this same patient.

behavior and level of consciousness following significant facial trauma. The "battered child" complex must be considered a possibility when the historian's account does not correlate with the extent of the child's injury. This suspicion must be addressed if unexplained bruises, burn marks, or repeated traumatic incidents appear in the child's medical history or are discovered upon physical examination.

RADIOGRAPHIC EXAMINATION

The diagnosis of facial fractures is made primarily by clinical examination. Radiographs should be considered diagnostic aids and should be used to confirm the clinical impression and to help assess the extent of the damage. Since many fractures of the jaws occurring in children are of the greenstick variety, they may be difficult to identify on radiographs. The presence of tooth buds may further obscure fractures on radiographs, and for these reasons radiographs should not be used as primary diagnostic tools (Figs. 27–5 and 27–6).

A complete facial series of radiographs should include left and right lateral oblique views of the mandible to observe the mandibular bodies and the ramus, a Towne view to identify condylar injuries, a posteroanterior view to observe the mandible and midface, a Waters view for midfacial and nasal fracture identification, and a submental vertex view for visualization of the zygomatic arches. The panoramic radiograph of the maxilla and the mandible, another invaluable diagnostic aid, may eliminate the need for some other radiographs if the suspected fracture is detected. Computerized tomography (CT) especially with three-dimensional reconstruction, is another valuable diagnostic tool and can be especially useful when greater detail of suspected injuries is desired.

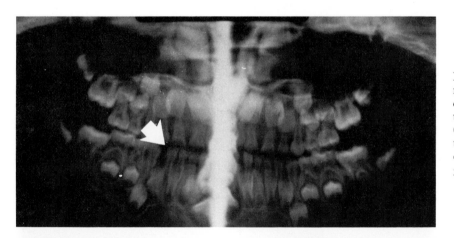

FIGURE 27–5. Developing tooth buds make it difficult to appreciate the presence of an open, complete fracture of the right parasymphysis region of this 6-year-old child. A diastema between the mandibular right cuspid and the lateral incisor *(arrow)* is the only radiographic indication of a fracture.

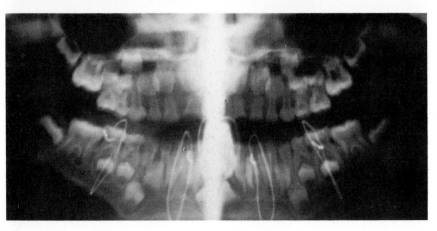

FIGURE 27–6. This radiograph demonstrates the result of a closed reduction of the fracture in Figure 27–5. An occlusal splint held in place by three circum-mandibular wires allowed the patient to function while healing occurred.

FRACTURES

Alveolar Fractures

The most common fracture occurring in the facial skeleton of the child is the alveolar fracture. Interested readers should consult Chapter 15 for the management of such injuries.

Midfacial Fractures

NASAL FRACTURES

Fractures of the nasal structure that occur before growth is completed should be managed like those in the adult. Septal hematomas, if present, should be evacuated as early as possible to avoid damage to the cartilage. If displaced, the septum should be reduced to the midline. Resection of the septal cartilage can have devastating effects on subsequent facial growth, and this must be avoided under all circumstances (Figs. 27–7 and 27–8). The upper lateral cartilages normally insert on the undersurface of the nasal bones but sometimes telescope further when the nose fractures. Once these structures are reduced by applying caudal traction, the nasal bones can be elevated from an intranasal approach. Nasal packs can be placed to support the reduced nasal bones and septum during healing. Open reduction of isolated nasal fractures is almost always avoidable in the growing patient, and secondary revision should be deferred until complete maturation (Figs. 27–9 and 27–10). External splinting is helpful in controlling swelling so that protection may be provided to the area after reduction.

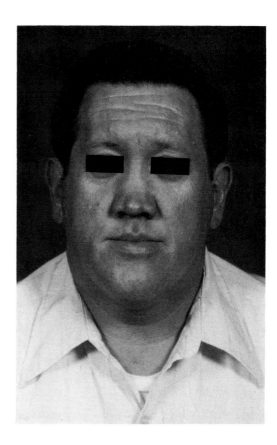

FIGURE 27–7. This 33-year-old man with severe middle face and nasal deficiencies demonstrates the effect of nasal septal resection performed during childhood subsequent to a nasal fracture.

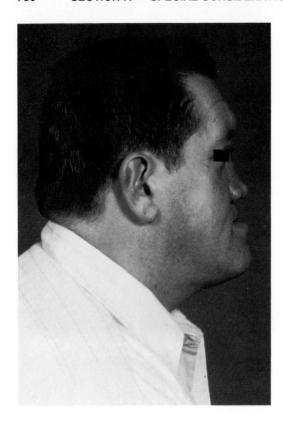

FIGURE 27–8. Side view of patient in Figure 27–7.

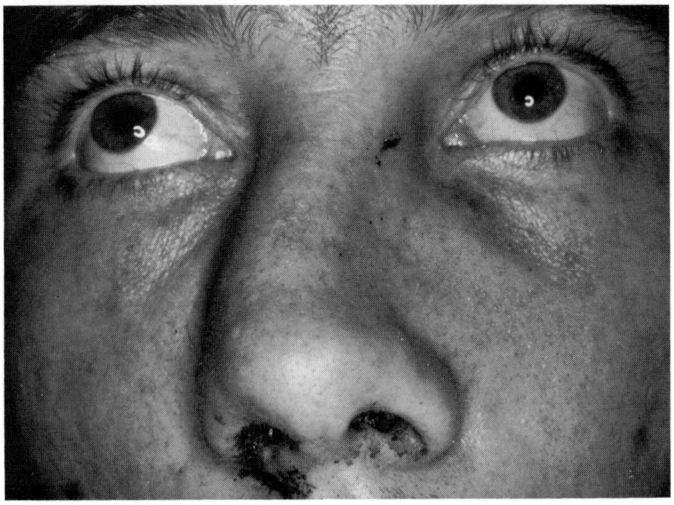

FIGURE 27–9. This 13-year-old sustained a grossly displaced nasal fracture in a diving accident.

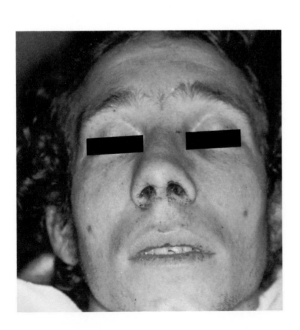

FIGURE 27–10. Closed reduction, as described in the text, successfully reduced the displaced nasal fracture.

MAXILLARY FRACTURES

The classic Le Fort fracture lines are rarely observed in the pediatric population.[12, 14, 31] Distinguishing characteristics of the child's maxilla include cancellous bone, unerupted teeth, and underdeveloped maxillary sinuses. The piriform aperture and zygomaticomaxillary buttress are much thicker structures in the child than in the adult, and subsequently, considerable force is necessary to disrupt the midfacial skeleton of the growing patient.

When a fracture occurs and malocclusion is present, almost without exception it can be managed well by closed reduction. Impressions can be taken, and models can be poured and sectioned to facilitate splint construction for a closed reduction. Surgical intervention into the tooth-bearing areas of the maxilla for placement of stabilization wires or plates increases the incidence of disruption of developing tooth buds and should be reserved for only the most unusual circumstances. The positions of developing maxillary teeth, especially cuspids, can be surprisingly cephalic. For this reason, piriform or infraorbital suspension wires are preferred. Occlusal grinding or postinjury orthodontic manipulation is highly effective in improving minor occlusal discrepancies, especially in the deciduous or mixed dentition stage; so even if perfect restoration of occlusion is not possible at surgery, minor discrepancies can usually be adjusted following surgery.

ORBITAL FRACTURES

Fractures of the orbit in children should be managed like those in the adult. Facial disfigurement, limitation of extraocular movements, prolapsed periorbita into the maxillary or ethmoid sinuses, and persistent diplopia are indications for open orbital exploration.

Complete ophthalmologic examination should precede orbital exploration. Exposure at the frontozygomatic region is performed through an incision in the eyebrow. Without shaving the brow, the incision is placed parallel to the lateral orbital rim (Fig. 27–11). The infraorbital rim, floor of the orbit, and medial orbital wall are approached through an incision placed in a natural fold in the inferior lid. In children, natural folds are not yet apparent, but incisions paralleling the eyelid margin and angling slightly inferiorly as the incision proceeds laterally do generally heal well and result in minimal scarring (Fig. 27–11). The incision is made through the skin ap-

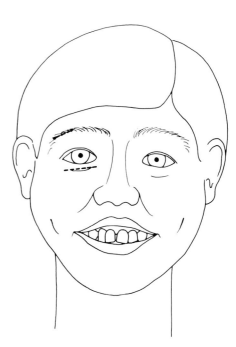

FIGURE 27–11. An incision placed in the eyebrow directly over the frontozygomatic suture provides access for open reduction and results in a concealed scar. The inferior orbital rim and orbital floor are approached through an inferior lid incision made approximately 7 mm under the inferior lid margin and labeled inferiorly as it courses laterally.

proximately 7 mm inferior to the lower lid margin, and the dissection is stepped through the orbicularis oculi muscle as it proceeds inferiorly toward the rim. Once the inferior orbital rim is reached, the periosteum over the rim is incised, and subperiosteal dissection exposes the orbital rim and floor as well as the lateral wall of the maxilla. If wires are placed in the inferior orbital rim, and the child's permanent teeth have not yet erupted, the possibility of injuring tooth buds exists. To avoid this risk, screws or wires should be placed in as cephalic a position on the rim as possible.

When orbital floor or medial wall fractures are present and the orbital contents are prolapsed into the maxillary or ethmoid sinus, the prolapsed periorbita should be retrieved, and the floor or wall should be supported with a bone graft to avoid enophthalmos. Although alloplasts have been used to support the orbital floor or medial wall, autogenous bone grafts harvested from the parietal eminence or the lateral cortex of the mandible eliminate the need for those materials and their possible adverse sequelae. If alloplasts are utilized, they should always be stabilized to adjacent bone to avoid migration and associated problems.

NASAL-ORBITAL-ETHMOID FRACTURES

Growth of the middle face is dependent upon growth of the anterior cranial fossa (sphenoid) orbit and the nasal septum. When open reduction of the nasal-orbital-ethmoid region is undertaken, periosteum is removed from the nasal and orbital bones, and this alone has the potential to inhibit subsequent growth. It is the author's experience that precise reduction in this area is more important for cosmetic considerations than for the possible adversities resulting from periosteal stripping and its effect upon later growth. The cosmetic sequelae from less than adequate reduction of these fractures in children is difficult to improve later in life. Open reduction of the nasal-orbital-ethmoid complex can be done with minimal disturbance to the nasal septum, and under no circumstance should the nasal septum be dissected or resected.

The region can be approached through an existing laceration, by extending the inferior lid incision superiorly on the lateral nasal bone, through incisions made over the nasal dorsum (Fig. 27–12), or by a coronal incision (Fig. 27–13). Unquestionably, the coronal incision provides the most acceptable cosmetic result.

The coronal incision is placed behind the hairline, in the scalp, and begins at the level of the ear. Sometimes the incision extends into the preauricular region if greater

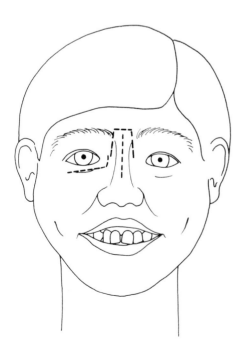

FIGURE 27–12.   A variety of incisions can be utilized to approach the nasal-orbital-ethmoid regions, including a mid-dorsal incision, extension of the inferior lid incision made superiorly onto the nasal bones, or a trapezoidal incision.

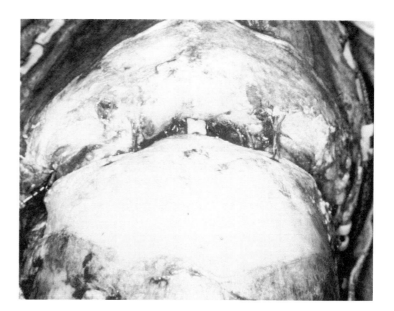

FIGURE 27-13. Unquestionably, the coronal incision offers the widest exposure to the midface and nasal-ethmoid regions.

exposure is required. The incision is carried to the level of the periosteum and temporalis fascia, and the dissection proceeds anteriorly toward the forehead in this bloodless, supraperiosteal plane. Prior to making the incision, normal saline can be injected to distend the plane, making the dissection easier. Hemostatic clips can also be placed on the edges of the flap to control bleeding from the scalp vessels, or electrocautery can be used. Once the forehead is reached, the periosteum is incised, and the entire middle face, nose, and orbits can be exposed in the subperiosteal plane. Bleeding from the skull or facial bones can be controlled with bone wax.

Precise reduction of the medial orbital rim, frontal process of the maxilla, and medial canthus is necessary to assure the restoration of aesthetics and lacrimal func-

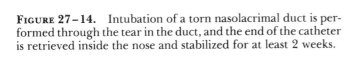

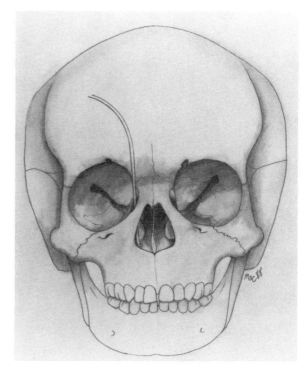

FIGURE 27-14. Intubation of a torn nasolacrimal duct is performed through the tear in the duct, and the end of the catheter is retrieved inside the nose and stabilized for at least 2 weeks.

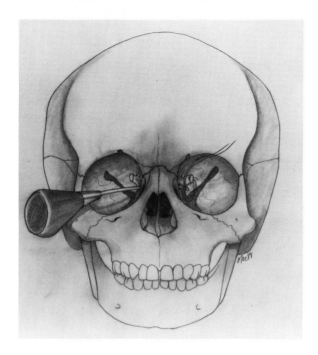

FIGURE 27–15. A transnasal canthopexy has been performed bilaterally by placing a figure-of-eight suture through the medial canthus on one side, passing it transnasally through the frontal process of the maxilla, and suturing it to the opposite canthus.

tion. If the nasolacrimal duct is torn, it should be cannulated and splinted for at least 2 weeks. This procedure is done by intubating the duct with a catheter through the laceration and retrieving it inside the nose (Fig. 27–14). If the medial canthus is detached or has retracted with a small fragment of bone, it must be reduced and held in place. A transnasal canthopexy surface is necessary when the canthus is displaced (Fig. 27–15 and 16). Children do not tolerate internal or external splinting well; therefore, it is important to attempt to reduce and fixate the nasal bridge and medial canthus without the use of splints. Occasionally, bone grafts placed on the medial orbital wall or on the nasal bridge are helpful in supporting these structures, especially when comminution has occurred (Fig. 27–17). Although bone plates provide a rigid

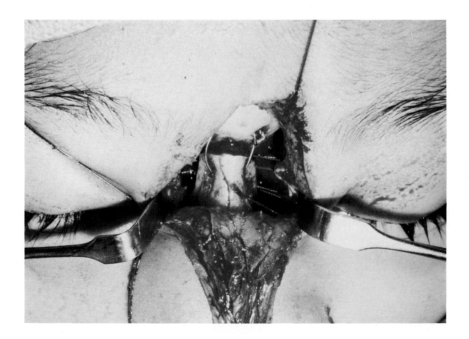

FIGURE 27–16. This clinical photograph demonstrates a bilateral medial canthopexy done with a trapezoidal incision.

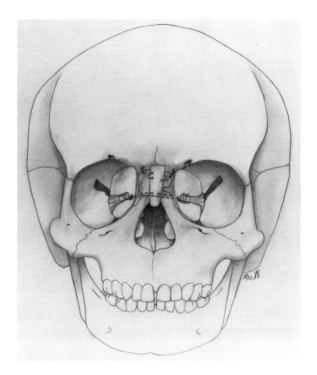

FIGURE 27–17. Bone grafts are often helpful to support the medial orbital wall or nasal bridge when reducing nasal-orbital-ethmoid fractures.

structure to support unstable fractures, especially in children, they may adversely affect growth, and for this reason the author does not favor their use in the growing patient when an alternative is available.

Case Report

A fall from a tractor, with the tire of the tractor subsequently passing over this 5-year-old boy's face, resulted in a severe midfacial fracture and a depressed skull fracture. Immediate neurosurgical intervention was necessary, and at the completion of this procedure, the patient's condition was unstable. The operation was terminated, and he was transferred to an intensive care unit, where he remained comatose for almost 4 weeks. By the fourth week, he had regained consciousness and was taken to surgery to reduce his nasal-orbital-ethmoid complex and to attempt to reduce the maxilla. Presurgical evaluation indicated severe disruption of the entire nasal-orbital-ethmoid complex and asymmetric displacement of the maxilla (Figs. 27–18 to 27–21).

An open reduction of the nasal-orbital-ethmoid region was performed through a midline incision. Mobilization of the frontal process of the maxilla and the nasal bones and bilateral transnasal canthopexies adequately restored nasal bridge projection and the intercanthal distance. Attempts to reduce his maxilla and zygomatic complex bilaterally were unsuccessful because of rapid bone healing. Several days later, orthodontic appliances were placed on his maxillary teeth, and a face mask with elastic forces was utilized to bring his maxilla forward (Fig. 27–22).

Two years following injury, good restoration of facial aesthetics is observed, as well as maintenance of Class I occlusion (Figs. 27–23 to 27–25). Superimposition cephalometric radiographs demonstrate anterior and vertical development of the midface and lower face since the accident (Fig. 27–26). Continued monitoring of his facial growth is necessary, and interventional orthodontic or surgical treatment will likely be necessary in the future.

This case illustrates several points worthy of emphasis. Immediate reduction of his facial fractures would have been much easier and more predictable. Unfortunately, his life-threatening neurologic condition prohibited this undertaking. The 4-week delay in treatment compromised efforts to reduce his facial fractures adequately, since healing had already occurred. Precise reduction of the nasal-orbital-ethmoid region, as described previously, has resulted in a satisfactory cosmetic outcome without significant interference with midfacial growth. Conservative manipulation of the tooth-bearing region of his maxilla has restored and maintained a

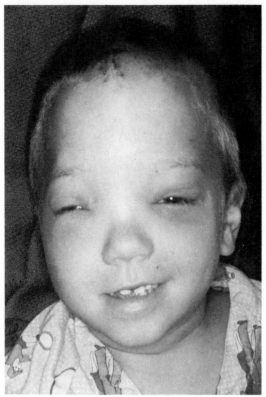

FIGURE 27–18.   Severe disruption of the entire middle face and nasal-orbital-ethmoid region is evident in this 5-year-old child. Notice the severe widening of the intercanthal region and the flat nasal bridge.

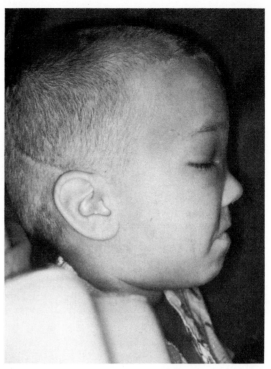

FIGURE 27–19.   Profile view of patient in Figure 27–18 demonstrates retrodisplacement of the midface and complete lack of nasal bridge support.

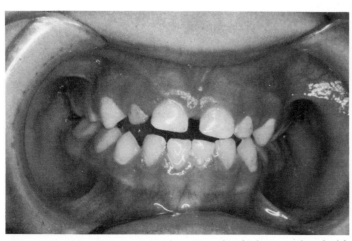

FIGURE 27–20.   Asymmetric Class III malocclusion associated with the injuries.

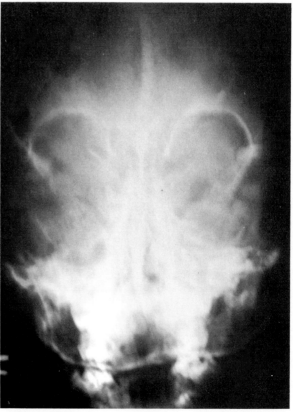

FIGURE 27–21.   This Waters view radiograph reveals complete disruption of the entire middle face.

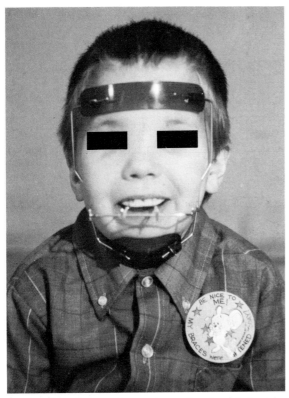

FIGURE 27–22. A face mask was fitted, and elastics with the forward traction on the face bow nonsurgically corrected the malocclusion resulting from maxillary fracture.

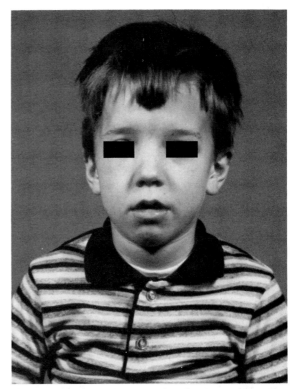

FIGURE 27–23. Open reduction of the nasal-orbital-ethmoid region through a nasal mid-dorsal incision and bilateral inferior lid incisions permitted adequate reconstruction of the intercanthal, nasal, and orbital regions.

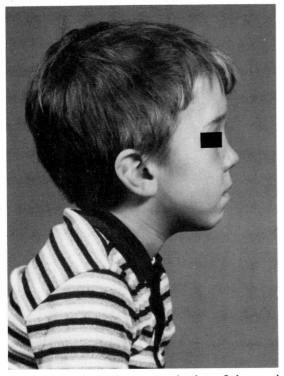

FIGURE 27–24. Adequate projection of the nasal bridge and middle face has been restored.

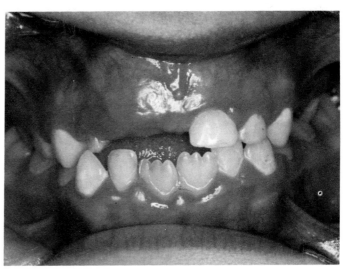

FIGURE 27–25. The patient continues to demonstrate a Class I occlusion through the mixed dentition stage.

FIGURE 27–26. Superimposition celphalometric tracings demonstrate continued downward and forward development of the middle face, 2 years after the injury.

Class I occlusion without interfering with dental development. Tears of the nasolacrimal apparatus were not appreciated at the time his facial fractures were reduced. Subsequent chronic epiphora and dacryocystitis necessitated dacryocystorhinostomy 9 months after reduction of the facial fracture.

ZYGOMATIC ARCH FRACTURES

Isolated zygomatic arch fractures occur from a direct blow over the area, and these are uncommon injuries in the growing patient. The authors prefer to reduce

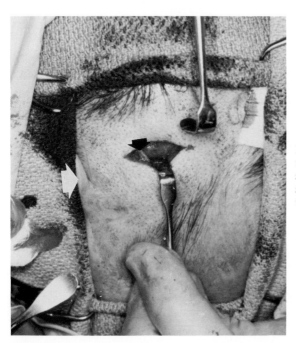

FIGURE 27–27. The depressed zygomatic arch is approached through a 2-cm incision placed in the scalp anterior to the ear and above the level of the lateral canthus. The white arrow identifies the anterior portion of the ear. The black arrow indicates an incision through the temporalis fascia.

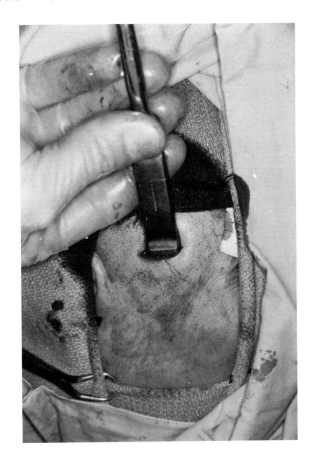

FIGURE 27–28. An instrument is inserted deep to the temporalis fascia and is passed beneath the depressed zygomatic arch, which will allow it to be elevated.

these fractures using an incision placed in the hair-bearing area of the scalp, above the lateral canthus level and anterior to the tragus (Gillies approach). After shaving the scalp over the area, a horizontal or an oblique incision is made to minimize the risk of injury to the frontal branch of the facial nerve. The incision is made to the level of the temporalis fascia (Fig. 27–27). The fascia is identified and incised, and an instrument (e.g., a Kelly clamp, double-ended periosteal elevator, urethral sound) is inserted under the fascia and passed below the fractured arch (Fig. 27–28). Laterally directed force on the end of the instrument will reduce the fracture. It is important to pass the reducing instrument deep to the temporalis fascia, since this is the most superficial plane that runs deep to the arch.

Postoperative trismus is expected, and the patient should be encouraged to exercise the mandible by opening widely, protruding, and performing lateral excursion.

Mandibular Fractures

FRACTURES OF THE MANDIBULAR CONDYLE

Fractures of the mandibular condyle that occur during childhood have the potential to result in progressive growth disturbances of the face.[1, 11, 32–36] Two mechanisms account for the pathogenesis of facial asymmetry following a condylar fracture in a growing patient. Immediately after the injury, the mandible deviates to the affected side if dislocation of the proximal segment occurs (Fig. 27–29). This deviation results from shortening of the ramus and is considered the static mechanism. The progressive mechanism results from the altered muscle-bone interaction secondary to the positional alteration of the mandible. If the mandible is left to function in its altered (unreduced) position, the body on the affected side will eventually bow while

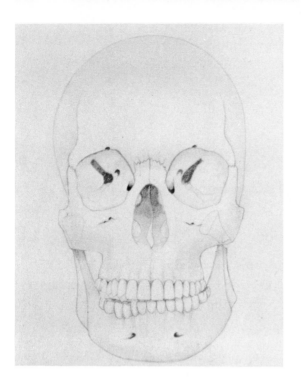

FIGURE 27–29.   Deviation of the mandible toward the affected side and an open bite on the affected side occur following a condylar fracture if the segments are displaced. This is the static mechanism responsible for facial asymmetry following a condylar fracture and results from shortening of the ramus.

the unaffected side flattens, the chin will deviate more to the affected side, and the ramus remains shortened on the affected side (Fig. 27–30). The masseter muscle and soft tissue envelope on the affected side become fuller than on the nonaffected side. Even the orbits, zygomas, and temporal bone may be affected. These deformations are difficult to eliminate and require extensive surgery if left until maturation.

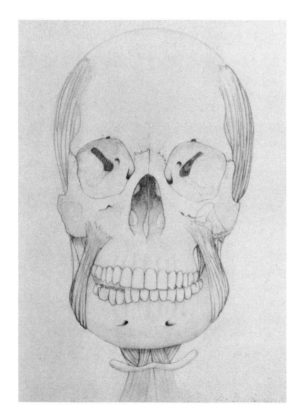

FIGURE 27–30.   The progressive mechanism responsible for facial asymmetry following a condylar fracture is secondary to the altered muscle-bone interaction that causes the body of the mandible to bow and the chin to deviate more to the affected side while the body of the mandible flattens on the nonfractured side.

To date, the world's literature and statistics reported from large series of childhood facial fractures suggest closed reduction, careful control of mandibular position, and restoration of mandibular function to be the method of choice for treating this injury.[7-10,13-15,37,38] Long-term retrospective reviews of patients who sustained condylar fractures conducted by Gilhuus-Moe and Lund indicate that conservative management of such fractures results in approximately 76 per cent of the patients having no growth disturbance after the injury.[33-35] Scrutiny of their data does not reveal the association of any particular fracture pattern with a higher instance of abnormal growth following injury. Walker's classic study of condylar fractures conducted on a primate model indicates that closed reduction of this injury resulted in the safest and most predictable outcome from both a functional and a growth potential perspective.[39] His findings are supported by other similar studies.[40,41]

Although some authors have reported satisfactory short-term results after the open reduction of "avulsive" condylar injuries in the growing patient, long-term data are not yet available to support this surgical approach.[17-19] Furthermore, the data of Lund and Gilhuus-Moe indicate that it is impossible to predict which patients will grow abnormally following a condylar fracture. In addition, the problems of reducing and stabilizing a condylar fracture and the effect of the surgery on subsequent growth make the effectiveness of this procedure questionable. Only long-term controlled studies will clarify the issue.

Moss' studies suggest that the role of the "functional matrix" is more important than the concept of the condyle's acting like a primary growth center when considering mandibular growth.[4] Other studies conducted by Moss conclude that growth of the mandibular condyle is secondary to and compensatory for the downward and forward mandibular position resulting from jaw function and growth of the middle face.[5]

Condylar fractures occurring during childhood often are not diagnosed. After reviewing records from the University of North Carolina Dentofacial Deformity Program, we concluded that approximately 10 per cent of the patients evaluated had evidence of old condylar fractures. Most of these fractures were undiagnosed at the time of injury, and many of the patients had only vague recall or no recall of ever injuring their jaws or face.[42] These facts led us to conclude that condylar fractures occur more frequently during childhood than reported, without significant pain or noticeable jaw dysfunction, and that many parents and health care providers frequently overlook this injury. These fractures are discovered only later in life, when facial asymmetry and malocclusion become more apparent.

The signs and symptoms of the condylar fracture in a growing child are identical with the diagnostic findings in the adult. Asymmetric malocclusion, anterior open bite, deviation of the mandible on opening or closing, preauricular pain, swelling, limitation of movement, blood in the ear canal, and submental laceration should alert the practitioner to the presence of condylar fracture[21,31,43] (Figs. 27–31 to 27–33).

Treatment. Since the osteogenic and tissue-healing potential of the child is greater than that in the adult, generally less time is required for immobilization. In fact, prolonged immobilization after condylar fractures in children is associated with a greater potential for ankylosis than in the adult and should be avoided.[14] It has been suggested that the hematoma that forms at the fracture site stimulates osteogenesis and that this may be responsible for the ankylosis following condylar fractures. Early mobilization discourages fibrosis and bone fusion and restores the muscle-bone stimulation necessary for continued symmetric growth.[7,44,45]

Once a condylar fracture has occurred, the proximal segment is usually displaced medially and anteriorly by the force of the lateral pterygoid muscle, and the remaining ramus shortens. As time progresses after the injury, the displaced proximal segment resorbs, and the condylar stump remodels by resorption and apposition. Additional remodeling takes place in the glenoid fossa. There is a critical time frame following this injury after which additional appositional remodeling does not occur, which is the reason why immediate reduction of occlusion and mandibular position is

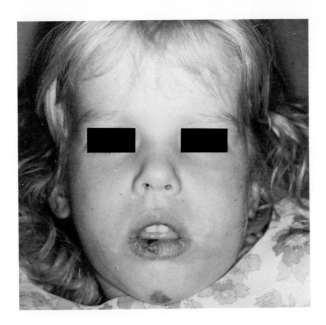

FIGURE 27–31.   This 3-year-old child fell from her tricycle and sustained bilateral mandibular condylar fractures. The chin contusion and lip lacerations should alert the examiner to the possibility of condylar fractures.

FIGURE 27–32.   Asymmetric malocclusion and an anterior open bite are consistent findings with this injury.

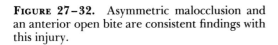
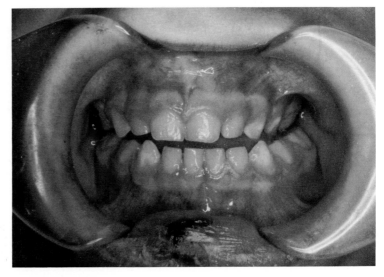

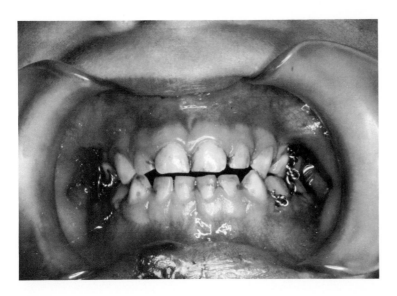

FIGURE 27–33.   Closed reduction has been performed with circumdental eyelet wires and intermaxillary fixation. Immobilization for 1 week, followed by restoration of function while controlling mandibular position with elastics, produced a satisfactory resolution for this difficult problem.

FIGURE 27–34. An example of a functional appliance that has been designed to restore mandibular position and occlusion. This appliance is helpful after the acute management stage, when function is restored, to maintain the forward and symmetric position of the mandible.

necessary for proper restoration of ramus height and for symmetric growth to continue. Experience suggests that the critical time is the first 6 months after the injury. Functional appliance therapy has been useful in maintaining occlusion and mandibular position during the immediate postinjury phase (Fig. 27–34). If the mandibular position and occlusion can be maintained for 6 months, most often mandibular growth will occur symmetrically. After this critical period has elapsed, the use of a functional appliance to change the asymmetric mandible has not been effective.

The goal of managing condylar fractures in the growing patient is to restore mandibular symmetry, occlusion, and function without interfering with future

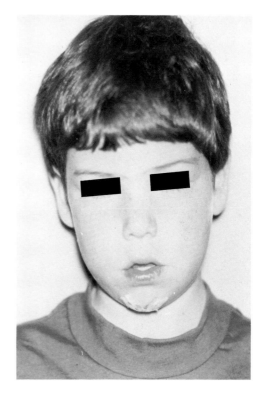

FIGURE 27–35. This 8-year-old boy fractured both mandibular condyles in a skateboard accident. Note the absence of facial asymmetry but the presence of a chin laceration.

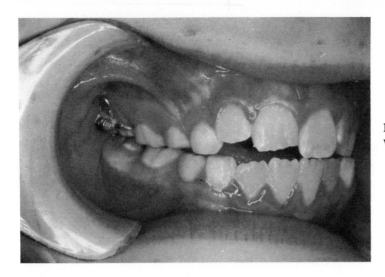

FIGURE 27–36. There is no malocclusion associated with the bilateral condylar injury.

growth. If a condylar fracture is identified and malocclusion is not present, immobilization is not necessary. Careful observation during the postinjury period is critical. If change occurs, intermaxillary fixation or some other means of controlling the occlusion and mandibular position (functional appliances) should be employed (Figs. 27–35 to 27–38).

When malocclusion or mandibular asymmetry accompanies a condylar fracture, reduction of the occlusion and mandibular position is achieved with intermaxillary wire fixation or elastic traction. Arch bars can usually be placed on the deciduous dentition, but often they require additional support from circum-mandibular, piriform, or circumzygomatic wires. Orthodontic appliances may be helpful in the mixed dentition stage. If the occlusion is easily reduced and the discomfort is not significant, elastic therapy can be maintained and jaw movement encouraged. If discomfort or another accompanying fracture is present, immobilization with wire fixation is indicated, but for a brief period only.

The most critical aspect of care after a condylar fracture in a growing patient is restoration of function. This restoration minimizes the risk of ankylosis and encourages symmetric growth. If immobilization with wire fixation has been utilized, the wire should be removed and controlled function with elastics begun shortly after surgery. If accompanying fracture management demands immobilization, function should be reinstituted in 1 week or no later than 2 weeks following the condylar injury. As a general rule, the younger the child, the earlier the physical therapy should be instituted. Vigorous opening-closing, lateral, and protrusive movement should be

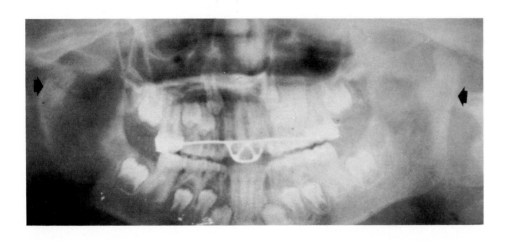

FIGURE 27–37. Panoramic radiograph reveals bilateral condylar fractures *(arrows)*.

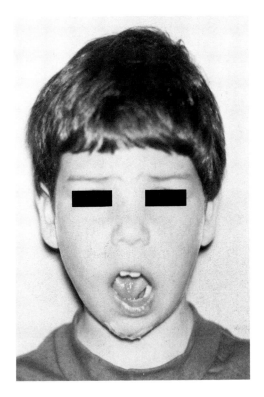

FIGURE 27–38.   The patient could function and reproduce his mandibular position without difficulty, so no immobilization was employed. Careful monitoring of the mandibular position and occlusion during the first 6 months and continued observation until maturation are necessary.

encouraged. The exact site of the condylar fracture, the amount of displacement of the proximal segment, and the level of attachment of the lateral pterygoid musculature will determine the presence or absence of lateral pterygoid muscle function on the affected side.

Ongoing observation of the occlusion of patients who have had condylar fractures must be emphasized. Periodic observation until complete maturation is warranted, and it is wise to involve an orthodontist in this aspect of care.

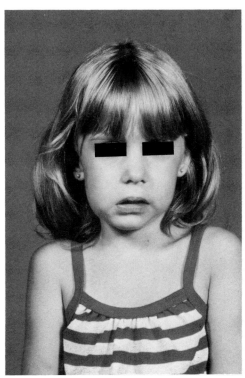

FIGURE 27–39.   This 5-year-old girl has an old condylar fracture that was unrecognized at the time of injury. The static and progressive mechanisms are responsible for her facial asymmetry, which affects her lower face, orbits, zygomas, and temporal regions.

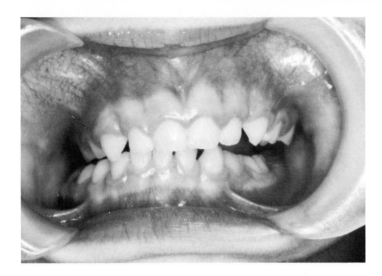

FIGURE 27–40. The asymmetric malocclusion associated with the old condylar fracture in this same 5-year-old patient.

The management of old condylar fractures (greater than 6 months following injury) by orthodontic or functional appliance therapy has not been successful in restoring mandibular position or symmetry even in the pediatric patient. Our experience indicates that surgery to reposition the mandible before growth is completed restores symmetry to the face, and we have observed favorable facial growth after this treatment. Surgical restoration of mandibular position during childhood improves facial symmetry and eliminates the need for more involved surgery later in life (Figs. 27–39 to 27–45).

MANDIBULAR BODY AND SYMPHYSIS FRACTURES

Fractures of the mandibular body and symphysis region in the growing patient occur adjacent to developing teeth and are almost always compounded into the oral cavity. These fractures must be treated with antibiotic therapy, reduction of the occlusion, and stabilization. Greenstick fractures in this area are common, and much displacement is usually not encountered. Even when significant displacement is present, these fractures usually snap into place and are self-retained by the occlusion or the fracture interfaces (Figs. 27–46 to 27–49).

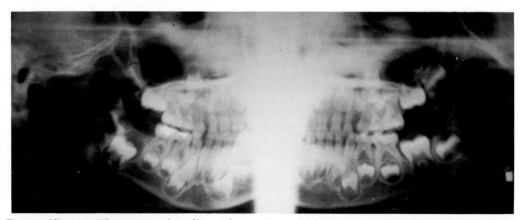

FIGURE 27–41. The panoramic radiograph reveals an old fracture of the right mandibular condyle.

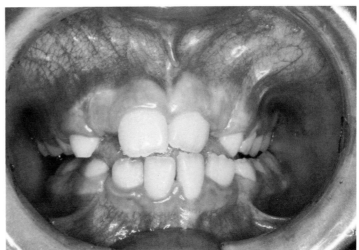

FIGURE 27–42. This posteroanterior radiograph demonstrates the skeletal asymmetry associated with the old condylar fracture.

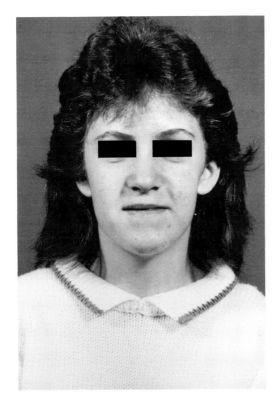

FIGURE 27–43. At age 6, bilateral sagittal osteotomies in the mandibular ramus were performed to improve the mandibular position. This photograph was taken at age 11 and reveals that the asymmetry has been improved.

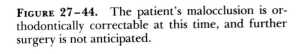

FIGURE 27–44. The patient's malocclusion is orthodontically correctable at this time, and further surgery is not anticipated.

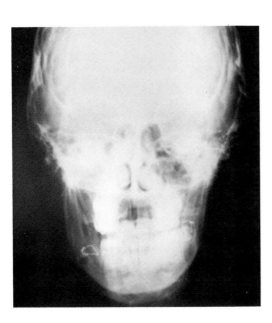

FIGURE 27–45. The posteroanterior cephalometric radiograph demonstrates an improved skeletal symmetry, especially when compared to Figure 27–42.

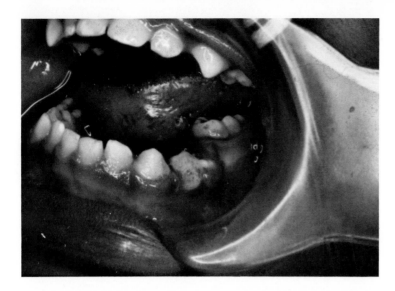

FIGURE 27–46. A 21-month-old child was struck by an automobile and sustained open and displaced fractures of the left mandibular body, as can be appreciated from the occlusal photograph.

Open reduction of the symphysis or body of the mandible in the pediatric patient is seldom necessary. When it is indicated, it is usual to have adequate distance between developing tooth buds and the inferior border of the mandible, so that interosseous wires or bone plates can be placed without interfering with dental development. The intraoral approach for the placement of intraosseous wires or plates is the method of choice, since it eliminates visible scars and possible injury to the facial nerve.

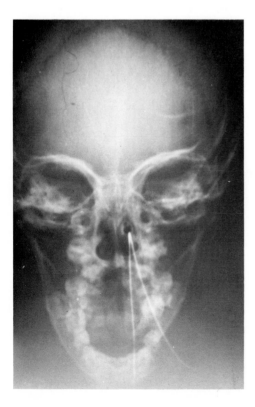

FIGURE 27–47. The posteroanterior radiograph demonstrates the amount of displacement of the fracture. Note the presence of teeth in the proximal segment, which will help to maintain the position of the reduced fracture.

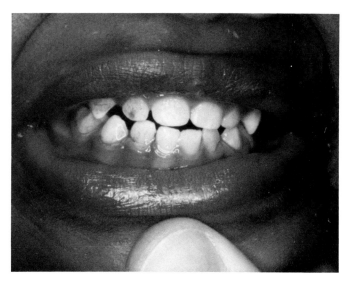

FIGURE 27–48. Three weeks after injury, the restored occlusion is observed. Immediate closed reduction in the emergency room resulted in retention of the segments by the fracture interfaces and the occlusion without the need to immobilize the mandible further. A soft diet during the postinjury state was suggested, and the patient was administered penicillin for 1 week.

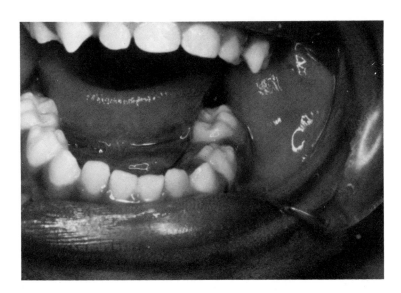

FIGURE 27–49. Open-mouth view of patient in Figure 27–48.

FIGURE 27–50. Panoramic radiograph of an 11-year-old child who had a history of mandibular fracture at age 4. The treating practitioner performed an open reduction extraorally and inserted a wire in the midportion of the body of the mandible, which interrupted the premolar development. If the wire had been appropriately placed at the inferior border, the interference problem could have been avoided.

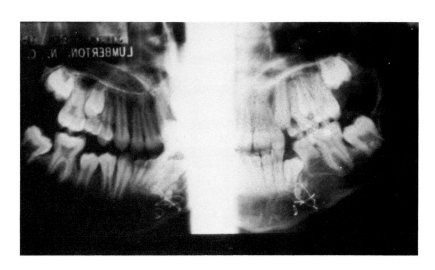

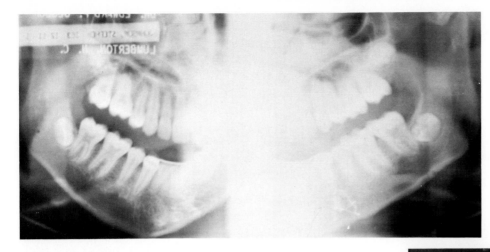

FIGURE 27–51. Four years after, transplantation of a premolar from the opposite side and orthodontic treatment have satisfactorily resolved the occlusal problem.

FIGURE 27–52. This 9-year-old boy fell from his bicycle and sustained multiple mandibular fractures, as is evidenced by facial swelling and disruption of his dental arches.

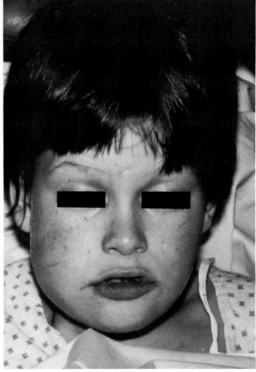

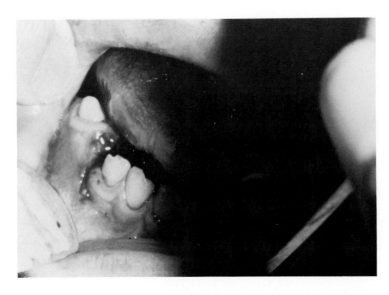

FIGURE 27–53. Same patient as in Figure 27–52.

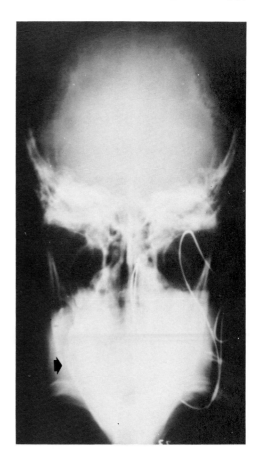

FIGURE 27–54. The posteroanterior radiograph demonstrates displacement of the right mandibular angle fracture.

Closed reduction of mandibular body or symphysis fractures is advocated because of the potential risk that open reduction poses to the developing tooth buds (Figs. 27–50 and 27–51). In addition, the effect of surgery upon subsequent growth must be considered, taking into account the disruption of soft tissue and periosteum necessary to perform an open reduction. Almost all fractures in these regions in the pediatric population are amenable to closed reduction (Figs. 27–52 to 27–57).

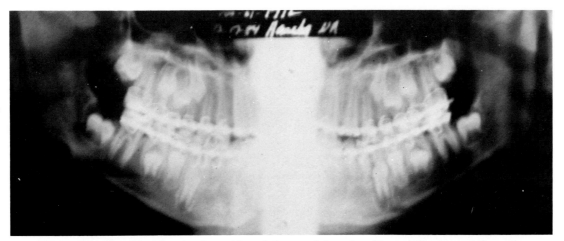

FIGURE 27–55. Closed reduction with arch bars and 4 weeks of immobilization satisfactorily resolved the situation. Notice the minimal displacement of the right proximal segment, which is of no consequence.

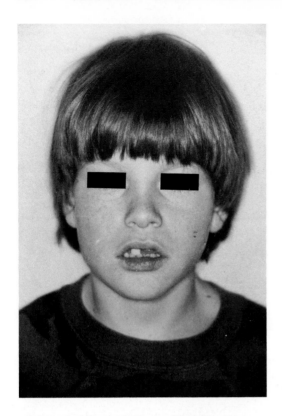

FIGURE 27–56. Good restoration of lower facial aesthetics and occlusion is seen 6 months following injury.

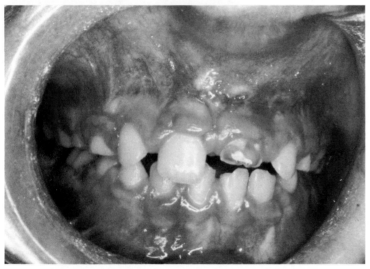

FIGURE 27–57. Intraoral view of patient's occlusion from Figure 27–56.

REFERENCES

1. Boyne PJ: Osseous repair and mandibular growth after subcondylar fractures. J Oral Surg 25:300, 1967.
2. Brodie AG: On the growth pattern of the human head from the third month to the eighth year of life. Am J Anat 68:209, 1941.
3. Hotz RP: Functional jaw orthopedics in the treatment of condylar fractures. Am J Orthod 73:365, 1978.
4. Moss MI, Rankow RM: The role of the functional matrix in mandibular growth. Angle Orthod 39:95, 1968.
5. Moss ML, Salintyn L: The primary role of functional matrixes in facial growth. Am J Orthod 55:566, 1969.
6. Proffit WR: Contemporary Orthodontics. St Louis, CV Mosby, 1986.
7. Graham GG, Peltier JR: The management of mandibular fractures in children. J Oral Surg 18:416, 1960.
8. Hagan EH, Huelke DF: An analysis of 319 case reports of mandibular fractures. J Oral Surg 19:93, 1961.
9. Khosla VM, Boren W: Mandibular fractures in children and their management. J Oral Surg 29:116, 1971.

10. Lal D: Management of fractures in the lower jaw in children. Oral Surg 12:1413, 1959.
11. Leake D, Habal MB, Murray JE: Long-term follow-up of fractures of the mandibular condyle in children. J Plast Reconstr Surg 47:127, 1971.
12. McCoy FJ, Chandler RA, Crow ML: Facial fractures in children. J Plast Reconstr Surg 37:209, 1966.
13. Rakower W, Protzell A, Rosencrans M: Treatment of displaced condylar fractures in children: Report of cases. J Oral Surg 19:517, 1961.
14. Rowe NL: Fractures of the facial skeleton in children. J Oral Surg 26:505, 1968.
15. Waite DE: Pediatric fracture of jaw and facial bones. Pediatrics 51:551, 1973.
16. Furman EB: Specific therapy in water, electrolyte and blood-volume replacement during pediatric surgery. Anesthesiology 42:187, 1975.
17. Hendrix JH, Green B: Open reduction of mandibular condyle. J Plast Reconstr Surg 23:283, 1959.
18. Hoopes JE: Open treatment of fractured mandibular condyle in children using a post-auricular approach. J Plast Reconstr Surg 46:357, 1970.
19. Peskin S, Laskin DH: Contribution of autogenous condylar grafts to mandibular growth. Oral Surg 20:517, 1965.
20. Broadbent TR: A method of naso-mandibular fixation in children and edentulous adults. J Plast Reconstr Surg 14:148, 1954.
21. Rowe NJ, Killey HC: Fractures of the Facial Skeleton. 2nd ed. London, Livingstone, 1968.
22. Bennett EJ: Fluids for Anesthesia and Surgery in the Newborn and the Infant. Springfield, IL, Charles C Thomas, 1975.
23. Kiesewetler WB: Pre- and Post-operative Care in the Pediatric Surgical Patient. Chicago, Year Book Medical Publishers, 1956.
24. Weil WB: Fluid and Electrolyte Metabolism in Infants and Children: A Unified Approach. New York, Grune and Stratton, 1977.
25. Winters RW: Principles of Pediatric Fluid Therapy. Boston, Little, Brown, and Company, 1982.
26. Winters RW: The Body Fluids in Pediatrics. Boston, Little, Brown, and Company, 1973.
27. Mason EE: Fluid, Electrolyte and Nutrient Therapy in Surgery. Philadelphia, Lea and Febiger, 1974.
28. Masiak MJ: Fluids and Electrolytes Through the Lifecycle. Norwalk, CT, Appleton-Century-Crofts, 1985.
29. Brown BR: Fluid and Blood Therapy in Anesthesia. Philadelphia, FA Davis, 1983.
30. Bjork A: Facial growth in man, studied with the aid of metallic implants. Acta Odontol Scand 13:9, 1955.
31. Shultz RC: Facial Injuries. Chicago, Year Book Medical Publishers, 1970.
32. Coccan PJ: Restitution of mandibular form after condylar injury in infancy. Am J Orthod 55:32, 1969.
33. Gilhuus-Moe O: Fractures of the Mandibular Condyle in the Growth Period. Norwegian Monographs on Medical Science. Oslo, Universitetsforlaget, 1969.
34. Gilhuus-Moe O: Fractures of the mandibular condyle in the growth period. Acta Odontol Scand 29:53, 1971.
35. Lund K: Mandibular growth and remodelling process after condylar fracture. A longitudinal roentgencephalometric study. Acta Odontol Scand 32 [Suppl 64], 1974.
36. MacLennan WD: Fractures of the mandible in children under the age of six years. Br J Plast Surg 9:125, 1956.
37. Blevine C, Gores RJ: Fractures of the mandibular condyloid process: Results of conservative treatment in 140 patients. J Oral Surg 19:392, 1961.
38. Chalmers J Lyons Club: Fractures involving the mandibular condyle: A post-treatment survey of 120 cases. J Oral Surg 5:45, 1947.
39. Walker RV: Traumatic mandibular condyle fracture dislocations. Effect on growth in Macaca rhesus monkey. Am J Surg 100:850, 1960.
40. Hayes AM: Histologic study of regeneration of the mandibular condyle after unilateral condylectomy in the rat. J Dent Res 46:483, 1967.
41. Heurlin RJ, Gans BJ, Stuteville OH: Skeletal changes following fracture dislocation of the mandibular condyle in the adult rhesus monkey. Oral Surg 14:1490, 1961.
42. Proffit WR, Vig KW, Turvey TA: Early fracture of the mandibular condyles: Frequently an unsuspected cause of growth disturbances. Am J Orthod 78:1, 1980.
43. Lovasco JH, Laskin DM: Facial growth after condylectomy. J Oral Surg 36:685, 1978.
44. Ellis D: Fractured mandible in a five year old. Oral Surg 33:348, 1972.
45. Thomson HG, Farmer AW, Lindsay WK: Condylar neck fractures. J Plast Reconstr Surg 34:452, 1964.

CHAPTER 28

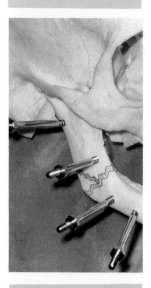

ORAL AND MAXILLOFACIAL TRAUMA IN THE GERIATRIC PATIENT

RICHARD F. SCOTT, D.D.S., M.S.

The geriatric patient with oral and maxillofacial injuries presents special problems and challenges in management. Principles of treatment are in accord with the general rules of fracture reduction and soft tissue management discussed elsewhere in detail in this text; however, associated medical problems and either the partial edentulous or the complete edentulous condition often complicate the situation. Customary methods of immobilization, such as intermaxillary fixation utilizing the dentition, may not apply, and alternative approaches are needed. Healing of facial fractures may require a longer time, and the incidence of complications, such as nonunion, may be higher. This chapter discusses these special issues of managing oral and maxillofacial injuries in the geriatric patient (Fig. 28–1).

EPIDEMIOLOGIC CONSIDERATIONS

Incidence of Facial Trauma in the Aging Patient

Specific data on the incidence of facial trauma in the aging patient are lacking in the current literature. However, information can be gained by reviewing reports on facial trauma that do not restrict themselves to specific age groups. In a review of 580 patients with a total of 935 mandibular fractures occurring from 1972 to 1978, Olson and colleagues[1] reported a peak incidence between the ages of 20 and 29 years. There were 41 fractures seen in patients between the ages of 40 and 49, 24 between the ages of 50 and 59, and 20 in those 60 years and older. Bochlogyros[2] reviewed 1521 mandibular fractures occurring in 853 patients from 1960 to 1980. Patients ranged in age from 6 weeks to 82 years. The peak incidence in male patients occurred between the ages of 20 and 29, and the peak incidence in females was between the ages of 10 and 29 years. There were 75 patients with fractures between the ages of 40 and 49 (61 men, 14 women), 58 patients between the ages of 50 and 59 (44 men, 14 women), 23 patients between the ages of 60 and 69 (15 men, 8 women), and 8 patients 70 years and older (2 men, 6 women). Thus, 18.9 per cent of the patients were 40 years of age or older. Ellis and associates[3] reviewed a total of 3462 mandibular

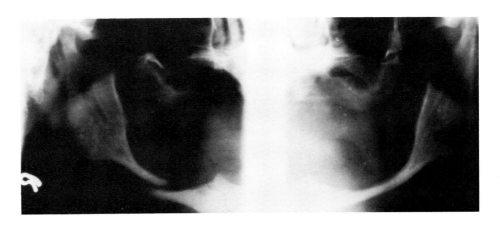

FIGURE 28–1. Panoramic radiograph demonstrating a fracture through the body region of an extremely atrophic mandible in an edentulous patient. Such fractures present special problems in management.

fractures in 2137 patients from 1974 through 1983 and demonstrated a similar trend in regard to age distribution. In a prospective study, James and colleagues[4] found 14.6 per cent of 253 patients with mandibular fractures to be 41 years of age or older (11.5 per cent aged 41 to 60, 3.1 per cent aged 61 and older).

Fractures of the maxilla or zygomatico-orbital complex show a similar distribution relative to age, although the literature contains fewer reports. Ellis and associates[5] reviewed 2067 patients with a total of 2160 zygomatico-orbital fractures from 1974 through 1983. Ages ranged from 3 to 76 years, with the majority of patients being males between the ages of 10 and 40, with a peak incidence occurring in those 20 to 30 years old. Female subjects accounted for 19.8 per cent of the patients studied and showed a peak incidence between the ages of 30 and 40 years. Approximately 30 per cent of the male patients studied were over the age of 39. Approximately 44 per cent of the female patients studied were older than age 39. In fact, in this report, it was concluded that in women zygomatico-orbital fractures were more prevalent in older age groups than they were in men. In an interesting report appearing in 1984, Zachariades and coworkers[6] investigated 1791 fractures involving the facial skeleton. Of these, 5.2 per cent (93 cases) occurred in edentulous patients. There were 27 cases of fractures of the zygomatico-orbital complex in this group and 66 edentulous patients with fractures of the mandible or Le Fort–type fractures (3.68 per cent of the fracture cases). Of this edentulous group, 70 per cent were men and 30 per cent were women. The age span of this edentulous group was 38 to 86, with 50 per cent of cases occurring between the ages of 50 and 70.

Common Mechanisms of Injury

The most frequent causes of fractures of the facial skeleton have been enumerated by many authors. They generally include motor vehicle accidents (including motorcycle accidents), altercations, falls, athletic injuries, and industrial accidents. The same causes apply to the aging patient; however, the frequency in each category changes as the patient ages. For example, in regard to motorcycle accidents resulting in mandibular fractures, Olsen and colleagues[1] reported two patients in the 40- to 49-year-old group and none over the age of 49, while there were 38 such fractures in those under the age of 40 in their study. The same authors also reported that in a total of 52 mandibular fractures occurring in patients over the age of 40, 23 were due to automobile accidents and 27 to altercations. The incidence of industrial accidents resulting in facial injuries also decreases as more of the patients reach retirement age. The same reasoning applies to athletics as a cause of injury. The leading causes of fractures of the facial skeleton in the aging patient are altercations, falls, and automobile accidents. Bruce and Strachan,[7] in an analysis of 216 patients with fractures of the endentulous mandible (aged 40 or older), reported that altercations accounted for 31 per cent, falls for 30 per cent, and automobile accidents for 28 per cent. Marciani and

Hill[8] reviewed 53 patients with fractures of an edentulous mandible. Of these, 43 per cent were involved in motor vehicle accidents, 19 per cent in altercations, and 17 per cent in falls. The mechanism of fracture must be quantified in light of the geographic location of the study group. For example, in large, industrialized areas with high rates of unemployment and low availability of automobiles for personal use, motor vehicle accidents as a cause of facial fractures will decrease and other causes, such as altercations, will predominate. Such results were seen by Ellis and colleagues,[3,5] who reviewed mandibular and zygomatico-orbital injuries.

Type and Severity of Injury

Zachariades and colleagues[6] reported that in 66 edentulous patients with either fractures involving the mandible or Le Fort–type fractures of the maxilla, the majority of fractures were found in the mandible — 104 fractures in 62 patients. Most of the mandibular fractures (44, or 42 per cent) were found in the condylar region, and one third of these were bilateral. Other fracture sites included 22 (21 per cent) of the ascending ramus or angle, 26 (25 per cent) of the mandibular body, and 12 (11.5 per cent) of the symphysis. Also in this group were six Le Fort type II and two Le Fort type III fractures. In all, there were 112 fractures in 66 patients. Twelve per cent of the patients had associated facial lacerations, and 12 per cent had associated cerebral concussions. In comparison, Bruce and Strachan[7] reported that in 216 patients with fractures of an edentulous mandible, 65 per cent occurred in the body region, 5 per cent in the symphysis region, 18 per cent in the ramus or angle region, and 12 per cent in the condylar region. Again for comparison purposes, Marciani and Hill[8] reported that in 53 patients with 96 fractures of the edentulous mandible, 67 per cent occurred in the body or angle region. These figures regarding distribution of fractures in the edentulous mandible correspond approximately with the figures seen in other studies,[1-4] in which no distinction was made on the basis of the remaining dentition. One may suggest, however, that there is a trend toward increased numbers of fractures in the edentulous mandibular body region and angle. These areas are where the greatest degree of atrophy occurs. This observation is consistent with the comments of Bruce and Strachan.[7] In an analysis of 146 patients with fractures of the edentulous mandibular body, they noted that the height of the mandibular body at the site of fracture was less than 10 mm in 45 per cent, between 10 and 20 mm in 40 per cent, and greater than 20 mm in 15 per cent.

TISSUE CHANGES IN THE AGING FACE

Soft Tissue Changes

QUALITATIVE TISSUE CHANGES

Soft tissue changes in the aging face result in characteristic anatomic changes. They begin to occur around the age of 30 and then progress steadily into the 80s and 90s. In the orbital areas, there is a progressive weakening of the orbital septum, and by age 50 the lateral canthus begins to slant downward. By the age of 60, these changes result in the illusion of decreased eye size. Skin lines at the lateral canthus have appeared and accentuate the process. Forehead wrinkles become more noticeable around the age of 40 and then deepen with progressive aging. In the nasal area, there is a deepening of the nasolabial folds, which becomes more pronounced between the ages of 50 and 80. Also during this time there is a gradual drooping of the nasal tip. Changes in the perioral area are accentuated with the loss of teeth and thus the loss of support for the upper and lower lips. This change is magnified as alveolar bone resorption follows tooth loss. These alterations are manifested by a downward drooping of the commissures, which is magnified if tooth replacement has not maintained the proper vertical dimension of occlusion. A drooping of the lower lip occurs and is often accompanied by an accentuation of the labiomental fold. Vertical wrinkles emanating from the upper and lower lips appear around the age of 60 and become more pronounced. Also beginning in the 50s there is some resorption of adipose and subcutaneous tissues in the cheeks and temporal areas. This resorption continues to become more pronounced as the patient ages.

The aging skin shows a generalized thinning of the epidermis, and there is less function in the skin appendages. A decrease in sebaceous gland activity occurs.[9] The thickness of the dermis decreases as a result of loss of elastic and collagen fibers. Collagen synthesis is reduced, and fibrocytes are relatively inactive in aged skin.[10] A decrease in hyaluronic acid production, leading to a low water-binding capacity, also occurs.[10] As the skin becomes grossly thinner, underlying blood vessels are much better visualized.

Changes in the mechanical properties of skin accompany these underlying modifications. Loss of elasticity is demonstrated easily by stretching the skin and noting its delayed response in regaining its former configuration. Differences in the stress-strain curve for skin of young and old individuals have been demonstrated and attributed to loss of elastic fibers.[11]

Practically, these changes have some significance in the trauma patient. The thinning of the epidermis and dermis, combined with the decrease in subcutaneous fat, makes the skin more vulnerable to injury, as it has inadequate cushioning to withstand external physical trauma. On the other hand, facial scars in the older patient tend to mature faster and have a shorter erythematous and hypertrophic phase than those seen in the younger patient or child. In addition, concealment of incision lines in open reduction techniques may be easier owing to the accentuation of the lines of facial expression, contour lines, and lines of dependency in the aged patient.

Skeletal Tissue Changes

QUALITATIVE TISSUE CHANGES

Various qualitative changes in the underlying facial skeleton may occur in the elderly patient. Some of these will be discussed in detail further on. However, the most striking alterations occurring in the jaws are those associated with tooth loss. These deserve special attention.

Changes Secondary to Tooth Loss

INCIDENCE OF EDENTULISM

The jaws are unique in regard to the types of changes that occur from a structural standpoint after tooth loss. Although all skeletal tissue may be subject to certain qualitative changes associated with aging, such as osteoporosis, the jaws actually undergo morphologic changes manifesting as atrophy with quantitative loss of osseous tissue. The problem is well known to all members of the dental profession and is one of large magnitude. It has been estimated that about 25 to 30 million people in the United States are edentulous in one or both jaws[12-14] and that most wear dentures. Periodontal disease affects nearly 80 per cent of our adult population, and more than 50 per cent of the population becomes edentulous by the age of 60.[15] In addition, the life expectancy in the United States has increased from 68.2 years in 1950 to 74.7 years in 1985 and is projected to increase to 78.1 years by the year 2020. Further, the percentage of the population over the age of 65 has steadily increased since 1950. Added to this is the fact that many senior citizens are leading more active lifestyles than they were 30 years ago. Because of these factors, the clinician may encounter an increasing percentage of elderly and edentulous patients in the facial trauma group.

PHYSIOLOGY OF EDENTULOUS BONE LOSS

The physiology of bone loss—in particular, alveolar bone loss—remains an enigma. It is generally believed that alveolar bone relies on the presence of existing dentition for its maintenance. Once the dentition is lost, resorption of the alveolar processes ensues. Much of the mechanism for this process remains unknown. Its impact, however, is heavily felt. Atwood and Coy[13] have described the physical, psychologic, and economic problems that result for millions of people throughout the world as the result of a major, complex oral disease that is chronic, progressive, irreversible, and disabling. The mechanisms that control this process remain unknown.

Generally, most investigators have relied heavily on the concept that biomechanical forces serve as a control mechanism and are thus responsible for bone remodeling. The concept traditionally holds that tension forces result in bone deposition and pressure forces result in bone resorption. In essence, the belief is that an imbalance of forces applied to bone causes stimulation of osteoblasts or osteoclasts or both. Remodeling of bone ensues until the forces are brought into balance and equilibrium returns. Further remodeling then ceases until the time a new imbalance occurs. However, as Enlow[15] points out, this is far from a complete explanation of the process. It does not adequately explain what specific control mechanisms are involved in the process. That is to say, although stress can trigger the remodeling process, the actual subsequent control of that process is not yet understood. A variety of control mechanisms may be involved. These include heredity, hormonal factors, local pH, enzymatic agents, local oxygen tensions, bioelectric potentials, local induction phenomena, and others.[15]

It is also not clear why remodeling of alveolar bone should differ from that in other areas of the jaws. That differences are present is clear (Fig. 28–2). Manson and Lucas[16] have shown that generalized remodeling activity occurs at a much higher rate in alveolar bone than in the adjacent corpus of the mandible. In addition, more active

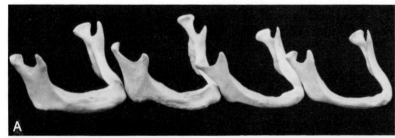
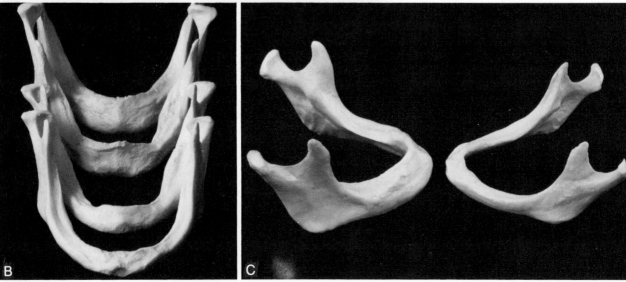

FIGURE 28–2. Loss of alveolar bone following tooth loss. *A,* Progressive bone loss as seen from a sagittal view. *B,* Progressive bone loss as seen from a frontal view. *C,* Comparison of a mandible that has recently become edentulous *(left)* with an edentulous mandible of long standing.

rates of deposition and resorption have been shown for alveolar bone than for non–tooth-bearing bone tissues by Baumhammers and Stallard.[17] These differences may have to do with the fact that alveolar bone is much more vascular and porous than the basal bone tissue.

Long-term denture wearing has been associated with increased alveolar bone resorption. Tallgren[18] has demonstrated continued resorption of alveolar bone under these circumstances. She has also noted that alveolar resorption is approximately four times greater in the mandible than in the maxilla and that similar changes are not noted in the adjacent basilar bone, cranial base, or upper face.

The underlying causes and the control of alveolar bone loss remain unknown; it is an area requiring much additional investigation. Until such information is available, little hope for controlling or delaying the process exists.

ANATOMIC CHANGES AND CONSIDERATIONS IN THE EDENTULOUS PATIENT

J.C. Bradley's work in the early 1970s has contributed to our knowledge of significant changes, related to aging, that occur in the mandible.[19] This knowledge has had practical importance in the management of mandibular fractures in the geriatric patient. Bradley performed angiographic studies on the mandible in cadavers and patients. He found that in many older individuals an inferior alveolar artery could not be found and in others the vessel was greatly reduced in size.[19] Bradley postulated that arteriosclerotic changes accounted for this finding and demonstrated that changes in the inferior alveolar artery preceded those in the carotid arteries by 15 years. These vascular changes may be a result of tooth loss, with the arterial supply to the mandible becoming less functional as the teeth are lost and bony atrophy occurs. However, the correlation between these factors was present but not great.

Bradley also demonstrated the presence of a periosteal plexus of vessels along the inferior border of the mandible made up of branches of the buccal, lingual, and facial arteries.[19] This plexus was also described by Cohen[20] in 1960. It is suggested that this plexus contributes the major part of the blood supply to the mandible and that stripping off this periosteum in open reductions of the atrophic mandible may seriously compromise blood supply and increase the incidence of nonunion across the fracture site. Because of these anatomic changes, Bradley advocated a supraperiosteal dissection with wire or plates placed over the periosteum when open reduction of an atrophic mandible is necessary.[19]

Recently, Pogrel and colleagues[21] again investigated the patency of the inferior alveolar artery via external artery angiography with digital subtraction. Eighty-four suitable angiograms were accumulated, 51 from men and 33 from women. The mean age of the patients was 58 years. Of those patients under 58 years old, the artery could be traced beyond the mandibular foramen into the mandibular canal in 24 of 42 patients. In those patients over the age of 58, the artery could be traced in only 18 of 42 cases. The artery was seen less often in elderly men than in elderly women. There was a statistically significant decrease in the patency of the artery in patients with a positive medical history of atherosclerosis.

Another anatomic factor of importance is the position of the inferior alveolar neurovascular bundle in extremely atrophic mandibles. Because of bone atrophy, the bundle may lie on the superior aspect of the residual ridge just below the mucosa. As Bruce suggests, the intraoral approach might therefore be more hazardous to the bundle than the extraoral approach.[7]

Significant atrophy is less often encountered in the maxilla than in the mandible and may be localized or diffuse. However, Branzi and Quintarelli[22] have shown that the maxillary artery may be more prone to atheroma than any other artery and that occlusion of the maxillary artery may lead to periodontal disease. A common example of localized maxillary atrophy is seen in the anterior maxilla when the patient has been edentulous except for the presence of mandibular anterior teeth.

Further, as maxillary alveolar bone is lost, the distance between the maxillary sinus floor and the residual ridge decreases, and the ratio of sinus space to bone increases. The lateral wall of the maxillary sinus is often quite thin, and the combination of these factors can produce a severely comminuted Le Fort type I, or "eggshell," fracture.

SYSTEMIC CONSIDERATIONS

When dealing with the geriatric patient, particular emphasis must be placed on the possibility of systemic disease that may complicate or alter the treatment of maxillofacial injuries. Diseases of the cardiovascular system are more common in the older patient. Atherosclerotic disease producing hypertension and coronary artery involvement may be accompanied by a history of angina pectoris or myocardial infarction. A recent history of infarction may preclude treatment or may permit only the least invasive therapy. Similarly, pulmonary diseases such as pulmonary emphysema or pulmonary hypertension are more likely to be encountered in the elderly patient. Discussion of the perioperative management of these conditions is not within the scope of this chapter. Suffice it to say that a high level of suspicion for the presence of such conditions should be maintained by the clinician. Special disease states may have a direct effect on the healing of osseous tissues. Such diseases as osteoporosis, renal failure, and diabetes mellitus fall into this category.

Osteoporosis

The basic clinicial manifestation of osteoporosis is a deficiency of bone mass. It is estimated that osteoporosis leads to over 150,000 hip fractures annually. It is also estimated that 25 to 30 per cent of all white women in the United States will experience an osteoporosis-related fracture by the age of 65.[23] The most frequent presentation of osteoporosis is in postmenopausal, elderly women. Following menopause, there appears to be an accelerated rate of bone resorption compared with bone deposition for a period of 4 to 7 years. Estrogen deficiency is believed to play a critical role in this process.

Before the diagnosis of postmenopausal osteoporosis or senile osteoporosis is made, other underlying disorders resulting in a secondary osteoporosis must be ruled out. Conditions to be ruled out include general malnutrition, calcium deficiency, malabsorption syndrome, alcoholism, excessive antacid intake, prolonged corticosteroid therapy, and diabetes mellitus. A thorough systems review, as well as complete blood count and differential and determination of serum calcium, phosphorus, and alkaline phosphatase levels, is appropriate. Radiographic survey of the facial bones can show a decreased bone density and a reduction in the normal trabecular pattern of bone; however, these changes will show up only after a 30 to 50 per cent decrease in mineral content and are thus somewhat late findings. Such patients are susceptible to fractures after even relatively minor trauma. Fracture healing may be prolonged owing to inadequate matrix formation for normal ossification. The treatment of osteoporosis has revolved around employment of four basic chemotherapeutic agents. These are (1) sodium fluoride, (2) estrogens, (3) anabolic steroids, and (4) calcitonin. Calcium, vitamin D_2, and congeners have also been employed. At this time, however, a cure for osteoporosis remains elusive.

Renal Failure

The majority of patients with chronic renal failure will eventually show manifestations of bone disease referred to, in this instance, as renal osteodystrophy. The severity of the presentation may range from osteomalacia, caused by a deficiency of the active form of vitamin D, to osteitis fibrosa cystica, resulting from renal-induced hyperparathyroidism. Osteomalacia is characterized by a defect in the process of mineralization of bone matrix. This factor distinguishes it from osteoporosis and results in an excess of nonmineralized or inadequately mineralized osteoid. Poor bone healing results. Secondary, or renal-induced, hyperparathyroidism results as phosphate clearance decreases with declining renal function. As the serum phosphate levels rise, there is a corresponding fall in serum ionized calcium levels. This resulting hypocalcemia stimulates the parathyroid glands to secrete additional parathyroid hormone (PTH). The PTH acts on osseous tissue to raise the serum calcium levels. In addition, the hydroxylation of 25-hydroxycholecalciferol (25-OHD) to 1,25-dihydroxycholecalciferol (1,25-[OH]$_2$D), the biologically most active form of vitamin D, is kidney dependent. Deficiency of 1,25-(OH)$_2$D results in diminished calcium absorption from the gut and produces hypocalcemia.

The combination of these processes produces early histologic changes in bone. In late disease, cystic lesions or giant cell tumors may appear in the mandible as well as other bones. Fracture healing is compromised.

The successful management of fractures in the patient with chronic renal failure is dependent on the regulation of the underlying disease. Appropriate consultation with renal specialists is mandatory. Therapy is directed primarily at control of and return to normal phosphorus levels. Low-protein diets are instituted to restrict phosphate intake and are supplemented with phosphate-binding agents, such as aluminum hydroxide, which decrease absorption of phosphate from the gut. Persistent hypocalcemia is treated with calcium supplementation and vitamin D preparations. A discussion of the long-term management of chronic renal failure with peritoneal dialysis, hemodialysis, or transplantation is beyond the scope of this chapter.

Diabetes Mellitus

Diabetes mellitus is the most common of the metabolic disorders and affects approximately 2 to 5 per cent of the American population. Multiple etiologic factors are responsible for this disorder. Several of these factors become significant in the group of patients under discussion. Age, obesity, inactivity, various drugs, and injury all affect glucose tolerance. In the patient with facial injuries and longstanding diabetes mellitus, the clinician should be alert to the possibility that complications may develop during the course of treatment.

Obvious considerations include the perioperative management of insulin requirements in the insulin-dependent patient. Various regimens have been advocated. One common practice is to begin an intravenous infusion of 1 L of 5 per cent glucose in water prior to surgery and to administer one half to one third of the usual morning intermediate insulin dose. Postoperatively, glucose levels are monitored in the recovery room, and regular insulin is administered on an as-needed basis. Postoperative inactivity increases the demand for insulin, and a return to the patient's routine insulin requirements may be delayed until more normal daily activities can be resumed. In addition, patients with facial fractures will often have postoperative dietary restrictions, perhaps as the result of intermaxillary fixation. Attention must be directed to coordinating dietary intake with insulin requirements. Dietetic consultation is appropriate.

Although infections do not necessarily occur with more frequency in diabetic patients, when they do occur, they can be severe and difficult to control. Polymorphonuclear leukocytes and macrophages are less active against bacteria and migrate in abnormal patterns in the insulin-deficient patient. Thus, poorly controlled diabetic patients may be more susceptible to nosocomial infections.

Atherosclerosis and renal disease are also considerations in the patient with longstanding diabetes mellitus. Atherosclerosis tends to be more advanced at an earlier age in the diabetic patient and may affect local healing when atrophic jaw fractures are being treated, as well as increase suspicion of concomitant coronary vessel disease. Diabetic renal disease may lead to the clinical picture discussed previously under "Renal Failure."

Chronic Drug Therapy

It is also important for the clinician to bear in mind that many of the geriatric patients seen for the treatment of maxillofacial injuries will present with various drug histories. As the average life expectancy increases, elderly patients constitute a growing percentage of the population. It is currently estimated that there are more than 25 million persons in the United States aged 65 and older, with this number increasing annually. There is little doubt that the incidence of chronic medical problems is higher in this population of patients. Many of these conditions are managed with drug therapy, and several of these drugs may have a direct effect on the treatment of patients with maxillofacial injuries. Examples of such drugs include chronic corticosteroid therapy, chronic heparin therapy, and anticonvulsant therapy. Chronic alcohol ingestion may also complicate healing and management.

Corticosteroids are used to treat a variety of conditions. These include substitution therapy in adrenal insufficiency and therapeutic uses in nonendocrine diseases, such as rheumatoid arthritis, systemic lupus erythematosus, allergic diseases, pemphigus, chronic ulcerative colitis, chronic active hepatitis, sarcoidosis, and thrombocytopenia, to name a few. It is important to keep in mind that osteoporosis and vertebral compression fractures are well-documented complications of corticosteroid therapy. Bones with a high degree of trabeculation are generally more affected. The mechanism for this is believed to be a direct effect on osteoblastic activity by corticosteroids and an indirect effect produced by their inhibition of calcium absorption by the intestine. This inhibition, in turn, results in an increased release of PTH. PTH has been shown to increase the effect of osteoclasts. The net effect is both a decreased formation and an increased resorption of bone.[24] A comparison of 128 asthmatic patients receiving long-term corticosteroid therapy with a group of 54 asthmatics not receiving long-term corticosteroids showed that 14 patients (11 per cent) in the first group had a total of 58 documented fractures, whereas no fractures were seen in the second group. Measurements of bone density were reduced in the first group.[25]

As mentioned previously, patients on long-term heparin therapy may show altered osseous tissues. Avioli[26] states that osteoporosis and spontaneous fracture may occur in patients who have received 15,000 units or more of heparin daily for over 6 months. Perhaps more frequently encountered is the patient who is on long-term therapy with one of the oral anticoagulants. These drugs are prescribed for prevention of thromboembolic disease and may be used in patients with cerebrovascular disease manifesting as recurrent transient ischemic attacks, in patients with a history of rheumatic heart disease and, perhaps most frequently, for secondary prophylactic treatment in patients with a positive history of venous thrombosis and pulmonary embolism.

When managing patients with maxillofacial injuries who have received long-term therapy with anticoagulants, various drug interactions must be kept in mind. The use of acetylsalicylic acid should be avoided, thereby avoiding impairment of platelet aggregation and untoward enhancement of the anticoagulant. Acetaminophen, which does not interact with the anticoagulant, is a reasonable alternative. In addition, metronidazole and trimethoprim-sulfamethoxazole have been shown to enhance the effect of anticoagulants, and in such patients, they must be used with caution. On the other hand, barbiturates increase the clearance of oral anticoagulants and thus decrease their action.[27] The benzodiazepines have no interaction with the oral anticoagulants.

Drugs used in anticonvulsant therapy may also have an effect on osseous tissues. Long-term use of phenytoin,[28] phenobarbital, and primidone has been shown to be associated with osteomalacia, probably because of an accelerated elimination of vitamin D.[29] This osteomalacia usually responds well to high levels of vitamin D administration.

Nutritional Considerations

Maintenance of nutritional requirements in the patient with maxillofacial trauma should be an integral part of the overall treatment plan. A detailed discussion of nutritional considerations in the trauma patient is presented in Chapter 4. Injury to osseous and soft tissues of the oral cavity region makes dietary intake difficult, and the situation may be compounded by regional edema, postinjury infections, and pain. Utilization of intermaxillary fixation techniques and intraoral splints makes feeding even more cumbersome. These considerations apply to facial injuries in patients of all ages but take on even greater importance in the elderly patient. Injury and operative trauma initiate a metabolic response requiring an acute increase in energy demands. The ease with which this increased demand is met depends on a number of factors, including the following:

1. Extent of the injury
2. Extent of the surgical intervention
3. Age
4. Pretrauma nutritional status
5. Presence of any preexisting nutritional deficiencies

Following injury and surgical correction, glycogen stores are consumed within a period of 24 to 36 hours. Subsequent demands for glucose are met through the process of gluconeogenesis via catabolism of protein, primarily protein from skeletal muscle and visceral protein.

The magnitude of this catabolic phase and its impact on the incidence of postoperative complications can be diminished with appropriate preoperative nutritional assessment and postoperative management of the patient's dietary intake. Preoperative nutritional assessment is critical, as several investigators have demonstrated that deficiencies may alter the response to surgery.[30-32] Others have documented deficiencies in randomly selected patients admitted to the hospital. Leevy and colleagues[33] showed that 59 per cent of randomly selected patients in a municipal hospital had a deficiency in circulating vitamins, including folic acid. Bollet and Owens[34] demonstrated a 35 per cent incidence of low serum albumin levels in patients admitted to the medical service. These figures must be viewed in light of the fact that serum albumin levels fall apparently only after significant protein depletion has occurred. Investigations have shown that hypoproteinemia interferes with wound healing,[35] can delay callus formation in fractures, and increases the incidence of infection.[36,37] Others have revealed an increased incidence of postoperative complications in patients with a pre-existing protein-calorie malnutrition when compared with surgical patients who have a normal preoperative nutritional status.[38]

Identification of protein-calorie–deficient patients can be accomplished via an extensive history, physical examination for evidence of muscle and fat wasting, and laboratory testing. Laboratory tests include serum albumin levels, prealbumin and retinol-binding protein levels, and lymphocyte counts.[39] The status of the cellular immune responses may also be estimated by recall skin antigen testing and total lymphocyte count. Indications of malnutrition include a serum albumin level less than 3.4 g/dl, a total lymphocyte count of less than 1500, and an unintentional weight loss of 10 per cent of the body weight. Deviation of the patient's body weight from calculated body weights should be recorded. It should be kept in mind that caloric requirements in healthy, active adults increase 50 to 60 per cent following major surgical procedures and that the potential for deficiencies is greater during the convalescence period after surgery of the oral cavity region. Requirements may be further increased if the patient with facial injuries has been unable to maintain normal intake between the time of injury and the time of surgical treatment.

Jones[40] reported that approximately 150 g of protein plus 3000 nonprotein calories (kilocalories) should be provided daily during convalescence from surgery. Another method of meeting caloric and protein needs is to supply 35 kcal/kg/day for maintenance and 45 kcal/kg/day for anabolism. Nitrogen intake should approximate 1 g of nitrogen per 150 nonprotein calories in the average patient.[41] Most commercially prepared enteral feeding formulae and dietary supplements approximate the correct nitrogen-calorie ratios, and their postoperative use should be strongly considered. It has been shown by Olejko and coworkers[35] that balanced nutrient intake, resulting in improved nitrogen retention and maintenance of body weight, can be achieved in orthognathic surgical patients postoperatively when commercially prepared dietary supplements are given at a level of 50 per cent of estimated caloric requirements (708 to 944 ml/day). If feeding by the oral route is impossible or contraindicated, nasogastric tube feeding should be employed.

SPECIAL CONSIDERATIONS IN MANAGING FACIAL TRAUMA IN THE GERIATRIC PATIENT

Soft Tissue Injuries

The basic principles of managing soft tissue injuries, as discussed in Chapter 23, apply to the geriatric patient as well.

Fractures of the Partially or Completely Edentulous Maxilla

In the geriatric patient, the decision-making process in the management of facial fractures must include not only what type of treatment to employ but also whether or not to treat. Associated medical problems may increase the risk of surgical intervention beyond a reasonable limit. The degree of intervention and the duration of general anesthetic required to complete the intervention must be evaluated with regard to pre-existing medical conditions. It is better to restrict planned intervention based upon sound evaluation of the patient's ability to withstand such surgical insult prior to initiation of treatment than to be hindered by untoward complications during treatment. When complications occur, treatment is compromised, and, in retrospect, a less invasive approach at the beginning may have yielded the better result. For example, some authors believe that elderly patients tolerate intermaxillary fixation poorly and that it may interfere with respiratory function. It has also been shown that edentulous patients are less able to generate normal masticatory forces and may, therefore, be less likely to displace fractures after reduction.[6]

Traditional concepts regarding the use of craniomaxillary suspension in maxillary fractures may be inappropriate in the geriatric patient. In a recent review of midfacial trauma, 14 of 21 patients were treated with maxillomandibular fixation alone, that is, without craniomaxillary suspension. None of the 14 showed facial elongation or nonunion. Complications occurred in six patients, three in each group. With craniomaxillary suspension, the principal complication was palatal tipping, whereas that with nonsuspension was open bite.[42] In the edentulous patient, minor degrees of open bite as well as tipping may be accommodated by a new prosthesis. In the sample of edentulous patients reported by Zachariades,[6] there were eight midface fractures, six Le Fort type II, and two Le Fort type III. Only one of the eight was treated with surgical intervention, namely, interosseous wiring and elevation of the zygomatic arch via a lateral orbital approach. This was an 80-year-old patient who, unfortunately, developed postoperative pneumonia and died. Satisfactory results were obtained in the other seven patients. Others have reported satisfactory union of maxillary fractures in the edentulous patient when active treatment was withheld for medical reasons.[43]

Once the decision to actively treat maxillary fractures is made based upon adequate assessment of the risk-benefit ratio for a particular patient, treatment may still be complicated by inadequate dentition, thus making stabilization and immobilization of reduced fractures difficult. Treatment is enhanced by utilization of pre-existing prosthetic appliances and subsequent maxillomandibular fixation. This practice helps not only to ensure postoperative occlusal relations but also to establish correct anteroposterior position of the maxilla and, in a situation involving a midline palatal fracture, the correct transverse reduction of the fixation.

Stabilization of the maxillary prosthesis can be accomplished in a variety of ways. These include suspension from the malar abutments or from circumzygomatic wires brought into the oral cavity. Both techniques are dependent on stable zygomas. Often, an anterior nasal spine wire must be used concomitantly to prevent downward displacement of the prosthesis from the anterior maxillary ridge. Wires may be secured to the prosthesis via holes drilled through the acrylic base or to segments of arch bars added to the prosthesis preoperatively with cold-cure acrylic. The latter technique facilitates maxillomandibular fixation when similar arch bar segments have been added to the mandibular prosthesis (Fig. 28–3).

Circumpalatal wiring has also been advocated to secure the prosthesis to the maxilla.[16] These wires are passed from the anterior maxillary vestibule into the nasal fossa and then traverse the palate in a sagittal plane. They are brought into the mouth again at the junction of the hard and soft palates by perforating the tissue in this region with the passing awl. Then they are brought anteriorly under the prosthesis and secured to the free ends in the anterior vestibule. An improvement in this technique avoids the presence of the wires along the intraoral palatal aspect by placing two holes in the acrylic at the distal extension of the prosthesis. Each end of the single wire is passed through these holes so that the free ends are pointing up. These ends are then brought anteriorly along the nasal floor and exit in the anterior vestibule, where they are again passed through previously drilled holes in the denture base and secured.

Transalveolar wires have also been used to secure a maxillary prosthesis. Owing

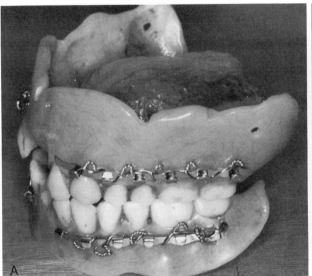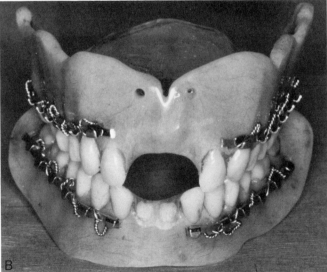

FIGURE 28–3. Utilization of existing dentures for reduction and stabilization of jaw fractures. A, Note that portions of arch bars have been applied to the dentures with cold-cure acrylic. Also note that holes have been placed through the denture flanges to facilitate wire placement. B, Note the removal of anterior maxillary and mandibular teeth from the dentures to facilitate postoperative feeding.

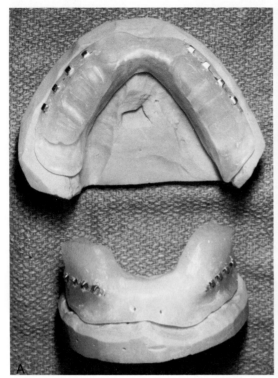

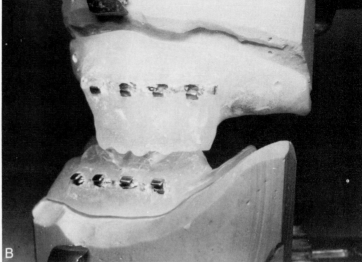

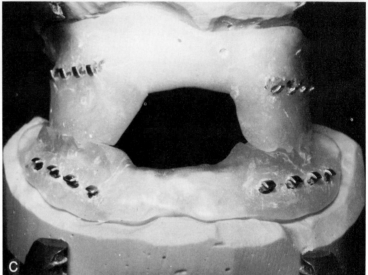

FIGURE 28-4. Fabrication of Gunning splints for reduction and stabilization of jaw fractures in the edentulous patient. *A,* Maxillary and mandibular splints in place on study models. *B,* Models and splints in place on an articulator to help ensure correct vertical dimension and occlusion. Note that the splints have been designed so that the occlusal surfaces interdigitate to provide definite seating and proper relationships at the time of insertion. *C,* Frontal view of mounted models and splints. Note the arch bar placement and the anterior feeding port.

to the thin nature of the alveolus, especially in areas of atrophy, this technique may prove inadequate, as the transalveolar wires may pull through the thin bone.

When a pre-existing denture is unavailable, Gunning splints may be fabricated from preoperative study models. Care must be taken in the fabrication of such splints to ensure the correct vertical dimension of occlusion (Fig. 28-4). It is prudent to include some form of soft lining material in the fabrication of these appliances to help guard against frictional irritation and pressure sores of the mucosa. When dentures or splints are used to obtain maxillomandibular fixation, consideration should be given to removing several of the anterior teeth from the denture or an area of acrylic from the anterior splint to facilitate postoperative feeding (Fig. 28-4C).

Recently, rigid fixation techniques utilizing miniplates have been used with increasing frequency in managing midface fractures. The basic principles that apply to younger age groups pertain to the geriatric patient also. These are discussed in Chapter 33.

The utilization of plates in transverse or Le Fort type I fractures of the edentulous maxilla is complicated by the lack of osseous tissue available. Atrophy of the alveolar ridges, coupled with pneumatization of the maxillary sinuses, may preclude the utilization of rigid fixation in these patients. It is interesting that the incidence of transverse fractures in the edentulous population compared with Le Fort type II and

Le Fort type III fractures may be low. This finding has led at least one author to speculate that in edentulous patients the line of least resistance in the maxilla is moved farther up toward the Le Fort II and Le Fort III fracture levels.[6] It may also relate to the lack of forces transmitted to the adjacent bones via existing dentition. The bone, in terms of its quality and quantity, at the Le Fort II and III levels is generally comparable to that of younger patients, and standard principles of rigid fixation apply. The clinician must weigh the desirability of perhaps avoiding maxillo-mandibular fixation with the use of rigid fixation against the possibility of greater morbidity from prolonged exposure to general anesthesia and increased operating time.

Fractures of the Partially or Completely Edentulous Mandible

The same considerations involving the decision to treat or not treat discussed previously apply to managing mandibular fractures in the geriatric patient. It may require more diagnostic acumen to know when not to operate and to recognize the indications for conservative patient management.[44]

There is still disagreement among surgeons regarding the proper management of the fractured edentulous mandible. Treatment options include open versus closed reduction, rigid versus nonrigid fixation, transosseous versus extraskeletal fixation, and immobilization versus no immobilization.

CLOSED REDUCTION

Proponents of closed reduction techniques emphasize the following:

1.   Increased hazards of open reduction in the edentulous and atrophic mandible
2.   Increased morbidity of prolonged surgical techniques and exposure to general anesthesia in the elderly
3.   Decreased vascularity in the atrophic mandible (as discussed previously)
4.   The incidence of local complications, such as nonunion, following open reduction
5.   The acceptability of results in regard to function with less than ideal anatomic reduction

In a review of 146 fractures of edentulous mandibles by Bruce and Strachan,[7] the number of nonunions was reported at 31 (20 per cent). Of the 31 nonunions reported, 25 of the fractures were originally treated by open reductions and 6 were treated by closed reduction. Eighteen of the nonunion cases involved bilateral fractures. These authors believed that open reduction interfered with limited vascularity and was more likely to result in nonunion. They also advised that all fractures of edentulous mandibles should be stabilized but felt that a denture or acrylic splint wired to the superior surface of the atrophic mandibular ridge added little to reduction or stabilization. They recommended supplemental methods, such as utilization of the Morris appliance.[7] Marciani and Hill[8] also advocated closed reduction of fractures of the atrophic mandibular body. These authors stated that the major factors contributing to the difficulty of repair of fractures in the atrophic, edentulous mandible are the location of the fracture, the height of the horizontal ramus, and the patient's systemic condition. Although recognizing the treatment limitations of closed reductions, that is, nonanatomic reduction, they advocated closed techniques for fractures of the body in thin, atrophic mandibles (less than 20 mm). Open techniques should be reserved for fractures involving larger edentulous mandibles. Comminuted fractures should not be opened. Fundamental to their arguments for closed reduction is the work of Bradley and Cohen[19,20] (discussed previously).

Closed reduction techniques generally involve the use of pre-existing dentures for stabilization and immobilization. If dentures are unavailable, Gunning splints may

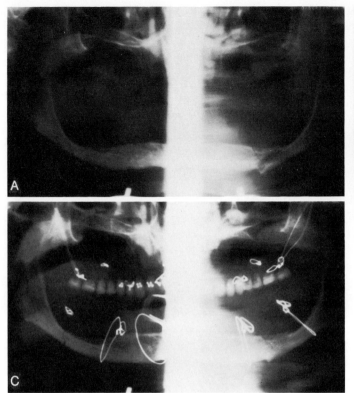

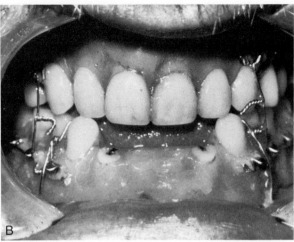

FIGURE 28–5. *A,* Panoramic radiograph of bilateral midbody fractures of the mandible in an edentulous patient. A moderate amount of atrophy of the mandible is present, with minimal displacement of the fractured segments. *B,* Postoperative photograph of patient with dentures in place and intermaxillary fixation applied. Note the circum-mandibular wires and the creation of a feeding port. The maxillary denture is held in place by circumzygomatic wires bilaterally. *C,* Postoperative panoramic radiograph of same patient demonstrating good reduction of the fractures.

be used. In either case, the appliance is held in place with circum-mandibular wires (Fig. 28–5). The other method of closed reduction involves employment of extra-skeletal pin fixation. Erich reported satisfactory healing in 15 edentulous patients with bilateral mandibular fractures with utilization of the patient's dentures.[45] Reduction via extraoral skeletal fixation has been reported by others.[46–48] The biphasic pin technique is a frequently used and effective system.[49] In this technique, pins are placed proximal and distal to the fracture in predrilled holes prepared through cutaneous stab incisions and are used to help reduce the fracture. Stabilization is then achieved by fabricating a nonyielding stabilizer bar of cold-cured acrylic and securing it to the pins (Fig. 28–6).

Difficulties and shortcomings exist with both methods of closed reduction. The patient's existing dentures may be poorly adapted to the alveolar ridge and may be ineffective in maintaining reduction. In patients with relatively little ridge resorption and a well-fitting denture, the prosthesis provides stabilization in three planes: from the superior, buccal, and lingual aspects. However, where significant resorption has occurred, little or no stabilization is provided from the lingual or buccal aspect (Fig. 28–7). Thus, fractures with some component of lateral displacement may be ineffectively stabilized with this technique. Obviously, similar considerations apply to the use of Gunning splints. In addition, fractures located proximal to the most distal extension of the denture or splint are not adequately stabilized with this technique.

Treatment with biphasic pins offers the advantage of being able to avoid maxillomandibular fixation but may prove to be difficult in atrophic mandibles. Some problems that may arise are inadequate quantities of bone for placement of pins and poor reduction of fractures in the severely atrophic body region. It should be kept in mind that a mandible 6 mm in height, reduced with only a 3 mm-margin of error, has lost 50 per cent of needed bone-to-bone contact (Fig. 28–8).

Another problem that may occur is the entrapment of soft tissue at the fracture line. Intraoperative postreduction radiographs should be employed routinely in such cases. While some stress that no open reduction should accompany the use of the

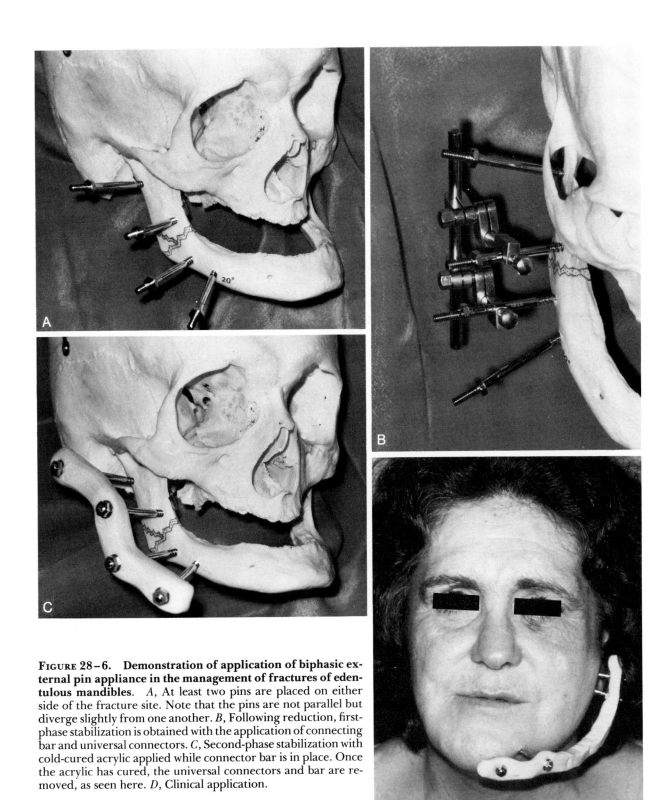

FIGURE 28–6. **Demonstration of application of biphasic external pin appliance in the management of fractures of edentulous mandibles.** *A,* At least two pins are placed on either side of the fracture site. Note that the pins are not parallel but diverge slightly from one another. *B,* Following reduction, first-phase stabilization is obtained with the application of connecting bar and universal connectors. *C,* Second-phase stabilization with cold-cured acrylic applied while connector bar is in place. Once the acrylic has cured, the universal connectors and bar are removed, as seen here. *D,* Clinical application.

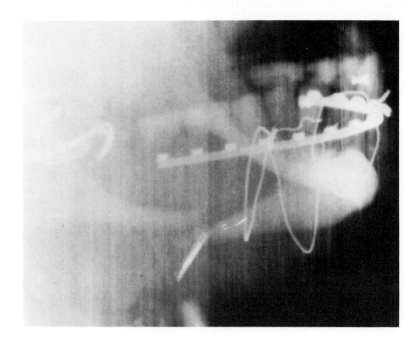

FIGURE 28-7. Lateral oblique radiograph demonstrating inadequate reduction and stabilization of a midbody fracture in an atrophic mandible treated by closed reduction utilizing the patient's denture and circum-mandibular wires.

biphasic appliance,[7] others advocate intraoral open procedures to visualize adequately the reduction obtained.[50] Other complications, although rare, have been reported. These include osteomyelitis[48] and parotid fistula formation.[51]

Another form of closed reduction that has been employed in treating fractures of the edentulous mandible is that of intramedullary pinning. This technique consists essentially of introducing a Steinmann pin (5/64 inch or 3/32 inch) or Kirschner wire (0.035 inch or 0.045 inch) lengthwise through the mandibular fragments once the fracture has been reduced. The wire is usually introduced into the bone via a small stab incision placed in the cutaneous tissue over the chin region. Bisi[52] reported satisfactory results in 23 of 24 patients treated with this method. He concluded that this technique should be considered the first treatment of choice for fractures of the body and most fractures of the angle of the edentulous mandible. However, Obwegeser and Sailer[53] state that treatment of the extremely atrophic mandible with this method is absolutely unacceptable.

OPEN REDUCTION

Proponents of open reduction techniques cite the following:

1. Necessity for direct visualization of the fractured segments to ensure adequate reduction of the atrophic bony margins
2. Increased need for stabilization of reduced fragments

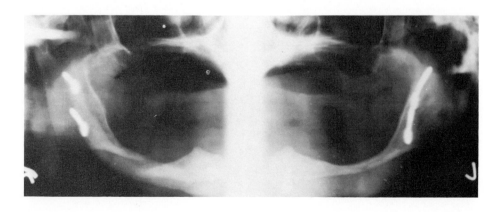

FIGURE 28-8. Panoramic radiograph of a midbody mandibular fracture demonstrating inadequate reduction and stabilization following treatment with the extraoral biphasic pin appliance.

Open techniques have been used in conjunction with biphasic pin placement and intramedullary pinning but more often involve placement of transosseous wires, titanium mesh trays, compression clamps, bone plates, or bone grafts.

Open techniques for the reduction of mandibular fractures in the edentulous patient have been discussed by various authors.[6-8,43-44,53-57] Generally, the same principles and techniques that are employed in the dentulous jaw and younger patient apply here as well. These techniques are discussed in detail in Chapter 16. There are, however, some special considerations in performing open reductions of the atrophic mandible. As referred to previously, the work of Bradley[19,58] and others[20,21] has shown significant changes in the vascular supply to the atrophic mandible, with greater dependence on periosteal supply. Because of this, stripping of the periosteum should be kept to a minimum during open procedures. Consideration may be given to placing transosseous wires over the periosteum rather than dissecting it free from the underlying bone. In addition, because of the often encountered exposed inferior alveolar neurovascular bundle lying superior to the residual alveolar crest and just submucosally, the surgeon must proceed with caution in intraoral open reductions to avoid damage to this structure.

Transosseous wiring alone is inadequate to stabilize fractured segments (Fig. 28–9). Consequently, it is most often used in conjunction with intermaxillary fixation utilizing splints or the patient's dentures (Fig. 28–10). To avoid the need for intermaxillary fixation, more rigid fixation techniques have been sought. Block and Boyne[57] advocate the use of a fine malleable metallic mesh tray for stabilization of fractures of atrophic, edentulous mandibles. They reported success in more than 14 cases (Fig. 28–11) and cited the following advantages:

1. Elimination of the need for intermaxillary splints
2. Fixation and stabilization in three planes
3. Elimination of the need for intermaxillary fixation
4. A selection of areas for screw placement through the mesh

The use of compression bone plates or lateral compression clamps has also been advocated. Proponents of these techniques note that lack of stability at the fracture site is the main cause of nonunion. In addition, compressive forces at the fracture site are believed to stimulate osteogenesis.[59] Reduction in the time of fixation required for healing has been reported.[60] Norkus and colleagues cited good results using the lateral compression clamp in 13 of 15 patients.[61] Kline also reported on the use of lateral compression clamps.[62]

Development of the self-tightening compression plate by Luhr in 1968 led to a renewed interest in utilizing bone plates for stabilization of mandibular fractures, especially in edentulous patients (Fig. 28–12).[63] Luhr considers fractures of the edentulous or insufficiently dentulous mandible as an indication for open reduction and application of compression plates. For fractures of the completely dentulous mandible, with certain exceptions, Luhr still prefers more conservative treatment.

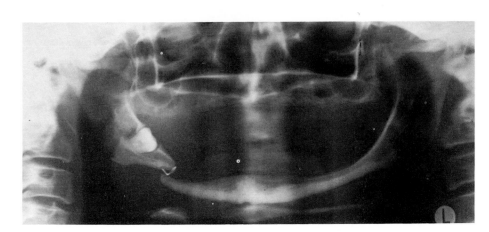

FIGURE 28–9. Panoramic radiograph demonstrating inadequate stabilization of a posterior body mandibular fracture treated with open reduction and transosseous wiring without intermaxillary fixation in an edentulous patient.

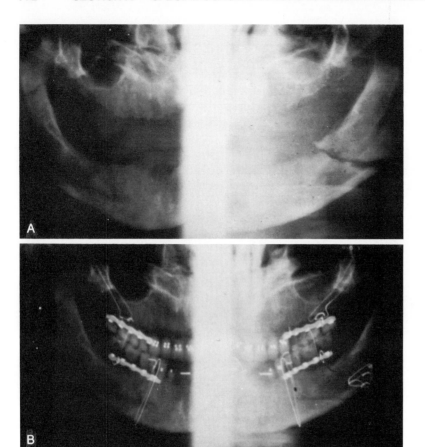

FIGURE 28–10. *A*, Panoramic radiograph showing an angle fracture of an edentulous mandible on the patient's left side. *B*, Post-treatment panoramic radiograph showing good reduction and stabilization. Transosseous wiring was employed in addition to immobilization, utilizing the patient's existing dentures. Note that the fracture is at the most distal extension of the mandibular denture.

He states that about 35 per cent of all mandibular fractures seen by himself and his coworkers are now treated by compression osteosynthesis.[63] In more than 500 fractures treated with the compression screw system, the overall rate of infection was no greater than that with strictly conservative treatment of fractures. With such techniques, the need for maxillomandibular fixation is generally eliminated. Rigid internal fixation by means of lag screws[64] and via open axial intramedullary wire placement[65] has also been advocated.

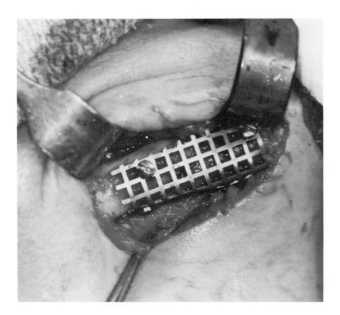

FIGURE 28–11. Open reduction of a mandibular fracture in an edentulous patient utilizing metal mesh tray for stabilization and immobilization of the fracture.

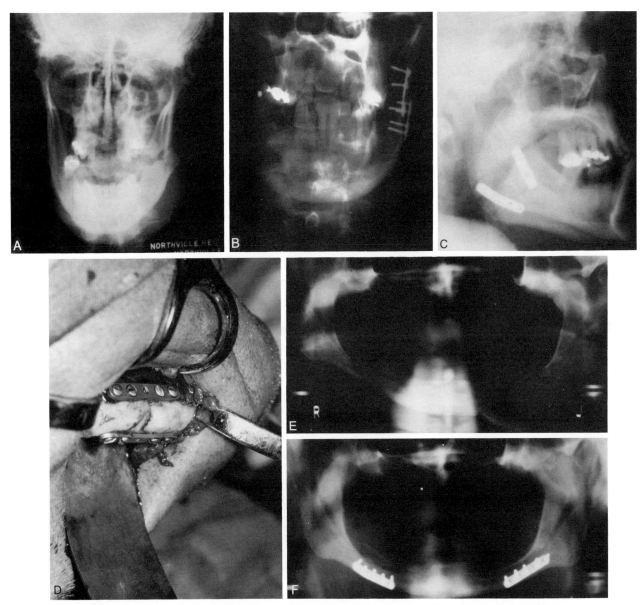

FIGURE 28–12.   Utilization of bone plates in the management of fractures of partially or completely edentulous mandibles.   *A–C,* A mandibular angle fracture in a partially edentulous patient treated by placement of inferior and superior bone plates. Further immobilization was not required and, in fact, was contraindicated in this psychiatric patient. *D,* Reduction, stabilization, and immobilization of a mandibular fracture in an atrophic, edentulous patient. Medial and lateral plates were employed for increased stability. *E and F,* Bone plates used in the treatment of bilateral fractures in an atrophic, edentulous mandible. No additional methods of immobilization were employed.

BONE GRAFTING OF ATROPHIC, EDENTULOUS RIDGES

Maxillary Bone Grafts

Utilization of bone grafts in the initial management of maxillary fractures in the geriatric patient has not been practiced widely, and its indications are very limited. Its use has been reserved for the rare instances of nonunion following primary management or for avulsive injuries. Stabilization of maxillary fractures is less difficult to maintain than that for mandibular fractures owing to the nonmobile nature of the maxilla in function and the limited effect of muscle pull, which can contribute to displacement. In addition, the need for augmentation of the edentulous maxilla for purposes of eventual prosthetic rehabilitation is limited compared with the same need in the edentulous mandible.

Mandibular Bone Grafts

Utilization of bone grafts in the primary management of fractures of the atrophic mandible has been advocated by several authors. In 1973, Obwegeser and Sailer[53] recommended the use of autogenous iliac crest, rib grafts, or, occasionally, deep-frozen rib grafts to treat fractures of the atrophic, edentulous mandible. In their opinion, intraoral open reduction techniques are always indicated in treating fractures of the edentulous mandible, the only exception being the fracture with no dislocation of the segments and an intact periosteum acting like a splint for the fractures. In such cases, they recommended conservative closed reduction. For mandibles with moderate degrees of atrophy, they believed that direct interosseous wiring, with or without additional splint support, or stabilization with bone plates can lead to successful outcomes. However, in patients who present with significant atrophy, they believed such methods to be inadequate.

Obwegeser and Sailer[53] also feel that treatment of the extremely atrophic mandible with intramedullary pin placement is totally inadequate. Their recommendation is open reduction via an intraoral incision extending from the retromolar triangle to the midline. The bone graft, which has been previously contoured to the desired augmented shape of the mandible, is placed on the atrophic ridge and extends at least 2.5 cm anterior and posterior to the fracture. It is secured to the mandible with circum-mandibular wires, at least two anterior and two posterior to the fracture site. When ribs are utilized, the authors recommend that two ribs be harvested, each 14 to 16 cm in length. The first is contoured and placed over the crest of the residual mandible, as in augmentation procedures. The second is split longitudinally, and then each half is contoured. One half is placed on the buccolabial aspect, and the other half is placed on the lingual aspect of the mandible. They are held in place with additional circum-mandibular wires. The soft tissue closure may require scoring of the periosteum to obtain tight closure without tension. The authors have not found it necessary to utilize additional splinting techniques with acrylic splints, intermaxillary fixation, extraoral appliances, or bone plates. Future prosthetic rehabilitation over the augmented ridge may require secondary vestibuloplasty procedures.

In 1979, Woods and colleagues[54] reported a similar technique. Successful results were obtained in the nine cases reported. Two patients required application of external pins to supplement stabilization. Both of these patients were reported to be very muscular men. Eight of the nine patients underwent secondary vestibuloplasty and lowering of the floor of the mouth approximately 6 months after fracture healing for prosthetic rehabilitation.

An extraoral approach via a submandibular incision has also been used for grafting procedures.[55] With this approach, however, generalized augmentation of the mandible is limited owing to access, and only grafting at the fracture site is attempted (Fig. 28 – 13).

Donor Site Considerations

Grafting procedures involve the use of either autologous bone or freeze-dried bone. Autologous bone is generally harvested from the iliac crest, the rib cage, or the calvarium. Selection of the donor site is influenced by a number of factors, including the amount of bone required, the corticocancellous ratio of donor bone, donor site scarring, the surgeon's preference, and donor site complications.

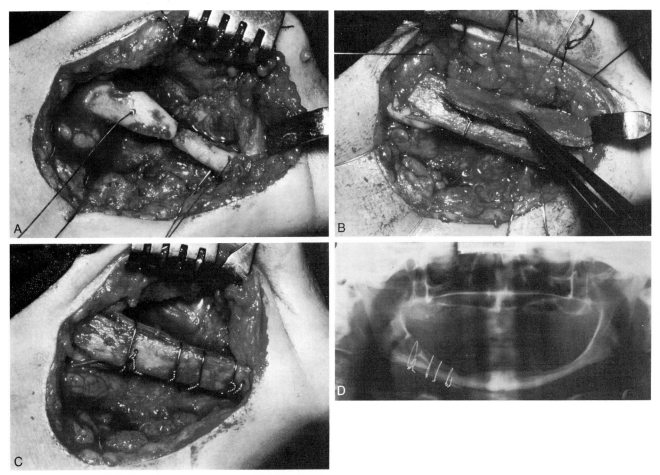

FIGURE 28-13.   **Atrophic mandibular fracture treated with autologous rib graft.**   *A*, Fracture approached via submandibular incision and segments reduced with the aid of transosseous wires. *B*, Split rib being placed on medial and lateral aspect of mandible and extending several centimeters beyond the fracture site in an anteroposterior direction. Initial wires used for reduction of fracture are now placed through rib graft and are used for stabilization of the graft. Note that additional circum-mandibular wires are also in place. *C*, Graft in place and circum-mandibular and transosseous wires tightened. *D*, Postoperative panoramic radiograph demonstrating graft in place and good reduction and stabilization of the fracture.

ILIAC CREST AS THE DONOR SITE

Utilization of the iliac crest for bone grafting of the fractured, atrophic mandible provides adequate amounts of bone, both cortical and cancellous, with minimal scarring, which can be hidden within the margins of underclothing. A variety of complications have been associated with this procedure. These include anesthesia or paresthesia associated with the donor site,[66-71] wound breakdown,[66,68] postoperative pain,[66-72] gait disturbances,[72] contour defects,[66,68] adynamic ilius,[73] stress fracture of the ilium,[74] hernias through the donor site,[69,75-78] and ureteral injury.[79] Of these, the first five are most frequently encountered.

Anesthesia or paresthesia has classically been associated with injury to the lateral femoral cutaneous nerve of the thigh. This nerve arises from the posterior branches of the second and third lumbar nerves. The nerve appears at the lateral border of the psoas muscle and crosses the iliacus muscle deep to its fascia. It may be single or in several branches. It courses anteriorly toward the anterior superior spine of the ilium and passes beneath the inguinal ligament superficial or deep to the sartorius muscle. It is generally several centimeters below the anterior superior iliac spine at this point. It then divides into anterior and posterior branches. The anterior branch supplies sensation to the skin and subcutaneous tissues on the lateral aspect of the front of the thigh as far as the knee. The posterior branch supplies the skin and subcutaneous tissues over the lateral part of the buttock and the proximal two thirds of the lateral aspect of the thigh. Since the nerve passes either deep to or through the inguinal ligament, it is difficult to injure it if proper techniques are employed.

In the surgical approach to bone harvesting from the ilium, the lateral femoral cutaneous nerve can generally be avoided by keeping the incision and bone harvest 1 cm posterior to the anterior superior iliac spine. The incidence of injury is reportedly low. Laurie and colleagues,[68] reporting on 60 patients with iliac crest bone harvesting, noted an 8.3 per cent incidence of hyperesthesia or anesthesia at 1 year postoperatively. Keller and Triplett[72] reviewed 160 consecutive cases of iliac bone harvesting and reported only 2 cases of neurologic disturbances. One was believed to be due to operative positioning of the patient, as the neurologic deficit was not anatomically explainable on the basis of the surgical injury. The problem resolved over 12 months. The other patient also showed resolution at 12 months.

More likely candidates for injury at the time of surgery are the lateral cutaneous branches of the subcostal and iliohypogastric nerves, both of which supply sensation to the skin overlying the gluteus medius and gluteus minimus muscles. The lateral cutaneous branch of the subcostal nerve crosses the crest of the ilium several centimeters behind the anterior superior spine of the ilium. The lateral cutaneous branch of the iliohypogastric nerve crosses the iliac crest at the junction of its anterior and middle thirds and distributes posterior to the lateral cutaneous branch of the subcostal nerve. Marx[80] suggests that confusion in terminology has led to attributing postoperative paresthesia solely to damage to the lateral femoral cutaneous nerve.

Wound breakdown has been shown to be associated with incision placement. Laurie and colleagues[68] reported that in their 60 cases 21 per cent of the patients with incisions over the crest showed delayed healing, whereas all of the patients with medial or lateral incisions showed primary healing.

Postoperative pain at the donor site has been reported to persist for a mean of 6 weeks, with 10 per cent of patients having pain at 2 years.[68] Of interest to the current topic, Keller and Triplett[72] examined age as a factor in the incidence and duration of postoperative complications. They reported postoperative pain at 2 weeks in 43 per cent of patients responding to a questionnaire who were less than 30 years old and in 52 per cent of patients older than 30 years of age. At 3 months postoperatively, the incidence of residual pain at the donor site in these patients was 5 per cent and 17 per cent, respectively. They also noted that many of the older patients, especially those undergoing grafting procedures for purposes of mandibular ridge augmentation, associated the harvesting procedure with the onset of joint and tendon stiffness several years after the jaw operation.

Postoperative gait disturbances may be dependent on surgical technique and approach. Harvesting from the mediosuperior aspect of the ilium preserves the laterosuperior contour of the crest and avoids stripping of the gluteus medius and gluteus minimus. These muscles act together to abduct the femur and rotate the thigh medially, both important aspects of walking. Stripping of their attachments to the lateral aspect of the ilium results in the so-called "postoperative gluteal gait." Harvesting from the medial aspect of the ilium, however, involves detachment of the iliacus muscle. This muscle helps flex the thigh but has little effect on rotary movements. Keller and Triplett compared the medial approach in 75 patients with the lateral approach in 60 patients.[72] Five per cent of the patients in the medial approach group reported difficulties with ambulation up to 8 weeks after surgery, compared with 10 per cent in the lateral approach group. At the 3-month postoperative check, 0 per cent reported problems in the medial approach group compared with 10 per cent in the lateral approach group. They concluded that sparing the gluteal muscle attachments to the lateral cortex yields fewer ambulation problems postoperatively and decreases later disturbances of gait. The incidence as well as duration of postoperative ambulation difficulties was also seen to be higher in the older group of patients, irrespective of surgical approach.

Contour defects of the donor site are associated with full-thickness grafts remov-

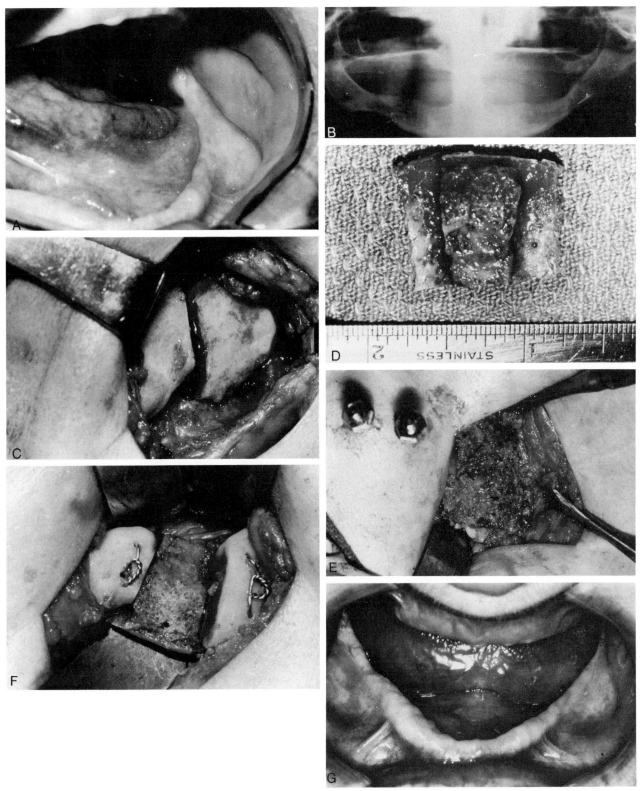

FIGURE 28–14. *A,* Intraoral view of a patient with a malunion of a mandibular fracture. Note lateral displacement of the proximal segment and vertical displacement with impingement of the left ramus on the maxillary tuberosity region. The patient was unable to wear a prosthesis. *B,* Panoramic radiograph of same patient showing malunion on the left side. There is also some malunion on the right side; however, this was not as clinically significant. *C,* Patient treated with osteotomy on the left side to allow for repositioning of segments. *D,* Autologous bone harvested from the patient's iliac crest and contoured into a **T** shape of the proper dimension to place between the osteotomized segments. *E,* Graft in place and held with transosseous wires. *F,* Cancellous bone packed around the grafted site. Note that biphasic pins are in place for postoperative immobilization. *G,* Postoperative intraoral view showing improved contour and ridge relationships. The patient was able to proceed to successful prosthetic restoration.

ing both cortices and the crest itself. They can be avoided by preservation of either the mediosuperior aspect or the laterosuperior aspect of the crest.

RIB AS THE DONOR SITE

Rib grafts for the treatment of atrophic mandibular fractures have been used with success.[53] One or more ribs, usually the fifth, sixth, or seventh, may be harvested from either chest wall. Either a lateral thoracotomy incision or a short submammary incision may be utilized. For purposes of fracture management, the short submammary incision will suffice. Even if simultaneous ridge augmentation is performed, adequate amounts of bone may generally be obtained from this approach. Ten-centimeter sections of bone can be obtained without difficulty, and even 17-cm lengths can be obtained from this approach.[81,82] The incision is carried down through skin and subcutaneous tissue. The underlying pectoral muscles are incised, and an incision is made through the periosteum overlying the rib. The Doyen elevator is used to free the periosteum from the rib. After the appropriate amount of rib is harvested, the periosteum is carefully closed, followed by the muscles.

Complications from rib harvesting include chest infections, wound breakdown, and pneumothorax. In a report on complications in 793 craniofacial operations, Whitaker and coworkers[82] reported that the incidence of pneumothorax after rib removal was as high as 20 to 30 per cent. James and Irvine[81] reported on 41 patients who underwent 52 partial rib resections. Complications directly associated with the rib harvest developed in eight patients (19.5 per cent). Five patients developed postoperative chest infections, one patient had pneumothorax, and two patients experienced wound breakdown. The incidence of chest infection was seen to diminish when active, early postoperative physical therapy was given.

POSTOPERATIVE COMPLICATIONS

The types of postoperative complications seen in the management of facial fractures in the elderly patient are the same as those in any age group. Infection, nonunion, malunion, and delayed healing are the most common.

In the edentulous mandible, nonunion is encountered at a rate as high as 20 per cent.[7] The management of nonunion most often involves the grafting of bone to the area of defect. Malunion is also encountered and is usually managed with an osteotomy, either as the sole procedure or in conjunction with bone grafting (Fig. 28–14).

Infection can also occur. Management follows the general guidelines of adequate debridement, establishment of drainage, and appropriate antibiotic coverage based on culture and sensitivity studies of the organisms involved in the production of the infection. There is some evidence that infections of the fractured edentulous jaw are less common than those of dentulous jaws.[83] However, compounded fractures of edentulous mandibles with loss of an intact, overlying mucosa should alert the clinician to guard against contamination of the fracture site.

Delayed healing is encountered in the elderly, and it is generally considered necessary to maintain immobilization of the fractured segments for a longer time than in the young. The correct period of immobilization varies with each patient and with the type and severity of the fracture encountered. However, 6 to 8 weeks is generally adequate for initial callus formation and primary calcification. If internal rigid fixation is employed in the management of these fractures, immobilization of the jaws may be avoided.

REFERENCES

1. Olson RA, Fonseca RJ, Zeitler DH, Osborn DB: Fractures of the mandible: A review of 580 cases. J Oral Maxillofac Surg 40:23, 1982.

2. Bochlogyros DN: A retrospective study of 1,521 mandibular fractures. J Maxillofac Surg 43:597, 1985.

3. Ellis E, Moos KF, El-Attar A: Ten years of mandibular fractures: An analysis of 2,137 cases. Oral Surg 59:120, 1985.

4. James RB, Fredrickson C, Kent JN: Prospective study of mandibular fractures. J Oral Surg 39:275, 1981.

5. Ellis E, El-Attar A, Moos KM: An analysis of 2,067 cases of zygomatico-orbital fracture. J Oral Maxillofac Surg 43:417, 1985.

6. Zachariades N, Papavassiliou D, Triantafyllou D, et al: Fractures of the facial skeleton in the edentulous patient. J Maxillofac Surg 12:262, 1984.

7. Bruce RA, Strachan DS: Fractures of the edentulous mandible. The Chalmers J. Lyons Academy Study. J Oral Surg 34:973, 1976.

8. Marciani RD, Hill OJ: Treatment of the fractured edentulous mandible. J Oral Surg 37:569, 1979.

9. Pochi PE, Strauss JS: The effect of aging on the activity of the sebaceous gland in man. In Montagna W (ed): Advances in Biology of the Skin. Vol 6. Oxford, England, Pergamon Press, 1965, pp 121–126.

10. Carlisle KS, Montagna W: Aging model for unexposed human dermis. J Invest Dermatol 73:54, 1979.

11. Larrabee WF, Sutton D, Carlisle KS: A histologic and mechanical study of aging skin. In Ward PH, Berman WE (eds): Plastic and Reconstructive Surgery of the Head and Neck. Vol 1. St Louis, CV Mosby, 1984.

12. Nakamoto RY: Bony defects on the crest of the residual alveolar ridge. J Prosthet Dent 19:111, 1968.

13. Atwood DA, Coy WA: Clinical, cephalometric and densitometric study of reduction of residual ridges. J Prosthet Dent 26:280, 1971.

14. United States Public Health Publication No. 1000–11–7, Washington, DC, US Dept of Health, Education and Welfare.

15. Enlow DH: Alveolar bone: Review of literature. In Lang BR, Kelsey CC (eds): International Prosthodontic Workshop. Ann Arbor, MI, The University of Michigan School of Dentistry, 1973.

16. Manson JD, Lucas RB: A microradiographic study of age changes in the human mandible. Arch Oral Biol 7:761, 1962.

17. Baumhammers A, Stallard RE: Retention and remodeling of H³-proline labeled matrix of cementum, dentin, and bone. Int Assoc Dent Res Prog Abstr 43:149, 1965.

18. Tallgren A: The effect of denture wearing on facial morphology: A seven year longitudinal study. Acta Odont Scand 25:563, 1967.

19. Bradley JC: Age changes in the vascular supply of the mandible. Br Dent J 132:142, 1972.

20. Cohen L: Further studies into the vascular architecture of the mandible. J Dent Res 39:936, 1960.

21. Pogrel MA, Dodson T, Tom W: Arteriographic assessment of patency of the inferior alveolar artery and its relevance to alveolar atrophy. J Oral Maxillofac Surg 45:767, 1987.

22. Branzi A, Quintarelli G: Ulteriore contribute allo studio anastomoistologico delle modificazioni dell'arteria muscellare interna nelle varia età dell'uomo. Riv Ital Stomat 11:1, 1956.

23. Chestnut CH, Kribbs P: Osteoporosis: Some aspects of pathophysiology and therapy. Prosthet Dent 48:4, 1982.

24. Goodman AG, Gilman LS, Gilman A (eds): The Pharmacological Basis of Therapeutics. 6th ed. New York, Macmillan, 1980, p 1487.

25. Adinoff AD, Hollister JR: Steroid induced fractures and bone loss in patients with asthma. N Engl J Med 309:265, 1983.

26. Avioli LV: Heparin-induced osteopenia: An appraisal. Adv Exp Med Biol 52:375, 1975.

27. Levy G, O'Reilly RA, Aggeler PM, Keech GM: Pharmacokinetic analysis of the effect of barbiturate on the anticoagulant action of warfarin in man. Clin Pharmacol Ther 11:372, 1970.

28. Symposium (various authors). In Woodbury DM, Penry JK, Schmidt RP (eds): Antiepileptic Drugs. New York, Raven Press, 1972.

29. Young RE, Ramsay LE, Murry TS: Barbiturates and serum calcium in the elderly. Postgrad Med 53:212, 1977.

30. Larsen RB: Dietary needs of patients following general surgery. Hospitals 39:133, 1965.

31. Holden WD: Nutrition. In Cole WH, Zollinger RM (eds): Textbook of Surgery. 9th ed. New York, Appleton-Century-Crofts, 1970, pp 157–163.

32. Riegel C, Koop CE, Drew J, et al: The nutritional requirements for nitrogen balance in surgical patients during the early post-operative period. J Clin Invest 26:18, 1947.

33. Leevy CM, Cardi L, Frank O, et al: Incidence and significance of hypovitaminemia in a randomly selected municipal hospital population. Am J Clin Nutr 17:259, 1965.

34. Bollet AJ, Owens S: Evaluation of nutritional status of selected hospitalized patients. Am J Clin Nutr 26:931, 1973.

35. Olejko TD, Fonseca RJ: Pre-operative nutritional supplementation for the orthognathic surgery patient. J Oral Maxillofac Surg 42:573, 1984.

36. Stein TP, Buzby GP: Protein metabolism in surgical patients. Surg Clin North Am 61:519, 1981.

37. Drucker WR, Howard PL, McCoy S: The influence of diet on responses to hemorrhagic shock. Ann Surg 181:698, 1975.

38. Mullen JL, Steinberg JJ: Pre-operative nutritional assessment. Compr Ther 7:6, 1981.

39. VanLandingham SB, Dey JC, Symmons RE: Nutritional support of the surgical patient. Surg Clin North Am 62:321, 1982.

40. Jones NB: Dietary needs of the oral surgery patient with comparison of dietary supplements. J Oral Surg 28:892, 1970.

41. Spanier AH, Shizgal HM: Caloric requirements of the critically ill patient receiving intravenous hyperalimentation. Am J Surg 133:99, 1977.

42. Sofferman RA, Danielson PA, Quatela V, et al: Retrospective analysis of surgically treated LeFort fractures: Is suspension necessary? Arch Otolaryngol 109:446, 1983.

43. Welsh LW, Welsh JJ: Fractures of the edentulous maxilla and mandible. Laryngoscope 86:1333, 1976.

44. Degnan EJ: Mandibular fracture in the geriatric patient: Problems in treatment planning. Report of case. J Oral Surg 28:438, 1970.
45. Erich JB: Treatment of bilateral fractures of the dentulous mandible. Plast Reconstr Surg 9:33, 1952.
46. Ricciardelli LA, Moloney PL, Doku HC: External biphasic pins for fixation and immobilization of a mandibular bone graft: Report of case. J Oral Surg 27:362, 1960.
47. Baumgarten RS, Desprez JD: The Morris biphasic external splint for mandible fixation. Plast Reconstr Surg 50:66, 1972.
48. Sachs R, Goracy E, Cheies L, et al: Osteomyelitis following fixation of a mandibular fracture with biphasic pins. J Oral Surg 31:923, 1973.
49. Morris JH: Biphase connector, external skeletal splint for reduction and fixation of mandibular fractures. Oral Surg 2:1382, 1949.
50. Obwegeser HL: Die extrorale Nagelung zur Behandlung von Frakturen im Kiefer Gesichtsbereich: Heutiger Standpunkt zur Indikation, Kontraindikation und Technik. Schweiz Z Militarmed 45:49, 1968.
51. Laskin D: Parotid fistula after the use of external pin fixation: Report of a case. J Oral Surg 36:621, 1978.
52. Bisi RH: The management of mandibular fractures in edentulous patients by intramedullary pinning. Laryngoscope 83:22, 1973.
53. Obwegeser HL, Sailer HF: Another way of treating fractures of the atrophic edentulous mandible. J Maxillofac Surg 1:213, 1973.
54. Woods WR, Hiatt R, Brooks RL: A technique for simultaneous fracture repair and augmentation of the atrophic edentulous mandible. J Oral Surg 37:131, 1979.
55. Boyne PJ, Upham C: The treatment of long standing bilateral fracture non and malunion in atrophic edentulous mandibles. Int J Oral Surg 3:213, 1974.
56. Cooper J, Rojer CL, Rosenfeld PA: Management of mandibular fractures using biphasic pins and mandibular splints. Laryngoscope 92:1042, 1982.
57. Block C, Boyne PJ: Use of a metal intraosseous fixation device for treatment of fractures of atrophic edentulous mandibles. J South Calif State Dent Assoc 40:996, 1972.
58. Bradley JC: A radiological investigation into the age changes of the inferior dental artery. Br J Oral Surg 13:82, 1975.
59. Richter HE, Boyne PJ: New concepts in facial bone healing and grafting procedures. Oral Surg 27:557, 1969.
60. Boyne PJ, Morgan FH: Evaluation of a compression intraosseous fixation device in mandibular fractures. Oral Surg 33:696, 1972.
61. Norkus RG, White NS, Thomas RF, Schulhof J: Application of a lateral compression clamp in the management of mandibular fractures. Oral Surg 39:2, 1975.
62. Kline SN: Lateral compression in the treatment of mandibular fractures. J Oral Surg 31:182, 1973.
63. Luhr HG: Compression plate osteosynthesis through the Luhr System. In Kruger E, Schilli W: Oral and Maxillofacial Traumatology. Vol 1. Chicago, Quintessence Publishing Company, 1982.
64. Niederdellmann H: Rigid internal fixation by means of lag screws. In Kruger E, Schilli W (eds): Oral and Maxillofacial Traumatology. Vol 1. Chicago, Quintessence Publishing Company, 1982.
65. Fries R: Intramedullary wire fixation. In Kruger E, Schilli W (eds): Oral and Maxillofacial Traumatology. Vol 1. Chicago, Quintessence Publishing Company, 1982.
66. McCain JP: A retrospective study of the donor site in bone grafts from the ilium: A review of 70 cases (abstract). Presented at the 60th Annual Meeting of the American Association of Oral and Maxillofacial Surgeons, Chicago, 1978.
67. Keathley CJ: Post-operative morbidity of iliac crest donor sites in preprosthetic surgery patients (abstract). Presented at 64th Annual Meeting of the American Association of Oral and Maxillofacial Surgeons, Atlanta, 1982.
68. Laurie SWS, Kaban LB, Mulliken JB, et al: Donor site morbidity after harvesting rib and iliac bone. Plast Reconstr Surg 73:933, 1984.
69. Cockin J: Autologous bone grafting complications at the donor site. J Bone Joint Surg [Br] 53:153, 1971.
70. Edelson JG, Nathan H: Meralgia paresthetica: An anatomical interpretation. Clin Orthop 122:255, 1977.
71. Weikel AM, Habal MB: Meralgia paresthetica: A complication of iliac bone procurement. Plast Reconstr Surg 60:572, 1977.
72. Keller EE, Triplett WW: Iliac bone grafting: Review of 160 consecutive cases. J Oral Maxillofac Surg 45:11, 1987.
73. James JD, Geist ET, Gross BD: Adynamic ileus as a complication of iliac bone removal: Report of two cases. J Oral Surg 39:289, 1981.
74. Guha SC, Poole MD: Stress fracture of the iliac bone with subfascial femoral neuropathy: Unusual complications at a bone graft donor site. Case report. Br J Plast Surg 36:305, 1983.
75. Reid RL: Hernia through an iliac bone graft donor site: A case report. J Bone Joint Surg [Am] 50:757, 1968.
76. Challis JH, Lyttle JA, Stuart AE: Strangulated lumbar hernia and volvulus following removal of iliac crest bone graft: A case report. Acta Orthop Scand 46:230, 1975.
77. Cowley SP, Anderson LD: Hernias through donor sites for iliac bone grafts. J Bone Joint Surg [Am] 65:1023, 1983.
78. Oldfield MC: Iliac hernia after bone-grafting. Lancet 1:810, 1945.
79. Escalas F, Dewald RL: Combined traumatic arteriovenous fistula and ureteral injury: A complication of iliac bone grafting. Case report. J Bone Joint Surg [Am] 59:270, 1977.
80. Marx R: Controversies in mandibular reconstruction. Presented at the Chalmers J. Lyons Academy of Oral Surgeons, Winter Meeting, Detroit, Michigan, 1988.
81. James DR, Irvine GH: Autogenous rib grafts in maxillofacial surgery. J Maxillofac Surg 11:201, 1983.
82. Whitaker LA, Munro IR, Jackson IT, Salyer KE: Problems in craniofacial surgery. J Maxillofac Surg 4:131, 1976.
83. DeAmaratunga NA: Comparative study of the clinical aspects of edentulous and dentulous mandibular fractures. J Oral Maxillofac Surg 43:3, 1988.

CHAPTER 29

BIOMATERIALS FOR CRANIAL, FACIAL, MANDIBULAR, AND TMJ RECONSTRUCTION

JOHN N. KENT, D.D.S., and DALE J. MISIEK, D.M.D.

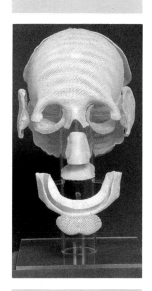

The alloplasts used for cranial, mandibular, maxillary, nasal, zygomatic, orbital, and temporomandibular joint (TMJ) reconstruction or augmentation following trauma include solid or mesh metals, solid or porous polymers, hydroxylapatite (HA), or a combination of these materials in porous forms. Surgical-grade metals and metallic alloys used for reconstruction or contour correction include titanium and titanium alloys, 316L stainless steel, and chrome-cobalt-molybdenum alloys. Although metals are quite biocompatible and readily fix to bone, their fabrication to exact anatomic requirements and modification at the time of surgery may limit their use in facial reconstruction, but they are quite useful for temporary and permanent correction of mandibular and TMJ deformity. With improvement of polymer and ceramic materials, particularly porous forms, most facial augmentations with biomaterials for correction of traumatic, developmental, and congenital defects have been achieved with silicone rubber, Proplast, and, more recently, solid and porous forms of HA. This chapter presents the biochemical and physical characteristics of most commonly used materials, their clinical application, technical details of frequently performed procedures, tissue reactions, and follow-up data. Experiences with biomaterials for the correction of deformities secondary to congenital and neoplastic disease are frequently described herein, since the principles of correcting the same deformities secondary to trauma are identical or similar in nature. This chapter attempts to point out the important contributions to common clinical applications of biomaterials from the specialties of neurosurgery, ophthalmology, oral and maxillofacial surgery, otorhinolaryngology, and plastic surgery.

Selection of an alloplastic material for cranial, facial, or mandibular reconstruction involves two important considerations. First, physical properties dictate how such materials may be adapted to the deficit and whether any functional load can be applied to it. Second, biocompatibility of the material will determine whether the alloplast, in its loaded or unloaded clinical adaptation, will be tolerated by the host tissues. In this chapter, we consider each material individually—polymer, metal, and ceramic—describing biochemical and physical properties, implant–host tissue interactions, and clinical applications.

TISSUE REACTION TO IMPLANT MATERIALS

Testing Methods

In assessing the performance of a permanent implant, the effect of the body tissues on functional properties of the implant and the cellular effect on near and distant tissue must be examined simultaneously. The terms "biofunctionality" and "biocompatibility" are used to distinguish these two categories of implant performance. The capability of a material in one category does not imply acceptability in the other. A metallic mandibular prosthesis or ceramic implant may fail because of functional problems relative to weaknesses in physical characteristics but may have no evidence of tissue intolerance; conversely, successful functional implants may be surrounded by pathologic tissue.[1-3] In some instances, cytotoxicity and implant dysfunction are simultaneous; for example, the polymer articulating surface of an orthopedic implant may undergo chemical exacerbation of the wear tendency, leading to unacceptable wear performance and particulate debris, which causes pathologic conditions.[4-6]

As with any surgery, after the implantation of an alloplast, acute inflammation ensues.[7] During normal wound healing, fibrous encapsulation around all implants and fibrous ingrowth into porous implants may occur. Techniques widely used for biocompatibility in small animals include examination of tissue thickness and cellular features. The absence of cytotoxicity may be misleading, since tissue thickness and potential reaction also depend on the mechanical interaction of the implant with adjacent tissue.[8,9] Methods of evaluating implant materials in small animals require surgical precision, modification of the device to fit the test animal's anatomy, histologic analysis of regional and distant tissue, and evaluation in the appropriate number of animals for the appropriate time. All of these methods are usually obtainable and predictable, except that implant devices may become structurally defective when designed to small animal specifications. The potential biocompatibility of an implant material can rapidly be determined by in vitro screening analysis prior to animal testing to eliminate unqualified materials[10] (Table 29–1). The particulate form of the material is placed in a pseudoextracellular fluid at 115°C for 62 hours. This time-temperature superposition may provide a simulation of long-term animal implantation but will not prove the functional safety of the test material. The fluid can be spectrographically analyzed for chemical by-products, which can be quantitatively measured. The fluid can also be used as a precursor of a tissue culture medium in which the behavior of explanted mammalian cells can be observed. A strong positive correlation may be observed between any generated chemical products and the cytotoxicity of the tissue culture medium prepared with the same fluid. These techniques provide a first-stage biocompatibility screen for new implant materials. If successful, second-stage tests are done to ascertain specific physical requirements, the standards of which have been defined by the American Society of Testing and Materials (ASTM). These tests should expose the material to those mechanical requirements encountered with in vivo function, utilizing a fluid medium approximating the ionic and proteinaceous content of body fluid. Favorable results are then tested in animals to confirm biocompatibility, and when indicated, the material is tested in a simulated and loaded (if pertinent) biofunctional application. When possible, this process of testing both parameters is finally repeated in human clinical trials.

Influence of Chemical and Mechanical Factors

The thickness of encapsulation and the amount of ingrowth will depend upon the mechanical, chemical, and physical chemistry of the implant interface as well as the stability of the implant at the clinical site. These parameters range from inertness to reactivity in the chemical sense, from stiffness to softness in the mechanical makeup,

TABLE 29-1.   BIOCOMPATIBILITY SCREENING RESULTS OF RESIN EXPOSED TO PSEUDOEXTRACELLULAR FLUID (PECF) FOR 62 HOURS AT 115°C AND 30 POUNDS PER SQUARE INCH ABSOLUTE

POLYMER	TISSUE CULTURE RESPONSE*	TOTAL CH$_3$, CH$_2$, AND CH IN PECF VIA INFRARED ANALYSIS MPM† EQUIVALENT n-HEXANOL
Chopped graphite fiber	+1	Not detectable
Silicone rubber (Dow Corning)		
372 Nonreinforced	+1	5
372 Reinforced—fabric	+1	5
Polyethylene‡ (specific gravity: 0.96)	+1	17
Vitreous carbon frit	+1 to +2	Not detectable
Polytetrafluoroethylene (PTFE)		
bleached fiber	+1 to +2	Not detectable
Fluorinated ethylene propylene		
(FEPT-160)	+1 to +2	Not detectable
Polyphenylene oxide (grade 731)	+1 to +2	27
Polyethylene (specific gravity: 0.96)	+2	Not detectable
Acrylic molding powder (V-415)	+2	Not detectable
Polyphenylene oxide (grade 534–801)	+2	17
Polyphenylene oxide (specific gravity:		
0.925)	+2	17
Fluorinated ethylene propylene		
(FEPT-100)	+2	23
Ionomer (1550)	+2	142
Polypropylene (grade 114, food grade)	+2	198
Vinylidine fluoride (grade 200)	+2 to +3	3
Nylon (grade 101)	+2 to +3	14
Ionomer (grade AD 8043)	+2 to +3	30
Cellulose propionate	+3	81.7
Polystyrene (HH401) (grade 300)	+3	168
Nylon (grade 38)	+4	12
Polyvinyl chloride (grade 5430)	+3 to +4	277
Polyurethane (grade 58093)	+4	89
Polyurethane (grade 16139)	+4	328
Polyvinyl chloride§	+4	514
ABS resin (grade X7-1000)	+4	516

* Scale: +1 = some vacuolization and growth inhibition but nominally as control cultures; +2 = moderate vacuolization, morphologic changes, and growth inhibition; +3 = severe growth inhibition and vacuolization; +4 = total growth inhibition.

† Moles per million.

‡ University of Texas, Austin, Drug/Plastic Research Laboratory, negative standard.

§ University of Texas, Austin, Drug/Plastic Research Laboratory, intensely toxic standard.

From Homsy CA: Biocompatibility in selection of materials for implantation. J Biomed Mater Res 4: 341, 1970; with permission.

and from solid to porous or woven body in regard to physical properties.[10,11] In addition, other factors such as mobility, for example, can promote thicker fibrous encapsulation and less fibrous ingrowth.

Chemically, some materials are inert and others are reactive; generally, chemical inertness is desired, although there are important examples of useful alloplasts that have major reactivity, such as resorbable polymer sutures and certain ceramics and glasses. Chemical reactivity includes (1) the process of reactants (alloplast, body milieu) reacting through electron exchange to form new chemical entities; (2) a physical-chemical reaction wherein the surface electrochemical morphology of the implant is engaged by the electrochemical polarity of biologic elements, with strong adherence sequelae; and (3) dissolution of constituents of an alloplastic surface, which then react chemically with biologic elements.[11]

Mechanically, materials range from stiff to soft; softness may be favored in nonloading situations when implants interface with soft tissue. This softness minimizes interfacial trauma from any relative motion between implant and tissue. In physical form, there are solids and various porous structures. Porous alloplasts, depending on the clinical setting, may be soft, since initial ingrowing tissue will be soft. Exceptions include skeletal applications or intraosseous implants, which are rigidly fixed and are not subject to cyclic mechanical loading.

When an implant is inert and solid, the process of normal wound healing leads to formation of a fibrous tissue capsule around the implant. The thickness of such a capsule is variable, depending on the mechanical and physical chemistry of the interface. For example, this capsule is usually very thin when there is little or no relative motion at the interface, such as with a stable fracture fixation plate; however, it can become quite thick if a nonunion develops in this instance or if it surrounds a necessarily mobile implant, such as that used for breast reconstruction. Mechanical stimuli leading to mobility encourage tissue thickness, which can be characterized by macrophages and giant cells in soft tissue and bone, as discussed further on.

Even such a simple change as the degree of wettability of an implant surface by body fluid and the surface morphology can have a profound effect. For example, the surface of a rough metallic fracture plate is easily wet by water (hydrophilic) and may have only a one- or two-layer-thick fibrous tissue interface between the surface of the metal and adjacent bone. If the surface, however, is made of a smooth, hydrophobic material, such as fluorocarbon polymer, with a reduction in the microroughness, the fibrous tissue encapsulation may be 50 to 100 μm thick. The interfacial reaction between implant and adjacent tissue or fluid is critical to the biotolerance of an implant (whether metal, ceramic, glass, or polymer) and its potential to yield a chemical entity that can move from the implant into the surrounding tissue.

Chemical reactions at the implant interface, independent of the material itself, can occur. Charged surface domains may have electron transfers that produce chemical product entities and may elicit inflammation when in contact with cellular elements.[12] Reactions between implant bodies, such as polymers, and the body tissues occur as a function of the potential energy of the reaction. Typically, the route from the implant and body fluid reactants to the final reaction products requires the surmounting of a reaction barrier[11] (Fig. 29–1). The higher the barrier, the less reactive are implants. This reaction may be chemical or physical-chemical or may be a leaching phenomenon. The reaction barrier is strongly influenced by the chemical features of the implant. The barrier is increased by higher interelement bond energies: silicone-oxygen or carbon-fluorine rather than carbon-carbon. Lower electron availability increases the barrier, as do morphologic factors of the polymer molecule having to do with shape, charge, and length of a polymer chain. Such polymers as silicone rubber, Teflon fluorocarbons, and ultra high molecular weight polyethylene have high reactive barriers.

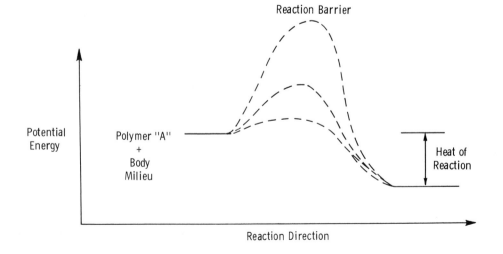

FIGURE 29–1. Plastic biocompatibility and biofuntionality. (From Homsy CA, Kent JN, Hinds EC: Materials for oral implantation — biological and functional criteria. J Am Dent Assoc 86:817, 1973, with permission.)

Porous Implant Systems

Attempts to adapt porous materials to implantation purposes produce more physiologic interaction between the implant and the host. Nonporous and porous implants tend to be isolated by the body within a membranous sheath; however, the porous implant may be receptive to the ingrowth of tissue, leading to a more or less effective integration of the implant with the host.[11]

As early as 1943, screws of cobalt-based alloy used as tooth implants were evaluated in primates.[13] A screw provides an increased surface area for interaction between implant and tissue and is viewed as a precursor of the surface–porous implant system. One would expect to find that an implant exhibiting either macromechanical or micromechanical stabilization and provoking little or no tissue reaction would exhibit improved mechanical stabilization because of the increased area of mechanical support. The use of a screw-type endosseous implant in dentistry was followed by the introduction of macroperforations into the implant to encourage through-and-through tissue and bone growth.

The use of macroperforations to improve the fixation of orthopedic endoprostheses was demonstrated by Moore.[14] Prostheses for the proximal femur were designed with a few large fenestrations in the stem portion of the prosthesis, which would reside within the femoral canal. Although this approach provided an improvement in function, the innovation of total hip joint arthroplasty required further improvements in the stabilization of the implant through the use of a rapid-curing acrylic polymer formulation. This measure permitted a much larger area of interface between the prosthetic element and adjacent host tissue and bone.[15]

Surface macroirregularities and macroperforations are evidently limited in effecting implant-host integration; this observation is suggested by the degree of unpredictability reported for subperiosteal and endosseous dental implants.[16] Encapsulation of such implants in fibrous connective tissue is commonly reported; epithelial downgrowth is variable in degree and most likely depends on implantation technique, bone damage or resorption, mechanical stress, and the dental hygiene of the patient. Symptomatic orthopedic endoprostheses usually show radiographic signs of motion in spite of apparent bone growth through perforations in the stem.[17] Potential advantages of microporosity are the much greater surface area of mechanical interdigitation between implant and tissue over which more positive and uniform interlocking may be obtained; improved vascularity of tissue immediately apposed to the implant; and more rapid fixation.[18]

Tissue will grow into structures that provide pore diameters greater than 20 μm. Increasing the pore size and the percentage of porosity enhances the degree of ingrowth; pore sizes greater than about 100 μm permit calcification in osseous structures in the absence of mobility. Early experimental results with rigidly fixed or intraosseous ceramics indicate both tissue and bone ingrowth to depths of 500 to 1500 μm in less than a month after implantation.[19]

Some clinically successful implanted skeletal prostheses must accommodate motion and load bearing as early as 1 week after insertion and substantial load bearing within 2 to 3 weeks. Porous systems are sensitive to relative motion between the unyielding matrix of the implant and any ingrowing tissue with load stress. Such motion restricts tissue ingrowth and encourages capsulation. The mechanical properties of these porous systems vary widely, depending on the porosity and pore size. Ideally, tensile strength and the modulus of elasticity of these porous structures should be made to approach the values reported for cortical bone. Metals and ceramics exceed these values, a controversial fact sometimes implicated in implant failure. Others suggest that these mechanical properties should approximate those of fibrous tissue, which must develop within the implant before any bone can form.

Homsy suggested that the stability of an implant would be optimized if the interface between a prosthesis and supporting bone or tissue does not introduce a sharp plane of mechanical property discontinuity; rather, the interface should be a zone of gradual conversion with fibrous connective tissue from the structure and properties of the apposed tissue to those of a porous polymer surface on the prosthesis.[11] Under these conditions, transmission of load stress between the prosthesis and the supporting tissue would tend to occur uniformly and at correspondingly low values of average unit stress. Therefore, ingrowing tissue would undergo little trauma because of the small motion of the prosthesis with respect to apposed tissue. These considerations have been suggested to be essential to the fixation of an implant under conditions in which dynamic stress is to be supported, for example, with joint prostheses, mandibular implants, or endosseous and subperiosteal denture supports. In this model, the porous polymer, functioning as an intermediate transmission of reducing stress between bone and prosthesis, must provide long-term stability without excessive motion, which could lead to fragmentation, loosening, and histologic failure.

In practice, however, most successful skeletal implants do have an abrupt change in mechanical properties at the tissue interface. Furthermore, tissue reaction leading to bone resorption rapidly occurs if motion and load exceed the physiologic or mechanical limitation of a polymeric intermediate zone. That interface may not provide a gradual conversion from the mechanical properties of the implant to those of the tissue. In addition, tensile and compressive strength, as well as elasticity, may be quite different.

The early innovators in prostheses for the cardiovascular system understood the importance of a low-modulus (resilient) implant for effective anastomoses to dynamically stressed tissue. More than 30 years ago, the concept of porous implants of synthetic polymers either in patch or in tubular forms for filling defects in the circulatory system was introduced.[20] Prostheses of Teflon, for example, that exhibit relatively open weaves develop organized fibrous tissue ingrowth within a few weeks after implantation.

The need for optimizing the design parameters for low-modulus stabilizing interfaces for prostheses was discussed by Homsy and others two decades ago.[11] Porous, resilient (low-modulus), and biocompatible coatings for prostheses may provide a desirable type of stabilizing interface with tissue and bone. The necessary bulk mechanical properties are provided by the core material, since high-modulus strength requirements may not be compatible with effective surface stabilization. Such a coating would become rapidly infiltrated with fibrous tissue; therafter, the diffuse distribution of stress through the coating would be a physiologic stimulus to the maturation of the tissue into appropriate stress-supporting structures (Fig. 29–2). As mentioned previously, however, the low-modulus polymer porous system may also fail for mechanical reasons. These porous materials are discussed separately further on.

Cellular Response

It should be clear that basic interactions between alloplast and host tissues need to be addressed at the cellular level. During the first few weeks after implantation, histiocytes and polymorphonuclear leukocytes gradually diminish, and fibrocytes form and express collagen. Histiocytes are less prominent in bone than in soft tissue, whereas the rate of collagen encapsulation may be more pronounced in soft tissue than in bone. The presence of these histiocytes or macrophages and their aggregated forms, foreign body giant cells, is a benign reaction seen in all implants as an extension of normal wound healing. Their presence has been noted in successful implants as long as 20 years after implantation. If, however, these cellular elements dominate, persist, and increase, this reaction becomes problematic. These observations are noted with medical-grade implants of silicone rubber, Teflon, and polyethylene polymers, cobalt-chromium alloys, and other materials.

The body protects itself from foreign materials via its immune system. One of the most important elements of the immune system is the macrophage. Ultimately, the

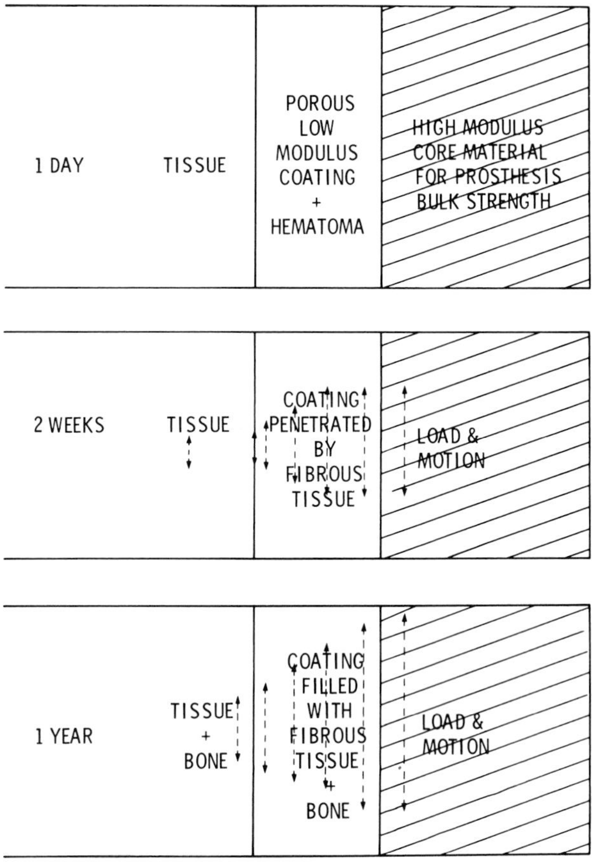

FIGURE 29-2. Low-modulus system stabilization. (From Homsy CA, Kent JN, Hinds EC: Materials for oral implantation —biological and functional criteria. J Am Dent Assoc 86:817, 1973; with permission.)

reaction of the macrophage to an alloplast will govern the global tissue reaction to the implanted material.

All tissue macrophages probably originate from bone marrow via differentiation from the monoblast (Fig. 29-3A). The macrophages are then distributed by the circulation to various organs and tissues throughout the body. It is important to note that macrophages are found in normal tissues, not in response to inflammation, and perform phagocytic functions (i.e., liver, lung, lymph nodes, spleen, and bone marrow). Histiocytes and type A cells are macrophages normally found in connective tissue and synovium, respectively (Fig. 29-3B).

The response of connective tissue macrophages to implanted materials occurs outside the lymphoreticular system. It primarily involves free macrophages, that is, histiocytes, macrophages, inflammatory exudates, and macrophages found in serosal cavities. Macrophages, like other elements of the immune system, respond to immunogenic materials, resulting in inflammation. Macrophages also respond to nonimmunogenic surfaces — that is, implanted foreign materials — by a poorly understood mechanism. These macrophages may become activated, thus initiating the entire biochemical sequence of inflammation.

Studies on blood monocytes and macrophages have shown that the cytoplasmic granules contain stored acid hydrolases and therefore can be called lysosomes.[21] Acid phosphatase was one of the first lysosomal enzymes histochemically demonstrated in macrophages.[22] A large number of acid hydrolases have now been identified. They include β-glucuronidase, β-galactosidase, and acid phosphatase. Neutral proteases, such as plasminogen activator, collagenase, and elastase, occur in smaller amounts.[23]

Although macrophages clearly have a vast range of hydrolytic activity, their storage compartment is probably less prominent than that of the polymorphonuclear phagocytes. The potential for sustained synthesis of lysosomal enzymes and the relative longevity of macrophages, however, make them a potent source of hydrolytic activity.

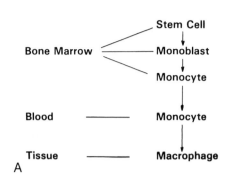

ELEMENTS OF THE MONONUCLEAR PHAGOCYTE
SYSTEM

A

DIFFERENTIATION OF MACROPHAGES

TISSUE	CELL TYPE
Liver	Kupffer Cell
Connective Tissue	Histiocyte
Lung	Alveolar Macrophage
Synovium	Type A Cell
Bone	Osteoclast
Inflammation	Foreign Body Giant Cell

B

FIGURE 29–3.   *A*, Elements of the mononuclear phagocyte system. *B*, Differentiation of macrophages.

An important functional characteristic of the macrophage is the ingestion of particulate matter, such as bacteria or dead cells, by phagocytosis. Foreign body implant material poses special problems. Contact between a wandering macrophage and a foreign surface may occur purely by chance, or the macrophage may be guided to the site by chemotaxis. Clinically, immunogenic particles, such as bacteria, will be coated with the C3b component of serum and specific immunoglobulin G (IgG) molecules and will be phagocytosed. Events associated with implants are not as well understood, except that hydrophobic materials, such as polytetrafluoroethylene and roughened plastics, are more easily taken by macrophages than are hydrophilic materials, which are preferred by fibroblasts.[24] Most implant materials, when exposed to protein, will adsorb the protein onto the implant surface. Hemoglobin, for example, is adsorbed in patches on polytetrafluoroethylene, while it forms a uniform layer 1.5 mm thick on platinum.[25] Under clinical conditions, the surface encountered by macrophages is not simply the implant material, but one that is modified by adsorption of a variety of multilayered high molecular weight protein molecules.[12] Particulate matter that is toxic, such as some metals and silica, as well as the physical shape may affect the release of lysosomal enzymes, producing the chronic damaging reactions. Other factors seem likely to influence the macrophage response to implant material. They are not well substantiated but do include surface area particle size and shape, total mass, and surface roughness and related free surface energy.

Little is known about the role of phagocytosis of particulate implant materials in the activation of macrophages. Studies by Rae do not indicate that titanium, titanium alloy, methylmethacrylate, or carbon in particulate forms cause a release of enzymes as great as that caused by a known inflammatory agent, such as zymosan.[12] Little is known about the mediators of inflammation that are released from macrophages after contact with implant materials. The most likely, in addition to lysosomal enzymes, are prostaglandin, complement, lymphocyte-activating factor, and others that have fibroblast-stimulating activity.[12] The role of these mediators of inflammation in the response of tissues to implant materials is poorly understood. A few macrophages, not associated with an inflammatory response, are normally found on an intact implant surface. However, large numbers of multinucleated giant cells opposed to polymer debris indicate that macrophages play an active role before fusing to form these giant cells. A general finding is that small polymer particles are phagocytosed by macrophages, while larger particles evoke the giant cell reaction. When large quantities of debris are present, a confluence of sheets of macrophages and giant cells leads to early fibrosis.[26] These findings are more frequently seen with wear debris of polytetrafluoroethylene and polyethylene than with carbon or metals. The macrophage response to polylactic acid, a biodegradable suture material usually absorbed by 63 days, is self-limited and poorly understood regarding the mechanism of the inflammatory response.

When a macrophage is in contact with an implant material, as a result of either phagocytosis of particulate matter or attachment to a surface, its survival is dependent on both the chemical and the physical nature of that material. Mouse peritoneal macrophages used to assess the toxicity of pure particulate metals show that titanium, chromium, and molybdenum were phagocytosed and produced no abnormal morphologic changes or release of lactate dehydrogenase (LDH). In contrast, particles of cobalt, nickel, and cobalt-chromium alloy caused marked changes in cell morphology and release of LDH.[27]

There have been only very few similar investigations on materials used for implants. Rae monitored the release of lysosomal enzyme markers and the cytoplasmic enzyme LDH from macrophages exposed to particulate preparations of the following materials: carbon fiber, aluminum oxide ceramic, polymethylmethacrylate, titanium, and titanium-aluminum-vanadium alloy.[28] When compared with the effects of the positive controls, silica and zymosan, all of the previously named materials, with the exception of the ceramic, produced only low levels of acid hydrolase release and did not affect cell viability as measured by LDH release. The ceramic material produced a marked release of the lysosomal enzyme markers and LDH. This finding was surprising, since the cells showed that they had extensively phagocytosed the material and retained an otherwise normal morphology. The release of acid hydrolases and other products by macrophages at the implant surface is important in mediating the events of chronic inflammation. Some materials may act directly on the macrophage, while others act through the immunologic involvement of lymphocytes[12,29] (Fig. 29–4A and B).

There is little doubt that inflammatory giant cells are formed in response to some implant materials, particularly polymers, as a result of the fusion of macrophages.[30,31] A supply of newly emigrated monocytes, the precurser of the macrophage, is essential to the enlargement of multinucleated giant cells.[32,33] Macrophages that have already phagocytosed indigestible material tend not to fuse into giant cells.[34]

Mechanisms of fusion of macrophages include mediation by the immune system, the recognition of an abnormal macrophage surface by young macrophages, or fusion of macrophages as a result of phagocytic activity. The last mechanism also includes

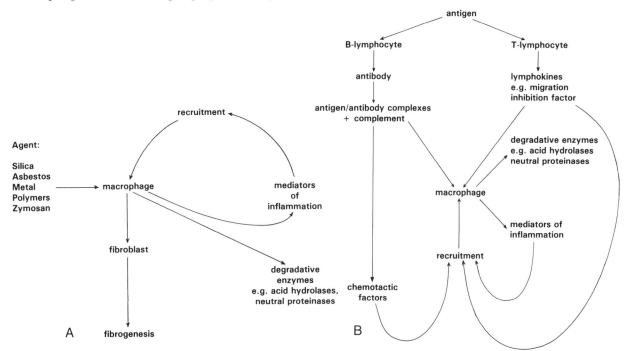

FIGURE 29–4.   A, Summary of direct effects of inflammatory materials on macrophages.[12,29] B, Summary of indirect effects of inflammatory agents on macrophages via the action of lymphocytes.[12,29] (Modified with permission from Rae T: The macrophage response to implant materials — with special reference to those used in orthopedics. CRC Crit Rev Biocompat 2:97, 1986. Copyright CRC Press, Inc., Boca Raton, FL.)

the possibility of attachment to a particulate surface too large to phagocytize, which is regarded by some as "frustrated phagocytosis," perhaps more relevant to the response to implant materials.[30]

Macrophages play an important role in the repair of damaged tissues, whether by accident or by design, during the surgical procedure of implanting a prosthesis. Their immediate role is in wound healing, but at a later stage, they become involved in the remodeling of bone in response to the presence of an implanted material.

Osteoclasts derived from circulating monocytes are generally associated with bone resorption. Macrophages and perhaps other cells may indirectly play a role in resorption.[35,36] There are both similarities and differences between the macrophage and the osteoclast. Their secretory products of collagenase, lysosomal enzymes, and prostaglandins are fundamental in resorption. Cell characteristics of the osteoclast, such as membrane ruffling and multiple nuclei, are not associated with the macrophage.[37,38] The claim that giant cells and macrophages directly cause bone resorption is not supported by the scientific literature. In the human body, osteoclasts are responsible for bone resorption, not foreign body giant cells. Chambers states that while osteoclasts are formed by the fusion of monocyte precursors, these mononuclear cells do not appear phenotypically related to giant cells or macrophages.[39] They also exhibit different enzyme activities than do macrophages or giant cells. However, there is increasing evidence that the macrophage and fibroblasts play a role in removing collagen fibrils once demineralization is initiated by the osteoclast.[40] Their guidance to a site of active bone resorption secondary to mobility of the implant or unacceptable load may be of importance in the overall process of bone resorption. Mechanical stimuli, such as mobility and the surface roughness of the tissue interface, may also stimulate macrophage response.

Both the osteoclast and the macrophage polykaryon (multinucleated foreign body giant cell) have a common precursor, the macrophage.[30] Since a foreign body giant cell granuloma reaction to polymer debris may be found in weight-bearing joints containing polyethylene or polytetrafluoroethylene, is it possible to say that macrophages and giant cells directly act as osteoclasts and effect bone resorption? There is little evidence to support this theory.[12] A more plausible scientific explanation for TMJ bone resorption is the excessive mechanical forces produced with increased weight-bearing loads as well as the force created by the clenching of teeth and by bruxism. However, prostaglandins and lymphokine, an osteoclast-activating factor, both released by cellular elements of a granuloma, are potent stimulators of bone resorption. Interestingly, in high concentrations, prostaglandins promote bone formation. Recent evidence also suggests that abnormal mechanical forces produced by bruxism and so on can initiate bone resorption. Bone remodeling induced by physical stress is prostaglandin E_2 mediated.[41] Increased prostaglandin E_2 causes local bone loss, bone resorption, and periodontal disease.[42] Therefore, excessive mechanical loads lead to increased prostaglandin E_2 production by bone, which in turn activates osteoclasts, whose actions lead to local bone loss and resorption.

There is little evidence to suggest that immunologic events are prominent in the response to implanted materials. Although macrophages, macrophage polykaryons, and fibroblasts are prominent features of the response to some materials, lymphocytes, plasma cells, and other immunocompetent cells are not normally involved. Exceptions may be lymphocytes and plasma cells involved in the response to infection or the sensitivity of experimental animals and some patients to components of implanted materials. Hypersensitivity may develop from cobalt or nickel in total hip replacement and other clinical applications. There appear to be large gaps of knowledge and misunderstandings of the macrophage response to implanted materials. Little is known about implant materials, even though the recognition of surfaces and particles of biologic origin by immunologic mechanisms is well understood. How do macrophages recognize materials with biologically featureless surfaces, such as metals and polymers, their free surface energies, and hydrophobic or hydrophilic differences? Clearly much basic research at the cellular level remains to be done.

IMPLANT MATERIALS

Requirements of Implant Materials

The general features of an alloplast for cranial, facial, or mandibular reconstruction should satisfy the following criteria:

1. Nonimmunogenic
2. Strength and resilience to restore hard tissue form where function is required
3. Bendability, moldability, or carvability to allow for intraoperative adaptation
4. Stable and nonreactive surface, whether loaded or not
5. Modulus of elasticity similar to that of connective tissue at the implant-tissue interface

Specific requirements for an ideal facial implant material have been defined by Kent[43,44]:

1. The material is readily available in block and precarved forms, can be repeatedly steam autoclaved, and is easily carved.
2. It can be bent or molded to improve bone interface and overlying facial contour. Therefore, it should be a low-modulus material permitting deformation to clinical requirements. The material should not have "memory" characteristics that may lead to mobility, extrusion, or resorption.
3. Surface but not total porosity for rapid tissue ingrowth and immediate stabilization on bone and surrounding soft tissue is desirable.
4. Deformation or resorption of bone beneath implants from soft tissue and muscle tension should not be clinically significant.
5. Redistribution of soft tissue overlying the face of implant materials should be minimal so that the clinician can predictably determine implant size.
6. The healed tissue implant matrix should have gross physical characteristics approaching those of grafted bone with supple overlying soft tissue and skin.
7. There should be no objectionable color characteristics of the materials when used in areas with thin skin coverage.
8. Material should be easily excised if the surgical result is not satisfactory or additional augmentation is necessary.
9. Although the materials need not be osteogenic, they should be osteoconductive or osteophilic to satisfy the clinical requirement of tissue ingrowth and stabilization.
10. The implant, of course, would be highly biocompatible, exerting no local or distant cytotoxic effects.

Although no single implant material satisfies all requirements for a facial or cranial augmentation, several polymers and ceramics satisfy many clinical requirements (Table 29–2). The discovery of plastic polymers opened a new era in tissue implantation. The characteristics of these polymers are dependent on the various chain formations of different macromolecular monomer components.

Acrylic Resins

Polymers of methacrylate esters were developed in the 1930s as external prosthetic biomaterials. This development was an extension of the employment of polymethylmethacrylate (PMMA) as a substitute for inorganic glasses. The properties of transparency, high toughness and strength, and ease of processing led to the use of PMMA as a denture material in 1933.[45] The use of PMMA as an internal implant

TABLE 29–2.   COMMONLY USED FACIAL ALLOPLASTS: CLINICAL CONSIDERATIONS

Feature	HA Proplast,*	Silicone Rubber,*	Acrylic,*	Porous Acrylic,*	Porous Polyethylene	Dense Hydroxyl-apatite†	Porous Hydroxyl-apatite†	Teflon*	Polyamide Mesh†
Surface porosity	+	−	−	+	+	−	+	−	+
Modulus of elasticity	+	−	−	−	−	−	−	−	+
Memory	+	−	−/+	−/+	−/+	−/+	−/+	−	+
Adaptability	+	+	+	+	−	−	−	+	+
Color	+	+	+	+	+	+	+	+	+
Ease of removal	−	+	+	−	−	+	−	+	−
Osteophilic	+	−	−	−	−	+	+	−	−
Displacement	+	−	−	+	+	+	+	−	+
Bone resorption	−	−	−	−	−/+	+	+	−/+	−/+
Soft tissue reaction	+	+	−	−	+	+	+	+	+
Degradation	+	+	+	+	+	+	+	+	−

* Unloaded application.
† Loaded or unloaded.
+ = advantage; − = disadvantage.

biomaterial began during World War II, when Zander applied the material to cranial defects[46] (Tables 29–3 and 29–4).

Polymerization of methylmethacrylate (MMA) is initiated by free radicals, intermediates that have an unpaired electron. Propagation of chains, once initiated, is extremely fast, linking thousands of monomers into a single polymer in a matter of seconds. The "heat-cured" acrylic is achieved by heating a mixture of MMA with benzoyl peroxide. The heat decomposes the benzoyl peroxide, which produces a phenyl radical. Room temperature–cured acrylics are commonly accelerated by N,N,-dimethyl-p-toluidine, light, radiation, oxygen, and environmental heat.

The medical-grade acrylic resin is generally available as a two-component system: a powder of small PMMA spheres and beads and a liquid monomer. The monomer polymerizes and links together the pre-existing polymer. The polymerization reaction is strongly exothermic, with maximal temperatures reaching as high as 120°C.

Reactions of host tissues to PMMA are varied and are related to the various components (i.e., monomers, comonomer, catalysts, plasticizers, and so forth), the thermal by-product of curing, and the physical aspects of the material itself. Toxicity, hypersensitivity, and systemic effects are generally related to the unreacted components, while the heat of curing and the physical properties of the material will produce localized tissue reactions.

Unpolymerized monomer, accounting for less than 1 per cent of the composition of "heat-cured" polymers and up to 2 to 4 per cent of "cold-cured" polymers, can have systemic toxic effects.[47] The lungs appear to function as a major clearing organ, while degenerative changes can be seen in the liver and kidneys.[48] Transient, moderate-to-severe hypotension, pyrexia, and cardiac arrest have been observed immediately after inserting PMMA bone cement with unbound monomer in the medullary canal of the femur for total hip replacement. Cardiac arrest is an erratic occurrence and may be related to surgical techniques that introduce fat or air into the blood stream with resultant embolic sequelae.[49] In humans, it appears that the maximal monomer blood level, about 1 mg/100 ml, is well below the level at which systemic effects were found in animal studies. Other low molecular weight constituents (i.e., accelerators, stabilizers, plasticizers, and so on) have been evaluated, but no toxic effects directly attributable to them have been reported.[50]

Hypersensitivity to the MMA monomer has been a topic of great discussion over the years. A type of contact mucositis has been attributed to residual monomer with

TABLE 29-3.   COMPOSITION OF CLINICALLY AVAILABLE POLYMERS

NAME	CHEMICAL FORMULA
Polymethylmethacrylate	
Polymethylsiloxane	
Polyethylene	
Polypropylene	
Polytetrafluoroethylene	
Polyethylene terephthalate	
Polyamide	

oral prostheses, but the polymer has never been implicated as a cause of any hypersensitivity, either externally or internally. Other low molecular weight constituents, such as benzoyl peroxide and tertiary amines, can be considered possible allergies, but to date no clinical reports have implicated these substances.[51]

Disadvantages of solid, heat-cured acrylics include difficult handling; problems with thermal, electrical, and x-ray conductivity; and their requirement for significant preoperative preparation. Self-curing forms (bone cement), mixed and polymerized

TABLE 29-4.   MECHANICAL PROPERTIES OF CLINICALLY AVAILABLE POLYMERS

NAME	TENSILE STRENGTH (N/M^2)	ELONGATION AT FRACTURE (%)	YOUNG'S MODULUS (N/M^2)	SHEAR Modulus (N/M^2)
Polymethylmethacrylate	7.0×10^7	5	3.0×10^8	1.1×10^9
Polymethylsiloxane	0.5×10^7	600	—	—
Polyethylene	3.0×10^7	800	4.0×10^8	1.4×10^8
Polypropylene	3.5×10^7	500	—	—
Polytetrafluoroethylene	2.3×10^7	600	5.0×10^8	1.8×10^8
Polyamide	8.5×10^7	90	2.8×10^9	1.0×10^9
Polyurethane	3.8×10^7	800	1.2×10^7	3.5×10^6

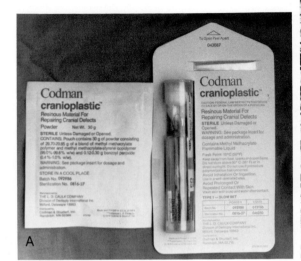
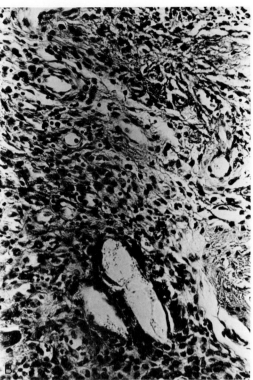

FIGURE 29–5. *A,* Methylmethacrylate for cranioplasty. *B,* Mechanical instability of implants stabilized with acrylic cement results in adjacent chronic inflammation with a granulomatous foreign body reaction to small acrylic particles, which are seen throughout this high-power (100×) section. (Courtesy of Dr. Hiromo Shoji, Professor of Orthopedics, LSU School of Medicine, New Orleans.)

in situ, can be adapted directly to contours of the cranial defect, whereas preformed materials are not as applicable. The two most commonly used commercial products of cold-curing acrylic for reconstruction of cranial deformities are Simplex (Howmedia International, Rutherford, NJ) and Cranioplast (Codmon and Shurtleff, Randolph, MA) (Fig. 29–5A). They are both composed of MMA, but the former contains a radiopaque additive.

Physical influences of acrylic resins relate primarily to two areas: tissue reactions to wear particles and local reaction to the heat of the in situ curing of the resin. Mechanical insufficiency, or wear, results in loose particles that can be found in adjacent soft tissues. These give rise to a foreign body reaction termed "acrylosis"[52,53] (Fig. 29–5B). This granulomatous type of foreign body reaction can be severe, and the perivascular lymphatics are usually unable to clear the particles, thus sustaining the problem. Ultimately, bone resorption and implant loosening or mobility will occur, leading to clinical failure.[54] Reactions to curing temperature, though of concern, seem not to outweigh the benefits of the acrylic resin as a cement or repair material. In vivo experiments have found temperatures at the bone-resin interface to range from 45 to 70°C.[55] The large discrepancy relates to a multitude of unpredictable parameters, which vary from case to case. Ultimately, the maximal temperature reached at the resin-tissue interface must cause local damage. Since body protein has been shown to coagulate at 56°C and bone collagen at 70 to 72°C, the curing temperature as well as the time it is maintained will determine the probability of tissue damage.

Long-term histologic reactions to acrylic resins are well documented in the orthopedic literature. After several years of function, the successful acrylic femoral implant will have a connective tissue capsule surrounding it that contains foreign body giant cells. Most authors feel this capsule is derived from mechanical loading and is not due to the bioincompatibility of acrylic polymers.[49] This theory is supported by clinical reports of cranioplasties in which stable implants and resorption-free bone around these minimally stressed implants are the rule[56] (Fig. 29–6A).

The concept of anchoring acrylic via porous attachment has been proposed because of the combined advantages of moldability and porosity. To prepare in situ self-curing cement with pores, an aqueous gel based on carboxymethyl cellulose is dispersed through the dough of the traditionally composed acrylic bone cement. The dispersed gel coalesces into an interconnected filament network, which is ultimately dissolved in and resorbed by the biologic environment, with resulting pores in the range of 300 to 1000 μm. The aqueous gel also acts as an efficient heat sink, thus reducing the notorious temperature peak that occurs during polymerization of acrylic cement. Compared with solid acrylic bone cements, the porous cement displays lower strength and stiffness; thus, clinical applications of this material should be confined to areas in which high loads and stresses are not expected. Histologically, porous implants are surrounded by a fibrous connective matrix containing a fair number of blood vessels. This aspect of porous implants is opposed to the traditional solid cement, which is characterized by fibrous encapsulation[57,58] (Fig. 29–6A to D).

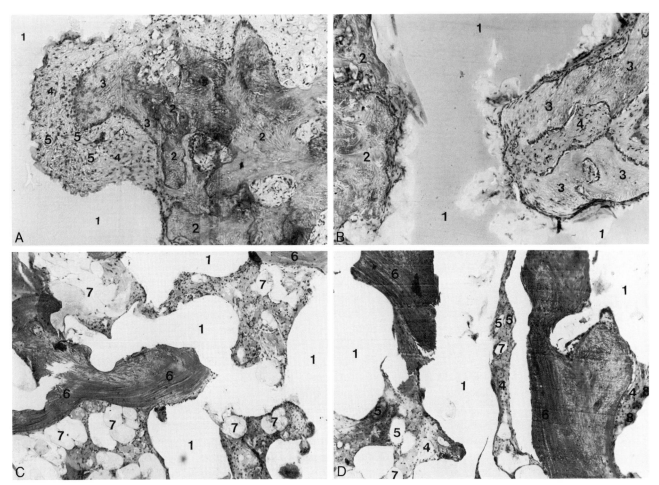

FIGURE 29–6. *A,* Starting bone ingrowth into superficial pore of porous polymethylmethacrylate (PMMA) implant after 3 weeks. *B,* Bone in pore of implant at 6 weeks. *C,* Bone in more centrally located pore after 20 weeks. *D,* Implant after 26 weeks. All photomicrographs are enlarged 25× (negative). Staining was hematoxylin–toluidine blue–acid fuchsin. *Key:* 1 = PMMA implant material; 2 = original bone; 3 = ingrown bone lined with osteoblasts; 4 = ingrown soft tissue; 5 = blood vessel; 6 = mature ingrown bone; 7 = fat cell; 8 = multinucleated giant cell. (Courtesy of Dr. P. J. van Mullem, Department of Oral Histology, University of Nijmegen, School of Medicine and Dentistry, the Netherlands.)

Clinical applications of acrylic resins in craniofacial reconstruction or augmentation have primarily been in the area of dental and maxillofacial prosthetics. Dental implants, submucosal augmentation, and contour correction of the jaws have been attempted, but clinical results have been less than satisfactory. Acrylic resins have been used in orbital wall and floor defects with some success, and intraocular lenses have been developed from this material.[59-61] The material is most widely used for the repair of cranial defects and the correction of contour with the use of either precured or in situ curing resins.[60-64]

Silicone Rubber

Silicone first became available commercially in 1943, and by the late 1940s, subdermal implantation for a variety of needs was begun. Its widespread use is due primarily to its many excellent physical characteristics, such as thermal stability, oxidative stability, nonwetting, extreme inertness, and retention of flexibility through wide temperature changes (Tables 29–3 and 29–4).

Silicone rubbers are formed from the basic building block, dimethylsiloxane, with small contributions from other organic side chains (i.e., vinyl and phenyl). Condensation polymerization can produce a high molecular weight molecule that has a highly polar Si-O-Si backbone that contributes to its flexibility. These molecules are cross-linked or vulcanized by chemically coupling the chains at widely separated points, thus retaining the flexibility of the original polymer chain. The process is initiated by the heat breakdown of a catalyst, dichlorobenzoyl peroxide, into free radicals, which can activate the organic side groups, thus forming cross-links.[65] A filler, finely divided silica, approximately 15 to 20 per cent by volume, is used to give silicone rubber enhanced mechanical properties.[66,67]

Physical properties depend on the exact composition of the silicone rubber and the curing procedure. Tensile strengths range from 25 to 100 MN/m^2, extensibility from 100 to 600 per cent, and hardness from 25 to 80 (Durometer).[66] Heat stability is a major advantage, allowing autoclavability and long shelf life. Most water-soluble materials as well as weak and strong acids and bases will have little or no effect on the silicone rubber at room temperature. The major disadvantage to silicone rubber is its relatively low tear resistance.

The biocompatibility of silicone rubbers is excellent. Toxic effects on any body tissue or fluid are almost nonexistent; although experimental evidence indicates that silicone acts as a hapten-like incomplete antigen,[68] this has not been shown to affect biocompatibility. Histologically, fibrous encapsulation occurs with no adhesion to the fibrous sheath (Fig. 29–7A and B). Though superior to many polymers, silicone rubber is thrombogenic, but this feature is due primarily to the silica filler. Gradual deterioration of the silicone rubber can occur,[69] which may be caused by the absorption of lipids from the blood, thus reducing the physical properties of the rubber. Lipid absorption is accelerated by abrasive wear, producing microcracks, which can produce late postoperative failures, especially in loaded functional applications. Abrasive wear alone can result in the failure of subdermal silicone rubber implants. Calcific deposits can also affect the surface of the implant, reducing mechanical properties.[70] When silicone implants are used in functional applications (joints, for example), a giant cell reaction can be seen locally in connective tissue and synovium, with no focal necrosis. Adjacent lymph nodes exhibit similar phenomena, but distinct or distant metastases have not been recorded[71] (Fig. 29–7D and E).

Medical applications of silicone rubber in the face fall into two major categories: contour alteration and joint rehabilitation. A variety of bulk and preformed silicone rubber implant devices with or without polymer fabric have been used to augment chin, zygomatic, and nasal deficiencies.[72-86] Preformed silicone is commercially available for many applications (McGhan; Wright Dow Corning, Arlington, TN; Byron, Tucson, AZ), while room temperature–vulcanizing (RTV) silicone may be used to customize implant shapes for specific deformities[86,87] (Fig. 29–7F). In the nose, silicone is used in custom implant form to reconstruct the dorsum, nasal tip, and columella. Implant migration is often seen here.[88] The nasal septum has also been repaired with silicone in sheet form, with major problems occurring with implant migration and extrusion. Facial reconstructions, including those involving the frontal, malar, and chin regions, have used silicone widely[89,90] (Fig. 29–7G to J). Silicone rubber, however, exhibits "memory" and therefore must conform to bone contour in the "relaxed" state, since bending the material may lead to extrusion or bone resorption. Sheeting to reconstruct the orbit secondary to traumatic floor defects has enjoyed widespread use, but extrusion and the need for extraocular muscle repair make it a less than optimal material in this area. Its use as an interpositional material in cases of TMJ ankylosis has had a long and controversial history. Many feel that silicone is an ideal material to prevent reankylosis and promote function, but repeated reports of functional failure because of fragmentation may indicate that its use here may be limited (see "TMJ Reconstruction," further on).

To minimize problems with implant stability, the use of porous silicone implants[91] and silicone bonded to Dacron[92] with Silastic Medical Grade Adhesive Type A (Wright Dow Corning) has been reported (Fig. 29–7K and L). Utilization of a porous form of silicone can be successful only in an area with minimal or no functional load or tissue movement applied to it. If it is used in other areas, problems with tearing and fracturing of the silicone will occur owing to the poor tensile strength of the material. Dacron bonded to silicone has aided in stabilization and is available in preformed combinations or can be custom made by bonding RTV silicone to Dacron in a mesh or felt form.

Medical-grade fluid silicone is clear, colorless, and odorless and has an oily lubricant feel to it. Its properties are unaffected by indefinitely prolonged storage at room temperature or exposure to sunlight and microorganisms. Wide-range thermal stability allows repeated steam autoclaving without significant alteration, but the material should never be gas sterilized because of its absorptive properties. Except for very rare idiosyncratic reactions, major problems reported to have resulted from injections of liquid silicone are explicable by qualitative and quantitative factors of misuse and by injections into unsuitable locations. Qualitative factors of misuse are intentionally added adulterants; injection of unpurified, industrial-strength silicone; and accidental contamination of large volumes stored with surfaces exposed or kept in rubber-stopped bottles or in contact with other materials that may have altered or decomposed. Complications following injections are known to depend upon the nature and amount of contaminants. The main quantitative consideration is the injection of excessive amounts of fluid in a particular site.[93]

The eventual tissue response to fluid silicone is fibroplastic, resulting in slightly increased local collagen deposition to the immediate surrounding area. Fibrosis is limited and does not become extensive. This is the case even with depositions of large volumes, providing the tissue has not been compressed and lymphatics and blood vessels are not encroached upon.[94]

Fluid silicone may be injected to lift depressed scars that result from various causes, provided they are not bound down by strong fibrous adhesions. Small volumes are effective for the vertical and oblique frown lines in the glabella region, and nasolabial folds can be lifted by repeated injections of silicone to a moderate amount of a few milliliters. Sunken facial contours on the upper cheeks can be effectively augmented, but excessive volume should not be injected. Depressed defects of the dorsum of the nose, like saddle nose deformity, minor degrees of nasal asymmetry, and defects of the nasal tip following rhinoplasty may be cosmetically improved by the introduction of small amounts of fluid silicone.[95,96] The injection of fluid silicone has a limited role in augmentation of the chin for correction of minor degrees of microgenia[94] and for optimizing the contour of the chin after a solid silicone implant is placed.

Restoration of facial contour has also been used in hemifacial atrophy.[97-99]

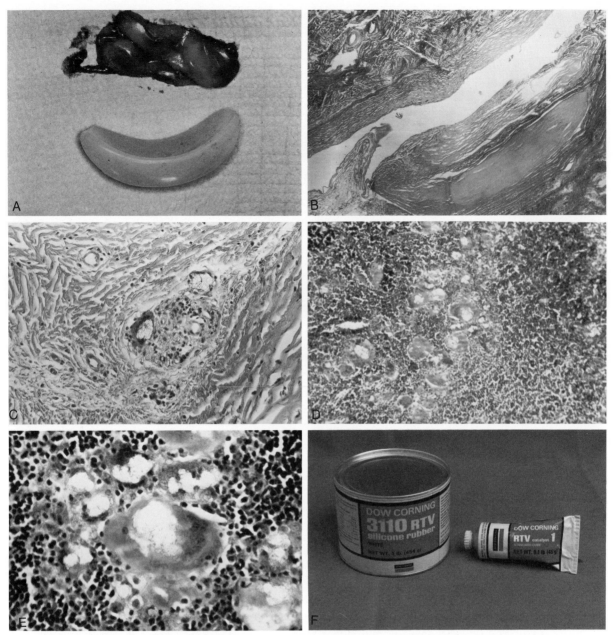

FIGURE 29–7. *A,* Tissue response to a clinically asymptomatic removed silicone rubber chin implant because of bone resorption. *B,* Histologic study reveals fibromembranous tissue with marked fibrosis, hyalinization, and chronic inflammation of skeletal muscle. *C,* Higher magnification of foreign body reaction to particles in skeletal muscle. *D, E,* Reaction of silicone rubber in submandibular lymph node seen at a magnification of 40× *(D)* and 100× *(E). F,* Room-temperature vulcanizing silicone rubber. *G, H,* Chin (gel-filled and solid) and malar silicone rubber implants. *I, J,* McGhan chin and malar silicone rubber implants. *K,* Dacron sheeting for silicone rubber implant fixation. *L,* Medical-grade adhesive type A. *(D* and *E* courtesy of Dr. Randy Malloy, Lafayette, LA.)

Illustration continued on opposite page.

Augmentation should proceed gradually to reduce the possibility of drift of fluid silicone and overcorrection, since the cumulative volume injected may be considerable. Migration of fluid is usually not a problem following proper procedures.

Still larger volumes of fluid silicone may be required for restoration of facial contours in progressive lipodystrophy.[97,98] Injections of fluid silicone have also been effective in augmenting flattened hemifacial contour in cases of first and second

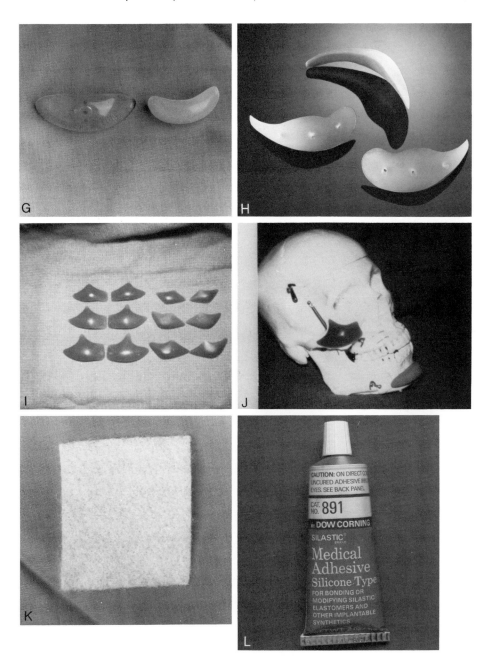

FIGURE 29–7. *Continued*

branchial arch syndrome.[94,99–101] Additional improvement of the appearance of the face has been achieved by silicone augmentation in patients treated by dermabrasion, rhytidectomy, and blepharoplasty.[102,103]

Polyethenes

The polyethenes comprise a group of polymers made from (ethene-type) monomers and include polyethylene and polypropylene. They are classified as flexible, crystallizable chain structures.[104] An amorphous polymer will have chain rigidity determined by the nature of the repeating units in the chain, and in particular, it will be increased by the presence of double bonds, cyclic structures, and certain appended groups or branches attached to the chain. Increased chain rigidity will increase melting point, dimensional stability, resistance to degradation, tensile strength, and glass transition temperature. These polymers are frequently characterized by properties related to processing or to end use rather than by the more fundamental properties of polymer physical chemistry[105] (Tables 29–3 and 29–4).

The first major classification of polyethenes is polyethylene. Commercial polymerization of ethylene gas was introduced by ICI, Ltd., in 1939 to produce what is now referred to as low-density polyethylene (LDPE). The reaction takes place in an autoclave at pressures between 15,000 and 45,000 psi. Oxygen or peroxide is used to initiate polymerization. Under these conditions, the ethylene reacts with itself in a process involving free radicals generated by the initiator molecules to form a polymer that has a high degree of side chain branching. The specific gravity of this material ranges from 0.910 to 0.935. In the early 1950s, another type of polyethylene, referred to as high-density polyethylene (HDPE), was made by low-pressure polymerization (below 1500 psi) in the presence of heterogenous initiator systems. This polymer is a substantially linear molecule with very few side chain branches; thus, a higher density is obtainable, and the range of specific gravity is from 0.940 to 0.970.

The polymer consists of a large number of ethylene units linked together to form a chain macromolecule. LDPE is a highly branched polymer. The chain branches tend to reduce crystallinity, thus increasing the percentage of amorphous material present, and the crystalline-amorphous ratio affects the properties considerably.[105,106] For example, a high percentage of amorphous material results in lower yield strength, lower stiffness, lower softening point, increased stress crack resistance, and better low-temperature brittleness.

The grade of polyethylene that has had the major effect upon surgery has a molecular weight of approximately 4×10^6 and is referred to as ultra high molecular weight polyethylene (UHMWPE). UHMWPE has dominated developments in total joint replacement surgery for the past two decades. This has happened because the use of polytetrafluoroethylene as an acetabular cup prosthesis showed unacceptable wear and tissue irritation.[107]

At the present time, the LDPEs are generally used in non–load-bearing applications. The LDPEs are seldom used in their pure form. Because of this, it is essential to separate tissue reactions arising from additives from those related to the polymer itself. Several publications have confirmed that there is very little tissue reaction to block polyethylene.[108–110] Implantation of cylinders in rabbits produced a fibrous pseudomembrane that was moderately cellular and vascular.[111] Particles are conducive to a more severe reaction.[112] With LDPE, there have been a wide range of uses reported in the ophthalmic, reconstructive, and cardiovascular surgery areas, as well as in neurology, in tendon repair, and in the manufacture of contraceptive devices.

A porous sponge form has offered new possibilities for reconstruction in non–load-bearing areas (PlastiPore, Richards Manufacturing Company, Memphis, TN; Medpor, Porex, Fairburn, GA). Its most widespread use has been in the middle ear; when the implant is placed here, it becomes embedded by a connective tissue network, with no chronic or acute inflammation. A drum-to-foot plate prosthesis (total ossicular replacement prosthesis [TORP]) and a drum-to-stapes prosthesis (partial ossicular replacement prosthesis [PORT]) result in a columella of living tissue, and it is reported that hearing gains are retained.[113] Multinuclear giant cells are noted to be present histologically, but there is a distinct absence of particulate matter in these cells. Porous polyethylene has been used with various pore sizes. Experimentally, it was noted that with pore sizes less than 100 μm there was a failure to allow for fibrous tissue or bony ingrowth into the implant. Such a failure results in fragility, instability of the material, and potential for infection and extrusion.[114] When larger pore sizes, in the 100- to 200-μm range, are used, the material has been shown to be successful in correcting facial and skull defects, in reconstructing the external ear, in reconstructing the trachea, and in rebasing the vocal folds.[115]

Ultra high molecular weight polyethylenes produce a low level of tissue response in bulk form.[111] The plastic flow of polymer away from highly compressed areas indicates that creep is a factor involved in the failure of UHMWPE. Body fluids may also lead to stress corrosion, resulting in further cracking, and finally, fretting has been seen in situ. Modifications to improve UHMWPE as an implant material have been successful. Gamma irradiation to produce cross-linking increases both the coefficient of friction and the wear rate. Surface hardness increases with the irradiation, resulting in a 30 per cent improvement in abrasion resistance.[116] However, this hardness is mainly a surface effect, since the bulk of the polymer is approximately eight times less cross-linked than the articulating surface. Other methods of altering the physical properties of UHMWPE include reinforcement with carbon fibers to improve mechanical properties.[117] With a volume of 10 per cent by weight of carbon fibers, there is an increased resistance to compressive loading and increased tensile strength. In addition, the reinforced polymer showed less compressive creep, and wear testing in joint simulators also showed an advantage over unreinforced material. A 20 per cent fiber volume gives even better mechanical properties.[118] Although carbon fiber has been used and shown to be effective in increasing the mechanical properties of UHMWPE, the effects of particles that are abraded from the prosthetic joint surface may be quite different, and therefore, caution still must be taken in recommending it as an articulating surface in a load-bearing joint.

Polypropylene is another of the polyethenes that have been used in medicine. The advantages are that with a high melting point (165 to 176°C) steam autoclaving is permitted and that the material is dimensionally stable and exhibits less creep under load than does polyethylene. Experimental implantation of sheets of polymer into rat abdominal wall and into joints of dogs showed only the formation of a fine, fibrous avascular capsule.[119] The use of polypropylene in a ball-and-socket joint design has been rejected because the meshlike wear particles can cause adverse tissue reactions. This observation is reinforced by the finding that polypropylene filaments have been shown to degrade when implanted subcutaneously in hamsters.[120]

Other variations include polyethylene terephthalate (Dacron), which has long been used as a vascular replacement material. Dacron in craniofacial reconstruction has been used as a reinforcement material with silicone rubber, as mentioned previously, as well as a contoured scaffolding in conjunction with a polyurethane elastomer to reinforce the polyethylene terephthalate mesh (OsteoMesh, XOMED, Inc., Gainesville, FL).[121–124] When used in this fashion, the mesh has been successful in restoring contour yet is easily adaptable at the time of surgery by trimming with scissors and can be used in conjunction with autogenous bone or bone replacement to obtain ultimately a physiologic reconstruction of craniofacial and mandibular defects (Fig. 29–8).

Polytetrafluoroethylene

Polytetrafluoroethylene, or PTFE (Teflon), is a long-chain, halogenated carbon polymer made by polymerization of tetrafluoroethylene gas at a high temperature and pressure. It is chemically inert with no known solvent, noncarcinogenic, resistant to corrosion, nonadherent, and able to be sterilized (Tables 29–3 and 29–4).

When Teflon is implanted, there is an initial inflammatory response with a predominance of aggregated histiocytes or giant cells. If the material is not loaded and the grafted area matures, giant cells become rare and are replaced with fibrous tissue.

Teflon comes in several forms. Sheeting of various thicknesses was initially developed for custom contouring at the time of surgery. It was indicated for nasal maxillary hypoplasia, for malar and infraorbital rim deficiency, following orbital wall or floor disruption, following partial mandibular resections, and for non–weight-bearing joint replacement.[125] Most of these indications are no longer valid, since newer implant materials with improved mechanical properties have replaced Teflon sheeting as a facial contour or joint replacement material. Its most common current application in the face is for repair of orbital floor fractures.[126–130] It is available for orbital

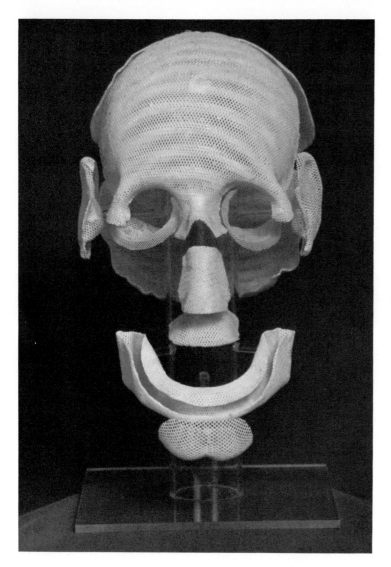

FIGURE 29–8. Cranial and mandibular porous Dacron cloth stiffened with polyurethane trays for reconstruction.

floor continuity in sheets that are 1.245 mm thick made of a white, feltlike material that does not wet.

Teflon has also been used in an injectable form consisting of pure particles of 50 to 100 μm suspended in a 50 per cent glycerin solution. The primary use for injectable Teflon is in paralyzed vocal cords.[131-135] Its use in facial augmentation had enjoyed limited success in the treatment of nasal deformities[136] and chin augmentation.[137] Viscosity of the compound results in technical difficulties related to injection and establishment of regular symmetric contours. Smaller, selected sites for injection have been shown to give better results then restoration of larger contour deficiencies, especially where muscle tension in associated tissues may cause early displacement prior to adequate implant encapsulation.

Proplast.   Proplast (Novamed Inc., Houston, TX) is a porous, low-modulus implant material that has been marketed in three forms. The basic material that forms the porous matrix of Proplast is PTFE perfluorocarbon polymer. It is found in Proplast in the form of both a fiber and a resin. The resin serves to fuse the fibers into the three-dimensional matrix. PTFE polymer is insoluble in all solvents and is resistant to chemical attack from almost all chemicals, save liquid sodium at an elevated temperature. It also has unique nonadhesion and antifrictional properties[138] (Tables 29–3 and 29–4).

Proplast I (gray) is a composite of PTFE and particulate carbon; Proplast II (white) is a composite of PTFE polymer and aluminum oxide fiber (Fig. 29–9A and B). A third generation of Proplast implant material, also white, is a composite of PTFE and synthetic HA. In all of these composites, the second ingredient coats the surface of the PTFE matrix and provides unique surface properties that facilitate the ingrowth of host tissue into the porous matrix. Fluorinated ethylene propylene (FEP), a dense, nonporous polymer chemically related to PTFE, has been laminated to Proplast I and II to provide an articular surface for TMJ interpositional disc and fossa prostheses (Fig. 29–9C to F). The pore size for Proplast I and II or HA-Proplast is 50 to 400 μm. Dendritic pore interconnections are 150 to 200 μm. The pore volume of Proplast implant materials constitutes 70 to 90 per cent of the total material volume. The histologic response to Proplast in a number of species has been studied in soft

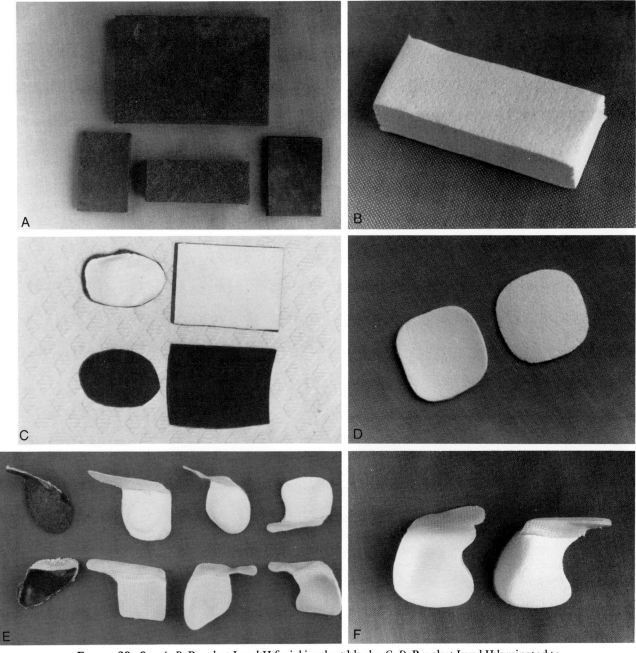

FIGURE 29–9. *A, B,* Proplast I and II facial implant blocks. *C, D,* Proplast I and II laminated to fluorinated ethylene propylene (FEP). *E,* Proplast II laminated to FEP and *F,* Proplast-hydroxylapatite (HA) laminated to polyethylene for glenoid fossa prostheses.

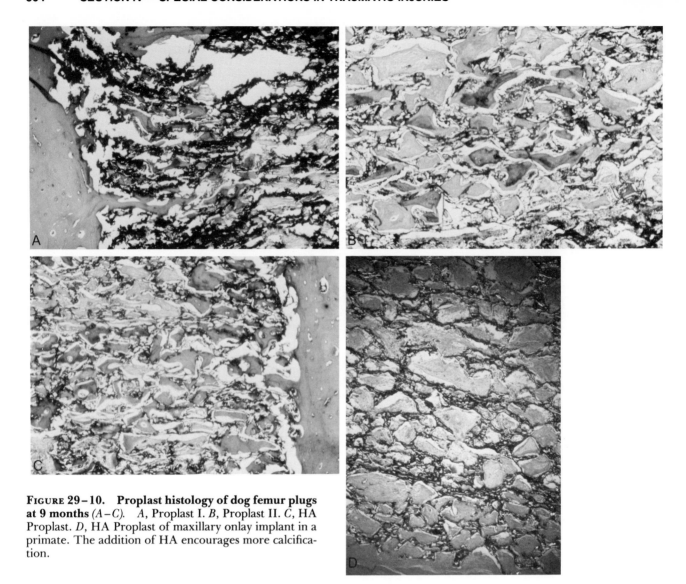

FIGURE 29–10.   Proplast histology of dog femur plugs at 9 months (*A–C*).   *A*, Proplast I. *B*, Proplast II. *C*, HA Proplast. *D*, HA Proplast of maxillary onlay implant in a primate. The addition of HA encourages more calcification.

tissue and osseous sites.[139–143] Initially, granulation tissue characterized by budding capillaries, histiocytes, multinucleated giant cells, fibroblasts, and collagen is present. Implants placed in bone have fewer histiocytes and giant cells than do those placed in soft tissue sites. In addition, the amount of collagen is inversely proportional to the number of giant cells and histiocytes present. Complete filling of Proplast implanted in bone with dense collagen may occur within 12 weeks. A variable but usually small number of macrophages and giant cells remain associated with these implants throughout their duration, unless motion and load are generated at the interface. The presence of these cells is not surprising, since it is known that macrophages have an affinity for hydrophobic surfaces.

Proplast I and II demonstrate the formation of osteoid variably within their porosity when they have been placed adjacent to an osseous surface. This formation occurs in implant locations where relative motion between the implant and adjacent osseous tissue is minimal or absent. The rapidity of the formation of such osteoid is also variable, depending upon the implant site. However, a zone of fibrous tissue may be present between the outer surface of the implant and the osseous tissue[139,140,143–146] (Fig. 29–10*A* to *D*). Proplast-HA composite, which is formed with synthetic HA, on the other hand, has been found to fill rapidly with mature lamellar bone within 3 to 6 months when placed within relatively mechanically quiescent implant locations. It would appear that the known ability of synthetic HA to facilitate bone formation from a fibrous tissue matrix is expressed in the Proplast-HA formation.[147,148]

As with other polymer and carbon materials, in vitro biotoxicity studies and animal experiments have shown Proplast as an onlay material to be highly compatible and free from (observable) systemic and local toxic side effects.[149] The behavior of Proplast and other polymers at the cellular level with joint loading is discussed under "TMJ Joint Reconstruction," further on.

The advantages of a porous implant material, such as Proplast, over solid polymers are the improved stabilization on or in bone by virtue of rapid tissue ingrowth rather than only fibrous encapsulation; a lower modulus characteristic similar to that of soft tissue, which permits material to be bent or molded to appropriate contours; easy wettability; light weight; radiolucency; and ease of carving. Proplast sheeting of 1 to 3 mm permits the repair of defects of irregular depth. Proplast is stable to temperatures greater than 392°F and can be sterilized by steam autoclaving up to three times. When laminated to UHMWPE, repeat autoclaving or a temperature above 250°F is not recommended. The disadvantages include the macrophage response discussed earlier, a slightly increased incidence of infection with intraoral use if contamination occurs during surgery, and decreased pore size and therefore less tissue ingrowth if the material is loaded or mishandled (compressed). The use of antibiotics is helpful, as described in the clinical section. The manufacturer states that Proplast is not indicated as an implant (1) by itself in weight-bearing or articulating bony surfaces where compressive loading is likely (TMJ), (2) over sinus cavities, (3) where there is insufficient underlying bone or soft tissue to prevent collapse in the event of external pressure, (4) in patients with systemic disorders that may compromise tissue ingrowth or normal wound healing, (5) in recent areas of infection, (6) in patients with a phobia for implant material, or (7) in gas or cold sterilization.

The applications of silicone rubber for craniofacial augmentation and defect filling have been extended by Proplast implant materials.[11,142,143,150-178] Proplast is available in block, preformed, or customized implants for chin, mandible, premaxilla, zygoma, orbit, and nasal augmentations[142,143,151,152,156-160,163,166,168,172,174,179] (Figs. 29-11 to 29-13). Silicone rubber sizers may be used for determining the correct implant pocket size, thereby reducing contamination and compression from excessive try-in and manipulation of the material.

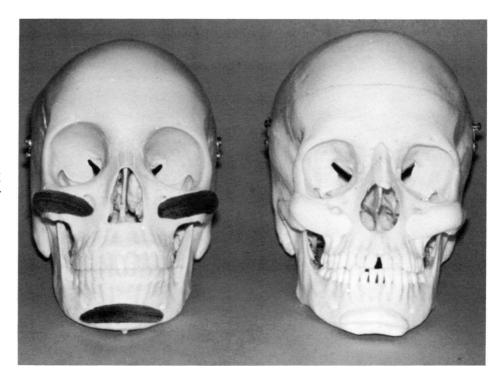

FIGURE 29-11. Proplast I and II and HA Proplast for facial augmentation.

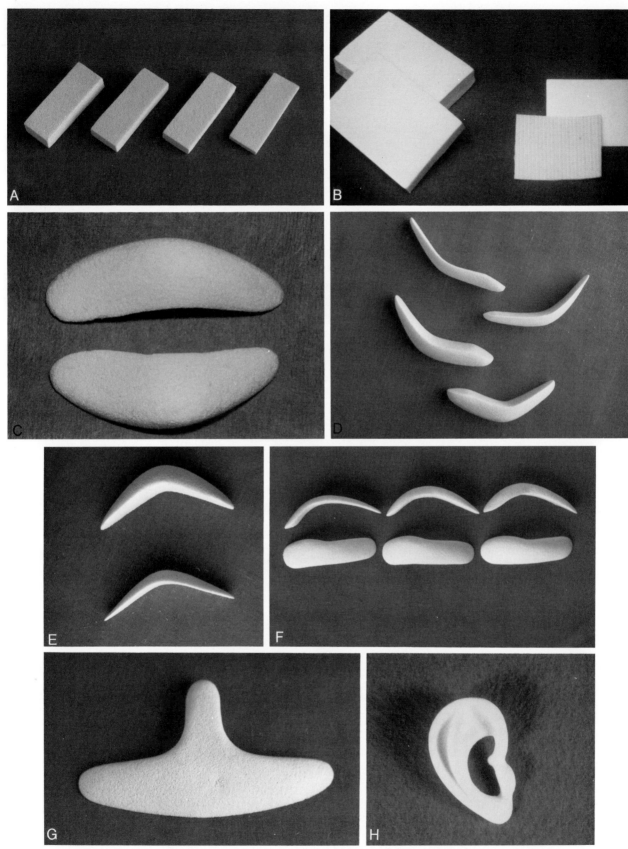

FIGURE 29–12.   *A,* Block HA Proplast. *B,* Block and Proplast laminated to reinforced FEP. *C, D,* HA Proplast Kent high-low zygomatic implants. *E,* HA Proplast laterally extended malar implants. *F,* Whitaker malar implants. *G,* HA Proplast periorbital implant. *H,* HA Proplast external ear prosthesis.

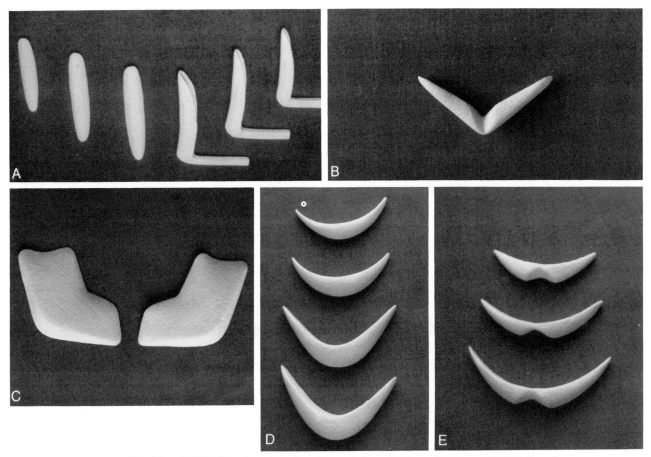

FIGURE 29–13. *A,* HA Proplast dorsal onlay and dorsal columellar strut. *B,* HA Proplast premaxilla. *C,* HA Proplast Whitaker mandibular angle implants. *D,* HA Proplast Kent chin implants. *E,* HA Proplast Freeman chin implants.

Since 1972, Proplast precarved material and block material carved at the time of surgery have been placed for chin and facial augmentation through both intraoral and extraoral approaches in outpatient and hospital inpatient procedure.[43,152,163] One early study (1975) demonstrated a 97 per cent cumulative success rate in nearly 400 patients in 14 teaching institutions and private practice centers.[161,162] Infection (10 cases) was the primary cause of failure, most likely from the contamination of the material during or following intraoral surgery. Infusion of antibiotics by a simple vacuum technique and additional experience with intraoral technique decrease the incidence of failure.[151] There have been no reported facial implant failures because of material cytotoxicity, tissue incompatibility, or systemic toxicity.

Because of the desire to promote rapid tissue ingrowth with microporous implant materials without the risk of contamination, studies have been performed to examine tissue ingrowth characteristics by infusing Proplast blocks with saline, autogenous plasma, and plasma with antibiotics before subperiosteal implantation into the maxilla and mandible in primates.[142,143] Previous studies and gross clinical inspection of Proplast infused with plasma implanted subcutaneously in rats had suggested an accelerated ingrowth of tissue and stabilization of the implant material.[180,181] Primate studies, however, indicate that presurgical infusion of the implant material with plasma may actually retard tissue density as well as evoke a more extreme local cellular response.[143] However, the cellular response was not significantly altered, and the ingrowth of tissue was similar when dry blocks were compared with those infused with antibiotic solution. In another study comparing local cellular response and tissue ingrowth densities in Proplast I and II implants in infraorbital rim and inferior border defects of the mandible in primates, no significant differences were noted between these two implant materials.[142]

In 1986, Proplast was modified; HA particles, replacing the aluminum oxide particles, were fused to PTFE fibers. Proplast I and II and HA-Proplast were placed in the femur and over the facial bones of dogs.[147,148] In the femur, histologic examination revealed fibrous tissue ingrowth at 4 weeks into Proplast I and II. However, the PTFE-HA composite evidenced a peripheral osteoid zone that was approximately 1 mm thick and more prominent adjacent to the intracanal cancellous bone. At 3 months, maturation of fibrous tissue was seen with all three composites. However, the peripheral osseous zone in the Proplast II material was osteoid, whereas the PTFE-HA composite demonstrated dense lamellar bone and osteoid throughout the plug at the levels adjacent to cancellous bone. At 6 months, the PTFE-HA composite showed dense lamellar bone in 25 per cent of its porosity, 50 per cent osteoid, and 25 per cent fibrous tissue. This finding is in contrast to the Proplast II composite, which demonstrated primarily osteoid in only 25 per cent of its porosity, with the remainder being fibrous tissue. On the face of dogs, the HA-Proplast implants demonstrated a similar increase in calcified tissue at the interface when compared with Proplast I and II (Fig. 29–10D). Bone density within the center, however, was not as great as with those implants placed in the femur.

These observations from pilot studies show that the PTFE-HA composite resulted in a greater proliferation of dense lamellar bone with the presence of haversian canals and osteoid. The ease of handling and carving and the osteoconductive nature of the HA make the PTFE-HA composite a more attractive candidate for facial implant use in non–stress-bearing skeletal reconstruction.[182,183]

Polyurethanes

The polyurethanes were originally introduced in Germany in the early 1900s and revealed outstanding abrasion and flexural fatigue resistance. In the mid 1950s, polyurethanes were implanted in the form of rigid foams for bone replacement (Fig. 29–8A) and as bone adhesives; the soft foams were used for heart valve suturing rings, vascular grafts, and catheter cuffs; and the elastomer was employed for cast heart valve leaflets and components of artificial heart assist devices (J. Jackson, Inc., Alexandria, VA). As is true with most of the synthetic polymers, the polyurethanes consist essentially of varied arrangements of polymeric molecules that share a common structure — the urethane group[184] (Tables 29–3 and 29–4).

A wide array of polyurethanes thus are possible. This selection is obtained by combining different groups through hydrogen bonding of adjacent molecular chains. Polyester versions are hydrolytically unstable owing to highly strained molecular configurations, whereas the polyethers are relatively insensitive to moisture. Medical experience has been successful primarily in the polyether class. The flexible segments provide the polymer with elastic recovery properties, and the hard segments provide intermolecular sites for secondary bonding. In addition, polyester polyurethane was found to change in its molecular structure drastically when implanted for periods up to 6 months.[185] The polyether polyurethanes are capable of long-term implantation with no significant physical changes occurring over periods in excess of 3 years.[186] Surface cracking indicating degradation secondary to stress has been shown not to have adverse effects in animal models,[187] except those experiencing chronic mechanical stress.[188,189]

Polyamide

Polyamide mesh, a derivative of polyamide, has been used successfully in facial augmentation by several authors.[190,191] This thermoplastic organopolymer is made up of a chain of frequent amide groups and based on phenol; it is chemically related to nylon and Dacron. Properties of heat stability and low tissue sensitivity make Supramid (J. Jackson, Inc.) a good alloplastic implant material. A moderate foreign body reaction is seen initially and is replaced by the growth of fibrous tissue in and around the fibers.[192] This infiltrate anchors the material and imparts an overall soft tissue texture. Long-term stability may be compromised by the finding that Supramid is degraded by the tissue[193,194] (Tables 29–3 and 29–4).

Supramid has been used both by itself and in combination with autogenous tissue ingrowth as an onlay material for the chin, nasal dorsum, and maxilla.[195-197] The problems with implantation of Supramid are difficulties in contouring and handling and in placement of the material at the time of surgery. An "autoalloplast" concept has evolved in which a rolled piece of Supramid is implanted in a secure area and incorporated with fibrous tissue for a 6-week period. At 6 weeks, the mesh material is harvested and reimplanted elsewhere in the body.[198] This approach is particularly interesting, as the material does take on the characteristics of soft tissue and is relatively resistant to infection. Stucker and colleagues contend also that they have successfully treated infection without removal of the implant on numerous occasions.

Calcium Phosphate Ceramics

Hydroxylapatite $[Ca_{10}(PO_4)_6(OH)_2]$ and related calcium phosphates are a new concept: hard tissue prosthetic materials that interact with, and may ultimately become an integral part of, living bone tissue. HA is used as a tableting agent in pharmaceuticals, as a calcium food supplement, as an anticaking agent in baked goods and table salt, and as the principal source of phosphate ion for the chemical industry.[199] Since HA (calcium and phosphate ions) has long been recognized as the principal mineral component of bone, research has been done in preventive fluoridation, in the development of the diphosphonates, and in the development of a bone graft substitute in dental, maxillofacial, and orthopedic surgery.[200]

Calcium phosphates have been used as bone graft substitutes in a variety of applications, such as HA particles under dentures to function in alveolar ridge augmentation, submerged root forms to prevent postextraction alveolar ridge resorption, block and particle forms when used as augmentations, and spacers with orthognathic and craniofacial procedures[201-221] (Fig. 29–14A to D).

All current calcium phosphate biomaterials can be classified as polycrystalline ceramics. Their material structure is derived from individual crystals that have been fused together at the crystal grain boundaries by a high-temperature (1100 to 1300°C) process called "sintering."[222,223] HA and tricalcium phosphate (TCP) $[(Ca_3(PO_4)_2]$, the latter usually having a β-Whitlockite crystal structure, have been the most widely investigated.

HA ceramics in either porous or dense forms can serve as permanent bone implants, showing virtually no tendency to bioresorb in vivo, while porous TCP ceramics have a tendency to bioresorb in a more or less unpredictable fashion when implanted in hard tissues.[224-226] The unpredictable bioresorption of TCP may limit its use, since porous TCP implants in vivo frequently cannot be distinguished radiographically from surrounding bone. If significant amounts of this material remain unresorbed or partially resorbed without bone maturation, it may be to the long-term biomechanical detriment of the reconstruction if it is a stress-bearing area.

The main limitation of calcium phosphate implant materials is their mechanical properties. Like most ceramics, these materials are quite brittle and have low impact resistance and relatively low tensile strength. The mechanical properties of calcium phosphate ceramics versus currently used metallic materials and bone are detailed in Table 29–5. Porous calcium phosphates have properties similar to those of cancellous bone, while the dense materials are significantly stronger than cortical bone. However, because dense calcium phosphate ceramics are much less compliant than is

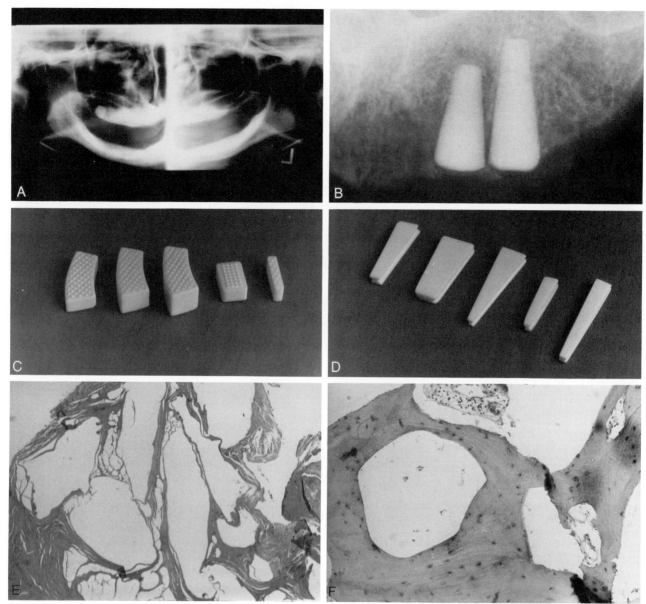

FIGURE 29-14. Particulate and block form of HA used for *A,* alveolar ridge augmentation, *B,* alveolar ridge preservation, and *C,D,* orthognathic and craniofacial reconstruction. Biopsy of human alveolar ridge at 3 years with *E,* HA alone or *F,* HA mixed with autogenous cancellous iliac bone for ridge augmentation. *G,* Bone adaptation to waffled HA primate facial onlay block. *H,* EDAX pulse image of calcium density *(left)* and corresponding back-scatter electron micrograph *(right)* of a dense HA particulate embedded in new bone near old bone interface. *I,* Electron micrograph of a decalcified bone-HA interface (D) showing remnants of HA implant crystals still attached to the amorphous bonding zone (BZ). A collagen fibril (C) is seen running parallel to the bonding zone and implant surface. *J,* Direct-transmission electron micrograph of an undecalcified, ultrathin section of a bone-HA implant interface, prepared by ion-beam micromiling.[201,212] Biologic apatite is deposited directly on the surface of the implant in a perpendicular palisade fashion. The white space represents the area perforated by the ion beam. *K,* Problems with permanent porous implant materials. *(H–K* courtesy of Dr. Michael Jarcho, San Diego.)

Illustration continued on opposite page.

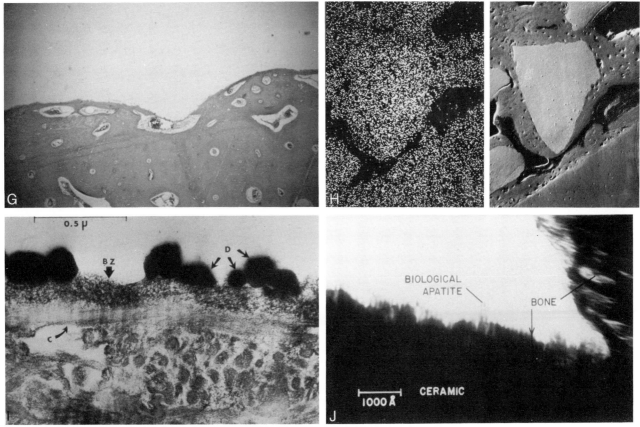

PROBLEMS WITH PERMANENT POROUS
IMPLANT MATERIALS

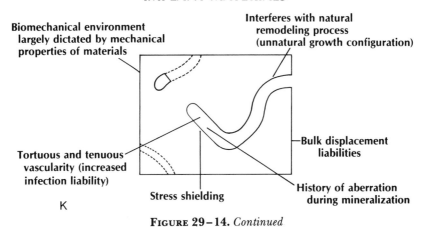

FIGURE 29–14. *Continued*

bone (an elastic modulus of a 1×10^7 psi versus 2×10^6 for bone), they cannot withstand the rigors of implant sites that would be expected to endure significant bending, torsional, or impact forces.

These "new concept" calcium phosphate biomaterials are distinguished from previous hard tissue implant materials by their basic biologic profile, which suggests they are the most biocompatible hard tissue implant materials known. This profile includes the lack of local or systemic toxicity, inflammatory or foreign body response, and intervening fibrous tissue between implant and bone when the implant is fixed directly on bone (Fig. 29–14E to G). They have an apparent ability to become directly bonded to bone by what appears to be natural bone-cementing mechanisms, with bone deposited directly on the surfaces without the presence of a fibrous tissue

TABLE 29-5. THE MECHANICAL PROPERTIES OF BONE AND METALLIC AND CALCIUM PHOSPHATE IMPLANT MATERIALS

MATERIAL	COMPRESSIVE STRENGTH (10^3 PSI)	TENSILE STRENGTH (10^3 PSI)	MODULUS (10^6 PSI)
Bone			
Cortical bone	20	10.0	2
Cancellous bone	6–9	0.5	—
Metals			
316L stainless steel	—	80–145	30–40
Cobalt-chromium alloy	—	97	30
Titanium	—	50	16
Calcium phosphate			
Dense	30–130	10–28	5–15
Porous	1–10	0.4	—

capsule. In one study of dense HA implants placed in artificially created defects in dog femora, calcification processes were observed to occur at normal rates immediately adjacent to the implants (Fig. 29–14*H*), and after 6 months, mineralization within the implant sites was comparable to that of surrounding bone.[227] In the inner pores of these materials, however, the rate of tissue infiltration and maturation becomes significantly retarded.

Calcium phosphate implant materials also display a complete lack of local or systemic toxicity because they can release only calcium and phosphate ions. Analysis of serum and urinary calcium and phosphate levels and/or Sequential Multiple Analyzer (SMA) 12 parameters carried out in conjunction with studies of a bioresorbable TCP material implanted in puppies (palate)[228] and dogs (orbital bone, iliac bone, mandible;[229] subcutaneous, intramuscular, femur;[230] spine)[231] and with nonresorbable HA in dogs (alveolus)[232,233] produced normal results. Tissue pathologic studies on major organs have been performed, including fine-detail kidney radiography, and no abnormalities or pathologic calcifications were noted.[228,230]

Probably the most remarkable feature of calcium phosphate implants is their ability to become directly bonded to bone without the need for porosity. Numerous investigators have observed this bone-bonding phenomenon, which is manifested by the inability to remove even dense or nonporous HA implants from surrounding bone without breaking the implant or the surrounding bone.[227–238]

Studies of the structure of the bonding zone between bone and HA ceramics using electron microscopic and other electron optical techniques have revealed a narrow band (500 Å to 2000 Å wide) devoid of collagen fibers but containing an amorphous organic ground substance[239,240] (Fig. 29–14*I*). Crystals of biologic apatite were found to be embedded in this ground substance,[241] arranged in an orderly perpendicular palisade array directly on the surface of the HA implant (Fig. 29–14*J*).[227,238] The bone immediately adjacent to the bonding zone is normal in appearance and contains its usual complement of ground substance, collagen fibrils, and bone mineral.[231,238–242] These observations of the bonding zone are very similar to those that have been made for natural bone-cementing substance, and the bonding zone has been characterized as having an amorphous ground substance that becomes demineralized.[243]

Calcium phosphate implants, composed of the same chemical substance as natural bone mineral, not only "fool" living bone cells into reacting as if they were natural autogenous materials but also "fool" the intercellular matrix into bonding these materials to living bone. Therefore, it naturally follows that the factors that govern the "take" of a conventional bone graft also play a role in the success or failure of calcium phosphate implants. Initial stabilization is required; otherwise, migration of the implant from a bony site into adjacent soft tissue occurs, and the implant is sequestered by a quiescent fibrous tissue capsule. The infiltration of an HA particle mass by fibrous tissue yields a very tough, almost bonelike structure, which plays a role in the use of HA for alveolar ridge augmentation.

Some think that these materials may stimulate osteogenesis,[244,245]; however, experiments involving millipore chambers[246] or implantation into nonbony tissues suggest these materials do not induce bone formation but instead serve as highly suitable substrates for hard tissue growth.

Viable autogenous cancellous bone has consistently outperformed calcium phosphate implants in histologically determined healing rates of periodontal lesions (dogs),[247] spinal fusions (dogs),[231] and segmental replacements (rabbits)[248]; however, the results clearly point to using the material as an autograft extender.[247]

A possible explanation for this difference in histologically observed healing rates between dense and porous materials is as follows (Fig. 29–14K). All of these materials impose upon infiltrating tissue an unnatural pathway that must be followed if the porous implant is to become fully invested with bone. Since bone is a tissue that is notorious for proliferating and remodeling according to its own overall biomechanical dictates, it is expected to travel these unnatural pore pathways with some reluctance. Most bony structures also require some degree of mechanical stimulation to maintain vitality. One must question the long-term fate of bone residing deep within the pores of a rigid ceramic structure, an environment virtually devoid of mechanical stress. In addition, the vascular system that supplies precursor fibrous tissue, and eventually bone, must follow the same tortuous pathway to get deep within such blocks. It would be expected that such a vascular system would be inefficient, both in its support of cell function and in its ability to serve as a conduit for systemic antibiotics, if infections arise at the implant site.

In support of this theory is a study wherein the calvaria of rabbits were implanted with porous blocks of a bioresorbable TCP material. Twenty-four hours prior to sacrifice (3 months), the animals were injected with radiolabeled calcium. Radioisotope analysis revealed that the uptake deep within the porous implant was approximately one-tenth that of surrounding bone; at the periphery of the implant, however, the rates of uptake were about one-half that of surrounding bone.[249] In one dog study, using a porous block form of HA derived from marine coral as an interpositional "sandwich graft" for alveolar ridge augmentation, the longest term sample evaluated (40 weeks) still contained large areas within the porous implant that were devoid of osseous or soft tissue.[250] In another dog study using this same porous HA material in block form as an onlay graft for alveolar ridge augmentation, the authors noted both a slow pattern of bone ingrowth and the fact that the noninfiltrated ceramic was crushed when the animals (initially on a soft diet) were returned to a solid diet 1.5 years after implantation.[251]

The preceding discussion on the perceived and verified limitations of the use of porous block forms of calcium phosphates clearly raises questions about their long-term suitability for use in humans. The ideal porous calcium phosphate implant material would appear to be one that is bioresorbable, with resorption rates closely matching hard tissue infiltration and replacement rates. No such material has yet been reported in the literature.

CLINICAL APPLICATIONS

General Considerations

Correction of traumatic deformity or augmentation requires adequate skin and mucosal covering to ensure acceptance of the implant without excessive tension. In severe cases, transplantation of skin and soft tissue may be necessary before alloplastic implantation can be accomplished. If there is a large area of underlying osseous tissue missing, bone grafting is usually preferred. The degree of functional stress or load at the recipient site and the likelihood of future trauma must be considered. Even the best-tolerated alloplast will respond unfavorably with undesirable tissue response when subjected to unusual stress and trauma. In planning augmentation with an alloplast, preoperative records are necessary and should include radiographs, photographs, and, if necessary, a facial moulage.[252]

The extraoral approach offers the advantages of accurate placement and ease of access to most areas of the facial skeleton. The incisions in the skin can be placed so that scars are hidden in natural wrinkles and creases under the chin, around the nose, or in hair-bearing areas of the scalp, eyebrows, or sideburns. Alexander suggests the following guidelines for placement of an implant.[252] The skin or mucosal incision should be placed at some distance from the site of the implant to avoid adhesions of the scar to the implant, with distortion of the skin or mucosa. The implant should lie in healthy tissue away from regions of excessive scarring or areas of irradiation. The implant should be buried as deeply as possible in a supraperiosteal pocket or should be placed directly on bone if the implant is porous or osteophilic. Implants should not be placed in areas where trauma, motion, loading, or tension on the tissue could cause migration or extrusion of the implant. Preoperatively determined landmarks and measurements should be used to ensure accurate placement. Then the implant should be sutured, wired, or screwed in position. After the closure, a firm pressure dressing should be placed to minimize formation of a hematoma or a seroma.

The following information is generally applicable to all facial implants. Informed consent, benefit and risk, indications, handling and technique, and follow-up material provided by the manufacturer must be understood. Proper surgical procedures and techniques and management of the patient are necessarily the responsibility of the medical professionals. Each surgeon must evaluate the suitability of the procedure and the implant for each patient based upon currently accepted practices and techniques, knowledge, individual judgment, and experience. The surgery should be as atraumatic as possible. The proper size of the implant must be determined for the individual patient by the surgeon.

The success of these implants and the procedure of which they are a part is heavily dependent upon the physical characteristics of the implant, the biologic response, proper preparation and handling, clinical experience, and postoperative management of the patient (Table 29–2). Frequent scalpel blade changes are necessary when modifying implants. "Feathering" edges to avoid step changes in implant profile reduces the possibility of palpating the edges of the implant. Initial stabilization can be accomplished by suturing, by wiring, or by the judicious use of screws. A broad, firm contact of the implant with underlying bone enhances stabilization of the implant by allowing tissue ingrowth. Whenever possible, the incision should be away from the implant to avoid closure directly over the implant. Double-layer closures— "watertight" ones—are preferred, particularly with intraoral techniques. Compression of implant pores should be avoided. Appropriate antibiotic protocol should be followed before and after surgery as well as antibiotic soaking or vacuum impregnation (Proplast) of the implant upon implantation.

Potential complications associated with surgical procedures must always be discussed with the patient prior to the decision to proceed with surgery. These include, but are not limited to, infection; poor reaction to medication, anesthesia, or surgical procedures; poor wound healing; hematoma; serous fluid accumulation; motor or sensory nerve damage or irritation; neuralgia; loss of sensation; intolerance by the patient of any foreign implant; continued pain or other symptoms; changes in surrounding tissue; implant migration; extrusion or structural failure; explantation; or additional surgical intervention.

Owing to the wide variety of patients' physical responses to implant surgery and the differences in surgical techniques and medical treatments, as well as the possibility of the complications of trauma, patients must be advised that these should not be considered lifetime implants and that explant surgery may be indicated at any time.

Custom Implants

Although stock or preformed implants are most frequently used in craniofacial and mandibular reconstruction, fabrication of the implant utilizing facial moulage, wax or clay models, and molds may provide the most accurate aesthetic correction. Several techniques are available for the construction of the facial moulage.[252,253] The use of irreversible hydrocolloid and plaster of paris is preferred, since these materials are readily available. The patient is placed in a semireclining position. Towels are draped around the face to prevent spillage of the impression material (Fig. 29–15A). The hair that may be included in the impression is coated with petrolatum or water-soluble lubricant to prevent locking (Fig. 29–15B). The periphery of the area is isolated, and rubber tubing or straws are placed in the nostrils to ensure air exchange (Fig. 29–15B). A thin mix (50 per cent more water) of alginate is applied to the face and reinforced with gauze strips or paper clips (Fig. 29–15C and D). The reinforced alginate mix is then topped with quick-set plaster (Fig. 29–15E). The patient is asked to wrinkle his or her face to enable removal of the impression, which is poured in either plaster or acrylic (Fig. 29–15F and G). This facial moulage is used in the planning and fabrication of custom-made or carved implants.

On the full-face moulage, a model of the implant is fashioned with clay or wax (Fig. 29–15H and I). When the desired size and shape are obtained, the model and the moulage are lubricated. A plaster impression is made of the model while it is on the moulage. The implant model can be tried on the patient to confirm proper contours (Fig. 29–15J). The model is then lifted from the moulage and placed in the impression mold, and both are lubricated. Plaster is again poured over the top of the mold. This step creates the second half of the final mold that is used for construction of the implant (Fig. 29–15K). The mold is then used for creation of an acrylic model or the implant itself. Certain materials, such as Proplast, are trimmed from bulk material under sterile conditions by the manufacturer or surgeon, using an acrylic, wax, or clay model as a guide (Fig. 29–16A and B). Others, such as silicone rubber and MMA, are prepared from the mold in cook book fashion, as follows.

Silastic Medical-Grade Elastomer 382 is the RTV silicone rubber most frequently used. The RTV rubber is weaker than the heat-vulcanizing types, but it is easier to use, and it can be molded in sites where heat cannot be tolerated. Once vulcanized, silicone rubber retains a "memory" of the original form and can be subsequently heat autoclaved without losing shape.[86,87,89,90,254] Silastic Medical-Grade Elastomer 382 is made by mixing two separate liquids: an opaque viscous elastomer base and a catalyst (Dow Corning Catalyst M). The elastomer base is composed of dimethylpolysiloxane polymer and silica filler and vulcanizes at room temperature without giving off heat when being directly molded into a defect. Several drops of a catalyst are added to the creamy liquid; it is mixed thoroughly and poured into both sides of the mold. The working time is approximately 10 minutes, and vulcanization is completed in 30 minutes. After the implant has cured, it is removed from the mold, the flash is trimmed, and the implant is fenestrated for tissue fixation. Handling is done only with washed gloves to avoid contamination by skin oils. The implant is then placed on the moulage; measurements are made from its perimeter to obvious anatomic landmarks so that accurate placement can be made at the time of surgery. The implant may be further modified by adaptation to a facial skeleton in selected cases. Ultrasonic cleaning and steam autoclaving of the implant are next done.

Craniofacial reconstruction with computer-assisted prosthesis implant designs is a recent technologic development. Since the early 1970s, computerized tomography (CT) has revolutionized the evaluation of skeletal deformities from congenital as well as traumatic causes. However, until recently, scans provided only a two-dimensional view, and one had to look at multiple slices to appreciate the entire scope of the area of injury or deformity (Fig. 29–17A). This practice, associated with the tried-and-true technique of facial moulage, allowed for the reconstruction of facial contour deformities with semiprecise implants that could mimic the necessary contour changes.

Text continued on page 820.

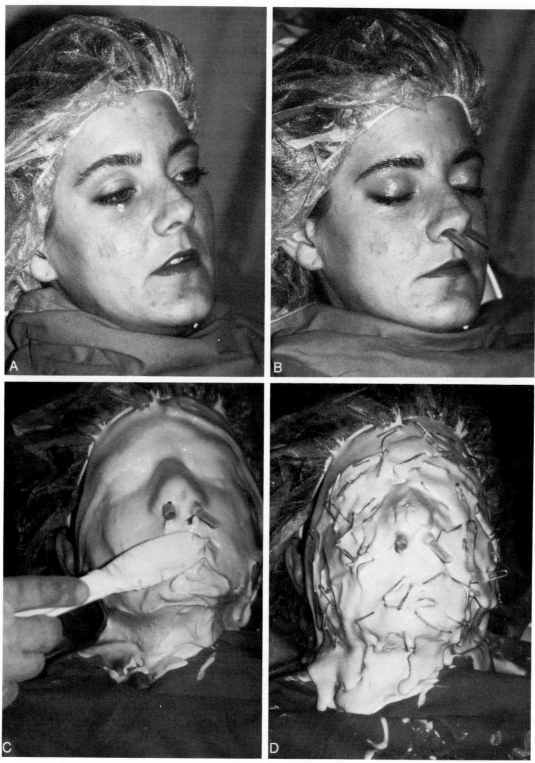

FIGURE 29–15. Facial moulage technique. *A,* With the patient semireclined, towels are draped and a bonnet is placed to prevent spillage of impression material onto clothes or into hair. *B,* If a temporal or frontal defect crosses the hairline, the hair may be included by coating it with a petrolatum or water-soluble lubricant to prevent locking. A straw can be cut and inserted into the nares for breathing if the mouth and nose are both to be included. *C,* A thin mix of impression material is applied evenly over the face. *D,* Prior to setting, gauze strips or paper clips are incorporated.

Illustration continued on opposite page.

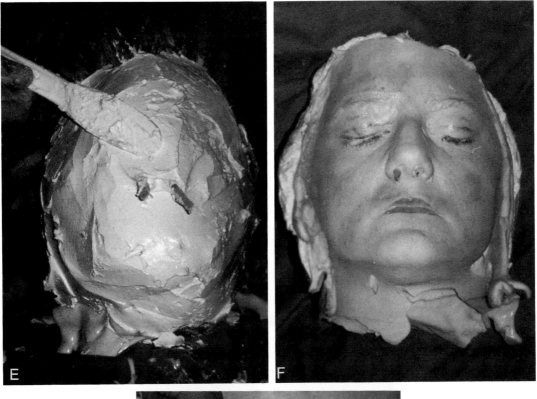

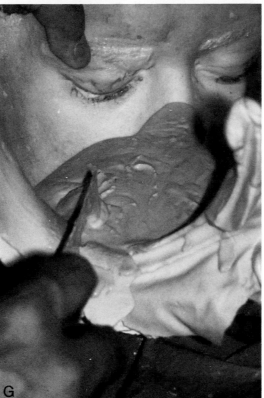

FIGURE 29–15. *Continued.*   *E, F,* Quick-set plastic is applied to the gauze or paper clip over the impression material. This will allow for the plaster and impression material to be removed as a single unit. When the impression material and plaster are set, the patient is asked to wrinkle her face to remove the moulage. The photograph of the moulage is actually concave rather than convex, as the photograph appears owing to depth of field. *G,* The moulage is then poured in either plaster or acrylic.

Illustration continued on following page.

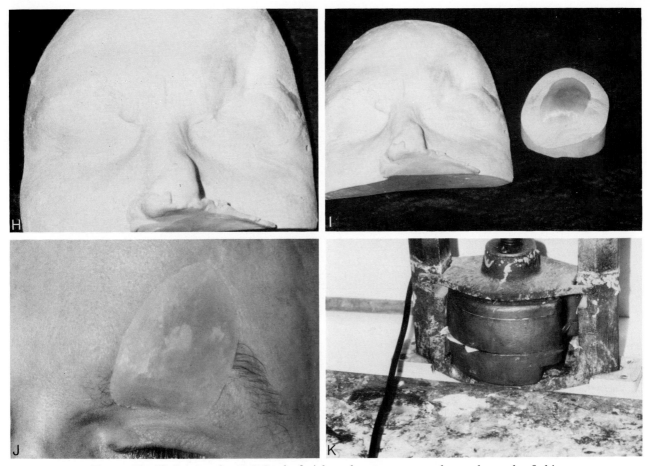

FIGURE 29–15. *Continued.*   *H, I,* On the facial moulage cast, wax or clay can be used to fashion a model for the implant. *J,* The implant model can be tried on the patient to confirm proper contour. *K,* A pressurized heat "flasking" technique is used to fabricate a surgical implant from the model utilizing acrylic, silicone rubber, and so on.

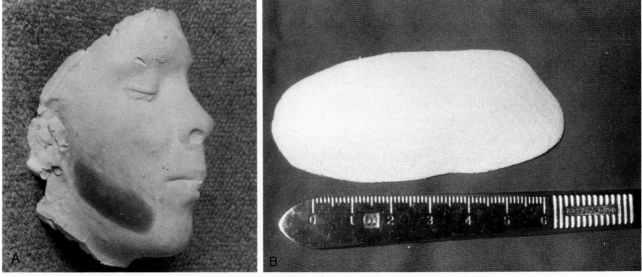

FIGURE 29–16.   *A,* Wax-up on facial moulage for right mandibular skeletal deficiency. *B,* Custom Proplast implant.

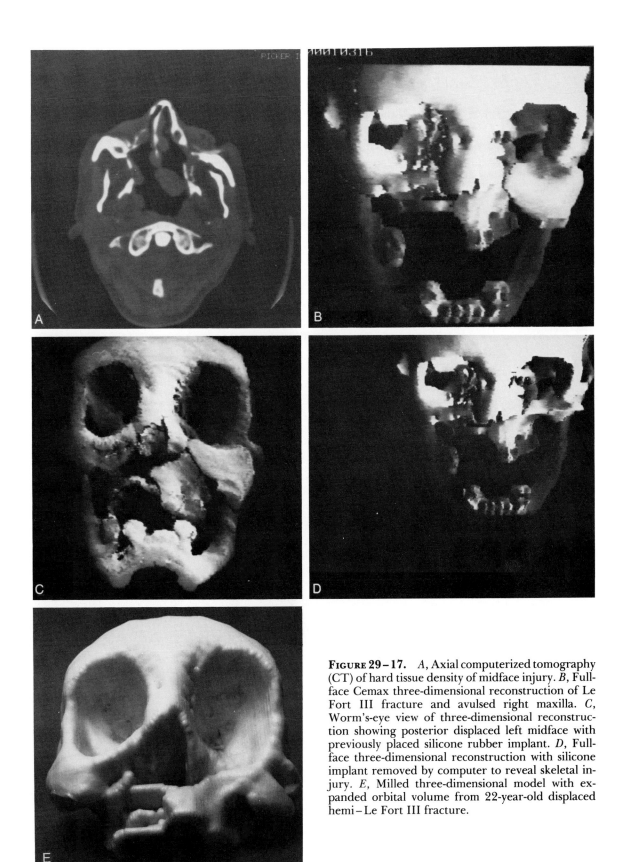

FIGURE 29–17. *A,* Axial computerized tomography (CT) of hard tissue density of midface injury. *B,* Full-face Cemax three-dimensional reconstruction of Le Fort III fracture and avulsed right maxilla. *C,* Worm's-eye view of three-dimensional reconstruction showing posterior displaced left midface with previously placed silicone rubber implant. *D,* Full-face three-dimensional reconstruction with silicone implant removed by computer to reveal skeletal injury. *E,* Milled three-dimensional model with expanded orbital volume from 22-year-old displaced hemi–Le Fort III fracture.

However, these implants had limitations because accurate adaptation to underlying bony structures was difficult, if not impossible, to attain owing to the irregularity of the intervening connective tissue below the skin. Such implants required extensive modification at the time of surgery, and only in the hands of a very skilled surgeon would the ultimate result be satisfactory.

Currently, with the advances in hardware and software available to the radiologist, it is possible to take information from these two-dimensional scans and create a composite three-dimensional image that can be viewed in multiple directions (Cemax Medical Systems, Santa Clara, CA; ISG Technologies, Toronto, Canada).[255-257] These images can be viewed on a monitor that allows the observer to rotate the image in any plane to view the inner or outer aspects of the deformities from any angle (Fig. 29–17B to D). A further application of this technology has been to take the three-dimensional information and, via a computer-controlled milling device, produce accurate models of the facial skeleton, including the deformities that are often masked by soft tissue (Fig. 29–17E). The computer will also reproduce what may have been lost by recreating symmetry if an asymmetric problem exists. This process can create a template that may be used to guide implant fabrication for precise customization prior to any surgical procedure.[258,259]

A specific protocol is necessary for scanners and must be adhered to in order to produce usable images and models. The maximal quality of these images is obtained from high-resolution, close-interval scanning in areas where there are no motion or

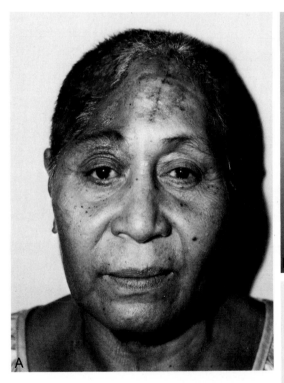

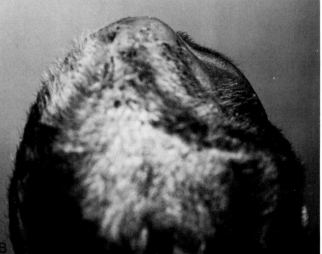

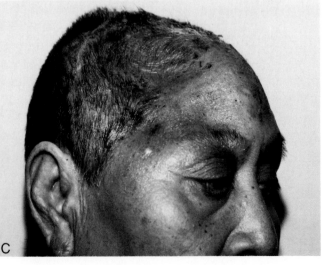

FIGURE 29–18.   Three-dimensional reconstruction of orbitocranial defect.   *A–C*, Patient prior to reconstructive surgery, showing right orbitocranial defect resulting from tumor extirpation. *A*, Anteroposterior (AP) view, *B*, bird's-eye view, and *C*, right three-quarters view are seen.

Illustration continued on opposite page.

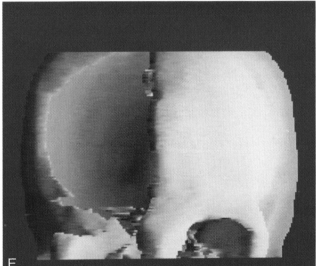
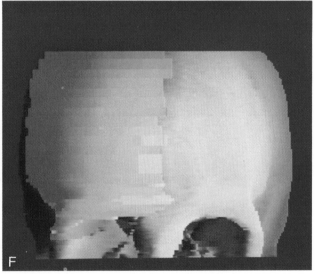

FIGURE 29–18. *Continued.* *D,* Cemax 1000 computer imaging system for three-dimensional reconstruction of CT images. *E,* Photograph of computer-generated three-dimensional image showing bony defect, right three-quarters view. *F,* Photograph of computer-generated image, with model to correct anatomic defect, right three-quarters view.

Illustration continued on following page.

distortion artifacts. It is necessary for the original scan data to be analyzed by available software so that three-dimensional images and models may be produced. The specific requirements of the scan include close-interval, contiguous cuts in the region where detail is needed. In the region of the cranium, face, orbital wall, and TMJ, the slice thickness should be no greater than 2 mm and the table increment should be no greater than 2 mm. A low-dose protocol is desirable, and any metal implants or other prostheses that may be close to the area of interest should be removed, or if this is not possible, the scan should be adjusted to avoid these objects.

It is very important to minimize the patient's movement and to maximize the symmetry of the patient when he or she is positioned in the scanner. Restraints are advised, and sedation may be necessary, since the average scan may be quite lengthy. Compatible scanners include multiple common models that are currently available in

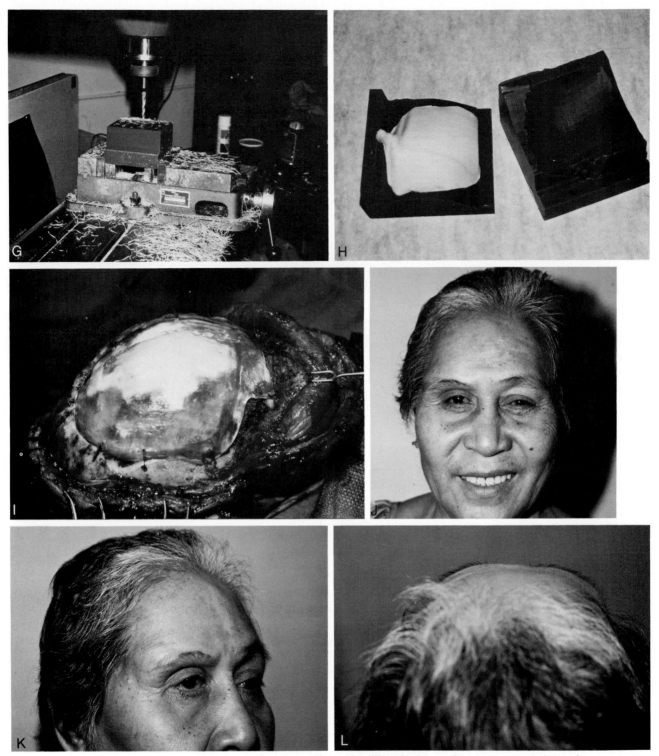

FIGURE 29–18. *Continued.*   *G*, Computer-directed milling device used to create "negative" of bony defect. *H*, The computer-generated hybrid resin model and the wax mold from which it was produced. Hybrid resin model is used to form methylmethacrylate prosthesis. *I*, Intraoperative photograph showing methylmethacrylate implant in position and precisely filling the anatomic defect. *J–L*, Postoperative photographs of *J*, AP view, *K*, bird's-eye view, and *L*, right three-quarters view. (Courtesy of Dr. Bryant Toth, Pacific Presbyterian Medical Center, San Francisco, CA.)

hospital radiology departments in the community. As long as these specific requirements are adhered to, quality scans and accurate models can be produced and become an invaluable asset to the diagnosis and treatment of deformities of the face and cranium (Fig. 29–18A to L).

Cranial Augmentation

Appropriate planning includes neurosurgical consultation and the presence or availability of the neurosurgeon for the procedure. Anterior skull defects occur as a result of traumatic, inflammatory, neoplastic, congenital, and surgical conditions.[260] Indications for restoration may be cosmetic or protective, or the procedure may be done for the relief of pain. Cosmetic reconstruction is often necessary in view of the social unacceptability of a defect, particularly in a non–hair-bearing area; defects under temporal muscle or hair-bearing areas are less significant cosmetic problems. These lateral defects are often correctable by muscle transposition,[261] which can be done with a cranial flap. The scar of this flap could be unaesthetic in a bald patient, and therefore, a tunneling dissection through a small incision would be a better cosmetic choice.

Depending upon the location and size of the skull defect, there is often concern on the part of the patient about possible injury to the underlying brain. Such concern may result in severely limited activity and may reduce the quality of life. Examples of patients who would be affected include normal children at play, patients with seizures, and patients involved in any contact occupation (for example, athletics or heavy industry). Other patients may complain of tenderness or pain or may even feel painful pulsations. These symptoms may be associated with defects of any size, located anywhere on the skull.

The timing of the cranioplasty after injury is important. In younger patients, the osteogenic potential of the outer periosteal layer of dura persists until age 5 or 6 years. After this point, there is little or no spontaneous regeneration of the cranium. Although controversy exists, any delay in older children is usually based only on the presence of overt or latent infection and on the condition of the overlying scalp.[262] In adults, accepted standards recommend waiting 6 months to 1 year after penetrating wounds and after a wound infection.[263,264]

Whenever anterior cranial augmentation is undertaken, the choice of material is between an alloplast and bone, or a combination may be used. Alloplastic materials include metal plates,[264] MMA,[265] silicone rubber,[266] HA,[260] and Proplast,[171,174] while autogenous materials include bone, dermis, fat, and cartilage.[267-271] Advantages of alloplasts include the availability of the material, the ease of the surgical procedure, nonresorbability, and superior cosmetic results. The main disadvantages are possible foreign body reaction and the potential for infection, which may produce fistulae, slippage, extrusion, granulomas, and erosion.[263,272] Furthermore, the most commonly used material, MMA, may fracture.[273] The incidence of complications with MMA has been reported to range from 2 to 12 per cent in 2 years.[274,275]

The advantages of autogenous bone grafts include tissue tolerance and the presence of a viable reconstruction matrix. Iliac bone and ribs are preferred. The disadvantages include unpredictable resorption with compromised aesthetics, the potential for early infection, donor site morbidity, and the inability to obtain enough bone for large defects.[276,277] Studies in animals have quantified the difference in resorption between cranial, or membranous, bone and endochondral bone used as onlay grafts.[278] Resorption ranged from 50 per cent in adults to 75 per cent in immature animals. The best results were obtained with autogenous membranous bone, such as that which occurs over the convexity of the skull. Variable resorption patterns have also been shown with demineralized bone.[279]

Several considerations enter into the selection of materials for reconstruction of cranial defects, especially when both plates of the skull have been lost. In view of the proximity to vital structures, such as the eyes and meninges, the potential for early or late infection with any material can be a serious problem. Although acrylic cranioplasties are believed to be associated with a higher infection rate than is bone, Manson and associates, in a study of patients with large cranial defects involving the frontal bone, frontal sinus, nose, and orbit, did not support the contention that there is a clear superiority of reconstructive material, bone versus acrylic, despite a history of previous bone infection.[265] No patient with an isolated cranial reconstruction experienced an infection, despite location in the area of the frontal sinus or the use of acrylic material. All patients experiencing infection underwent simultaneous reconstruction of the frontal cranium and nose and three- or four-wall reconstruction of the orbit; in these patients, the frontal sinus had previously been eliminated and a bone infection had previously been present. The risk factors associated with cranioplasty were timing and whether cranial vault reconstruction was in communication with previously infected ethmoid sinuses and the nose. Protection of the intracranial contents from external trauma by a hard, solid material is desirable.

Softer materials, such as silicone rubber or Proplast, are not utilized in full-thickness calvarial defects but can be used to augment the existing bony table defect created by trauma or cranial bone graft donor sites (Fig. 29–19A to D). The material

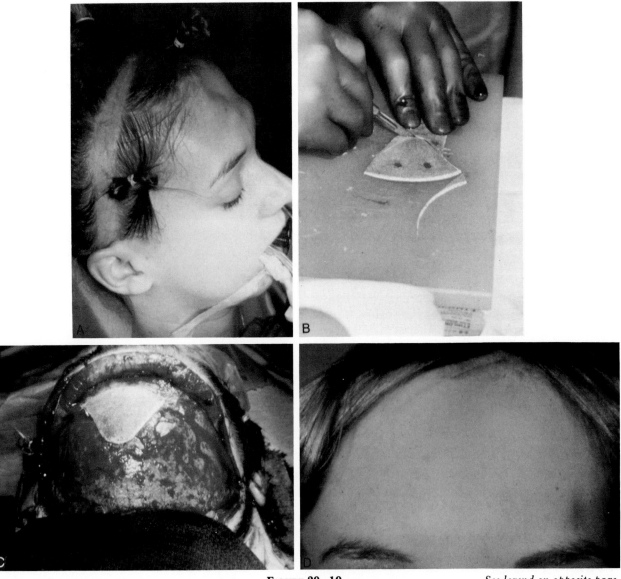

FIGURE 29–19.   *See legend on opposite page.*

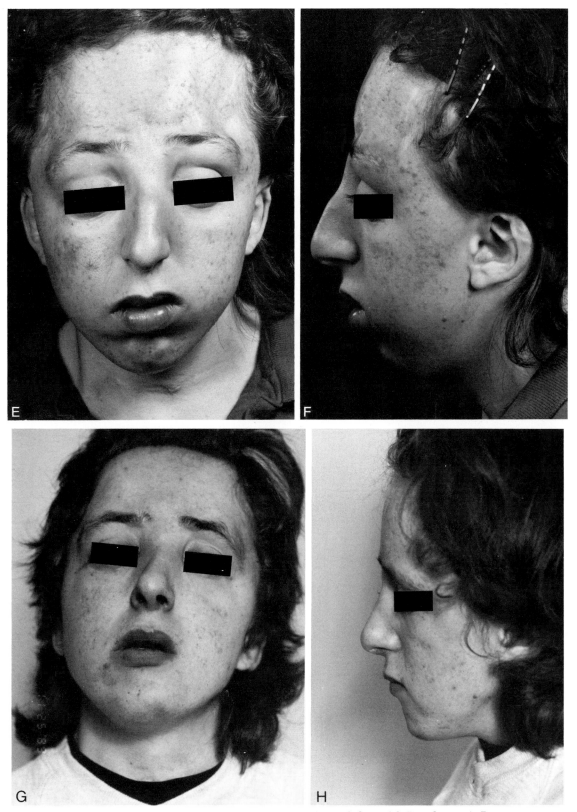

FIGURE 29–19. *Continued.*   **Correction of frontal bone defect with Proplast.**   *A,* Preoperative view. *B, C,* Operative views showing carving and placement of Proplast. *D,* Postoperative appearance. (*A–D* courtesy of Dr. Bromley Freeman, Houston, TX.) Patient had previously undergone a Le Fort III osteotomy for Crouzon's disease and hypertelorism. *E,* Postoperative full-face and *F,* profile views prior to corrective surgery on lateral canthus, nose, chin, and forehead. *G,* Full-face and *H,* profile views after correction, which included methylmethacrylate (MMA) cranioplasty. (*E–H* courtesy of Dr. Barry Zide, New York.)

should not undergo resorption or settle into the underlying bone. Although a mechanical adaptation to bone may be satisfactory, bonding to bone by the material or incorporation of a bone graft into the host site is preferable. Finally, secondary revisions of the restorative material should not compromise the primary result.

Acrylic. As a cranioplasty material, MMA is strong, has a density similar to that of bone, and possesses a low thermal conductivity, similar to that of cortical bone. It is moderately well tolerated by soft tissue, bone, and dura, and it is radiolucent except when additives are used to make it radiopaque. Bone growth or resorption of adjacent bone or cement itself in this application is uncommon.

Methylmethacrylic mixing at surgery with polymerization in situ is the most common application. The mixing time should take about 2.5 to 3.0 minutes. Unbound monomer is lost by evaporation; therefore, mixing techniques that encourage its evaporation are desirable. The material should be beaten as rapidly as possible. The mixing and fitting time together can last up to 7 minutes; hardening takes another 7 minutes.[280] The material should be worked until it is tacky before being implanted. When being molded in situ, it should be worked from the center out, avoiding folding and lapping. Maximal strength is obtained in 1 week. Fracture can occur at the laminations created by the blood-cement interfaces. Wire mesh placed at the doughy stage may strengthen the implant. Loosening of the implant may occur from the effect of the high heat of polymerization on bone in contact with the curing cement. The burned bone later resorbs, leaving the specimen slightly too small. The MMA should therefore undergo most of its cure outside the body before being finally molded in situ. Irrigation with cool saline will reduce this excess heat at the interface.[287]

In successful frontal recontouring with bone cement, there must be adequate forehead skin coverage. Loose bone, as well as all residual mucous membrane and granulation tissue, should be removed. A contraindication to the implantation of MMA may be exposed sinus mucosa or communication with nasal or ethmoid mucosa. Obliteration of the frontal sinus by stripping the lining may be necessary if the nasofrontal duct is not functional. The cavity then fills with fibrous tissue or may be filled surgically with an autogenous free fat graft. When resection of the frontal sinus is indicated, bilateral ablation is less conspicuous than unilateral ablation. Reconstruction of a unilateral defect is more difficult because of problems in achieving symmetry. Integrity of the dura is essential if the posterior wall is absent before one can introduce bone cement. Curing MMA in contact with the brain can induce sufficient cortical irritation to cause seizures. Coverage of the implant with periosteum should be accomplished when possible, but it is not essential. The overlying skin and subcutaneous tissue flap, however, must be replaced accurately, as this will contribute to the ultimate symmetry of the facial features. A pressure dressing completes the procedure[280,281] (Fig. 29–19E and F).

Hydroxylapatite. Cranioplasty with HA can be used over dura with no clinical evidence of adverse reaction.[260] Animal studies using HA as a cranioplasty material have also demonstrated a high degree of biocompatibility and lack of inflammatory response in the meninges[220,282] (Fig. 29–20A to D). The resulting firm HA mass offers some protection to the underlying brain, especially when the HA is mixed with autogenous bone. Another advantage of HA is the ability for it to be adjusted or reaugmented without the likelihood of infection. The disadvantages in the use of HA include hematoma formation and control of the particulate material. Extracranial augmentation of HA blocks and particles evaluated by El Deeb and Roszkowski[220] revealed that the HA granules become stable within 3 to 4 weeks but that there is loss of some augmented height owing to settling of the material within a subpericranial pocket. The HA blocks maintained the augmented cranial contours, but 25 per cent of them exhibited mobility. Histologic evaluation revealed no evidence of inflammation or bone resorption with either the HA granular or block form. HA granules were separated from each other and from the bone interface by a layer of collagen fibers, and the blocks were also surrounded by a fibrous capsule. There was no evidence of

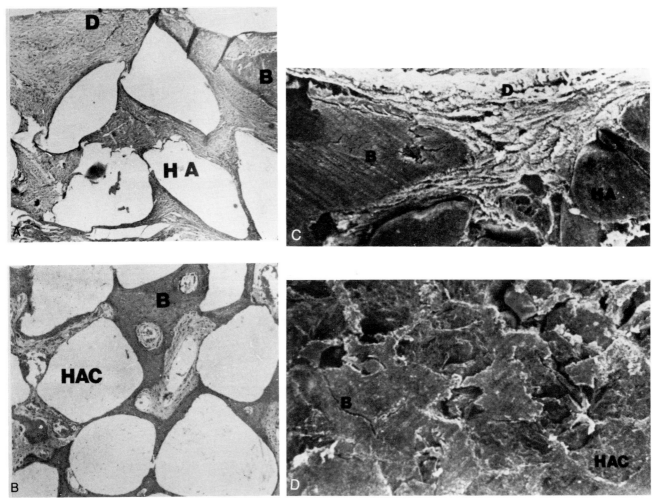

FIGURE 29–20. *A*, Light micrograph of a cat craniotomy site with an HA implant stained with hematoxylin and eosin. The HA implant site shows dense, fibrous connective tissue between individual HA particles Magnification 40×. D = dura; B = bone; H = HA particle ghost. *B*, Light micrograph of a craniotomy with HA collagen implant stained with hematoxylin and eosin. The HAC implant sites were highly vascular and had a predominance of bone as the connective tissue between the particles. Magnification 40×. B = bone; HAC = HA particle ghost of the HAC implant. *C*, Scanning electron microscope (SEM) view of the craniotomy with HA implant. The HA particles are seen after sectioning with a diamond saw. The particles (HA) are seen to be in direct contact with the dura (D). Dense, fibrous connective tissue lies between the implant particles. Bone (B) is shown on the left. Magnification 75×. *D*, SEM of a craniotomy site with HAC implant. The HAC implant site reveals the implant particles surrounded by bone (B) and difficult to distinguish. The implant-bone interface appears devoid of fibrous tissue. Magnification 75×. (Courtesy of Drs. Marilyn Zimny and Lester Machado, Department of Anatomy, Louisiana State University Medical Center, New Orleans.)

bonding between HA granules, and the bone-HA interface was separated by an intervening fibrous layer. Since no cranial defect was created in this study and since mobility by manipulation of the smooth blocks was possible, it was not surprising to note a lack of bone interface—in contrast with the results of other investigators. Holmes and Hagler,[283] however, assessed the potential of a porous HA matrix to serve as a cranial defect bone graft substitute. Specimens retrieved at 3, 6, 12, 24, and 48 months maintained cranial contour, but little apparent bone ingrowth was seen in most graft specimens. The implant specimens were composed of 39.3 per cent HA matrix, 17.2 per cent bone ingrowth, and 43.5 per cent soft tissue ingrowth. Holmes noted that the final requirement for the clinical application of any biomaterial is that it be easy to shape, embrace, and fixate. Lacking the elastic contribution of collagen in bone, the HA implant is brittle and prone to fracture while being shaped, wired, or pressed into place. The porosity of the implant at its surface prevents it from gliding smoothly through a soft tissue passage. Increased surgical exposure of the implant site may thus be required.

The surgical method of HA cranioplasty is technique sensitive, as are all cranioplasty techniques. Scalp flaps and tunneling incisions must be designed to be outside the defect, behind the hairline, and never parallel to previous wounds and scars. Old scar incisions may be used, but care must be taken not to incise the dura. Tunneling procedures should be done cautiously under direct vision with a headlight. After careful subperiosteal separation of the skin from the dura, direct inspection should ensure that there are no tears. Delivery of HA in confined areas is done with a syringe (Fig. 29–21A to C). Larger amounts of HA, with or without autogenous bone, are placed through a coronal flap and slightly overcontoured. Iliac bone strips are placed

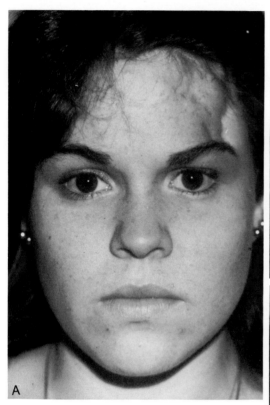

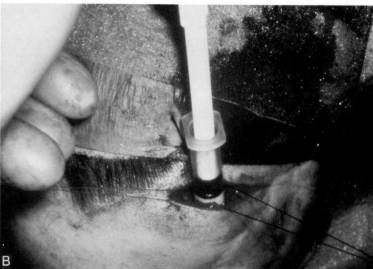

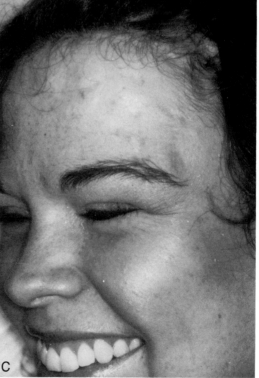

FIGURE 29–21. *A,* Preoperative, *B,* intraoperative, and *C,* postoperative correction of frontal bone defect with HA particles and scar revision. (*A* and *B* from Zide MF, Kent JN, Machado L: Hydroxylapatite cranioplasty directly over dura. J Oral Maxillofac Surg 45:481, 1987; with permission.)

in large defects to avoid dural compression and provide a solid base for an HA-bone combination.

Drains are not used because of the potential loss of HA particles and the possibility of bacterial contamination and HA particle migration. Hematoma migration is preventable in most cases with pressure dressings. A firm pressure dressing of external acrylic or plaster bandage should be maintained for 3 to 4 weeks to preserve contour. The wearing of hats or restricting bands should be avoided. Zide, Kent, and Machado reported seven patients with noticeable defects of their frontal bone who underwent reconstruction with dense HA particles with or without autogenous bone placed directly over the dura. The results indicate that HA is well tolerated over dura; no meningitis occurred with follow-up of 1.0 to 3.5 years. The clinical response was excellent, and complications were minor, generally related to particle control and settling.[260]

Zygoma Reconstruction

Depression of the malar eminence or zygoma most commonly occurs after untreated or inadequate reduction of zygomatic complex fractures at the zygomaticofrontal suture, at the infraorbital rim, at the malar buttress, and along the temporal process of the zygoma. Facial deformities resulting from a malunited zygomatic complex are common and are the result of comminuted segments, concomitant facial trauma, or neurologic or higher priority injuries that delay or compromise primary facial repair.[284]

The most common complaint is persistent periorbital flattening and accompanying discrepancies. Commonly stated reasons for this flattening are severity of injury, length of time from injury to primary open reduction, comminution of the maxillary and orbital bones, scar bands, masseteric muscle pull or muscular actions of facial expression, inadequate reduction using two-point fixation only, maxillary antral packing that provided inadequate support, lack of reduction because the fracture was marked by edema, and treatment that was delayed because of other injuries.[285-287]

Discrepancies associated with displacement of the zygoma may include distraction of the orbital floor, causing cosmetic as well as visual problems. The resulting volume expansion of the orbit may create enophthalmos, which may be difficult to correct because of fat herniation, atrophy, scar formation, and settling of the orbital tissues. The visual axis may be malaligned, causing persistent diplopia. Soft tissue may accompany the malunited bone and cause displaced canthi, change in facial lines or folds, and epiphora.[258]

The physical examination should be systematic and thorough, with concentration on details around the problem area. Particular attention should be directed to canthal positions and attachment, enophthalmos, level of pupils, scars and tissue loss, ectropion, lacrimal dysfunction, ocular movements, and depression of the globe. The ophthalmologist should document visual acuity, ocular axis and movements, slit-lamp examination, ocular pressure, and funduscopic examination to provide a solid preoperative data base.

In addition, the vascular supply to the area may be lessened, compromising reconstruction. Angiography or fluorescence may be useful to determine the availability of adequate vascular pedicles for skin flaps and incision planning. Facial photographs should be included to document the deformity and to aid in preoperative study (Fig. 29–22A to E). These should include frontal, lateral, superior, and angled views. It may also be beneficial to use a facial moulage to compare the defect with the normal side.

The radiographic survey should be directed toward exact location, displacement, and identification of fragments of the remaining hard tissue. Useful radiographs include panoramic, Waters', submental vertex, Caldwell's, and lateral skull views (Fig. 29–22F). The submental vertex and lateral cephalogram, if properly

FIGURE 29–22. *A–E,* Multiple facial views of malunited zygomatic complex (ZMC) deformity secondary to trauma. *F,* Waters' view demonstrating frontozygomatic and orbital rim deformity. (*F* from Block MS, Kent JN: Correction of vertical orbital dystopia with a hydroxylapatite orbital floor graft. J Oral Maxillofac Surg 46:420, 1988; with permission.)

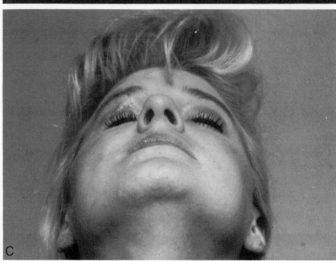

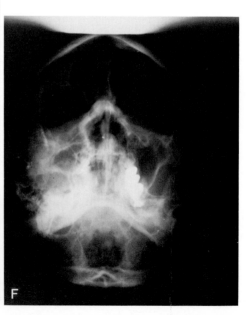

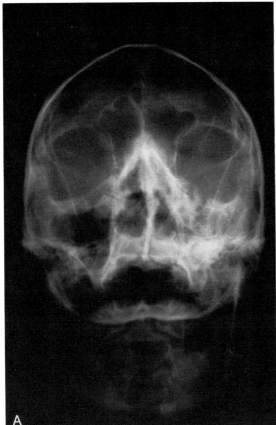

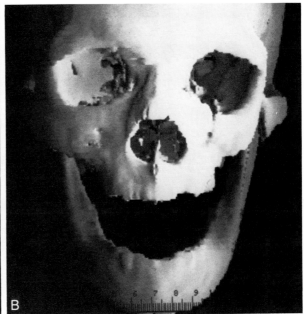

FIGURE 29–23. *A*, Posteroanterior (PA) radiograph of ZMC fracture. *B*, Cemax three-dimensional reconstruction.

oriented, may confirm anteroposterior discrepancies and orbital rim positions. When such studies are indicated, one may advance to facial tomograms and CT. With newer CT programs, image enhancement and enlargement may result in visualization of very small fragments (Fig. 29–23*A* and *B*). After the examination is completed, a specific treatment plan can be sequentially formulated. The aesthetic augmentation of the depressed malar complex should be timed to avoid conflict with the correction of any problem that would predispose the patient to infection. Such problems include root tips, fractured teeth, oroantral fistulae, or infected fracture sites.

In addition to the zygomatic eminence, the contour of its peripheral extensions, the inferior orbital rim, the lateral orbital rim, and the zygomatic arch must all be considered before the choice of implant material and surgical approach is made. In planning the shape of the implant, the zygomatic eminence should always be the most projecting part. As a general guide, this projection should lie in an angle formed by lines drawn on the face from the outer canthus to the lateral oral commissure and from the base of the nasal ala to the tragus of the ear. The zygomatic prominence should lie in the posterosuperior quadrant (Fig. 29–24*A* to *F*).

There are three approaches to correcting the asymmetry of the zygomatic complex: (1) osteotomy of the zygomatic complex, (2) both osteotomy and alloplastic or autogenous augmentation, and (3) augmentation alone with either autologous or alloplastic material.

Zygomatic complex osteotomy techniques have been extensively discussed by Perino and associates[284] and by Kawamoto.[289] The indications for osteotomy include zygomatic complex unit displacement, resulting in expansion of orbital volume, neuropraxis, entrapped orbital contents, zygomatic arch collapse, or difficulty in opening the mouth (Fig. 29–25*A* and *B*). Osteotomy techniques may at times necessitate the use of a bone graft, especially in cases of late reconstruction with severe displacement. The disadvantages of osteotomy are, therefore, the added osseous

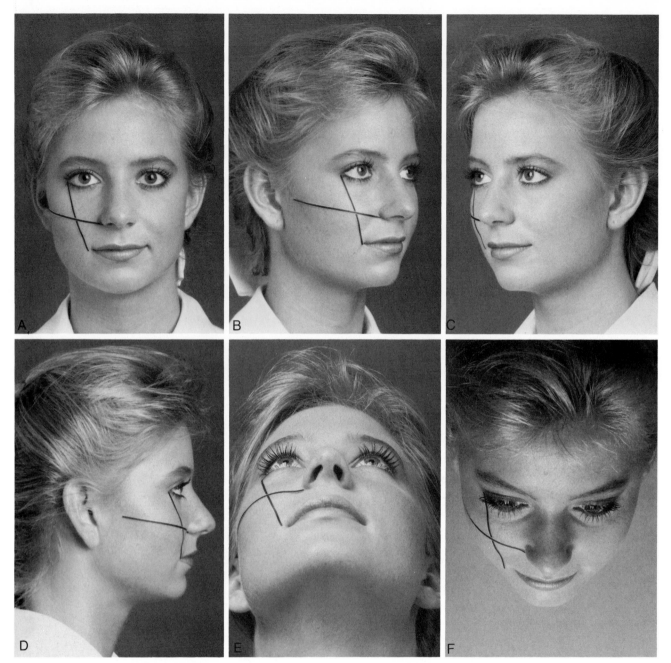

FIGURE 29–24.   *A–F,* Prominence of the ZMC shown in multiple facial views.

surgical procedure, morbidity from the bone graft donor site, possible ocular or orbital sequelae from late mobilization of the zygomatic complex, difficulty in stabilization, and variable relapse potential associated with resorption of segments or grafts. In addition, patients with severe scarring and loss of bone structure without functional loss may not be suitable candidates for osteotomies. These defects might be better treated with implants.

Zygomatic complex osteotomy and alloplastic or autogenous augmentation may be performed on the same patient. However, Perino and associates note that onlay augmentation may remove the last vestige of blood supply from the facial pedicle to the zygoma.[284] To prevent infection and to enhance precision, augmentation is probably best done secondarily.

Onlay grafts and alloplastic materials have been used for decades. In the 1950s,

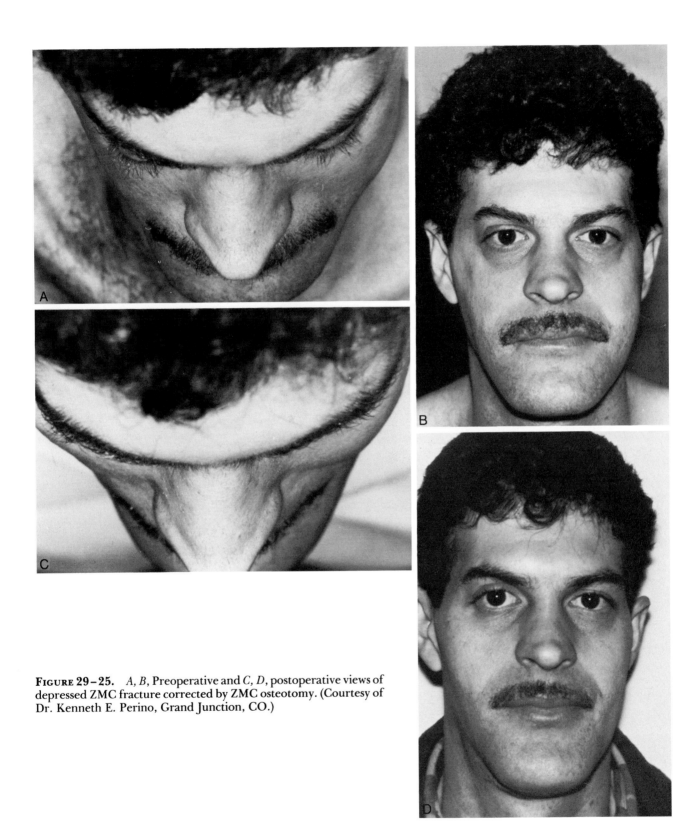

FIGURE 29–25. *A, B,* Preoperative and *C, D,* postoperative views of depressed ZMC fracture corrected by ZMC osteotomy. (Courtesy of Dr. Kenneth E. Perino, Grand Junction, CO.)

Converse and Dingman advocated the use of autogenous bone for onlay augmentation in the face.[290-294] However, variable resorption of grafts placed along the lateral maxilla and orbital floor has limited the use of this technique.[288,294] In addition, soft tissue defects with resulting scar contraction and tension will add to the resorption of these onlay bone grafts. Free fat grafts and cartilage grafts have shown variable results with morbidity associated with the donor sites.[295] Microvascular transfer of ribs, with and without soft tissue, has proved a viable option with proper selection of patients and technical expertise.[296]

Biomaterial augmentation of the zygomatic complex includes several materials. The principal advantages of these alloplasts are less complicated surgery and decreased morbidity.

Silicone Rubber.   Deformities of the zygomatic complex can be corrected with preformed silicone rubber implants, blocks, or molding a custom RTV silicone rubber implant. Silastic (Wright Dow Corning) medical-grade silicone rubber is available in both forms. The types used for carving come in blocks of varying hardness. These can be cut with a scalpel and then finely contoured and smoothed with a motorized dermabrader.

The implant can also be fabricated from a moulage of a facial defect. These devices can be made either from heat-vulcanizing silicone rubber or from RTV medical-grade silicone rubber. With the latter, the volume of the implant can be augmented at the time of surgery with freshly cured or cut surfaces that bond to each other. Prefabrication of the moldable material over skin or on a facial moulage is helpful; however, intraoperative adjustments of the implant are necessary, since exact details of the bone defect cannot be produced (Fig. 29–26A to D).

Silicone implants are placed in the malar region via either transoral or extraoral approaches. Their main disadvantage is the lack of adaptation to exact bony morphology during surgery. Carving silicone rubber to the exact shape is difficult and may leave rough edges. The material cannot be molded or bent to the confines of the surgical defect because of "memory." Custom fabrication on a model made from three-dimensional imaging techniques may be preferable.

Compression or bending of the material increases soft tissue tension and subsequent extrusion. Stabilization of the silicone rubber implant is accomplished by direct suturing or wiring to bone or soft tissue via holes placed through the rubber. The lack of stabilization from large holes rather than surface porosity may result in mobility, extrusion, or bone resorption.

Proplast.   Preformed Proplast facial implants and blocks are available for augmentation of the zygoma and periorbital rim areas[151,164,166,167,169,172,174,179,183] (Figs. 29–27 and 29–28). The documented clinical advantages of Proplast include the implant's rapid stabilization to bone by tissue ingrowth, ease of sculpture to a modified shape, sufficient firmness to maintain desired contours, and flexibility for close adaptation of large porous surface areas to underlying bone contour. It is easily carved and contoured during surgery, allowing for accurate adaptation to irregular bony margins and corners without return to its original shape. Primate studies have demonstrated a high tissue ingrowth density and rate with respect to vacuum impregnation with antibiotic solutions.[142,143]

Proplast zygomatic implants are designed to wrap around the body of the zygoma, extending from the zygomaticotemporal suture to the canine fossa. Notched (infraorbital nerve region) implants and the more commonly used longer (55-mm) Kent high-low profile implants provide the surgeon with a choice of augmentation height as well as thickness. In 1972, Kent described their subperiosteal placement through the intraoral route and their securing to the orbital rim.[151,152] More recently, Whitaker adopted the intraoral route and modified these zygomatic implants by increasing the length by 5 mm.[167] His early experiences parallel the long-term stability and satisfaction on the part of the patient experienced by Kent. Complications, occurring in approximately 2 per cent or fewer cases, include infection, malposition, and dissatisfaction of the patient.[151,167,179,183]

As with any alloplastic material, inadequate closure of oral incisions or exposure

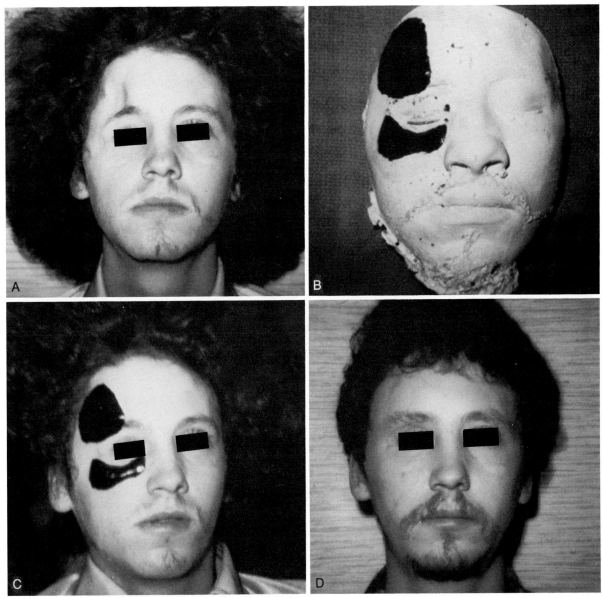

FIGURE 29–26. *A*, Right ZMC and frontal bone deficiency on patient following trauma. *B*, Wax-up of ZMC and frontal bone deficiency on facial moulage. *C*, Wax-up on preoperative face. *D*, Postoperative correction with RTV silicone rubber. (Courtesy of Dr. T. William Evans, Columbus, OH.)

of the implant to the maxillary sinus and nasal cavity jeopardizes implant survival. With antiseptic cleansing of the oral cavity and infusion with antibiotic before handling, the infection rates of intraorally placed implants are minimal (2 per cent).[151,167]

Hydroxylapatite. Augmentation of the facial bones with HA is of recent interest following its widespread use for deficient atrophic ridge and space maintainers in orthognathic surgery. Waite and Matukas described the use of HA particles mixed with microfibrillar collagen and blood to yield a cohesive mixture that can be sculptured to correct deficiency over the zygomatic bones.[213] Eleven cases followed for 6 to 22 months were studied retrospectively, and the augmentation was found to remain stable and aesthetically pleasing (Fig. 29–29*A* to *C*). The control of particles as well as the uniformity of bilateral augmentation, particularly when both frontal and lateral aspects of the zygoma require symmetric augmentation, is a concern.

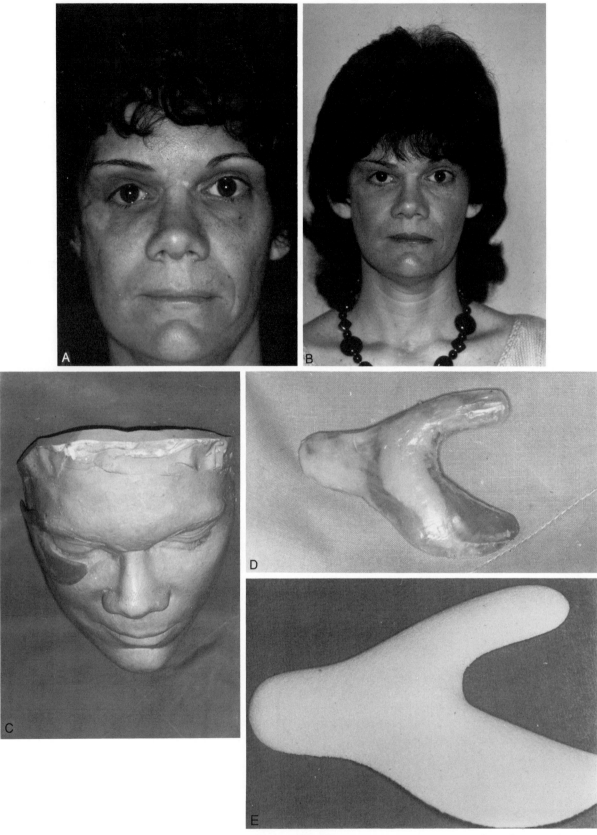

FIGURE 29–27.   *See legend on opposite page.*

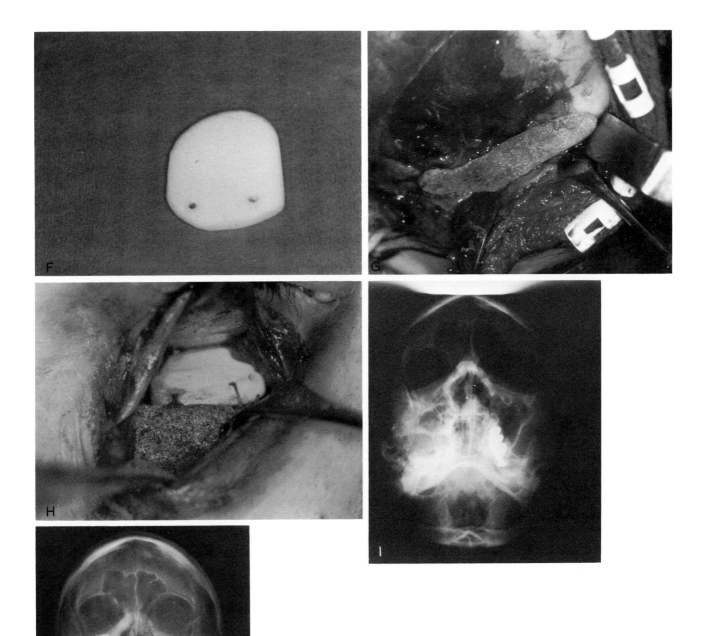

FIGURE 29–27. *Continued.* Reconstruction of right depressed ZMC with enophthalmos. *A,* Preoperative full face. *B,* Postoperative full face. *C,* Facial moulage with wax correction. *D,* Wax pattern. *E,* Custom Proplast ZMC implant. *F,* HA orbital floor block. *G,* Coronal approach for placement of Proplast implant. *H,* Infraorbital view of both implants. *I,* Preoperative and *J,* postoperative Waters' view. (*E* and *H* from Block MS, Kent JN: Correction of vertical orbital dystopia with a hydroxylapatite orbital floor graft. J Oral Maxillofac Surg 46:420, 1988; with permission.)

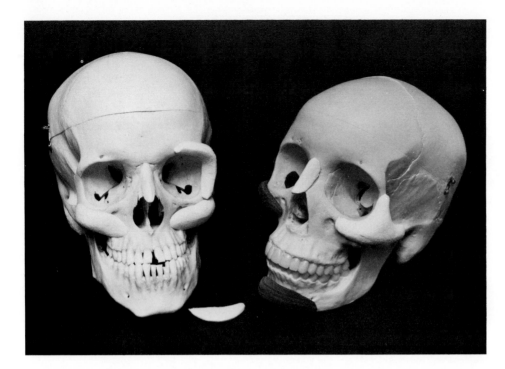

FIGURE 29–28. Preformed Proplast facial implant for correction of periorbital or ZMC deficiency.

Wolford and colleagues[218] described the use of porous HA blocks for midface augmentation in which two blocks stabilized with bone screws were required to augment the infraorbital region (Fig. 29–30A to E). Lateral augmentation of the zygomatic complex was apparently not possible because of the difficulties in shaping and stabilizing brittle, curved segments of HA. It appears that small, single-planed defects are more ideal for this material.

El Deeb and Holmes[297] studied porous HA blocks and black Proplast I in monkeys. Subperiosteal pockets were created bilaterally over the zygomatic and mandibular regions in six rhesus monkeys. The animals were sacrificed postoperatively at each interval 3, 6, and 12 months, respectively. The implants were retrieved en bloc and halved. Half of each specimen was examined histologically, and the other half was used for histometry scanning under electron microscopy. Clinical evaluation revealed that porous HA implants were more stable than Proplast implants. The Proplast implants showed the presence of giant cells and the complete encapsulation by infiltration with fibrovascular connective tissue. The porous HA implants were united to the underlying cortex by bony ingrowth.

The authors correctly state that their comparative data can contribute to the selection of clinical implants. Strangely, though, this study failed to use either Proplast with aluminum oxide or Proplast-HA; rather, it used Proplast I, a material essentially discontinued a decade ago for facial augmentation. Clearly, manipulation of a soft, flexible polymer by the animal permits a microrelative mobility and may encourage a limited, persistent, giant cell response, as noted by the author, while rigid fixation of ceramic blocks does not. It is interesting that no clinical complications were reported with either material. The authors further note that a number of clinical criteria, not studied, are equally important in selecting an implant material. Such factors as ease of carving and shaping, ease of placement and fixation, quality of underlying bone adaptation and overlying soft tissue coverage, degree of natural feel, and impact resistance are important.[297] These clinical factors would favor a deformable, low-modulus material, such as silicone rubber or Proplast, over a hard, brittle material, such as HA, for zygomatic reconstruction.

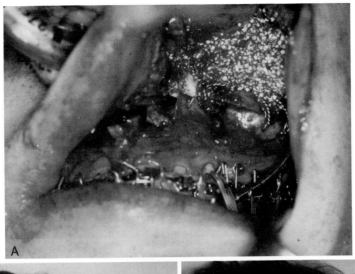

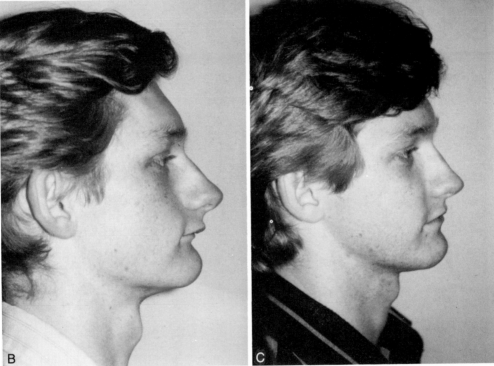

FIGURE 29–29.   *A*, HA particles used to correct ZMC deficiencies. *B*, Preoperative and *C*, postoperative views following correction, including Le Fort I downgraft and mandibular advancement.

Zygomatic Augmentation: Operative Technique

Intraoral Approach.   Zygomatic augmentation is usually performed with the patient under general anesthesia. The following technique described by Kent for Proplast augmentation of bilateral congenital deficiency also generally applies to traumatic deformities and to other materials.[151,167] The mouth is prepared with a nonsoap povidone-iodine (Betadine) wash followed by a saline irrigation. Local anesthesia with epinephrine is used to establish hemostasis.

A 1-inch horizontal incision is made through the mucosa slightly lateral to the depth of the vestibule on the lip side above the canine and premolar teeth (Fig. 29–31*A*). The incision is extended obliquely through the small muscles of facial expression and then through the periosteum at the base of the zygomatic bone. The periosteum is reflected superiorly over the infraorbital and lateral orbital rim, with care taken to avoid exposure

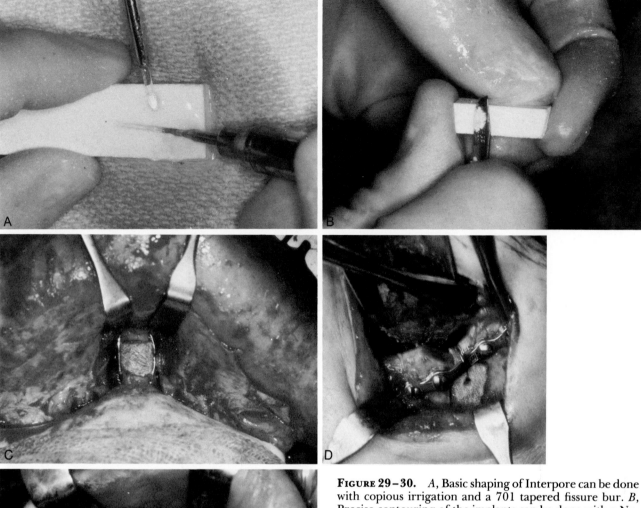

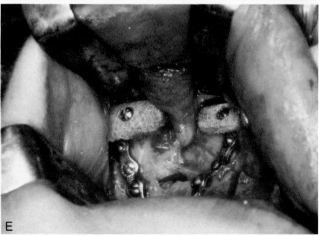

FIGURE 29–30. *A,* Basic shaping of Interpore can be done with copious irrigation and a 701 tapered fissure bur. *B,* Precise contouring of the implants can be done with a No. 15 blade under copious irrigation. *C,* Through a bicoronal flap, the Le Fort III midface osteotomy was performed with grafting of the nasofrontal area. *D,* Through a subciliary approach, a modified Le Fort III midface osteotomy is demonstrated on the left side of the orbit. An osteotomy was performed vertically through the lateral orbital rim and zygomatic buttress area. The Interpore graft is seen along with the bone plate in this 8-mm modified Le Fort III midface advancement. *E,* An Interpore onlay augmentation of the infraorbital rim is observed. Two pieces were inserted on each side of the infraorbital nerve. The implants are stabilized with bone screws. (Courtesy of Dr. Larry M. Wolford, Baylor College of Dentistry and Baylor University Medical Center, Dallas.)

of periorbital fat, and medially over the maxilla to the nasal bone (Fig. 29–31*B*). The infraorbital nerve is identified and preserved. Periosteum and muscle are left attached to the maxilla below the plane of the incision to act as a barrier to the inferior displacement of the implant. The periosteum is then reflected over the lower lateral orbital rim and laterally around the zygoma, over the entire surface of the zygomatic arch to the zygomaticotemporal suture line (Fig. 29–31*C*). The dissection is supraperiosteal over the maxillary sinus, where bone may be absent in traumatic deformities. The implant is trimmed to ensure proper, but not overexcessive, augmentation over the lateral aspect of the zygomatic arch, the prominence of the zygoma, and the paranasal area. This step may require thinning the implant over the arch or the paranasal areas in uncorrected traumatic zygomatic complex fractures. Carving is done with a No. 10 or 15 blade, usually on the bone side of the implant.

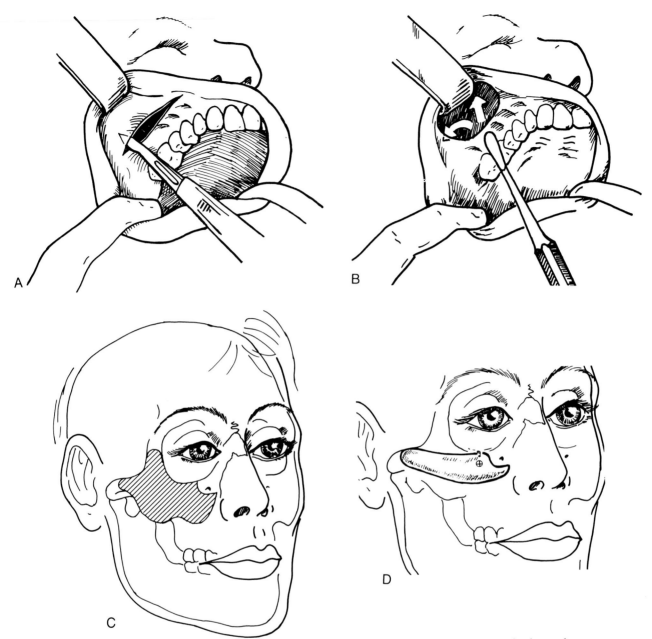

FIGURE 29–31.   *A–D,* Drawing of surgical ZMC augmentation with Proplast and other polymers (see text).

The implant is then impregnated with concentrated antibiotic solution, such as 1 g of cephalosporin in 100 ml of saline, and is trimmed before preliminary insertion. Insertion and removal of the implant before final trimming should be minimized. The edges of the zygomatic implant should remain feathered to avoid being palpable. Notching of the implant for the infraorbital nerve is usually necessary. After implantation, insertion of a thin periosteal elevator over and beneath the implant at its posterior limit will ensure proper placement without curling of the thin, feathered edge. Stabilization of the posterolateral half of the implant is provided by the pocket over the zygomatic arch. Inferior displacement is prevented by stabilization of the medioanterior half with 1–0 or 2–0 sutures through bone, as follows:

A superiorly directed hole is made through the lateral aspect of the infraorbital rim. The free end of a 1–0 or 2–0 polyglycolic-polylactic acid suture is passed through the hole, and the needle is then passed through the bone side of the superior edge of the implant. Alternatively, stabilization has also been achieved with wire or a bone screw into the body of the zygoma (Fig. 29–31D).

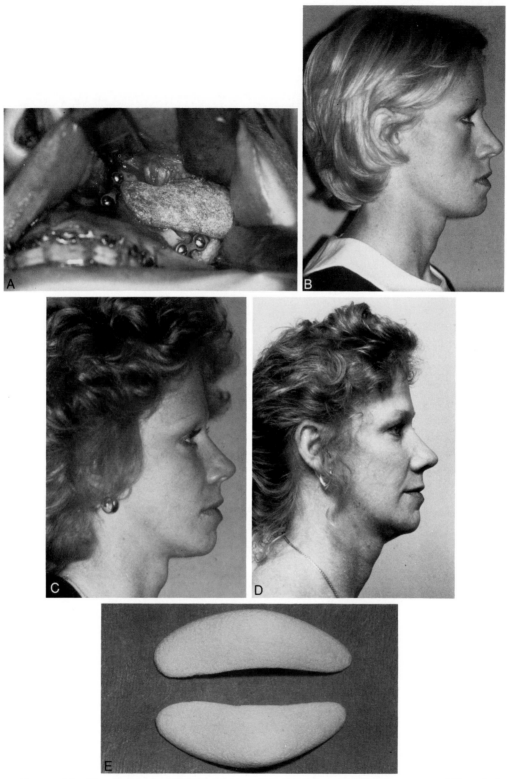

FIGURE 29–32.   *A*, Proplast ZMC implant and Le Fort I osteotomy to correct midface deficiency. *B*, Preoperative, *C*, 2-year postoperative, and *D*, 15-year postoperative profile following Proplast zygomatic augmentation. *E*, High-low profile zygomatic Proplast implants.

Simultaneous augmentation with Le Fort I osteotomies is possible (Fig. 29–32A). The implant should be trimmed so that the inferior edge in the canine fossa does not extend over the edge of the osteotomy line. Although the incidence of infection from sinus exposure is low, patients should be advised of increased infection risk in this instance. Antibiotic impregnation and wash through the procedure are necessary. Two-layer closure through muscle and mucosa with closely approximating interrupted sutures is required to prevent postoperative dehiscence or infection. Good oral hygiene measures are necessary during the immediate postoperative period. Systemic antibiotics are used for 10 days, at which time sutures are removed. The Proplast implants (Kent high-low profile or Whitaker) are preferred, since they extend into the canine fossa.

With the high-low implant, the maximal thickness of the implant at the zygoma prominence is off center, so that an implant providing maximal thickness superiorly on one side (high profile) can be flipped and used on the opposite side to provide maximal augmentation inferiorly (low profile) (Fig. 29–32B to E).

Extraoral Approach. Augmentation of the zygoma, maxilla, and lateral and supraorbital rims is performed by the extraoral approach with the use of general anesthesia. Local anesthesia with epinephrine is used for hemostasis. A subperiosteal surgical pocket is created to receive the implant by a traditional approach through the eyebrow, infraorbital crease, or eyelid. In trauma patients with anterior maxillary wall defects, the surgical pocket dissection should be supraperiosteal to avoid exposing the implant to sinus fluids. A bone base is required to support most of the implant. The implant is impregnated with antibiotic solution and trimmed before preliminary insertion. The edges of these implants should be feathered to avoid being palpable. Immediate postoperative stabilization of the implant is achieved by passing a suture or wire through the edge of the implant and overlying soft tissue or by securing it to bone with a suture, wire, or screw.

The Deficient Orbit

Orbital floor, rim, and roof defects have been reconstructed with a variety of autogenous and alloplastic materials. Defects caused by trauma may require reconstruction for both cosmetic and functional reasons. Small defects may be covered with soft tissue grafts, while larger ones require bone, cartilage, or alloplastic replacement.

Surgical procedures generally required for defects of the orbital roof include packing the frontal sinus and residual cavity with fat or muscle, establishing proper drainage from the sinus to the nose, and reconstructing the roof with autogenous bone or bone graft substitutes such as HA.[298]

Enophthalmos and superior sulcus deformities are extremely common findings after removal of an eye because of trauma. The causes are primary volume deficiency, tissue laxity with inferior settling of the muscle cone, and, possibly, fat atrophy.[299] The ocular globe has a volume of approximately 7.3 cc. When it is removed, there is a 7.3-cc volume deficit in the orbit. Most implanted spheres and ocular prostheses have a volume of 2 cc each, with a combined volume of 4 cc. This situation results in an overall volume deficit of 3 cc.[300]

Vertical orbital dystopia (VOD) is a condition in which the globe is vertically malpositioned. Although most of the causes are congenital (unilateral or asymmetric craniosynostoses, hemifacial microsomia-microphthalmia, hypoplasia of the lesser wing of the sphenoid bone, and facial clefting syndrome), neoplasms (fibrous dysplasia, antrum carcinoma, gliomas and intracranial tumors, frontal-ethmoid sinus tumors, von Recklinghausen's disease, and angiomatoses) and trauma (orbital floor and wall fractures and radiation injury) may account for more than 25 per cent of cases.[301] It is sometimes associated with other facial deformities.

Vertical orbital repositioning will alter the patient's orbital axis. In an adult, normal stereoscopic vision is within 40 seconds of the visual arc.[302] If differences exist in the vertical or horizontal level of the eyes, the patient corrects image disparities on the retinas by either abnormal compensatory eye movement (phoria) or a retinal response (fixation disparity). Compensatory muscle movement may accommodate for a significant amount of image disparity, with a central sensory mechanism compensating for the remaining disparity. However, if images are torsionally disparate — that is, one image rotated in relation to the other — the patient compensates and achieves fusion by central sensory mechanisms.[303] Because torsional changes can be compensated for by central mechanisms, a major objective of the surgical correction of VOD should be repositioning of the globe in a rotational arc with the optic foramen as its centroid.

Late enophthalmos, a frequent finding in VOD caused by an unrepaired zygomatic or orbital blow-out fracture, can also result in aesthetic problems and functional impairment. The sunken appearance of the superior sulcus and the depressed globe are obvious cosmetic defects (Fig. 29–33A to D). Functional impairment of the eye that includes restriction of motion and diplopia is a common complaint. Early repair

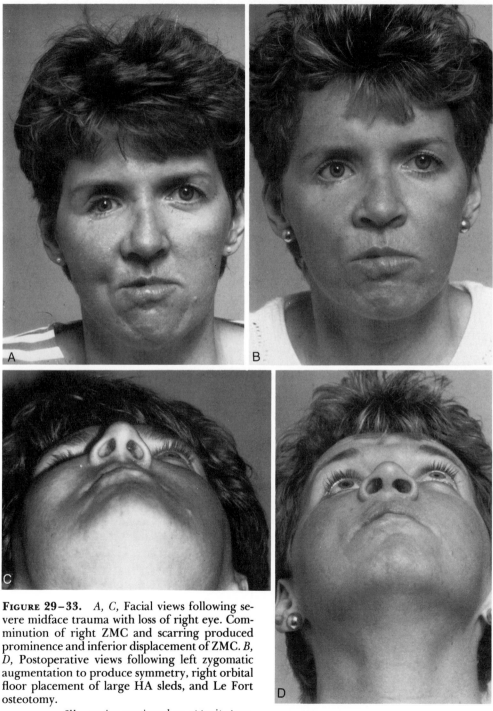

FIGURE 29–33. *A, C,* Facial views following severe midface trauma with loss of right eye. Comminution of right ZMC and scarring produced prominence and inferior displacement of ZMC. *B, D,* Postoperative views following left zygomatic augmentation to produce symmetry, right orbital floor placement of large HA sleds, and Le Fort osteotomy.

Illustration continued on opposite page.

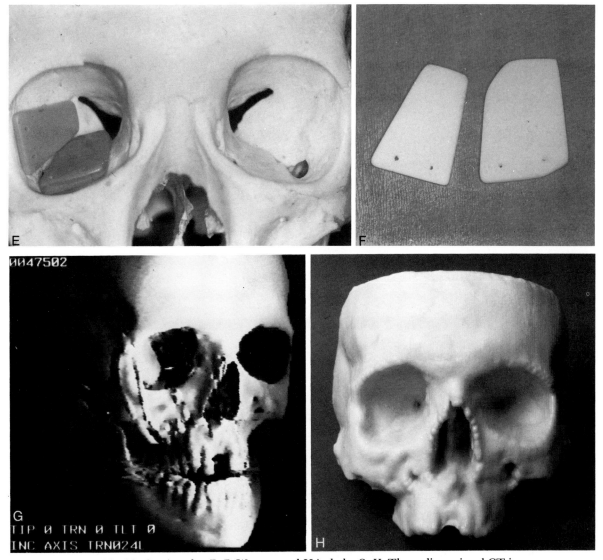

FIGURE 29–33. *Continued.   E, F,* Wax-up and HA sleds. *G, H,* Three-dimensional CT images and milled model.

Illustration continued on following page.

of zygomatic and orbital fractures before scar contracture and fat atrophy is necessary but may be uncertain, since the only parameter for measuring the adequacy of treatment is the late cosmetic and functional result.

In the seeing eye, the placement of silicone rubber, MMA, Teflon, cartilage, fascia, and bone, as well as osteotomy, has been used[284,289,304–312] (Fig. 29–34). However, autogenous material may resorb, alloplasts may migrate and cause undesirable tissue reaction and contraction, and the osteotomy may constitute only a crude, nonreproducible method for the correction of late enophthalmos. Patients with comminuted orbital-zygomatic fractures may not be candidates for such osteotomy techniques because of malunion or multiple bone fragments.

Hydroxyapatite has been recently advocated as a nonresorbable bone graft substitute without the shortcomings of either bone grafts or other alloplasts.[313] The use of stable, inert, and nontoxic measurable material like dense HA also allows the placement of volume-measured implants, with reproducible results (see Fig. 29–33A to L). This procedure can be done by simply placing the final carved blocks in a syringe of saline and measuring the water displacement.

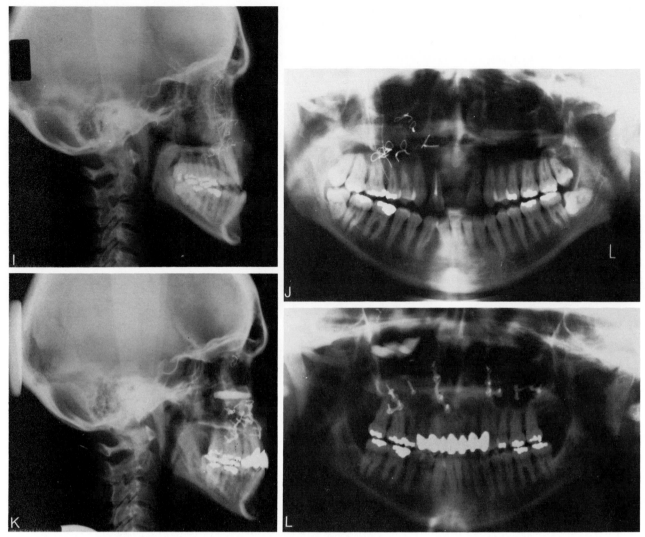

FIGURE 29–33. *Continued.*   *I, J,* Preoperative cephalometric and panoramic radiographs. *K, L,* Postoperative cephalometric and panoramic radiographs.

Several procedures are advocated to restore volume deficit, some of which place implant materials in the superior sulcus. Such materials include dermal fat, fascia lata, acrylic implants, and superior silicone implants.[314-317] Problems with these implants include decreased upper eyelid mobility, instability of the implant, and inferior settling with time.[300]

Alternatively, materials are placed on the orbital floor, raising the orbital contents to fill the superior sulcus deformity. They include subperiosteal glass beads, bone plates in the subperiosteal space, RTV silicone rubber, and, more recently, HA blocks.[87,299,318,319,333] Wedge-shaped sleds of acrylic and silicone on the orbital floor are also recommended to move the sphere anteriorly and superiorly.[320-322] Efforts to prevent anterior implant migration include wiring the implant to the bony orbit.[322]

A century ago, Lang recognized fracture of the orbital floor following blunt facial trauma.[323] The anatomic and physiologic changes in the orbital floor and orbital contents following trauma, requiring orbital floor exploration, are well known.[127,288,324-328] Treatment is somewhat varied and controversial. Prior to 1950, acute orbital floor fractures were stabilized with maxillary antrum packing, either gauze or balloons, through a Caldwell-Luc approach.[127] A variety of materials have been used for the past 40 years as a result of direct surgical approach to the orbital floor in reconstructing these fractures. They include sheeting of Teflon, Silastic,

Supramid, Marlex Mesh, tantalum, acrylic, Gelfilm, polyethylene, glass, lyophilized dura, homogeneous and autogenous cartilage, and bone.[126-130,326-331] Again, autogenous grafts have traditionally been the material of choice, although they have been criticized for unpredictable resorption and donor site. Alloplastic materials have steadily increased in spite of the complications of infection, extrusion, and implant displacement.[332]

Long-term treatment results for re-establishing orbital floor continuity following trauma by Polley and Ringer[333] and by Aronowitz, Freeman, and Spira[334] demonstrate a very low incidence of complications with the use of Teflon sheeting (1.245 mm). The incidence of implant infection, extrusion, or displacement is reported to be low (0.4 per cent).[333] The rate of later complications—diplopia and enophthalmos—is reported to be slightly higher. Gauze packing of the antrum is associated with a higher infection rate of Teflon orbital implants and is no longer recommended.[334] These findings support the use of Teflon as a safe and effective material for the reconstruction of orbital floor defects following blunt facial trauma.

The extent of orbital floor damage determines whether silicone, Teflon, or other polymer sheeting should be used for reconstruction. For minor fractures with an intact periosteum, no reconstructive material is needed. In larger defects with periosteal disruption, with or without antral mucosal disruption, alloplastic sheeting reconstruction can be undertaken. In enophthalmic situations with extensive fractures involving nearly the entire orbital floor, in which volume must be restored, autogenous bone is generally preferred (Fig. 29–34).

Surgical Approach to the Orbital Floor

The surgical approach to the orbital floor has undergone many modifications over the past 25 years. Direct incision over the inferior orbital rim was replaced by a slightly higher incision in the inferior lid crease. The inferior lid crease incision was then replaced by a blepharoplasty subciliary incision in the early 1970s. In the early 1980s, the inferior fornix approach to the orbital floor, which had been described by Tessier, was modified by McCord, who added a lateral canthotomy and inferior cantholysis.[335] This addition to the inferior fornix approach described by Tessier provided much wider exposure of the orbital floor and inferior medial wall. In addition, this surgical dissection allowed exposure of the entire lateral orbital rim and wall above the zygomaticofrontal suture line. Thus, through one skin incision of only 10 to 12 mm, the surgeon could now repair extensive orbital floor fractures as well as displaced fractures at the zygomaticofrontal suture.

Experience with this surgical exposure soon proved that this was the method of choice for all surgical procedures requiring exposure of the orbital floor and medial wall. Consequently, orbital decompression for thyroid orbitopathy is also best performed through this surgical exposure.

Inferior Fornix and Lateral Cantholysis Incision.* The inferior fornix and lateral canthal area are infiltrated with lidocaine or bupivacaine with 1:200,000 epinephrine. The lateral canthus is incised, and the inferior crus of the lateral palpebral tendon is incised, which allows complete detachment of the lower lid from the lateral orbital rim (Fig. 29–34A to C). At this point, the surgeon has two choices for exposure of the orbital floor. One can incise the conjunctiva and retractors of the lower eyelid in the inferior fornix, which places the incision behind the orbital septum. The advantage to this incision is that it is more direct, and the disadvantage is that orbital fat will be found on both sides of the incision. The other alternative is to incise the conjunctiva and retractors at the lower tarsal border (Fig. 29–34D). This incision will allow dissection of a skin muscle flap along the anterior surface of the orbital septum to the inferior orbital rim (Fig. 29–34E). The disadvantage to this exposure is that it is technically more difficult

---

* Furnished by Darrell E. Wolfley, M.D., Professor of Ophthalmology, Director of Oculoplastic Surgery, Louisiana State University Eye Center, LSU School of Medicine, New Orleans.

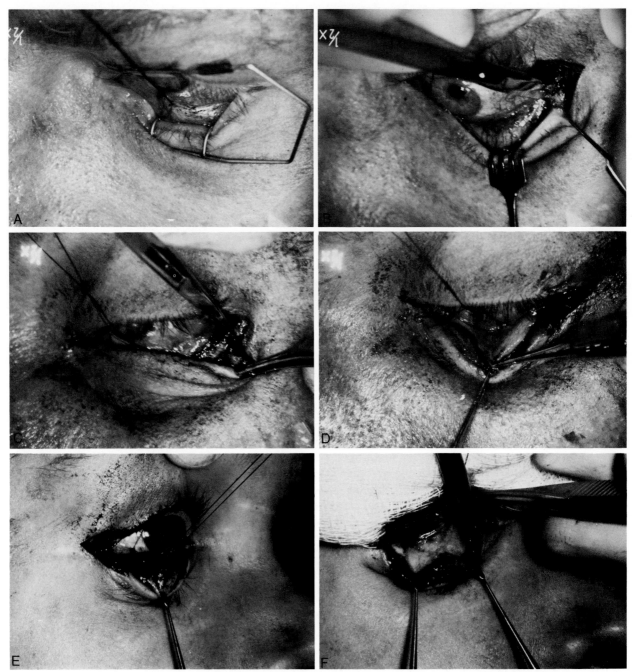

Figure 29–34. *A*, A 4–0 silk suture passed under the tendon of the inferior rectus muscle allows for testing of forced duction during surgical procedures. *B*, Incision of lateral canthus and incising crus of lateral palpebral tendon. *C*, Inferior crus of lateral palpebral tendon now incised, allowing displacement of lateral portion of lower eyelid. *D*, Conjunctiva incised at lower tarsal border. *E*, Plane of dissection along anterior surface of orbital septum with 4–0 silk suture used for retraction of posterior lamella of eyelid, which includes conjunctiva, capsulopalpebral fascia, and orbital septum. *F*, Further dissection of plane between postorbicularis fascia and orbital septum. Dissection is carried to the origin of the orbital septum at the periosteum of the inferior orbital rim. *G*, Incision of periosteum along inferior orbital rim, with reflection of periosteum. *H*, Elevation of periosteum along medial orbital floor reveals anterior edge of fracture. *I*, Rongeurs are used to enlarge fracture for better visualization of orbital contents within maxillary sinus. *J*, Supramed Extra implant, 0.6 mm in thickness, is being placed along orbital floor to re-establish the barrier between the periorbital area and the maxillary sinus. *K*, Double-armed 5–0 Vicryl sutures attached to the fibrous remnants of the lateral palpebral tendon for reconstructing the lateral canthal angle. *L*, Plain gut sutures (6–0) are utilized to reapproximate the conjunctival edges of the inferior fornix. (Courtesy of Dr. Darrel E. Wolfley, New Orleans.)

Illustration continued on opposite page.

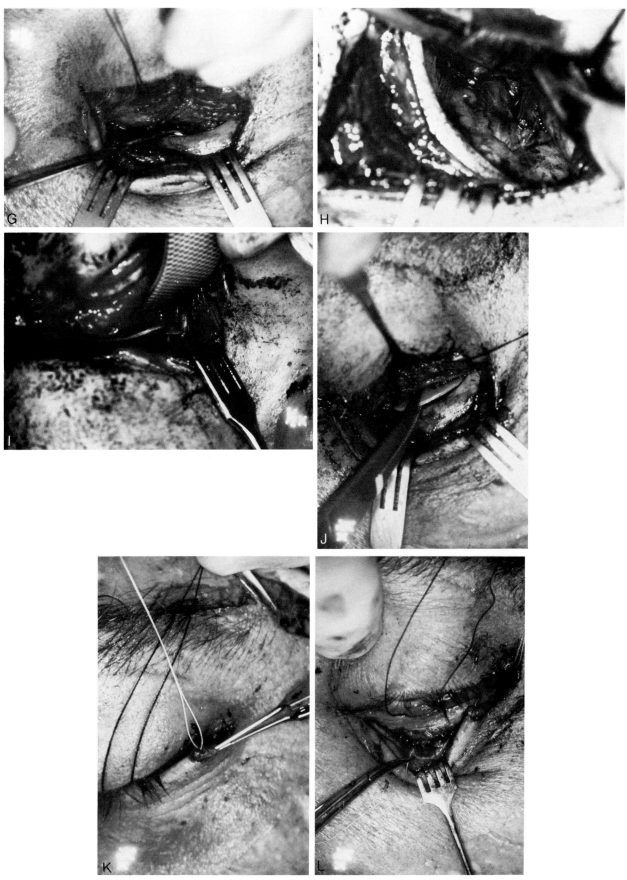

FIGURE 29–34. *Continued*

and has the potential for more extensive damage to the orbicularis muscle and subsequent scarring. The advantage is that the orbital fat remains behind the intact orbital septum (Fig. 29–34*F*).

Once the inferior orbital rim is exposed, the orbicularis muscle and submuscular fat are cauterized, and the periosteum is incised on the anterior surface of the infraorbital rim (Fig. 29–34*G*). The periosteum is then reflected in both anterior and posterior directions. The inferior reflection of the periosteum will allow closure of the periosteum after repair of the fracture. The superior and posterior reflection along the orbital floor is most easily started laterally. As this reflection reaches the medial orbit, the inferior oblique muscle and nasolacrimal duct are at risk. The inferior oblique muscle will elevate with the periosteum, and the nasolacrimal duct must then be avoided. The posterior reflection of the periosteum will reveal the orbital fracture in the posterior medial floor (Fig. 29–34*H*). Extensive trauma will create a fracture that extends laterally through the infraorbital groove. However, most fractures will be localized medial to the infraorbital nerve.

It is often helpful to enlarge the anterior position of the fracture to allow direct observation of the prolapsed periosteum and orbital fat (Fig. 29–34*I*). The orbital fat and torn periorbita should be elevated into the orbit for the entire 360-degree circumference of the fracture. With fresh fractures, this is generally accomplished with a combination of retraction with malleable retractors and direct elevation with bayonet forceps or hemostats. With older fractures, this elevation of orbital contents into the orbit may require sharp dissection to separate the periorbita from the mucoperiosteal surface of the maxillary sinus. Sharp dissection may also be required along the lateral edge of the fracture in the area of the infraorbital nerve. Once the orbital contents have been elevated into the orbit from the medial to the lateral edge of the fracture, the orbital floor can be reconstituted. Most orbital blow-out fractures can be satisfactorily repaired with stiff alloplastic implants. Supramid Extra in thicknesses of 0.4 to 0.8 mm is very functional for such repair (Fig. 29–34*J*). The implant should rest on secure bone several millimeters medial, lateral, anterior, and posterior to the fracture. The implant must be thick enough to resist indentation by the pressure of the orbital contents.

It is generally not necessary to fix the orbital implant to the bony orbital rim. The implant can be held adequately in place by closing the periosteum along the infraorbital rim with 4–0 or 5–0 Vicryl sutures. The lateral canthal angle is then reconstructed with a double-armed 5–0 Vicryl suture through the fibrous tissue lateral to the lateral edge of the tarsus (Fig. 29–34*K*). This suture is brought through the superior crus of the lateral palpebral tendon and temporarily tied. If the lateral canthal angle is adequately repositioned, the suture is loosened and the conjunctiva is closed with several interrupted 6–0 plain gut sutures (Fig. 29–34*L*). The Vicryl suture is then pulled up and permanently tied, and the lateral canthal angle is reapproximated with a 6–0 Prolene suture. The orbicularis muscle in the lateral canthal incision is then closed with 6–0 Vicryl sutures, and the skin is closed with a small monofilament suture.

This same exposure can be used to elevate the periosteum along the lateral orbital rim for fixation and bone plating of zygomaticofrontal suture separation. This procedure will generally require incision of the periosteum along the lateral palpebral tendon with the periosteum as it is reflected along the lateral wall. The periosteum is then closed, and the lateral canthal angle is reconstructed as previously described.

Medial wall fractures can be exposed through this same surgical dissection. However, if the preoperative CT scan reveals significant prolapse of orbital contents into the ethmoid sinuses, it is virtually impossible to reposition the orbital contents into the orbit through the inferior fornix approach. Consequently, an additional exposure above is required to reposition medial orbital contents adequately into the orbit and to reconstitute the medial orbital wall with alloplastic or autogenous materials.

This additional exposure of the medial orbital wall can be achieved through a bicoronal forehead flap, through an upper lid crease incision and dissection, or through a lateral nasal-brow incision. For cosmetic reasons, the lid crease incision or bicoronal flap is preferable. If lacerations are found in the glabellar or nasal area, these lacerations can be used to expose the medial wall.

Alloplastic Nasal Reconstruction

Nasal augmentation presents several particular problems because of the nose's unique position of prominence on the face. It is susceptible to microtrauma and major blows and is the most obvious abnormal structure when asymmetry or disfigurement is present. The nose is divided into two major regions, the first being the upper half, which is made up of the bony pyramid of the nasal bone. This region is firm and has a very thin soft tissue covering; therefore, deformities are not easily masked by overlying connective tissue. The lower half of the nose is highly mobile and again has very thin soft tissue coverage. This area is subject to frequent stress owing to its mobility, which can often result in dislodgment and extrusion of an implant, as was previously described with silicone rubber. Alloplastic materials are frequently tried with limited success in the nose, since there is no one material that fulfills all of the needs for nasal implants.[336] These needs are support, which requires a firm implant, and contour restoration, which requires a soft, malleable implant. Autogenous cartilage is probably the most versatile and desirable implant, particularly when the lower half of the nose is involved. However, cartilage may not always be available in large enough quantities for augmentation, and it is difficult to carve precisely, particularly when

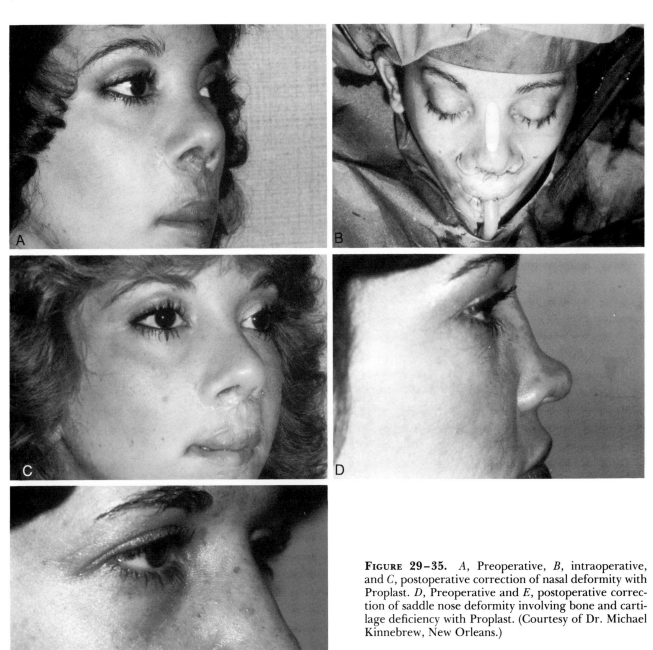

FIGURE 29–35. *A*, Preoperative, *B*, intraoperative, and *C*, postoperative correction of nasal deformity with Proplast. *D*, Preoperative and *E*, postoperative correction of saddle nose deformity involving bone and cartilage deficiency with Proplast. (Courtesy of Dr. Michael Kinnebrew, New Orleans.)

cartilage is stacked upon itself for bulk. Finally, when cartilage is morselized to remove memory, often small particles may become free and have a tendency to shrink or resorb.

Augmentation of the upper half of the nose has been tried in various ways, and it appears that Proplast offers advantages because of its firmness and its adaptability to the underlying bony structure and overlying soft tissue (Fig. 29–35A to E).[161,169] Proplast has been shown to be easily sculpted and comes in precarved nasal dorsal implants for the purpose of reconstructing the saddle nose deformity. Once implanted and infiltrated with host tissue, the implant itself has a low migration and extrusion rate but may become infected if exposed postoperatively to nasal fluids or subjected to trauma. Silicone rubber is also used; however, extrusion because of memory and lack of tissue ingrowth requires exact adaptation and encapsulation (Fig. 29–36A to D).

For the lower half of the nose, where upper lateral cartilages and the nasal dorsal cartilage are encountered, a more flexible implant that can withstand a lot of mobility without displacement or extrusion is required. Supramid may be the most versatile allograft for this purpose. Advantages include ready availability, infection resistance, and soft tissue simulation. The primary difficulty with Supramid is in placement and

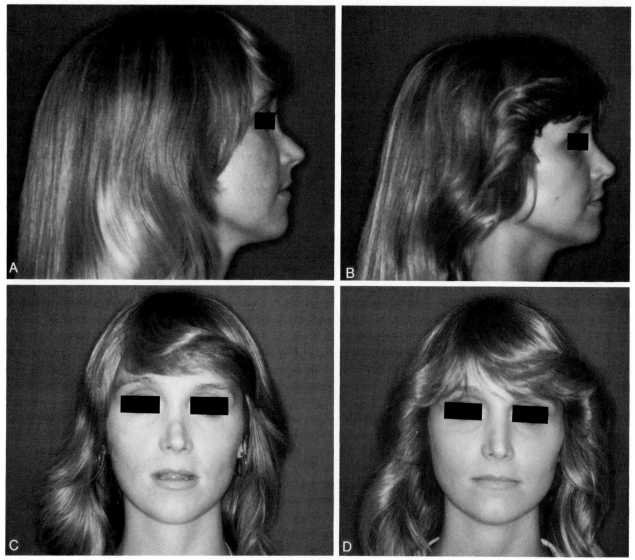

FIGURE 29–36.   *A*, Preoperative and *B*, postoperative profile of saddle nose deformity repaired with silicone rubber onlay. *C*, Preoperative and *D*, postoperative full-face views. (Courtesy of Dr. Michael Kinnebrew, New Orleans.)

contouring. Finally, Supramid may be compromised by long-term resorption, which may have a deleterious effect on earlier results.

The placement of any implant material in the nose requires proper planning and proper exposure. The following discussion will describe the proper exposure of the lower and upper lateral cartilages as well as the nasal dorsum via an internal nasal approach. In the severely deformed nose, an external approach is far superior, since skeletonization and reconstruction under direct vision lead to more satisfactory results. Variations on these techniques are certainly acceptable, since there are many different ways to approach the surgical dissection and exposure of the nose. However, the principles of adequate exposure and release of overlying soft tissue tethering are critical to provide for redraping of the soft tissue and adequate stabilization of the implants that are placed.

Nasal Reconstruction: Operative Technique

Internal Approach.[337,338]   After either adequate general anesthesia and endotracheal intubation or sufficient depth of intravenous sedation, a local anesthetic with epinephrine is injected into the nose for both anesthesia and hemostasis. It is important to achieve block anesthesia of the external nasal branches of the infratrochlear nerve, the infraorbital nerve, the internal nasal branches of the nasociliary nerve, and the nasal branch of the anterior superior alveolar nerve. Small volumes of local anesthesia should be injected so as not to distort the nose significantly and prevent contouring of the implant and draping of the soft tissue. The patient should be prepared and draped appropriately, and beginning with exposure of the right nostril, the dissection can begin. The right ala is retracted, and the caudal border of the lower lateral cartilage is identified. An intercartilaginous incision is then made between the alar and upper lateral cartilage to allow for subsequent retraction (Fig. 29–37A and B). For maximal exposure,

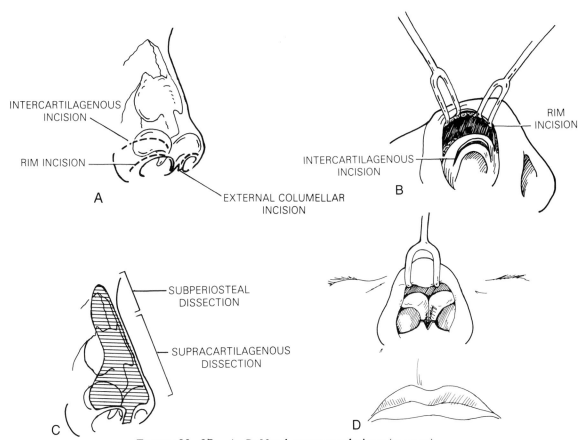

FIGURE 29–37.   *A–D,* Nasal surgery technique (see text).

a similar intercartilaginous incision should be made on the left side. Again, supracartilaginous dissection to the nasal bones and then subperiosteal dissection to the root of the nose should be accomplished (Fig. 29–37C). At this point, the two planes of dissection should be confluent over the midline and down to the nasal tip to provide for adequate mobilization of overlying soft tissue and adequate exposure of bone. The nasal implant can now be modified and placed, the tissues can be redraped, the intercartilaginous incisions can be sutured, and the nose can be dressed with an external stent to prevent hematoma formation and early dislodgment of the implant.

If access to the lower lateral or alar cartilages is necessary, then in addition to the intercartilaginous incision, a rim incision is made near the caudal border of the lower cartilages. Dissection, both blunt and sharp, is carried above the alar cartilage in a subcutaneous fashion, staying on the alar cartilage to expose it as far laterally and medially as possible. In addition, a transfixation incision can be made, separating the membranous from the cartilaginous septum and thus exposing the entire cartilaginous skeleton of the lower half of the nose. At this point, all intervening scar tissue should be removed, and the cartilaginous framework should be identified and examined for deformity. If implants are used to correct these deformities, precise contouring will be required, since the thinness of the tissues in this region will accentuate any contour abnormalities. Securing the implants to the existing cartilage or to the overlying skin can be performed with 5–0 or 6–0 nonresorbable sutures to tack the tissue in place. At this point, the nose should then be re-examined with the soft tissue passively in place and draped, and the final contour adjustments should be made. After this, the area can be sutured, closing both the intercartilaginous and the rim incisions. The nasal tip should be taped to support the tip and align the cartilages. In addition, an external nasal dressing should be applied to prevent any lateral displacement of the lower half of the nose in the initial healing phase. The external nasal dressings used in both instances of dorsal implants as well as lower half implants should be applied with no pressure exerted. This measure is to prevent a pressure necrosis of skin over the implants, thus increasing the risk of infection and extrusion. These nasal dressings should be left in place for approximately 7 to 10 days to secure the initial adaptation of the overlying skin to the underlying implant and skeleton. Internal nasal packing is usually not necessary for this type to work. Only if osteotomies are associated with an implantation procedure should internal nasal packings be considered. In addition, if a significant amount of septal work is done to straighten a traumatically deviate septum, internal nasal packing should be performed. This packing should be maintained for approximately 2 to 3 days to prevent septal hematoma formation as well as dislodgment or displacement of the surgically straightened nasal septum.

External Approach.[339] An external approach to the nose will probably be the indicated method of reconstructing the traumatized or severely malformed nose. This approach will allow the operator the greatest exposure to determine the exact structure and orientation of underlying cartilage and bone as well as to facilitate placement of grafts to yield a satisfactory result. The surgical technique begins following the induction of general anesthesia. Presurgical markings are made prior to the injection of local anesthetic with epinephrine and the intranasal application of cocaine. Bilateral alar margin incisions are made along the rim and are continued down along the columella approximately one third of the way toward the base of the columella (Fig. 29–37D). At this point, these bilateral incisions are connected across the skin of the columella, utilizing an inverted **V** incision. The dissection over the lower lateral cartilages should be made as close to the underlying cartilage as possible to minimize bleeding. The dissection should extend as far laterally on the lower lateral cartilage as possible, but the lateral attachments of the alar tissues should not be disrupted. At this point, excessive soft tissue asymmetry involving the supratip tissues should be corrected. Defatting and excision of scar tissue can be done under direct vision with little difficulty. The lower lateral cartilages are then identified and are isolated from each other in the midline to provide for realignment and suturing at the midline to refine the nasal tip. It is at this point that cartilage grafts or implants or both may be placed around the lower lateral cartilages, in the columella, and at the nasal tip for augmentation. In the area extending upward to the base of the nasal bone, obvious asymmetry can be corrected with osteotomies. Deficiencies can be identified and accurately reconstructed with dorsal implants with the use of direct contouring and fixation to underlying bone.

The Deficient Chin

Preformed chin implants may be indicated for those patients with a contour-deficient chin that is the result of a developmental condition or an acquired one, such as trauma, infection, or tumor. Chin deficiency associated with trauma occurs from local tissue loss but more commonly results from condylar fractures and complications that produce posterior facial height shortening and backward rotation of the mandible.

Binder and colleagues retrospectively reviewed 539 cases of chin augmentation done over a period of 9 years and using different materials and routes of insertion.[340] The types of materials utilized in varying numbers were the acrylics, silicone rubber, fine silicone sponge, Proplast, Supramid, and the silicone gel-filled bag with and without Dacron backing. Each implant was rated on its ability to fulfill most adequately the aesthetic and functional requirements of chin augmentation.

Acrylic chins are hard, nonwettable, inert compounds that are difficult to sculpt. Exact conformation to the chin cannot be achieved, and displacement is common, even when the implant is perforated for tissue ingrowth. Silicone rubber implants are easier to sculpt and to conform to the chin contour. Their contour, however, may allow for palpability, and displacement may occur unless a Dacron backing is present for tissue ingrowth. The porous or sponge implants, which include fine silicone sponge, Proplast, and polyamide mesh (Supramid), share common features but also retain specific problems unique to each material. The general advantages of porous implants are the ease of insertion, the ability to provide a natural feel to the mandible, and the enhanced capacity for fixation by tissue ingrowth.

Proplast offers advantages over silicone sponge. Its wettability to body fluids allows better tissue ingrowth. It has a unique ability to fix to bone, and when placed subperiosteally, its position on bone is stable and is difficult to move. Susceptibility to infection, when the implant is placed through the mouth, is higher in Proplast than in any of the other common chin implants. Supramid allows fibrous ingrowth and has a particular ability to blend into the surrounding tissues. It is also difficult to remove.

A silicone gel-filled bag prosthesis with the addition of Dacron mesh to enhance fixation is preferred by many cosmetic surgeons. Minimal changes in the permeability of the capsule around silicone gel-filled breast prostheses are known to occur, allowing the inner gel to dissolve into the surrounding tissues. The clinical significance of this phenomenon and its extrapolation to chin implants are not known.

Early reports suggested that the migration of silicone rubber and acrylic chin implants into bone from soft tissue tension, particularly when the implants are used for chin contour augmentation, is greater when the implants are placed subperiosteally than supraperiosteally.[341,342] However other factors, such as the size of the implant, high placement over softer alveolar bone, and material differences like softness and flexibility, more likely contribute to bone resorption. Bell[73] and Spira[343] noted, however, that after approximately 12 months resorption appeared to be a self-limiting phenomenon with silicone rubber. In our own experience, the migration of Proplast implants into bone is usually complete after 12 months. Recent studies by Freidman and colleagues,[344] Dann and Epker,[165] and Kent and associates[151] have noted implant migration into bone. The thinning of soft tissue over the chin of most implants occurs in the presence of existing facial deformity and other factors such as lip incompetence or hyperactive mentalis muscle and scarring.[151] Concomitant mandibular advancement or autorotation of the mandible with maxillary osteotomy is also important in determining the extent of chin implant migration into bone and the percentage of augmentation relative to implant thickness (Fig. 29–38A to E).

Peled and colleagues[345] placed silicone implants in the nasal, cheek, and chin areas of children with the Down syndrome to improve facial appearance. Clinical and radiologic follow-up evaluation revealed significant crater-like bone resorption in the mandibular symphysis in 75 per cent of the cases. All of these implants were removed, and the bone showed regrowth to the presurgical state. No sign of bone damage was present in the malar or nasal area.

Pressure on chin implants placed too high over the soft alveolar bone may cause root resorption. Skin slough is a rare complication caused by a prolonged tight immobilization pressure bandage over implants. Rejection of the implant, a rare

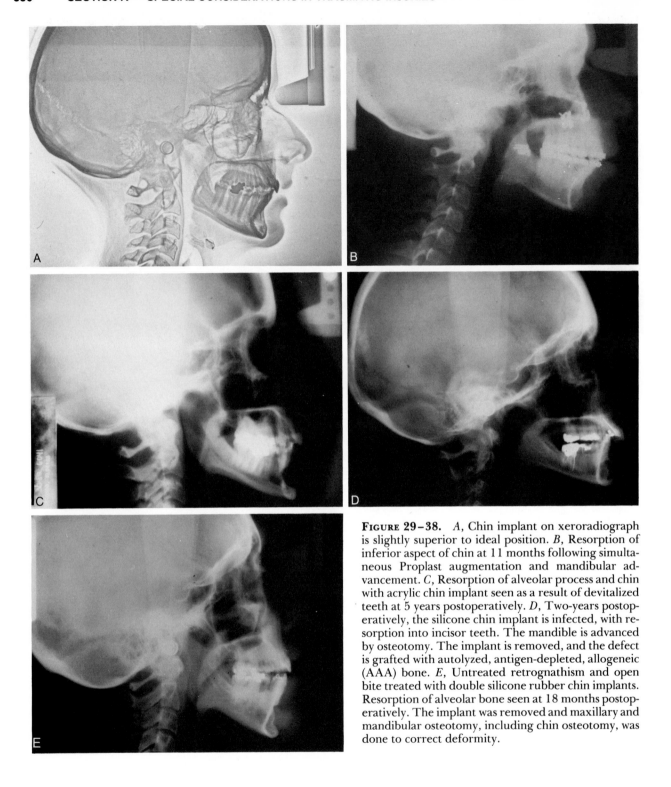

FIGURE 29–38. *A*, Chin implant on xeroradiograph is slightly superior to ideal position. *B*, Resorption of inferior aspect of chin at 11 months following simultaneous Proplast augmentation and mandibular advancement. *C*, Resorption of alveolar process and chin with acrylic chin implant seen as a result of devitalized teeth at 5 years postoperatively. *D*, Two-years postoperatively, the silicone chin implant is infected, with resorption into incisor teeth. The mandible is advanced by osteotomy. The implant is removed, and the defect is grafted with autolyzed, antigen-depleted, allogeneic (AAA) bone. *E*, Untreated retrognathism and open bite treated with double silicone rubber chin implants. Resorption of alveolar bone seen at 18 months postoperatively. The implant was removed and maxillary and mandibular osteotomy, including chin osteotomy, was done to correct deformity.

occurrence, is due to either hematoma or infection. Risk of rejection can be minimized by meticulous attention to hemostasis, aseptic techniques, prophylactic antibiotics, and detailed closure, particularly if the intraoral route is used. Late removal of implants is usually related to the size of the implant, activity of surrounding musculature, failure of the implant to undergo fixation to surrounding tissues, and bone resorption.

Insertion of chin implants is via either the intraoral or the extraoral route. Most surgeons report the same or a slightly higher rate of infection and extrusion when the implants are placed through the intraoral route. The extraoral approach is easier to perform and produces less postoperative discomfort; however, the cosmetically noticeable smaller incision offers limited exposure.

Recent reports have attempted to define factors affecting the long-term stability of Proplast chin augmentation. In an early study by Kent and Westfall, 94 per cent of 150 patients received chin and zygomatic implants through the intraoral route.[151] All implants were placed subperiosteally and fixed to either underlying bone or overlying soft tissue by resorbable sutures. Serial cephalograms in patients who had undergone chin augmentation and who were followed for up to 96 months were measured for changes in implant thickness, overlying soft tissue thickness, superior implant migration, and posterior implant migration into bone.

The thickness of the chin implants was 98 to 100 per cent of the original thickness. The superior migration of the implant material was not found to be clinically significant except in some patients with concomitant mandibular advancement or vertical maxillary excess.[151] In these patients, posterior migration into bone, the primary clinical concern of all types of implant materials, was greater in those undergoing mandibular advancement and in those with uncorrected skeletal open bite or vertical maxillary excess (Fig. 29–38E). Increasing soft tissue tension in patients who have undergone mandibular advancement osteotomies or correction of vertical maxillary excess or open bite would account for most cases of alloplastic migration into the chin. Soft tissue tension may also occur from inadequate pocket preparation, failure to detach or release periosteum along the inferior border, oversized implants, scarring from trauma or infection, lip incompetence, and coexisting dentofacial deformities. Placement of implants directly over the pogonion—the most dense bone over the symphysis—rather than over the alveolar process would limit migration of implant material into bone. However, postoperative loss of chin contour is due to the thinning of overlying soft tissue as well as to the posterior migration of the implant into bone.[151] This information is significant to the clinician, since, for example, selection of a 10-mm implant would produce a 7-mm augmentation over the long term.

Chin Augmentation: Operative Technique

Intraoral Technique. Intraoral techniques and the shapes of Proplast chin implants were developed by Kent in 1972.[151,161,162,179] The chin implants, ranging in size from 6 to 12 mm, wrap around the symphysis, tapering just below the mental foramen (Fig. 29–39A). Freeman chin implants, similar in shape, are dimpled at the midline.[174] The following technique, specific for Proplast, generally applies to other implants. Genioplasty may be performed with the patient under local anesthesia and sedation or with the patient under general anesthesia. The mouth is prepared with a nonsoap povidone-iodine (Betadine) wash followed by saline irrigation. A local anesthetic with epinephrine is injected over the mandibular symphysis and inferior border area for hemostasis. A horizontal incision, 1-inch long or one-half the implant length, is made through the mucosa midway between the depth of the vestibule and the wet line of the lower lip. The body of the mentalis muscle is sharply incised, leaving sufficient bulk of the muscle attached to the mandible for a two-layer closure. The periosteum is incised immediately above the most prominent aspect of the symphysis (the pogonion). This incision is carried obliquely posterior to the inferior border below the cuspid-premolar roots. Care is taken to avoid and protect branches of the mental nerve. There should be no reflection of muscle or periosteum over the alveolar process. Intact soft tissues in this area minimize the superior movement of the implant toward the vestibule. Generous periosteal stripping over the symphysis and *beneath* the inferior border to the molar region is essential to develop adequate pocket size and permit submental tissue advancement (Fig. 29–39B). Vertical relieving incisions through the periosteum are occasionally needed in large advancements, such as when implants are placed over an advanced horizontal osteotomy segment (Fig. 29–39C and D). The submental tissues are now easily advanced to permit closure over the implant without tension. The implant is impregnated with antibiotic solution and trimmed before preliminary insertion. Concentrated antibiotic impregnation of all facial Proplast is best accomplished by placing the implant in a large (60-ml or larger) irrigation syringe with an adequate amount of sterile antibiotic solution (e.g., 1 g of cephalosporin in 100 ml of normal saline) to cover the implant (Fig. 29–39E). The

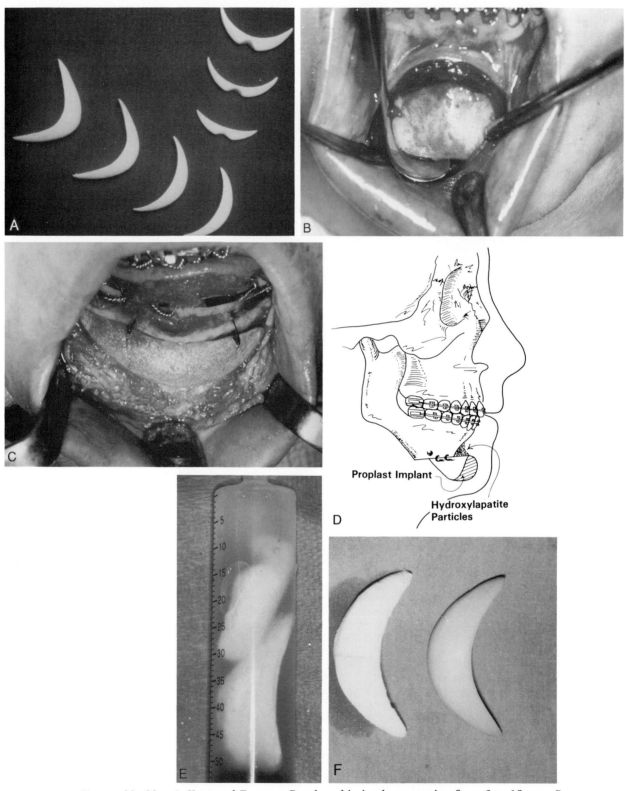

FIGURE 29–39. *A,* Kent and Freeman Proplast chin implants ranging from 6 to 12 mm. *B,* Reflection of periosteum over symphysis and beneath inferior border. *C, D,* Combination of Proplast implant with horizontal osteotomy for large advancement of chin. *E,* Vacuum impregnation of Proplast implants.

Illustration continued on opposite page.

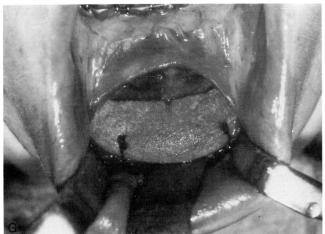
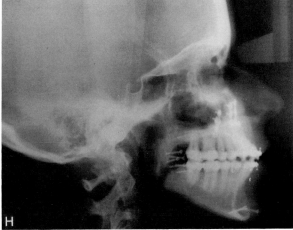
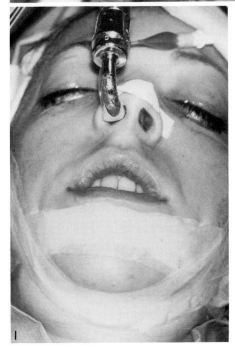

FIGURE 29–39. *Continued.* *F–H,* Chin implant with silicone rubber sizer secured with either *G,* sutures or *H,* screws. *I,* Pressure dressing following chin implantation.

syringe is held in a vertical position with the open end pointed up. The implant, along with an air bubble, will now be at the open end of the syringe. All air is expelled from the syringe. The open end of the syringe is occluded with the finger, and the plunger is retracted several times, creating a vacuum. Air is again expelled from the syringe, and the above process is repeated until no further air bubbles are elicited from the implant. The implant will sink when full of solution. The midline of the implant is marked with a scalpel to ensure symmetry. Silicone sizers may be used to determine the extent of chin augmentation and to minimize the handling of Proplast (Fig. 29–39F). To minimize bone resorption, the implant is centered over or slightly below the pogonion. For the best stabilization, the implant is placed subperiosteally. Then 2–0 or 3–0 polyglycolic acid suture or nonresorbable suture or wire is passed through a hole, made at the inferior border midline and 1.5 cm on each side of the midline, and through the implant for stabilization (Fig. 29–39G). Two or three bone screws may also be used (Fig. 29–39H).

Antibiotic wash (1 g of cephalosporin in 1000 ml of saline) is used throughout the procedure. A final antibiotic wash is usually done once the implant is placed, with the more concentrated solution used in vacuum impregnation. Careful approximation of muscle, followed by placement of closely interrupted sutures through the mucosa, is necessary to prevent postoperative asymmetric chin animation, chin droop, or dehiscence or infection. One-half-inch tape over gauze is placed horizontally along the labiomental fold and vertically beneath the chin for 5 days to help ensure the final position of the implant and to prevent hematoma formation (Fig. 29–39I). Systemic antibiotics are used for 10 days. Good oral hygiene measures are necessary during the immediate postoperative period (Fig. 29–40A to E).

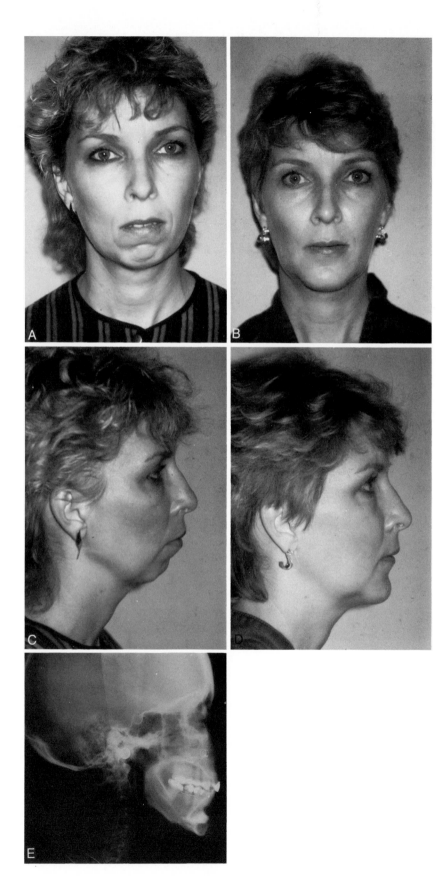

FIGURE 29–40. *A*, Preoperative and *B*, postoperative full-face views, and *C*, *D*, profile views with *E*, 5-year postoperative cephalogram of chin implant placed over horizontal osteotomy segment and HA particles to soften labiomental crease.

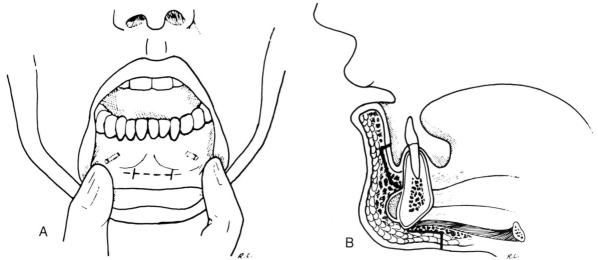

FIGURE 29–41. *A*, Location of intraoral incision on lip side of vestibule. *B*, Intraoral and extraoral dissection to the mandibular symphysis.

Extraoral Technique. Genioplasty by the extraoral submental approach may also be performed with the patient under local anesthesia and sedation or with the patient under general anesthesia. Local anesthetic with epinephrine is injected in the mandibular symphysis area and inferior border area for hemostasis. A short, curved incision, approximately 1 inch, is made through the skin and subcutaneous fat in the submental region, parallel and slightly posterior to the inferior border of the symphysis (Fig. 29–41*A* and *B*). The flap is undermined to the outer superior aspect of the inferior border, where muscle and periosteum are incised and reflected to create a subperiosteal pocket over the symphysis. The remainder of the technique is similar to that used for the placement of the implant through an intraoral incision.

The Deficient Mandibular Angle and Inferior Border

Mandibular angle and border deficiency occurs in congenital and developmental abnormalities such as hemifacial microsomia, micrognathism, steep mandibular plane angles with mandibular retrognathism, maxillary excess, and open bite (Fig. 29–42*A* to *C*). Acquired deficiencies most commonly occur after trauma to or surgery on the ramus and condyle. Proximal segment rotation in either instance with or without backward rotation of the body of the mandible commonly leaves a vertical and lateral deficit at the angle. Contour correction is possible through the intraoral route but is more frequently performed with the extraoral submandibular or retromandibular technique (Fig. 29–43*A* to *H*).

Mandibular ramus angle and inferior border implants made of preformed HA and Proplast or customized implants of silicone rubber and Proplast fabricated from facial moulage or three-dimensional imaging techniques are used for correction of traumatic and congenital defects in these areas as well (Figs. 29–44*A* to *E* and 29–45*A* to *K*).

Mandibular Angle Augmentation: Operative Technique

Intraoral Technique. Mandibular angle augmentations are performed with the patient under local or general anesthesia. A povidone-iodine (Betadine) wash similar to that described for chin or zygomatic augmentation is done. Epinephrine is injected over the lateral aspect and angle of the ramus. A vertical incision identical with that used for a vertical ramus osteotomy is made in the buccal sulcus. The incision is carried obliquely down to bone, contacting it along the anterior border of the ramus. The periosteum is

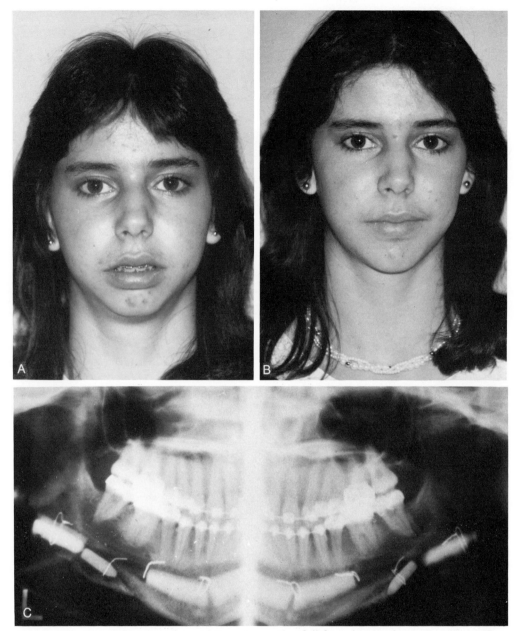

FIGURE 29–42. *A,* Preoperative and *B,* postoperative full-face views and *C,* panoramic radiograph showing augmentation of the entire inferior border with HA blocks.

reflected to the inferior border, the posterior border, and superiorly to the height of the defect. A curved elevator is used to clear the soft tissue off the posterior and inferior border and the angle of the mandible. Release of the pterygoid-masseter sling may be necessary for inferior extension of the implant. Careful undermining of the sling with a long, curved hemostat will allow for incision of these fibers, protecting the facial nerve (Fig. 29–46).

On the basis of preoperative clinical assessment, with the use of measurements from the patient, photographs, cephalograms, panoramic radiographs, or three-dimensional imaging, the implant thickness is selected. The implant is inserted into the pocket to widen and vertically extend the mandibular angle. The implant must sit precisely on bone, and the anterior edges should be feathered to avoid being palpable. Extension toward the mental foramen is possible, but augmentation is difficult below the mental nerve when using the angle implant. The implant is vacuum impregnated with antibiotic solution, as previously described for chin and zygomatic implants. Bone screws are placed obliquely through the implant and the borders and angle of the mandible to secure the implant. Frequent comparison with the opposite angle to ensure symmetry is

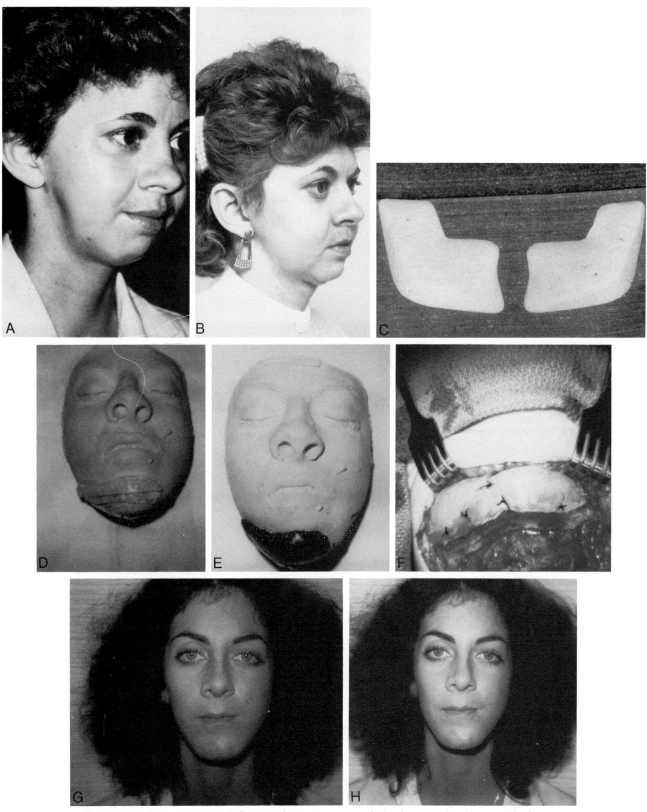

FIGURE 29–43. *A,* Angle deficiency from resorption following mandibular condyle fracture and ramus osteotomies. *B, C,* Correction of angle deficiency with HA Proplast Whitaker angle implants. In another patient correction of right inferior border of mandible with a deformity secondary to condylar hyperplasia. *D,* Wax-up on moulage. *E,* RTV silicone rubber prosthesis. *F,* Intraoperative view of silicone rubber augmentation through extraoral approach. *G,* Preoperative view and *H,* postoperative view following extraoral placement of prosthesis and Le Fort I osteotomy and mandibular osteotomy. (*D–H* courtesy of Dr. T. William Evans, Columbus, OH.)

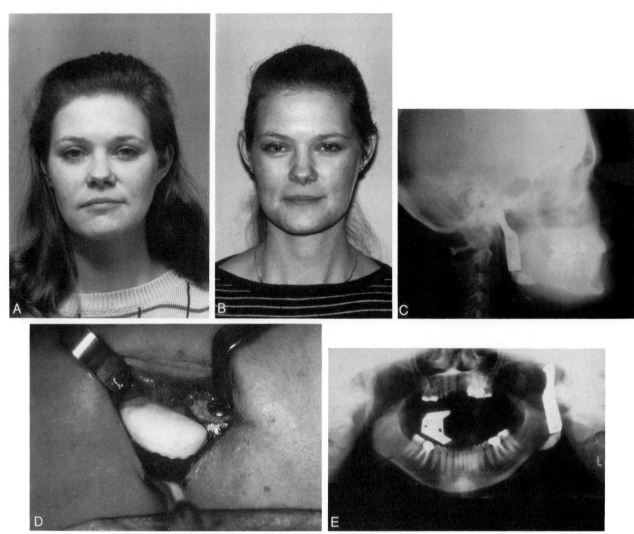

FIGURE 29–44.   **Patient with unilateral trauma to the mandibular condyle followed by condylar resorption, loss of ramus vertical dimension, and ankylosis.**   *A*, Preoperative and *B*, postoperative full-face photographs. *C*, Postoperative cephalogram after reconstruction with total joint prosthesis and HA block wired to the angle. *D*, Removal of wires over HA block demonstrating bony union to dense HA. *E*, Five-year post operative panoramic radiograph with 45-mm opening.

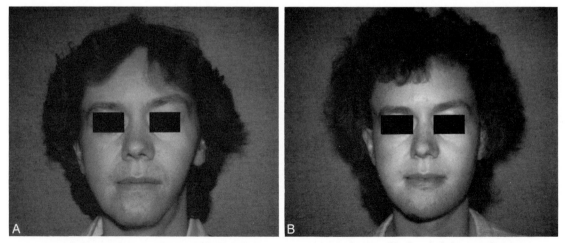

FIGURE 29–45.   *A*, Preoperative and *B*, postoperative left mandibular deficiency of ramus, angle, body, inferior border, and chin.

Illustration continued on opposite page.

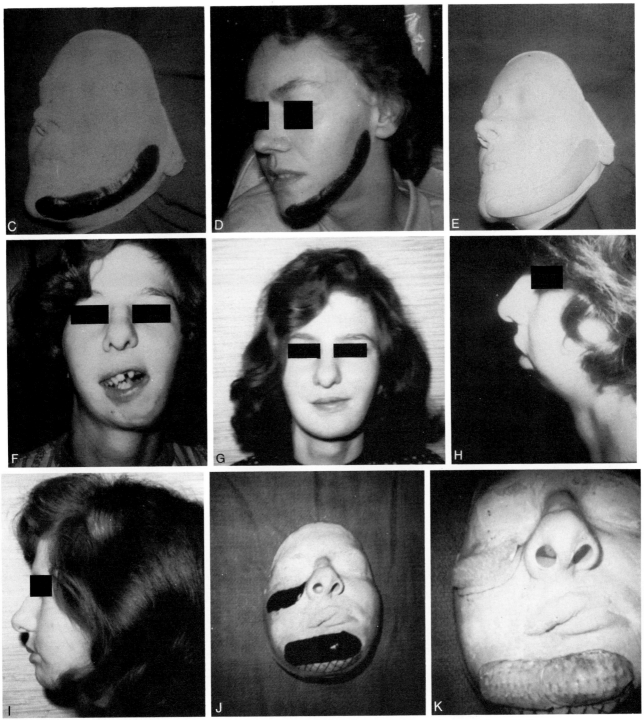

FIGURE 29–45. *Continued.*   *C, D,* Wax-up of deformity on facial moulage and face. *E,* Custom silicone rubber implant. *F,* Preoperative and *G,* postoperative views of another patient with severe right hemifacial hypertrophy and mandibular micrognathism corrected by facial bone osteotomies and implants. *H,* Preoperative and *I,* postoperative profile views. *J, K,* Wax-up and custom silicone rubber implants to correct chin and malar deficiencies. (Courtesy of Dr. T. William Evans, Columbus, OH.)

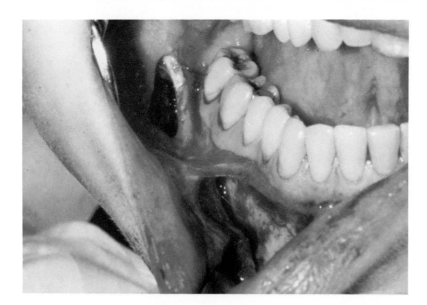

Figure 29–46. Intraoral angle, inferior border, and parasymphyseal dissection for alloplastic augmentation.

important. Closure and postoperative management are handled as described for chin and zygomatic augmentation.

Extraoral Technique. With the patient under general anesthesia, the entire face is prepared and draped, exposing the lobe of the ear and the commissure of the mouth to allow for maintenance of anatomic orientation as well as observation of facial nerve stimulation. The patient is evaluated with the head in a straight upright position. The mandibular angle and inferior border are drawn on the face, and the submandibular incision line is marked in a natural skinfold one to two fingerbreadths below the area of the mandible that needs to be exposed. Salivary contamination from the mouth is avoided by the use of parasympatholytic agents and gauze placed in the buccal and labial vestibule.

Local anesthetic solution with epinephrine is injected for hemostasis immediately subcutaneous to the incision line. An incision of necessary length for implant placement is made to the platysma muscle. The platysma is divided with a mosquito hemostat to the superficial layer of the deep cervical fascia. The marginal mandibular branches of the facial nerve are identified at this level with the use of a nerve stimulator. The cervical fascia is incised and retracted superiorly. The masseter muscle and periosteum are then exposed and incised at the inferior border level. The facial artery and vein are identified and ligated if necessary. By stretching the elements of the pterygomasseteric sling medially and laterally to the angle and inferior border, a No. 15 blade can be used to divide this directly to the inferior border. Subperiosteal dissection will expose the posterior border, angle, lateral ramus, and posterior mandibular body through this incision. The implant is then impregnated or soaked with antibiotic solution and placed over the mandible, as described previously with the intraoral technique. Augmentation done anteriorly below the mental foramen is easier with this approach. Bone screws are used to secure the implant. If the retromandibular approach is used, the skin incision is centered slightly below or at the angle of the mandible, curving behind the angle. The dissection at its most posterior limit is along the level of the parotid-masseteric fascia. Dissection through the deep cervical fascia is done with a sharp hemostat and a nerve stimulator. The incision at this level and subsequently through the masseter is at or slightly above the angle of the mandible and is frequently between the buccal and mandibular branches of the facial nerve.

Closure of the pterygomasseteric sling may not be possible or desirable if the inferior border has been extended. The platysma is reidentified and closed, if possible, and the skin is approximated in routine fashion.

Alveolar Ridge Reconstruction

The principles and techniques of reconstructing the alveolar ridge of the maxilla and mandible after trauma are described in *Preprosthetic Oral and Maxillofacial Surgery;* techniques include soft and hard tissue grafting, osteotomies, dental implants,

ALVEOLAR RIDGE RECONSTRUCTION

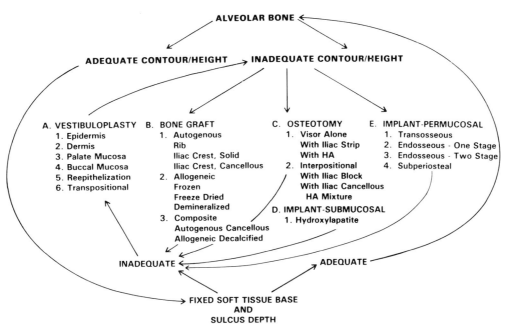

FIGURE 29–47.   Methods to reconstruct the deficient alveolar ridge.

bone plates, and use of HA.[346] The use of biomaterials is limited to the last three methods. Bone plates are described in Chapter 33 of this text. HA applications for reconstruction of the traumatic or avulsed ridge follow the same guidelines as reconstruction of the atrophic alveolar ridge.

A variety of procedures can be used to reconstruct the alveolar ridge. The indications for surgery are based on the remaining ridge height and contour and the adequacy of the fixed soft tissue base and sulcus depth (Fig. 29–47). Also important in the mandible is the resistance to fracture.

Selection of a corrective procedure should not be determined by any specific ridge height measurement but rather by the degree and type of anatomic deficiency. Vestibuloplasty procedures, such as the buccal and labial sulcus extensions with or without skin, dermis, or mucosal grafting, as well as lowering of the floor of the mouth, are helpful only if there is adequate alveolar ridge height and convex ridge form. Complete resorption of the soft alveolar bone to dense basilar bone would contraindicate soft tissue vestibuloplasty and indicate hard tissue augmentation. Those methods to increase alveolar ridge height and retention of dentures in the past included onlay bone grafting and inlay or interpositional bone grafting as well as the use of metallic dental implants.

Onlay bone grafts in the form of rib and iliac crest grafts with or without a vascularized pedicle can produce a tremendous increase in ridge height but have serious drawbacks.[347] Grafted bone may not produce a uniformly level ridge because its form is poor and resorption is unpredictable.[348] At least 40 to 60 per cent of grafted bone may be resorbed during the first 1 to 2 years and 60 to 100 per cent by the end of 3 to 5 years.[349-351] The success of these grafts is that they add basal bulk or horizontal width to a thin mandible or maxilla. Resorption of onlay bone grafts is such a serious problem that patients are faced with a series of multiple denture relines, many weeks and months without dentures, an increased expense over other techniques, and possible donor site complications, such as pneumothorax and prolonged hip pain. Allogeneic bone and demineralized bone eliminate the problem of donor site complications, but problems of infection from dehiscence, varying degrees of resorption, and, again, multiple denture problems (such as numerous relines, discomfort, and time without dentures) are similar to those experienced with autogenous grafts.[352] Vestibuloplasties, usually necessary to provide a firm, fixed soft tissue covering over grafted bone, are generally not possible for 4 to 6 months, until revascularization of the bone graft and formation of a viable periosteum occur.

Visor and interpositional osteotomy techniques with grafts are an improvement over onlay bone grafting, with less postoperative resorption and loss of ridge height and contour.[353,354] However, donor site morbidity, limited vertical height, lateral resorption or deficiency (visor), frequent relines, and prolonged periods of inability to wear a denture are still significant disadvantages.

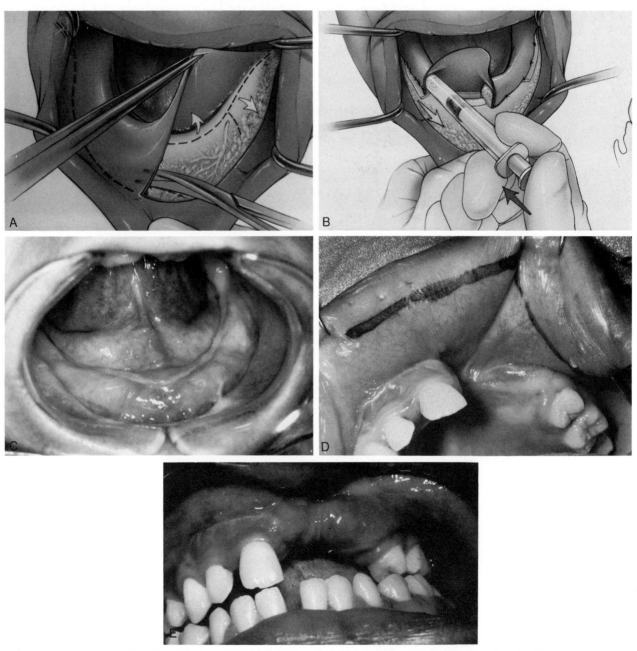

FIGURE 29–48.   Mucosal flap technique.   *A*, Mucosal flap, with the incision just inside the lower lip and cheek, is raised from the retromolar areas bilaterally to the lingual aspect of the ridge crest. The periosteum is incised and reflected as indicated. *B*, Closure of mucosal flap as HA is injected. *C*, Postoperative result. *D*, Mucosal flap procedure used for reconstruction of anterior maxillary traumatic defect. *E*, Postoperative result.

Clinical trials using particulate forms of HA for ridge augmentation were initiated at Louisiana State University in 1978. After evaluating atrophic ridge types and a variety of surgical techniques, an alveolar ridge classification (Classes I to IV) based on the severity of the deficient mandibular and maxillary alveolar ridges was developed by Kent to standardize and determine surgical approaches, material usage, and the clinical performance of HA under denture function.[355-357] The material was placed alone or in combination with finely crushed autogenous cancellous bone via a subperiosteal tunneling technique to obtain improvement in alveolar ridge height and form. Results on more than 300 patients from 1978 to 1984 have shown the material to be simple, effective bone substitute to improve ridge height and form for denture function.[346,355-357] An estimated 20,000 patients in the United States received HA ridge augmentation between 1982 and 1984.

Tunneling techniques, open procedures, tissue-expanding techniques, and HA used with interpositional osteotomies have been proposed to augment the alveolar ridge[211,356-366] (Figs. 29–48 to 29–51). The literature describing these techniques, including the role of splints and so on, as well as supporting animal studies on both dense and porous particles and blocks, is voluminous. After 1984, the incidence of total alveolar ridge augmentation with HA dramatically declined as the success of osteointegrated implants provided improved methods of denture retention with fewer complications. Complications after total HA augmentation include principally migration and displacement of particles from overfill and containment problems.[357] Soft tissue pain, irregular ridge form, mental nerve dysesthesia, and denture instability are additional problems. The current management of deficient alveolar ridge is with dental implants placed anteriorly in the mandible with or without posterior

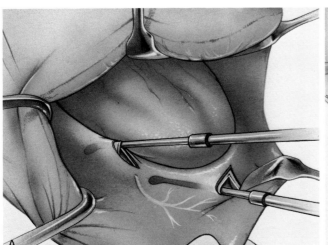

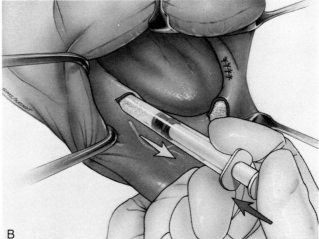

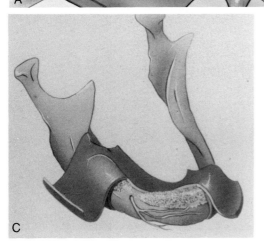

FIGURE 29–49.   *A*, Tunneling technique for mandibular HA ridge augmentation. Combined mucosal tunneling with periosteal elevation through vertical midline and posterior crestal incisions to avoid mental nerve exposure. *B*, Injection of HA. *C*, HA not deposited in area of mental nerve.

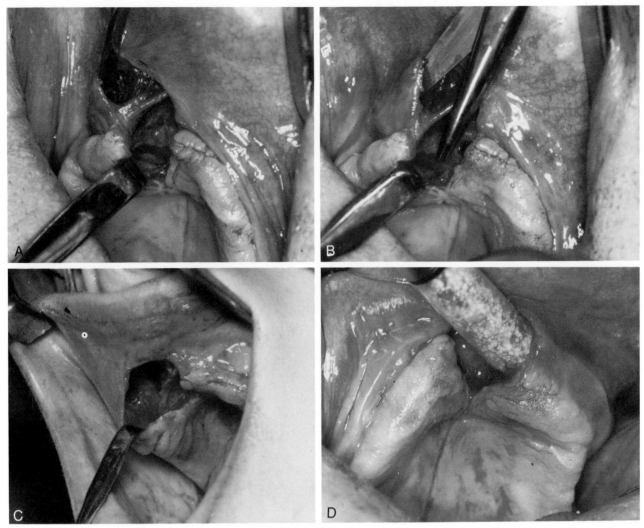

FIGURE 29–50. *A,* Technique for HA reconstruction of Class IV maxillary deficiency. Mucosal dissection and subperiosteal reflection have been done. *B,* Periosteum cut at crestal tissue junction. *C, D,* HA injected in large tissue pocket.

HA[367,368] (Figs. 29–52 and 29–53). Maxillary deficiency is corrected primarily by HA or bone grafts, or both, placed anteriorly, with implants placed posteriorly through sinus grafting procedures[369] (Fig. 29–54*A* and *B*). Suffice it to say, HA particles are primarily used only in small amounts through simple techniques for ridge atrophy. Open procedures utilizing flaps and tunneling techniques are recommended for major traumatic defects.[358]

Recent studies by Mehlisch and colleagues and by Collins have evaluated alveolar ridge augmentation material composed of purified fibrillar collagen and particulate HA.[214,370] In a study of 77 patients and 99 reconstructed ridges, this material provided superior placement and ease of manipulation.[214] Particle migration, displacement, or loss of ridge height was rare. Moreover, the rapid development of rigid firmness and stability allowed for the loading of dentures within 3 to 6 weeks. Prosthodontistic evaluations and surveys of satisfaction on the part of the patient showed great satisfaction with denture fit, comfort, aesthetics, speech, and ability to masticate.

Block and Kent have studied augmentation with HA combined with demineralized bone.[204,215] Thirty mongrel dogs underwent ridge augmentation with 3 ml of HA alone (HAO), HA combined with autogenous bone (HAB), or HA combined with demineralized bone (HAD). Bone was not found in the HAO-augmented ridges

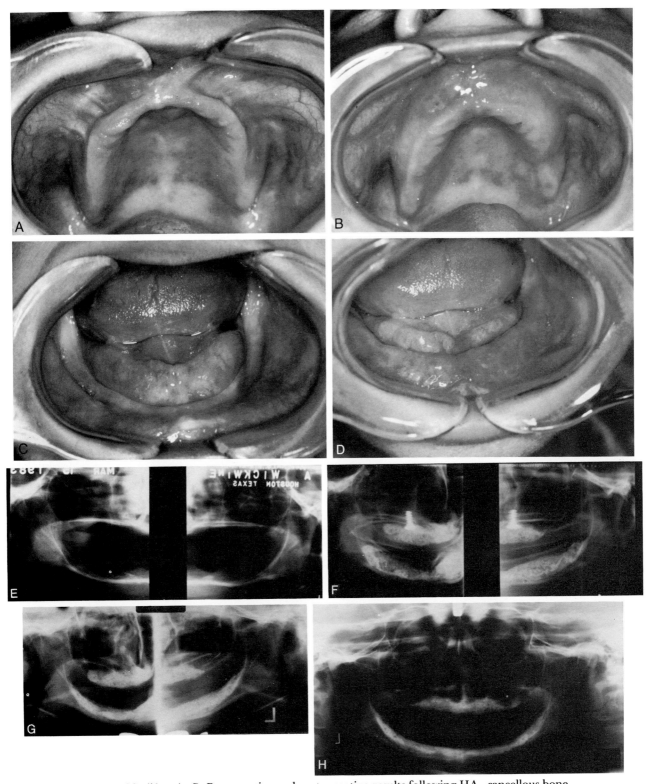

Figure 29–51. *A–D,* Preoperative and postoperative results following HA–cancellous bone reconstruction of Class IV maxillary and mandibular deficiencies. *E–H,* Preoperative, immediate postoperative, 6-month postoperative, and 6-year postoperative panoramic radiographs of HA–cancellous bone reconstruction of Class IV maxillary and mandibular deficiencies.

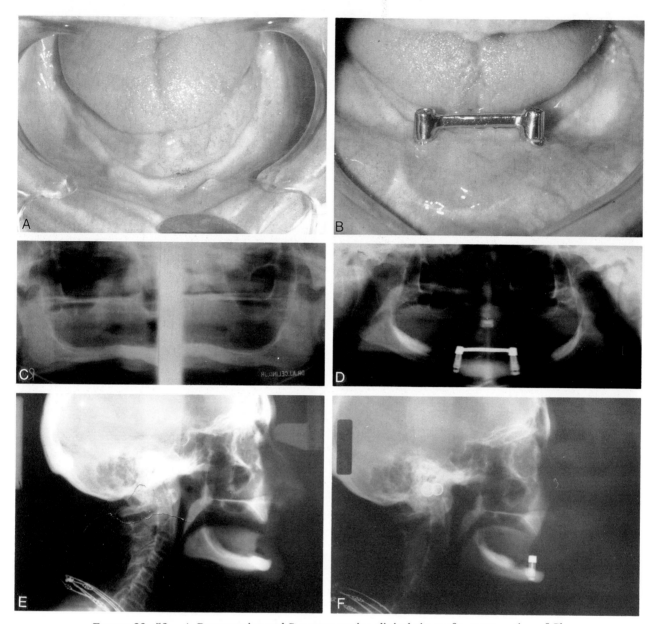

FIGURE 29-52.   *A,* Preoperative and *B,* postoperative clinical views of reconstruction of Class IV mandibular deficiency with HA-coated implants and posterior HA. *C,* Preoperative and *D,* postoperative panoramic radiographs of reconstruction with HA-coated implants and posterior HA. *E,* Preoperative and *F,* postoperative cephalometric radiographs.

through 52 weeks, bone was found in the HAB-augmented ridges by 12 weeks (Fig. 29-55*A*), and the HAD-augmented ridges showed bone formation after 26 weeks (Fig. 29-55*B* and *C*). This study demonstrates that demineralized bone can induce osteogenesis within the HA-augmented ridge in dogs, but it is delayed when compared with HAB augmentations.

Radiographic studies by Kent and associates and by Block have analyzed the postoperative maintenance of ridge height augmentation and have also elucidated differences between Class III and IV atrophic ridges with respect to the use of HA alone and HA combined with autogenous bone.[201,202,205] Those reports show that very good maintenance was found to be in excess of 90 per cent of the original augmentation height and that there was no statistically significant difference between the results with HA alone and the results with HA and bone augmentation. Clinically, this is an important observation, since the decrease in ridge height following the use of

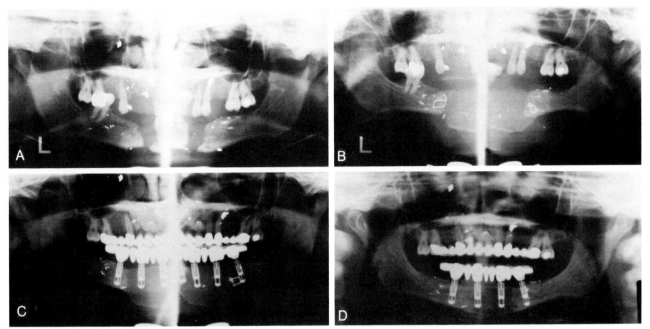

FIGURE 29–53. *A*, Radiograph of gunshot wound that destroyed entire symphysis. *B*, Reconstruction of symphysis with vascularized osteomyocutaneous iliac crest graft. *C*, HA-coated implants placed 2 months following reconstruction. *D*, Five-year result.

onlay autogenous bone grafts alone has been approximately 60 per cent through 2 years of follow-up, with increasing resorption revealed in longer follow-up studies.

Preliminary studies by Zide and coworkers exploring the biomechanical behavior of different ratios of autogenous bone and HA used to correct major continuity defects suggest that ratios of 1:4 to 1:1 (HA to autogenous bone) yield strength comparable to that of autogenous grafts alone up to 6 months in dog mandibles.[371] Since autogenous bone grafts for the reconstruction of continuity defects are known to undergo significant postoperative resorption, the use of HA in these grafts may limit the bone resorption because of the nonresorbability of HA and its direct biomechanical influence on bone, which may minimize bone resorption as a result of biologic apatite attachment.

Porous HA particles and blocks (Interpore 200) have been used for augmentation of atrophic residual mandibular ridges with clinical and radiographic follow-up for at least 2 years (Fig. 29–56*A* and *B*). Hupp's and McKenna's study of 15 patients showed no evidence of migration or resorption of the blocks.[210] However, most

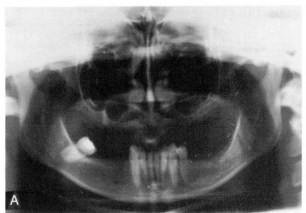
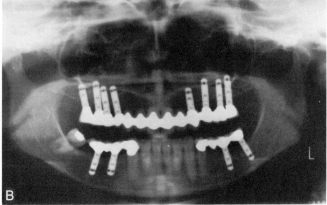

FIGURE 29–54. **Sinus bone graft with Ha-coated implants.** *A*, Preoperative and *B*, 3-year postoperative radiographs.

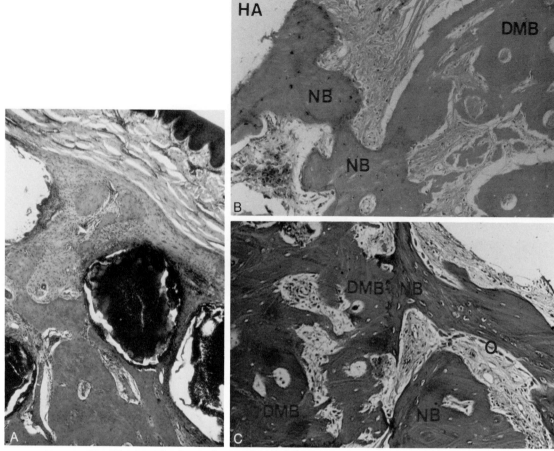

FIGURE 29–55. *A*, Histology of HA mixed with autogenous iliac cancellous bone in a dog's alveolar ridge at 12 weeks. *B, C,* Histology of HA mixed with demineralized bone in a dog's alveolar ridge at 26 weeks. In *B*, new bone (NB) is seen on the ghost of a HA particle, arising from demineralized bone (DMB). In *C*, the center of the ridge shows osteoblastic (O) activity producing new bone (NB) from the surface of demineralized bone (DMB).

suffered complications with ulcerations over the blocks, persistent exposure, suture line dehiscence leading to exposure infections, and chronic pain. Skin grafts took only partially, and 37 of the original 45 blocks required complete removal.[210] Similar findings have been reported by Piecuch and colleagues[372] and by Peterson.[373]

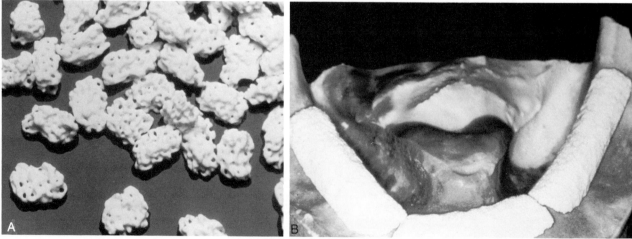

FIGURE 29–56. *A*, Porous, particulate HA (Interpore 200) for ridge reconstruction. *B*, Interpore 200 blocks contoured for alveolar ridge reconstruction.

Facial Bone Reconstruction Using Hydroxylapatite

Traditionally, autogenous and homogenous corticocancellous bone grafts have been inlayed or onlayed to enhance stability and improve function and cosmetics with orthognathic, craniofacial, and other reconstructive procedures. The desire to avoid a second surgical site as well as to reduce operating time and risk of infection and relapse has led to the development and use of dense HA blocks and particles. A discussion on HA in these procedures is included, since the biologic principles of osteotomies for secondary repair of trauma defects are no different.

Prospective clinical trials were performed by Kent and colleagues from 1982 to 1985 to evaluate HA blocks and particles for use in orthognathic and reconstructive surgery.[206,207] The particles were dense HA, 20 to 40 mesh (Calcitite particles and Orthoblocks, Calcitek, Inc., Carlsbad, CA). When the need for containment of the particles was anticipated, a surgical splint was used, or microfibrillar collagen (Avitene, Aricon, Inc., Humacao, PR) or plaster of paris was added to the HA. The blocks consisted of textured, dense HA (TDH) (Calcitek, Inc.) in rectangular, triangular, trapezoidal, and curved shapes with a variety of dimensions for interpositional and onlay application in orthognathic and craniofacial surgery. Initially, they consisted of a dense HA ceramic with two opposing porous surfaces, 1 mm deep, containing pores 150 to 400 μm in diameter. The porous layers were reduced in depth to a "monolayer" of hemispherical cells, 100 to 300 μm in diameter, for initial grip, stabilization, and prevention of slippage while allowing positive displacement of two bone segments (Fig. 29–57A). When subsequent animal studies showed that a roughened, nonporous surface provided adequate mechanical stability, waffle texturing the surface of a dense block provided a greater gripping surface area for strong mechanical stability and bonding to bone than did a smooth surface (Fig. 29–57B). These textured, dense blocks were easily contoured in the operating room with medium-grit diamond burs, wedged in place, and, when necessary, transosseous encircling wires were used for stabilization. Bone plates were employed to facilitate the technique in 1984, late in the study.

Hydroxylapatite particles were placed in 43 patients in a total of 54 procedures.[206] Follow-up periods ranged from 4 to 40 months. The amounts of HA ranged from 3 to 75 g. Complications with the use of particles occurred exclusively in the primary reconstruction of large mandibular continuity defects, such as those occurring after hemimandibulectomy. In patients with continuity defects, the HA particles were mixed with autogenous bone, 1 g of HA to 4 cc of finely ground iliac cancellous

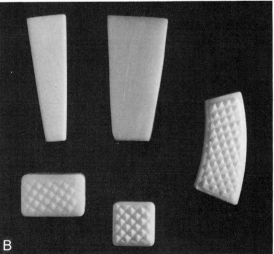

FIGURE 29–57. *A*, Porous/dense/porous Calcitite Orthoblock. *B*, Nonporous, waffled Calcitite Orthoblock.

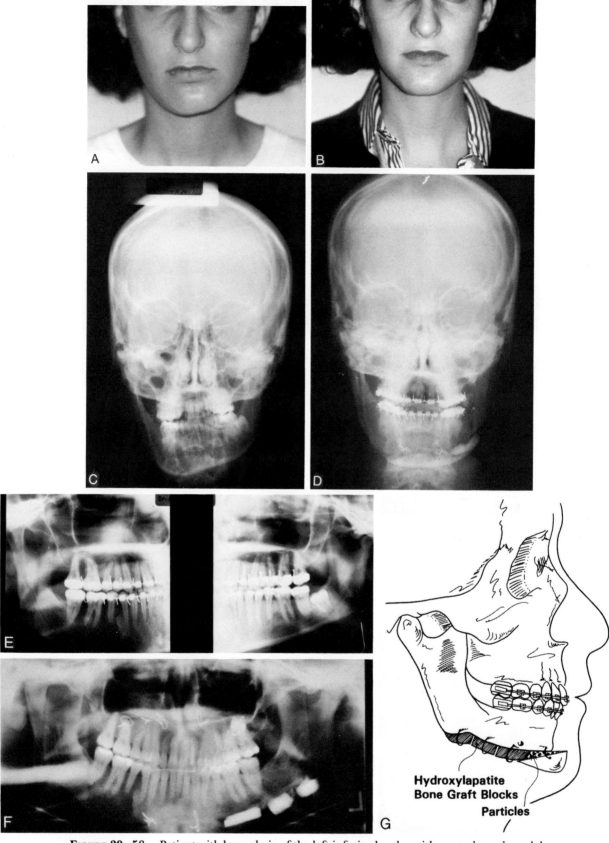

Hydroxylapatite Bone Graft Blocks

Particles

FIGURE 29–58. Patient with hypoplasia of the left inferior border with contralateral condylar hyperplasia. Le Fort I osteotomy, ramus osteotomies, genioplasty, and left inferior border augmentation with HA blocks. *A*, Preoperative PA radiograph. *B*, Postoperative PA radiograph. *C*, Preoperative panoramic radiograph. *D*, Postoperative panoramic radiograph. *E*, A combination of particles and blocks may be necessary to achieve a smooth contour. (Calcitek, Inc., Carlsbad, CA.)

bone chips, and were placed in titanium cribs. Intraoral dehiscence, with loss of some graft material, occurred in four patients. One hundred twenty blocks were placed in 55 patients with or without autogenous iliac crest bone grafts for orthognathic surgery procedures. Follow-up ranged from 4 to 36 months.

No TDH blocks were lost or removed because of undesirable tissue reaction or infection.[206] Four complications with the blocks were noted. Displacement during maxillomandibular fixation occurred in three patients with Le Fort I osteotomy. Long-term results and stability were not affected in two of these patients, but postoperative mobility required an additional grafting procedure in the third patient. In a fourth patient, dehiscence of the mucosa over one block placed at the pterygoid plate for maxillary advancement was visible 8 weeks postoperatively. The protruding portion of the block was trimmed, and the wound healed without further complication. Radiographic stability studies demonstrated relapse rate of 0 to 20 per cent, depend-

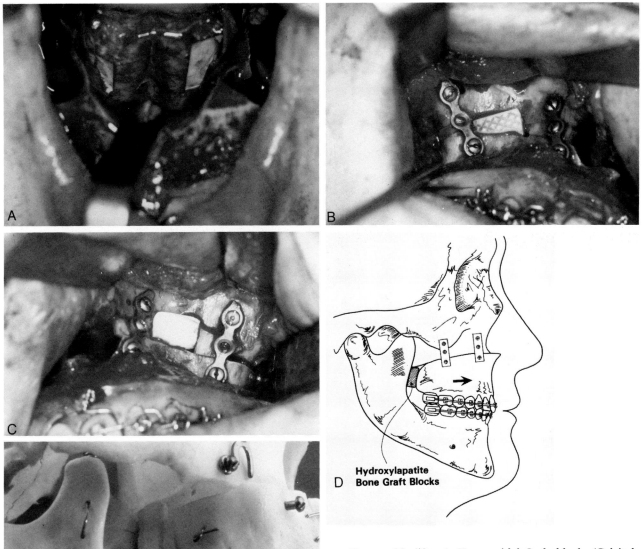

Figure 29–59. *A*, Trapezoidal Orthoblocks (Calcitek, Inc., Carlsbad, CA.) placed in parasagittal cuts to maintain transverse widening following a segmental Le Fort I osteotomy. *B, C*, Le Fort I downgraft using interpositional dense HA Orthoblocks. *D, E*, Le Fort I advancement using dense HA Orthoblocks wedged between the posterior maxillary wall and the pterygoid plates.

ing on the procedure, a significant improvement over that with autogenous bone grafting techniques. The fixation of Calcitite blocks was dictated by the clinical conditions. A waffled or ground surface block may be wedged, wired, or plated. Examples include inferior border onlays (Fig. 29–58*A* to *G*), widening of the palate (Fig. 29–59*A*), Le Fort I downgraft (Fig. 29–59*B* and *C*), Le Fort I advancement with or without step osteotomy at the zygomatic buttress (Fig. 29–59*D* and *E*), and genioplasty downgraft (Fig. 29–60*A* to *I*) and advancement (Fig. 29–61*A* to *D*). Our clinical experience strongly suggests that Calcitite HA blocks or particles adequately serve as space fillers and onlay graft substitutes, without retarding bone growth. Bone grafts along some areas of the osteotomy lines, however, are necessary whenever

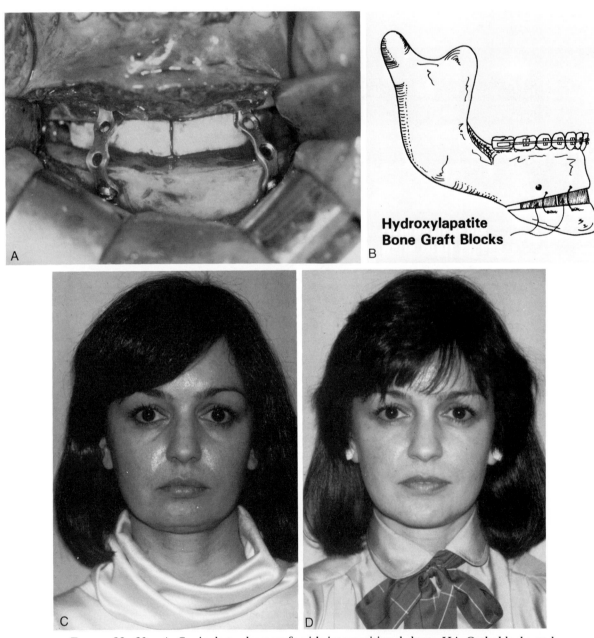

FIGURE 29–60. *A*, Genioplasty downgraft with interpositional dense HA Orthoblocks and plate fixation. *B*, Genioplasty downgraft with interpositional dense HA Orthoblocks with wire fixation. *C*, Preoperative and *D*, postoperative full-face views of a patient with vertical symphyseal hypoplasia and retrogenia.

Illustration continued on opposite page.

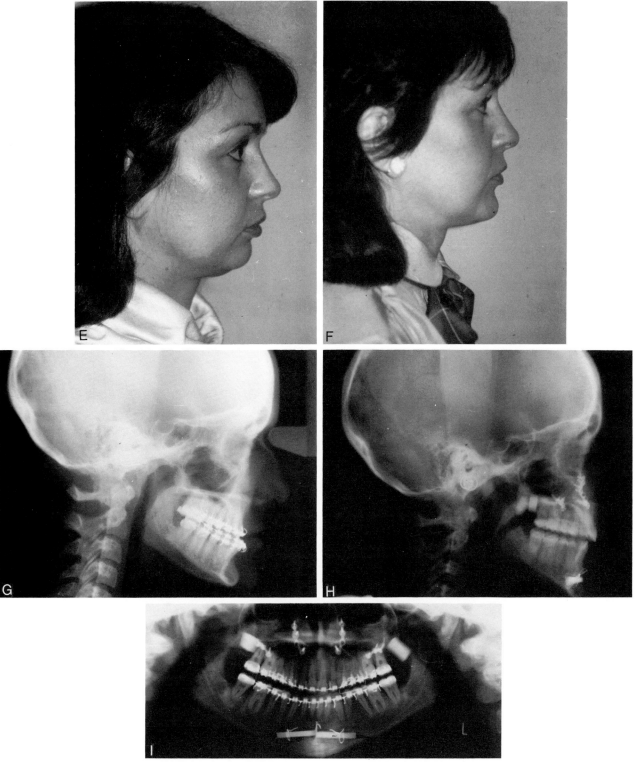

FIGURE 29–60. *Continued.* *E,* Preoperative and *F,* postoperative profile of vertical symphyseal hypoplasia. *G,* Preoperative and *H,* postoperative lateral radiographs of vertical facial deformity, including hypoplasia corrected with maxillary and mandibular osteotomies and a genioplasty downgraft with symphyseal interpositional dense HA Orthoblocks and wire fixation. *I,* Postoperative panoramic radiograph.

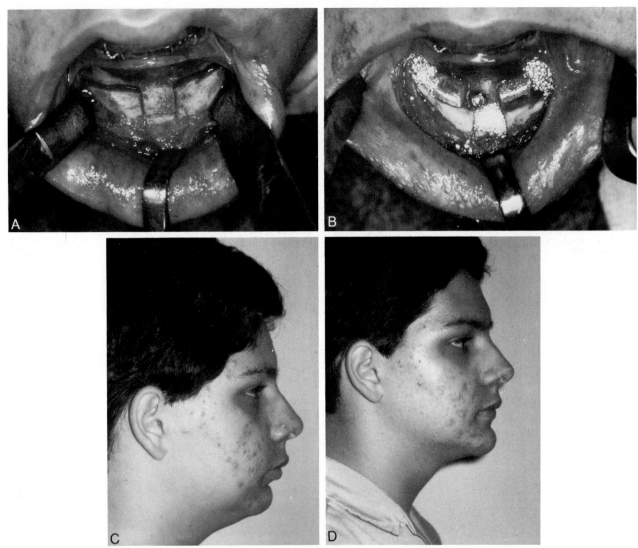

FIGURE 29–61.   *A*, Genioplasty downgraft and advancement with tenon and mortise technique. *B*, Porous/dense/porous HA Orthoblocks used to maintain the downgraft and particulate HA (Calcitite) used for establishing contour. *C*, Preoperative and *D*, postoperative profiles of genioplasty downgraft and advancement with HA block stabilization and HA particle contour fill.

functional stress is significant. For example, HA blocks alone may not be adequate for Le Fort I downgraft (Fig. 29–62*A* to *D*) or Le Fort III advancement (Fig. 29–63*A* to *F*), since it is not known if the ceramic will withstand long-term shear forces without the resiliency of autogenous bone. In contrast, Le Fort I advancement procedures in which bone-to-bone contact is present along some areas of the lateral maxillary walls do not require autogenous bone. Similarly, a downgrafted symphyseal border in genioplasty will do well with only an HA-bone interface, since shear forces are negligible.[206]

Wolford and associates[218] in 1987 also reported a prospective study in which HA was used as a bone graft substitute in orthognathic surgery (Fig. 29–64*A*). In Wolford's study, coralline porous HA was placed in 92 patients using 355 blocks (Interpore 200, Interpore, Inc., Irvine, CA). Follow-up ranged from 8 to 24 months, and a variety of maxillary, mandibular, and midface osteotomies were performed (Fig. 29–64*B* to *F*). Stabilization with wedging and wiring of the blocks was similar to that in Kent's study, except that fixation with bone screws was done whenever indicated. The incidence of infection was higher with porous HA owing to the exposure of porous blocks to nasal and sinus fluids. Because of the brittle nature of porous HA, rigid skeletal fixation was necessary to prevent transmission of masticatory forces and implant fracture during early phases of wound healing. Seventeen biopsies in nine patients who received porous HA blocks demonstrated 48.5 per cent HA matrix, 18.0 per cent bone ingrowth, and 33.5 per cent soft tissue or vascular space. The HA matrix surface area averaged 9.4 mm^2/mm^3, with 62.1 per cent of the surface covered by appositional bone ingrowth (Fig. 29–65A to D). The nine exposed implants contained connective tissue ingrowth only at their margins, with little or no bone present.[212]

Several factors determine the success of the HA bone graft substitute in orthognathic or reconstructive surgery. These factors include the nature of the hard tissue interface, the clinical indication for supplemental autogenous bone, the method of fixation, the duration of immobilization, the structural integrity and biomechanics of the material at the graft site, the incidence of complications, and the short- and long-term stability.

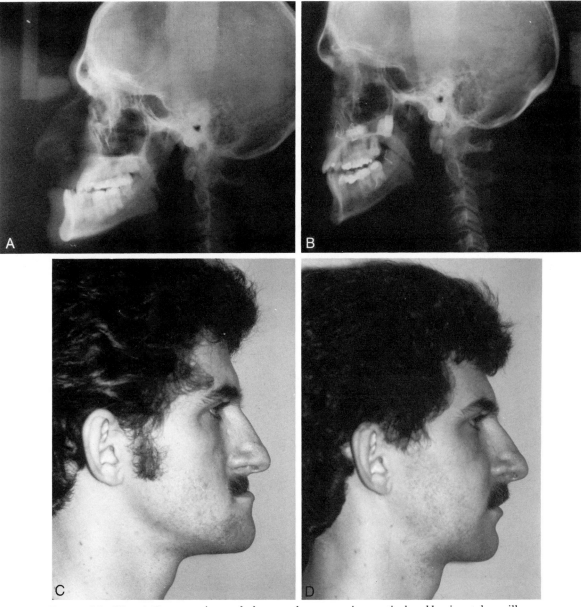

FIGURE 29–62.   *A*, Preoperative cephalogram demonstrating vertical and horizontal maxillary hypoplasia with mandibular prognathism. *B*, Five-year postoperative cephalogram following Le Fort I advancement and downgraft with autogenous iliac cancellous bone and HA blocks and mandibular set backs. *C*, Preoperative and *D*, 5-year postoperative profile views of corrected vertical and horizontal maxillary hypoplasia and mandibular prognathism.

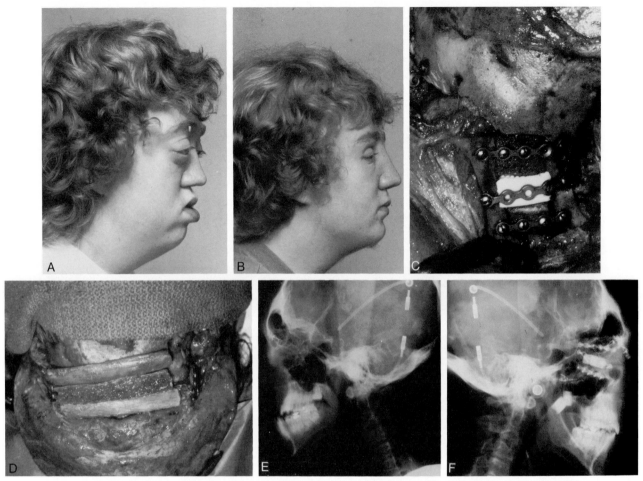

FIGURE 29–63. *A*, Preoperative and *B*, 2-year postoperative profile views following Le Fort III osteotomy for correction of Crouzon's disease. *C*, Use of autogenous bone with dense HA blocks and plates at the lateral orbital rim to maintain a 14-mm midfacial advancement. *D*, Onlay rib grafts used to augment the supraorbital bar and frontal bone. *E*, Preoperative and *F*, postoperative cephalometric radiographs illustrating the position of the dense HA blocks in the pterygomaxillary fissure and the lateral orbital rim regions. Note resorption of onlay rib grafts for frontal augmentation.

Bone chemically bonds to the HA surface by a natural bone-cementing substance if the HA graft is inlayed or onlayed with intimate bone contact.[225] Separation may not occur at the interface, even when established implants are purposely fractured after 3 weeks of healing. Mobility of the interface will delay healing and encourage fibrous connective tissue formation.

The selection of nonporous forms of HA rather than porous ones for some applications is based on a critical review of animal and clinical evidence reporting over a decade of experience. It is recognized that bone grafts, during their avascular period, and porous implant materials, be they HA, other ceramics, or polymer composite and metals, have a greater potential to become infected with intraoral applications than do nonporous materials as a result of the wicking effect of the interconnecting pores.[44,206] In the present surgical applications, the transient exposure of the implants to bacterial contamination is often unavoidable owing to the intraoral surgical approach and possible postoperative incision dehiscence. In addition, in some cases (downgrafts and maxillary widening), permanent communication of the implants with nasal sinus cavities may take place. Nonporous, dense implants, which have the lowest potential for infection, would appear to be more suitable than porous ones in oral applications.

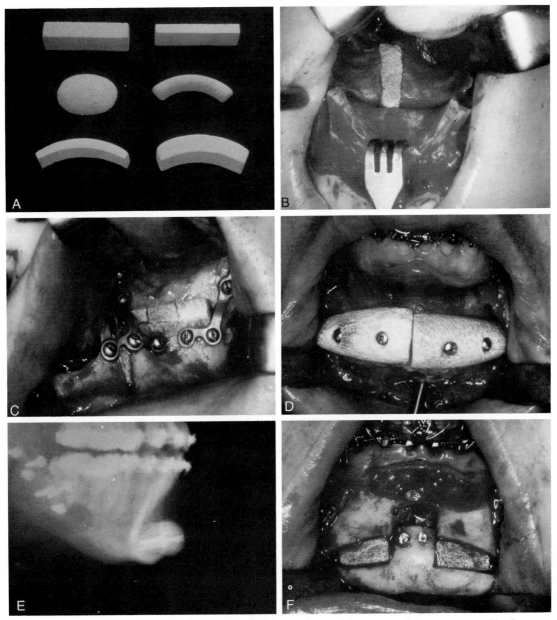

FIGURE 29–64. *A,* Shapes of Interpore 200 for orthognathic surgery. *B,* Interpore used in the midline of an expanded maxilla inserted from the nasal side. *C,* Maxillary advancement with grafting at the maxillary step area as well as between the advanced maxillary wall and the stable wall. Rigid fixation utilizing four bone plates is necessary to provide adequate stability to enhance healing and connective tissue (bone and soft tissue) ingrowth. *D,* Chin implants or bone or both must be contoured so that there is maximal bone-implant interface to facilitate bone growth into the implants. One bone screw in each segment is usually satisfactory to provide adequate stabilization. The holes through the Interpore material must be made slightly larger than the diameter of the shaft of the screw so that the implants are not fractured as the screws are inserted. *E,* An Interpore chin augmentation as seen radiographically. Note the bone screws stabilizing the implants. *F,* Downgraft of the chin with Interpore 200 blocks using the tenon and mortise technique. (Courtesy of Dr. Larry M. Wolford, Baylor College of Dentistry and Baylor University Medical Center, Dallas.)

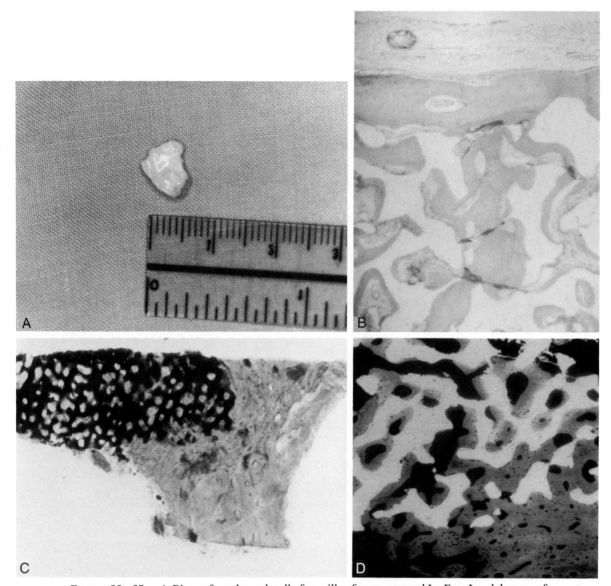

FIGURE 29–65.   *A,* Biopsy from lateral wall of maxilla after segmental Le Fort I and downgrafting. Interconnected clear spaces are left after removal of implant matrix by decalcification. Hematoxylin and eosin; original magnification 40×. *B,* Implant pores contain bone and fibrovascular tissue ingrowth. Connective tissue and bone occupy pores within the HA matrix represented by interconnected clear spaces. The antral surface of implant spaces is covered with a layer of bone and mucosa. *C,* Biopsy from lateral wall of maxilla after segmental Le Fort I advancement. Bone ingrowth extends throughout the portion of the implant contained within the osteotomy defect. The portion of implant extending into overlying soft tissue has less bone ingrowth (toluidine blue and alizaren red). *D,* SEM appearance of implant shown in *A.* Implant appears white, bone is gray, and soft tissue and vascular spaces are black owing to their different back-scattered electron densities. Haversian canals and osteocyte lacunae are easily seen. Original magnification 40×. (Courtesy of Dr. Larry M. Wolford, Baylor College of Dentistry and Baylor University Medical Center, Dallas, and Dr. Ralph E Holmes, University of California, San Diego.)

From the point of view of biomechanical suitability, the dense HA implants, with compressive strengths greater than 25,000 psi, are more than adequate for these applications.[225] Dense HA ceramics have proved to serve as permanent implants, showing no tendency to bioresorb even after prolonged periods of implantation (more than 7 years in humans). In contrast, porous HA implants have compressive strengths of approximately 1000 psi. Although some authors have suggested that porous HA implants can ultimately develop adequate strength by virtue of tissue growth,[374] others have reported a slow pattern of bony ingrowth, with the implants becoming crushed even after prolonged periods of implantation (1.5 years).[251] The prolonged time for bone growth into porous ceramic blocks may limit the use of these blocks in clinical situations that require early stability and function. This is particularly true when load may be significant. One type of "permanent" porous HA (coral HA) has been reported to undergo approximately 30 per cent biodegradation after only 1 year of implantation.[375] The current surgical indications seek permanent changes in contour or bony relationships to maintain occlusal balance. Dense HA blocks eliminate the biomechanical uncertainties associated with porous HA implants. However, porous HA blocks are easier to trim and may be more adaptable than dense HA blocks. Brittle ceramic with holes drilled through it carries a higher risk of fracture when dense blocks are used than when porous blocks are used. Dense and porous HA onlays are both brittle and may be less desirable for chin or zygomatic augmentation, since contour varies from patient to patient, requiring a bendable alloplast.[209]

Mandibular Reconstruction

The reconstruction of the contour-deficient, discontinuous, or absent mandible has been a problem that has challenged the reconstructive surgeon for centuries. Defects from trauma, infection, neoplasm, and congenital malformation all pose similar challenges to rehabilitation. Problems that can arise as a result of these defects include loss of masticatory function; loss of speech articulation; loss of support; interference with the functions of the tongue, sublingual and submandibular glands, hyoid bone, and tracheal structures; loss of an intact swallowing mechanism; loss of a supratracheal airway; and loss of facial form. Without the return of a functional anatomy, serious psychosocial problems will undoubtedly follow.[376]

The goals of mandibular reconstruction are tailored to the individual case, based on the functional deformity presented. Rehabilitation necessitates the re-establishment of the proper continuity and form of the mandible. This process includes skeletal, muscular, joint, soft tissue, and dentoalveolar considerations.[377]

The literature is replete with reports of autogenous and even heterogenous mandibular replacement. Bone grafting will succeed when movement at the graft site is minimal or absent. Stabilization is a necessary adjunct in the mandible, since resistance to the movement of grafts during function can be achieved only with a rigid framework that maintains arch continuity and prevents deformation secondary to muscle pull and scar contracture.[378] For optimal healing, regardless of the type of bone graft employed for reconstruction, alloplastic materials are necessary to complement natural replacements, and it is to this area that we will limit our discussion.[379]

ALLOPLASTIC MATERIALS

A brief review of the literature concerning alloplastic materials reveals that mandibular replacements are traditionally divided into three groups: medical polymers, ceramics, and metals. Recent advances and the availability of different types of alloplastic materials, along with the research and technology related to their use, have made many alloplasts ideal adjuncts for mandibular replacement.[380]

Medical Polymers. Polymers are not often mentioned as definitive treatment modalities for mandibular reconstruction. Celluloid[381] and gutta-percha[382] were often used in the early 1900s for stabilization in patients who had undergone hemimandibulectomy or in those patients who had had a significant segment of mandible removed. Vulcanized rubber[383] was used for prostheses that were fashioned as removable rather than implanted for continuity re-establishment and function. Polyethylene, polyurethane, and polyethylene derivatives, such as Dacron, have been used but lack sufficient strength to serve alone as the mandibular replacement.[384,385] Acrylic has been used since the 1940s for bone replacement and involves both single-stage autopolymerization techniques[386,387] and two-stage techniques with custom implant fabrication.[388] In addition, metal-acrylic combinations have been employed to increase the physical properties of the acrylic by reinforcement with metals. Silicone rubber has had limited use in mandibular continuity reconstruction and is usually used in combination with Dacron, wires, metal plates, and screws.[389] The primary contributions of silicone rubber to mandibular reconstruction are its use in gap arthroplasties in ankylosed TMJs and its use in augmentation of the contour-deficient chin in retrognathic or microgenic patients.[390] Teflon has been used but, again, was found to lack the inherent strength necessary for maintenance of mandibular continuity and function.[391] Proplast, a derivative of Teflon, has not been used for reconstructing continuity defects of the mandible but rather has primarily been involved in joint rehabilitation as well as onlay augmentation in the deficient alveolar deformity.[43,44,151,152,163]

Ceramics.   Ceramics have been used since the late 1800s, when it was common to use plaster of paris to fill cystic defects of bone.[392] Plaster of paris is still employed if resorption and replacement with bone are deemed necessary.[393] However, in most cystic cavities, bone will fill in on its own, and replacement with a material requiring resorption and replacement only increases infection potential at the site of operation. Ceramic materials such as aluminum oxide and calcium aluminate have been used alone or in conjunction with bone to augment the volume of grafted material that could be placed in an area to provide a reconstruction to this section of the mandible.[394] More recently, HA has been advocated in particulate and block form as well as a coating for metals; this material is discussed in more detail in a previous section of this chapter.

Metals.   Metals first came into prominence for mandibular reconstruction in the early 1900s. Gold, aluminum, silver, and bronze have all been used in wire as well as plate form to reconstruct sections of the mandible or entire mandibles.[395] Iron, steel, copper, zinc, and nickel steel wire also were tried in various combinations but were found to have either inadequate strength or intolerable tissue reactions to be viable implant material.[395]

Wires were the earliest form of metals used for mandibular reconstruction, and these could be twisted to form an angle or an articular surface and were easily adaptable at the time of surgery.[396] However, the strength of single and braided wires has marked limitations, and contour restoration could be accomplished only in one dimension, since no bulk was provided for three-dimensional mandibular contour reconstruction. More recently, pins molded to hold two mandibular fragments together have been advocated as temporary prostheses to prevent collapse and fibrosis of the unconnected mandibular segments.[397–400]

Cast metal implants became available in the 1930s, when cobalt-chromium and related alloys were used for skeletal reconstruction.[398,401] Cobalt-chromium is still used today in a variety of forms, since it is very strong and well tolerated for use in alveolar (Fig. 29–66A to F), mandibular body and angle, and TMJ reconstruction[401–408] (Fig. 29–66G to M). Stainless steel has enjoyed widespread use for TMJ replacement and mandibular fixation in the form of plates and screws, with or without bone grafts (Fig. 29–66N). Stainless steel mesh prostheses have been used, particularly when concomitant bone grafting is performed[404] (Fig. 29–66O). Similarly, titanium and titanium alloys have been used for this purpose and have gained a lot of popularity because of their light weight, bendability, strength, and tissue compatibility[410] (Fig. 29–66P to S). Tantalum, used in a sheet or mesh form, is a very strong and permanently self-supporting metal; however, it is very difficult to adapt to specific contours at the time of surgery, particularly in the mandibular angle and symphyseal regions, and it fractures after long-term function (Fig. 29–66T). The incidence of fracture eventually led to discontinuing it for reconstruction.

Secondary mandibular reconstruction following trauma will likely fall into three

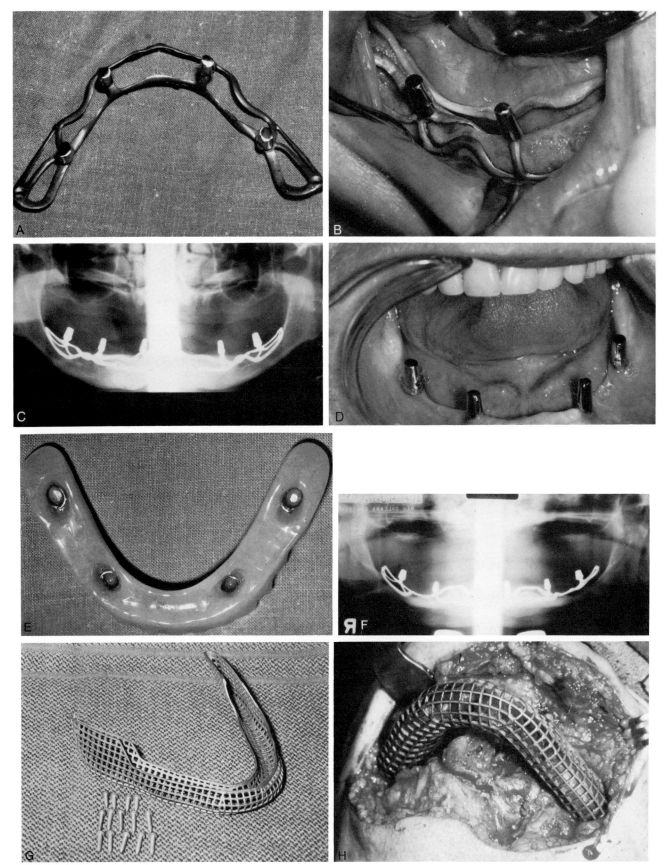

FIGURE 29–66. *A, B,* Cobalt-chromium custom cast subperiosteal implant used for replacement of lost mandibular alveolar bone. *C–E,* Fifteen-year postoperative panoramic radiographic, and clinical view of well-fitting, functional subperiosteal implant. *F,* Five-year postoperative panoramic radiograph of subperiosteal implant with bone resorption and clinical mobility. *G, H,* Cobalt-chromium custom cast mesh for mandibular reconstruction.

Illustration continued on following page.

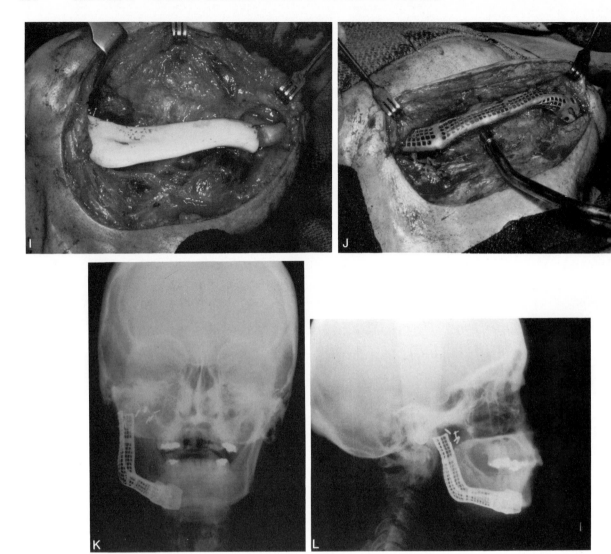

FIGURE 29–66. *Continued.   I,* Silicone space maintainer placed at initial surgery when the mandible is resected. Impressions taken at the initial surgery allow for a custom cast metal implant to be fabricated. *J,* Custom cast chrome-cobalt prosthesis placed at the second operation to restore mandibular form and temporomandibular joint (TMJ) function. *K, L,* PA and cephalometric radiographs showing excellent restoration of contour and form with the cast metal prosthesis.

Illustration continued on opposite page.

categories: stabilization of fracture nonunion, repair of small continuity defects (1 to 2 cm), and reconstruction of large continuity defects with or without TMJ reconstruction.[376–397,409] Our experience has shown that metals have consistently provided the adaptability and strength necessary to restore contour and provide function when used in combination with bone grafts.

Various metals have already been mentioned as having been used successfully in mandibular reconstruction. The most widespread and versatile of these metals, deserving further elaboration, include 316L stainless steel, cobalt-chromium alloys, and titanium. To understand the advantages and disadvantages of these more fully, we must look at their physical and chemical properties as they relate to biocompatibility and clinical adaptability.

Type 316L stainless steel.   This metal is at present the most widely used surgical implant alloy (Fig. 29–66N). The primary constituents of 316L are essential trace elements that exist in body fluid under precise physiologic regulation and with precise function.[410] This alloy represents a major improvement in biocompatibility over

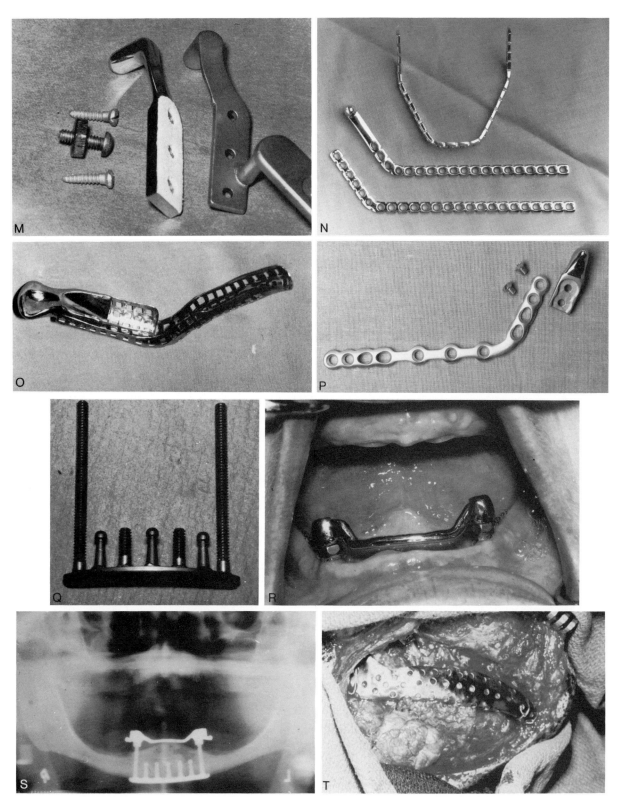

FIGURE 29–66. *Continued.*   *M,* Cobalt-chromium cast mandibular condyle implant used in conjunction with a polymer fossa for VK-I total TMJ reconstruction. *N,* Stainless steel mandibular reconstruction plates (Synthes) used for TMJ, ramus, and body reconstruction. *O,* Stainless steel adjustable mesh tray (3M) for mandibular angle and condyle reconstruction. *P,* Wurzburg pure titanium mandibular reconstruction plate. *Q, R,* Staple Mandibular Bone Plate fabricated from titanium, 6 per cent aluminum and 4 per cent vanadium alloy. *S,* Radiograph showing application of Staple Mandibular Bone Plate. *T,* Tantalum sheeting conformed to a tray for mandibular reconstruction. (*K* and *L* courtesy of Dr. Bob Gross and Dr. Randall James, Shreveport and Denver.)

TABLE 29-6. PROPERTIES OF SURGICAL-GRADE METAL ALLOYS

PROPERTY	STAINLESS STEEL ASTM F56(316L)	CO-CR (VITALLIUM) ASTM 75	TITANIUM (PURE) ASTM F67	TITANIUM-6,4 ASTM F136
Tensile strength (N/m²)	6.5×10^8	6.9×10^8	7.1×10^8	10.0×10^8
Ultimate tensile strength (psi)	80,000	95,000–105,000	90,000	125,000–130,000
Yield strength (N/m²)	2.8×10^8	4.0×10^8	4.7×10^8	9.7×10^8
0.2% Yield strength (psi)	35,000	65,000	80,000	115,000–120,000
Hardness	$R_B 85-95$	$R_C 25-35$	$R_C 100$	Depends on surface finish
Young's modulus (N/m²)	21×10^{10}	24×10^{10}	12×10^{10}	12×10^{10}
Modulus (0.2%) (psi)	$17.5-57.5 \times 10^6$	32.5×10^6	40×10^6	60×10^6
Maximal strain (%)	55	8	18	10
Fatigue limit (N/m²)	2.8×10^8	3.0×10^8	3.0×10^8	—
Elongation at fracture (%)	45	8	30	12

previous metals. However, it is not the absolute inertness of the metal that is responsible for the nonreactivity; rather, it is the slow release of toxic metal ions that may have long-term adverse effects after surgical implantation.[411]

Stainless steel is the predominant biomedical implant alloy because of its early development,[412] history of success, ease of fabrication, variety of mechanical properties (Table 29–6), and corrosion behavior. Four main classes of stainless steel can be produced by alloying: ferritic, martensitic, austenitic and precipitation-hardenable. By alloying various elements to iron in different combinations, the resultant metal alloys will have distinctly different properties.[413]

The desirable properties of an implantable alloy include primarily corrosion resistance, malleability, and strength. In Table 29–7, the elemental makeup of 316L stainless steel is outlined. This alloy falls within the austenitic range, which has the best

TABLE 29-7. COMPOSITION OF SURGICAL-GRADE METAL ALLOYS (WEIGHT %)

ELEMENT	STAINLESS STEEL ASTM F56(316L)	CO-CR (VITALLIUM) ASTM 75	TITANIUM (PURE) ASTM F67	TITANIUM-6,4 ASTM F136
Carbon	0.08 (Max.)	0.35 (Max.)	0.10 (Max.)	0.08 (Max.)
Manganese	2.00 (Max.)	1.00 (Max.)	–	–
Phosphorus	0.03 (Max.)	–	–	–
Sulfur	0.03 (Max.)	–	–	–
Silicon	0.75 (Max.)	1.00 (Max.)	–	–
Cobalt	–	Bal. (57.4–65)	–	–
Chromium	17–20	27–30	–	–
Nickel	10–14	2.50 (Max.)	–	–
Molybdenum	2–4	5.7	–	–
Iron	Bal. (59–70)	0.75 (Max.)	0.50 (Max.)	0.25 (Max.)
Oxygen	–	–	0.45 (Max.)	0.13 (Max.)
Aluminum	–	–	–	5.5–6.5
Vanadium	–	–	–	3.5–4.5
Titanium	–	–	Bal. (99+)	Bal. (88.5–92)

Max. = maximum; Bal. = Balance

corrosion resistance of the four classes of stainless steel. Chromium, carbon, nickel, manganese, and molybdenum are the primary elements that make up this alloy. For the steel to be fully austenitic, these elements are combined with iron specifically to increase corrosion resistance at the expense of mechanical strength when compared with the other classes of stainless steels. Quality control is necessary, since a chromium or nickel content that is too low or a molybdenum content that is too high will promote other phases of stainless steel, which have inferior corrosion resistance. In addition, carbon, which itself promotes austenite, in relatively low concentrations precipitates in the form of chromium carbides, again adversely affecting corrosion resistance.

Chromium, one of the main components of 316L stainless steels, is easily passivated. The intent of alloying chromium to iron is to produce a combination that will take on the passive properties of the chromium. This passive state for iron will occur with a minimal chromium content of 12 per cent.[414] This degree of passivity can be further increased by the addition of nickel, molybdenum, and silicone.[415]

When a metal or alloy has a relatively low corrosion rate in a strongly oxidizing environment, it is considered passive. This state is due to the formation of a passive surface film; there are two theories for the ability of this surface film to resist corrosion.[416] These are the oxide film[417,418] and the adsorption[419] theories of passivity. The oxide film theory, generally acknowledged to account for this corrosion-resistant behavior, promotes a protective film that forms on the metal or alloy and tenaciously adheres to the metal surface. This film acts as a physical barrier that separates the metal or alloy from its corrosive environment, impeding the transport of metal cations into solution.

For austenitic stainless steel, findings have shown that increased fineness of polishing produces an increased thickness of the film layer,[420] while the chromium content of the layer remains similar to that of the alloy itself.[421] With potentiostatic passivation, in which chromium, molybdenum, and silicone content and film thickness appear to be potential and time dependent, corrosion resistance is greatest with minimal film thickness (10 to 50 Å).[415,422,423] Therefore, surface treatment appears to be very important in film composition and ultimate in vitro corrosion resistance.

The design, processing, and handling of metallic implants significantly influence in vivo corrosion and stress corrosion behavior. Factors include design deficiencies, faulty manufacturing processes, surface treatment, manipulating and contouring implants at placement, and defects produced during implantation.[424-431] Metallurgical analyses of failed orthopedic implants show fatigue to be the major cause of failure.[426] Fatigue will occur when corrosion has sufficiently weakened an area of the implant that is subject to functional mechanical stress. Defects in implants that would lower corrosion resistance include the following: high inclusion content; porosity and impurities in welded structures; cracks due to cold rolling, pitting, and poorly sunk screw holes; and molybdenum content below 2 per cent, an ASTM specification.[432-434]

Corrosion products of stainless steel have also been associated with local tissue changes and potential systemic effects. Four categories of systemic effects include carcinogenic effects,[435,436] metabolic effects,[437,438] immunologic effects,[439] and bacteriologic effects.[440] Although stainless steel is the least corrosion resistant of the metallic implant materials currently used, the reaction is usually localized and rarely requires removal of the implant.[411]

Cobalt-chromium alloys.   In 1735, cobalt was isolated as a metal, but not until the early 1900s did metallic cobalt begin to find some industrial uses. Because in its pure form it is not particularly ductile or corrosion resistant, it did not enjoy widespread use.[441] Haynes[442] began to develop a series of cobalt-chromium alloys that had good corrosion resistance because they contained chromium. These alloys had good mechanical properties, and with the addition of other elements—iron, tungsten, and molybdenum—good high temperature properties and abrasion resistance increased their industrial usage (Table 29–7).

In the early 1930s, Erdle and Prange[443] patented an alloy and casting technique for the preparation of metallic dental castings. This alloy, Vitallium, was introduced to dentistry as an alternative to gold alloys.[444] By the late 1930s, Vitallium was used for the first time in orthopedic surgery for the fabrication of hip arthroplasty cups[445] and for internal fixation plates.[446] Since then, cobalt-chromium alloys have been the most widely used base metal casting alloy in prosthetic dentistry and have become one of the three major surgical metallic materials, along with stainless steel and titanium.

Metallic cobalt mechanically is harder than most pure metals and can have high yield and tensile strengths (Table 29–6). Chemically, the cobaltous ion (Co^{2+}) is basic and stable in aqueous solutions, but the cobaltic ion (Co^{3+}) is a powerful oxidizing agent and is very unstable. Electrochemically, cobalt is not easily passivated and exhibits poor corrosion resistance.[441]

Cobalt-chromium alloys such as cobalt-chromium-carbon, cobalt-chromium-molybdenum, cobalt-chromium-nickel, and cobalt-chromium-nickel-molybdenum have all been developed to take advantage of the mechanical properties of metallic cobalt while enhancing corrosion resistance (Table 29–6). Early observations regarding corrosion resistance were related to the cast alloys. Casting porosities and cracks led to crevice corrosion in situ, where the implants are bathed in a saline environment.[447,448] The wrought alloy has been shown to have superior corrosion resistance in this regard.[449,450] With recent endeavors in coupling different alloys in joint prostheses, galvanic corrosion, produced by contact between dissimilar metals, has become a concern. With the use of passivated alloys, it has been argued that coupling will not result in galvanic corrosion,[451] but it has been shown that this argument is not valid for combinations involving stainless steel.[452]

Cobalt is an essential trace element functioning with vitamin B_{12}. Free cobalt has no function, and 80 per cent of dietary intake is excreted unabsorbed, with the remainder eliminated via the urinary tract. Raised cobalt levels have been shown to produce a respiratory alkalosis, which can in turn stimulate erythropoietin production in the kidney. In addition, absorbed cobalt has been shown to be located in heart muscle, where in rare instances a cobalt cardiomyopathy can result.[453,454]

Chromium is an essential dietary element that is required in low concentrations. Storage is largely confined to the reticuloendothelial system, but in tissues, levels are extremely variable and normal levels are difficult to define.[455] Though mechanisms of chromium toxicity are not well known, high oral doses have been documented to cause nephrogenic and cardiogenic shock.[456] Chromate dust can cause contact ulcerations of skin and nasal mucosa and may produce pneumoconioses and an increased risk of bronchial cancer.

Like chromium, molybdenum and nickel are also essential trace elements. Toxic effects, too numerous to mention here, are well described in both animals and humans. Actual levels of these elements following implantation of a surgical-grade alloy are not known, but because corrosion rates are very low, it can only be presumed that the local and systemic levels of each of these elements are extremely low.[457–459]

Cobalt-chromium alloys have been processed for bioimplantation by several methods. Cast, wrought, and powder metallurgy processing methods have all been developed for use specifically to take advantage of the superior mechanical strength, corrosion resistance, and biocompatibility. Cast microstructures have large grains, large carbide particles, and severe chemical inhomogeneity, while the wrought alloys, when not worked, will have a finer microstructure and are harder and stronger, with similar ductility.[460] Powder processing offers the advantage of an even finer microstructure and chemical homogeneity and thus results in improved chemical and mechanical properties.[461]

These improvements in processing methods make cobalt-chromium alloys desirable in condylar and total joint systems in which manipulation of the implant is minimal or not required (Fig. 29–66G and M). Unfortunately, the inherent mechanical strength and hardness of these alloys make them very difficult to adapt to the unpredictable contour requirements of mandibular reconstruction. Custom casting methods have been employed with success[403,404] but may have limited application when exact contours cannot be accurately predetermined.

Titanium. Although originally discovered in 1791, titanium was not considered useful owing to the difficulty in extracting the metal from the metal ore. Not until the 1930s, when the first commercially feasible extraction process was developed, was it realized that titanium is quite a ductile and useful metal. With further improvements in the processing of large quantities of titanium, interest in its use for industrial and medical applications became widespread. The weight of titanium is 60 per cent that of steel; furthermore, it has a wide range of mechanical properties, has very high corrosion resistance, and is readily machined and manufactured into a variety of shapes and forms. Probably its greatest limitation is cost, restricting its industrial applications to those in which high strength-weight ratios are required. Surgical applications of titanium, in which cost-benefit ratios are lowest, have stimulated more research directed at one metal than any other in history.[462]

In 1940, the first time titanium had been implanted in laboratory animals, it was shown that not only was it as well tolerated as cobalt-chromium alloys and stainless steel but also it had a tendency for bone to grow into contact with it.[463] Further studies indicated that titanium had excellent tissue tolerance[464] as well as excellent corrosion resistance.[465] Orthopedic and neurosurgical applications soon followed, but full acceptance of pure titanium as an implant material was held back, since its strength was still inferior to that of stainless steel and cobalt-chromium alloys. The alloying of titanium to aluminum and vanadium has resolved many of the early mechanical deficiencies and has made it a viable alternative for most orthopedic applications (Table 29–7).

Mechanical properties of titanium show an exceptional weight-strength ratio. The Young modulus is approximately half that of either stainless steel or cobalt-chromium alloys, implying greater flexibility. Titanium has excellent ductility and tensile strength; yield strength and fatigue limits are equal to or greater than those of stainless steel and cobalt-chromium alloys (Table 29–6).

Corrosion resistance is probably one of the most exceptional properties of titanium. Of note is that titanium is virtually uncorrodible in neutral solutions, including saline, which makes it desirable for medical implant applications. This corrosion resistance is due to a passive titanium dioxide layer that forms spontaneously with exposure to air. This thin (150 Å) layer is compact and prevents any further oxidation of the underlying metal at ambient temperatures.

Despite this high corrosion resistance, titanium can still be found in the adjacent soft or hard tissues.[466,467] However, general corrosion phenomena do not fully explain this clinical finding. Pitting and crevice corrosion does not occur with titanium, nor is galvanic or stress corrosion seen under physiologic conditions.

Toxicologically, titanium appears to be very benign.[468] Particles found in tissues adjacent to implants in humans were not associated with neutrophils, granulation tissue, or necrotic debris, and multinucleated giant cells were very rare.[467] From these observations, it appears that there is little or no harmful effect of titanium in local tissues. Hypersensitivity to titanium has not been described,[469] and thrombogenicity has not been noted.[470]

The behavior of the titanium (6 per cent)–aluminum (4 per cent)–vanadium alloy is very similar to that of pure titanium. Although there are improved mechanical properties (Table 29–6), the same passive titanium dioxide layer imparts similar corrosion resistance. Thus, the titanium (6 per cent)–aluminum (4 per cent)–vanadium alloy is tolerated by tissues equally as well as pure titanium, while improving upon the mechanical properties of the latter. This feature has made the alloy preferable to pure titanium for orthopedic and maxillofacial applications (Fig. 29–66*H* and *I*).

METHODS OF RECONSTRUCTION

From this discussion, metals appear to be a necessary adjunct to mandibular continuity reconstruction, regardless of the size of the defect. In addition, when the

TMJ is involved, metallic reconstruction may be a superior alternative to biologic replacements, such as vascularized or nonvascularized rib grafts.

Repair of Small Defects.   Small defects (1 to 2 cm) in the symphysis or body regions of the mandible are often the result of infections or fracture nonunions. Metal plates are ideal for this application because they can provide rigid stabilization. Placing the plates in the edentulous mandible may allow for only approximate restoration of ideal alignment and spacing; however, with the use of ridge alignment and facial symmetry as a guide, satisfactory results can be achieved (Fig. 29–67A to I). In the

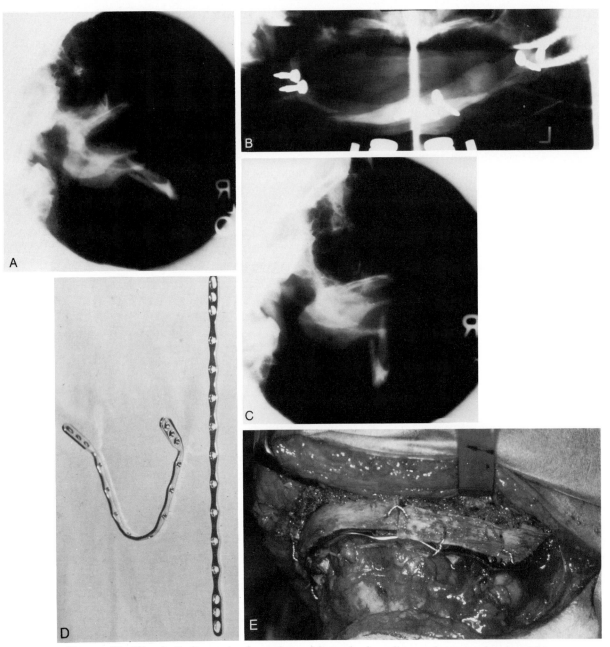

FIGURE 29–67.   *A*, Radiograph of a patient with total edentulism and severe alveolar ridge resorption who suffered *B*, bilateral mandibular body fractures and was treated initially with biphasic pin fixation without primary bone grafting, which the patient refused. *C*, Following removal of biphasic pin fixation, a bilateral nonunion with resultant "bucket handle" deformity occurred. *D*, Stainless steel Richards bone plate bent to conform to the mandible. *E*, Iliac crest and rib grafts harvested to reconstruct the nonunion as well as the deficient alveolar ridge.

Illustration continued on opposite page.

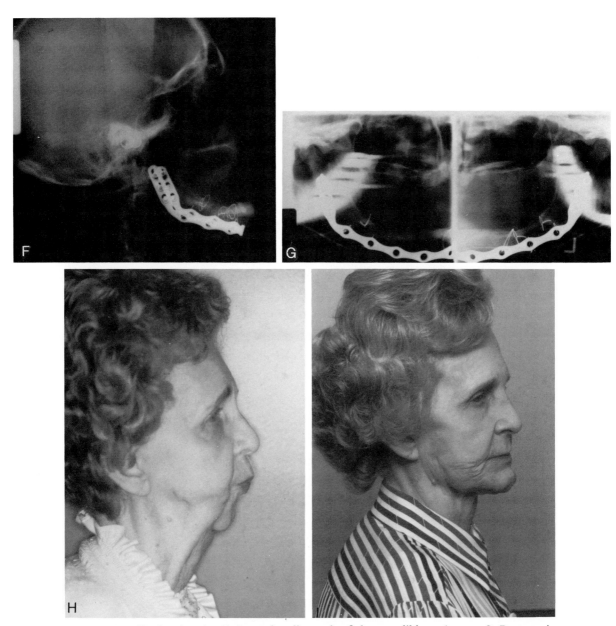

FIGURE 29–67. *Continued.* *F,* Lateral radiograph of the mandible at 1 year. *G,* Panoramic radiograph at 6 years. *H,* Preoperative profile view. *I,* Postoperative profile view.

dentate or partially edentulous mandible, the dentition should allow for more accurate realignment of bony segments (Fig. 29–68*A* to *G*).

For reconstruction in conjunction with particulate cancellous bone marrow (PCBM) grafts, an extraoral route is preferred to avoid oral contamination of the grafted bone. This practice will additionally allow for placement of the plate close to the inferior border, so that the denser basal bone may be engaged for rigidity, the plate may be positioned below the mental and inferior alveolar neurovascular bundles and tooth roots, and the metal may be kept as far away as possible from the oral environment to avoid potential intraoral dehiscence and interference with denture prostheses when present. Metal plates offer an advantage over mesh trays in this instance, since more rigid fixation can be applied, PCBM graft confinement is provided by adjacent bone and soft tissue, and lingual periosteal stripping is not necessary for placement.

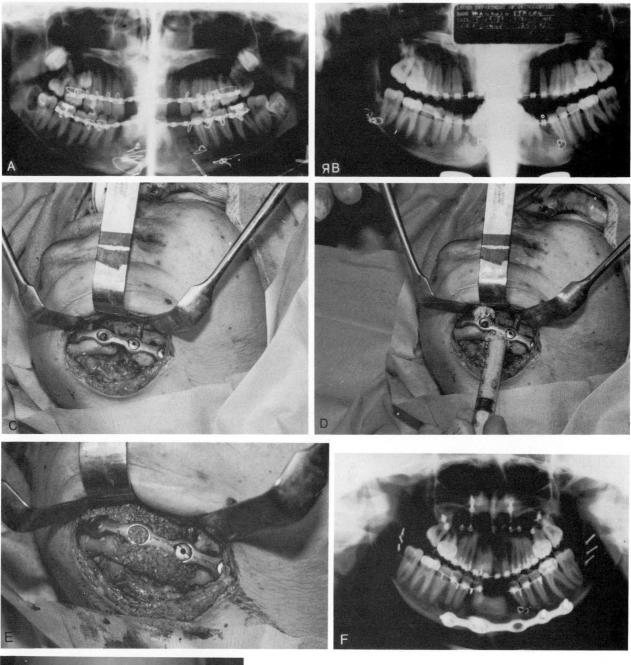

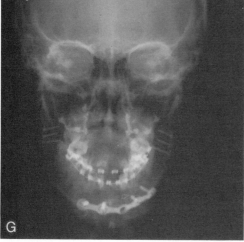

FIGURE 29–68. *A*, Sixteen-year-old patient involved in a motor vehicle accident who suffered multiple fractures of the mandible, including bilateral condylar neck fractures, right angle fracture, and comminuted left parasymphyseal fracture. *B*, Six months following initial injury, there was a transverse symphoseal collapse, which was the result of infection and bone loss with nonunion of the parasymphyseal fracture. *C*, Intraoperative view showing recreation of symphyseal transverse dimension and titanium reconstruction plate fixation. In addition, bilateral sagittal ramus osteotomies and Le Fort I osteotomy were performed to correct a retrognathic–open bite deformity. *D, E,* AAA bone graft placed in continuity defect. *F, G,* Postoperative radiographs showing fixation of mandibular fragments and re-establishment of symphyseal form.

To provide the necessary fixation and stability, the metal plate must be stabilized with a minimum of two screws in each bony fragment. The screws must be bicortical, placed perpendicular to the outer cortex. Most reconstruction plate systems require tapping the screw holes prior to placement of the screws. Self-tapping screws may bind in the bone, causing damage to the head of the screw or screwdriver or actual shearing off of the screw head.

Stainless steel, cobalt-chromium, or titanium plates may be used with equal success under these conditions. Titanium plates will be easier to adapt for a passive bone fit, while cobalt-chromium plates, because their superior mechanical strength allows for a thinner plate, will have a lower profile on the bony surface.

Metal plates may eliminate the need for intermaxillary immobilization, but dietary restrictions are still necessary. Full liquids or semisoft foods should be recommended for up to 3 months to allow for bone healing. At 6 months, the decision can be made to remove the bone plate if bone continuity has been re-established.

Repair of Large Defects.   In large mandibular continuity defects, involving greater than 2 cm of lost bone, one must observe similar preoperative considerations for providing functional symmetry and ridge relationships as were noted for smaller defects. Again, an extraoral approach to prevent oral contamination is preferred unless an intraoral incision either is unavoidable or can be made not to lie over the bonegraft, thus averting an extraoral scar. In some instances, scar contracture may necessitate bringing in soft tissue to replace deficient intraoral soft tissue. Vascularized grafts from the iliac crest, scapula, and fibula may be necessary to serve the dual purpose of soft and hard tissue reconstruction.

The decision to use a metal plate versus a mesh tray will often depend on the type of bone graft to be used to reconstruct the continuity defect. If there is adequate intraoral soft tissue coverage and scar contracture is minimal, a mesh tray can be used in a trough configuration (Fig. 29–69A to I). Here it will contain a PCBM graft in addition to stabilizing the bone fragments. Mesh trays have openings that allow for revascularization of the bone graft. Stainless steel mesh is the most easily contoured to the symphysis and angle regions, since it comes in precontoured mandibular forms that may be cut and adapted at the time of surgery (Fig. 29–70A to H). Use of the mesh tray is ideal for later endosseous implant reconstruction, since the tray is away from the mouth and should not interfere with implant placement (Fig. 29–71A to L).

A metal plate, made of stainless steel, cobalt-chromium, or titanium, may also be used. Although adaptation may be easier than with a metallic mesh tray, securing or containing the bone graft may be problematic (Fig. 29–72A to G). If residual lingual plate or inferior border remains, this may work well with a PCBM graft, but in the absence of residual bone to help in keeping the graft in place, it is difficult to control migration and displacement of the grafted bone. Corticocancellous blocks, though inferior to densely packed PCBM, may be secured to the plate with wires or screws. Plates, however, are the material of choice when using a vascularized bone graft, since the solid piece of bone can be contoured to the place and secured without embarrassment to the vascular pedicle. If a plate is used, three or four screws should be placed in each remaining mandibular fragment to ensure stability and allow for postoperative opening.

Removal of the bone plate or mesh tray may be contemplated once bone healing has taken place. Often, these prostheses will contribute to facial form and contour, and it may not be advisable to remove them. Further, if unpredictable resorption and replacement of the bone graft leave large voids within the area of reconstruction, the mandible may be subject to pathologic fracture in these weakened areas.

Often, reconstruction of the mandible necessitates re-establishment of the functional TMJ complex. This procedure will require combining the principles just set forth for mandibular reconstruction, including stabilization and immobilization of bone grafts, with the creation of a new TMJ articulation. This latter feat is by no means simple, as will be evidenced in the discussion in the following section.

When a metal prosthesis is used to replace both mandibular form and TMJ

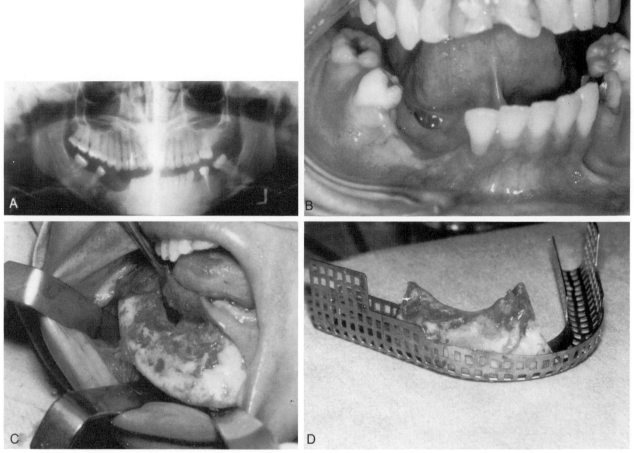

FIGURE 29–69. *A,* Preoperative panoramic radiograph of a 28-year-old woman with an ameloblastoma involving the right mandibular body and parasymphyseal region. *B,* Extraction of the bicuspid in the area of the tumor allowed for healing of the mucosa, leaving no exposed tumor, bone, or underlying connective tissue. *C,* An intraoral incision made in the buccal mucosa, away from bone, allowed for complete exposure of the mandible, from the angle around to the opposite parasymphyseal region. *D,* Resected mandibular segment used to contour a stainless steel mesh tray and to determine how much tray would be needed for fixation.

Illustration continued on opposite page.

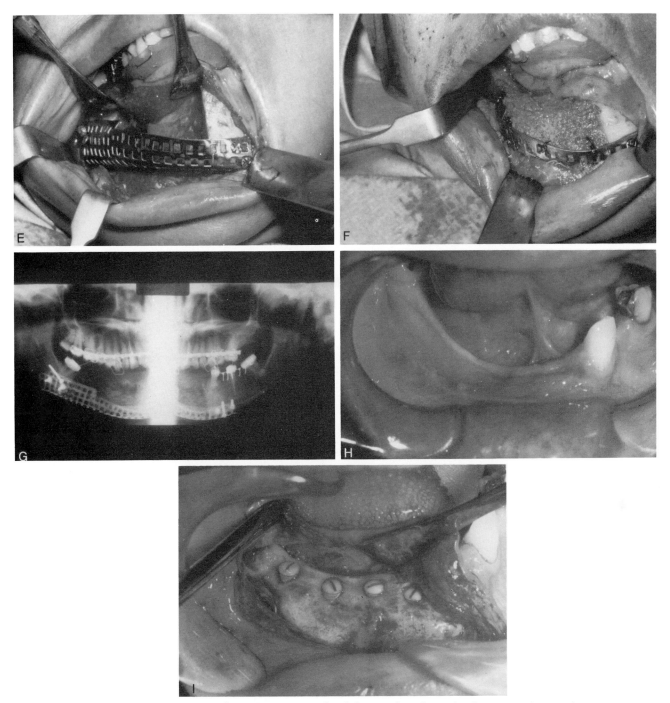

FIGURE 29–69. *Continued.* *E*, Precontoured stainless steel mesh tray in place, restoring continuity. Fixation of the tray is accomplished with bicortical screws. *F*, Particulate cancellous bone marrow (PCBM) graft used in the mesh tray to re-establish the bony contour of the resected portion of the mandible. *G*, Postoperative radiograph of reconstructed mandible. *H*, Six-month postoperative view of reconstructed mandible showing incision line in the buccal vestibule. *I*, Exposure of the bone graft at 6 months showed adequate bone for placement of HA-coated dental implants.

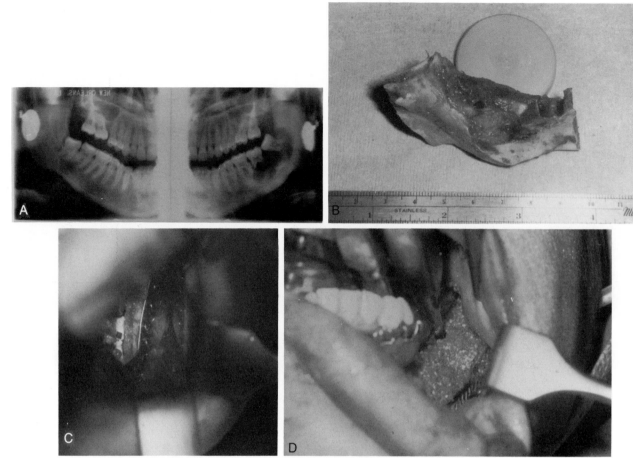

FIGURE 29–70. *A*, Preoperative panoramic radiograph of 25-year-old woman with an amelo-blastoma of the left mandibular angle. An intraoral approach was chosen because despite extraction of molar teeth in the area of tumor, mucosal healing did not take place to prevent intraoral contamination of a bone graft. *B*, Resected left mandibular body and ramus, leaving the posterior border and condyle in place. *C*, Screws used to secure stainless steel mesh tray to remaining bone at the mandibular angle. Screws were placed percutaneously. *D*, Combined PCBM-HA graft placed in the mesh tray to restore lost bony contour.

Illustration continued on opposite page.

function, permanence must be considered, since the prosthesis will be required for mandibular function from the time it is inserted. Again, access and the availability of soft tissue coverage, both intraorally and extraorally, will determine the nature of the bone graft used. If the defect involves only a mandibular ramus and condyle, it is possible to eliminate a bone graft entirely (Fig. 29–73*A* to *G*).

When a portion of the mandibular body is missing, reconstruction of this missing bone is essential for the later dental rehabilitation in which removable or fixed denture prostheses are required. A stainless steel mesh tray with a metal condylar attachment is recommended when a PCBM graft is used. As previously mentioned, the mesh tray will be able to contain the bone graft and provide proper contour to re-establish the form of the lost mandibular angle.

Attention must be paid to the TMJ articulation. If the TMJ disc can be maintained intact, function of the metal condyle against it may be preserved, but if not, metal-bone contact may cause erosion of the bony fossa and may result in pain and limitation of mandibular function (Fig. 29–74*A* to *K*).

More often than not, a prosthetic fossa articulation for a metal condyle will be

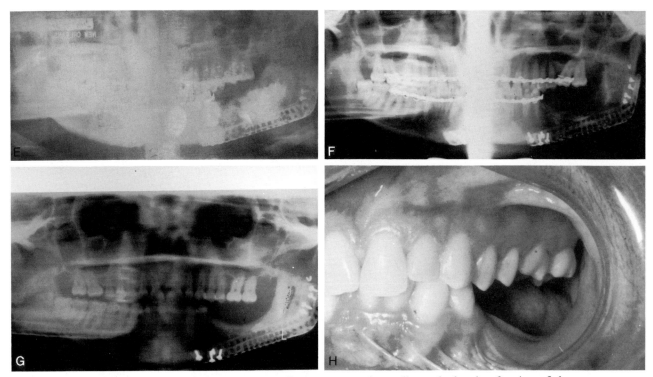

FIGURE 29-70. *Continued.* *E,* Immediate postoperative radiograph showing fixation of the mesh tray and position of grafted bone. *F,* Three-month postoperative radiograph showing remodeling of bone graft. *G,* Five-year postoperative radiograph. *H,* Five-year postoperative intraoral view of area to be restored with endosseous implants and fixed denture prostheses.

necessary. Plates that have a condyle component can easily be adapted to reform the condyle, ramus, angle, and body configuration. Again, plates do not work well with particulate bone grafts, but corticocancellous block grafts (Fig. 29-75A to L) and vascularized grafts (Fig. 29-76A to V) are well suited to this purpose.

If a metal prosthesis fails, it may be possible to resort to a costochondral condyle graft if the ramus is present either from the original defect (Fig. 29-77A to P) or from newly grafted bone. Usually, however, a new metal prosthesis can be adapted to this situation with or without the use of a glenoid fossa prosthesis. Each of the alloys previously discussed—stainless steel, cobalt-chromium, or titanium—is equally effective.

TMJ Reconstruction

Diseases and deformities of the TMJ necessitating surgical intervention include internal derangements, hypomobility or ankylosis, arthritides, and defects following infection, trauma, and removal of tumors. The nonsurgical management and surgical repair of internal derangements will be discussed only as they pertain to the use of biomaterials and related reconstructive procedures. Since a majority of TMJ problems result from postoperative arthroscopy and arthroplasty repairs of disc problems, arthritides, and trauma, a brief review of TMJ hypomobility and pain (etiology and deformity) is necessary to appreciate the role of biomaterials.[471-478] The repair of condyle and facial fractures with bone plates, screws, and pins is discussed in Chapter 33. *Text continued on page 917.*

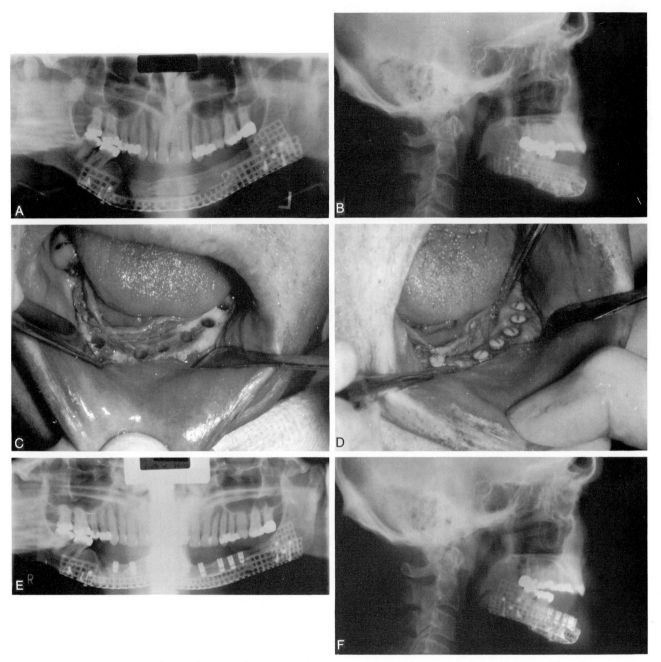

FIGURE 29–71.   Nine-month postoperative *A*, panoramic and *B*, cephalometric radiographs of a 62-year-old man with intramedullary squamous cell carcinoma of the mandible, which was reconstructed with a stainless steel mesh tray and combined PCBM-cortical graft from the iliac crest. The mesh tray was maintained to prevent pathologic fracture in the right parasymphyseal region as well as to provide chin contour. *C*, Intraoperative view of grafted bone prepared for placement of HA-coated dental implants. *D*, HA-coated dental implants in place. Postoperative *E*, panoramic and *F*, cephalometric radiographs of HA-coated dental implants. Implants are not placed to the depth of the mesh tray, since dense connective tissue rather than bone was formed here.

Illustration continued on opposite page.

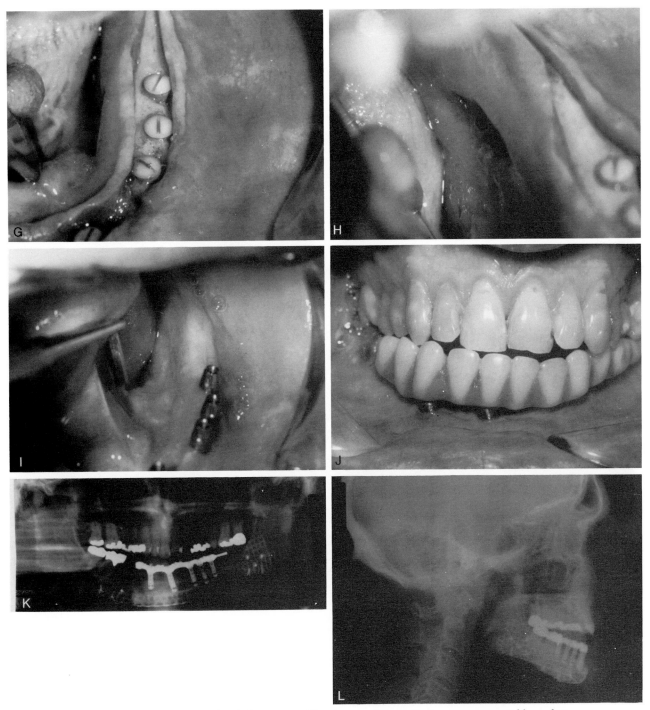

FIGURE 29–71. *Continued.* *G*, Exposure of implants at 8 months shows some crestal bone loss but good integration nonetheless. *H*, Manipulation of mucosa resulted in exposure of the mesh tray on the lingual surface of the mandible. *I*, The mesh tray was bent to readapt to the existing bony mandible, and the mucosa was allowed to granulate over the defect. This took approximately 1 month. *J*, Restored occlusion view, and *K*, panoramic and *L*, cephalometric radiographs showing complete reconstruction of mandible lost to neoplasm.

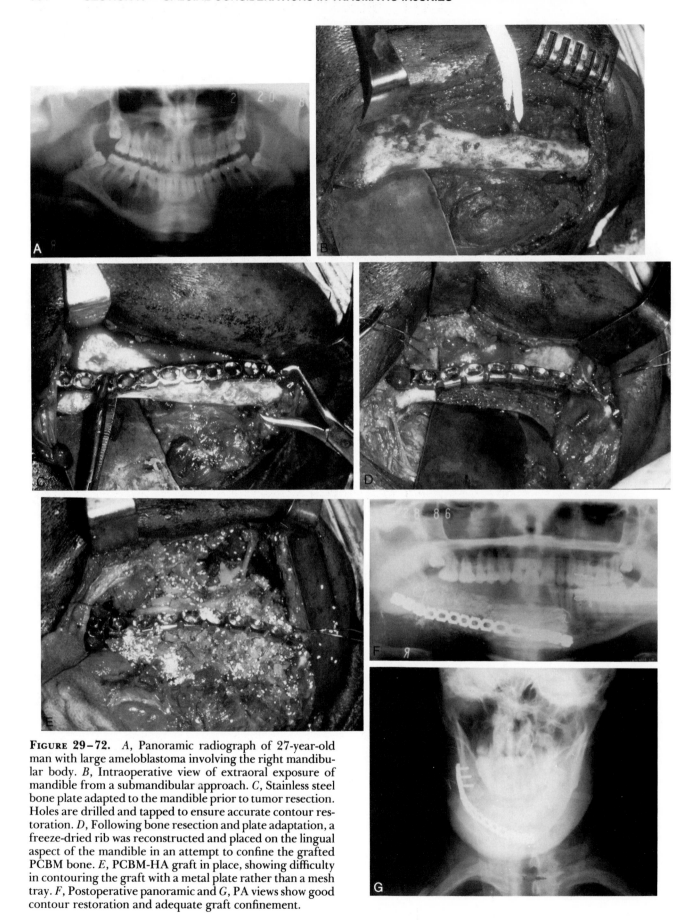

FIGURE 29–72. *A*, Panoramic radiograph of 27-year-old man with large ameloblastoma involving the right mandibular body. *B*, Intraoperative view of extraoral exposure of mandible from a submandibular approach. *C*, Stainless steel bone plate adapted to the mandible prior to tumor resection. Holes are drilled and tapped to ensure accurate contour restoration. *D*, Following bone resection and plate adaptation, a freeze-dried rib was reconstructed and placed on the lingual aspect of the mandible in an attempt to confine the grafted PCBM bone. *E*, PCBM-HA graft in place, showing difficulty in contouring the graft with a metal plate rather than a mesh tray. *F*, Postoperative panoramic and *G*, PA views show good contour restoration and adequate graft confinement.

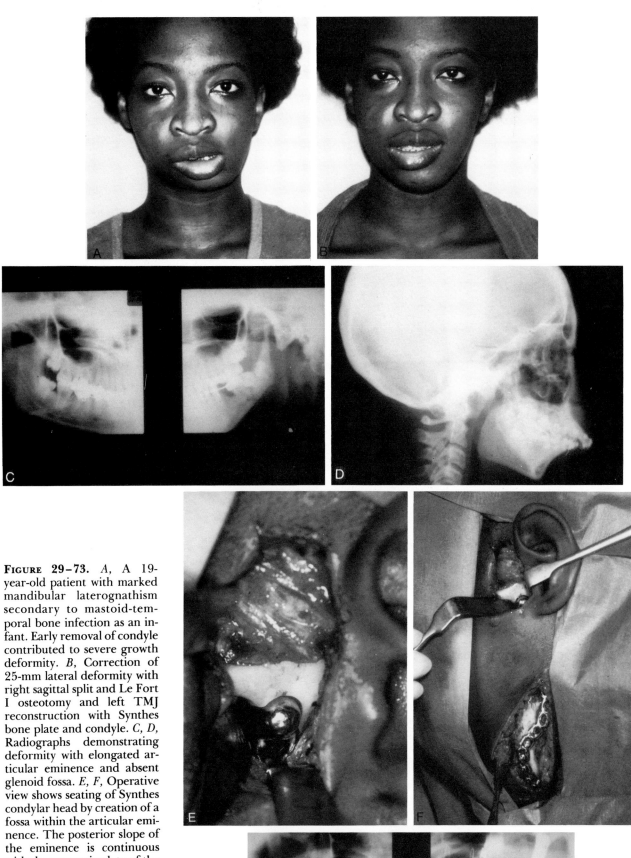

FIGURE 29–73. *A*, A 19-year-old patient with marked mandibular laterognathism secondary to mastoid-temporal bone infection as an infant. Early removal of condyle contributed to severe growth deformity. *B*, Correction of 25-mm lateral deformity with right sagittal split and Le Fort I osteotomy and left TMJ reconstruction with Synthes bone plate and condyle. *C, D*, Radiographs demonstrating deformity with elongated articular eminence and absent glenoid fossa. *E, F*, Operative view shows seating of Synthes condylar head by creation of a fossa within the articular eminence. The posterior slope of the eminence is continuous with the tympanic plate of the auditory canal. *G*, Postoperative radiograph.

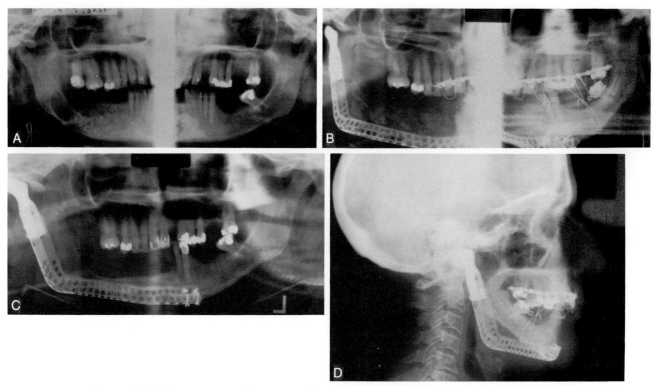

Figure 29–74. *A,* Preoperative panoramic radiograph of 56-year-old woman with ameloblastoma of right mandibular body and ramus. *B,* Postoperative panoramic radiograph shows reconstruction of mandibular body, ramus, and condyle with mesh tray prosthesis and metal condyle attachment. PCBM graft was placed to fill the entire contour defect. The metal condyle articulated directly on bone in the glenoid fossa. *C, D,* Three-year postoperative radiograph showing an intact mesh tray prosthesis with a fully remodeled bone graft. Note the apparent lack of mineralization in the tray in the region of the angle and posterior body. This phenomenon is occasionally seen because the metal prevents an adequate blood supply to support bone in these areas. Here, the grafted bone is resorbed and replaced with dense connective tissue. *E,* Because of right TMJ pain and limitation of motion as well as mobility of the tray in the symphysis, the prosthesis was removed. *F, G,* Lateral glenoid fossa resorption because of the bone-metal interface was seen intraoperatively. *H,* Since no bone graft was required, a stainless steel metal plate with attached condyle was secured to the reconstructed right mandible to re-establish a functional TMJ articulation. *I,* A glenoid fossa prosthesis was used for total TMJ reconstruction. This allowed for fossa reconstruction, providing an excellent articulating surface for the metal condyle. *J,* Postoperative panoramic and *K,* PA radiographs showing the metal plate in place and reconstructing the mandibular body, ramus, and condyle. Screws securing the glenoid fossa prosthesis can be seen in the zygomatic process of the temporal bone.

Illustration continued on opposite page.

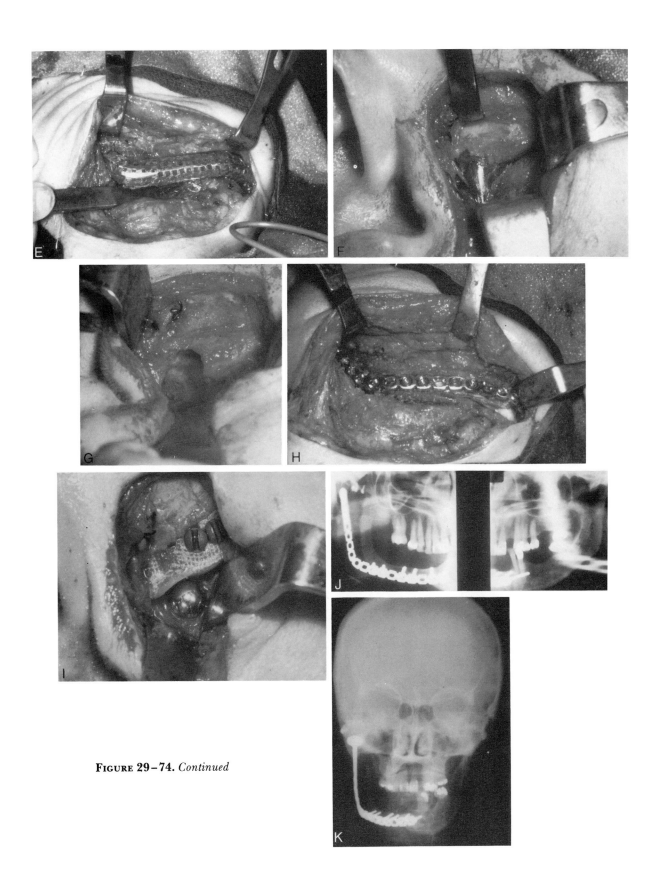

FIGURE 29–74. *Continued*

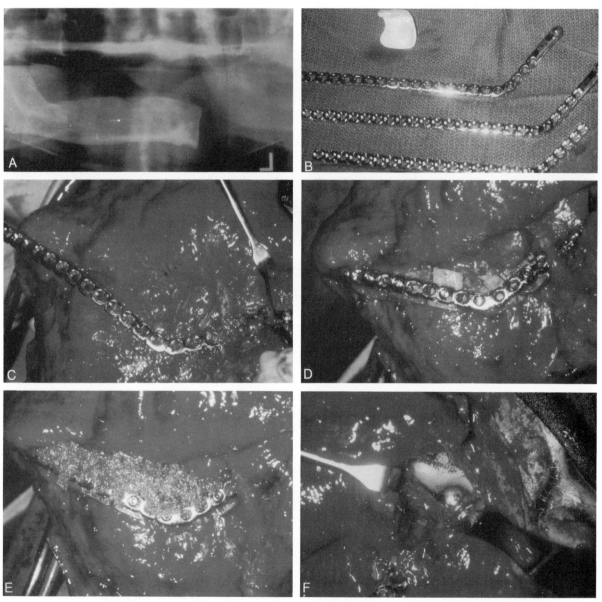

FIGURE 29–75.   *A,* Preoperative panoramic radiograph of 52-year-old man following resection of the left hemimandible for a squamous cell carcinoma. *B,* Synthes stainless steel mandibular reconstruction plates with and without condyle extensions. An HA-polymer glenoid fossa prosthesis used for total TMJ reconstruction is compatible with this and other metal condyle configurations. *C,* Intraoperative view shows plate being contoured in situ. *D,* Block corticocancellous bone grafts are secured to the plate with screws. *E,* PCBM-HA graft is used to fill in voids between the corticocancellous blocks as well as to add to the vertical augmentation of the mandibular body. *F,* Total TMJ reconstruction with metal reconstruction plate condyle and glenoid fossa prosthesis.

Illustration continued on opposite page.

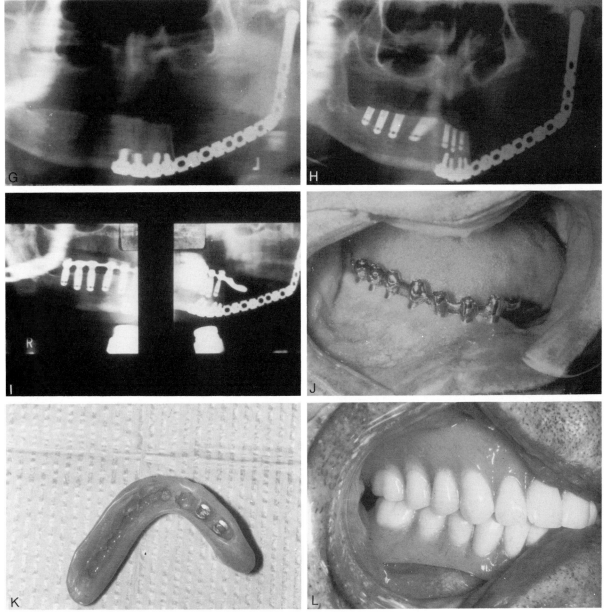

FIGURE 29–75. *Continued.* *G,* Postoperative panoramic radiograph. *H,* One-year postoperative radiograph showing placement of endosseous HA-coated dental implants in the residual ungrafted mandible. Though mineralization of the grafted portion of the mandible can be seen, it was transversely and vertically inadequate to accept placement of endosseous implants. *I–L,* Panoramic and clinical views of restored endosseous HA-coated implants with hybrid denture prosthesis.

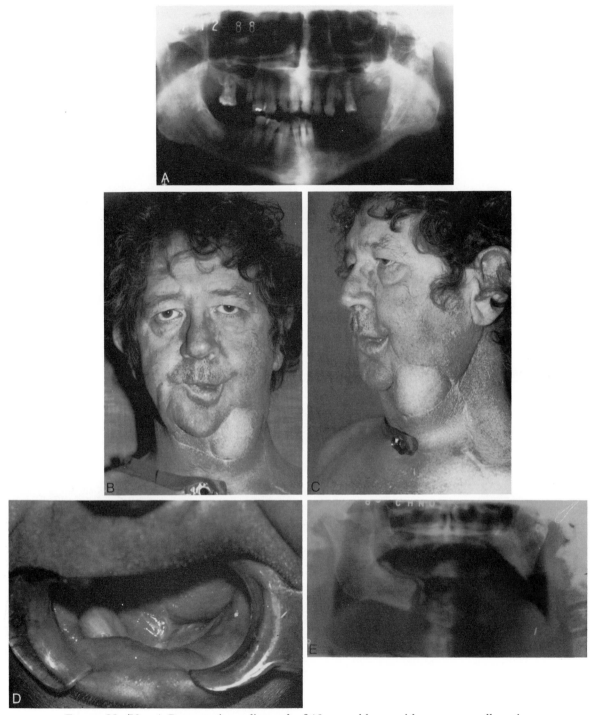

FIGURE 29–76. *A*, Preoperative radiograph of 46-year-old man with squamous cell carcinoma involving the floor of the mouth, mandible, and skin. *B–E*, Clinical and radiographic appearance following partial mandibulectomy and deltopectoral myocutaneous flap reconstruction. Scarring and tissue redundancy made conventional prosthetic rehabilitation impossible.

Illustration continued on opposite page.

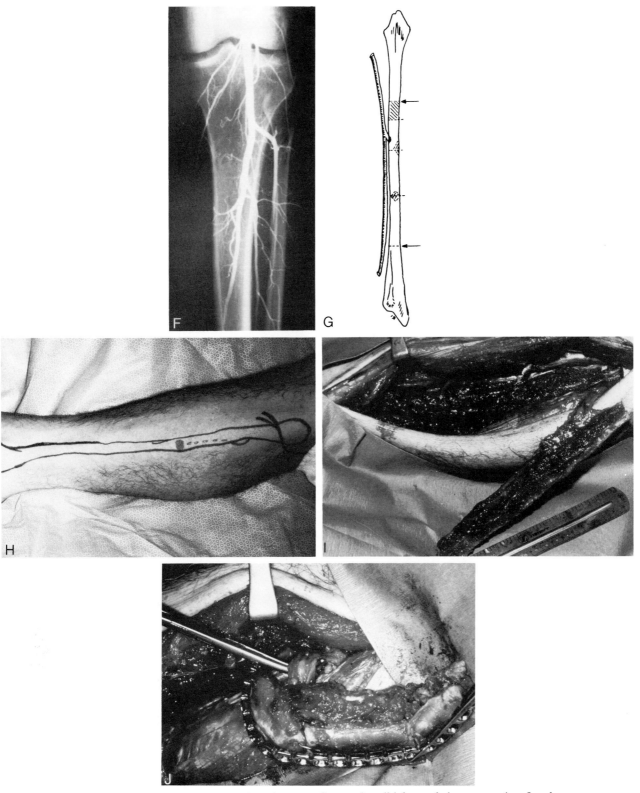

FIGURE 29–76. *Continued.   F,* Arteriogram of posterior tibial vessels in preparation for the harvesting of a vascularized fibula graft. *G,* Depending on the defect, as much as 25 to 30 cm of fibula can be harvested. *H, I,* Intraoperative views showing fibula harvesting. *J,* Osteotomizing of fibula prior to cutting the vascular pedicle will ensure viability of osteotomized segments.

Illustration continued on following page.

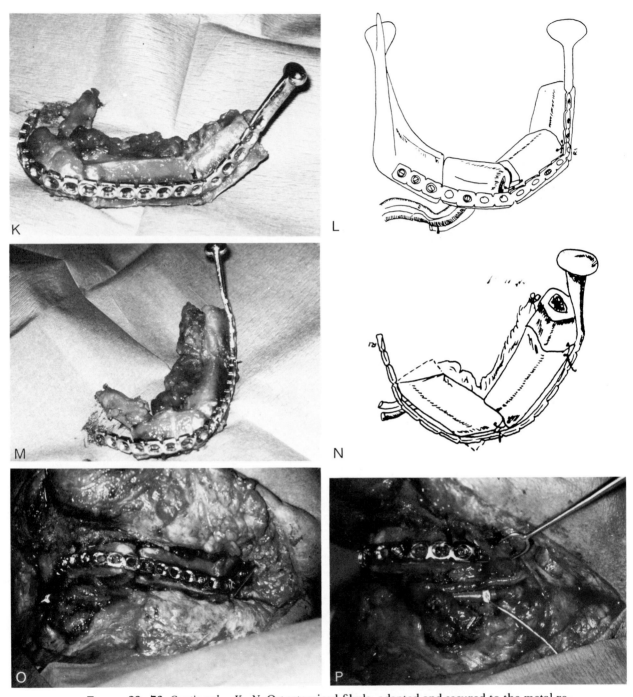

Figure 29–76. *Continued.* *K–N,* Osteotomized fibula, adapted and secured to the metal reconstruction plate with wires. *O, P,* Plate and fibula transferred to mandible, where microvascular anastomosis to the facial artery is carried out. *Q,* Postoperative panoramic radiograph and *R,* cephalometric radiographs. *S–V,* Postoperative clinical views at rest and in function.

Illustration continued on opposite page.

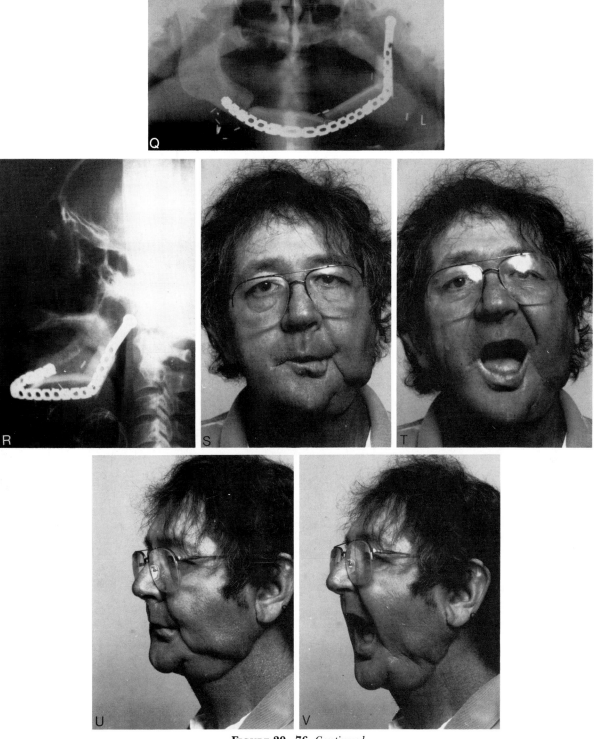

FIGURE 29–76. *Continued*

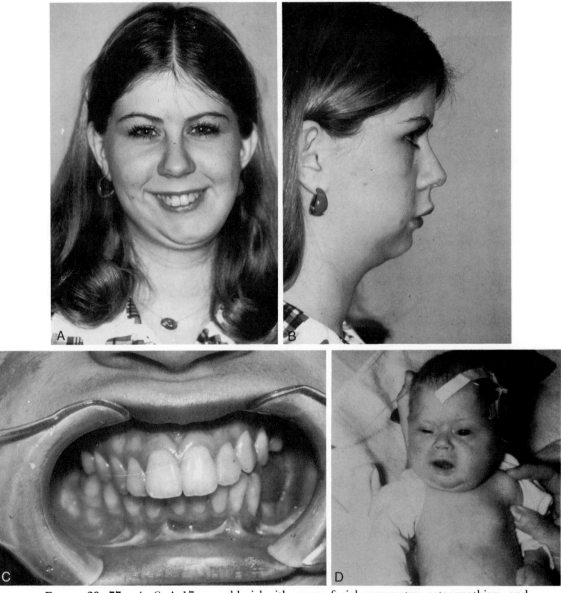

Figure 29–77. *A–C,* A 17-year-old girl with severe facial asymmetry, retrognathism, and malocclusion secondary to sepsis at multiple locations, including right TMJ, experienced as an infant, *D.*

Illustration continued on opposite page.

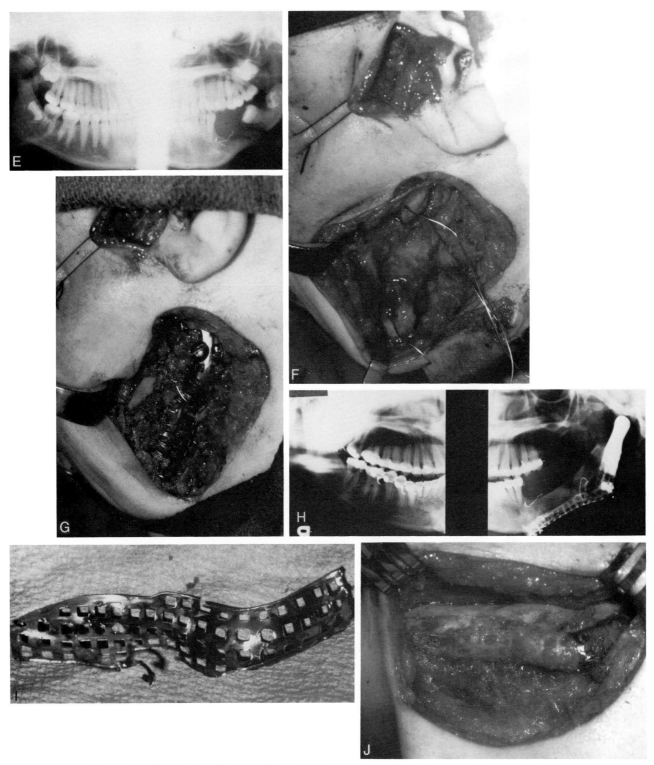

FIGURE 29–77. *Continued.*   *E,* Radiograph shows complete loss of ramus with nonunion of an island of the body of the mandible from previous reconstruction with bone grafts. *F, G,* Operative views showing placement of titanium mesh tray and condyle utilizing existing island of bone and particulate iliac crest graft. *H,* Postoperative radiograph at 2 years showing body of mandible restored with graft and ramus-angle area restored with existing bone island. At 3 postoperative years, patient desired removal of cobalt-chromium (Vitallium) tray because of bone screw irritation. Bone had grown over the inferior border of tray. *I, J,* Tray was removed with difficulty in two segments.

Illustration continued on following page.

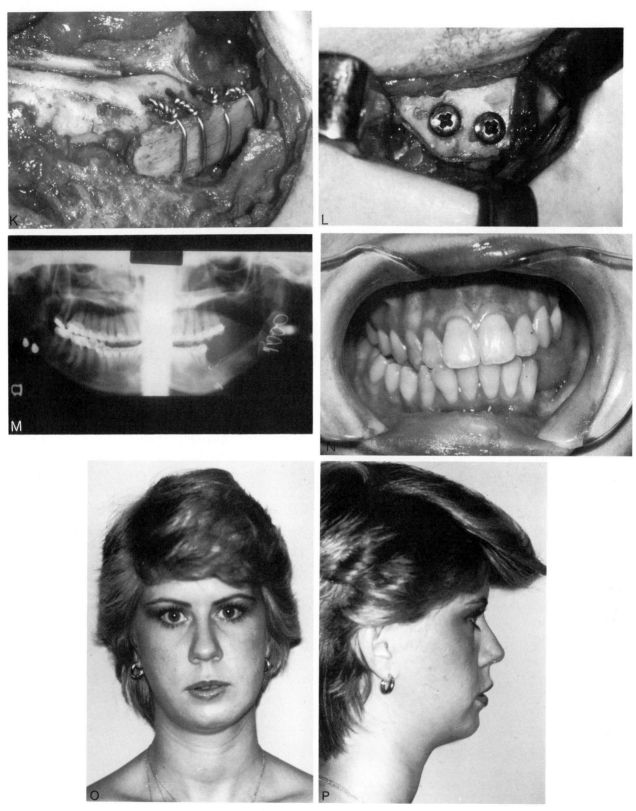

FIGURE 29–77. *Continued. K, L,* Condyles were reconstructed, with rib graft placed on posterior border. Sagittal split with extraoral bone screws was done to correct asymmetry further. *M,* Postoperative radiograph at 4 years showing orthodontic treatment. *N–P,* Occlusion and facial appearance at 6 years after surgery. Patient is doing well 12 years after surgery.

Etiology of TMJ Disorders

Intra-articular hypomobility may be either fibrous or bony in nature; it is more commonly unilateral than bilateral and is most frequently caused by TMJ surgical failures and trauma. Hypomobility, condylar resorption, malocclusion, and chronic pain associated with surgery for internal derangement (discectomy and high condylectomy), rheumatoid arthritis, ankylosing spondylitis, and infections extending to the joint from otitis, mastoiditis, and osteomyelitis are remaining etiologic factors (Fig. 29–78A to E). In most instances of hypomobility, the meniscus is displaced or destroyed. Patients with a history of chronic pain and multiple TMJ procedures usually have fibrosis of accessory ligaments and muscles surrounding the TMJ, leading to extra-articular hypomobility.

The pathogenesis of intra-articular hypomobility or ankylosis is one of progressive destruction or displacement of the meniscus and joint tissues, with narrowing of the joint space, replacement with granulation tissue between joint parts, and formation of fibrous connective tissue bands blending throughout the periarticular and capsular tissues, which leads to calcification and eventually actual fusion of the mandible to the glenoid fossa or articular eminence. Since the lateral pterygoid muscle

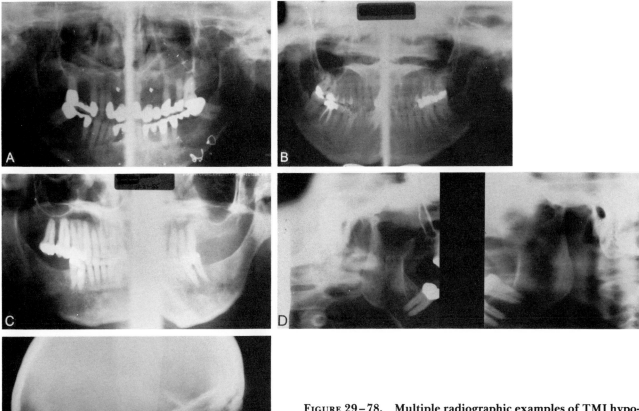

FIGURE 29–78.   Multiple radiographic examples of TMJ hypomobility.   A, Bilateral TMJ ankylosis following mandibular condyle fractures 20 years previously. B, Bilateral ankylosis following multiple TMJ surgeries. C, Left ramus condyle deformity with hypomobility 25 years after osteomyelitis of TMJ. D, Panoramic radiograph demonstrating advanced rheumatoid arthritis of left condyle and moderate rheumatoid arthritis of right. E, Cephalometric radiograph in rheumatoid arthritis showing open bite deformity.

attachment to the meniscus and condyle is usually destroyed or altered, protrusion of the jaw will be limited, if not absent, and lateral and protrusive excursions will be diminished even if mobility is restored. Ankylosis occurring before puberty leads to facial deformity, with deviation toward the affected side in unilateral cases and open bite with mandibular deficiency in bilateral cases. When the function of the jaw is impaired, the enveloping soft tissue matrix cannot influence growth of the mandible in its genetically determined downward and forward direction. In view of the major contribution to growth by the condylar head within the first few years of life, children should be operated upon with autogenous grafts as soon as possible, so that growth may take place by local remodeling (resorption and deposition) in response to soft

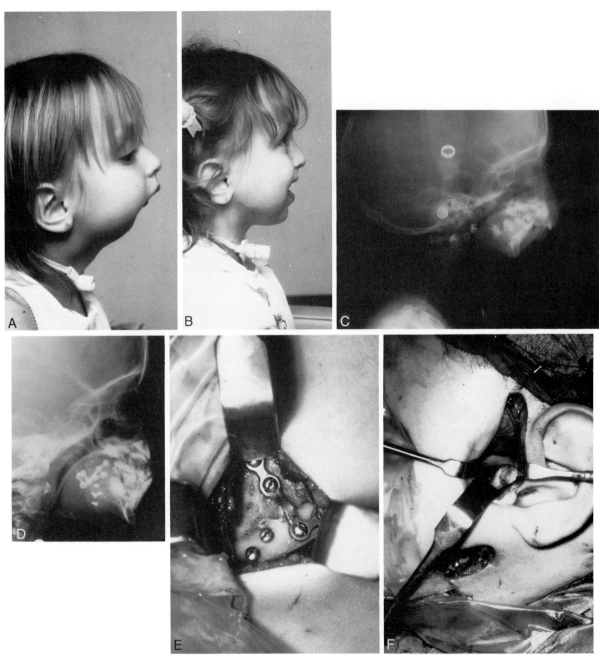

FIGURE 29–79.   Reconstruction of bilateral ankylosed condyle with rib grafts.   *A*, Preoperative and *B*, 1-year postoperative profile views in a child with tracheostomy in place since birth. *C*, Preoperative and *D*, postoperative radiographs. *E, F*, Intraoperative fixation with Wurzberg bone screws.

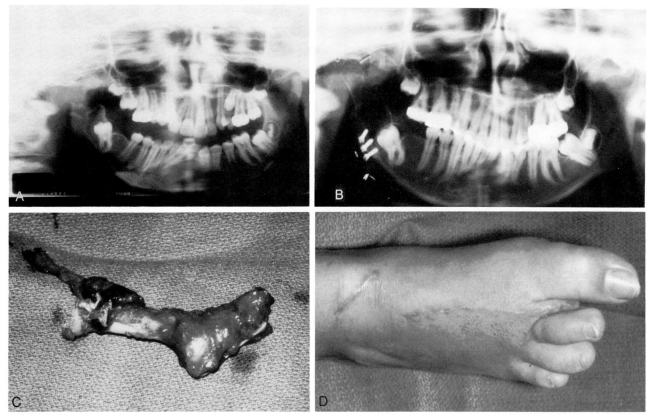

FIGURE 29–80. Reconstruction in a 12-year-old girl with vascularized second metatarsal. Condyle failed to develop following cleavage release of ankylosis at 18 months of age. *A*, Preoperative and *B*, 2-year postoperative radiographs. *C*, Metatarsal graft with dorsalis pedis vessels. *D*, Foot seen postoperatively.

tissue demands, which can occur only with a widely functioning mandible (Figs. 29–79 and 29–80).

Extra-articular hypomobility is caused by a variety of pathologic conditions involving the muscles of mastication and cranial nerves V and VII—trauma, tumors, and neurogenic diseases such as epilepsy, paralysis, and cerebrovascular accidents. Trismus of the muscles of mastication, resulting from infections, myofascial pain disorders, and even simple maneuvers such as dental injections, can lead to hypomobility. Clearly, the formation of fibrous adhesions along muscle pathways, whatever the cause, will lead to hypomobility. Of prime importance to arrive at the proper treatment is the differentiation between intra-articular and extra-articular ankylosis or recognition of the combination.

Three types of TMJ injury with broad overlap among them are contusion, dislocation, and fracture. In terms of assessment and treatment, they are among the most important and controversial of all maxillofacial injuries. Complications of TMJ trauma include occlusal dysfunction, disc displacement with degeneration or perforation or both, degenerative joint disease, ankylosis, and disturbed mandibular development.

The displaced disc, which is caused by repetitive microtrauma from bruxism, clenching, malocclusion, and so on, is influenced by genetic collagen deficiency, altered synovial fluid production, inflammation, metabolic altered collagen, and hypermobility. Early management consists of medication, diet modifications, splints, physical therapy, occlusal rehabilitation, and other measures. When nonsurgical measures fail, surgical intervention is necessary to repair or replace anatomic deficiencies in the face of pain, dysfunction, and pathology noted with appropriate diagnostic imaging. Disc displacement frequently leads to calcifications, arthritides, synovitis, adhesions, perforations, and fibrocartilaginous metaplasia of the bilaminar zone and articular cartilage.[479] All types of trauma to the disc and articular surfaces may cause collagen disruption, release of pain mediators in joint fluids, and inflammation, resulting in pain, loss of lubrication, and degeneration of surfaces. Abnormal joint loads accelerate surface wear through increased joint friction and compression, which are discussed further on.

In general, children are more susceptible to dysfunction and deformity owing to the high incidence of trauma to the chin, which is the most frequent childhood facial injury.[480] Fortunately, because of the incredible regenerative capacity of the immature condyle, most pediatric condylar trauma does not result in residual deformity (Fig. 29–81A and B). Nevertheless, prevention or appropriate nonsurgical or surgical intervention, as outlined by Kaban,[481] is the best method to avoid facial growth abnormalities. The most devastating sequela of condylar trauma in children is condylar hypoplasia, possibly resulting from interruption of the potential of the condyles to respond to the functional matrix.[482] Anatomically, the pediatric condyle is more susceptible to intracapsular injury. According to Rowe,[483,484] the immature, thinly covered, and highly vascular condyle may tend to burst open when a traumatic blow is applied. The result is a hemarthrosis containing multiple comminuted fragments of bone with a high osteogenic potential. However, for ankylosis to occur, direct condyle-fossa contact secondary to disruption of the disc must also be present.[485] In spite of this anatomic susceptibility, there is fortunately a low incidence of ankylosis in children. If bony ankylosis occurs in children, the treatment of choice is costochondral grafting to restore the condyle and ramus height. Fascia temporalis, perichondrium, or, more commonly, nothing is used to line the glenoid fossa.[481,486–489] Cleavage between the joint parts, rather than gap arthroplasty, is frequently recommended in children because of the potential for reankylosis, the lack of materials suitable for restoration of vertical dimension, and the inability to restore growth.

The cortical and trabecular framework of the adult condyle is more substantial than that of its pediatric counterpart; thus, the propensity for intracapsular fracture is reduced. Other forms of intracapsular trauma are hemarthrosis, meniscal tear, and meniscal displacement, which may occur alone or in conjunction with condylar fracture or dislocation. Ankylosis may occur, as described in experiments by Wheat[485] or as discussed by Lovasko and Laskin,[490] when disruption of the meniscal barrier occurs in conjunction with intracapsular hematoma or fracture. Meniscal tears or displacement as a result of extracapsular fracture or dislocation may lead to degenerative joint changes, pain, or hypomobility.[491] This situation may be mediated by a number of factors, including obstruction from disc displacement, generation of articular carti-

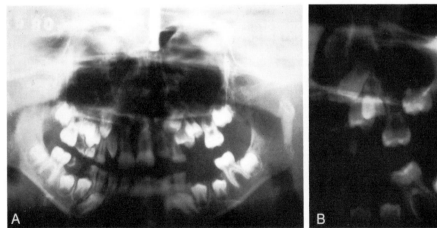
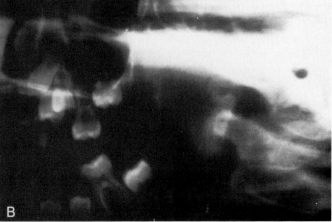

FIGURE 29–81.   *A*, Preoperative radiograph and *B*, radiograph 6 months after injury of a child with bilateral displaced condylar head fractures showing regenerative capacity of growing condyle.

laginous wear debris and inflammation from loss of the disc buffer, fibrosis, avascular necrosis, and condylar resorption mitigated by chemical and cellular mediators of inflammation. Although the need for discal repair in conjunction with open reduction of condyle fractures has recently been reported, the majority of condylar fractures are treated in a closed manner; thus, the occurrence of post-traumatic TMJ disc pathology is not uncommon.[492]

Biomechanical and Related Cellular Responses to Implant Materials

This discussion provides a limited account of the biomechanical factors that contribute to cellular and tissue responses to functioning biomaterials used in TMJ reconstruction, responses that cause hypomobility, pain, and bone resorption. Because of the anatomic and functional complexity of the TMJ, biomechanical analyses of the forces in this joint are difficult to compute. However, recently retrieved materials from reconstructed joints in patients often are indicative of the range of loads in the TMJ. For example, retrieved Vitek-Kent (VK) glenoid fossa or silicone rubber prostheses in patients with abusive parafunctional habits and poor occlusion indicate that these implants had a history of high functional stress and rate of wear, resulting in a dramatically reduced in situ service life. In patients in whom these implants were properly placed and the occlusion managed, with parafunctional habits eliminated or minimized, the implants were found to have an acceptable in situ service life.[493] Properly placed implants in patients with satisfactory occlusion in the absence of bruxism and clenching, with normal muscle activity, probably have a normal load imparted to the implant surface. Unfortunately, most patients with TMJ problems in need of disc surgery often have occlusal discrepancies and parafunctional habits leading to high joint loads, which are recalcitrant to treatment. In addition, systemic disease or localized osteoarthritic problems, preoperative and postoperative, can lead to irregular resorption of the condylar articulating surface. In both conditions, such overloading can abuse and cause increased wear and fragmenting of a joint implant.

Two entirely different types of articulation with a TMJ prosthesis can occur—rotation and translation with rotation. Most patients with disc replacement and a few patients with partial or total joint prosthesis have lateral pterygoid function and thus are capable of rotation and translation. Both movements apply force to the slope or even the height of the eminence, and in the depth or greatest concavity of the fossa. Engineering studies show that rapidly fluctuating loads lead to increased rates of wear when the polymer surface is convex such as with a polymer condyle.[494] This condition is reduced by placing the polymer on the concave surface, such as a polymer glenoid fossa.[495] Most patients with total TMJ reconstruction have minimal translation and increased rotation leading to an increased rate of polymeric wear.

Although polymer disc, condyle, or fossa implants normally manifest a benign response and excellent stabilization, they, like normal joint tissues, can succumb to abnormal biomechanical or pathologic conditions associated with TMJ function. Any articular replacement cannot be expected to reverse ongoing disease processes or compensate for previously failed procedures secondary to increased load. Improper placement or initial stabilization, excessive loading, placement against an irregular or remodeling surface, and an increased load history as a result of parafunctional habits can yield high stresses, resulting in displacement or abnormally high wear. Experience with orthopedic and TMJ total joint implant systems, which generally have a convex metallic surface against a concave polymer surface, has shown that all joint implant surfaces undergo wear. As discussed previously, the normal tissue reaction to polymers is a limited macrophage–giant cell response. Limited wear may be accommodated by lymphatic channels and the mononuclear phagocyte system.[12] When excessive wear and fragmentation leading to particulate polymer debris occur, a proportionally intense macrophage and giant cell response appears. Lymphadenopa-

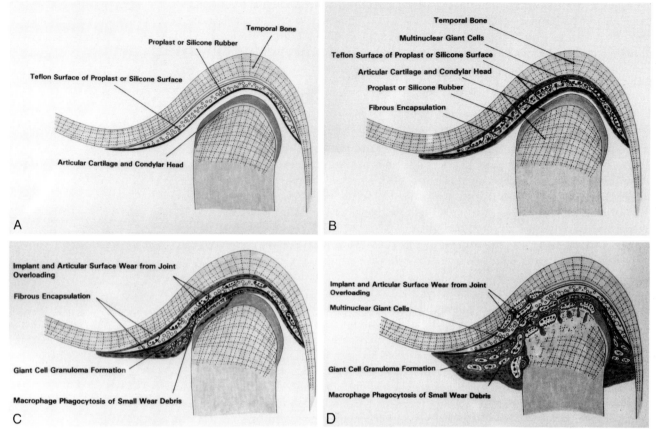

FIGURE 29–82.   Histopathologic sequence of polymeric articulating surface wear and bone resorption.   *A*, Orientation of polymer implant as a disc substitute. *B*, Normal formation of fibrous encapsulation with presence of multinucleated giant cells. These giant cells can be anywhere on the implant surface and initially are not associated with wear debris and chronic inflammation. *C*, Wear debris of the implant surface and condylar articular cartilage with phagocytosis and fibrosis. *D*, Late stages indicating implant perforation, bone resorption, and giant cell granuloma formation with central necrosis.

thy has also been reported.[496,497] Motion of the implant at any bone interface may also increase these cells. Small particles less than 5 μm are usually phagocytized by macrophages, and large debris is surrounded by giant cells (macrophage polykarons). As the system becomes overwhelmed, sheets of macrophages and their polykaryons develop into frank granulomas with peripheral fibroses and central necrosis[26] (Fig. 29–82*A* to *D*). Fibrosis results in a thick, scarred capsule that eventually reduces joint mobility. Although the exact role of macrophages and their chemotactic secretory products (lysosomal enzymes, prostaglandins, complement, lymphocyte-activating factor, and fibroblast-stimulating activity) in the failure of orthopedic implants has not been elucidated, data suggest that they contribute directly or indirectly via their secretions to degenerative joint changes, bone resorption, and loosening of a prosthesis.[12,36,37]

Loading or weight bearing appears to be the key in the development of bone resorption where particulate debris and reactive tissue are formed. Although most bone resorption is mediated by osteoclasts (another member of the mononuclear phagocyte system), macrophages assume features similar to those of osteoclasts when they are cultured with devitalized human bone.[35-40] These cells, attached to the particles, have a characteristic clear zone in their cytoplasm and secrete lysosomal enzymes.[498] In addition, macrophages are sensitive to both parathyroid hormone and calcitonin.[499] Major differences, however, are the lack of a ruffled membrane and the lack of multinucleation in the macrophage, both features so typical of the osteoclast.[36,37] Macrophages may also contribute to bone resorption via the secretion of collagenase and prostaglandins, both of which are known to play a role in bone resorption.[35] In cases in which sustained particle formation occurs, macrophage secretions may affect bone vitality. Prolonged local inflammation, mediated by plasminogen activation of bradykinin complement proteins and prostaglandins, may compromise the blood supply to bone and lead to avascular necrosis. Many of these same chemicals are potent stimulators of pain.

The behavior of artificial discs and other joint substitutes is governed by several events. Proplast in the joint, for example, when unloaded following placement, is invaded with a dense, collagenous infiltration. This occurrence is particularly true of bony onlay applications and when the mean interconnecting pore diameter is greater than 100 μm. This property of collagenization is important because tissue ingrowth into porous implants imparts important properties to the material that are thought to render it suitable for the stabilization of joint prosthesis or meniscus substitutes. Fontenot and colleagues have shown that tissue-integrated Proplast has a viscoelastic response to stress and strain that is similar to but less than that of a normal cadaver meniscus[500-502] (Fig. 29–83). Viscoelastic materials tend to distribute and reduce stresses within the material and over a contact surface. This property may help to moderate the normal sequelae of joint loading that can occur after placement of a prosthesis. An equally significant property is direct tissue continuity and encapsulation with ingrowth from the joint surface into Proplast, which permits eventual autostabilization of the implant. These two events are necessary for a successful implant.

Unfortunately, both autostabilization and a reduction of joint stresses by tissue encapsulation or ingrowth may not occur in the following clinical situation[503]: (1) failure to control abnormal loading from abusive parafunctional habits, (2) immediate and active postoperative physical therapy, and (3) failure to stabilize the implant properly. Under these conditions, tissue ingrowth into porous materials such as Proplast is minimal or absent. If incomplete tissue ingrowth develops and immediate protective encapsulation over the articular surface fails to occur, implant mobility follows. Cyclic abrasive loading of the fossa and condyle develops, leading to particulate debris and resorption, with the pathologic response progressing as described previously (Fig. 29–82A to D). In the case of nonporous implants, such as silicone rubber sheeting or blocks, the same process develops at a slower rate owing to a lack of an abrasive porous surface but leads eventually to the same state of biomechanical failure and tissue reaction. Although bone remodeling is often linked to implant placement, resorption is known to occur following any TMJ surgery and as a result of excess loading from parafunctional habits. Avascular necrosis may develop whether implants are used or not.[505] Implant success is clearly dependent on adequate control of these loading factors. Unfortunately, their placement is frequently used as a means

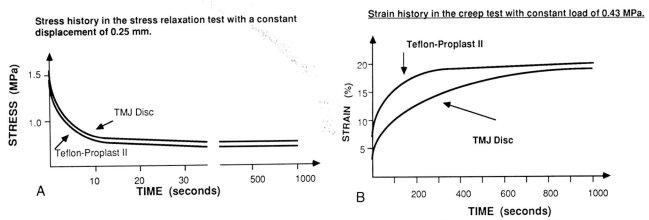

FIGURE 29–83. *A,* Mechanical stress relaxation and *B,* creep tests of human cadaver TMJ disc and Teflon-Proplast II that had been implanted in dogs.

of correcting these factors. No implant is better than the natural disc, which in many cases has been destroyed by these factors and/or disease prior to, during, or following surgery.

Disc Reconstruction

The approach to the treatment of residual post-traumatic disc injury is similar to the more common treatment of disc internal derangement that many actually believe occurs as a result of repetitive microtrauma to the joint. The 1984 American Association of Oral and Maxillofacial Surgeons *Criteria for TMJ Meniscus Surgery* states that surgery includes repositioning, repair, or replacement of the disc with or without articular contouring. Gross morphologic changes, such as deformation, calcification, and perforation, may lead to disc removal alone or disc removal with planned temporary or permanent implants, homogenous, or autogenous materials.[505,506] Histologic examination will reveal increased vascularity with cartilage formation, adhesions or frank fibrous synovitis, and loss of collagen fiber orientation.[504] Degeneration of the bony articular surfaces ensues with fibrillation and exposed subchondral bone. Myofascial pain is very common, and joint loading increases from parafunctional habits. Interpositional tissue and implant procedures are technique sensitive, and the joint response varies considerably because of this and postoperative biomechanics. These procedures are now reviewed.

DISC REPOSITIONING

Indications, detailed technique, and results of repositioning and repair of the disc are described in great detail by Dolwick and Sanders and will not be discussed here.[506] The surgical technique for this and disc replacement procedures is described in the following paragraphs and under "TMJ Surgical Techniques."

A technique for suturing the disc atop a mandibular condyle was recently described by Walker and Kalamchi[507] and is similar to the technique and postoperative management they employed for high condylectomy with silicone rubber replacement. Their study was carried out on 50 patients who had undergone TMJ surgery because of chronic joint pain, limited mouth opening, and joint noise. These patients were diagnosed as having internal derangement (disc displacement). The surgical technique consisted of performing a high condylectomy (2 to 4 mm), freeing the displaced disc, and suturing it to the condylectomy stump and the lateral capsule. Relief of pain, dysfunction, and hypomobility was obtained in 44 patients who were followed from 4 to 24 months and in 6 patients who were followed beyond 24 months.

The procedure of salvaging and repositioning a healthy disc over a condyle with osteoarthritis and an irregular cortical surface justifies the high condylectomy or shave. However, removal of 2 to 4 mm of condyle for disc repositioning and attachment in the absence of articular disease must be questioned and evaluated in comparison with routine disc repair without condylectomy.

DISC REMOVAL WITHOUT REPLACEMENT

In an extensive literature review of TMJ surgery, Merrill noted that the most common surgery for painful TMJ between 1900 and 1960 was disc removal without replacement.[508] Recent reviews of this subject have also been provided by Ioannides[509] and McCarty.[510] Meniscectomy without replacement was first reported by Lanz in 1909.[511] In 1956 Silver reported good results with 5-year follow-up on 44 patients but provided no clinical detail.[512] More recently, Silver reported a 30-year experience (range of 14 to 30 years) of 212 meniscectomies in which arthritic changes were observed in only 4 per cent of the joints.[513] All patients had at least a 30-mm opening. Of 10 bilateral cases 3 patients had recurrent pain and dysfunction. Reichenbach and Grimm[514] reported 85 per cent satisfaction with 48 patients but noted considerable joint noise and deviation with arthrosis. Mayer reported 70 per cent satisfaction with 22 patients, but all experienced hypomobility.[515] Similar results with pain have been reported by others.[516-518] In 1980, Brown reported 214 patients with a 40 per cent incidence of hypomobility and pain.[519] Of these patients, 15 per cent required additional surgery for pain. Eriksson reported at 29-year follow-up on 15 of Boman's patients; only 2 suffered from pain, and all had improved opening but radiographically showed degenerative changes.[518,520] Various animal studies by Sprinz (1954 and 1961), Lekkas (1973), Wheat and associates (1977), Yaillen and colleagues (1979), and Ioannides and Maltha (1983)[485,521-525] suggest that disc removal without replacement produces articular damage and that replacement with interpositional grafts or implants should be done. Block and Bouvier reported adverse responses of a joint that had undergone discectomy as well as the unoperated on joint in rabbits whose postoperative diet was coarse. Fibrocartilage thickness with a broadened, flattened condyle was seen in rabbits fed a coarse diet. These findings were not observed in rabbits fed a ground diet.[526,527] Block, Kent, Walters, and Misiek compared discectomy treatments in monkeys, which were as follows: no replacement, FEP-Proplast II, UHMWPE-Proplast HA, temporalis muscle flaps, and dermis. No significant differences were observed between groups after 5 months. Implant joints revealed surface erosion with polymer particles in synovial tissues, bone present in the Proplast HA layers, fibrous tissue present in Proplast II layers, and loss of glycosaminoglycoside (GAG) staining. Temporalis muscle flap joints had interposed soft tissue that was fibrous in appearance, loss of condylar GAG, and degenerative changes of the condyle. Dermis joints either maintained joint architecture or had subcondylar bone changes as well. Discectomy without replacement was usually better than any interpositional material, with dermis maintaining joint architecture better than temporalis muscle or the implants. There were joints in all groups that maintained the normal architecture or exhibited destruction.

Clearly, the control of important variables such as biting force patterns, diet, vascular insufficiency of the condyle from surgery, and loss of joint lubricant in the animal models influences the results of meniscectomized joints.[528] Of concern is commonly reported osteoarthritis with osteophytes, denudation of articular cartilage, hypomobility, and pain. In recent years, the adverse complications noted above with meniscectomy alone has led to the placement of autogenous, homogenous, and alloplastic interpositional materials. These were deemed necessary to separate the articular surfaces, reduce adhesions and degenerative changes, maintain vertical dimension, and reduce hypomobility, crepitation, and pain.

DISC REMOVAL WITH AUTOGENOUS AURICULAR CARTILAGE PLACEMENT

Autogenous auricular cartilage as a disc replacement was first described by Perko in 1973.[529] Other reports by Rudelt[530] and Witsenburg and Freihofer[531] expressed satisfactory results with limited follow-up. Recently, Ioannides and Freihofer[509] reported on 17 patients (22 joints) with a follow-up of 1 to 6 years, with a mean of almost 3 years. All patients showed a decrease in symptoms and improved function. Short intermaxillary fixation improved the mandibular opening. Matukas and Lachner,[532] in a preliminary report, followed 22 patients (35 joints) from 3 to 24 months. The primary indication for surgery was pain (TJM pain and headache) after either nonsurgical or surgical treatment. In 19 joints, meniscectomy with implants had been performed previously. In most of those patients, these symptoms had increased with chewing and talking. Relief of pain was achieved in all but two patients, and the average interincisal opening increased from 28 to 33 mm. No patients required additional surgery. An experience by Kent and associates with 18 patients (27 joints) followed from 6 to 17 months yielded equally good results for improvement of pain, hypomobility, and chewing ability.[533]

In 1987, Tucker evaluated the performance of auricular cartilage as well as a control of no replacement following disc removal in monkeys up to 6 months. The cartilage graft showed viability with fibrous tissue ingrowth. However, less condylar degenerative signs were seen compared with the control.[534]

Articular cartilage is biologically inert but does require perichondrium on at least one side to maintain viability and integrity. Cartilage has a low metabolic rate with low nutritional requirements. It is quite suitable without a vascular supply. Placement is critical because of its elastic memory. The donor site is in the same operative field and

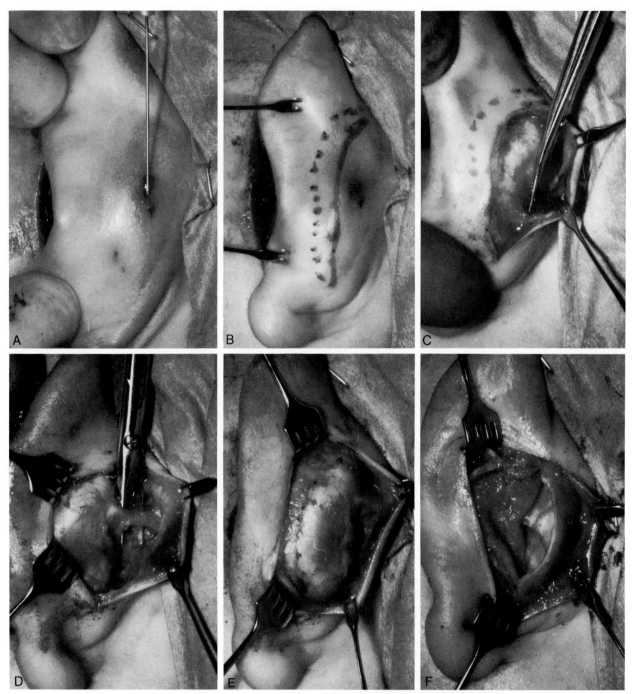

FIGURE 29–84.   Technique for replacement of TMJ disc with auricular cartilage.   *A,* Infiltration of local anesthetic with 1:100,000 epinephrine over posterior and anterior surfaces of conchal cartilage. *B,* Antihelix *(dotted line)* and incision line *(solid line). C,* Supraperichondrial dissection over conchal cartilage. *D,* Ligamentous attachment lateral to crura of helix. *E,* Incision along dotted line is made opposite the inner aspect of the antihelix. *F,* Incision with supraperichondrial or subperichondrial dissection.

Illustration continued on opposite page.

can be secured through the same incision if a postauricular approach is used. However, devitalization of portions of the ear is a concern with the postauricular approach when patients have had previous preauricular incisions.

Auricular Cartilage Graft Technique (Fig. 29–84A to J).   After necessary joint surgery is completed through a preauricular approach, a curved skin incision is made on the back of the ear over the posterior concha just opposite the inside of the antihelix to maintain outer ear integrity. This same incision is used for both taking the graft and then entering the joint through a postauricular approach. The outer layer of perichondrium is left on the graft, and the skin is dissected down to the mastoid fascia to the base of the crus of the helix. The cartilage is incised along the line of the skin incision, and the cartilage, including the inner layer of perichondrium, if preferred, is dissected from the inner skin. The graft measures 15 × 25 mm — 20 × 35 mm. If the graft is relatively flat, it is probably best placed in the joint with the vertical length in an anteroposterior direction to cover the condyle, fossa, and articular eminence following meniscectomy or implant removal. Normally, the graft will have a well-defined cup, and it is usually placed

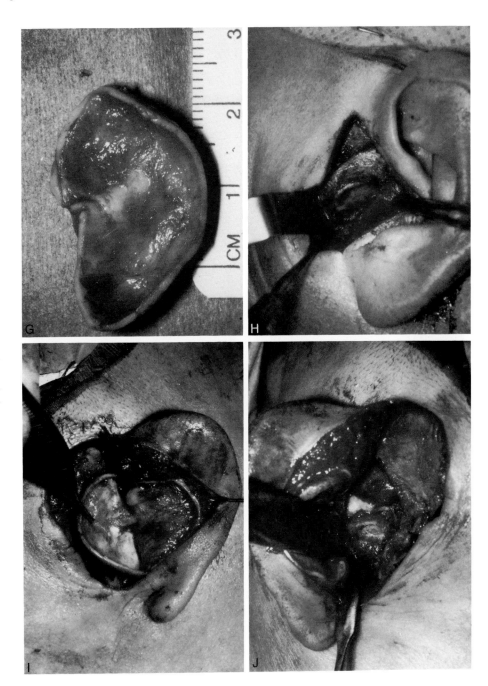

FIGURE 29–84. *Continued.* *G,* Resected conchal cartilage measuring 30 mm × 18 mm. *H,* Ventral surface of cartilage over condyle. *I,* Conchal cartilage harvesting combined with postauricular approach. *J,* Convex surface of cartilage viewed with concave surface over condyle in postauricular technique.

with the outer rim running mediolaterally and cupping the posterior aspect of the condyle. The graft is usually secured with one or two 4–0 polylactic acid sutures to the lateral capsule or bilaminar zone with an RV-1 needle. Occasionally, no sutures are necessary if the graft remains ideally positioned on observed full joint function. The graft may also be secured to the glenoid fossa/articular eminence with sutures through the roof of the zygomatic arch. Hemostasis is carefully controlled, and the skin incision is closed with running 5–0 chromic sutures after the joint is closed. No drains are placed; rather, cotton roll or balls saturated with mineral oil are packed into and behind the outer ear, and a mastoid dressing is applied.

DISC REMOVAL WITH AUTOGENOUS TEMPORALIS MUSCLE-FASCIA PLACEMENT

Temporalis fascia and muscle were first used by Golovine in 1898 for reconstruction following orbital exenteration.[535] Temporalis muscle was subsequently used for the repair of defects of the cranium, orbit, ear, and anterior skull base.[536–538] The superior portion of the temporalis fascia and muscle has been used as a pedicled flap between the condylar stump and articular fossa for correction of TMJ ankylosis.[539–543] It has also been used as a free graft for the repair of disc perforation (Fig. 29–85A to C) and traumatic perforation of the glenoid fossa after penetration of the condyle into the middle cranial fossa.[544] Its advantage is the close proximity of the TMJ with the donor site.

In a pedicle form, the temporalis muscle has been brought lateral to the zygomatic arch, the zygomatic arch has been sectioned to allow placement of the temporalis muscle in the TMJ, or the muscle has been brought medial to the arch, across the articular eminence and fossa, and sutured to the retrodiscal tissues (Fig. 29–86A and B). The pedicle technique described by Feinberg and Larsen[545] is similar to that used by Kent[546] and Tideman.[540]

Temporalis Fascia and Muscle Flap. Our technique develops a pedicled fascia, pedicled partial- or full-thickness muscle, or pedicled full-thickness fascia and muscle, with pericranium as a flap using the most posterior and horizontally oriented portion of the temporalis muscle above the arch.[546] The flap is brought medial to the arch and

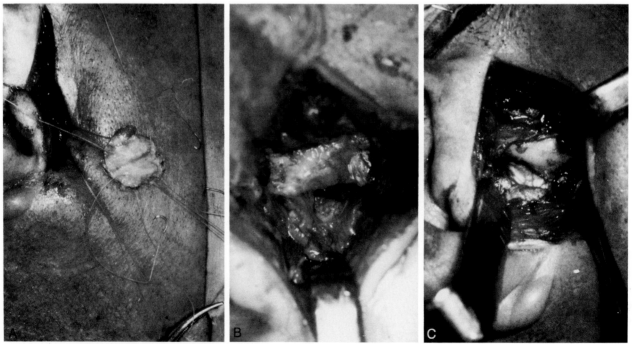

FIGURE 29–85. *A*, Temporalis fascia sutured over *B, C*, large, perforated disc in severe degenerative joint disease (DJD).

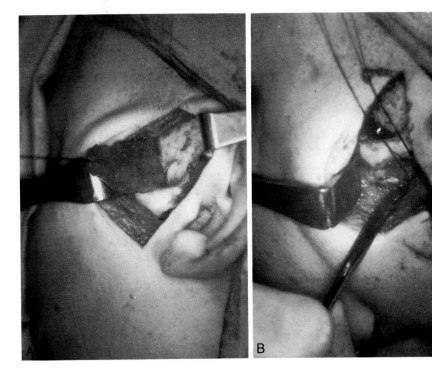

Figure 29–86. *A,* Full-thickness pedicled temporalis muscle graft to replace disc and loss of small vertical dimension from condylar resorption. Posterior fibers with suture pass pedicle beneath zygomatic arch. *B,* Pedicle sutured to retrodiscal tissues.

sutured to the medial posterior and lateral retrodiscal tissues, positioned with its pericranial side against the articular eminence and fossa. The flap is therefore pedicled off the muscular branches of the anterior and posterior deep temporal artery. Selection of the thickness of the flap is based on the amount of vertical dimension lost within the TMJ after placing the teeth in occlusion. The loss may be due to a nonrepairable disc to failed alloplastic implants or autogenous interpositional materials or to cleavage or small gap arthroplasty procedures for the correction of ankylosis.

The TMJ is approached through a modified temporal preauricular incision described by Al-Kayat and Bramley,[547] with a 2- to 3-cm superior extension above the ear. As patients with TMJ disorders frequently have bulging of the temporalis muscle lateral to the vertical plane of the zygomatic arch, care must be taken to avoid incising the deep layer of the temporalis fascia if it is to be used as a pedicled flap rather than a free graft. The periosteum over the superior and medial side of the arch must be reflected to the temporozygomatic suture line for access and for identifying the anterior and inferior extent of the incision through the muscle. A 2-cm horizontal section of the posterior fibers of the fascia or muscle or both, with or without pericranium, is mobilized so that the posterior incised margin of the flap is located just above the helix of the ear. Once the flap is elevated, it is rotated as it is brought beneath the zygomatic arch and pulled posteriorly into the joint so that the fascia side opposes the mandibular condyle and the muscle or pericranium side opposes the glenoid fossa. A 1–0 or 2–0 suture through the posterior aspect of the flap may be used to assist the maneuver of drawing the flap through the medial aspect of the arch and placement into the glenoid fossa. Stripping of the periosteum on the superior and medial aspects of the zygomatic arch facilitates the flap repositioning, frequently without the need for pull-through suture assistance. The flap is then sutured to the retrodiscal tissue from a medial to lateral direction with three or four 4–0 Vicryl sutures on an atraumatic needle. Drains are usually not placed, as an adequate mastoid pressure dressing placed for 72 hours should prevent hematoma formation.

The results of Feinberg and Larsen,[545] 19 joints in 13 patients with a follow-up of 13 months, and those of Kent and associates,[546] 25 joints in 18 patients with the longest follow-up of 42 months, have been encouraging but the treatments have not been without some complications. The pedicled temporal fascia and muscle flap is preferred as an alternative disc replacement material when significant vertical dimension has been lost and lateral pterygoid function of the mandibular condyle has not been compromised. Generally, these patients did not have as much pain relief postoperatively as patients with auricular cartilage or dermis. However, the muscle flap did have more preoperative joint disease and loss of vertical dimension. The use of free temporalis fascia, dermis, or auricular cartilage is preferred when the disc is removed and significant vertical dimension loss of the mandibular condyle is not evident. An advantage of the temporal fascia and muscle procedure, in contrast to dermis harvesting, is the availability of local tissue. The viability of a pedicle flap is superior to that of free grafts, such as dermis or free fascia. Degradation of the flap and replacement of the muscle by fibrous connective tissue could be viewed as a disadvantage. Certainly, hypomobility and return of the patient's pain because of excessive scar formation binding the articular head of the condyle are possible. Its formation and function as a pseudodisc as a result of the replacement of muscle by fibrous connective tissue may enable it to withstand increased load within the TMJ; however, the function is less and immediate hypomobility and pain are greater than with auricular cartilage or dermis grafts. Postoperative physical therapy and medication to relieve pain and muscle spasm are necessary. The postoperative opening reported by Feinberg and Kent verifies this compromise.[545,546] The usual complications of bleeding, trauma to the temporalis muscle, including the nonflap areas, disruption of the flap at its suture line to the retrodiscal tissues, and failing to incise an adequate length of the muscle flap are major disadvantages. Temporal muscle spasms and tendinitis with headaches are a common postoperative complaint for a few months.

DISC REMOVAL WITH AUTOGENOUS DERMIS PLACEMENT

In 1962, Georgiade reported the use of dermis in patients treated for internal derangement symptoms of clicking, locking, and pain.[548] In this report, the dermis was sutured in position to cover the condylar head after removal of the meniscus. Dermis grafting has also been reported in the successful treatment of ankylosis.[549-551] In 1984, Zetz and Irby reported the use of dermis grafting in treating patients with perforations of the TMJ meniscus.[552] The dermis was sutured over the perforation in the superior joint space. In 1986, separate studies by DeChamplain and associates and Tucker and colleagues evaluated this technique of suturing dermis in the perforations of the meniscus in monkeys.[553,554] The dermis showed a capacity to form a healing area in the perforated monkey meniscus. The ability of synovial cells to migrate over the dermal graft was interpreted as a positive finding indicating a return to a more anatomically normal joint. In 1989, Eppley and coworkers, using rabbits, compared sutured and grafted methods of disc repair, dermis and temporalis fascia grafts, and methods of sutured and laser-assisted graft fixation[555] on surgically created defects made anterior to the retrodiscal tissue. Seven of nine dermal grafts became incorporated into or onto the disc, retaining their own tissue characteristics. Temporalis fascia grafts failed to induce disc healing in all nine animals. Sutured defects did not demonstrate healing, and the laser-assisted technique failed as well. Meyer reported 88 per cent success in a 3- to 8-year follow-up measuring pain control and function in 58 patients having repair or replacement with dermis grafting in TMJ surgery for internal derangement.[556] Neary and Walters reported that early dermis grafting appears to be successful in secondary reconstructive surgery of the TMJ when alloplastic disc material undergoes biomechanical failure.[557] They concluded that nearly 70 per cent of their patients had significant improvement in opening and pain relief.

The technique utilized for the securing of the dermis in the surgical site varies according to the amount of pathology and the design of the repair procedure. Suturing the dermis over the perforation in the superior joint space is the technique described by Zetz and Irby and used in the experimental studies by DeChamplain and associates and Tucker and colleagues. Dermis grafting after meniscectomy requires suturing the dermis to the residual attachment tissues after resection and removal of the meniscus (Fig. 29–87).

Dermis has been used throughout the twentieth century by surgeons for repair of hernias, tendon or ligament repair, correction of facial contour, and

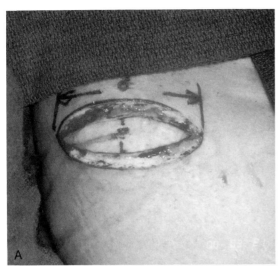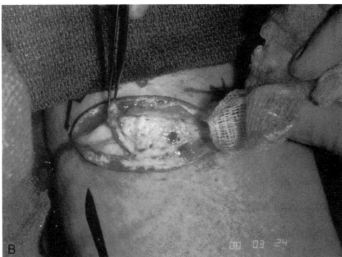

FIGURE 29–87.   *A, B,* Harvesting dermis from buttock for disc replacement.

arthroplasties.[558-562] Transplanted dermis has the capacity to form epithelial cysts from surviving epithelial appendages. This potential problem has been reported in the TMJ.[563] Studies have demonstrated the eventual disintegration and disappearance of hair follicles (at approximately 3 weeks) and sebaceous glands (at approximately 1 week), but the long-term survival of sweat glands.[564] In that same study, capillary circulation was noted in the dermis free graft. Histologic studies show that dermis remains essentially dermis with large amounts of collagen and elastin, allowing mobility and suppleness to remain. The strength characteristics of dermis are reported to be superior to those of fascia; dermis is able to resist forces from all directions, while fascia can resist forces in only two planes. Transplanted dermis is stable, with dimensional resorption limited to approximately 20 per cent.[565] Donor site morbidity (pain, cosmetic defect, and infection) are major concerns. Adhesions and fibrosis leading to hypomobility and pain are minor complaints.

The recent popularity of all autogenous grafting is due to improved postoperative management of the patient and avoidance of the alloplastic tissue reaction, described in the next section.

DISC REMOVAL WITH ALLOPLASTIC DISC REPLACEMENT

Alloplastic disc replacement has a recent history with swift and remarkable widespread use in the past two decades.[508] Advantages appeared to be several, such as avoidance of donor site morbidity, easy access and trimming, reduced surgery time, less immediate postoperative pain, and early return to normal function. Two of the most widely used materials for disc replacement have been silicone rubber and Proplast-Teflon sheeting, the former as a temporary or permanent device and the latter as a permanent device. One of the earliest reports of alloplastic replacement of the TMJ disc was provided by Gordon in 1958.[566] He placed polyethylene caps and reported good results; however, long-term follow-up was not available.

Silicone Rubber.   Silicone rubber sheeting or blocks have been used longer and more frequently than any interpositional implants or meniscal repair material. As anticipated, early reports of silicone rubber showed that most forms became encapsulated by a fibrous connective tissue. Particulate debris with macrophage and foreign body giant cell clustering was observed only under load or if trimming debris was left in the wound.[567,568] The early clinical applications were primarily in orthopedic weight bearing or loading or in soft tissue reconstructive procedures. Reactions to silicone rubber are widely known and have been summarized.[71,75]

In 1969, Hansen and Deshazo[569] reported good results 3 years following menis-

FIGURE 29–88.   Silicone rubber with fabric reinforcement used as disc substitute in TMJ.

cal repair with silicone rubber. Kreutziger and Mahan[570] described the use of silicone rubber sheeting in 1975, and Alpert in 1978[571] described success in four patients after using Silastic tubing for interpositional arthroplasty.

Silicone implants became a very popular disc replacement material following a report presented by Sanders to the AAOMS Clinical Congress in 1981[572] (Fig. 29–88). Bessette and coworkers[573] described a partial meniscectomy procedure for retention of the anterior meniscus and replacement of the posterior non–load-bearing portion of the meniscus with silicone carved to replace the thickness and shape of the resected disc in 62 patients. They reported that 87 per cent of their patients were improved 1 year after surgery and 62 per cent had an increased range of motion. In addition, 10 implants placed in monkeys were histologically evaluated at 1 and 3 months. Chronic inflammation with macrophage and giant cell response was noted in 6 of 10 animals. Although no adverse condylar changes were noted, remodeling of both condyle and fossa was seen. The meniscectomy of this study, however, differs from the usual meniscectomy in that only the posterior aspect of the disc and the bilaminar zone were removed and replaced with silicone rubber, preserving the anterior aspect of the disc for load bearing. Ryan reported 89 per cent success in 150 patients using Dacron-reinforced silicone rubber. Minimal criteria for implant success were noted, but the follow-up was only an average of 1.5 years.[574] Kalamchi and Walker[575] reported resolution of preoperative signs and symptoms in 63 of 68 patients treated with silicone and high condylectomy; follow-up ranged from 6 months to 14 years, with 30 per cent being followed for greater than 5 years.

Another modification of silicone used as a disc replacement material was introduced by Wilkes in 1982 via personal communication to Westesson[576] and possibly others. This method, as described by Hall,[577] relies upon the temporary placement of 0.020-inch Dacron-reinforced silicone into the glenoid fossa from the anterior to posterior recess, with removal 3 to 4 months after placement. The goal of this therapy is to stimulate the growth of encapsulated connective tissue that would mature into fibrocartilage and thus prevent the formation of fibrous adhesions. Eighty-five per cent of patients (34 of 40) reported by Hall had good relief of pain, and the mean postoperative range of motion was 40 mm, a 9-mm increase over the preoperative mean. The danger of this technique lies in the retention of silicone debris after removal of the temporary implants (Fig. 29–89A to D). In 1985, Dolwick and Aufdemorte reported that the biomechanical properties of silicone are not ideal for use in the TMJ.[578] They reported the histologic findings of eight patients who required implant removal because of pain or dysfunction (Fig. 29–90A to D). Their study described fragmented silicone within granulomatous tissue removed from the joint as well as silicone distributed diffusely throughout a parotid lymph node. In 1987, Westesson and colleagues[576] reported radiographic findings consistent with destructive lesions of the mandibular condyle in 6 of 20 patients who had received temporary silicone disc replacement implants. Histologic assessment of tissue retrieved from a

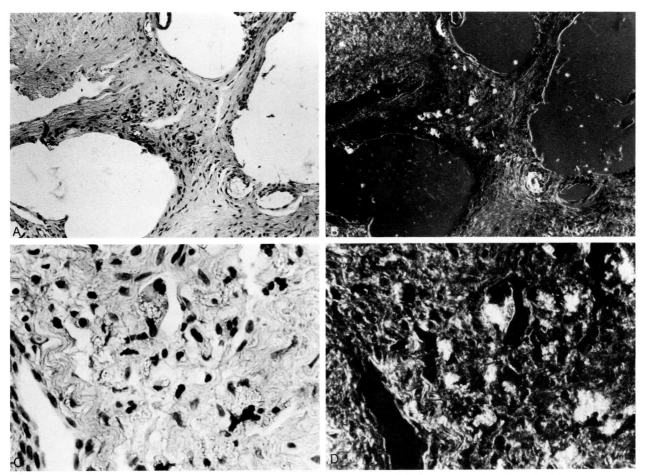

FIGURE 29–89. *A–D*, Temporary silicone rubber and tissue removed at 4 months. Multiple sections of soft tissue reveal fragments of polypoid cartilage partially covered by synovium and showing fragmentation. Fragments of fibroligamentous tissue showing focal foreign body granulomatous reaction to nonrefractile material. Sections of decalcified material reveal polypoid and fragmented cartilaginous tissue, including thickened and fibrotic synovial tissue. *A, B,* Low-power (10×) views and *C, D,* high-power views (40×) using bright-field and dark-field techniques are shown.

patient who had been reoperated on revealed particulate silicone wear debris associated with foreign body granulomas and resorption of underlying cartilage and bone (Figs. 29–89 and 29–91). The same findings are seen with Proplast particles (Fig. 29–92). In 1982, Gallagher and Wolford[579] reported that 3 of 10 Silastic implants required removal because of lateral displacement. It is interesting that they also reported satisfactory use of plain Proplast blocks without an articulating surface of Teflon in interpositional arthroplasty situations. The length of follow-up was not adequate to determine the presence of articular wear debris and tissue reaction.

Proplast-Teflon. Another material used at first in high condylectomy and then as a meniscal replacement implant was a composite of Proplast and Teflon.[580] Initially, the material was a combination of Proplast I with a dense, nonporous Teflon surface. A meniscectomy was not performed; instead, the Proplast surface was sutured to the meniscus, and the Teflon surface was allowed to articulate against the condyle after a high condylectomy.[581,582] Simultaneous implant translation with the condyle and the disc was possible. Gliding motion between the implant surfaces was minimal, since the disc was not removed (Fig. 29–93A to F). Significant loading of the TMJ was not realized, and the early success with this material, approximately 80 per cent, led to the development of Proplast-Teflon interpositional implants (PTIPIs) as meniscus replacements in the early 1980s. They were a combination of Proplast II

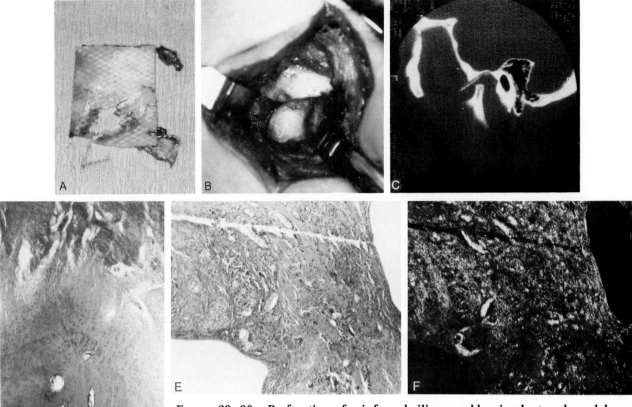

FIGURE 29–90.   **Perforation of reinforced silicone rubber implant and condyle and fossa resorption at 2-year follow-up.**   *A, B,* Intraoperative views. *C,* CT of joint. *D,* Histopathology of decalcified bone and soft tissue and associated fibromuscular tissue and synovium show moderate chronic inflammation with *E,* foreign body giant cell reaction and *F,* particles refractile to polarized light.

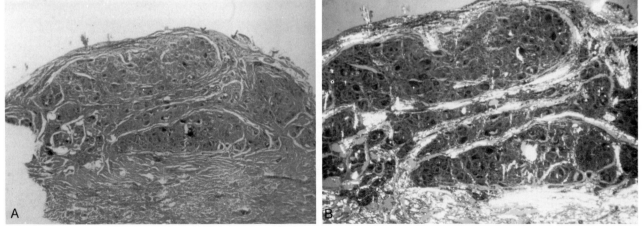

FIGURE 29–91.   *A, B,* Patient had a failed silicone rubber disc replaced with a Proplast-Teflon implant and rib graft. The failed Proplast implant was replaced with a dermis graft. Dermis was removed because of continued pain and resorption. Particulate debris is found in the dermis. *A,* Hematoxylin and eosin and *B,* dark-field photomicrographs (10×). Benign fibroligamentous tissue includes skeletal muscle and portions of cartilage. The larger fragment shows complete replacement by dense foreign body granulomatous reaction to both doubly refractile and nonrefractile particles.

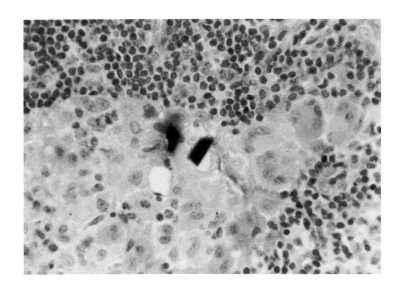

FIGURE 29–92. Lymph node hyperplasia and inflammation seen with carbon particle in macrophage.

laminated to Teflon FEP, a dense, nonporous material that provided a bearing surface for condylar articulation (Vitek, Inc.). PTIPIs were available as sheeting or as preformed implants embedded with or without polyaramid fabric in thicknesses from 1.3 to 4.3 mm (Fig. 29–94A and B). These devices attached to the glenoid fossa, encouraging tissue ingrowth and eliminating a superior joint space. Their use was widespread and included placement over loaded, shaved, or diseased condylar surfaces as were silicone implants. This practice is now seriously questioned, since condylar loading and remodeling vary, resulting in implant breakdown, tissue reaction, and bone resorption (Fig. 29–95A to D). Suggestions for proper PTIPI and silicone rubber replacement, as well as postoperative patient management, have been provided by the manufacturer[583] and have been discussed by Merrill.[508]

The first report describing PTIPI placement after meniscectomy was presented by Kiersch in 1983.[584,585] He reported 173 cases with an average of 4.36 years of preoperative pain and included subjects with degenerative joint disease, displaced or perforated meniscus, and rheumatoid arthritis. He reported an excellent result (43 per cent), good result (39 per cent), adequate result (11 per cent), and poor result (7 per cent) for this group of patients. Merrill conducted a survey in 1985 on TMJ surgery experience and found that 17 of 47 responses favored Proplast and 5 favored silicone rubber. A repeat survey in 1987 showed a very low preference for any alloplastic implant.[586] In 1986, 322 surgeons participated in a Vitek survey offered to the membership of the AAOMS, the results of which are given in Table 29–8.[587] This study asked surgeons to identify the number of satisfactory and unsatisfactory results with meniscectomy and silicone rubber, Proplast-Teflon, autogenous tissue replacement as well as meniscus repairs. Success rates for all procedures were nearly 80 per cent or greater. The length of follow-up, however, was not provided.

The tissue response to Teflon observed by early investigators is controversial. In 1963, Calnan evaluated several polymers for reconstruction and concluded that one form of smooth Teflon was the least reactive and was without significant permanent giant cell production. All materials were encapsulated with fibrous connective tissue.[588] Charnley had used Teflon as early as 1960[589] for hip replacement and concluded that the Teflon coefficient of friction approached that of articular cartilage.

However, early evaluation of one form of Teflon (PTFE) for orthopedic weight bearing by Charnley in 1963[590] and by Leidholt and Gorman in 1965[591] showed that surface abrasion and particulate debris caused an intense foreign body giant cell response with granuloma formation, bone resorption, and implant fracture. Lymphadenopathy from abrasion and wear particles of Proplast-Teflon TMJ disc has been reported.[496]

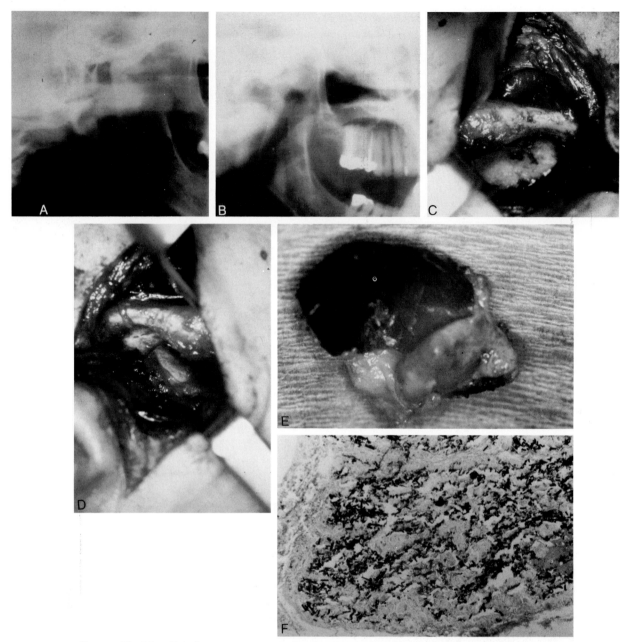

FIGURE 29–93.   **Proplast nonporous Teflon laminate placed over condyle surface after high condylectomy with no removal of meniscus.**   *A,* Preoperative radiograph of joint. *B,* Radiograph 10 years after surgery, showing some loss of condylar height and width from high condylectomy and function over implant. *C,* Normal glenoid fossa and *D,* intact cortical articulating surface of remaining condyle. *E,* Proplast implant and tissue. *F,* Histologic section of ingrown and encapsulated tissue shows extensive fibrous connective tissue and minimal inflammatory cells.

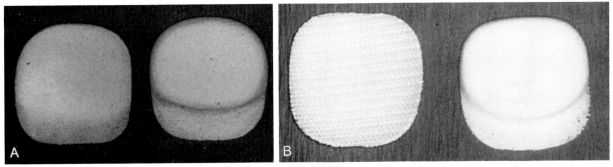

FIGURE 29–94. *A*, Nonreinforced Proplast II–nonporous Teflon interpositional implant. *B*, Reinforced (polyaramid fabric) Proplast II–nonporous Teflon interpositional implant.

FIGURE 29–95. *A*, Proplast II–nonporous Teflon implant placed after meniscectomy against healthy cortical surface of the condyle. *B*, Proplast II–nonporous Teflon implant placed after meniscectomy against shaved condyle with medullary bone exposed. Failure would be expected here owing to unpredictable condylar remodeling. *C*, Proplast II–nonporous Teflon implants reinforced with polyaramid fabric placed against healthy cortical surface of condyle. Satisfactory result at 3 years. *D*, Proplast II–nonporous Teflon implant reinforced with polyaramid fabric placed against shaved condylar head. Unpredictable condyle resorption and ultimate failure again can be expected.

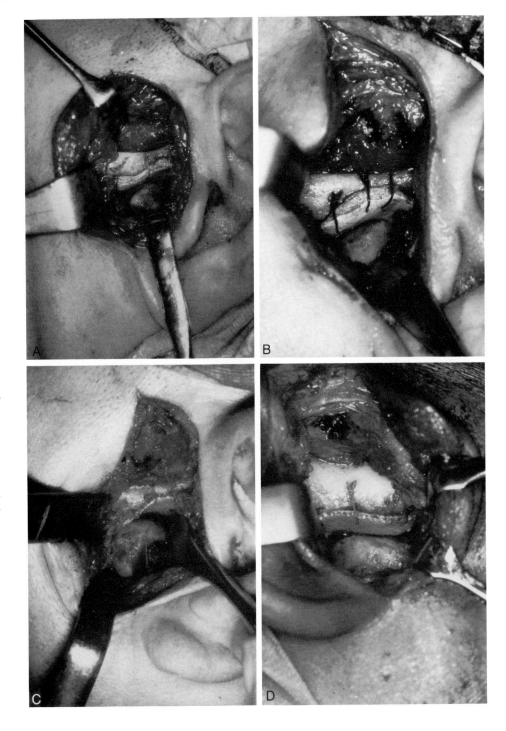

TABLE 29–8.   VITEK TMJ SURVEY RESULTS*

Type of Procedure	Number of Surgeons Reporting	Number of Procedures	Mean Number of Operations/ Surgeons	Mean % Satisfactory†	Standard Error for Mean % Satisfactory
Meniscus repair without interpositional material	268 (83.2%)	7053	29.0	85.7	1.1
Meniscectomy using silicone rubber sheeting	117 (36.3%)	958	9.5	79.3	1.7
Meniscectomy using Proplast– nonporous Teflon laminates	259 (80.4%)	4686	19.6	91.5	1.0
Meniscectomy using autogenous or homogenous tissue	50 (15.5%)	356	7.9	82.9	1.7

The total number of responders was 322. ( ) = per cent of total survey responders.

* Summary statistics for number of operations and reported percentage of satisfactory results for four types of procedures.

† Each surgeon's report contributes equally to the mean value of percentage of satisfactory results for each procedure.

By 1972, Homsy had developed Proplast, a porous composite of Teflon and carbon, to encourage tissue ingrowth and stabilization, since it was generally felt that motion from mechanical stimuli contributed to adverse tissue reaction.[138–140] The large pore volume would allow for bone ingrowth to obtain stability. The presence of giant cells was noted by Homsy and felt to be transient, or at least not harmful in small numbers, and related to motion and mechanical stimuli. Recently, a number of clinicians specializing in TMJ disorders and radiologists have reported a significant incidence of condylar resorption, pain, and malocclusion from the use of Proplast-Teflon disc replacement.[592–598] Apparently, the degree of motion and mechanical stimuli or anticipated load within the TMJ exceeded the tolerance of material and expectation of the manufacturer.

In 1987, Heffez and colleagues[592] discussed preoperative and postoperative clinical and radiographic findings in 12 patients who underwent meniscectomy and replacement with PTIPIs. Clinical assessment after a mean follow-up of 11.8 months revealed that six patients had an excellent result, two had a good result, one had some improvement, and one had a poor result; there were no postoperative occlusal changes reported. Their radiographic assessment comparing preoperative tomograms and postoperative CT scans showed severe postoperative remodeling of the condyle, glenoid fossa, and eminence in 8 of 11 joints. Fossa adaptation was good in 9 of 12 joints. Eminence adaptation was poor in 7 of 12 joints. Only one patient with a persistent clenching habit required implant removal in which the postsurgical clinical result was not changed by removal of the implant. Overall, symptoms were not synonymous with osseous changes. Fossa erosion produced a large intra-articular space of connective tissue, which maintained vertical dimension. Although the authors remarked that their radiographic findings were more severe and differed from those reported by Eriksson and Westesson in patients with discectomy alone, it is possible that these differences can in part be explained by the fact that their radiographs were obtained less than 1 year after surgery, during a period of obligatory postmeniscectomy remodeling. Eriksson and Westesson obtained their results an average of 29 years postoperatively, when anatomic stability had been achieved.[592,599] On the other hand, resorption of the TMJ bony surfaces may not allow eventual favorable remodeling, particularly in the face of tissue reaction from a worn or fragmented implant surface.

In 1987, Bronstein[593] reported a tomographic comparison of 20 joints treated with silicone implants and 18 joints treated with PTIPIs. One PTIPI was removed. Radiographic changes of the condyle in the PTIPI group were more severe, but most patients had an acceptable clinical progress. Unfavorable results with 55 Proplast implants were reported by Florine and colleagues in 1988.[594] Using a tomographic evaluation, this paper compared joints that had undergone either discoplasty or discectomy with PTFE placement. It is interesting that the implants were described as being laminates of Proplast porous PTFE or dense, smooth PTFE rather than having FEP on the articular surface, which provides improved wear characteristics under joint function. Stretching exercises were begun 1 or 2 days postoperatively, which may be contraindicated, since early physical therapy interferes with connective tissue stabilization of the implant, encapsulation, and the development of viscoelastic properties. Nine of 15 patients who received bilateral PTFE implants developed open bites. Severe condylar and fossa resorption was common. Since changes in TMJ morphology after discoplasty and discectomy alone are not similar, it was difficult to derive comparative conclusions from the two populations presented for study in this paper. However, the results showed 34 joints with severe condylar changes and 16 joints with moderate condylar changes out of 82 that were treated with PTFE. The developing open bite malocclusions and bone resorption of the joint suggest that this material alone, without the benefit of FEP on the articular surface and without the benefit of adequate connective tissue integration (because of early loading from active and aggressive physical therapy), is not, as the authors state, able to withstand forces generated in the TMJ. Patients' comfort, function, and satisfaction were high and did not correlate with the condylar degeneration.

Others have noted similar results with Proplast-Teflon.[595–598,600–602] In 1986, McBride presented the results achieved with Proplast-Teflon implants that were placed in 245 joints of 144 patients, with a mean follow-up of 34 months. Eighty-four per cent of the implants were bilateral. Eighty-seven per cent of the patients exhibited mild-to-moderate symptoms of osteoarthritis. Seventy-five per cent of the patients had nonreducible discs, and 24 per cent had perforations. Relief of symptoms was excellent in 75 per cent of the patients and good, fair, or poor in the remaining 25 per cent. Seventeen per cent of the implants were removed. The postoperative symptoms of the group with good or poor results (25 per cent) were essentially the same as their preoperative symptoms: 38 per cent had joint pain, 46 per cent had joint noise, and 48 per cent had headaches. However, 67 per cent of the joints had noticeable or measurable condylar resorption, ranging from 1 mm (13 per cent) to 1 to 3 mm (23 per cent) to over 3 mm (31 per cent). Patients in the last group developed open-bite deformity.[601]

Estabrooks and colleagues conducted a retrospective review of 301 meniscectomies with Proplast-Teflon implants.[602] Factors such as interincisal opening, occlusion, joint sounds, joint degeneration, and satisfaction on the part of the patient were examined. In 55 per cent of the joints, the disc was displaced without reduction, and 44 per cent had perforation. In 77 per cent of the joints, degenerative disease was noted in one of the articular surfaces. The overall surgical success rate was 88.7 per cent, with an average follow-up period of 33 months. Although many patients demonstrated significant condylar degeneration at 1-year follow-up, such change did not necessarily result in symptomatology or joint dysfunction. Only 10 per cent of implants were removed. Estabrooks felt that minimal postoperative therapy and condylar motion, which allowed tissue encapsulation of the Teflon and ingrowth into the Proplast, contributed to the success.[602]

Animal Studies of Disc Replacement.   Small animal studies of TMJ polymer disc replacements are sparse, since the physical properties of most implants are not adequate for small joints. In 1986, Timmis and associates[603] used New Zealand rabbits in which 8 were used as control subjects (joints opened, washed out, and closed without discectomy) and 32 were used as experimental subjects, all of which underwent discectomy followed by placement of disc implants. All animals were maintained with Teklad pellets and water at will, and subjects from each group were sacrificed at 2, 8, and 20 weeks. The control specimens had intact discs and minor degeneration of the articular surfaces at 2 and 4 weeks but displayed none of the changes seen in other species after discectomy.[604] In the group treated with silicone rubber, all implants were encapsulated, and silicone particulate debris associated with foreign body responses, characterized by both giant cells and macrophages, was present at all times. Resorptive changes of the articular surfaces were present at 2, 4, and 8 weeks but appeared to stabilize by 20 weeks. Displaced implants were present in both the 4- and the 8-week groups. Particulate debris and foreign body responses were also associated with Proplast-Teflon at all survival times, with necrosis appearing by 20 weeks. Displaced implants were present at 4, 8, and 20 weeks, and tearing of the implants was present in each group. Marked bone resorption with osteoclast activity persisted through 20 weeks. The control subjects did not undergo discectomy; thus, changes in fossa or condylar morphology that might occur as a result of that procedure alone were not evaluated or compared with those observed in control specimens.

No data concerning the thickness of the rabbit discs removed are provided. Human implants of 1-mm Dacron-reinforced silicone rubber and 1.3-mm PTIPI thicknesses were used. This factor may have a significant influence on the results, since the average disc thickness for the rabbit is only 0.3 mm, which is 3.3 times less than the silicone rubber and 4.3 times less than the PTIPIs.[604] Changes of this magnitude severely overload the joint and result in early mobility and displacement, leading to accelerated implant fatigue, wear, and bone resorption. In addition, active and early postoperative function is noncontrollable. The animals were placed on pellets rather than a soft diet postoperatively, the chewing of which can have a negative effect on soft tissue encapsulation of silicone rubber and encapsulation with infiltration, which is necessary for the development of viscoelastic properties in PTIPIs.

El Deeb also evaluated these implant materials in monkeys.[605] The TMJ menisci in animals were replaced with Proplast-Teflon in one side and silicone rubber in the contralateral joint for up to 6 months. Postoperative gross examination revealed that the Proplast was more stable than the silicone rubber. In all cases, there was a thick fibrotic layer between the implants and the condylar surface. This fibrotic layer was not uniform in thickness and was thicker in the Proplast implant than in the silicone rubber. The TMJ condylar surface showed various degrees of degenerative joint changes as well as bony exostosis with all implants. Histologic evaluation of the Proplast showed many foreign body giant cells present at 3 months. At 6 months, the Proplast implants were invaded from the non-Teflon side by foreign body giant cells and histiocytes. The implants showed intense giant cell response at 6 weeks, 3 months, and 6 months. At 1 year, the intensity of the response had decreased with the silicone rubber but had increased with the Proplast. Again, the human implants used in this study are twice the thickness of the removed animal disc.

The results of these two animal studies may not represent a normal, unloaded, restored joint, but, rather they intentionally portray the effects of severe loading on these implants and on joint morphology resulting from differences in thickness between the meniscus and the implants. Nevertheless, knowing the effects of such increased loading, which produces reactive soft tissue, bone changes, and implant mechanical failure, is beneficial, since increased load forces are now strongly suspected, but not quantified, in the pathologic human joint. Excess loading of polymer surfaces against bone unquestionably initiates the process of implant wear, fragmentation, and displacement, leading to severe soft and hard tissue reactions. As stated previously, a limited macrophage and giant cell response occurs with all polymers. However in the highly successful use of polymer implants such as silicone rubber, Teflon, Proplast, and MMA for unloaded applications of facial, breast, orbital floor repair and skeletal augmentation, these cellular findings, noted on removal of the implant after very long-term follow-up with no clinical problems, are not increasingly persistent or problematic.

Multicenter Study of Proplast-Teflon Implants. Because of the recent (1983 to 1986) extensive use of Proplast-Teflon implants by oral and maxillofacial surgeons and the impact of animal studies, a large multicenter study of these implants was done.

A four-page data base furnished by Kent and Spagnoli was completed by seven oral and maxillofacial surgeons who had reconstructed 680 TMJs in 465 patients following disc removal through 1987 (Table 29–9).[503] All patients were treated outside Louisiana by these surgeons, spanning all U.S. AAOMS districts. Of the patients, 96 per cent were female. Of the 680 joints, 584 (85.9 per cent) had functioning Proplast-Teflon implants, while 96 (14.1 per cent) were removed. Of the 96 removed implants, 16 were unilateral and 80 were bilateral. Patients who continued to function with their implants had an average of 33 months of postoperative follow-up; however, the average span of time prior to implant removal was only 20 months. Follow-up ranged from 6 to 76 months, with a weighted average follow-up of 31.9 months. Twenty-eight per cent required unilateral implant placement, and 72 per cent required bilateral placement. The incidence of removed implants, unilateral and bilateral, was 8.5 per cent and 16.2 per cent, respectively (Table 29–9A).

Table 29–9 shows that 540 (92.4 per cent) of the joints with functioning Proplast-Teflon implants are asymptomatic; however, 44 (7.6 per cent) are symptomatic, with associated pain or decreased range of motion or both. Three hundred sixteen (58.5 per cent) of the asymptomatic and 19 (43.3 per cent) of the symptomatic joints did not have evidence of occlusal or condylar changes, whereas 185 (34.2 per cent) of the asymptomatic and 19 (43.3 per cent) of the symptomatic joints had condylar but not occlusal changes. Occlusal and condylar changes were present in 39 (7.3 per cent) of the asymptomatic and 6 (13.4 per cent) of the symptomatic joints. The significance of this data is discussed further on.

Conditions associated with removal of 96 implants are described in Table 29–9C. Remarkably, 9, or 9.4 per cent, of the removed implants came from asymptomatic joints without clinical or radiographic criteria for removal. The reason given by patients was the fear of problems described by lawyers and newspaper accounts of lawsuits. Of the joints, 14.5 per cent had a history of trauma *after* Proplast-Teflon implant placement. Implant mobility or displacement was detected in 11 per cent of the joints, and 3 per cent of the joints were compromised by infection. Signs associated with implant removal include pain (80 per cent), malocclusion (39 per cent), and hypomobility (35 per cent).

Operative findings associated with wear and stability of the 96 removed implants, together with gross observations of the intracapsular tissues, are recorded in Table 29–9D. Although 30 per cent of the removed implants had no observable wear, Teflon wear only was present in 4 per cent and perforation into Proplast was found in 39 per cent of the removed implants. Intracapsular granulomatous tissue was associated with 27 per cent of the retrieved implants. Twenty-two per cent of the implants were encapsulated on their superior side, and 61 per cent were encapsulated on the inferior side. Condylar, fossa, and eminence resorption was observed in 46 per cent, 23 per cent, and 9 per cent of these joints, respectively. A smooth, hard, cortical condyle was present in 29 per cent of the joints, whereas a rough, irregular, cancellous, resorbed condyle was observed in 31 per cent. Reconstructions with total joint prostheses or rib grafts, temporalis flaps, or dermis and cartilage grafts, along with osteotomies following implant removal, were reported (Figs. 29–96 and 29–97).

The preoperative diagnosis influenced the results (Table 29–9E). Trends show that joints associated with myofascial pain, disc displacement without recapture, condylar resorption, and clenching, bruxism, or malocclusion had a relative increase in frequency in patients with Proplast-Teflon implant removal. In contrast, diagnoses such as disc displacement with recapture, disc perforation, degenerative joint disease, rheumatoid arthritis, and bony ankylosis were not related to an increased frequency of implant removal. Although fibrous ankylosis was not associated with an increased frequency of implant removal when the diagnosis was made prior to any surgery, it was associated with a slight relative increase in removal when the diagnosis was made at the time of implant placement.

The effects of procedures performed prior to Proplast-Teflon implant surgery and of condylar surgery performed at the time of implant placement are interesting.

TABLE 29-9. PROPLAST-TEFLON INTERPOSITIONAL IMPLANT STUDY

A. Patient Profile

Patients: 465	Male 4%	Female 96%
Joints: 680		
Unilateral:	188	(27.6%)
Bilateral:	492	(72.4%)
In Place: 584	(85.9%)	
Unilateral:	172	(29.4%)
Bilateral:	412	(70.6%)
Removed: 96	(14.1%)	
Unilateral:	16	(16.6%)
Bilateral:	80	(83.4%)

Incidence of unilateral removed: 8.5%   Average follow-up of implants in place: 33 mo
Incidence of bilateral removed: 16.2%   Average follow-up of implants removed: 20 mo

Follow-up range: 6–76 mo   Average age of patients with implants in place: 33 yr
Weighted average follow-up: 31.9 mo   Average age of patients with implants removed: 30 yr

B. Patient Status of In-Place Proplast-Teflon Implant (PTI) ($N = 584$)

	Asymptomatic ($N = 540$)		Symptomatic* ($N = 44$)	
No condylar or occlusal change	316	(58.5%)	19	(43.3%)
Condylar but no occlusal changes	185	(34.2%)	19	(43.3%)
Condylar and occlusal changes	39	(7.3%)	6	(13.4%)
	540	100%	44	100%

* Pain and decreased range of motion.

C. Reasons for PTI Removal ($N = 96$)

Pain	77	(80.2%)
Condylar resorption	64	(66.6%)
Malocclusion	38	(39.6%)
Hypomobility	34	(35.4%)
Trauma	14	(14.6%)
Mobility/displacement	11	(11.5%)
Legal	9	(9.4%)
Infection	3	(3.1%)

D. Operative Findings at PTI Removal ($N = 96$)

Wear into Proplast	38	(39.6%)
No wear	30	(31.3%)
Teflon wear only	4	(4.2%)
Fractured	14	(14.6%)
Displaced	10	(10.4%)
Loose	9	(9.4%)
Buckled	3	(3.1%)
Encapsulated inferior surface	59	(61.5%)
Encapsulated superior surface	22	(21.8%)
Condylar resorption	44	(45.8%)
Fossa/eminence resorption	31	(32.3%)
Rough, irregular condyle	30	(31.3%)
Smooth, cortical condyle	28	(29.2%)
Granulomatous tissue	26	(27.1%)

E. Diagnosis Before TMJ Surgery ($N = 680$)

	PTI in Place	PTI Removed	All
Disc displacement without recapture	62.5%	87.5%†	66.0%
Myofacial pain dysfunction (MPD)	33.5%	69.8%†	38.67%
Disc displacement with recapture	29.5%	21.8%	20.7%†
Degenerative joint disease (DJD)	29.2%	27.0%	28.9%†
Disc perforation	28.9%	28.1%	28.8%†
Clenching, bruxism, and malocclusion	12.5%	46.8%†	17.3%
Fibrous ankylosis	4.1%	2.1%	3.8%
Condylar resorption	1.5%	4.1%†	1.9%
Rheumatoid arthritis	0.68%	0	0.58%†
Bony ankylosis	0	0	0

† Trends.

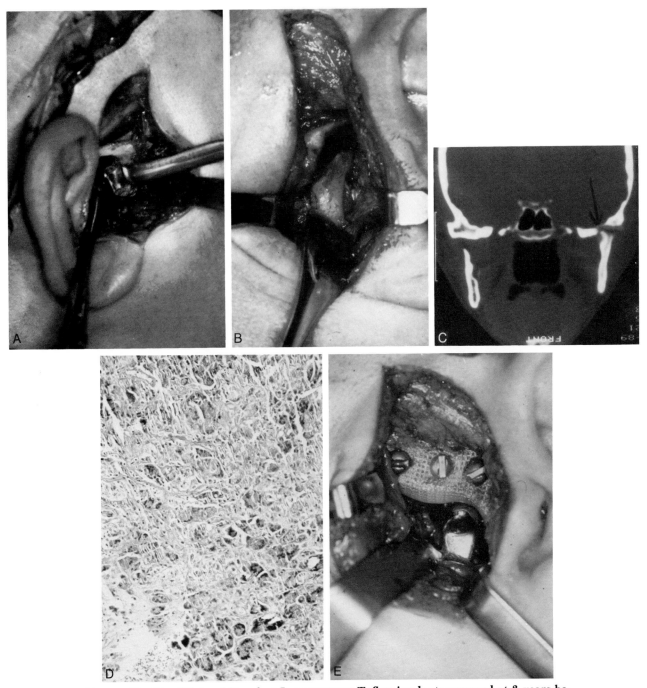

FIGURE 29–96. Bilateral Proplast I–nonporous Teflon implants removed at 3 years because of pain, condylar resorption, and development of a hypomobility, open bite deformity. *A,* Proplast I–nonporous Teflon implant is rolled up and displaced. *B,* Condyle and fossa resorption noted following implant removal. *C,* Preoperative CT demonstrating both condyle and glenoid fossa resorption with near perforation of the glenoid fossa into the middle cranial fossa. *D,* Extensive foreign body giant cell reaction to wear debris. *E,* Reconstruction with VK-I total TMJ system with coronoid process bone graft to reinforce glenoid fossa thinning.

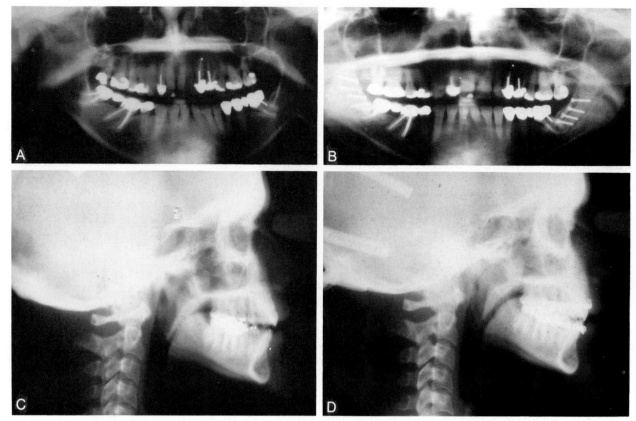

FIGURE 29–97. *A*, Preoperative and *B*, postoperative radiographs showing Proplast I–nonporous Teflon implants that failed because of trauma 2 years after placement. Reconstruction consisted of bilateral temporal muscle flaps with sagittal ramus osteotomies to correct bite and restore function. *C*, Preoperative and *D*, postoperative radiographs of bilateral Proplast II–nonporous Teflon implants. Pain, hypomobility, and open bite developed 2 years postoperatively. Implants were removed intact, leaving a normal-appearing dense, fibrous sheath between each condyle and glenoid fossa. A Le Fort I osteotomy was done to correct the open bite.

Although 84 per cent of patients participated in nonsurgical therapy, few surgical procedures were performed on these joints prior to implant placement. Only 62 joints had had previous surgery (plication in 95 per cent). In 30 per cent of these, the implant was removed, nearly twice the removal rate for the entire study. In contrast, joints that underwent condyle shaving at the time of implant placement did not have an increased frequency of implant removal. A total of 320 joints, or 48.5 per cent of all patients in the study, had some form of condyle shaving. Only 30, or 9 per cent, of the 330 joints that had condyle surgery required removal of the Proplast-Teflon implant.

Of concern are those patients with condylar or occlusal changes or both (Table 29–9B). Since continued condylar destruction is possible owing to joint loading and reaction to polymer debris, maximal implant removal could increase to 50 per cent. Some of these patients may even become symptomatic following implant removal and soft tissue grafting with temporalis muscle, ear cartilage, or dermis. In our own experience, more than 50 per cent of approximately 75 referred implant patients have proceeded to major joint reconstruction. When implants are removed, thorough debridement of the periarticular tissue is necessary for successful soft tissue grafting. Our experiences are good with ear cartilage and temporalis fascia or muscle and less favorable with dermis. Tissue reaction noted at implant removal includes fibrous encapsulation of polymer debris with giant cell granuloma formation as the debris increases. Biopsy of surrounding periarticular tissue demonstrates the reaction. Formation of cartilage or bone is possible, leading to significant hypomobility.

Preauricular and submandibular lymphadenopathy with small polymer debris occurs. The joint reaction may persist if debris removal is inadequate. Foci of polymer particles will be seen, and degeneration, fragmentation, and fibrous or even osseous transformation will occur in the soft tissue grafts.

Conclusion. The current problems of alloplast, either temporary or permanent, may outweigh its use as a disc replacement. Loading factors are difficult to quantify, and the resulting biomechanical failure leads to complications that exceed those of autogenous disc replacement. Active and early physical therapy appears to prevent stabilization and adequate encapsulation of implants, making them vulnerable to articular wear. Painful synovitis and destructive arthritic changes develop. Granulomatous reactions occur, leading to condylar resorption, increased pain, and malocclusion. Close clinical follow-up is mandatory. Squeaking noises and myofascial pain dysfunction indicate excess loading and probably surface damage to the implant. Radiographic changes of the articular cortices probably indicate destruction rather than favorable remodeling. Either magnetic resonance imaging (MRI) or tomographic studies are suitable. Soft tissue reaction is readily identified by the MRI.[598] Displacement and surface changes can be seen on MRI and CT. Persistent pain, swelling, hypomobility, and condylar resorption, particularly in the face of developing malocclusion, warrant exploration and complete removal.

As noted previously, there seems to be a large pool of data on implants ranging from acceptable to very poor results. However, late condylar resorption is a concern even with acceptable results. It is noted that uncorrected or uncontrollable clinical conditions may prevent satisfactory disc replacement therapy in some patients, whether the alloplastic implant is used or not. Regardless, these experiences with the current materials, techniques, and postoperative management seriously question alloplastic disc replacement.

TMJ Surgical Techniques

Preauricular Approach.[506] Surgical approaches and their relationship to the facial nerve are shown in Figure 29–98. With the patient supine and the head turned approximately 60 degrees opposite the side that is being operated on, a cotton pledget soaked in antibiotic ointment is placed in the external auditory canal. The hair in the temporal region is shaved 2 inches above the zygomatic arch. The ear and preauricular skin are prepared and draped so that the ear, eyebrow, and lateral canthus of the eye are exposed; in this way, the surgeon may observe stimulation of the facial nerve. A sterile plastic drape may be used to keep hair out of the surgical field. The incision is outlined at the junction of the facial skin with the helix of the ear, using natural skinfolds whenever possible. Prior to incision, cord anesthesia-containing epinephrine is injected for hemostasis. To facilitate manipulation of the condyle and mandible, a large towel clamp is placed percutaneously to engage the mandibular angle posterior to the facial artery and vein and below the mandibular canal.

The incision is made and extended through the skin and superficial fascia to the depth of the temporalis fascia (Fig. 29–99A). Electrocautery or a heated scalpel is necessary to control bleeding and facilitate dissection. The superior portion of the flap is extended anteriorly along the temporalis fascia by blunt dissection. This flap also is developed inferiorly, adjacent to the external auditory canal. The surgeon must keep in mind that the canal cartilage runs inferomedially and the dissection should parallel the cartilage. The lateral capsular ligament can be identified by the presence of a large vein that may cross in the region of the articular fossa. This vein should be dissected out, clamped, and ligated or cauterized, since inadvertent division may cause excessive bleeding and retraction of the vein into the soft tissues posterior to the mandibular condyle. Starting at the root of the zygomatic arch, an incision is made superiorly and anteriorly through the superficial temporal fascia at a 45-degree angle extending to a point 2 cm above the arch (Fig. 29–99B). This incision is made only through the superficial layer of the deep temporal fascia, except when the bone of the zygomatic process of the temporal bone is encountered. Here a periosteal incision is made. This layer is elevated in an anterior and inferior direction in this plane directly down to the zygomatic process of the temporal bone and zygomatic arch (Fig. 29–99C and D). The capsule is thus exposed following subperiosteal elevation over the zygomatic arch. This practice will allow the branches of the facial nerve to be retracted forward and away from the area of dissection.

With the condyle distracted inferiorly, a local anesthetic solution with epinephrine can be injected to balloon the superior joint space. With this space identified, scissors or a scalpel may be used to enter the upper joint space, paralleling the contour of the fossa and leaving periosteum attached to the bony fossa to facilitate closure at the conclusion of the procedure. The capsule is then reflected laterally (Fig. 29–99E). The upper joint space and the disc and its attachments can be visualized and inspected with regard to position, movement, and integrity. Utilizing a large towel clip, the position of the disc can be observed with the condyle in function, and any dyskinesia can be visualized. The disc can be repositioned, and mandibular movements can be duplicated again with the towel clip to see whether or not the dyskinesias previously noted are eliminated. This practice will also allow for inspection of the anteromedial aspect of the disc to look for perforations or tears, which may determine the course of action for the remainder of the procedure (Fig. 29–99F and G). If access is limited by an enlarged lateral tubercle of the articular eminence, an osteotomy of the process may improve access (Fig. 29–99H).

The lower joint space may be entered by incising the disc along its lateral attachment to the condyle within the lateral aspect of the superior joint space (Fig. 29–99I). The lower joint space is opened, and observation of the inferior aspect of the disc as well as the contour of the condylar head may be made (Fig. 29–99J). Brisk bleeding, if encountered, may be controlled by clamping of the posterior attachment should allow the surgery to proceed in a fairly dry field. If the disc is partially displaced, a wedge of the retrodiscal region can be removed, and plication of the disc posteriorly and laterally will reposition it properly (Fig. 29–99K and L). If the disc is inspected and noted to be nonreducible or perforated and nonrepairable, it may be excised, and a local temporalis fascia or muscle free or pedicle flap, a dermis graft, an auricular cartilage graft, or an alloplast may be placed with or without recontouring (Fig. 29–99M to P). Our preferences are shown in Figures 29–84 to 29–87. Once the disc has been either repositioned or replaced, the condyle again can be placed into function utilizing the towel clip at the mandibular angle. Direct observation of the repositioned or replaced meniscus should reveal satisfactory function prior to closure.

The lower and upper joint spaces are thoroughly irrigated with saline, and any evidence of bleeding should be controlled with electrocautery or ligation. The lower joint space is closed by suturing the disc or graft back to its lateral condylar attachment. Again, when this is performed, the mandible should be placed in function to observe the relationship to the bony fossa condyle. If this relationship is satisfactory, the upper joint space is finally irrigated, hemorrhage is controlled, and the lateral capsular ligament is sutured, plicating the disc or graft both laterally and posteriorly (Fig. 29–99Q and R). The subcutaneous tissues are thoroughly irrigated, and deep closure with resorbable

Text continued on page 954.

FIGURE 29–98. *A, B,* Surgical approaches to the TMJ and landmarks as they relate to the facial nerve. Key: T = tragion point; FT = frontal division of temporal branch where it crosses the malar arch; A = most anterior concavity of the bony auditory canal; B = most inferior point on the bony auditory canal; PG = post glenoid tubercle; F = facial nerve bifurcation into temporal-facial and cervical-facial branches; A-FT = 2.0 cm (0.8–3.5); B-F = 2.3 cm (1.5–2.8); PG-F = 3.0 cm (2.4–3.5); FT-L = most posterior branch of frontal lies 4 cm posterior to lateral canthus on the T-L line; M-C = mastoid to commissure of lip; T-L = tragion to lateral canthus.

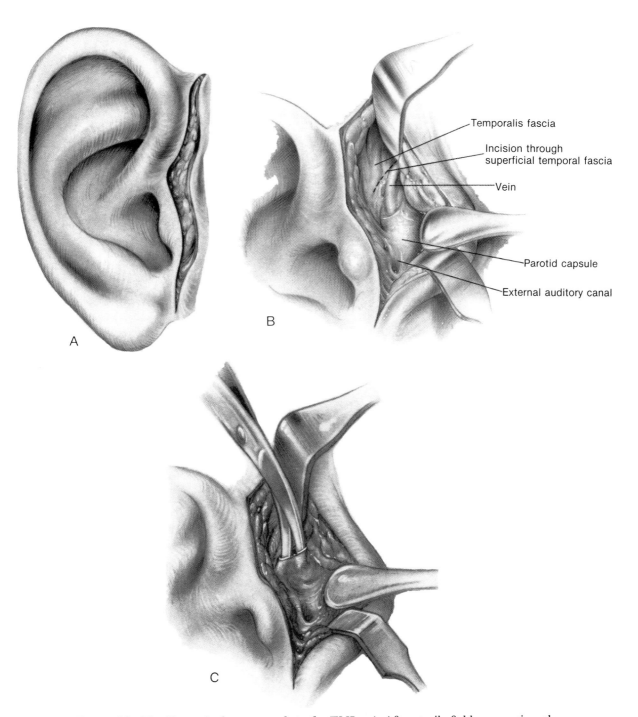

FIGURE 29–99.   **Preauricular approach to the TMJ.**   *A,* After sterile field preparation, the preauricular incision is made through skin and subcutaneous tissue to the depth of the temporalis fascia. *B,* Blunt dissection clears the temporalis fascia, and an oblique incision is made through the superficial layer of the temporalis fascia, extending to bone at the zygomatic process of the temporal bone. This incision should parallel the temporal branches of the facial nerve. *C,* Blunt dissection exposes the lateral aspect of the glenoid fossa and TMJ capsule. Overlying tissue is incised posteriorly and reflected anteriorly.

Illustration continued on following page.

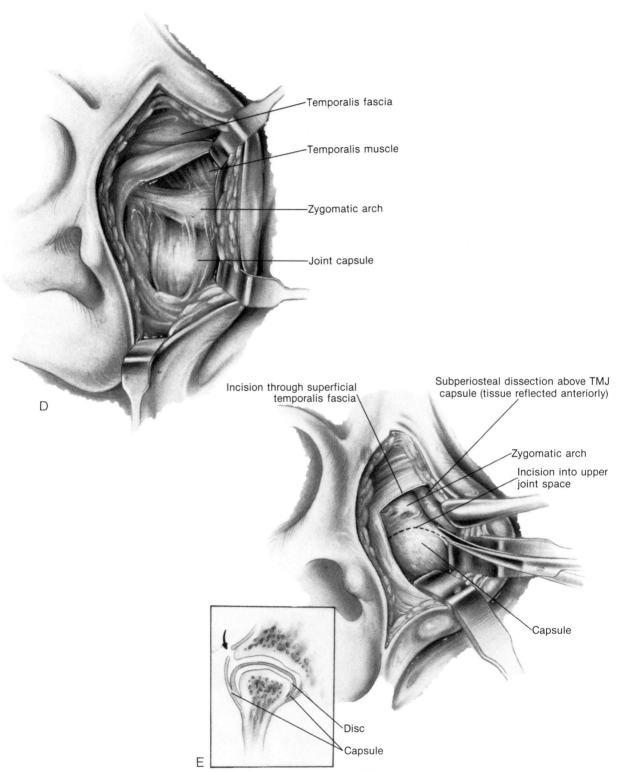

FIGURE 29–99. *Continued. D,* The TMJ capsule should be exposed at least to the articular eminence, both anteriorly and inferiorly. *E,* Distracting the condyle inferiorly, the superior joint space is incised anteroposteriorly, paralleling the fossa and eminence. The inset shows the incision in the frontal plane.

Illustration continued on opposite page.

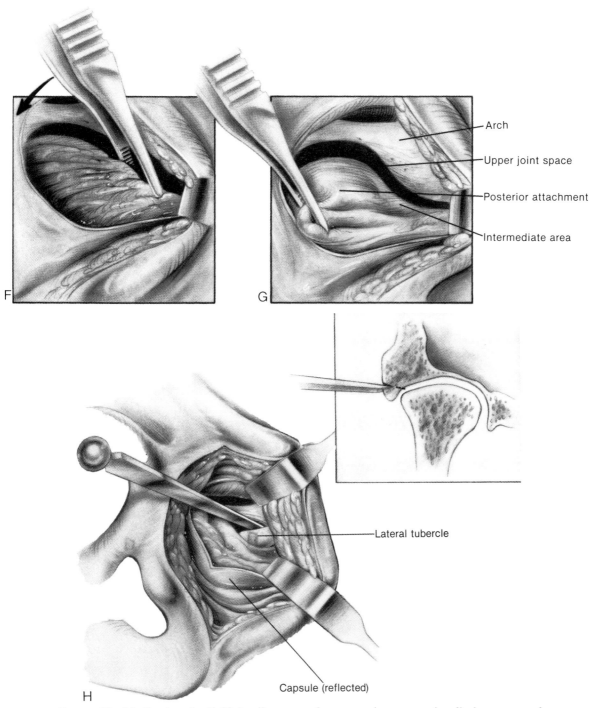

FIGURE 29–99. *Continued.* *F,* If the disc cannot be seen owing to anterior displacement and does not reduce with condyle movement, the disc can be pulled posteriorly by grasping the posterior attachment *G.* This allows the surgeon to examine the disc and determine treatment options. *H,* Occasionally, the lateral tubercle of the fossa will obstruct vision and access into the superior joint space. Removing the lateral tubercle with an osteotomy will often improve vision and access.

Illustration continued on following page.

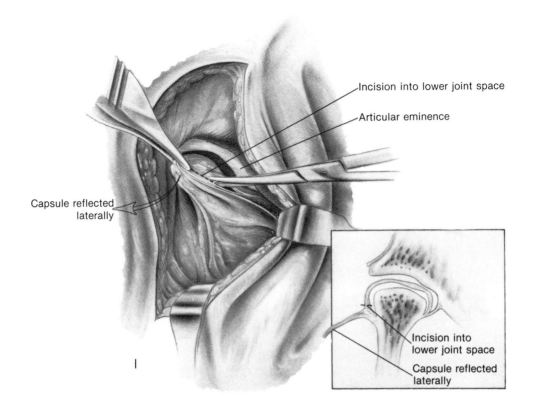

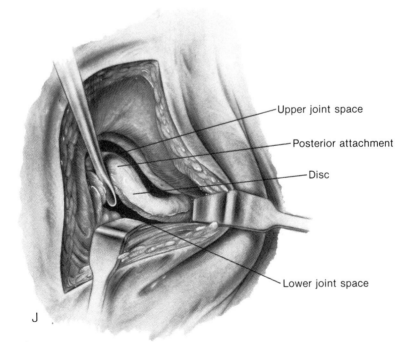

FIGURE 29-99. *Continued. I,* The lower joint space is opened by incising at the junction of the disc and the lateral capsule and posterior attachment. *J,* By inferior distraction of the condyle, the upper joint space, disc, lower joint space, and condylar head can all be visualized.

Illustration continued on opposite page.

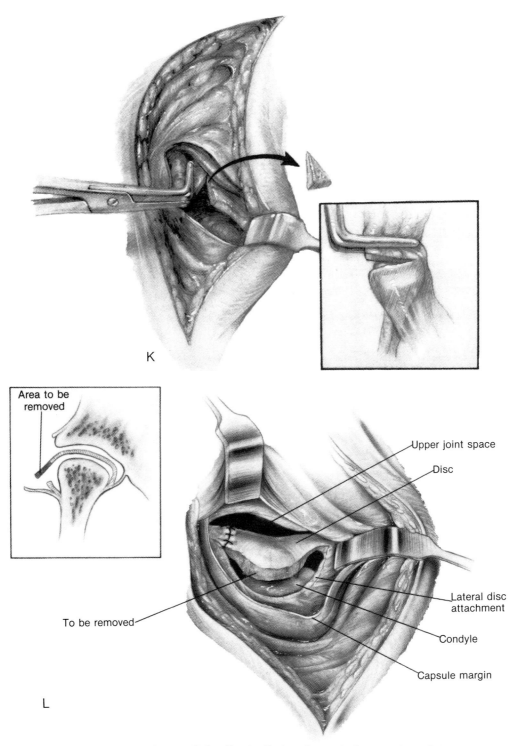

FIGURE 29–99. *Continued. K,* If the disc is displaced anteriorly, a wedge of tissue can be removed from the posterior attachment, allowing the disc to rotate posterolaterally for reduction of the displacement. *L,* The repositioned disc should fit tightly over the condylar head, allowing rotation but not translation of the condyle against the disc.

Illustration continued on following page.

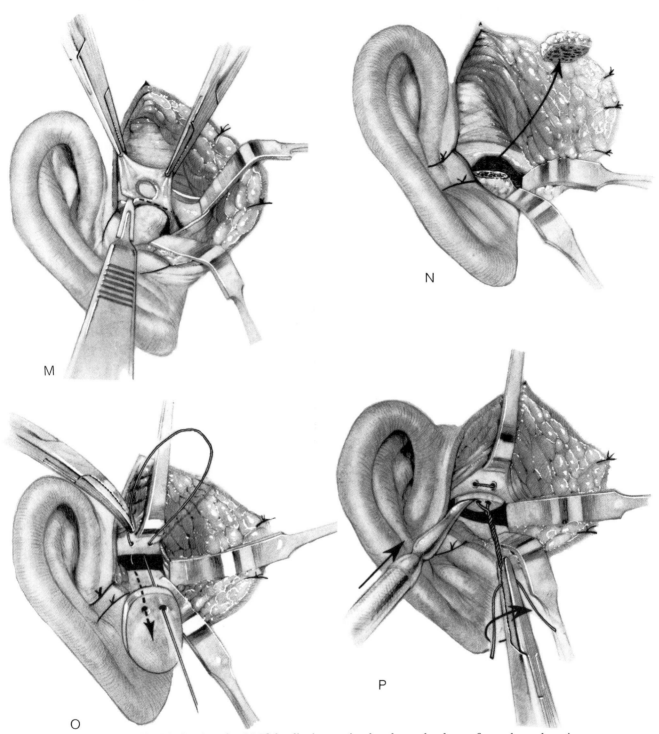

FIGURE 29–99. *Continued.*   *M,* If the disc is examined and noted to be perforated or otherwise nonfunctional, it must be completely excised, particularly anteromedially. *N,* High condylectomy can be performed if condylar degeneration is excessive. Every effort should be made to avoid cancellous marrow exposure. Excessive condylar removal can result in immediate and long-term vertical dimension changes as well as occlusal problems. *O,* If an interpositional alloplast is used to replace a disc following meniscectomy, the alloplast must be contoured to fit the fossa and articulate with the condyle during excursions. Finally, the alloplast must be secured to the lateral fossa to prevent functional displacement. *P,* Nonresorbable sutures, such as stainless steel wire or Mersilene, are used to secure the alloplast into the fossa. Movement of the alloplast may impair joint function as well as accelerate alloplast wear or fatigue.

Illustration continued on opposite page.

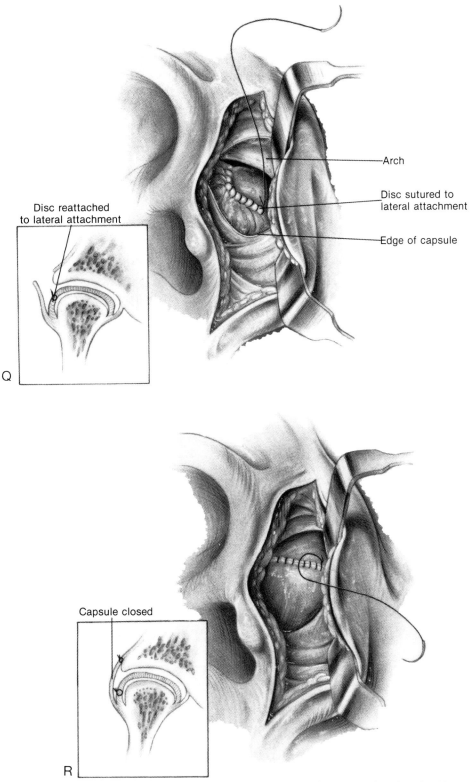

FIGURE 29–99. *Continued.   Q,* The lower joint space is closed, reapproximating the disc to the lateral capsule. *R,* The upper joint space is closed with the repair of the lateral capsule.

suture is performed in a simple-interrupted fashion to eliminate dead space. A subcutaneous closure using resorbable suture should approximate the wound margins, and either a simple, continuous skin closure or a subcuticular closure can be performed with 6 – 0 nylon sutures. The external ear canal is then inspected, the previously placed cotton is removed, and the canal itself is irrigated with saline or peroxide to remove any blood. Antibiotic ointment is placed on the incision. A Telfa or Adaptic dressing is placed over the incision, and gauze is used to apply pressure to the incision and operative area prior to dressing the area with either a mastoid or a facioplasty dressing.

Preauricular Temporal Approach.   The preauricular temporal approach described by Al-Kayat and Bramley[547] in 1978 differs from the traditional preauricular approach described by Rowe in 1972[606] in the positioning of the skin incision and the dissection through the temporal fascia. This approach utilizes a question mark – shaped incision, which begins about a pinna's length away from the ear anteriorly and superiorly just within the hairline (Figs. 29 – 98 and 29 – 100A and B). The incision curves posteriorly and inferiorly well posterior to the temporal vessels until it meets the upper attachment of the ear. The incision then follows the attachment of the ear and just endaurally, as described by Rowe. The temporal incision is carried through the skin and superficial fascia to the level of the temporal fascia.

Blunt dissection is continued in this plane inferiorly to a point 2 cm above the zygomatic arch where the temporal fascia splits. Starting at the root of the zygomatic arch, an incision is made superiorly and anteriorly through the superficial temporal fascia at a 45-degree angle extending to this point 2 cm above the arch.

Once inside this layer (pocket), the periosteum on the zygomatic arch can be incised safely and turned forward as one flap with the outer layer of the temporalis fascia and superficial fascia containing the nerve. The surgical plane (pocket) can be developed anteriorly as far as the posterior border of the frontal process of the malar bone.

In proceeding downward from the lower border of the arch, tissues lateral to the TMJ capsule are reflected. The capsule is incised to enter either joint space and expose the condyle and its neck. Since the bifurcation of the facial nerve may be only 2.4 cm in an inferioposterior direction from the posterior glenoid tubercle, the dissection should not extend below the lower attachment of the ear.

Face Lift Approach.   In 1983, Zide and Kent[491] described the face lift approach for subcondylar fractures. The scar may be more esthetic, and the technique combines preauricular with retromandibular techniques to provide greater exposure of the fracture. Edema from the injury should be resolved to facilitate the dissection through the parotid gland.[607] The preauricular aspect of the face lift approach is in the natural crease anterior to the pinna. Under the lobe of the ear, the incision continues in the lobular fold and extends posteriorly on the posterior surface of the auricle (Figs. 29 – 98 and 29 – 100 C). The undermining of the face is accomplished in the subdermal fatty layer. In this approach, the decision must be made whether to dissect out the facial nerve first or merely to bluntly dissect through the parotid gland and masseter muscle. If the patient is heavier, dissection of the facial nerve trunk and branches may be necessary to avoid damage. The facial nerve, trunk, and branches may need to be dissected out using one of the three methods described. All three methods described by Zide and Kent rely on cutaneous anatomic landmarks.

1.   The method described by Ressner in 1952[608] relies on the consistent relationship of the temporal branches of the facial nerve to the zygomatic arch. Ressner uses this relationship in performing parotidectomies; it has also proved to be useful in determining the approach for open condylar reduction. A line is drawn from the lateral canthus of the eye to the tragion point. The temporal nerve branches, usually two, cross the superior aspect of the zygomatic arch 3 or 4 cm posterior to the lateral orbital rim at the canthal line level.[609]

2.   Roscic in 1980[610] described a method which involves finding the main trunk of the facial nerve. A line is drawn from the mastoid process to the corners of the mouth. After superficial dissection, the parotid gland is dissected off the auricular cartilage, mastoid process, and the sternocleidomastoid muscle. Care must be taken not to enter the parotid capsule. At the mastoid process, a curved clamp placed against the bone is used to separate tissue and dissect anteriorly and medially into the retromandibular fossa. The nerve trunk is then found — glistening white when exposed, lying under the reference line previously mentioned.

3.   This method utilizes the findings of Al-Kayat and Bramly.[547] Briefly, the temporal branch of the facial nerve crosses the zygomatic arch (0.8 to 3.5 cm) anterior to the external auditory canal. In addition, the temporal branches are located anterior to a line drawn from the posterior glenoid tubercle to the bifurcation of the facial nerve, into the cervicofacial and temporofacial branches, which lie 1.5 to 2.8 cm inferior to the lowest

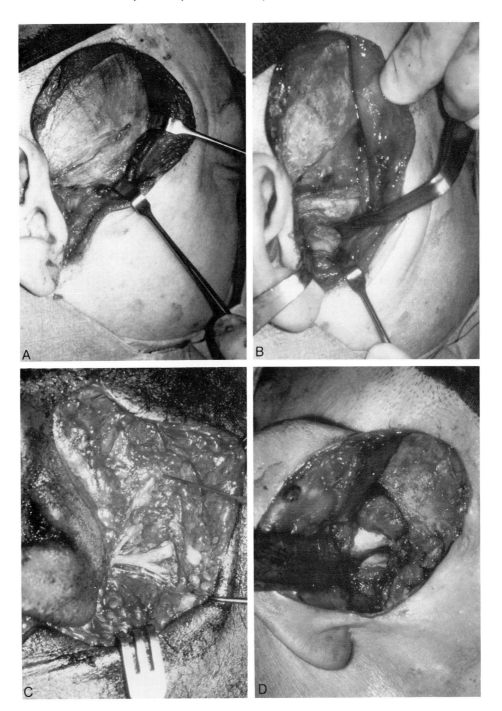

FIGURE 29-100. *A*, Temporal preauricular approach with 45-degree incision through the superficial layer of the temporal fascia down to the zygomatic process of the temporal bone. *B*, Reflection of fascia and periosteum over the arch, with the capsule excised and the condyle exposed. *C*, Modified rhytidectomy approach (see text). *D*, Postauricular approach (see text).

concavity of the bony external auditory canal and within 2.4 to 3.5 cm in an inferior direction from the lowest point of the glenoid tubercle. This latter finding helps in locating the main trunk of the facial nerve.

Postauricular Approach. Azhausen (in 1931),[611] Alexander and James (in 1975),[612] and Walters and Geist (in 1983)[613] have described the postauricular approach (Figs. 29–98 and 29–100D). An incision is made 3 to 7 mm posterior to the auricular flexure. This incision extends from a point approximately 5 mm posterior to the most superoanterior attachment of the auricle, then inferiorly to the mastoid process. The incision is carried to the subcutaneous tissue and postauricular muscles and down to the mastoid fascia anteriorly toward the external auditory canal. The canal is then incised 8 mm above the mastoid fascia after the canal is freed from the adjacent tissue. The tissue anterior to the canal is dissected free, and a 2–0 silk suture is passed through the anterior aspect of the canal and attached to the mastoid fascia posteriorly for retraction-dissection, and is continued superiorly to the external auditory canal to expose the outer layer of temporal fascia. The incision of the fascia and exposure of the subcondylar region are then carried out as previously described by Al-Kayat and Bramley.[547] Numerous advantages and disadvantages compared with the preauricular dissection are described.[612,613] However, this technique may not be indicated in patients with previous preauricular joint surgery because of possible devitalization of the external ear.

Intraoral Approach.   The intraoral approach initially described by Winstanly[614] for subcondylar osteotomies was recently described for condylar fracture reduction by Jeter and colleagues.[615] An incision is made in the soft tissue and periosteum overlying the external oblique ridge and extending down into the mandibular vestibule. A subperiosteal dissection is carried out, so that the entire lateral aspect of the ramus is exposed from the sigmoid notch to the angle of the mandible. It is important to release the periosteum underlying the posterior and inferior borders of the ramus to allow good access. A modified LeVasseur-Merrill fiberoptic retractor is inserted to expose the subcondylar fracture site.

Partial TMJ Reconstruction

The reconstruction of one articular surface, usually the condyle or a portion of it, is defined as a partial TMJ reconstruction.[616] Reconstruction of the condylar head attempts to restore both function to the TMJ and vertical dimension to the ramus. The use of autogenous, homogenous, and alloplast implant materials in intra-articular ankylosis is one of the oldest biomaterial applications involving the facial bones.

GENERAL PRINCIPLES

In adult interpositional arthroplasty, in which a section of the ankylosed bone is removed between the condyle neck and glenoid fossa, followed by placement of a variety of materials to produce a pseudoarticulation on either the superior or the inferior surface, is the most successful treatment for restoring mandibular function. The use of interpositional materials is necessary to maintain the vertical dimension of the mandibular ramus, to preserve the Class III lever situation that exists with normal TMJ anatomy, and to establish maximal mandibular opening.[617] In children, the use of thin interpositional material in the form of tissue or polymer sheets tented over the articulating stump of the mandible is generally preferred. A cleavage procedure, rather than a large ostectomy, is performed to preserve as much of the ramus as possible.[618] If mandibular function is restored and maintained, deviation of the jaw to the affected side at the completion of growth may be minimal. If function is compromised, the deformity will be greater.

BIOLOGIC MATERIALS

In 1860, Verneuil utilized a temporal muscle and fascia flap as an interpositional material to return function to the temporomandibular articulation and to prevent reankylosis[619] (Fig. 29–86). Initially, this was not a popular concept, and until 1894, when Helferich[620] revitalized Verneuil's technique, condylectomies and gap arthroplasties without interpositional materials, frequently leading to open bite, were the standard mode of therapy. Blair in 1914[542] and Murphy in 1913[543] advocated the temporal muscle and fascia interpositional arthroplasty, which then became the treatment of choice for ankylosis for the next 20 years. In 1934, Risdon,[621] gaining access to the condyle and ramus through a submandibular approach that now bears his name, utilized the detached masseter muscle as the interposed material, pulling it through the arthroplasty gap and suturing it to the medial pterygoid muscle.

Since the time that interpositional arthroplasty was popularized, many biologic materials have been used. Chromatized pig bladder mucosa,[622] preserved fascia lata,[623] bovine cartilage,[624] dermis,[548] and fresh fascia lata[625] have all been tried and have met with varied success. Although reankylosis was frequently avoided with these materials, TMJ function was compromised. Through atrophy and scarring, the vertical dimension of the ramus was not maintained, resulting in a posterior and clockwise rotation of the mandible. Thus, the mandible changes from a Class III to a Class I lever system, with the fulcrum moving from the temporomandibular articulation to the posterior dentition.[617] The result of this was relative retrognathism and apertognathism.

In 1928, Blair[626] introduced a composite costochondral rib graft for condylar reconstruction. This biologic transplant was felt to restore anatomically the functioning TMJ, and its use has been advocated over the years[627,628] (Fig. 29–101A to J). The idea that these, and other so-called transplanted "growth centers" (such as metatarsal[629] (Fig. 29–80), fibular head,[630] sternoclavicular,[631] and iliac crest),[632] provided a primary growth center in actively growing young patients[633] has been discounted by Sarnat and Muchnic,[634] Durkin,[635] Petrovic,[636] and Sorenson and Laskin.[637] Rather, the re-establishment of the "skeletal unit" within the "functional matrix," as described by Moss and Salentijn,[638] providing for "translative and transformative growth," accounts for successful use of these composite grafts in growing individuals. The use of biologic materials in hypomobile adult cases, however, may present serious limitations and complications: inability to restore or maintain ramus vertical dimension, displacement of grafted or transplanted material, unpredictable resorption or fracture of grafted bone, reduced mandibular function from necessary immobilization, recurrent ankylosis infections, and potential donor site complications. In spite of these possibilities, however, we believe autogenous grafts are preferred before puberty and in the initial reconstruction of most deformities in adults. In the adult patient with a history of multiple surgical failures, hypomobility, and infections, a vascularized rib graft or total joint prostheses can be used to reduce complications associated with unpredictable resorption and fractures of nonvascularized grafted bone. Biologic materials are therefore capable of physiologic adaptation in the TMJ. However, the process may be both favorable and unfavorable.

ARTIFICIAL MATERIALS

In an effort to improve TMJ function and minimize the aforementioned problems, a number of partial joint alloplastic materials have been suggested.[639] Interpositional arthroplasty materials include silicone rubber, acrylic, metallic condyle prostheses, and other polymers used as bulk material for pseudoarticulation in condylectomy or ankylosis.[478,640–649] Most nonmetallic implants are polymers. Polyvinyl sponge[650] allows bony ingrowth, but 20 to 30 per cent shrinkage in vivo can be predicted. Self-curing silicone rubber and MMA are also used to establish a pseudoarticulation with the mandible.[642] MMA[651,652] can be custom contoured at the time of surgery, but owing to its porosity, adsorption of proteins can produce a foreign body reaction. Furthermore, the continuous leaching of monomer from the acrylic implants induces a chronic low-grade inflammatory response. The principal disadvantage of all artificial TMJ materials is a complete lack of physiologic adaptability.

ARTHROPLASTY WITH SILICONE RUBBER

Silicone rubber in the form of carved blocks, ulnar head prostheses, or chin implants has been used for years[478,641,646,648] (Fig. 29–102). Walker has emphasized the use of a silicone rubber cap in arthroplasty over the past three decades.[478,575] In a recent report on the use of this polymer for disc and condylar head replacement in 68 patients followed for 1 to 15 years, 63 had an improvement with no recurrence of symptoms.[575] In their study, patients had several conditions present prior to surgery.

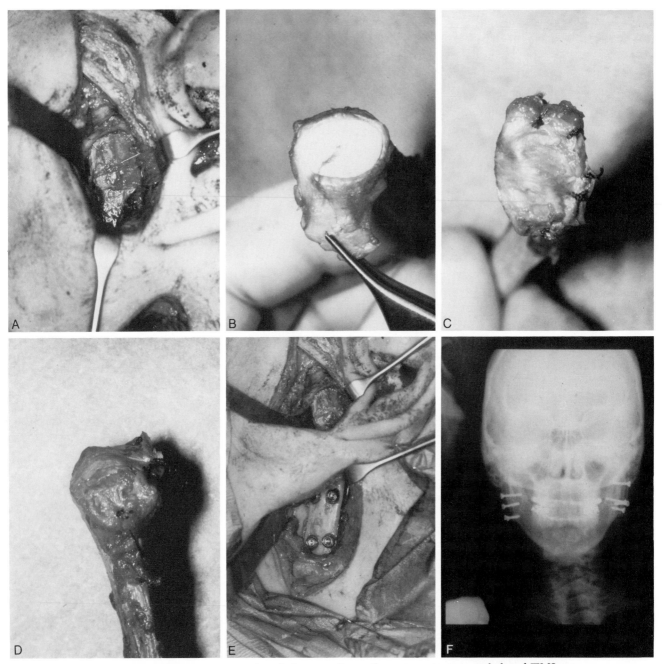

FIGURE 29–101.   *A–D*, Costochondral composite graft to reconstruct an ankylosed TMJ secondary to trauma. Note perichondrium sutured over the cartilage to provide a soft tissue interface between the graft cartilage and the bony fossa. *B*, Rib graft should be harvested to include 2 cm of cartilage. Perichondrium is incised on top of the cartilage and reflected to approximately 5 mm from bone junction. Excess cartilage is excised. *C, D*, Perichondrium is then sutured over remaining cartilage surface. *E*, Synthes bone screws used to secure the costochondral graft to the lateral ramus. The patient is allowed immediate function using guiding elastics. *F*, Postoperative PA radiograph showing costochondral reconstruction.

Illustration continued on opposite page.

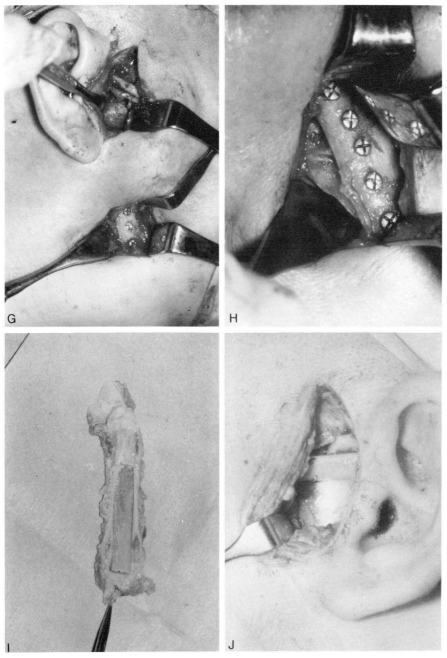

FIGURE 29–101. *Continued.*   *G, H,* Reconstruction of the condylar head following degeneration secondary to a failed interpositional implant. Also a free composite bone graft was placed in the glenoid fossa to repair reciprocal bone degeneration seen in this area. *I,* Rib graft with vascularized soft tissue pedicle. *J,* Perichondrium sutured over cartilage and intercostal artery anastomosed with facial artery.

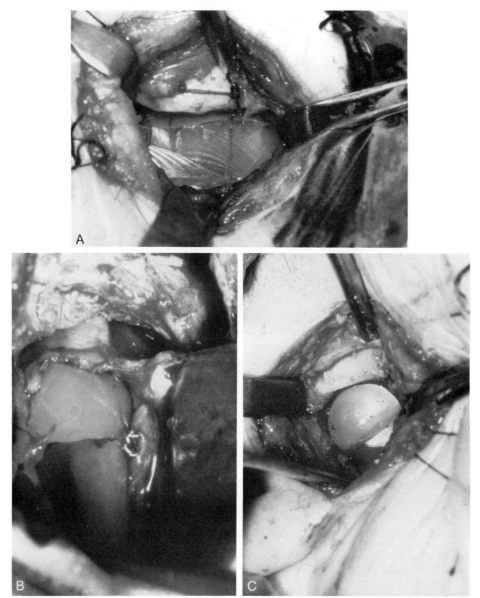

FIGURE 29–102. *A*, Carved silicone rubber block tied to the temporal bone with Mersilene suture, rather than wire, provides for an articulation between the implant and condylar stump. *B*, Silicone rubber chin implant wired to the condylar head provides for an articulation between the glenoid fossa and the implant. *C*, Ulnar head prosthesis with the stalk removed, used to cap the condylar stump and provide for an articulation between the implant and the glenoid fossa.

There was clinical and radiographic evidence of osteoarthritis associated with an unsalvageable disc, and there had been prolonged internal derangement of the TMJ associated with loss of pliancy, severe thinning, or other impairment of the disc, and there was failure of previous surgery on the TMJ, which included various implants placed in the joints. The technique of using silicone rubber in arthroplasty for degenerative disease is described here, since the procedure is similar to that used for hypomobility in trauma patients. Results with trauma patients may not be as good, since there may be a history of more extensive tissue damage as well as an increased number of surgeries.

Walker's Technique.   Walker's technique[575] includes a standard preauricular incision 5 to 6 cm in length, with alternate blunt and sharp dissection to the temporalis fascia; it is then extended inferiorly along the temporalis fascia to the zygomatic arch and upper extent of the capsule. The capsule is cleanly exposed approximately 1.0 to 1.5 cm in an inferior direction, and a vertical incision is made through the capsule to the condylar neck. The upper limb of this incision remains just superficial to the disc, so that opening of the upper joint space is avoided at this point. The periosteum and capsular attachments are freed around the condylar neck, and in so doing, the lower joint space is entered to expose the condyle. Approximately 2 to 4 mm of the vertical height of the condylar head or necessary ankylosed bone is excised using a No. 701 cross-cut fissure bur run under sterile saline irrigation. The raw condylar stump is then smoothed with a bone file or bur. The upper joint space is opened with a horizontal incision. If the disc is displaced, but otherwise salvageable, it is repositioned over the condylar stump and secured with 2–0 nonresorbable sutures.[507] Holes for the sutures are made through the posterior lateral cortex 3 mm below the cut edge of the condyle up through the medullary surface (Fig. 29–103A and B). If the disc is found to be perforated, displaced with loss of pliancy, or extraordinarily thin, it is excised. If previous surgery included disc removal and replacement with alloplastic material, the prosthesis is removed. The arthroplasty is now completed, using silicone rubber as an attachment to the top of the raw condylar stump. Again, two holes are drilled through the cortices of the condylar neck approximately 3 mm below the cut edge of the stump. One hole is started near the center of the condylar neck posteriorly, and the other hole is started near the lateral pole. A 3-mm or greater disc or cap, slightly larger than the top of the condylar stump, is then cut from a sheet or block of silicone and is secured with two separate 25-gauge stainless steel wires passed through the holes and then across the top of the silicone disc in a mattress fashion. The wires are tightened securely by twisting at the back of the condylar neck, firmly fixing the silicone disc atop the condylar stump for immediate function (Fig. 29–103C through I). The jaw is then moved in various excursions, including a wide-open position to be certain the condylar stump with attached silicone implant moves easily and without hindrance.

Walker emphasizes the role of postoperative physical therapy.[575] Arch bars are used with two or three small elastics at night for 3 months to hold the teeth in correct occlusion. The elastics are removed in the morning for full daytime use of the jaw. Jaw range of motion stretching and levering are progressively increased daily to exceed eventually an incisal clearance of 40 mm by 3 or 4 weeks after surgery. The rationale for holding the teeth and jaw in the correct position at night is to promote healing and maintain vertical dimension. Use of the jaw during the day may disrupt or delay healing but allows range of motion to increase progressively through the use of passive and active stretching movements. A progressively increasing range of jaw movement minimizes the restraint of tight scarring within the joint or similar restriction in the extracapsular area, which are probable causes of long-term tethering of the jaw and pain after surgery. All efforts are made to achieve wide opening of the jaw within the limits of the maturating scar tissue. Walker believes an incisal opening of 40 mm is regarded as the minimum toward which the physical therapy is directed.[575]

The postoperative physical therapy regimen is in agreement with that of Kent and others, except in patients who have limited or absent lateral pterygoid function. In such patients, inability of translation may physically limit their maximal opening to the 30-35 to mm range. Efforts to exceed this range produce pressure and myofascial pain in the soft tissues along the posterior border, angle, and condylar neck areas.[653]

Complications associated with silicone rubber block arthroplasty include inadequate wire stabilizations; bone resorption from soft tissue detachment, leading to loose wires; short- and long-term displacement of the prosthesis from polymer tearing at the wire site; polymer degradation with particulate matter and foreign body granulomatous reaction; and postoperative limitation of opening, with pain from excessive and poor compliance with physical therapy. Displacement may be more common when the implant is forced to move with the condyle. Stabilization of silicone rubber implants with the temporal bone, rather than the condyle, provides articulation at the condylar stump level.

Metallic implants used as a condylar cap that are relatively anatomic, such as stainless steel[654] (Fig. 29–104A to F), cobalt-chromium (Vitallium),[640,647,655,656] tantalum, and gold,[657] have been successful, but, again, problems arise. The stiffness or lack of working properties of these metals may not allow good bony adaptation intraoperatively. Although alloplasts such as metals allow for immediate function, poor stress distribution and improper stabilization and fixation may lead to bone resorption, fibrous encapsulation, and eventual loosening of the material.

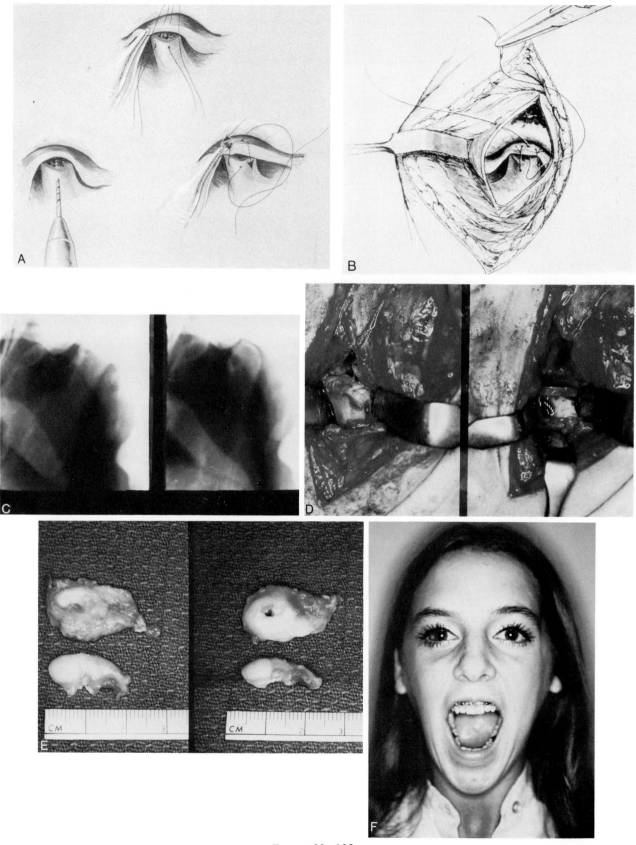

FIGURE 29–103.

See legend on opposite page.

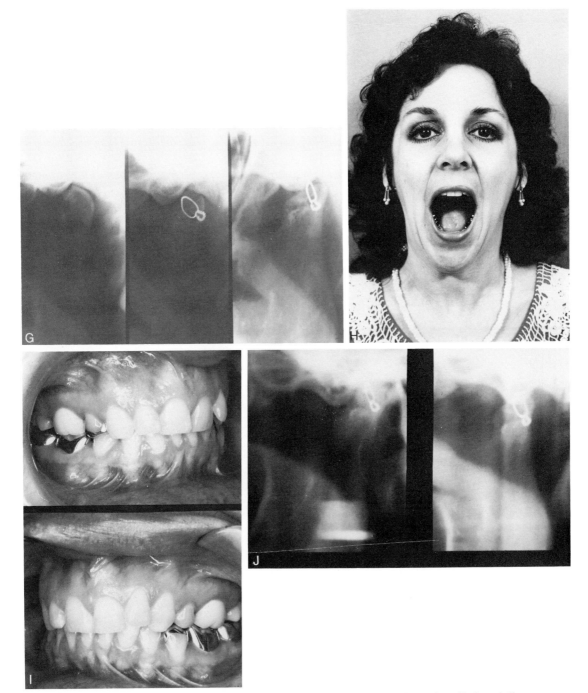

FIGURE 29–103.   *A, B,* Excision of condylar head and technique of securing displaced disc to condylar stump. *C,* Preoperative transpharyngeal radiographs of right TMJ in closed and open positions of jaw. *D,* Surgery on the right TMJ, July 18, 1974: mandibular condyle with osteoarthritic changes (a) and mandibular condyler stump with 3-mm-thick Silastic disc fixed atop the stump via interosseous wiring (b). *E,* Specimen: osteoarthritic condylar head and disc with perforation—condylar head and disc from below (a) and condylar head and disc from above (b). *F,* Postoperative facial view of patient with mouth opened widely to 42 mm at the incisal edges; physical therapy continued for 3 months to maintain wide incisal opening and good occlusion via the wearing of two small intermaxillary elastics at night while sleeping. Full daytime use of the mandible was required. *G,* Preoperative (6/21/74), immediate postoperative (7/24/74), and 7-year follow-up (8/28/81) transpharyngeal radiographs of right TMJ in open positions of the jaw. *H,* A 14-year follow-up facial view of patient with mouth open; 45-mm incisal opening. *I,* A 14-year follow-up view of occlusion, right and left. *J,* Follow-up transpharyngeal radiographs at 14 years of right TMJ in the closed and open positions of the jaw. (Courtesy of Dr. Robert V. Walker, Dallas.)

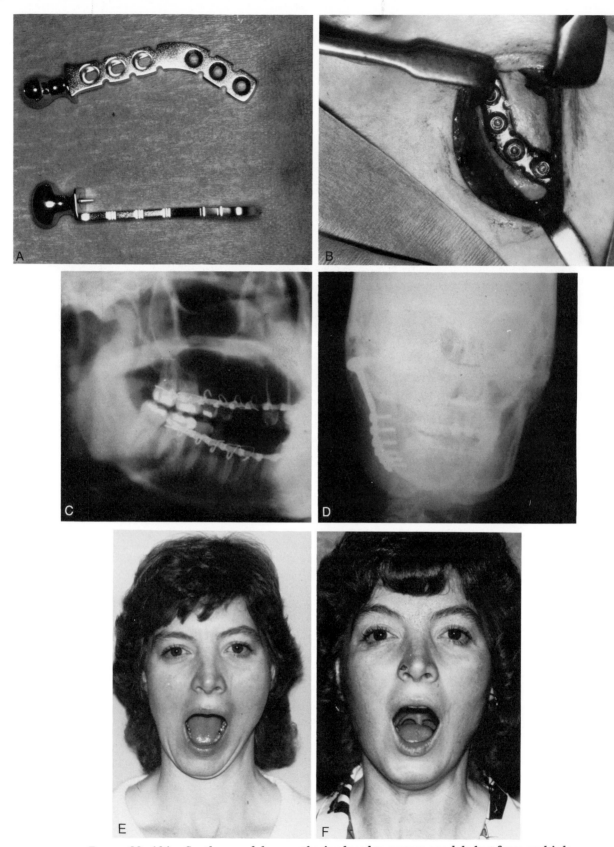

FIGURE 29–104.   **Synthes condylar prosthesis placed to restore condyle lost from multiple attempts at open reduction.**   *A*, Synthes 316 stainless steel condylar prosthesis. *B*, Prosthesis placed via retromandibular approach. *C*, Preoperative and *D*, postoperative reconstruction of condyle. *E*, Preoperative and *F*, 8-year postoperative follow-up of opening with mandibular symmetry.

CONDYLAR PROSTHESES

In the early 1970s, an anatomic metallic condylar prosthesis composed of a chrome-cobalt-molybdenum alloy, with the shank of the prosthesis coated with Proplast I or II, was proposed to improve stabilization[644,645,658-660] (Fig. 29–105A and B). The use of the prosthesis as described by Hinds and Kent was advocated for cases of hypomobility[658] (Fig. 29–106A to I), severe arthritides, and loss of the condyle in acquired deformities, such as neoplasms, infections, and trauma.[616,643,653,660] Its principal advantage over the interpositional polymers is primarily enhanced stabilization in patients with malocclusion and facial deformity, since vertical dimension defects may be significant. Placement of this type of prosthesis permits correction of the TMJ disorder as well as correction of existing facial asymmetry, mandibular retrognathism, or open bite. Immediate postoperative function was possible and, of course, encouraged in the patient with ankylosis. The shank had parallel flanges that fit into recesses cut into the lateral aspect of the mandibular ramus and was secured to the ramus with three or four self-tapping screws. In a 10-year retrospective survey by Kent of 109 prostheses placed in 80 patients, functional joint rehabilitation was successful in 87 per cent of the cases.[660] The principal use of the prosthesis (85 per cent) was in patients who had ankylosis from trauma and in patients who had undergone multiple TMJ surgeries. Complications included glenoid fossa resorption, hypomobility secondary to chronic pain, scarring, and noncompliance with physical therapy, as with other materials. Resorption of the glenoid fossa was minimal in the dense bone of an ankylosed fossa. However, significant fossa resorption was observed postoperatively in highly loaded joints, ramus lengthening, and rheumatoid arthritis (Fig. 29–107A and B). This prosthesis was later modified to serve as one of two components in the development of the Vitek-Kent (VK) total joint system.[616,653] The surgical technique for metallic condylar placement as part of the VK system is described further on.

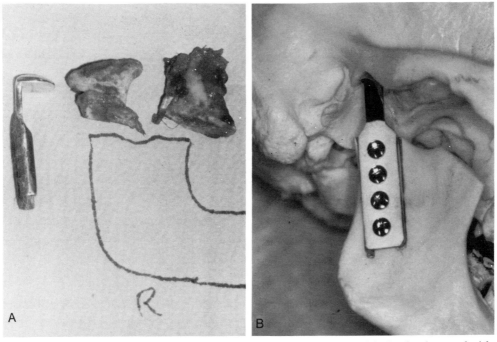

FIGURE 29–105. Cobalt-chromium (Vitallium) condylar prosthesis with the shank coated with A, Proplast I and B, Proplast II used primarily in bony ankylosis cases.

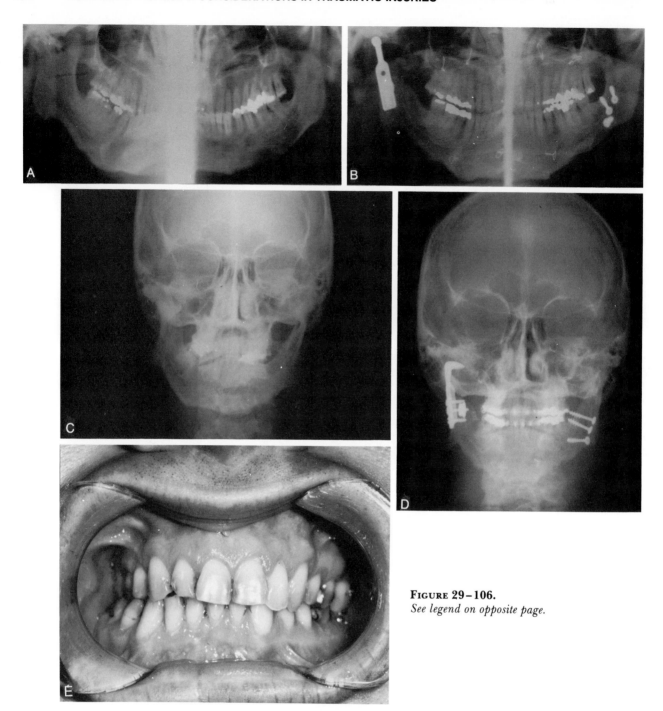

FIGURE 29–106.
See legend on opposite page.

GLENOID FOSSA PROSTHESES

Partial joint replacement has also been done with prefabricated, anatomically designed, glenoid fossa prostheses. Although these prostheses resurface the fossa and articular eminence, their articulation with the mandibular stump is similar to silicone rubber fastened to the temporal bone. Early prostheses were constructed from cast stainless steel,[661] chrome-cobalt,[640,656,662–667] and silicone rubber.[668–674] Robinson[661] first utilized a stainless steel, cuplike glenoid fossa implant for correction of ankylosis. This fossa implant, prefabricated from skulls, spanned the glenoid fossa and articular eminence and was secured into position by two stainless steel screws.

Christensen[640] recognized the need for further anatomic refinement of the alloplastic glenoid fossa. He made multiple castings of chrome-cobalt to cover the glenoid

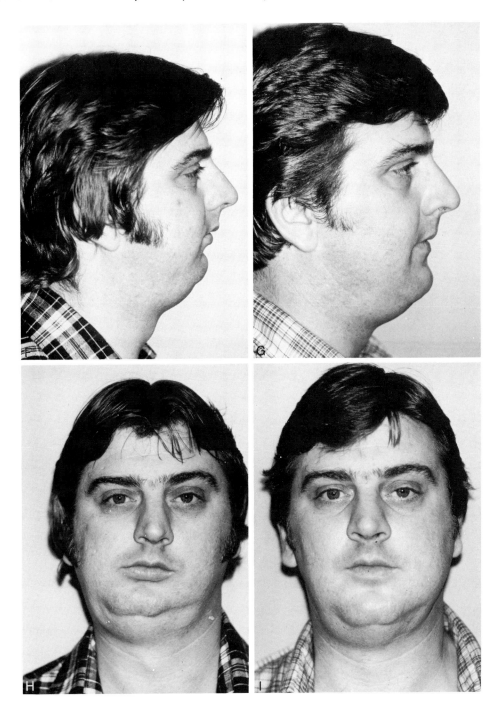

FIGURE 29–106. **Patient with 30-year history of ankylosis secondary to childhood trauma, resulting in facial asymmetry, retrognathism, and malocclusion.** Treatment consisted of rotation of maxillomandibular complex with lengthening of ankylosed side by Le Fort I downgraft osteotomy, condylar prosthesis, and sagittal split osteotomy. *A,* Preoperative and *B,* postoperative panoramic radiographs. *C,* Preoperative and *D,* postoperative PA radiographs. *E,* Occlusion both preoperative and postoperative. *F,* Preoperative and *G,* postoperative profile views. *H,* Preoperative and *I,* postoperative full-face views.

fossa, articular eminence, and adjacent zygomatic process on 20 skulls with different glenoid fossa sizes. The implant could be slightly modified intraoperatively with bending pliers and was secured with 5-mm screws. A vertical ramus osteotomy was performed to reposition the remaining condyle superiorly into the metallic glenoid fossa. Christensen reported successful arthroplasty for correction of fibrous and bony ankylosis in six patients with a follow-up of 15 months.

Morgan treated patients with TMJ disorders by recontouring the articular eminence and placing an articular eminence implant similar to the Christensen fossa implant.[662–664,667] He utilized a chrome-cobalt casting, designed from skulls, to restore the height and contour of the articular eminence, eliminate crepitation, act as a disc replacement, and separate the articular surfaces an appropriate distance to minimize bone erosion. When used for a disc replacement, the prosthesis was modified by

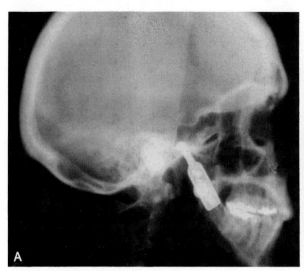

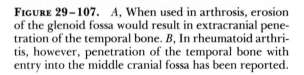

FIGURE 29–107. *A,* When used in arthrosis, erosion of the glenoid fossa would result in extracranial penetration of the temporal bone. *B,* In rheumatoid arthritis, however, penetration of the temporal bone with entry into the middle cranial fossa has been reported.

adding silicone rubber to provide complete fossa coverage. This device was secured to the zygomatic arch by three 5-mm chrome-cobalt screws. Morgan reported 132 TMJ operations on 90 patients over an 8-year period, with 86 per cent of patients reporting some improvement in pain relief.[664]

Robinson and Arnet described the use of a fine, closed-cell, sponge-type of silicone rubber for interpositional arthroplasty to treat eight patients with ankylosis.[668,669] They believed that resurfacing of the glenoid fossa with silicone rubber would prevent further bone erosion and ankylosis. The silicone rubber sponge was cut intraoperatively to fill, approximately, the joint's defect after excision of ankylosed bone. The sponge was contoured in such a way that the medial portion extended inferiorly to mechanically prevent lateral displacement of the sponge. Robinson reported good success with the sponge material and disappointing experience with solid silicone rubber used with interpositional arthroplasties. Silicone rubber has also been used for resurfacing of the glenoid fossa following traumatic dislocation of the condyle into the middle cranial fossa.[670,671] In addition, RTV solid silicone rubber implants have been constructed from skull molds.[672]

As described further on, under "Total TMJ Reconstruction," VK custom fossa prostheses made of Proplast (fossa surface) and Teflon FEP (condyle articulating surface) were developed in 1981 (Vitck, Inc.) (Fig. 29–108*A* and *B*). The glenoid fossa prosthesis portion of the VK total joint system was conceived as having a dual use — for articulation of a remaining condylar head or metallic condylar replacement. The selection of materials for the glenoid fossa interpositional device was guided first by the need for biocompatibility, second by the need for tissue ingrowth fixation for long-term stabilization, third, by a provision for immediate fixation to the zygomatic arch with screws, and fourth, by the ability of the surgeon to trim with ease the peripheral and superior aspects of the implant to accommodate the anatomy of a given patient. Soon after its introduction, oral and maxillofacial surgeons came to prefer a combination of glenoid fossa prosthesis with the condyle head prosthesis (a total joint system, described further on) to preclude any possibility of intrusion of the condyle head prosthesis into the fossa bone or the possibility of condylar head resorption. However, there remained a need for an articulating surface that would be

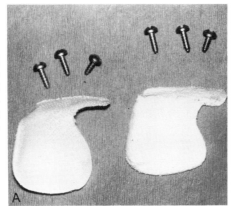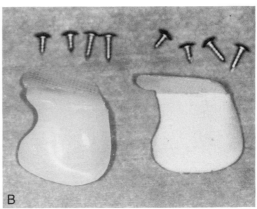

FIGURE 29–108. VK-I and VK-II glenoid fossa prostheses. *A*, Proplast II laminated to Teflon (VK-I). *B*, HA-Proplast laminated to ultra high molecular weight polyethylene (VK-II).

accommodating to the natural condylar head under relatively low TMJ loads, to allow for a degree of self-fitting of the natural condylar head, similar to a carved silicone rubber block. Therefore, the use of a VK fossa implant was similar to, if not identical with, the use of interpositional silicone rubber fossa or condylar head caps. Stabilization of the VK glenoid fossa prosthesis with screws, however, was an improvement over previous polymers. The development and characteristics of the fossa, including surgical technique, are described in the discussion of the VK total joint system.

Insertion of the VK glenoid fossa prosthesis *alone* was indicated to improve function, relieve pain, and restore vertical dimension loss of approximately 3 to 8 mm in patients with condylar erosion or condylectomy who had a history of meniscectomy with implant failures; in those with glenoid fossa and condylar erosion in degenerative joint disease, rheumatoid arthritis, and related arthropathies; in those with fibrous ankylosis, pain, and dysfunction secondary to trauma and previous TMJ surgery; and in those with bony ankylosis when arthroplasty with interpositional materials does not require condyle replacement.[616,653] Owing to its use over degenerative diseased condylar surfaces with intramedullary bone exposed, postoperative findings, however, resulted in a 20 to 40 per cent reoperation rate and are discussed further in the data on VK partial and total joint reconstruction (Fig. 29–109*A*). Articulation of a healthy, intact cortical surface of the condylar head (a rare finding with vertical loss) against a VK fossa prosthesis generally showed improved results (Fig. 29–109*B* to *E*).

Total TMJ Reconstruction

The use of both glenoid fossa and condylar prostheses, resurfacing or replacement of two articular surfaces, is defined as total TMJ reconstruction. Although the bony glenoid fossa or condylar head may not be deficient in many instances, protection against high-load bone erosion from polymer and metallic articular surface replacement is necessary.[616]

PROSTHESIS DESIGN CRITERIA

Fundamental mechanical, biologic, and surgical criteria for devices used in joint reconstruction should be considered in the design and manufacture of alloplastic implants. Primary requirements satisfying design specifications are outlined below.

Mechanical Requirements. The device must be mechanically strong enough to withstand functional loading with an adequate margin of safety designed into the device. Frictional forces transmitted through the prosthetic joint, which tend to place torsional stresses at the interface between articulating materials, should be minimized. The wear of any component of the device must be sufficiently low to give the

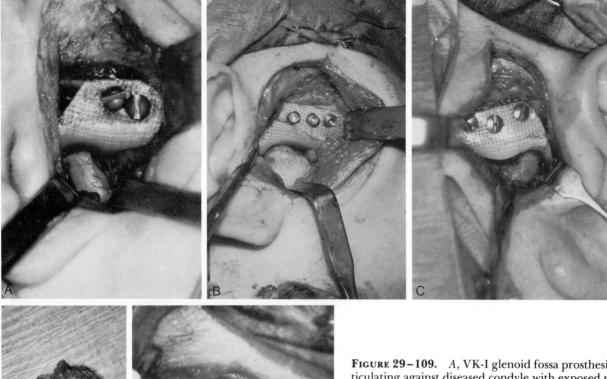

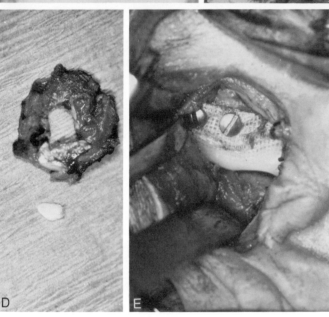

FIGURE 29–109. *A,* VK-I glenoid fossa prosthesis articulating against diseased condyle with exposed medullary bone. This resulted in abrasion of the fossa surface and particulate debris with inflammation necessitating removal of the implant. *B,* VK-I glenoid fossa prosthesis articulating against a condyle with a smooth, intact cortical surface. Satisfactory follow-up for 5 years has been achieved. *C,* VK-II glenoid fossa prosthesis articulating against a smooth, intact condyle, with its blood supply preserved with soft tissue attachments. Three-year follow-up of this patient yields a satisfactory result. *D, E,* Patient with advanced DJD with disc perforation and multiple osteophytes, who underwent reconstruction with a VK-II glenoid fossa prosthesis. Satisfactory follow-up at 3 years.

implant a long working life. The material selected for the fabrication of the device should be capable of proper sterilization without degradation of the mechanical properties or physical shape.

Biologic Requirements. All materials used must be acceptable to the body with no adverse short- or long-term effects. Wear of the device components will occur; all wear debris must be accepted by the body with no short- or long-term effects.

Surgical Requirements. The prosthetic components must be so designed that in conjunction with a few specialized insertion instruments the device can be placed easily and accurately. An acceptable salvage procedure must be available to deal with failures, which, almost inevitably, will occur.

Mechanical Properties. The mechanical properties of polymers used in joint reconstruction that are of major importance are the yield stress, creep resistance, and wear. The yield or flow stress is important and controls whether instantaneous plastic deformation will occur under a set of prescribed loading conditions. Plastic deformation is critical, since it can significantly increase wear and distort the implant. Under the influence of sustained loading forces, either compressive or tensile, polymers exhibit varying degrees of viscoelastic behavior, and their deformation under loading increases with time, a characteristic known as "cold flow." The static load-carrying capacity of a metal-polymer bearing assembly, such as a prosthetic joint, is governed by the magnitude of the compressive load to be supported. The bearing capacity is the mean surface pressure and is determined by dividing the applied compressive load by the projected support area of the bearing. For UHMWPE and polyoxymethylene (Delrin), the permissible mean surface pressure is 10 N/mm^2, whereas for PTFE it is only 2 N/mm^2.[672a] The limiting factor in a metal-polymer bearing in which the sliding partners move slowly or operate under fluid film lubrication, such as prosthetic joints, is the static load-carrying capacity of the bearing.

Materials Used.   Silicone rubber and metallic prefabricated glenoid fossa implants have been used along with titanium mesh condylar replacements for reconstruction in patients who have sustained deformed TMJ anatomy from previous surgery.[673] Combined fossa and condylar replacement has been reported by Kiehn and others on a patient with a history of multiple surgical procedures, including meniscectomy and metatarsal head implantation.[655] Following the example of orthopedic experiences for total joint reconstruction, Kiehn placed chrome-cobalt fossa and condylar prostheses using PMMA cement. The patient's glenoid fossa surface was roughened and undercut to gain mechanical retention of the fossa prosthesis with the cement. The condylar prosthesis was placed along a decorticated posterior ramus and was also cemented with MMA. The prostheses were also reported in a follow-up of 27 patients over a 4-year period in which four prostheses were removed because of infection, dislocation, or skin erosion.[665]

The use of MMA for stabilization of metallic condylar prostheses was also utilized by Kummoona.[666] An intramedullary channel in the condylar stump and ramus was prepared, and the prosthesis was cemented with MMA for internal stabilization. Kummoona's fossa implant, secured with screws to the zygomatic arch, and the condylar prosthesis were fabricated from chrome-cobalt, placing metal against metal for articulation. He reported on a successful 2-year follow-up of three cases using this technique.

VK TOTAL TMJ SYSTEM

In 1981, Kent designed the shape and contour of polymer glenoid fossa and metallic condylar head prostheses for total joint replacement, and Vitek selected material to optimize TMJ reconstruction and function on the basis of improved adaptability, stabilization, wear, and frictional characteristics.[616,653,660]

Design and Materials.   The fossa prosthesis mimics the slope of the articular eminence, the oval shape of the glenoid fossa, and its articulating surface. A review of the fossa anatomy and condylar function, as well as Oberg's classic study of the TMJ dimensions and areas of wear and degeneration, was instrumental in the design.[675-677] It then became apparent that a few carvable implants would serve the need for most patients. A prototype fossa prosthesis made of Proplast I at the bone interface and Teflon-carbon at the articulation site was developed to articulate with a previously developed metal condyle. The fossa implant extended anteriorly along the zygomatic arch, medially to the junction of the zygoma and the infratemporal crest of the greater wing of the sphenoid, and posteroinferiorly to protect the anterior portion of the external acoustic meatus. The actual fossa depth, measured perpendicular from a horizontal line parallel to the plane of the articular eminence, decreased proportionately to increases in the fossa thickness. In 1982, both VK-I condyle and fossa prostheses were developed (Figs. 29–110 to 29–112). The fossa prostheses contained Proplast II porous implant material to interface with the bony fossa, since it can be easily carved and modified to variable anatomic situations, can provide stabilization by tissue ingrowth, and can distribute force transmitted across the reconstructed joint. The Teflon FEP material of the inferior or articulating layer was

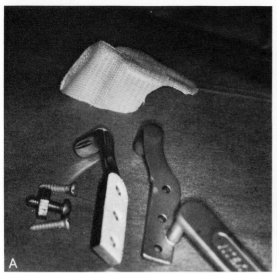

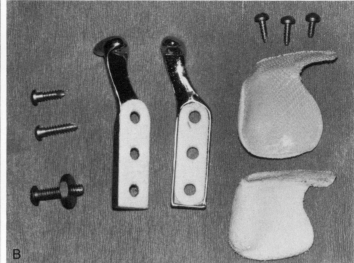

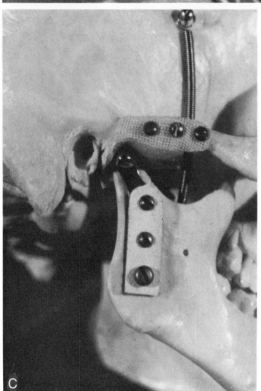

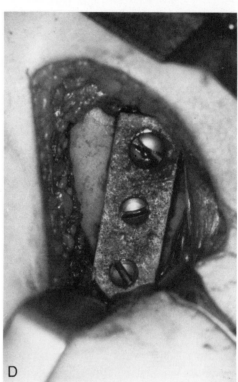

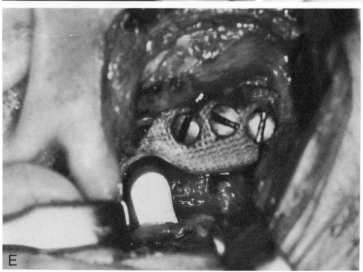

FIGURE 29–110. VK-I total TMJ system *A*, without and *B*, with lateral condylar extension *C*, VK-I total TMJ system with self-tapping screws, bolts, and nuts to secure both condyle and fossa to underlying bone. Intraoperative views show VK-I condylar prosthesis *D*, fixed to the lateral ramus and *E*, articulating with the glenoid fossa prosthesis. Here there is no lateral extension of the metal condylar head.

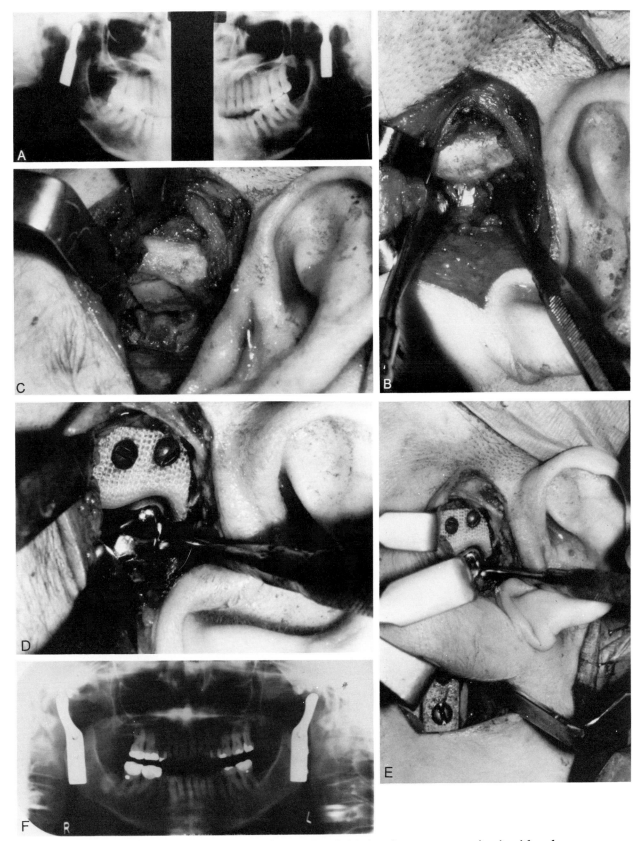

FIGURE 29–111. Patient with rheumatoid arthritis in whom reconstruction is with only a metallic condyle, producing erosion of the glenoid fossa and articular eminence with resultant open bite. *A*, Preoperative panoramic radiograph with condyle displacement and open bite. *B*, Operative view showing condyle embedded in the articular eminence. *C*, Articular eminence and fossa reconstructed with an iliac crest corticocancellous bone graft. *D, E*, Simultaneous total joint reconstruction with VK-I total joint system utilizing a condylar prosthesis with lateral extension. *F*, Three-year postoperative radiograph.

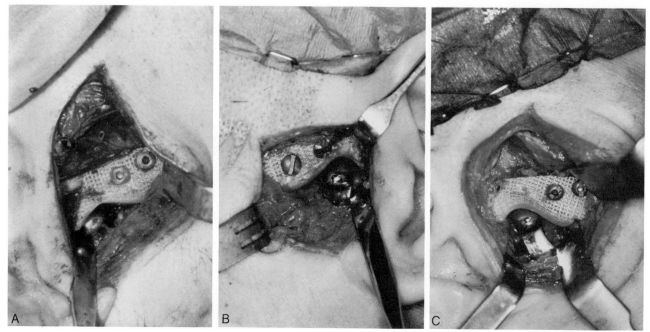

FIGURE 29–112.   *A*, Malpositioned condyle-fossa relationship. Condyle is set too far posteriorly in fossa. *B*, Malpositioned condyle showing medial point contact, requiring removal and condylar neck bending to establish an articulation. *C*, Correct condyle-fossa relationship with maximal metal-polymer articulation.

selected by Vitek in part on the basis of data from wear studies. The test methodology designed by Homsy in the late 1970s used the thrust washer principle wherein an annulus of experimental material is caused to rotate against a disc of mating material. The mating material was surgical chrome-cobalt-molybdenum alloy used to manufacture the VK TMJ condylar prosthesis. The test apparatus allowed oscillatory loading (square-wave) between test and mating materials at selected relative velocities, loading frequency, and absolute load stress. The mating and experimental materials were immersed in 37.5°C pseudosynovial fluid during these tests.[678]

It was assumed that the effective articular interfascial area between the TMJ condylar head and fossa is on the order of 1 cm²; therefore, the test load condition of 12 kg/cm² corresponding to a 12-kg total load across the TMJ was used. Under this test load, wear rates were determined using relative velocity between a metallic mating substance and a polymer experimental material of 5 cm/sec and a loading frequency of 36 cycles/min (Table 12–10). The wear data also demonstrated the problem of utilizing metal against metal, that is, galling.

Vitek selected the materials on the basis of reports indicating that the normal biting force in the adult human is approximately 21 kg.[679] The reactive force through both condyles is approximately 75 per cent of the biting force, and as much as 80 per cent of the reactive force may be borne by the contralateral condyle.[680] Therefore,

TABLE 29–10.   COMPARATIVE WEAR TEST DATA*

TEST MATERIAL	WEAR RATE (MM/100,000 CYCLES)
Teflon FEP polymer	0.018
Delrin acetal polymer	0.022
Acrylic polymer	0.111
Surgical chrome/cobalt/molybdenum (Cr/Co/Mo) alloy	Galling with catastrophic wear

* Load, 12 kg/cm²; relative speed, 5 cm/sec, 36 cycles/min; mating material, Cr/Co/Mo alloy.

the maximal force through a single condyle that corresponds to the normal biting force is calculated at 12.6 kg. Although this correlates with the test load that was used in evaluating wear performance of candidate materials, it is now believed that pathologic TMJ load may be significantly higher.

The combination of low wear behavior, minimal friction, and appropriate fabrication properties led to the selection of Teflon FEP for the articular surface of the VK-I fossa implant. This FEP layer was reinforced with polyamide fiber mesh for strength and dimensional stability. The mesh was not exposed on the articulating surface; it serves to limit the plastic flow (creep) inherent in all thermoplastic polymers and therefore limits distortion of the articulating surface. At the fossa depth, the FEP layer was approximately 2 to 3 mm thick, and the Proplast layer varied in thickness (4 to 6 mm) to allow for carving and adaptability to the natural fossa and restoration of condyle vertical dimension. A lateral flange consisting of polyamide mesh embedded in FEP polymer and integrally connected with the remainder of the implant allowed firm securing of the prosthesis to the zygomatic arch with three small transosseous metal screws. The articulating surfaces of the fossa prosthesis were coapted with the geometry of a newly developed VK-I chrome-cobalt condylar head to minimize contact unit stresses and wear. After 3 years of follow-up, it was recognized that failure due to cold flow and high rate of wear of the Teflon occurred in high-load situations and malalignment of the prostheses.

In 1969, Charnley and Kamangar reported on the wear rates of 100 stainless steel–PTFE total hip prostheses that had been removed from patients.[680a] Revision surgeries were necessary owing to the massive amounts of wear debris resulting in an undesirable tissue reaction. In many of the cases, the acetabular components had worn through. Charnley employed PTFE in 1958 because of its low coefficient of friction and relative chemical inertness. The mechanical properties of the material that affect wear rate are creep rate (or cold flow) and the yield and ultimate tensile strengths. High creep rates are particularly detrimental and explain the poor performance of PTFE. It is interesting to note that Charnley and Kamangar did not feel that cold flow was a significant problem with PTFE. However, it must be remembered that the static load-carrying capacity of PTFE is 2 N/mm². It was probably exceeded in many of the cases examined, and cold flow may have contributed a significant portion to the apparent wear. In addition, Charnley and Kamangar described an experiment in which a 22-mm steel ball had been loaded into a socket machined into a block of PTFE. Under a static load of 76.3 kg, no detectable deformity had manifested itself in a period over 7 years. Under this level of loading, the mean contact pressure in the bearing was slightly below the static load-carrying capacity of the material, and cold flow would theoretically have been expected to be excessive under these conditions.

In analyzing the mechanics of the TMJ, it is obvious that the contacting surfaces have radii of curvature; that is, the mandibular condyle has a convexity of specific radius, and the glenoid fossa has a concavity of specific radius. In designing a proper method for testing materials used in the reconstruction of the TMJ, the test apparatus should reflect the geometric similarities found in the joint. The thrust washer principle is a general method used as a means for comparison among materials; however, this method does not approximate the circumstances that the materials would be subjected to when implanted. In other words, the simple mechanical testing of the materials using the thrust washer method may have been inadequate, since it did not reflect the geometry of the joint and the character of stress and wear patterns that materials are subjected to when fabricated or molded to represent this type of geometry, that is, the concave polymer articulating surface, such as that found with the interpositional Proplast implant.

In 1986, the VK-II total joint system was developed with two basic changes[653] (Fig. 29–113A). First, the VK-II fossa implant has a superior layer of Proplast-HA that could also be carved intraoperatively to adapt to the natural, specific fossa architecture. Like other forms of Proplast (Proplast I and II), Proplast-HA utilizes a porous matrix of PTFE fibers. In Proplast-HA, synthetic HA is fused to the surfaces

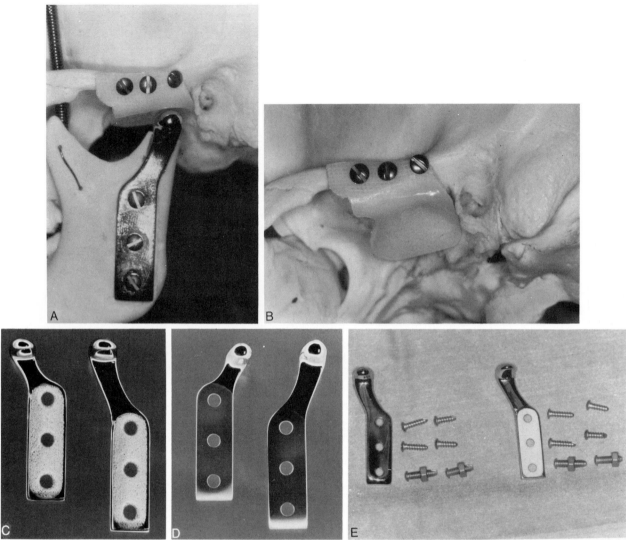

FIGURE 29–113. *A,* VK-II total TMJ system. *B,* VK-II glenoid fossa prosthesis secured to the zygomatic process of the temporal bone with self-tapping screws. *C, D,* VK-II condyles showing the medial side of 45- and 53-mm prostheses, which are HA-Proplast coated, and the lateral side of the prostheses. *E,* Self-tapping screws, bolts, and nuts used to secure the VK-II condyle to the ramus.

of a porous matrix of the PTFE fibers. Second, the inferior, articulating surface of the glenoid fossa implant was changed to medical-grade nonporous UHMWPE (Fig. 29–113B). Testing completed in 1985 demonstrated that UHMWPE, which is used as the articulating surface in total hip and knee implants, could be manipulated to provide an articulating surface of a glenoid fossa implant geometrically analogous to the Teflon FEP articulating surface. Friction and wear studies on prostheses using joint simulators have been carried out since 1967; wear testing was conducted using a TMJ simulator with metallic condylar head implant articulating against prototype UHMWPE fossae. The wear testing apparatus consisted of a motor-driven two-bar linkage connected with a mounting platform. A uniform and constant force of 12 kg/cm² was applied at the condyle-fossa interface by way of a preloaded spring. The linkage was designed to articulate the condylar head against the fossa to a degree that corresponded to about 35 to 40 mm of interincisional opening. The testing was conducted in 37°C normal saline. The test was run at 32 cycles/min. The results of the testing indicated that the wear and cold flow resistance of the UHMWPE articulating surface was eight times better than the Teflon FEP in articulation against a metallic condyle. The FEP fossae had wear through, whereas the UHMWPE fossae had no wear through and showed initial signs of wear earlier in testing, with a leveling off of wear. With this improved in vitro mechanical testing method, the effects of geometry, contact pressure, cold flow, and strengths of the materials were clearly illustrated, resulting in a change of the articulating surface materials from FEP to UHMWPE.

The use of the TMJ simulator, illustrating the effects of geometry and the resultant patterns of stress and wear in vitro, linked the findings reported by Fontenot and Kent in 1988.[493] This report published the results of articular surface wear of 15 retrieved FEP glenoid fossa prostheses that articulated against a prosthetic condyle (9) or a natural condyle (6). Macroscopic or visible wear was staged 0 to 4. Stage 0 was no visible polymer wear (2 implants); stage 1 was visible uniform wear only (8 implants); stage 2 was wear through the polymer into the fabric with less than 1 mm exposure (1 implant); stage 3 was wear exposing more than 1 mm of fabric (2 implants); and stage 4 was wear through the polymer surface and fabric into the proplast (2 implants). The average in situ service life was 30 months. Characterization of the surface wear by SEM analysis confirmed the staging of results with the naked eye. Average wear rates were 0.68 mm per year whereas the wear rate for retrieved UHMWPE acetabular cups from the hip are on the order of 0.1 mm per year.[672a]

Vitek subsequently recommended that because of possible condyle resorption and the results of orthopedic studies, use of the UHMWPE-Proplast glenoid fossa was limited to the total joint replacement with condylar head prosthesis. As with the previous fossa prosthesis, the VK-II implant is secured to the zygomatic arch with two or three small, self-tapping bone screws for immediate stabilization. Ingrowth into the porosity of the Proplast-HA material on the superior aspect of the implant assists in long-term stabilization of the implant.

The condylar prosthesis is fabricated from cast surgical-grade cobalt-chromium-molybdenum alloy (ASTM F-75) (Fig. 29–113C and D). The shank offers three holes for self-tapping bone screws and bolts for implant stabilization to the mandible (Fig. 29–113E). A 1-mm layer of ultraporous Proplast-HA implant material is fused to the medial side of the implant's shank for tissue ingrowth and long-term stabilization of the prosthesis.

Indications. Nonsurgical treatment of pathologic TMJs may consist of, but not be limited to, the use of splints, medications, rest, and rehabilitation involving physical therapy. When these and other more conservative surgical measures have failed to relieve pain and re-establish function of the TMJ, surgical treatment utilizing the VK total joint system may be indicated. Each surgeon must select the procedure that will provide pain relief and restoration of function, occlusion, and aesthetics, so that the procedure suits the needs of each patient, rather than making the patient suit the procedure. Generally, patients experience condyle and disc destruction, which may include glenoid fossa alteration, involving minor or major loss of condylar vertical height and diminished or absent lateral pterygoid muscle function.[616]

Kent has defined indications for the VK total joint system. They include severe malformation or destruction of the TMJ anatomy resulting from idiopathic condylar resorption; advanced rheumatoid arthritis with condylar resorption, open bite, and retrognathism; severe osteoarthritis with condylar collapse; ankylosis; tumors; trauma; and extensive condylar resorption following surgery for internal derangement or the above conditions. Such joints may exhibit significant functional impairment, resulting in pain, restricted motion, vertical deficiency of the ramus, and malocclusion and thus pose difficult problems in joint reconstruction[616] (Figs. 29–114 to 29–116).

In contrast, McBride believes that the best opportunity to resolve joint problems is with earlier total joint procedures rather than after multiple surgeries.[681] Failure of these early surgical procedures is usually associated with the development of additional degeneration. Each time an additional procedure is performed, the potential for obtaining optimal total joint results diminishes, particularly with relief of pain and improved function. Consequently, the repetitive use of surgical procedures on joints

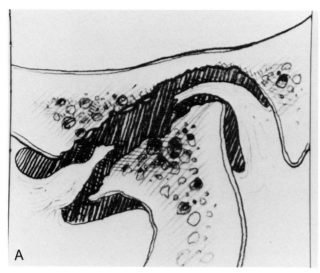

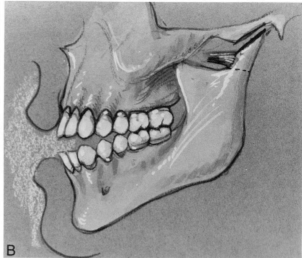

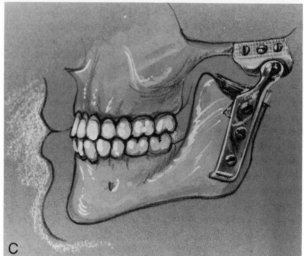

FIGURE 29–114. *A,* Severe DJD associated with anterior dislocation of the disc, perforation of the retrodiscal tissue, loss of condylar and fossa integrity, anterior spur formation, and shortening of the condylar head. *B,* Open-bite deformity from degenerative process described in *A.* The dotted line illustrates resection area of the condyle in preparation of total joint placement. *C,* VK-II total joint reconstruction with repositioning of remaining condylar stump and lateral pterygoid muscle. Technique described in Figures 29–125 and 29–126. (Courtesy of Dr. Kevin McBride, Dallas.)

that have failed to respond to similar surgical procedures in the past does not seem appropriate. McBride states that we must accept the limitations imposed by the degenerative joint processes and the general health and habits of patients and recognize that surgical failures are probably more appropriately attributed to the patient's physiologic failure associated with joint loading than to the specific technicalities of the soft tissue repair procedure.[681]

Since total joint reconstruction involves replacement of the condylar head and resurfacing of the articular fossa, its use implies the presence of uncontrollable degeneration of the mandibular condyle, a process that may have begun with displacement or perforation of the meniscus and chondromalacia of the articulating surface. Selection of other procedures is usually dependent on healthy articular surfaces, often difficult to determine.[681]

Magnetic resonance imaging may provide an effective mechanism for evaluating the physiologic status of the condyle.[682,683] The signal intensity from the medullary portion of the condylar head can be used as an indicator of the blood flow to the condylar head. The medullary portion of a normal condyle produces a bright white pattern (on a T_1-weighted image) owing to a high signal intensity corresponding to the high fluid volume in the medullary bone. The dense cortical shell of the condylar head appears black on the image owing to its low fluid concentration. The intensity of the medullary signal decreases as the degenerative process progresses. This relationship can be utilized in the process of determining which joints are appropriate candidates for total reconstruction.[681] As the vascularity of the condylar head decreases, it would seem that the potential for healing and stabilization of the degenerative process decreases. However, the exact degree of reduction of vascularity that must occur before irreversible condylar degeneration takes place has not been established.

McBride believes that once there has been sufficient degeneration of the condylar head to produce even a small anterior open bite, the potential for obtaining a stable, comfortable, and functional joint over an extended period is less with procedures other than total joint reconstruction. It may be possible to obtain good short-term relief of pain, improvement in function, and restoration of occlusion with other joint surgical procedures combined with orthognathic surgery. However, the natural progression of the degenerative process leads to recurrence of the open bite, increasing joint symptoms, and decreasing joint function in a high percentage of patients. When large anterior open bite is present, restoration of occlusion may demand simultaneous orthognathic and less involved joint surgical procedures. When compared with total joint reconstruction, the combined orthognathic and joint procedures offer no advantages with regard to potential complications, long-term stability, or comfort, function, or cooperation of the patient.

Problems.   Complications with and contraindications to total TMJ prostheses include hematoma; motor or sensory damage; hypomobility; malocclusion; continued pain; previous or new TMJ infections; limited capacity for cooperation during the postoperative phase; systemic diseases such as noncontrolled diabetes, cardiovascular diseases, or collagen disorders, which may lead to poor wound healing; and other systemic illnesses or conditions, such as allergic conditions, osteomyelitis, and other states that prevent satisfactory wound healing. Generally, many of these contraindications and complications apply also to autogenous materials for reconstruction of fossa or condyle.

With any spatial implant under load, it is essential that the surgical procedure result in an anatomy that approximates the natural joint as closely as possible. An improper relationship of artificial joint parts, too rapid or excessive joint loading, or improper postoperative physical therapy or follow-up can contribute to the failure of the total joint procedure or any TMJ procedure involving alloplast or autogenous tissues. The damage caused to any polymer implant material by such events can release fragments of the implant, which in turn can stimulate an inflammatory response and pain. A limited and normal macrophage response with giant cells is a common finding in the use of any polymer TMJ or facial implant material.

However, numerous and persistent macrophage responses with a large aggregation of histiocytes (foreign body giant cells) and granulomatous tissue have been observed when particulate debris of polymer implant materials (silicone rubber, fluorinated polymer, acrylics, and high molecular weight polyethylene) is generated within the TMJ following partial or total joint reconstruction (Fig. 29–117A and B). Lymphadenopathy has also been reported.[496,497] Prompt implant removal or revision surgery (or both) is recommended once examination has determined that these conditions exist. A guarded outlook is appropriate for any alloplastic TMJ reconstruction, particularly in patients with a history of previous surgical failures (Fig. 29–117C). The long-term conditions of articulating surfaces are not known. Since recent studies on various polymers have shown potential increased wear debris, patients with either Teflon or silicone rubber fossa prostheses should be closely monitored.

At surgery, implant articulating surfaces can be damaged, which can lead to failure of the procedure. Therefore, all articulating surfaces must remain smooth and free of debris, particularly after trimming. Care must be taken not to damage the articulating surfaces of the implant during handling and preparation procedures. The surgeon should examine the articulating surfaces immediately before wound closure. Shortened life expectancy of the implant can occur from (1) failure to trim the glenoid fossa implant to the proper anatomic dimension; (2) wear caused by debris left in the joint space or rough articulating surfaces; (3) failure to secure the implant

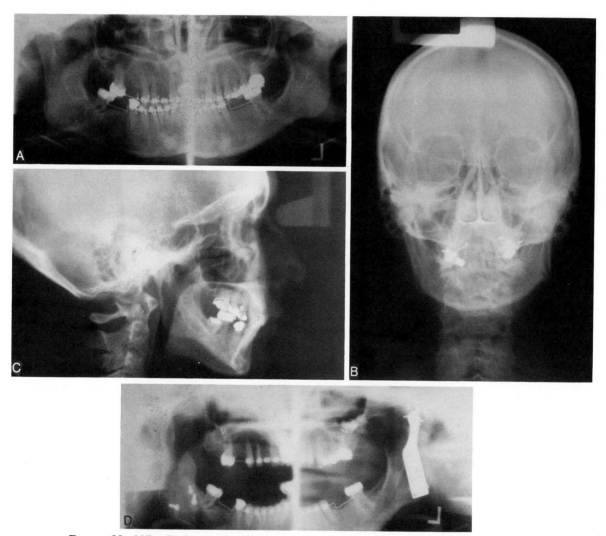

FIGURE 29–115.   Patient with a bony ankylosis and resulting maxillary and mandibular asymmetry and mandibular retrognathism.   Treatment consisted of orthodontics and surgery. Surgical procedures performed include a Le Fort I osteotomy with a unilateral HA block downgraft, a unilateral sagittal ramus osteotomy, and a unilateral total joint. Surgical workup involved setting the maxilla to the operated mandible. Rigid fixation was necessary for early mobilization. A comfortable 35-mm opening was obtained 2 weeks postoperatively and has been maintained for 3 years. *A*, Preoperative panoramic radiograph. *B*, Preoperative PA radiograph. *C*, Preoperative cephalometric radiograph. *D*, Postoperative panoramic radiograph with wide mandibular opening showing prosthesis translation. This is due to the attachment of the lateral pterygoid muscle to the prosthesis and sigmoid notch.

Illustration continued on opposite page.

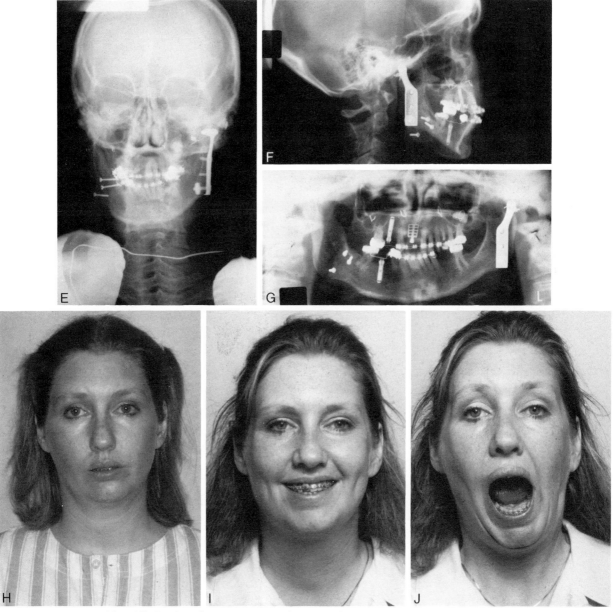

FIGURE 29–115. *Continued.*   *E,* Postoperative PA radiograph. *F,* Postoperative cephalometric radiograph at 3 years includes dental implants. *G,* Postoperative panoramic radiograph at 3 years. *H,* Preoperative full-face view. *I,* Postoperative full-face view. *J,* Postoperative opening.

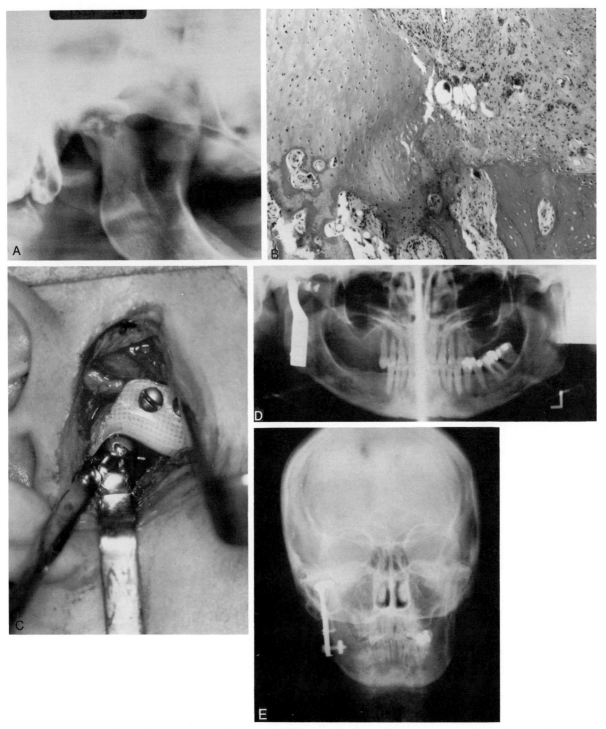

FIGURE 29–116.   A 45-year-old woman with untreated (surgical and nonsurgical) advanced DJD of the right TMJ.   At surgery, the right condyle was easily removed with rongeurs. Unilateral total TMJ reconstruction was performed with the VK-II total joint system. *A,* Preoperative panoramic radiograph showing severe condylar destruction and collapse of bony architecture. *B,* Histologic view of condylar head shows that fibrocartilage and the cortex of the articular surface are interrupted and ingrown with fibrovascular tissue. *C,* Intraoperative orientation of condyle prosthesis to cup of the glenoid fossa prosthesis. *D,* Postoperative panoramic radiograph at 4 years. *E,* Postoperative PA radiograph at 4 years.

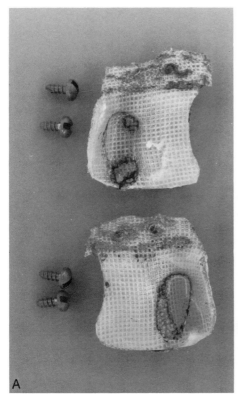

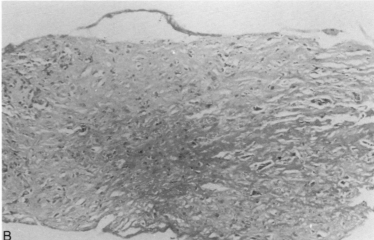

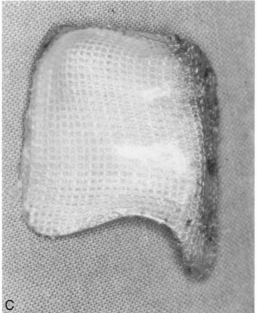

FIGURE 29-117. *A*, Bilateral VK-I glenoid fossa implants with excessive wear through Teflon into polyaramid fabric at 4.5 years. Patient had a history of multiple TMJ surgeries, clenching, and bruxism. *B*, Foreign body giant cell response to particulate surface wear debris from FEP articulating surface of VK-I glenoid fossa prosthesis. *C*, Normal VK-I glenoid fossa prosthesis removed 3 years postoperatively because of pain. Removal and replacement did not improve the pain in this patient with drug dependence.

properly, thus causing accelerated bone resorption from movement of the fossa or condylar components during function; and (4) malpositioning of the components, causing maladaptation of the condylar component vis-à-vis the fossa component (Fig. 29–112*A* and *B*).

VK-II TOTAL JOINT RECONSTRUCTION

Perioperative Preparation.[616] Proplast implants must be gas sterilized, cold sterilized, or irradiated because of the porous nature of Proplast material. Steam sterilization is necessary for 30 minutes at a temperature not exceeding 250°F. Total joint reconstruction is a technically sensitive surgical procedure. The success of this or any implant procedure is heavily dependent upon the proper preparation and handling of materials. The preoperative clinical examination must include assessment of facial form, with particular attention to anterior and posterior vertical height discrepancies. Patients with severe TMJ destruction often have facial deformities (mandibular asymmetry, retrognathism, open bite, and so on) secondary to chronic condylar resorption. Panoramic radiographs, TMJ tomograms, and CT, including three-dimensional model fabrication, are helpful (Fig. 29–118). Lateral cephalograms (or true lateral skull films) and prediction tracings are essential.

Initial cephalometric tracings are made as in the preoperative planning for most patients with dentofacial deformities (Fig. 29–119*A*). The S-curve of the glenoid fossa

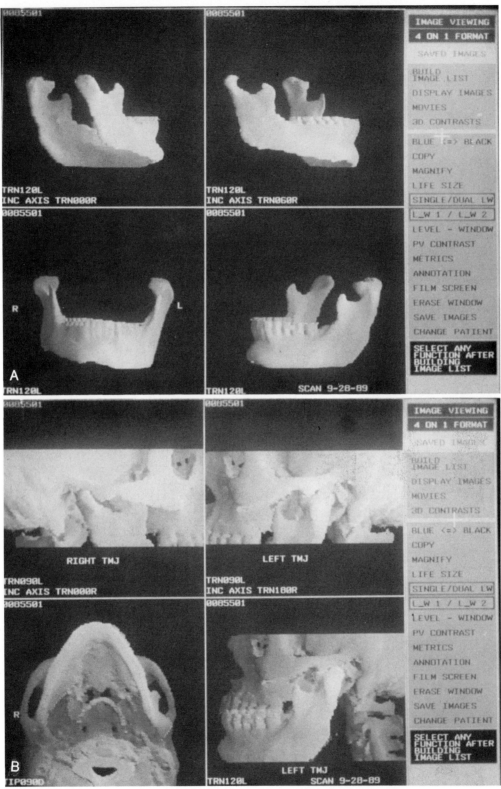

FIGURE 29–118. *A, B,* Three-dimensional CT reconstruction of mandibular asymmetry secondary to severe condylar hyperplasia. (Courtesy of Dr. Kevin L. McBride, Dallas.)

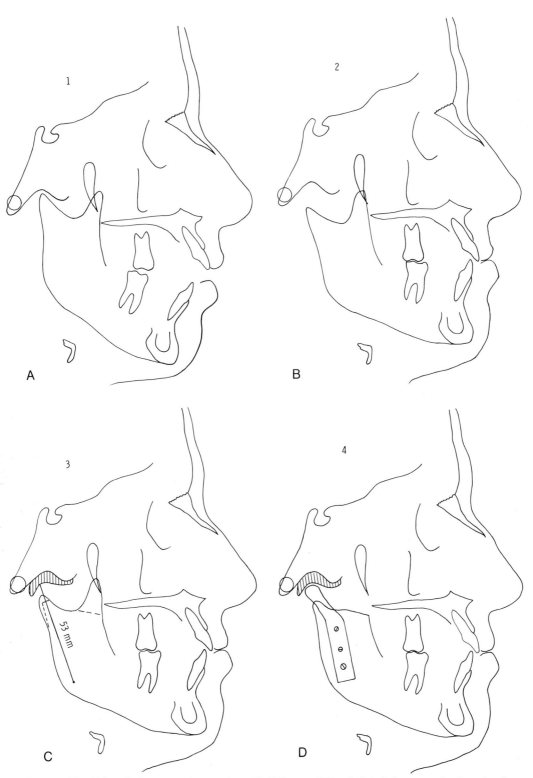

FIGURE 29–119. *A,* Preoperative tracing of TMJ, mandible, facial skeleton, and relaxed soft tissues. *B,* Correct mandibulomaxillary relations with estimated position of remaining condyle. *C,* Tracing the outline of the fossa implant. The distance from the fossa implant to the center of the mandibular angle determines the length of the metallic condyle. *D,* Total joint replacement.

and the articular eminence surfaces are traced. A second, or overlay, prediction tracing is drawn with all nonmovable parts of the facial skeleton (skull, maxilla, nose, and upper lip) (Fig. 29–119B). The prediction tracing is then rotated to visualize the mandible in proper occlusion and aesthetic form. The mandible, lip, chin, and condyle are then traced to complete the final postoperative prediction. The distance between the remaining condylar surface, or the anticipated condylar neck area following arthroplasty and condylectomy, and the glenoid fossa determines the thickness of the fossa prosthesis (Fig. 29–119B). Usually, a 6-mm fossa or occasionally a 9-mm fossa is used. For selection of a VK-II condylar prosthesis, a line is drawn on the prediction tracing from the anticipated articulation site on the fossa prosthesis to a point at the angle of the mandible 5 mm from the posterior and inferior borders (Fig. 29–119C). The longest VK-II condylar prosthesis that does not exceed the length of this line is then selected (Fig. 29–119D). An interocclusal acrylic splint is then constructed, with the study models placed in optimal centric occlusion. The patient is asked to use antibacterial facial and hair scrubs during the evening prior to surgery to decrease the potential for skin contamination.

Surgical Technique.[616] In the perioperative period, the patient is given large doses of steroids to minimize edema, as well as antibiotics against facial, ear, oral, nasal, and pharyngeal organisms. Intravenous cephalosporin (2 g initially, followed by 1 g every 6 hours for 72 hours) is preferred. The mouth and nose are packed, and antisialologue medication is administered before surgery and every 4 hours during surgery to reduce secretions. After shaving the preauricular area, the hair is retracted with a water-based jelly. The skin is dried thoroughly, and 2-inch silk tape surrounds the head beneath the occiput, including the endotracheal tube (Fig. 29–120A and B). The face is prepared with povidone-iodine (Betadine) soap and solution. The ear canal and eyelids are prepared with povidone-iodine (Betadine) solution only, and antibiotic-moistened cotton is placed in the ear canal. Disposable papers drapes are stapled to the skin; plastic drapes are avoided because they can promote skin excretions and hide potential seepage of fluid from the mouth and nose. Each side is draped separately in bilateral cases to avoid contamination as the head is rotated from one side to the other. A center drape, which is tented at the lateral canthus and oral commissure for observation of facial nerve stimulation, is placed for easy removal and entry into the mouth. The face is painted with povidone-iodine (Betadine) each time the drape is removed and replaced (Fig. 29–120C). If simultaneous orthognathic surgery is planned (maxilla or ramus on the opposite side), these procedures should be done before the total joint placement if possible. Surgery on the opposite-side ramus may be necessary before total joint placement.

A standard temporal-preauricular and retromandibular (preferred to the subman-

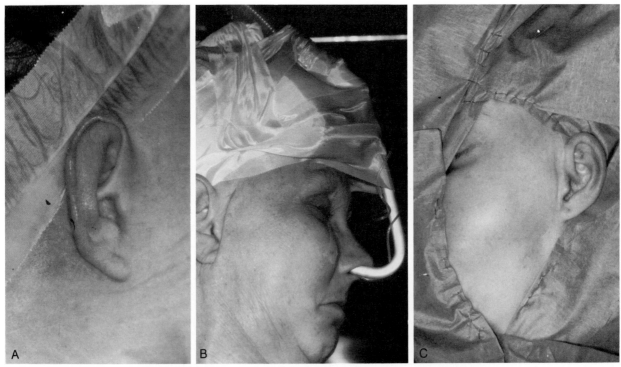

FIGURE 29–120. *A–C,* Surgical preparation of the face (see text).

dibular approach for greater access to the ramus) approach should be used to expose widely all aspects of the TMJ and mandible in total TMJ reconstruction (Fig. 29–121A). A "cleanout" of the fossa and articular eminence is required. The lateral pterygoid muscle is identified and tagged for attachment to the neck of the metallic condyle or sigmoid notch. A 4- or 5-cm retromandibular incision beneath and around the angle of the mandible is made to assist with or following the preauricular dissection. The dissection approaches the ramus between the marginal mandibular and buccal branches of the facial nerve. Care is taken to preserve the facial nerve. The pterygomasseteric sling is incised, and the lateral surfaces of the mandible, sigmoid notch, and coronoid process are exposed. Approximately 12 mm of vertical space within the fossa is required to place a total joint. Reduction of the remaining condylar head or neck may be required. It may be advisable to perform simultaneously a coronoidectomy to facilitate postoperative function and allow for rotation or advancement of the mandible when correcting open bite or retrognathism, if present. In patients with previous multiple joint surgeries, scarring from the base of the skull to the sigmoid notch and coronoid area must be released by stripping the superior surface of the ramus along its medial and lateral superior one-third area. Increased sizes of urethral sounds or slowly inflated tissue expanders are used to enlarge the pocket between the joint and ramus in badly fibrosed cases (Fig. 29–121B and C). Tight intermaxillary wire fixation using a previously applied arch bar and prepared occlusal splint is performed after the mandible is fully mobilized.

The fossa and condyle implants must be vacuum impregnated in a 60-ml syringe with an antibiotic solution (1 g of cephalosporin or other appropriate antibiotic in 100 ml of normal saline), using the technique described for facial augmentation with Proplast (Fig. 29–121D). An instrument tray of templates, special screws, and so on is necessary (Fig. 29–121E).

Sizers may be used for determining the correct size of the implant and may aid in proper trimming of the actual fossa implant. If necessary, the glenoid fossa implant may be adapted to the natural glenoid fossa by shaving the superior Proplast-HA surface. Alteration of the existing fossa–articular eminence anatomy is usually not necessary, except in case of severe resorption or bony ankylosis (Fig. 29–121F). Bleeding from the middle meningeal vessels may be encountered. Control of bleeding may be accomplished by local packing or ligation, as seen in Figure 29–121G to I. If fossa resorption has occurred, grafting with a carved coronoid process, iliac crest, or cranial graft may be necessary to fill in a thin or perforated fossa roof. Preoperative tomograms, CT, or MRI may strongly suggest this need (Fig. 29–111). Trimming of the medial and posterior edges of the implant may be necessary, since they may be slightly oversized. Trimming the anterior edge is necessary if the flange extends beyond the articular eminence. Care must be taken not to mechanically disrupt, reduce, or disfigure the smooth thickness of the UHMWPE on the articulating surfaces. Finally, the superior margin of the flange extension along the zygomatic arch is trimmed until it is flush with the superior edge of the zygomatic arch.

The glenoid fossa implant is checked for stability with the condylar template (Fig. 29–121J and K). The lateral surface of the ramus, at the remaining condylar neck, may have to be decorticated to improve surface adaptation or "fit" of the condylar implant template. Premature contact of the superiomedial aspect of the condylar template or lateral displacement of the fossa prosthesis when loaded with the template might indicate the need for additional trimming of the Proplast surface of the fossa prosthesis or bending of the condylar neck (Figs. 29–122 and 29–123). A 1.5 mm tapered fissure or wire-passing drill is used to place two or three holes for small, 4- to 7-mm, self-tapping bone screws through the flange of the glenoid fossa implant and the lateral portion of the zygomatic arch. The condylar template is used to mark screw holes and an L-shaped groove site for the condyle. The template should be placed as far posteriorly as possible to prevent damage to the inferior alveolar nerve when screw holes are made. A 2-mm L-shaped groove is prepared using fissure burs, and holes for self-tapping screws or bolts are made with the condylar implant seated in the L-shaped groove. The screw holes and bolt are prepared using a 2.2-mm and 2.5-mm drill, respectively, with the bolt and nut placed in the inferior hole. Final positioning of the condyle, however, must represent no premature contacts within the fossa. Large articulation contact areas between the two prostheses should be observed (Fig. 29–124A and B). The use of the McBride bending instrument to produce medial or lateral S-shape bending as well as rotation of the condylar head is helpful and may be essential (Figs. 29–123 and 29–124). Bending the metal may lead to cracking, however, which would require removal and discard. Back-up prostheses should always be available. Suturing the lateral pterygoid muscle insertion around the condylar neck or through a hole in the sigmoid notch is recommended to help in postoperative translation. An osteotomy of the remaining condylar head allows repositioning of the lateral pterygoid muscle, as described by McBride (Figs. 29–125 and 29–126). The wound is irrigated with the concentrated antibiotic solution and closed.

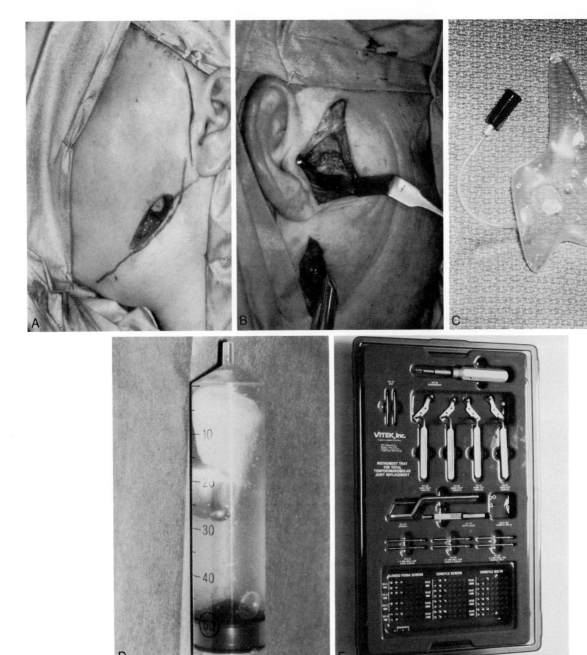

FIGURE 29–121. *A,* Retromandibular incision centered immediately beneath the angle of the mandible with dissection between the buccal and mandibular branches of the facial nerve gives the best access to the ramus and condyle area. *B,* Urethral sound used to expand scar tissue lateral to the condylar stump. *C,* A tissue expander may also be used to slowly expand the tissue lateral to the ramus. *D,* Vacuum impregnation of the condyle and fossa prosthesis with a concentrated antibiotic solution. *E,* Vitek instrument tray for total joint replacement. *F,* Extensive erosion of the articular fossa may necessitate bone removal along the root of the zygomatic arch and articular eminence to permit stable placement of the fossa implant level with the base of the skull. *G,* Erosion of articular fossa and removal of fibrous tissue may also lead to exposure of middle meningeal vessels. *H,* Normal bony fossa contour and position of middle meningeal vessels, (A). Fossa erosion and exposure of vessels (B). Extensive erosion and hemorrhage of vessels require control with oxidized cellulose or microfibrilar collagen (C). Thinned or perforated fossa requires bone grafting before inserting glenoid fossa prosthesis (D). *I,* If local measures fail to control middle meningeal bleeding, vessels can be ligated at the base of the skull slightly anterior and medial to the articular eminence. *J, K,* Glenoid fossa implant positioned and secured with screws using condylar template. (*F–K,* Courtesy of Dr. Kevin L. McBride, Dallas.)

Illustration continued on opposite page.

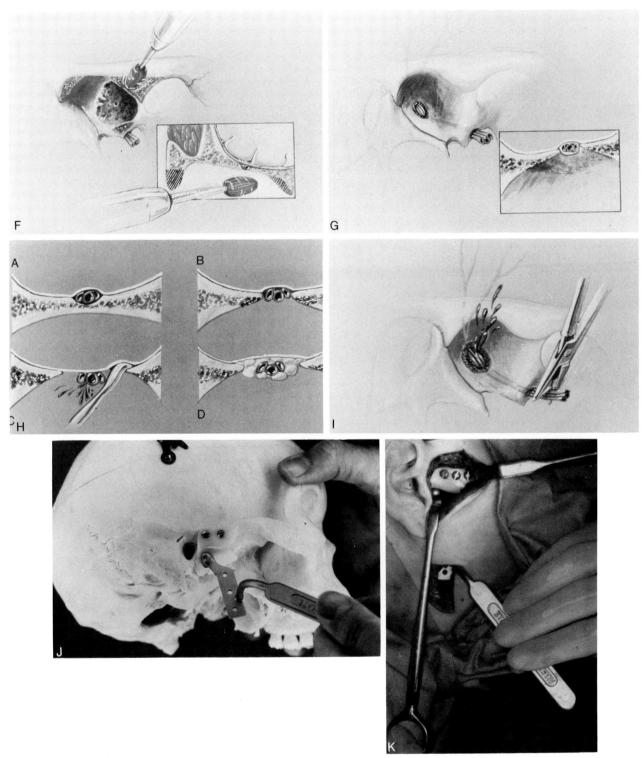

FIGURE 29–121. *Continued*

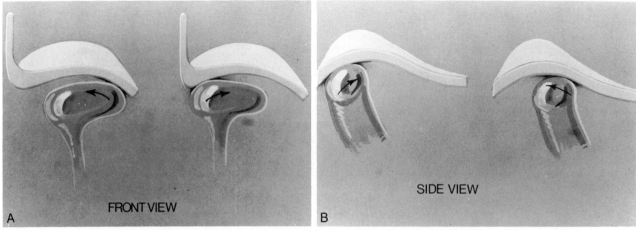

FIGURE 29–122. Improper relationship of condyle to fossa and necessary adjustments. Location of the condylar implant along the *A,* medial or lateral and *B,* posterior or anterior slope of the fossa implant will result in migration of the condylar implant to a more stable location in the center of the fossa, producing changes in the final occlusal position. (Courtesy of Dr. Kevin L. McBride, Dallas.)

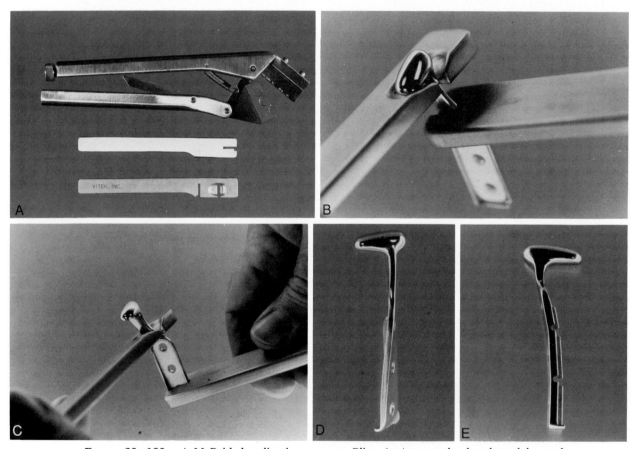

FIGURE 29–123. *A,* McBride bending instruments. Pliers *(top)* are used to bend condylar neck to move condylar head medially or laterally and tip medial pole up or down. Prosthesis shank may be made concave or convex. Plate benders twist the neck to move condylar head and pole anteriorly or posteriorly. Shank may also be twisted. *B,* McBride bending plates in position to twist the condylar head to permit rotation of the medial pole anteriorly or posteriorly. *C,* Application of McBride bending plates to permit twisting of the condylar implant shank. *D,* Long left VK-II condylar prosthesis with the inferior aspect of the shank twisted medially. *E,* Grooves cut in the posterior rail to facilitate bending of a right condylar implant with a concave bend in the shank. The neck has been bent to tilt the medial pole of the condylar head inferiorly.

Illustration continued on opposite page.

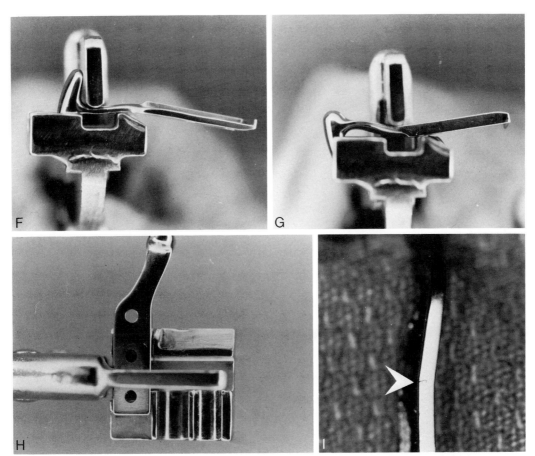

FIGURE 29–123. *Continued.* *F*, McBride bending pliers with long right VK-II condylar prosthesis in position to bend just below the condylar head. This will tip the medial pole of the condyle inferiorly and move the condylar head slightly medially. *G*, McBride bending pliers with 53-mm-long VK-II condyle in position to bend low on the condylar neck. This will move the condylar head laterally. *H*, Left VK-II condylar implant in position to create a concave bend in the inferior aspect of the shank. *I*, Excessive bending of the shank results in a fracture line, contraindicating implant placement. (Courtesy of Dr. Kevin L. McBride, Dallas.)

Immediate immobilization of the mandible is encouraged. Training elastics may be necessary for 7 to 10 days to assist in closing the mandible because of complete detachment of the muscles of mastication.

Postoperative Management.[616] A thorough follow-up program designed for gradual, controlled joint loading is necessary. A soft diet or one that involves no chewing for at least 2 months minimizes joint loading, with a gradual increase in food hardness as tolerated. Maximal mandibular opening several times each hour is necessary to obtain 30 to 35 mm by the third postoperative week. Lateral excursion and translation of the metallic condyle may be reduced or eliminated secondary to loss of lateral pterygoid muscle function unless its insertion is reattached. Deviation on opening is characteristic in unilateral cases. Patients should be cautioned not to open more than 35 mm, since dislocation is possible. The incidence of soft tissue pain may be greater when opening is forced beyond 35 mm in those patients unable to translate. Physical therapy agents (Fig. 29–127A and B) and procedures will be determined by the surgeon and therapist on the basis of diagnosis, history of previous procedures, preoperative and postoperative pain, myalgia, and response. Physical therapy may be necessary for several months to maintain the desired opening and to prevent fibrosis and hypomotility. The use of a continuous passive motion (CPM) machine is beneficial. Splints, nonsteroidal anti-inflammatory drugs, analgesics, and muscle relaxants may be helpful in reducing early joint loading and myalgia, controlling pain, and returning to normal function. Final occlusal adjustments should be delayed for 2 to 3 months after surgery.

The kinematic and functional requirements of a healthy masticatory system include stable occlusion with accompanying stable TMJs and dynamic mandibular mobility from the TMJ, with unrestrained range of motion and absence of pain. In the severely debili-

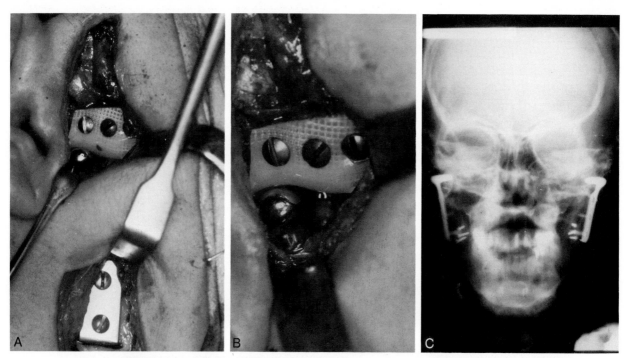

FIGURE 29–124. *A,* VK-II condyle fossa prostheses properly positioned. *B,* Metal condylar head articulating the glenoid fossa with maximal contact. *C,* Postoperative PA radiograph showing left metal condyle bent to adapt to anatomic contours.

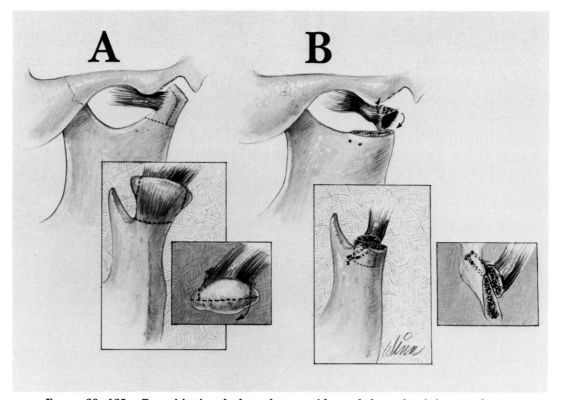

FIGURE 29–125. Repositioning the lateral pterygoid muscle by maintaining attachment to the anterior portion of the condylar head. *A,* The dotted lines illustrate the general line for sectioning the condylar head and maintaining a segment of bone attached to the lateral pterygoid muscle. *B,* The anterior portion of the condylar head is turned 90 degrees, so that the posterior edge of the reduced condylar head is adapted to the medial cortex of the condylar stump. A 26-gauge stainless steel wire is passed in mattress fashion through the anterior aspect of the condylar neck and the condylar segment. To develop a flat surface for the condylar implant, reduction of the lateral aspect of the condylar neck and ramus should be accomplished prior to wire placement. (Courtesy of Dr. Kevin L. McBride, Dallas.)

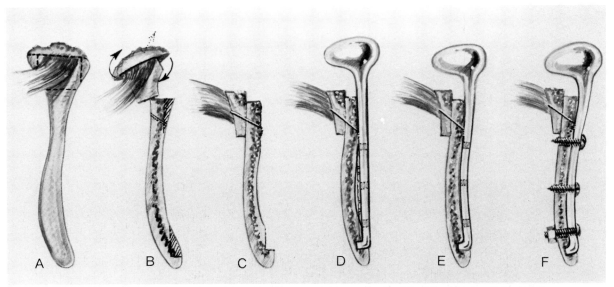

FIGURE 29–126.   Anterior view demonstrating repositioning of the lateral pterygoid muscle attached to a portion of the condylar head and bending of the condylar implant shank to adapt to the concave ramus.   *A*, Dotted lines indicate the portions of the condyle to be resected. *B*, The condylar segment attached to the lateral pterygoid muscle is repositioned inferiorly and anteriorly onto the medial aspect of the ramus. Bone is removed on the lateral aspect of the ramus from the condylar neck and mandibular angle regions to flatten the concave ramus and improve adaptation of the condylar implant. *C*, A mattress transosseous wire is placed to secure the lateral pterygoid muscle. *D*, The condylar implant is tried, and the ramus-implant contact is evaluated. *E*, The shank of the condylar implant is bent to adapt to the cancave ramus. *F*, The implant is secured with two screws and a bolt with a nut. (Courtesy of Dr. Kevin L. McBride, Dallas.)

tated TMJ requiring total joint replacement, reconstruction may provide joint and occlusal stability and some relief of pain. However, TMJ range of motion and mandibular mobility depend on postoperative rehabilitation and prosthesis design, as well as tissue deficiencies resulting from previous surgery.

Numerous experimental studies have indicated the beneficial effects of CPM on the healing of articular and periarticular tissues. Clinical studies by Salter and others have reported on the benefits of CPM in the postoperative management of various joint procedures. In particular, patients undergoing total knee arthroplasty, when managed postoperatively with CPM therapy, have an improved recovery rate by decreasing postoperative surgical pain, pain medication, and swelling. Wound healing is enhanced. The cumulative effect results in a shortened hospital stay.[684–699]

Poremba and Moffett and Sebastian and Moffett reviewed the history of orthopedic joint mobilization and the effects of CPM used on animals and on human ankle, knee, hip, finger, elbow, and shoulder joints. A prototype CPM for the TMJ is described.[700] In a second report, the results of CPM clinical trials on 13 patients (5 with and 8 without CPM) were described, noting maximal incisal opening with 5 days of use. Surgical procedures were arthroscopy and disc repair or dura implants. Postoperative opening of the CPM group was significantly improved over that of the control group after 6 weeks of observation.[701]

Fontenot and Kent have reported on the development, application, and clinical experience of a CPM device for the TMJ.[702] The CPM unit is a microprocessor-based electromechanical device that is designed to deliver and sustain low-force full-cycle oscillation of the mandible and TMJ (Fig. 29–127C to G). Movement of the motor shaft, which attaches to the mandible and maxilla, is under microcomputer control, which allows a variety of programmed parameters for motion. Attachment of the motor shaft to the mandible and maxilla ranges from custom acrylic splints to surgical arch bars. Impressions were frequently done intraoperatively because of hypomobility.

The CPM device (TransJaw R) (Vitek, Inc.) was used in postoperative rehabilitation over four years on 30 patients (51 joints) with the VK-II system[702] and 41 patients (71 joints) with arthroscopy or disc repair. The number of previous operations, preoperative and postoperative interincisal opening (IIO), patient age, sex, and duration of therapy are seen in Table 29–11.

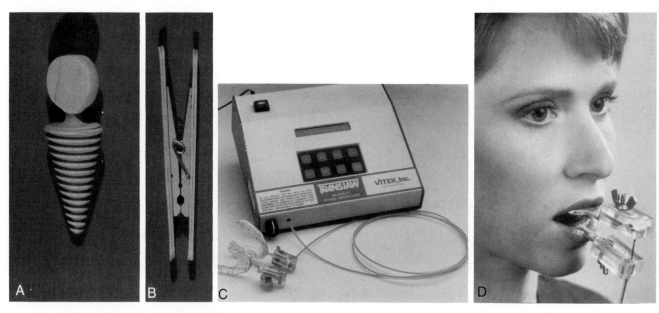

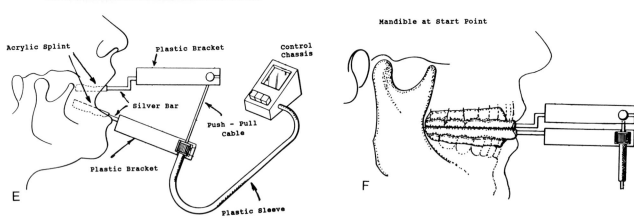

CPM Arrangement for the Temporomandibular Joint

Mandible at Start Point

Mandible at Maximum Span

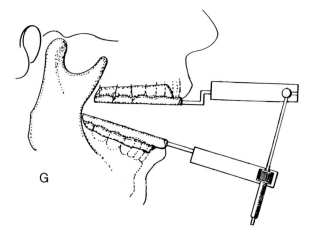

FIGURE 29–127. *A*, Lorenz wooden screw. *B*, Tongue blades glued to a clothespin. *C*, Continuous passive-motion (CPM) machine with splints. *D*, Maxillary and mandibular splints used in conjunction with CPM machine. *E*, CPM arrangement for the TMJ. The push-pull cable is coupled to the maxillary and mandibular plastic brackets. Movement of the push-pull cable is under microcomputer control, allowing the patient or surgeon to input parameters for mandibular motion. Schematic depicting the patient at *F*, the start point and at *G*, maximal span. A cycle is defined as the start point to maximum span and then the return to start point. Mandibular velocities in any one cycle range from 0.6 mm/sec to 1.3 mm/sec.

TABLE 29-11.   MULTI-CENTER CLINICAL TRIALS OF A CONTINUOUS PASSIVE MOTION DEVICE FOLLOWING TMJ SURGERY

	NEW ORLEANS	MIAMI	DALLAS
Patients (Sex)	17 (17F, 0M)	41 (35F, 6M)	13 (12F, 1M)
No. of TMJ procedures	28, All VK-II replacements	71	23, All VK-II replacements
Age (SD)	34.7 (7.8)	35 (9.3)	33.8 (8.8)
[Range]	[25–55]	[17–61]	[24–42]
Previous surgery	7.3 (4.8)	1.4 (1.2)	3.4 (2.0)
[Range]	[1–20]	[0–9]	[1–7]
Preop IIO (SD)	14.7 (9.0)	23.9 (8.6)	23.2 (8.8)
[Range]	[5–35]	[3–38]	[4–32]
Postop IIO (SD)	33.9 (7.4)	32.7 (6.2)	34.8 (5.4)
[Range]	[20–48]	[23–44]	[26–45]
Net IIO (SD)	19.2 (7.7)	8.9 (6.7)	12.2 (9.9)
[Range]	[10–38]	[1–19]	[2–32]
Duration of therapy (SD)	425.8 (347.0)	70.5 (47.5)	120.1 (87.0)
[Range], days	[21–1125]	[30–240]	[30–395]

IIO = Interincisal opening

Protocol for CPM Therapy

Phase I: CPM therapy to begin immediately after surgery for 14 days. CPM device is used as often as possible for a minimum of 8 hours per day. The span is set at 19 mm at a rate of 60 seconds per cycle, with the span gradually increasing to 40 mm.

Phase II: Therapy is continued to day 28, but the 8-hour requirement per day is relieved. The patient is encouraged to use the device at a span of 40 mm.

Phase III: Any CPM therapy beyond day 28 is long term. Here the CPM device is used as an adjunct to physical therapy.

The CPM physical rehabilitation program was instituted at 5 to 7 postoperative days and was divided into a multiphasic program. Phase I was 7 to 14 days with the use of the CPM device as often as possible for a minimum of 8 hours per day. In Phase II, the requirement of 8 hours per day was reduced to 4 hours, and therapy was maintained until day 28. Phase III was considered to be any amount of CPM therapy after day 28 and was used as an adjunct to physical therapy.[687,688] An overwhelming majority of arthroscopy and disc repair patients required only phase I or II treatment whereas over 80 per cent of total joint patients required long-term phase III treatment.

Before the development of CPM for the TMJ, the postoperative management of a patient with total TMJ arthroplasty generally was the province of a physical therapist or oral and maxillofacial surgeon or both, who increased the patient's range of motion by various combinations of active and active-assistive range-of-motion exercises, sometimes with the aid of mechanical devices, such as wedges and large wood or polymer screws. These treatments were essential for retraining the patient to return to normal masticatory and speech activities. However, the results of CPM for the TMJ appear to enhance the traditional roles of the physical therapist and surgeon in the care of patients undergoing total TMJ arthroplasty.

Follow-up results are encouraging, since the patients receiving total joint prostheses have conditions that are refractory to most forms of surgical therapy. Kent reported on a total of 182 TMJs reconstructed at Louisiana State University in 107 patients with VK-I or VK-II prostheses with a 6 to 72 month follow-up between 1982 and 1988[653] (Table 29–12). Before placement of the VK system, 335 previous surgical procedures (range of 1 to 15, average of 3.7) were done on 159 of the 182 joints by a variety of surgeons across the United States. The most common diagnoses before any surgery were internal derangement, degenerative joint disease, and condylar fractures (Table 29–12 B and C). The admitting diagnoses for partial and total joint procedures were primarily ankylosis and degenerative disease, with a high incidence of ramus vertical dimension loss. The majority of patients exhibited mandibular retrognathism and open bite deformity, requiring restoration of this ramus deficiency. Inferior and anterior movement of the mandibular angle required at surgery ranged from 4 to 12 mm. Table 29–12 D to H demonstrates success rates relative to

TABLE 29-12.   VK TOTAL JOINT RECONSTRUCTION (Kent)

A. VK System Placed in Patients with Previous TMJ Surgery

	VK-I	VK-II
Joints	108	51
Unilateral	30	11
Bilateral	78	40
Partial joints	37	4
Total joints	71	47
Patients	65	27

B. Previous Surgery History

Diagnosis	Before Any Surgery	On Admission for Total Joint
Internal derangement	48	0
DJD	25	42
Condylar fracture	23	0
Rheumatoid arthritis	9	9
Bony ankylosis	7	31
Other trauma	4	0
Idiopathic condylar resorption (ICR)	4	3
Fibrous ankylosis	0	67
Condylectomy	—	8
Bony fossa erosion	—	5
Prosthesis erosion	—	18
Condylar prosthesis, malposition	—	11
Vertical dimension loss	—	73

C. Type of Previous TMJ Surgeries

N = 335	Internal derangement	DJD	Diagnoses Condylar fracture	Others	Total
Disc repair	29	1	7	1	37
Discectomy alone	8	2	3	2	15
Discectomy with temporary Silicone	1	0	0	0	1
Discectomy with permanent Silicone	29	19	14	4	66
Discectomy with Proplast-Teflon	37	14	4	1	56
Discectomy with dermis	3	3	0	0	6
Condylar shave	39	25	19	9	92
Coronoidectomy	11	2	4	0	17
Eminectomy	4	3	1	0	8
Rib grafts	4	1	0	4	9
Osteotomy	12	6	5	1	24
Fossa prosthesis alone	13	1	3	0	17
Condylar prosthesis alone	8	2	10	6	26
Total joint	33	5	3	3	44
Steroid injections	7	0	0	0	7
Infection	1	0	0	0	3
Temporalis scarring	1	0	0	0	1
Morgan prosthesis	4	0	0	0	4

D. VK System Placed in Patients with No Previous TMJ Surgery

	VK-I	VK-II
Joints	18	5
Unilateral	6	1
Bilateral	12	4
Partial	4	1
Total	14	4
Patients	12	3

TABLE 29–12.   VK TOTAL JOINT RECONSTRUCTION (Kent) *(Continued)*

E. VK-I Partial Joint Follow-up

Yr	In Place	Removed	Interval Success Rate
0–1	41	5	88%
1–2	36	3	92%
2–3	33	2	94%
3–4	23	4	83%
4–5	12	1	92%
5–6	4	0	100%
Total	41	15	63.4% (80% if removed implants are only those from material failure)

F. VK-I Total Joint Follow-up

Yr	In Place	Removed	Interval Success Rate
0–1	85	6	93%
1–2	79	10	87%
2–3	67	2	97%
3–4	46	2	96%
4–5	25	2	92%
5–6	7	0	100%
Total	85	22	74.5% (88% if removed implants are only those from material failure)

G. VK-II Partial Joint Follow-up

Yr	In Place	Removed	Interval Success Rate
0–1	5	0	100%
1–2	5	0	100%
2–3	4	0	100%
Total	5	0	100%

H. VK-II Total Joint Follow-up

Yr	In Place	Removed	Interval Success Rate
0–1	51	3	94.1%
1–2	25	0	100.0%
2–3	5	0	100.0%
Total	51	3	94.1% (none removed for material failure)

I. Removal of Partial (P)/Total (T) Joint Prostheses

	Pain of Unknown Origin	Pain of Extensive Fibrosis	Pain of Fibrosis Erosion	Infection
VK-I	12 (4 P) (8 T)	5 (T)	14 (9 P) (5 T)	4 (4 T)
VK-II	(3 T)	0	0	0
Total	15	5	14	4

J. VK TMJ Reconstruction 1982–1990 (Kent)

	Yrs. Followed	No. Placed	No. Removed	Success Rate
VK-I Partial	7–8	41	16	61%
VK-I Total	7–8	85	29	66%
VK-II Partial	4–5	6	0	100%
VK-II Total	4–5	115	9	92%

prosthesis type and follow-up time from placement. VK-I partial joint and total joint procedures were successful in 63 per cent and 75 per cent of cases, respectively. When the data were calculated to include only implants removed because of material failure, the success rates were 80 per cent and 88 per cent, respectively. VK-II partial and total joint procedures were successful in 100 per cent and 94 per cent of cases, respectively. Their follow-up, however, is only 3 years. The increased success is due to more strict clinical criteria for partial joint reconstruction and improved fossa wear of UHMWPE in total joints. Reasons for removal, usually related to fossa prostheses, were chronic pain and fibrosis with or without Teflon erosion (Table 29–12).

Data provided by McBride (Table 29–13) indicate significant reduction of TMJ pain and headache with improved range of mandibular opening on 140 joints in 86 patients who were followed from 3 to 48 months.[703] As expected, 94 per cent of the patients were female, and 77 per cent of the joints were in patients having bilateral surgery (Table 29–13A). The majority of joints (77 per cent) required the longest condyle. When possible, the lateral pterygoid muscle was reattached with ostectomy and wiring (Fig. 29–125). More than one half of the fossa prostheses were polyethylene. Mandibular advancement and open-bite closure were accomplished in 13 and 64 patients, respectively (Table 29–13B). Joint pain was reduced significantly. The average preoperative joint pain level was measured at 4 (0 to 10 range). The average preoperative headache pain level was 6 (1 to 10 range). The postoperative joint pain scale rating averaged 1.2 (0 to 7 range) (Table 29–13C). Headache pain, slightly worse than the joint pain preoperatively, was reduced to nearly the same postoperative pain measurement (Table 29–13D). Although the average maximal interincisal opening remained unchanged from its preoperative measurement, the range of opening improved (Table 29–13E). Three fossa components were removed and replaced because of surgical infection (1), pain (1), and polymer debris (1). Six joints were re-entered to excise fibrous adhesions. Two condylar implants were removed — one for infection and one for pain. As discussed earlier, McBride's patients were operated on much earlier in the patient's surgical history than Kent's patients. Success rates would be expected to be higher and complications lower, since surgical risks are lower in this population. Continued follow-up of VK-I system with Teflon-FEP fossa and VK-II system with UHMWPE fossa indicates significantly better results with the polyethylene fossa (Table 29–12J). A review of these cases indicates nearly one-half of the removed Telfon-FEP fossas were due to material failure (wear) while no polyethylene fossas were removed for material failure.[704]

The follow-up data of the VK system indicate that several variables affect partial or total joint reconstruction. Prior surgery on the TMJ was directly associated with increased risk of reconstruction failure. In this series of patients, excessive joint loading, bruxism, poor occlusal support, malocclusion, excessive fibrosis from multiple procedures, and particularly chronic pain played major roles in determining total TMJ replacement success. Our data suggest that patients who have had sound previous surgical procedures accompanied by chronic pain should be told that complete relief of pain is not realistic. Surgical revision after placement of total joint prostheses as well as soft and hard tissue grafts should be resisted in the face of chronic pain with normal radiographic findings, acceptable mandibular function, and satisfactory occlusion. In the patient with a total joint reconstruction who has chronic pain, however, a simple exploration avoiding major revision surgery may be justified to rule out suspicions of implant tissue reaction. In a few patients, malposition of the metal condyle resulted in point contact and polymer wear. All patients with a VK-I system should be followed closely, since we have observed articular wear of the Teflon surface since 1985. Ultimately, we believe many will require removal after 10 years of follow-up. Removal and replacement with a VK-II fossa (polyethylene articular surface) are strongly indicated (Fig. 29–117A). In these patients with the Teflon fossa, a foreign body reaction with occasional granuloma was also found on histologic examination of retrieved joint tissue, with macrophages or giant cells attempting to phagocytose or encapsulate the polymer wear debris. In patients with partial joint recon-

TABLE 29-13. VK TOTAL JOINT RECONSTRUCTION (McBRIDE)

A. Data on 140 Joints: Average Age of Patient, 36 (range, 17-68)

Female	131	94%
Male	9	6%
Right	63	45%
Left	77	55%
Unilateral	32	23%
Right	9	6%
Left	23	16%
Bilateral	54	77%

B. Total Joint Sizes and Surgery Data

Condyles		
45 mm	33	24%
53 mm	107	76%
Lateral pterygoid muscle retained	29	21%
Fossae		
Small:	16	11%
Medium:	120	86%
Large:	4	3%
FEP fossa:	54	39%
Ultra high molecular weight polyethylene (UHMWPE) fossa	86	61%
No. of patients with mandibular advancement	13	15%
Average movement:	3 mm (range, 2-5 mm)	
No. of patients with an open bite closed	64	
Average movement:	2 mm (range, 1-6 mm)	

C. Joint Pain

	Patients	Average Joint Pain on 0-10 Scale	Range of Joint Pain
Preoperative	84	4	0-10
3-6 mo postoperative	60	1	0-7
6-12 mo postoperative	67	1	0-7
12-18 mo postoperative	32	1	0-7
18-24 mo postoperative	13	2	0-5
24-36 mo postoperative	11	2	0-6
36-48 mo postoperative	5	0	0-1

D. Headache Pain

	Patients	Average Headache Pain on 0-10 Scale	Range of Headache Pain
Preoperative	84	6	0-10
3-6 mo postoperative	73	1	0-7
6-12 mo postoperative	82	1	0-10
12-18 mo postoperative	39	1	0-8
18-24 mo postoperative	13	2	0-5
24-36 mo postoperative	12	2	0-10
36-48 mo postoperative	5	1	0-5

E. Maximal Interincisal Opening

	Patients	Average Opening, Maximal	Range of Opening
Preoperative	84	35	4-55
3-6 mo postoperative	74	33	20-43
6-12 mo postoperative	83	35	22-45
12-18 mo postoperative	39	36	26-44
18-24 mo postoperative	13	33	24-45
24-36 mo postoperative	12	36	23-41
36-48 mo postoperative	5	31	24-35

struction, Teflon fossa prosthesis wear was more frequent and was usually associated with postoperative condylar degeneration if medullary bone was exposed at surgery. Excessive joint loading and the formation of rough or sharp bony areas on the articular surface accelerated this process. In our opinion, strict indication criteria, such as an intact cortical surface of the condyle and avoidance of soft tissue detachment of the lateral and anterior poles, are necessary for placement of any polymer fossa against the natural condylar head. Finally, although the use of a glenoid fossa prosthesis as a disc replacement has been reported,[705] it is absolutely contraindicated because of thickness and increased loads resulting from ramus lengthening.

The use of a polymer glenoid fossa prosthesis with a metallic condyle has produced improved function in the rehabilitation of most adult patients with severe TMJ destruction. However, a total TMJ alloplastic joint should not be viewed as a panacea for complex TMJ problems. An accurate diagnosis must be established and the underlying causes of TMJ dysfunction elucidated prior to treatment planning. Medical and nonsurgical therapy, as well as more conservative surgical measures, must be exhausted. Destruction of joint parts, not dysfunction alone, may suggest total joint replacement. In most cases, vertical dimension forces along the fossa-condyle axis may be substantially increased from fibrosis, resulting in pain, hypomobility, and frequently open bite. Significant unknown compressive forces may exist in any patient with loss of condyle and protective buffering meniscus. Restoration of posterior ramus vertical dimension and correction of open bite or retrognathism may further increase joint loading. Reconstruction, therefore, should include suitable measures to resist erosive sequelae in natural fossa, remaining condyle, or implant articulation surfaces.

The Proplast-bone interface may allow for stresses to be dispersed by the fibrous tissue ingrowth to a large base of surrounding tissue. Once fibrous ingrowth occurs, long-term dependence upon the screws in the zygomatic arch may not seem to be critical. A few screws have been removed because of pain, and the removal of fossa prostheses in a few of our patients has demonstrated significant adhesion of the Proplast to the fossa and articular eminence. Relief of pain was not obtained. However, significant posterior displacement of the fossa prosthesis after screw removal in one patient produced major occlusal changes and dysfunction.

Successful total TMJ replacement is assessed by relief of pain and by re-establishment of masticatory function and aesthetics (Fig. 29–128A to P). Patients with less surgery or no previous surgery at all, such as those with loss of a condyle from trauma or advanced rheumatoid disease, have much better expectations than the chronic pain patient with a history of multiple joint procedures (Fig. 29–129). The disadvantages and limitations of any total joint replacement by alloplastic materials also include the lack of options if the prosthesis fails, and the availability and adaptability of replacement or future generation prostheses.[650] Although clinical requirements will vary widely when failures do occur, replacement with total joint prostheses (VK and Synthes, Davos, Switzerland) have been successfully performed. We have used Synthes condyles with spherical articulating surface against a VK fossa. However, this procedure provides less articular surface area contact between the implant parts (Fig. 29–130). A recent report by Sonnenburg and Sonnenburg clearly supports TMJ total joint indications, reconstructive experiences, and results with a Synthes mated fossa-condylar prosthesis[706] using a high-density polyethylene fossa and metallic condyle.

Improvement in materials and operative procedures has changed the design of total joint surface replacements in extremities.[707,708] The articulation of metal on metal creates erosion products and high stresses on the implant-bone interface, resulting in material failure and dislocation of the prostheses. However, the use of a metal femoral head against a geometrically conforming UHMWPE acetabulum minimizes erosion problems and high stress concentrations to the underlying bone during function.[708]

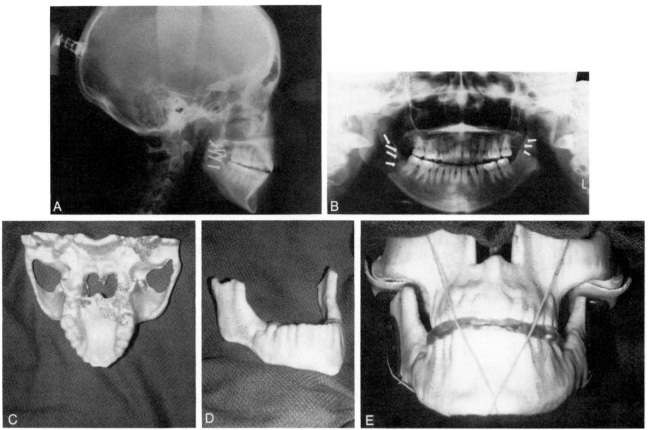

FIGURE 29–128.   This 25-year-old woman previously had 10 bilateral procedures by three different surgeons, with procedures including plications, implants, osteotomies, muscle flaps, grafts, and debridements prior to prosthetic total joint reconstruction. Because of the alteration of normal ramus anatomy and excessive degeneration of the bony fossa and condyle, it was elected to obtain three-dimensional CT of the mandible, maxilla, and temporal bones to fabricate custom prostheses. All metal from previous surgeries was removed, and all amalgam restorations were replaced with composite resins. From information obtained from the three-dimensional CT, models of the maxilla and mandible were milled. Stone models were made from alginate impressions of the milled models. These were then hand articulated to set the occlusion arbitrarily. An acrylic splint was fabricated to fit the milled models, and custom wax condyle templates were fashioned to fit the abnormal ramus anatomy against custom carved glenoid fossa prostheses. The wax condyles were cast in Cobalt-chromium (Vitallium) and polished from the neck up. The portion contacting the ramus was a plasma spray coating of HA. Custom HA-Proplast implants were also fabricated from the milled models to correct excessive antegonial notching secondary to previous orthognathic procedures. The preoperative opening was 11 mm, and the postoperative opening through the use of a CPM device reached a maximum of 52 mm, stabilizing at 45 mm. Unfortunately, the chronic pain that prompted many of the procedures has persisted. *A,* Preoperative cephalometric radiograph demonstrating open bite. *B,* Preoperative panoramic radiograph. *C,* Milled maxillary model showing abnormal glenoid fossa contour. *D,* Milled mandibular model. *E,* Frontal view of wax condyles with milled models in splint fixation.

Illustration continued on following page.

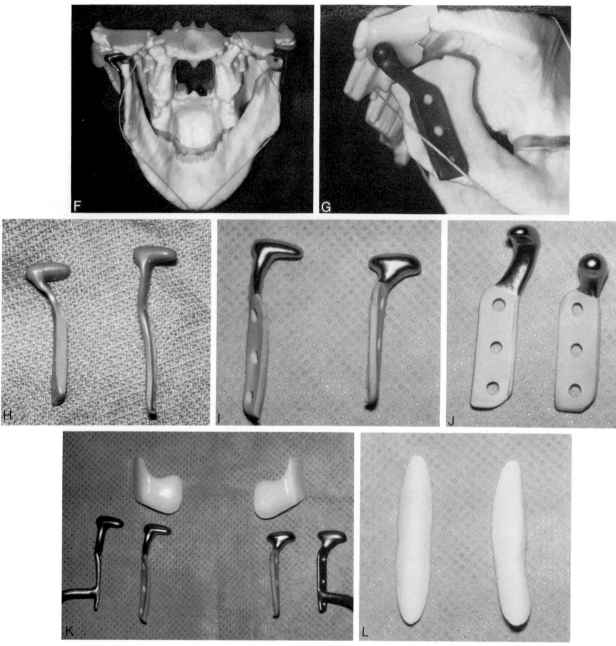

FIGURE 29–128. *Continued.* *F,* Posterior view of wax condyles showing abnormal condyle-ramus relationship on left. *G,* Wax condyle articulating against custom glenoid fossa prosthesis. *H,* Wax condyle templates prior to casting. *I,* Custom condyle prostheses coated with HA, side view. *J,* Custom condyle prostheses, facial view. *K,* Custom template, condyle, and fossa prostheses. *L,* Custom inferior border HA-Proplast implants.

Illustration continued on opposite page.

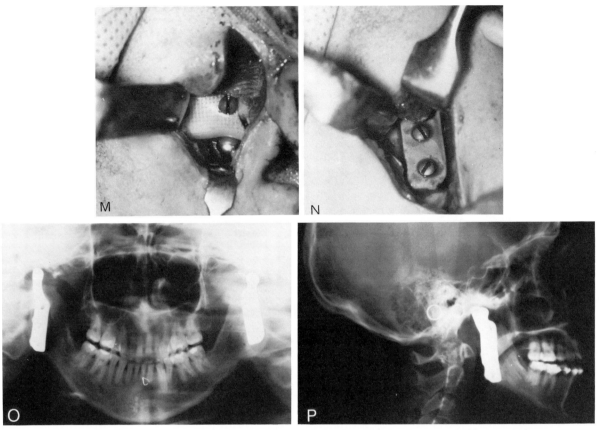

FIGURE 29–128. *Continued.*   *M,* Operative view of condyle articulating in glenoid fossa prosthesis. *N,* Operative view of condyle flush to lateral ramus. *O,* Postoperative panoramic radiograph. *P,* Postoperative cephalometric radiograph.

Surgery and reconstruction of the TMJ with a wide variety of techniques have now been discussed. The role of biomaterials may be significant, but they should be used only when other procedures, particularly those involving autogenous materials, are not justified because of an inferior benefit-risk ratio. Procedure selection may be based on the circumstances of the patient or surgeon. The surgical procedure, therefore, must fit the patient's needs, not vice versa.

A synopsis of our diagnosis of TMJ deformity and its reconstruction is given in Table 29–14. These principles also apply to the secondary treatment of condylar fracture complications.[709] They include the following:

1. Physical therapy by passive and active means must be tried in cases of minor dysfunction with pain and hypomobility, Although brisement under general anesthesia is used, the results are questionable and frequently counterproductive. Arthroscopic surgery to release adhesions in the upper joint space may be helpful in the patient who is compliant with physical therapy.

2. In cases of malocclusion with reasonable joint function and no significant pain and hypomobility, occlusal adjustment, restorations, and osteotomies are indicated based on the severity of occlusal deficit. The principle of secondary reconstruction because of malocclusion following condylar fractures is *not* to do TMJ procedures in the face of pain-free satisfactory movement. The treatment of significant occlusal deformity then becomes similar to the treatment of occlusal dysfunctions from developmental deformity.

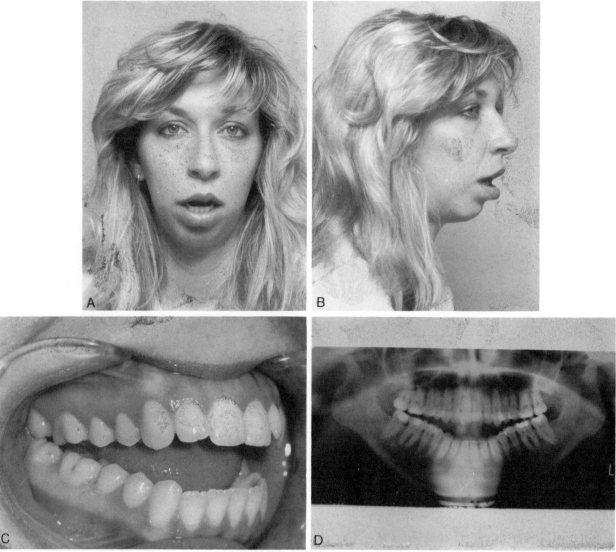

FIGURE 29–129.   **A 25-year-old patient with juvenile rheumatoid arthritis who had developed a severe open-bite deformity over a 10-year period.**   *A*, Preoperative full-face, *B*, profile, and *C*, occlusal views. *D*, Preoperative panoramic and *E*, cephalometric radiographs. *F*, Postoperative panoramic and *G*, cephalometric radiographs following reconstruction with bilateral VK-II total joint system, Le Fort I osteotomy, and genioplasty. Three-year postoperative *H*, profile, *I*, full-face, and *J*, occlusal views.

Illustration continued on opposite page.

3.   The presence of significant pain and hypomobility without malocclusion may be aided by arthroscopy but probably will require arthroplasty. Both procedures require release of adhesions in the upper joint space and a determination of the integrity and health of the disc.

4.   If the disc is displaced but otherwise normal, repositioning, even as a free graft, is recommended. Securing the disc to the condylar head is reasonable. However, deformed, calcified, or perforated discs require at least a partial, if not total, meniscectomy. Replacement with soft tissue grafts between the two bony articulating surfaces is generally preferred, although no use of interpositional graft has been suggested. Our experience with grafts suggests that auricular cartilage, temporalis fascia, and dermis are top choices. Homografts and alloplastic disc replacement are least preferred.

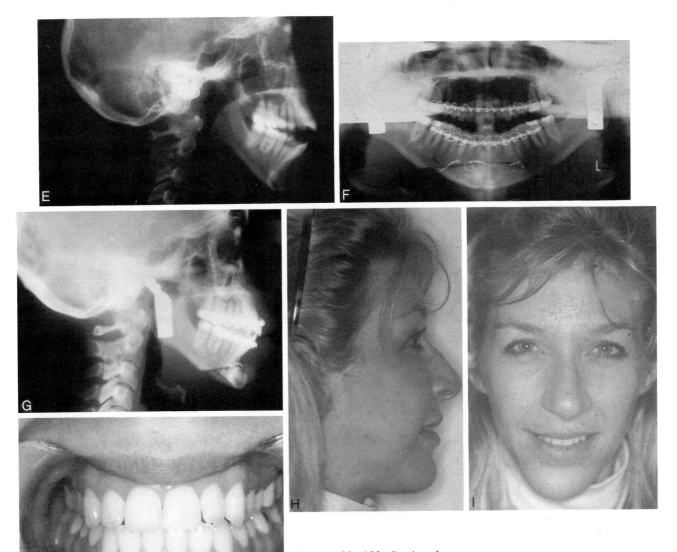

FIGURE 29–129. *Continued*

5. Minor vertical dimension problems involving loss of a few millimeters of condylar surface and disc (with lateral pterygoid muscle function not impaired) are treated by partial joint reconstruction. In these cases, the cortical surface integrity and health of the condyle may be questionable. Disc and adhesion removal with condylar shaving or high condylectomy is required. In the absence of malocclusion, grafting with pedicled temporalis muscle and fascia or sternal cartilage will restore more condylar height than will auricular cartilage or dermis. Osteotomy of the maxilla and soft tissue grafts (auricular cartilage, temporalis muscle or fascia, and dermis), however, will correct both significant vertical dimension problems and malocclusion. Follow-up is critical, since continued degenerative change is certainly possible. Implant devices, such as silicone rubber blocks and glenoid fossa prostheses, are least preferred because of excess loading, long-term stability problems, and surface wear. The result is generally an inflammatory tissue reaction caused by polymer particulate debris, pain, and condylar resorption.

6. Major vertical dimension loss (half or more of the condylar head) with reduced lateral pterygoid muscle function and malocclusion is reconstructed with ei-

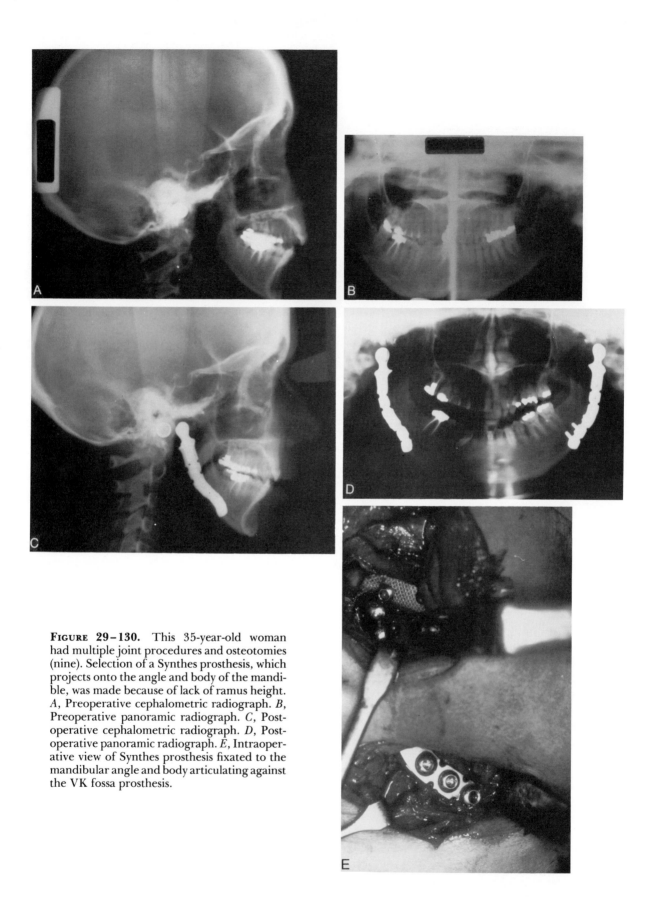

FIGURE 29–130. This 35-year-old woman had multiple joint procedures and osteotomies (nine). Selection of a Synthes prosthesis, which projects onto the angle and body of the mandible, was made because of lack of ramus height. *A*, Preoperative cephalometric radiograph. *B*, Preoperative panoramic radiograph. *C*, Postoperative cephalometric radiograph. *D*, Postoperative panoramic radiograph. *E*, Intraoperative view of Synthes prosthesis fixated to the mandibular angle and body articulating against the VK fossa prosthesis.

TABLE 29-14. DIAGNOSIS AND TREATMENT OF TMJ PATHOLOGY

DEFICIT	TREATMENT PRIORITY
Minor hypomobility and pain	Physical therapy, brisement, arthroscopy
Malocclusion in the absence of significant TMJ dysfunction and pain	Occlusal adjustments, restorations, osteotomies
Pain and hypomobility leading to fibrous ankylosis without malocclusion	Arthroscopy or arthroplasty with release of adhesions and physical therapy
Disc with pain and hypomobility	Repair and/or reposition if possible, including disc tied to condylar head: removal and replacement with (1) auricular cartilage, (2) temporalis fascia, (3) dermis, (4) homograft, or (5) implant devices
Minor vertical dimension loss, condylar surface and disc, possible malocclusion	Partial joint reconstruction with disc removal, high condylectomy, and (1) temporalis fascia and muscle, (2) sternal cartilage, (3) osteotomy of maxilla and soft tissue grafts (auricular cartilage, temporalis fascia, and dermis), or (4) implant devices
Major vertical dimension loss, disc and entire condylar head; no previous secondary procedures, significant malocclusion, loss of lateral pterygoid muscle function	Partial joint reconstruction with disc and condyle removal and (1) costochondral graft (vascularized optional), (2) total joint prosthesis, or (3) osteotomy of maxilla or posterior ramus border and soft tissue grafts (auricular cartilage, temporalis fascia, and dermis) and alloplastic angle replacement
Major vertical dimension loss, disc and entire condylar head with a history of chronic pain, hypomobility, malocclusion and unsuccessful secondary surgical procedures	Total joint prosthesis; partial joint reconstruction with (1) vascularized bone grafts or (2) osteotomy of maxilla or posterior ramus border and soft tissue grafts (auricular cartilage, temporalis fascia, and dermis)

ther partial or total joint procedures. The absence of previous operations is an indication for selection of partial joint reconstruction procedures, such as costochondral grafts (vascularized or not) and osteotomies in combination with soft tissue grafting of the joint. Total joint reconstruction is also recommended after multiple previous surgical procedures. Maxillary or posterior ramus border osteotomies combined with soft tissue grafting to the joint (auricular cartilage, temporalis fascia or muscle, and dermis) are also suitable options. However, drastic reduction of articulating surface area may result in graft failure and additional condylar neck resorption secondary to increase in load per unit area of the remaining condylar stump. Cosmetic reconstruction with alloplast may be necessary to correct any mandibular angle deficit from autorotation.

7.   The last category is similar to the preceding one, but total joint procedures are more strongly indicated when the patient has had recurrent problems following numerous secondary alloplastic and autogenous procedures. Repositioning of the mandible with bone grafting procedures to correct retrognathism and open bite is vulnerable to relapse, ankylosis, and resorption because of muscle lengthening and scar contracture.

The selection of TMJ surgical procedures for reconstruction is therefore based on (1) the health of the mandibular condyle, (2) the degree of vertical dimension loss, (3) the presence or absence of satisfactory lateral pterygoid muscle function, (4) associated hypomobility, (5) malocclusion, (6) the number of previous surgical procedures, (7) pain, and (8) the preference of the patient.

The development of some alloplastic materials to replace the TMJ disc and condyle-fossa relationship is perhaps based on intuition or empiricism rather than sound biomechanical data. In that regard, such developments parallel the experience in orthopedics, that is, total hip or resurfacing techniques. The same can be said concerning autogenous materials, but revascularization and remodeling aid greatly in physiologic adaptation, a process not possible with implant materials. The incidence of reoperation on cases involving alloplastic materials may be no greater than that with cases involving autogenous materials. However, the destruction of joint parts is greater with the former, although the need for additional surgical intervention—that is, to relieve pain and improve function—is similar. The quest for acceptable materials to avoid donor site surgery and its complications as well as the fusion of joint parts that occurs with autogenous materials has led to increased usage of alloplastic materials. Large numbers of patients and the postoperative evaluation of these implant materials have been reported. The early success rates are usually high, but the long-term success is unknown. Confirmation of the long-term success of large series of autogenous materials is also lacking.

Alloplastic design, selection of materials, and surgical technique have led to controversial results and parameters for success, that is, pain-free normal function and occlusion in the face of bone resorption. Material design and choice, mechanical properties, interface biomechanics, selection of patients, surgical technique, postoperative management, condylar disease, and anatomy of the damaged joint will determine the long-term effects of prostheses. Biomechanical data are frequently gained by in vitro methods that do not always simulate the in vivo model. Loads generated in human pathologic conditions are thought to be greater, but the magnitude is not known. Materials, such as Teflon, Proplast, and Silicone rubber, are therefore frequently selected on the basis of nonpathologic loads. In fact, only in the past two decades have clinicians even suggested significant loading of the TMJ, let alone measuring either normal or pathologic conditions. Implant retrieval analysis and mathematical and experimental models are common in orthopedics but very new to the TMJ. They may provide evidence of implant functional limits and failure analysis.

Animal testing, commonly used for biocompatibility determination of tissue or cell toxicity, must include the degree and type of tissue ingrowth or encapsulation under mechanical load. Advantages of animal testing, therefore, include the effects of wear debris and the stability of prostheses in a joint. Disadvantages are a lack of long-term results, uncontrollable loading and postoperative management, miniaturization and design modification to fit small animal anatomy, and the physical limitations of material reduced in size. Extrapolation and correlations to the human situation may be difficult owing to small animal anatomy, bone structure, joint loading patterns, and functional activity. For example, animal studies may not accurately indicate tissue ingrowth rates or optimal pore size. Mechanical testing standards of materials are well known, as are conventional radiographic imaging and various histologic analyses. Retrospective human clinical studies, although admittedly deficient and plagued with variables, still provide critical information on the acceptability of implant materials, surgical indications and techniques, and the continued and long-term usage of these materials.

ACKNOWLEDGMENTS

We wish to acknowledge Nora Constantine, Cathy Daigle, Jacque Negrotto, and Jewel Robinson of the Word Processing Center for the preparation of this manuscript, as well as Bill Stallworth and Bryan Eschette of the Photography Department and Raymond Calvert of the Art Department at the LSU School of Dentistry. We appreciate the contributions of the following surgeons and scientists: Michael S. Block, D.M.D., M. Franklin Dolwick, D.M.D., Ph.D., T. Williams Evan, D.D.S., M.D., Mark G. Fontenot, D.D.S., M. Eng., Bromley Freeman, M.D., Bob Cross, D.D.S., Ralph Holms, M.D., Charles A. Homsy, Sc.D., Randall James, D.D.S., Michael Jarcho, Ph.D., Michael C. Kinnebrew, D.D.S., M.D., Kevin L. McBride, D.D.S., Lester Machado, D.D.S., M.D., Randolph Malloy, D.D.S., Ph.D., Victor J. Matukas, D.D.S., Ph.D., M.D., Kenneth E. Perino, D.D.S., Hiromo Shoji, M.D., Bryant A. Toth, M.D., P. J. van Mullem, Ph.D., Robert V. Walker, D.D.S., Paul J. Walters, D.D.S., Darrell E. Wolfley, M.D., Larry M. Wolford, D.D.S., Michael F. Zide, D.D.S., Barry M. Zide, D.D.S., M.D., and Marilyn Zimny, Ph.D., and all of the biomaterial companies who furnished material as listed herein.

REFERENCES

1. Carmen R, Kahn P: In vitro testing of silicone rubber heart-valve poppets for lipid absorption. J Biomed Mater Res 2:457, 1968.

2. Weightman B, Simon S, Rose R, et al: Environmental fatigue testing of Silastic finger joint prostheses. In Homsy C, Armeniades CO (eds): J Biomed Mater Res Symposium No. 3: Biomaterials for Skeletal and Cardiovascular Applications. New York: John Wiley & Sons, 1972, p 15.

3. Homsy CA, et al: Prevention of interfacial corrosion of SMO stainless steel applications. Clin Orthop 76:261, 1971.

4. Redler I: Polymer osteosynthesis. A clinical trial of ostamer in 42 patients. J Bone Joint Surg [Am] 44:1621, 1962.

5. Straub LR, King DE, Lambert CN: Final report of the committee for the study of femoral head prostheses. J Bone Joint Surg [Am] 41:883, 1959.

6. Smyth EHJ: The mechanical problem of the artificial hip. J Bone Joint Surg [Br] 40:778, 1958.

7. Marchant RE, Sugie T, Hiltner A, Anderson JM: Biocompatibility and an enhanced acute inflammatory phase model. In Fraker AC, Griffin CD (eds): Corrosion and Degradation of Implant Material: Second Symposium ASTM STP 859. Philadelphia, American Society for Testing and Materials, 1985, p 251.

8. Laing PG, Ferguson AB Jr, Hodge ES: Tissue reaction in rabbit muscle exposed to metallic implants. J Biomed Mater Res 1:135, 1967.

9. Homsy CA, Stanley RF, Anderson MS, et al: Reduction of tissue and bone adhesion to cobalt-alloy fixation appliances. J Biomed Mater Res 6:451, 1972.

10. Homsy CA: Biocompatibility in selection of materials for implantation. J Biomed Mater Res 4:341, 1970.

11. Homsy CA, Kent JN, Hinds EC: Materials for oral implantology — biological and functional criteria. J Am Dent Assoc 86:817, 1973.

12. Rae T: The macrophage response to implant materials — with special reference to those used in orthopedics. CRC Crit Rev Biocompat 2:97, 1986.

13. Bernier JL, Canby CP: Histologic studies on the reaction of alveolar bone to Vitallium implants. J Am Dent Assoc 30:188, 1943.

14. Moore AT: A metal hip joint, a new self-locking Vitallium prosthesis. South Med J 45:1015, 1952.

15. Charnley J: Acrylic Cement in Orthopedic Surgery. Baltimore, The Williams and Wilkins Company, 1970, p 10.

16. Adell R, Branemark PI, Hansson BO, et al: Intraosseous anchorage of dental prostheses, II. Scand J Plast Reconstr Surg 4:19, 1970.

17. Sarmiento A: Austin-Moore prostheses in the arthritic hip: Experiences with 224 patients. Clin Orthop 82:14, 1972.

18. Rhinelander FW, Rouweyha M, Milner JC: Microvascular and histogenic responses to implantation of porous ceramic with bone. J Biomed Mater Res 5:81, 1971.

19. Klawitter JJ, Hulbert SF: Application of porous ceramics for the attachment of load-bearing internal orthopedic applications. In Hall CW, et al (eds): J Biomed Mater Res Symposium No. 2: Bioceramics — Engineering in Medicine, Part 2. New York, John Wiley & Sons, 1972, p 161.

20. Voorhees AB, et al: Use of tubes constructed from Vinyon "N" cloth in bridging arterial defects. Ann Surg 135:332, 1952.

21. Bainton DF, Nicols BA, Farquhar MG: Primary lysosomes of blood leukocytes. In Dingle JT, Dean RT (eds): Lysosomes in Biology and Pathology. Vol 5. Amsterdam, North-Holland, 1976, 3.

22. Gomori PG: Distribution of acid phosphatase in tissues under normal and under pathogenic conditions. Arch Pathol 32:189, 1941.

23. Beck F, Lloyd JB: Histochemistry and electron microscopy of lysosomes. In Dingle JT, Fell HB (eds): Lysosomes in Biology and Pathology. Vol 2. Amsterdam, North-Holland 1969, p 567.

24. Van Oss CJ, Bernstein JM, Park BH, et al: Physiochemical aspects of phagocytosis and of some phagocytic disorders. In Milgram F, Albini B, (eds): Immunopathology, 6th International Convention of Immunology. Basel, S Karger, 1979, p 311.

25. Ratner BD, Horbett TA, Shuttleworth D, Thomas HR: Analysis of the organization of protein films on solid surfaces by ESCA. J Colloid Interface Sci 83:630, 1981.

26. Revell PA, Weightman B, Freeman MAR, Vernon-Roberts B: The production and biology of polethylene wear debris. Arch Orthop Trauma Surg 91:167, 1978.

27. Rae T: A study on the effects of particulate metals of orthopaedic interest on murine macrophages in vitro. J Bone Joint Surg [Br] 57:444, 1975.

28. Rae T: The biological response to titanium and titanium-aluminum-vanadium alloy. I. Tissue culture studies. Biomaterials 7:30, 1986.

29. Davies P, Allison AC: Secretion of macrophage enzymes in relation to pathogenesis of chronic inflammation. In Nelson DS, (ed): Immunobiology of the Macrophage. New York, Academic Press, 1976, 427.

30. Chambers TJ: Multinucleate giant cells. J Pathol 126:125, 1978.

31. Papadimitriou JM, Walters MNI: Macrophage polykarya. CRC Crit Rev Toxicol 6:211, 1979.

32. Mariano M, Spector WG: The formation and properties of macrophage polykaryons (inflammatory giant cells). J Pathol 113:1, 1974.

33. Chambers JT: Studies on the phagocytic capacity of macrophage polykaryons. J Pathol 123:65, 1977.

34. Papadimitriou JM, Sforcina D, Papaelias L: Kinetics of multinucleate giant cell formation and their modification by various agents in foreign body reactions. Am J Pathol 73:349, 1973.

35. Mundy GR, Altman AJ, Gondek MD, Bandelin DT: Direct resorption of bone by human monocytes. Science 196:1109, 1977.

36. Mundy GR, Varani J, Orr W, et al: Resorbing bone is chemotactic for monocytes. Nature 275:132, 1978.

37. Holtrop ME, King GJ: The ultrastructure of

the osteoclast and its functional implications. Clin Orthop 123:177, 1977.

38. Riaez LB: Local and systemic factors in the pathogenesis of osteoporosis., N Engl J Med 318:818, 1988.

39. Chambers TJ: The pathobiology of the osteoclast. J Clin Pathol 38:241, 1985.

40. Deporter DA: The possible role of the fibroblast in granuloma-induced bone resorption in the rat. J Pathol 127:61, 1979.

41. Smojen D, Binderman I, Berger E, Harell A: Bone remodeling induced by physical stress is prostaglandin E_2 mediated. Biochem Biophys Acta 627:91, 1980.

42. Jeffcoat MK, Williams WJ, Wechter WJ, Williams RC, et al: Flurbiprofen treatment of periodontal disease in beagles. J Periodont Res 21:624, 1986.

43. Kent JN: Clinical experiences with biomaterials in oral and maxillofacial surgery. Part 1, Chap 17. *In* Boretos, J and Eden, M (eds): Contemporary Biomaterials. Materials and Host Response, Clinical Applications, New Technology and Legal Aspects. Park Ridge, NJ, Noyes Data Corporation, 1984, p 254.

44. Kent JN, Zide MF: Wound healing: Bone and biomaterials. Otolaryngol Clin North Am 17:273, 1984.

45. Drury GD, Caress A, Corrin PG: The non-metallic denture bases. Br Dent J 59:130, 1935.

46. Penhale KW: Acrylic resin as implant for correction for facial deformities. Arch Surg 50:233, 1945.

47. McCabe JF, Basker RM: Tissue sensitivity to acrylic resin: A method of measuring the residual monomer content and its clinical application. Br Dent J 140:347, 1976.

48. Spealman CR, Main RJ, Haag HR, Larson PR: Monomer methylmethacrylate: Studies on toxicities. Ind Med 14:292, 1945.

49. Charnley J: Acrylic Cement in Orthopedic Surgery. London, E & F Livingstone, 1970.

50. DeWijn JR, Van Mullem PJ: Biocompatibility of acrylic implants. *In* Williams DF (ed): Biocompatibility of Clinical Implant Materials. Vol 2. Boca Raton, FL, CRC Press, 1981, p 99.

51. Turell AJW: Allergy to denture-base materials—fallacy or reality. Br Dent J 120:415, 1966.

52. Henrichsen E, Jansen K, Krogh-Poulsen W: Experimental investigation of the tissue reaction to acrylic plastics. Acta Orthop Scand 21:141, 1951.

53. Charvsky CB, Bullough PG, Wilson PD: Total hip replacement failure: A histologic evaluation. J Bone Joint Surg [Am] 55:49, 1973.

54. Feith R: Side effects of acrylic cement implanted into bone. Acta Orthop Scand, Suppl 161, 1975.

55. Meyer PR, Lautenschlager ET, Moore BK: On the setting properties of acrylic bone cement. J Bone Joint Surg [Am] 55:149, 1973.

56. Cabanela ME, Coventry MB, MacCarty CS, Miller EW: The fate of patients with methylmethacrylate cranioplasty. J Bone Joint Surg [Am] 54:278, 1972.

57. Van Mullem PJ, DeWijn JR: Bone and soft connective tissue response to porous acrylic implants. J Cranio-Max-Fac Surg 16:99, 1988.

58. Van Mullen PJ, DeWijn JR, Vaadrager JM: Porous acrylic cement: Evaluation of a novel implant material. Ann Plast Surg 21:576, 1988.

59. Janakarajah N, Sukumaran K: Orbital floor fractures and their treatment. Aust NZ J Ophthalmol 13:75, 1985.

60. Abrahams IW: Repair of orbital floor defects with premolded plastic implants. Arch Ophthalmol 75:510, 1966.

61. Wolfe FA: Correction of a lower eyelid deformity caused by multiple extrusions of alloplastic orbital floor implants. Plast Reconstr Surg 68:429, 1981.

62. Rietz K: One-stage method of cranioplasty with acrylic plastic, with a follow-up study. J Neurosurg 15:176, 1958.

63. Cabbabe EB, Shively RE, Malik P: Cranioplasty for traumatic deformities of the fronto-orbital area. Ann Plast Surg 13:175, 1984.

64. Van Gool AV: Preformed polymethylmethacrylate cranioplasties: Report of 45 cases. J Maxillofac Surg 3:2, 1985.

65. Van Noort R, Black MM: Silicone rubbers for medical applications. *In* William DE (ed): Biocompatibility of Clinical Implant Materials. Vol II. Boca Raton, FL, CRC Press, 1981, p 79.

66. Meals RN, Lewis FM: Silicones. New York Reinhold Plastics Application Series, 1959.

67. Braley S: The chemistry and properties of the medical grade silicone rubber. J Macromol Sci Chem 4:529, 1970.

68. Heggess JP, Kossovsky N, Parsons RW, et al: Biocompatibility of silicone implants. Ann Plast Surg 11:38, 1983.

69. Frisch EE, Langley NR: Biodurability evaluation of medical-grade high-performance silicone elastomer. *In* Fraker AC, Griffin CD (eds): Corrosion and Degradation of Implant Materials: Second Symposium. ASTM STP 859. Philadelphia, American Society for Testing and Materials, 1985, p 278.

70. Van Noort RT, Black MM, Harris B: Developments in the biomedical evaluation of silicone rubber. J Mater Sci 14:197, 1979.

71. Swanson AB, Maupin BK, Nalbandian RM, deGroot Swanson G: Host reaction to silicone implants: A long-term clinical and histopathologic study. *In* Fraker AC, Griffin CD (eds): Corrosion and Degradation of Implant Materials: Second Symposium, ASTM STP 859. Philadelphia, American Society for Testing and Materials, 1985, p 267.

72. Meyer RA, Gehrig JD, Funk EC, et al: Restoring facial contour with implanted silicone rubber. Oral Surg 24:598, 1967.

73. Bell WH: Correction of the contour deficient chin J Oral Surg 27:110, 1969.

74. Braley S: The silicones in maxillofacial surgery. Laryngoscope 78:549, 1968.

75. Brown J: Study and use of synthetic materials as subcutaneous prostheses. Plast Reconstr Surg 26:264, 1960.

76. Carlin G: Personally fabricated chin implants. Plast Reconstr Surg 51:121, 1973.

77. Cipcic J: Silicone implant correction of facial deformities. Laryngoscope 78:565, 1968.

78. Converse JM, Kawamoto HK, Wood-Smith D, et al: Deformities of the Jaws, Ch 30, pp 393, 772, 995, 1395. *In* Converse, JM (Ed.): Reconstructive Plastic Surg. Philadelphia, WB Saunders, 1977.

79. Millard R: Adjuncts in augmentation mentoplasty and correction rhinoplasty. Plast Reconst Surg 36:48, 1965.

80. Safian J: Progress in nasal and chin augmentation. Plast Reconst Surg 37:446, 1966.
81. Marble HB Jr, Alexander JM: A precise technique for restoration of bony facial contour deficiencies with silicone rubber implants: Report of cases. J Oral Surg 30:737, 1972.
82. Webster RC, White MF, Smith RC, et al: Chin augmentation: Subperiosteal and supraperiosteal implants. Aesthetic Plast Surg 1:149, 1977.
83. Mahler D: Chin augmentation, a retrospective study. Ann Plast Surg 8:468, 1982.
84. Beekhuis GJ: Augmentation mentoplasty with polyamide mesh. Arch Otolaryngol 110:364, 1984.
85. Habal MB: Prefabricated Silastic subdermal implants for facial reconstruction. J Fla Med Soc 62:36, 1975.
86. Wilkinson TS, Iglesias J: Room temperature vulcanizing Silastic in facial contour reconstruction. J Trauma 15:479, 1975.
87. Vistnes LM, Paris GL: Uses of RTV silicone in orbital reconstruction. Am J Ophthalmol 83:577, 1977.
88. Davis PKB, Jones SM: The complications of Silastic implants. Experience with 137 consecutive cases. Br J Plast Surg 24:405, 1971.
89. Bessette RW, Casey DM, Shatkin SS, Schaaf NG: Customized silicone rubber maxillofacial implants. Ann Plast Surg 7:453, 1981.
90. Craig RDP, Simpson W, Stanley W: The correction of facial contour defects by precision-made Silastic implants. Br J Plast Surg 28:67, 1975.
91. Bessette RW, Cooper T, Natiella J, et al: Histologic evaluation of pore size and shape in silicone implants in rhesus monkeys. Ann Plast Surg 7:447, 1981.
92. Schultz RC: Facial reconstruction with alloplastic materials. Surg Annu 12:351, 1980.
93. Selmanowitz VJ, Orentreick N: Medical-grade fluid silicone: A monographic review. J Dermatol Surg Oncol 3:597, 1977.
94. Rees RD: Silicone injection therapy. In Rees TD, Wood-Smith D (eds): Cosmetic Facial Surgery. Philadelphia, WB Saunders Company, 1973, 232.
95. Ashley FL, Braley S, Rees TD, et al: The present status of silicone fluid in soft tissue augmentation. Plast Reconstr Surg, 39:411, 1967.
96. Berman WE: Synthetic materials in facial contours. Trans Am Acad Ophthalmol Otolaryngol 68:876, 1964.
97. Ashley FL, Rees TD, Ballantyne DL, et al: An injection technique for the treatment of facial hemiatrophy. Plast Reconstr Surg 35:640, 1965.
98. Rees TD, Ashley FL: Treatment of facial atrophy with liquid silicone. Am J Surg 111:531, 1966.
99. Rees TD, Ashley FL: A new treatment for facial hemiatrophy in children in injections of dimethylpolysiloxane fluid. J Pediatr Surg 2:347, 1967.
100. Blocksma R: Experience with dimethylsiloxane fluid in soft tissue augmentation. Plast Reconstr Surg 48:564, 1971.
101. Blocksma R, Braley S: Implantation materials. In Grabb WC, Smith JW: Plastic Surgery. 2nd ed. Boston, Little, Brown and Company, 1973, 131.
102. Orentreich N: Preventive and therapeutic measures for aging skin. Proc Sci Sec Toilet Goods Assoc 41:37, 1964.
103. Sperber PA: Chemexfoliation and silicone infiltration in the treatment of aging skin and dermal defects. J Am Geriatr Soc 12:594, 1970.
104. Hastings GW: Biocompatability of polyethylenes and polypropylene. In Williams DF (ed): Biocompatibility of Clinical Implant Materials Vol II. Boca Raton, FL, CRC Press, 1981, p 43.
105. Bloch B, Hastings GW: Plastics Materials in Surgery, 2nd Ed. Springfield, IL, Charles C Thomas, 1972.
106. Richards RB: Polyethylene—structure, crystallinity, and properties. J Appl Chem 1:370, 1951.
107. Charnley J: Fluon as a bearing material. J Bone Joint Surg [Br] 45:622, 1963.
108. Evarts CM, Stoffe AD, McCormack L: Investigation of canine tissue reaction to TFE fluorocarbon resin, to high density polyethylene and to Vitallium. J Surg Res 10:91, 1970.
109. Roydhouse RH: Implant testing of polymerizing materials. J Biomed Mater Res 2:265, 1972.
110. Salthouse TN, Willigan D: An enzyme histochemical approach to the evaluation of polymers for tissue compatibility. J Biomed Mater Res 6:105, 1972.
111. Laling PG: Compatibility of biomaterials. Orthop Clin North Am 4:249, 1973.
112. Stinson NE: Tissue reaction induced in guinea pigs by particulate polymethylmethacrylate, polyethylene and nylon of the same size range. Br J Exp Path 46:135, 1965.
113. Shea JJ, Emmett JR: Biocompatible ossicular implants. Arch Otolaryngol 104:191, 1978.
114. Brown BL, Neel HB, Kern EB: Implants of Supramid, Proplast, Plasti-Pore, and Silastic. Arch Otolaryngol 105:605, 1979.
115. Berghaus A: Porous polyethylene in reconstructive head and neck surgery. Arch Otolaryngol 111:154, 1985.
116. Shen C, Dumbleton JH: The friction and wear behavior of irradiated very high molecular weight polyethylene. Wear 30:349, 1974.
117. Farling G, Bardos D: An improved bearing material for joint replacement prostheses: Carbon fibre reinforced UHMW polyethylene (abstract). In Mechanical Properties of Biomaterials. Conference of the Biological Engineering Society, Keele 1978.
118. Bradley JS: Carbon-Fibre–Enforced Plastics for Orthopedic Implants. Ph.D. Thesis, North Staffordshire Polytechnic, Stoke-on-Trent, England, 1980.
119. Calnan JS: Assessment of biological properties of implants before their clinical use. Proc R Soc Med 63:1115, 1970.
120. Liebert TC, Charloff RP, Cosgrove SL, McCuskey RS: Subcutaneous implants of polypropylene filaments. J Biomed Mater Res 10:939, 1976.
121. Leake DL, Habal MB: Osteoneogenesis: A new method for facial reconstruction. J Surg Res 18:331, 1975.
122. Maniscalo JE, Leake D, Halsal MB: Cranioplasty use of a combination graft. J Fla Med Assoc 63:869, 1976.
123. Habal MB, Leake DL: A new method for reconstruction of severe craniofacial deformities. Surg Gynecol Ostet 142:751, 1976.

124. Leake DL, Habal MB: Reconstitution of craniofacial osseous contour deformities, sequelae of trauma and post resection for tumors, with an alloplastic-autogenous graft. J Trauma 17:299, 1977.

125. Barron JN, Borchgrevink H, El Bayadi N: A report on Teflon. Br J Plast Surg 19:113, 1966.

126. Converse JM, Smith B, Obear MF, Wood-Smith D: Orbital blowout fractures: A 10-year survey. Plast Reconstr Surg 39:20, 1957.

127. Freeman BS: The direct approach to acute fractures of the zygomatic-maxillary complex and immediate prosthetic replacement of the orbital floor. Plast Reconstr Surg 29:587, 1962.

128. Browning CW, Walker RV: The use of alloplastics in 45 cases of orbital floor reconstruction. Am J Ophthalmol 60:684, 1965.

129. Quereau JVD, Souders BF: Teflon implant to elevate the eye in depressed fracture of the orbit. Arch Ophthalmol 55:685, 1956.

130. Keen RR: Orbital fractures treated with Teflon implants. In Transactions of the IVth International Conference on Oral Surgery. Copenhagen, Munksgaard, 1973, p 311.

131. Arnold GE: Vocal rehabilitation of paralytic dysphonia. Arch Otolaryngol 76:358, 1962.

132. Boedts D, Roels H, Cluskens P: Laryngeal response to Teflon. Arch Otolaryngol 86:562, 1967.

133. Goff WF: Teflon injection for vocal cord paralysis. Arch Otolaryngol 90:98, 1969.

134. Lewy RB: Responses of laryngeal tissue to granular Teflon in situ. Arch Otolaryngol 83:355, 1966.

135. Stone JW, Arnold GE: Human larynx injected with Teflon paste. Arch Otolaryngol 86:550, 1967.

136. Schell JJ: Polytef injection for nasal deformity. Arch Otolaryngol 92:554, 1970.

137. Landman MD, Strahan RW, Ward PH: Chin augmentation with polytef paste injection. Arch Otolaryngol 95:72, 1972.

138. Homsy CA: Biocompatibility of perfluorinated polymers and composites of these polymers. In Williams DF (ed): Biocompatibility of Clinical Implant Materials. Vol II. Boca Raton, FL, CRC Press, 1982, p 59.

139. Homsy CA, Anderson MS: Functional stabilization of soft tissue and bone prostheses with a porous low modulus materials system. In Biocompatibility of Implant Materials. Tunbridge Wells, Kent, England, Sector Publishing, 1976, p 85.

140. Homsy CA, Cain TE, Kessler FB, et al: Porous implant systems for prosthesis stabilization. Clin Orthop Rel Res 89:220, 1972.

141. Rhinelander FW, Oxon MA, Stewart CL, et al: Growth of tissue into a porous low modulus coating on intramedullary nails: An experimental study. Clin Orthop Rel Res 164:293, 1982.

142. Westfall RL, Kent JN, Homsy CA: A comparison of porous composite PTFE/graphite and PTFE/aluminum oxide facial implants in primates. J Oral Maxillofac Surg 40:771, 1982.

143. Kent JN, Westfall RL: Presurgical infusion of Proplast: Primate facial augmentation. J Oral Surg 37:637, 1979.

144. Janeke JB, Komorn RM, Cohn AM: Proplast in cavity obliteration and soft tissue augmentation. Arch Otolaryngol 100:24, 1974.

145. Shea JJ, Emmett JR: Biocompatibility ossicular implants. Arch Otolaryngol 104:191, 1978.

146. Kessler FB, Homsy CA, Berkeley ME, et al: Obliteration of traumatically induced articular surface defects using a porous implant. J Hand Surg 5:328, 1980.

147. Kent JN, Block MS, Prewitt JM III, Homsy CA: Femur defect healing of hydroxylapatite PTFE composites. American Association of Oral and Maxillofacial Surgeons Annual Meeting, Case Reports and Outlines, Anaheim CA, September, 1987, p 41.

148. Homsy CA, Kent JN, Block MS, et al: Effect of synthetic hydroxylapatite on tissue ingrowth into a soft, porous matrix. In Proceedings of Third World Biomaterials Congress, Kyoto, Japan, April 1988.

149. Homsy CA: Proplast: Chemical and biological considerations. In Rubin L (ed): Biomaterials in Reconstructive Surgery. St. Louis, CV Mosby 1982.

150. Kent JN, Westfall RL, Carlton DM, et al: Chin and facial augmentation with Proplast block: A seven year retrospective study. In Proceedings of First World Biomaterials Congress, Vienna, April 1980.

151. Kent JN, Westfall RL, Carlton DM: Chin and zygomaticomaxillary augmentation with Proplast: Long term follow-up. J Oral Surg 39:912, 1981.

152. Kent JN, Homsy CA, Gross BD, Hinds EC: Pilot studies of a porous implant in dentistry and oral surgery. J Oral Surg 30:608, 1972.

153. Freeman BS: Proplast. Plast Reconstr Surg 69:902, 1982.

154. Farrell CD, Kent JN: Clinical applications of Proplast in oral and maxillofacial surgery. Alpha Omegan, December 21, 1975.

155. Bell WH: Augmentation of the nasomaxillary and nasolabial regions. Oral Surg 41:691, 1976.

156. Bellinfante LS, Mitchell DL: Use of alloplastic material in the canine fossa–zygomatic area to improve facial esthetics. J Oral Surg 35:121, 1977.

157. Freeman BS: Proplast, a porous implant for contour restoration. Br J Plast Surg 29:158, 1976.

158. Moos KF, Jackson IT, Henderson D, Gibbs PM: The use of Proplast in oral and maxillofacial surgery. Br J Oral Surg 16:187, 1979.

159. Epstein LI: Clinical experiences with Proplast as an implant. Plast Reconst Surg 63:219, 1979.

160. Parks ML, Merrin ML, Kamer FM: Proplast chin augmentation. Presented at the 2nd International Symposium on Plastic and Reconstructive Surgery of the Head and Neck, Chicago, June 1975. Laryngoscope 86:1829, 1976.

161. Vitek, Inc., Data Sheet: 81001, March 1981, Houston.

162. Dow Corning Data Sheet 89-4, December, 1979.

163. Kent JN, Homsy CA, Hinds EC: Proplast in dental facial reconstruction. Presented at the 5th International Conference on Oral Surgery, Madrid, April 1974, and Oral Surg 39:347, 1975.

164. Hinderer UT: Malar implants for improvement of the facial appearance. Plast Reconstr Surg 56:157, 1975.

165. Dann J, Epker BN: Proplast genioplasty: A

retrospective study with treatment recommendation. Angle Ortho 47:173, 1977.

166. Block MS, Zide MF, Kent JN: Proplast augmentation for post-traumatic zygomatic deficiency. Oral Surg 57:123, 1984.

167. Whitaker LA: Aesthetic augmentation of the malar midface structures. Plast Reconstr Surg 80:337, 1987.

168. Whitaker LA: Facial proportions in aesthetic surgery. *In* Farkas LG, Munro IR (eds): Anthropometric Facial Proportions in Medicine. Springfield, IL, Charles C Thomas, 1987, p 103.

169. Silver WE: The use of alloplast material in contouring the face. Facial Plast Surg 3:81, 1986.

170. Sheen JH: Maxillary augmentation. *In* Aesthetic Rhinoplasty. 2nd ed. St. Louis, CV Mosby 1987, p 283.

171. Sheen JH: Cranial bone graft. *In* Aesthetic Rhinoplasty. 2nd ed. St. Louis, CV Mosby, 1987, p 383.

172. Nigro DM: Malar augmentation. Plast Recontr Surg 82:370, 1988.

173. Wolford LM, Oelschlaeger M, Deal R: Proplast as a pharyngeal wall implant to correct velopharyneal insufficiency. And Commentary. Cleft Palate J 26:119, 1989.

174. Freeman BS, Wiemer DR: Clinical uses of Proplast: Expectations and results. *In* Rubin LR (ed): Biomaterials in Reconstructive Surgery. St Louis, CV Mosby, 1983, p 494.

175. Bell WH, Jacobs JD: Surgical-orthodontic correction of maxillary retrusion by Le Fort I osteotomy and Proplast. J Maxillofac Surg 8:84, 1980.

176. Burton DJ, Berarducci JP, Scheffer RB: Proplast grafting: A new method for stabilization of maxillary advancements. Oral Surg 50:387, 1980.

177. Barton RT: The use of synthetic implant material in osteoplastic frontal sinusotomy. Laryngoscope 90:47, 1980.

178. Clark RP, Robertson JH, Shea JJ, Tomoda K: Closure of dural defects with Proplast. Am J Otol 5:179, 1984.

179. Preformed and Custom Implants, Vitek, Inc, June 1988, and NovaMed, Inc, July 1989.

180. Arem AJ, Madden JW: Soft tissue response to blood impregnated proplast. Plast Reconstr Surg 58:580, 1976.

181. Arem AJ, Ramussen D, Madden JW: Soft tissue response to Proplast: Quantitation of scar ingrowth. Plast Reconstr Surg 61:214, 1978.

182. Kent JN, Block MS, Homsy CA, et al: Femur defect healing of hydroxylapatite PTFE composites. *In* Case Reports and Outlines of Scientific Sessions, American Association of Oral and Maxofacial Surgeons, 69th Annual Meeting, Anaheim, CA, September 1987, p 41.

183. Kent JN: Reconstruction of facial contour with Proplast. Presented at Symposium on Bone Grafting: Biology and Application for Maxillofacial Indications, San Diego, December 1988.

184. Habal MB, Leake DL, Maniscalo JE, Kim J: Repair of major cranio-orbital defects with an elastomer-coated mesh and autogenous bone paste. Plast Reconstr Surg 61:394, 1978.

185. Boretos JW: The chemistry and biocompatibility of specific polyurethane systems for medical use. *In* Williams DF (ed): Biocompatibility of Clinical Implant Materials. Boca Raton, FL, CRC Press, 1981, p 127.

186. Mirkovitch V, Akutsu T, Kolff WJ: Polyurethane aortas in dogs. Three year results. Trans Am Soc Artif Intern Organs 8:79, 1962.

187. Boretos JW: Tissue pathology and physical stability of a polyether elastomer on three-year implantation. J Biomed Mater Res 6:473, 1972.

188. Parins DJ, McCoy KD, Horvath N, Olson RW: In vivo degradation of a polyurethane: Preclinical studies. *In* Fraker AC, Griffin CD (eds): Corrosion and Degradation of Implant Materials: Second Symposium, ASTM STP 859. Philadelphia, American Society for Testing and Materials, 1985, p 322.

189. Azycher M, McArthur WA: Surface fissuring of polyurethanes following in vivo exposure. *In* Fraker AC, Griffin CD (eds): Corrosion and Degradation of Implant Materials: Second Symposium, ASTM STP 859. Philadelphia, American Society for Testing and Materials, 1985, p 308.

190. Kornblut AD, Stark TW, Vap JG, deFries HO: The role of autografts, homografts, heterografts, and alloplastic implants in reconstructive head and neck surgery. Otolaryngol Clin North Am 15:147, 1982.

191. Stucker FJ: Autoalloplast: An experimental and clinical study. Arch Otolaryngol 108:130, 1982.

192. Dickinson JT, Joguss GW: Alloplastic implants 1972. Otolaryngol Clin North Am 5:441, 1972.

193. Beekhius GJ: Mersilene mesh to augment the nasal bridge. Am J Cosmet Surg 3:49, 1986.

194. Nackemson A, Nordwall A: Wound strength in a clinical material. Scand J Plast Reconstr Surg 9:93, 1975.

195. Stucker FJ, Hirokawa RH, Pruet CW: The autoalloplast — an alternative in facial implantation. Otolaryngol Clin North Am 15:161, 1982.

196. Beekhuis GJ: Augmentation mentoplasty with polyamide mesh. Arch Otolaryngol 110(6):364, 1984.

197. Fanous N, Webster R: Supramid tip implants in rhinoplasty. Arch Otolaryngol Head Neck Surg 113:728, 1987.

198. Stucker FJ, Hirokawa RH, Bryarly RC: Technical aspects of facial contouring using polyamide mesh. Otolaryngol Clin North Am 15:123, 1982.

199. McConnel D: Apatite. New York, Springer-Verlag, 1973.

200. Francis MD, Centner RL: The development of diphosphonates as significant health care products. J Chem Educ 55:760, 1978.

201. Kent JN, Zide MF, Quinn JH, et al: Correction of alveolar ridge deficiencies with nonresorbable hydroxylapatite. J Am Dent Assoc 105:993, 1982.

202. Kent JN, Zide MF, Quinn JH, et al: Alveolar ridge augmentation using nonresorbable hydroxylapatite with or without autogenous cancellous bone. J Oral Maxillofac Surg 41:629, 1983.

203. Quinn JH, Kent JN, Hunter RG, et al: Preservation of the alveolar ridge with HA tooth root substitutes. J Am Dent Assoc 110:189, 1985.

204. Block MS, Kent JN: Healing of mandibular

ridge augmentation using hydroxylapatite with and without autogenous bone in dogs. J Oral Maxillofac Surg 43:3, 1985.

205. Block MS, Kent JN: Long term evaluation of hydroxylapatite augmentation of deficient mandibular alveolar ridges. J Oral Maxillofac Surg 42:793, 1984.

206. Kent JN, Zide MF, Kay JF, Jarcho M: Hydroxylapatite blocks and particles as bone graft substitutes in orthognathic and reconstructive surgery. J Oral Maxillofac Surg 44:597, 1986.

207. Kent JN, Zide MF, Jarcho M, et al: Hydroxylapatite blocks for stability in orthognathic surgery. J Dent Res 64, International Association of Dental Research Abstract No. 367.

208. Kent JN, Finger IM, Quinn JH, et al: Hydroxylapatite alveolar ridge reconstruction: Complications and technique modifications. J Oral Maxillofac Surg 44:37, 1986.

209. Frame JW: The versatility of hydroxylapatite blocks in maxillofacial surgery. Br J Oral Maxillofac Surg 25:452, 1987.

210. Hupp JR, McKenna SJ: Use of porous hydroxylapatite blocks for augmentation of atrophic mandibles. J Oral Maxillofac Surg 46:538, 1988.

211. Gongloff RK: Use of collagen tube contained implants of particulate hydroxylapatite for ridge augmentation. J Oral Maxillofac Surg 46:641, 1988.

212. Holmes RE, Wardrop RW, Wolford LM: Hydroxylapatite as a bone graft substitute in orthognathic surgery: Histologic and histometric findings. J Oral Maxillofac Surg 46:661, 1988.

213. Waite D, Matukas VJ: Zygomatic augmentation with hydroxylapatite: A preliminary report. J Oral Maxillofac Surg 44:349, 1986.

214. Mehlisch DR, Taylor TD, Leibold DG, et al: Evaluation of collagen/hydroxylapatite for augmenting deficient alveolar ridges: A preliminary report. J Oral Maxillofac Surg 45:408, 1987.

215. Block MS, Kent JN, Ardoin RC, Davenport W: Mandibular augmentation in dogs with hydroxylapatite combined with demineralized bone. J Oral Maxillofac Surg 45:414, 1987.

216. Zide MF, Kent JN, Machado L: Hydroxylapatite cranioplasty directly over dura. J Oral Maxillofac Surg 45:481, 1987.

217. Mercier P, Zeltser C, Cholewa J, Djokovic S: Long-term results of mandibular ridge augmentation by visor osteotomy with bone graft. J Oral Maxillofac Surg 45:997, 1987.

218. Wolford LM, Wardrop RW, Hartog JM: Coralline porous hydroxylapatite as a bone graft substitute in orthognathic surgery. J Oral Maxillofac Surg 45:1034, 1987.

219. Rooney T, Berman S, Indresano AT: Evaluation of porous block hydroxylapatite for augmentation of alveolar ridges. J Oral Maxillofac Surg 46:15, 1988.

220. El Deeb M, Roszkowski M: Hydroxylapatite granules and blocks and an extracranial augmenting material in rhesus monkeys. J Oral Maxillofac Surg 46:33, 1988.

221. Cullum PE, Frost DE, Newland TB, et al: Evaluation of hydroxylapatite particles in repair of alveolar clefts in dogs. J Oral Maxillofac Surg 46:290, 1988.

222. Rao WR, Boehm RF: A study of sintered apatites. J Dent Res 53:1351, 1974.

223. Rejda BV, Peelen JGJ, deGroot K: Tricalcium phosphate as a bone substitute. J Bioengin 1:93, 1977.

224. DeGroot K: Bioceramics consisting of calcium phosphate salts. Biomaterials 1:47, 1980.

225. Jarcho M: Calcium phosphate ceramics as hard tissue prosthetics. Clin Orthop 157:259, 1981.

226. Jarcho M, Bolen CH, Thomas MB, and Bobrick, J: Hydroxylapatite synthesis and characterization in dense polycrystalline form. J Mater Sci 11:2027, 1976.

227. Jarcho M, Kay JF, Gumaer KI, et al: Tissue, cellular and subcellular events at a bone-ceramic hydroxylapatite interface. J Bioengin 1:79, 1977.

228. Mors WA, Kaminski EJ: Osteogenic replacement of tricalcium phosphate ceramic implants in the dog palate. Arch Oral Biol 20:365, 1975.

229. Ferraro JW: Experimental evaluation of ceramic calcium phosphate as a substitute for bone grafts. Plast Reconstr Surg 63:634, 1979.

230. Cameron HU, MacNab I, Pilliar RM: Evaluation of a biodegradable ceramic. J Biomed Mater Res 11:179, 1977.

231. Shima T, Keller JT, Alvira NM, et al: Anterior cervical discectomy and interbody fusion: An experimental study using a synthetic tricalcium phosphate. J Neurosurg 51:533, 1979.

232. Nery EB, Lynch KL: Preliminary clinical studies of bioceramics in periodontal osseous defects. J Periodontol 49:523, 1978.

233. Nery EB, Lynch KL, Hirthe WM, Mueller KH: Bioceramic implants in surgically produced infrabony defects. J Periodontol 46:328, 1975.

234. Sayler K, Holmes R, Johns D: Replamineform porous hydroxylapatite as bone substitute in craniofacial osseous reconstruction. J Dent Res 56:173, 1977.

235. Hassler CR, McCoy LG, Clarke LC: Studies on the degradability of large tricalcium phosphate segments. In Proceedings of the 2nd Annual Meeting of the Society for Biomaterials, Clemson, SC, 1976, p 88.

236. Denissen HW, deGroot K: Immediate dental root implants from synthetic dense calcium hydroxylapatite. J Prosthet Dent 42:551, 1979.

237. Kato K, Aoki H, Tabata T, Ogiso M: Biocompatibility of apatite ceramics in mandibles. Biomater Med Dev Art Org 7:291, 1979.

238. Kay JF, Doremus RH, Jarcho M: Ion micromilling of bone-implant interfaces. In Transactions of the 4th Annual Meeting of the Society for Biomaterials, 10th International Biomaterials Symposium, San Antonio, 1978, p 154.

239. Jasty V, Jarcho M, Gumaer KI, et al: Bone tissue response to dense hydroxylapatite disc implants in mongrel dogs: A light and electron microscopic study. Ninth Int Cong Elect Micros 2:674, 1978.

240. Jarcho M, Jasty V, Gumaer KI, et al: Electron microscopic study of a bone-hydroxylapatite implant interface. In Transactions of the 4th Annual Meeting of the Society for Biomaterials, 10th International Biomaterials Symposium, San Antonio, 1978, p 112.

241. Ogiso M, Kaneda H, Arasaki J, et al: Epithelial attachment and bone tissue formation on the surface of hydroxylapatite ceramics. First World Biomaterials Congress, Baden, Austria, 1980, 4.1.5. (abstract).

242. Denissen HW, deGroot K, Kakkes P, et al: Animal and human studies of sintered hydroxylapatite as a material for tooth root implants. First World Biomaterials Congress, Baden, Austria, 1980, 3.8.1. (abstract).

243. Ham AW, Cormack DH: Histology. 8th ed. Philadelphia, JB Lippincott, 1979, p 399.

244. Getter L, Bhaskar SN, Cutright DE, et al: Three biodegradable calcium phosphate slurry implants in bone. J Oral Surg 30:263, 1972.

245. Grower MF, Horan M, Miller R, Getter L: Bone inductive potential of biodegradable ceramic in millipore filter chambers. J Dent Res 52:160, 1973.

246. Boyne PJ, Fremming BD, Walsh R, Jarcho M: Evaluation of a ceramic hydroxylapatite in femoral defects. J Dent Res 57(A):108, 1978.

247. Levin MP, Getter L, Cutright DE: A comparison of iliac marrow and biodegradable ceramic in periodontal defects. J Biomed Mater Res 9:183, 1975.

248. Lemons JE, Ballard JB, Culpepper MI, Niemann KMW: Porous tricalcium phosphate ceramic for segmental lesions. First World Biomaterials Congress, Baden, Austria, 1980, 4.10.3. (abstract).

249. Hassler CR, McCoy LG, Rotaru JH: Long term implants in solid tricalcium phosphate. Proc 27th Ann Conf Eng Med Bio 16:488, 1974.

250. Finn RA, Bell WH, Brammere JA: Interpositional grafting with autogenous bone and coralline hydroxylapatite. J Maxillofac Surg 8:217, 1980.

251. Piecuch JF, Topazian RG, Wolfe S: Experimental ridge augmentation with porous hydroxylapatite implants. J Dent Res 62:148, 1983.

252. Alexander JM: Alloplastic augmentation of middle-third facial deformities. J Oral Surg 34:165, 1976.

253. Bessette RW, Casey DM, Shatkin SS, et al: Customized silicone rubber maxillofacial implants. Ann Plast Surg 7:453, 1981.

254. Chalian VR, Drane JB, Standish SM: Maxillofacial Prosthetics. Baltimore, The Williams and Wilkins Company, 1971, p 108.

255. Herman GT, Liu H: Three-dimensional display of human organs from compacted tomograms. Computer Graph Image Process 9:1, 1979.

256. Hemmy DC, David DJ, Herman GT: Three-dimensional reconstruction of craniofacial deformity using computed tomography. Neurosurgery 23:534, 1983.

257. Marsh JL, Vannier MW: The "third" dimension in craniofacial surgery. Plast Reconstr Surg 71:759, 1983.

258. Toth BA, Ellis DS, Stewart WB: Computer-designed prostheses for orbitocranial reconstruction. Plast Reconstr Surg 81:315, 1988.

259. Zinreich SJ, Mattox DE, Kennedy DN, et al: 3-D CT for cranial, facial and laryngeal surgery. Laryngoscope 98:1212, 1988.

260. Zide MF, Kent JN, Machado L: Hydroxylapatite cranioplasty directly over dura. J Oral Maxillofac Surg 45:481, 1987.

261. Jackson IT, Munro IR, Salyer KE, et al: Atlas of Craniomaxillary Surgery. St Louis, CV Mosby, 1982, p 46.

262. Erculei F, Walker AE: Post-traumatic epilepsy and early cranioplasty. J Neurosurg 20:1085, 1967.

263. Prolo D: Cranial defects and cranioplasty. In Wilkins RH, Rengachary SS (eds): Neurosurgery. Vol 2. New York, McGraw-Hill, 1985, p 1647.

264. Rish BL, Dillon JD, Meirowsky A: Metal cranioplasty: A review of 1030 cases of penetrating head injury. Neurosurgery 4:381, 1979.

265. Manson PN, Hoopes JE, Crawley WA, et al: Frontal cranioplasty: Risk factors and choice of cranial vault reconstructive material. Plast Reconst Surg 77:888, 1986.

266. Courtemanche AD, Thompson GB: Silastic cranioplasty following craniofacial injuries. Plast Reconstr Surg 41:165, 1968.

267. Hancock DO: The fate of replaced bone flaps. J Neurosurg 20:983, 1963.

268. Nadell J, Kline DG: Primary reconstruction of depressed frontal skull fractures including those involving the sinus, orbit, and cribriform plate. J Neurosurg 41:200, 1974.

269. Elkins CW, Cameron JE: Cranioplasty for traumatic deformities of the frontoorbital area. Ann Plast Surg 13:175, 1984.

270. Cabbabe EG, Shively RE, Malik P: Cranioplasty for traumatic deformities of the frontoorbital area. Ann Plast Surg 13:175, 1984.

271. Martin JW, Ganz SD, King GE, et al: Cranial implant modification. J Prosthet Dent 52:414, 1984.

272. Jobe R, Iverson R, Vistnes L: Bone deformation beneath alloplastic implants. Plast Reconst Surg 51:169, 1973.

273. Jackson IT, Hoffman GT: Depressed comminuted fracture of a plastic cranioplasty. J Neurosurg 13:116, 1956.

274. Cabanela ME, Coventry MD, MacCarty CS, et al: The fate of patients with methyl methacrylate cranioplasty. J Bone Joint Surg [AM] 54:278, 1972.

275. Henry HM, Guerrero C, Moody RA: Cerebrospinal fluid fistula from fractured acrylic cranioplasty plate. J Neurosurg 45:227, 1976.

276. Longacre JJ, DeStefano GA: Further observations of the behavior of autogenous split-rib grafts in reconstruction of extensive defects. Plast Reconst Surg 20:281, 1957.

277. Korlof B, Nylen B, Reitz K: Bone grafting of skull defects: A report of 55 cases. Plast Reconst Surg 52:378, 1973.

278. Wilkes GH, Kernahan DA, Christenson M: The long term survival of onlay bone grafts—a comparative study in mature and immature animals. Ann Plast Surg 15:374, 1985.

279. Ousterhout DK: Clinical experience in cranial and facial reconstruction with demineralized bone. Ann Plast Surg 15:367, 1985.

280. Schultz RC: Restoration of frontal contour with methyl methacrylate. Ann Plast Surg 3:295, 1979.

281. Schultz RC: Reconstruction of facial deformities with alloplastic material. Ann Plast Surg 7:434, 1981.

282. Machado L, Zide MF, Kent JN: Experimental evaluation of hydroxylapatite and hydroxylapatite in a collagen and crelatin matrix as cranioplasty implant materials.

American Association of Oral and Maxillofacial Surgeons Annual Meeting, Case Reports and Outlines, Washington, DC, 1985, p 27.

283. Holmes RE, Hagler HK: Porous hydroxylapatite as a bone graft substitute in cranial reconstruction: A histometric study. Plast Reconstr Surg 81:662, 1988.

284. Perino EK, Zide MF, Kinnebrew MC: Late treatment of malunited malar fracture. J Oral Maxillofac Surg 4:804, 1986.

285. Rowe NL, Killey HC: Fractures of the Facial Skeleton. 2nd ed. Edinburgh, E & S Livingstone, 1968.

286. Habelius L, Ponten B: Results of immediate and delayed surgical treatment of facial fractures with diplopia. J Oral Maxillofac Surg 1:150, 1973.

287. Karlan MS, Cassisi NJ: Fractures of zygoma: A geometric, biochemical and surgical analysis. Arch Otolaryngol 105:320, 1979.

288. Converse JM, Smith B, Obear MF, Wood-Smith D: Orbital blowout fractures: A ten-year survey. Plast Reconst Surg 39:20, 1967.

289. Kawamoto HK Jr: Late post-traumatic enophthalmos: A correctable deformity? Plast Reconst Surg 69:423, 1982.

290. Converse JM: Restoration of facial contour by bone grafts introduced through the oral cavity. Plast Reconst Surg 6:295, 1950.

291. Converse JM, Campbell RM: Bone grafts in surgery of the face. Surg Clin North Am 34:375, 1954.

292. Converse JM: Techniques of bone grafting for contour restoration of the face. Plast Reconst Surg 14:332, 1954.

293. Dingman RO: The use of iliac bone in the repair of facial and cranial defects. Plast Reconst Surg 6:179, 1950.

294. Conley JJ: Complications of Head and Neck Surgery. Philadelphia, WB Saunders Company, 1979, p 378.

295. Sailor HE: Experiences with the use of lyophilized bank cartilage for facial contour correction. J Oral Maxillofac Surg 4:149, 1976.

296. Seratin D, Reifkohl R, Thomas I, Georgiade NV: Vascularized rib—periosteal and osteocutaneous reconstruction of the maxilla and mandible: An assessment. Plast Reconst Surg 66:718, 1980.

297. El Deeb M, Holmes RE: Zygomatic and mandibular augmentation with Proplast and porous HA in Rhesus monkeys. J Oral Maxillofac Surg 47:480, 1989.

298. Allard RH, Swart JG: Orbital roof reconstruction with a hydroxylapatite implant. J Oral Maxillofac Surg 40:237, 1982.

299. Smith B, Obear M, Leone CR: The correction of enophthalmos associated with anophthalmos by glass bead implantation. Am J Opthalamol 64:1088, 1967.

300. McFarland JE, Seiff SR, Shorr N: Cyanocrylate-fixed silicone sleds in the orbit. Arch Opthalmol 105:704, 1987.

301. Edgerton MT, Jane JA: Vertical orbital dystopia—surgical correction. Plast Reconstr Surg 67:121, 1981.

302. Parks MM: Stereoacuity as an indicator of bifixation. In Strabismus Symposium, Giessen, Federal Republic of Germany, August 1966. Basel, S Karger, 1968, p 228.

303. Jampel RS: Ocular torsion and the function of vertical extraocular muscles. Am J Ophthalmol 79:292, 1975.

304. Bromberg BE, Rubin LR, Walden RJ: Implant reconstruction of the orbit. Am J Surg 100:818, 1960.

305. Bennett JE, Armstron JR: Repair of defects of bony orbit with methyl methacrylate. Am J Ophthalmol 53:285, 1962.

306. Bioghouts JMHM, Otto AJ: Silicone sheets and bead implants to correct the deformity or inadequately healed orbital fracture. Br J Plast Surg 31:254, 1978.

307. Dingman RO, Grabb WC: Costal cartilage homografts preserved by irradiation. Plast Reconst Surg 28:562, 1961.

308. LaGrange F: De l'anaplerose orbitaire. Bull Acad Natl Med (Paris) 80:641, 1918.

309. Converse JM, Cole G, Smith B: Late treatment of blow-out fracture of the floor of the orbit: A case report. Plast Reconstr Surg 28:183, 1961.

310. Mathog RJ, Mesi FA, Smith B: Post-traumatic enopthalmos and diplopia. In Mathog RJ (ed): Maxillofacial Trauma. Baltimore, The Williams and Wilkins Company, 1984, p 239.

311. Block, MS, Zide MF, Kent JN: Proplast augmentation for post-traumatic zygomatic deficiency. Oral Surg 57:123, 1984.

312. Block MS, Kent JN: Correction of vertical orbital dystopia with a hydroxylapatite orbital floor graft. J Oral Maxillofac Surg 46:420, 1988.

313. Zide MF: Late posttraumatic enophthalmos corrected by dense hydroxylapatite blocks. J Oral Maxillofac Surg 4:804, 1986.

314. DeVoe AG: Experiences with the surgery of the anophthalmic orbit. Am J Ophthalmol 28:1346, 1945.

315. Cutler NL: Fascia lata transplant for retrotarsal atrophy of upper lid following enucleation. Am J Ophthalmol 29:176, 1946.

316. Sugar HS, Forestner HJ: Methacrylic resin implant for sunken upper lid following enucleation. Am J Ophthalmol 29:993, 1946.

317. Callahan A: Miscellaneous adnexal conditions correctable by surgery. In Reconstructive Surgery of the Eyelids and Ocular Adnexa. Birmingham, AL, Aesculapius Publishing, 1966, p 227.

318. Spaeth PG: Superior sulcus deformity and ptosis. Int Ophthalmol Clin 10:791, 1970.

319. Hill JC, Radford CJ: Treatment of advancing enophthalmos. Am J Opthalmol 60:487, 1965.

320. Neuhaus RW, Shorr N: The use of room temperature vulcanizing silicone in anophthalmic enopthalmos. Am J Ophthalmol 94:408, 1982.

321. Spivey BE, Allen L, Stewart WB: Surgical correction of superior sulcus deformity occurring after enucleation. Am J Ophthalmol 82:365, 1976.

322. Soll DB: Correction of the superior lid sulcus with subperiosteal implants. Arch Ophthalmol 85:188, 1971.

323. Lang W: Traumatic enophthalmos with retention of perfect acuity of vision. Trans Ophthalmol Soc UK 9:41, 1889.

324. Kroll M, Wolper J: Orbital blowout fractures. Am J Ophthalmol 64:1169, 1967.

325. Sacks AC, Friedland JA: Orbital floor fractures: Should they be explored early? Plast Reconst Surg 64:190, 1979.

326. Crikelair GF, Rein JM, Potter GD, Cosman B: A critical look at the "blowout" fracture. Plast Reconstr Surg 49:374, 1972.

327. Roncevic R, Malinger B: Experience with various procedures in the treatment of orbital floor fractures. J Maxillofac Surg 9:81, 1981.

328. Mathog RH: Reconstruction of the orbit following trauma. Otolaryngol Clin North Am 16:585, 1983.

329. Constantian MB: Use of auricular cartilage in orbital floor reconstruction. Plast Reconstr Surg 69:951, 1982.

330. Goldman RJ, Hessburg PC: Appraisal of surgical correction in 130 cases of orbital floor fracture. Am J Ophthalmol 76:152, 1973.

331. Stark RB, Frileck SP: Conchal cartilage grafts in augmentation rhinoplasty and orbital floor fracture. Plast Reconstr Surg 43:591, 1969.

332. Wolfe SA: Correction of a lower eyelid deformity caused by multiple extrusions of alloplastic orbital floor implants. Plast Reconstr Surg 68:429, 1981.

333. Polley JW, Ringer SL: The use of Teflon in orbital floor reconstruction following blunt facial trauma: A 20 year experience. Plast Reconstr Surg 79:39, 1987.

334. Aronowitz JA, Freeman BS, Spira M: Long-term stability of Teflon orbital implants. Plast Reconstr Surg 78:166, 1986.

335. McCord CD: Orbital decompression for Graves disease — exposure through lateral canthal and inferior fornix incision. Ophthalmology 88:533, 1981.

336. Adams JS: Grafts and implants in nasal and chin augmentation — a rational approach to material selection. Otolaryngol Clin North Am 20:913, 1987.

337. Sheen JH: Esthetic Rhinoplasty. 2nd ed. St Louis, CV Mosby, 1987.

338. Meyer R: Secondary and Functional Rhinoplasty — the Difficult Nose. Orlando, FL, Grune & Stratton, 1988.

339. Johnson CM, Toriumi DM: Open Structure Rhinoplasty. Philadelphia, WB Saunders Company, 1990.

340. Binder WJ, Kramer FM, Parkes ML: Mentoplasty — clinical analysis of alloplastic implants. Laryngoscope 91:383, 1981.

341. Robinson M, Shuken R: Bone resorption under plastic chin implants. J Oral Surg 27:116, 1969.

342. Hinds EC, Kent JN: The chin. In Surgical Treatment of Developmental Jaw Deformities. St Louis, CV Mosby, 1972, p 206.

343. Spira M: Editorial to Jobe et al: Bone deformation beneath alloplastic implants. Plast Reconstr Surg 51:174, 1973.

344. Friedland JA, Coccaro DJ, Converse JM, et al: Retrospective cephalometric analysis of mandibular bone resorption under silicone rubber chin implants. Plast Reconstr Surg 57:144, 1976.

345. Peled IG, Wexler MR, Ticher S, et al: Mandibular resorption from silicone chin implants in children. J Oral Maxillofac Surg 44:346, 1986.

346. Kent JN, Jarcho M: Reconstruction of the alveolus ridge with hydroxylapatite. In Fonseca R, Davis H (eds): Preprosthetic Surgery. St Louis, CV Mosby, 1985.

347. Davis WH, Ward WB, Delo RI, et al: Long term ridge augmentation with rib grafts. J Maxillofac Surg 3:103, 1975.

348. Fonseca RJ, Clark PJ, Bunks EJ Jr, et al: Revascularization and healing of onlay particulate autologous bone grafts in primates. J Oral Surg 38:572, 1980.

349. Baker RD, Terry BC, Davis WH, Connole PW: Long-term results of alveolar ridge augmentation. J Oral Surg 37:486, 1979.

350. Wang JH, Waite DE, Steinhauser E: Ridge augmentation: An evaluation and follow-up report. J Oral Surg 34:600, 1976.

351. Fazili M, Vernooy, AM, Visser WJ, et al: Follow-up investigation of reconstruction of the alveolar process of the atrophic mandible. Int J Oral Surg 7:400, 1978.

352. Kelley JF, Friedlander GE: Preprosthetic bone graft augmentation with allogeneic bone: A preliminary report. J Oral Surg 35:268, 1977.

353. Peterson LJ: Augmentation of the mandibular residual ridge by a modified visor osteotomy. J Oral Maxillofac Surg 41:332, 1983.

354. Stoelinga PJW, Tideman H, De Koomen HA, et al: A reappraisal of the interposed bone graft augmentation of the atrophic mandible. J Maxillofac Surg 11:107, 1983.

355. Kent JN, Quinn JH, Zide MF, et al: Correction of alveolar ridge deficiencies with nonresorbable hydroxylapatite. J Am Dent Assoc 105:993, 1982.

356. Kent JN, Quinn JH, Zide MF, et al: Alveolar ridge augmentation using nonresorbable hydroxylapatite with or without autogenous cancellous bone. J Oral Maxillofac Surg 41:629, 1983.

357. Kent JN, Finger IM, Quinn JH, et al: Hydroxylapatite alveolar ridge reconstruction: Clinical experiences, complications and technique modification. J Oral Maxillofac Surg 44:37, 1986.

358. Barsan RE, Kent JN: Hydroxylapatite reconstruction of alveolar ridge deficiency with an open technique — a preliminary report. Oral Surg 59:113, 1985.

359. Bonomo DJ: Subperiosteal soft tissue expansion for ridge augmentation. Miniclinic of the Chicago Dental Society Review, 1986, p 34.

360. Lew D, Clark R, Shahbazian T: Use of a soft tissue expander in alveolar ridge augmentation: A preliminary report. J Oral Maxillofac Surg 44:516, 1986.

361. Block MJJ, Rose R: Der Subperiostale Gewebe-Expander als Hilfsmittel bei der Alveolar Kamm Plastik. Dtsch Z Mund Kiefer Gesichtschir 11:443, 1987.

362. Mercier P: Ridge form in preprosthetic surgery. Oral Surg 6:235, 1985.

363. Lew D, Amos EA, Unhold GP: An open procedure for placement of a tissue expander over the atrophic alveolar ridge. J Oral Maxillofac Surg 46:161, 1988.

364. Wittkampf ARM: Augmentation of the maxillary alveolar ridge with hydroxylapatite and fibrin glue. J Oral Maxillofac Surg 46:1019, 1988.

365. Witthampf ARM: Short term experience with superiosteal tissue expander in reconstruction of mandibular alveolar ridge. J Oral Maxillofac Surg 47:469, 1989.

366. Stoelinga PJW, Blijdorf PA, Egbert M, et al: Augmentation of the atrophic mandible with interposed bone grafts and particulate HA. J Oral Maxillofac Surg 44:353, 1986.

367. Kent JN, Block MS, Finger IM, et al: Biointegrated hydroxylapatite coated dental implants — five year results and observations. J Am Dent Assoc. In press.

368. Block MS, Kent JN, Kay J: Evaluation of hydroxylapatite-coated titanium dental implants in dogs. J Oral Maxillofac Surg 45:601, 1987.

369. Kent JN, Block MS: Simultaneous maxillary sinus floor bone grafting and placement of hydroxylapatite coated implants. J Oral Maxillofac Surg 47:238, 1989.

370. Collins AC: Use of collagen tubes containing particulate HA for augmentation of the edentulous atrophic maxilla. J Oral Maxillofac Surg 47:137, 1989.

371. Zide MF, Misiek DJ, Kent JN, Jarcho M: The evaluation of strength and resorption with different ratios of hydroxlapatite and bone in canine mandibular continuity defects (unpublished data).

372. Piecuch JF, Topazian RG, Skoly S, et al: Experimental ridge augmentation with porous hydroxylapatite implants. J Dent Res 62:148, 1983.

373. Peterson LJ: Late complications following residual ridge reconstruction with porous hydroxylapatite blocks. Presented at the 68th Annual Session of the AAOMS, New Orleans, September 1986.

374. Holmes R, Mooney V, Bucholz R, et al: A coralline hydroxylapatite bone graft substitute. Clin Orthop 188:252, 1984.

375. Holmes RE: Bone regeneration within a coralline hydroxylapatite implant. Plast Reconstr Surg 63:626, 1979.

376. DeChamplain RW: Mandibular reconstruction. J Oral Surg 31:448, 1973.

377. Margolis IB, Smith RL, Davis WC: Reconstruction of defects of the mandible. Surgery 79:638, 1976.

378. Maisel RH, Hilger PA, Adams GL: Reconstruction of the mandible. Laryngoscope. 93:1122, 1983.

379. Pearl RM, LePore V, Hentz VR, Sarig A: An approach to mandibular reconstruction. Ann Plast Surg 21:401, 1988.

380. Parel SM, Drane JB, Williams EO: Mandibular replacements: A review of the literature. J Am Dent Assoc 94:120, 1977.

381. Erndt J: Prosthesis after jaw resection. Arch Clin Chir 52:210, 1968.

382. Small IA, Kautman M, Abramson B, et al: The search for a mandibular substitute. Sinai Hosp Detroit Bull 9:243, 1961.

383. Scudder CL: Tumors of the Jaws. Philadelphia, WB Saunders Company, 1912, p 354.

384. McDowell F, Ohlwiler D: Mandibular resection and replacement: Collective review. Int Abstr Surg 115:103, 1962.

385. Blocksma R, Braley S: Implantation materials. *In* Grabb WC, Smith J (eds): Plastic Surgery. Boston, Little, Brown, and Company, 1968, p 111.

386. Healy MJ, et al: The use of acrylic implants in one stage reconstruction of the mandible. Surg Gynecol Obstet 98:395, 1954.

387. Caorsi VA: Cited in Healy MJ, et al: The use of acrylic implants in one stage reconstruction of the mandible. Surg Gynecol Obstet 98:395, 1954.

388. Van Reenen PF: The use of acrylic implants after extensive mandibular resection. J Dent Assoc S Afr 19:367, 1964.

389. Leake D, Habal MB, Murray JE, et al: Custom fabrication for mandibular reconstruction. Oral Surg 33:879, 1972.

390. Brown JB, Fryer MP, Kollias P, et al: Silicone and Teflon prostheses including full jaw substitution. Am Surg 157:932, 1963.

391. Small I, Brown S, Kobernick S: Teflon and Silastic for mandibular replacement: Experimental studies and reports of cases. J Oral Surg 22:377, 1964.

392. Peltier LF: The use of plaster of paris to fill defects in bone. Clin Orthop 21:1, 1961.

393. Calhoun NR, Greene CW, Blackledge GT: Effects of plaster of paris implants on osteogenesis in the mandibles of dogs. J Dent Res 42:1244, 1963.

394. Smith L: Ceramic plastic material as a bone substitute. Arch Surg 87:653, 1963.

395. Carruthers FW: Historical review of metals used in orthopedic surgery. South Med J 34:1223, 1941.

396. Blair VP: Cited in Small IA, et al: The search for a mandibular substitute. Sinai Hosp. Detroit Bull. 9:243, 1961.

397. Olson DB: Intermediate and reconstructive care of maxillofacial missile wounds. J Oral Surg 31:429, 1973.

398. Venable CS, Stuck WG: The effects on bone of the presence of metals, based on electrolysis: An experimental study. Ann Surg 105:917, 1937.

399. La KY, Love JM, Perry CJ: Use of the Kirschner wire for mandibular reconstruction. Arch Otolaryngol Head Neck Surg 14:68, 1988.

400. Shuker S: Inter-ramii intraoral fixation of severely comminuted mandibular war injuries. J Maxillofac Surg 13:282, 1985.

401. Weisman S: Metals for implantation in the human body. Oral Implant 2:5, 1971.

402. Lane SL, Hoffman B, Lane JV: Vitallium implant for hemimandible. Am J Surg 96:768, 1958.

403. Markowitz NR, Cutone GA, Merrill R, et al: Immediate permanent reconstruction of a mandibular continuity defect with use of a chromium-cobalt alloy. J Am Dent Assoc 98:943, 1979.

404. Nahum AM, Boyne PJ: Restoration of mandible following partial resection. Trans Am Acad Ophthalmol Otolaryngol 76:957, 1972.

405. Freeman BS: The use of Vitallium plates to maintain function following resection of the mandible. Plast Reconstr Surg 3:73, 1948.

406. Conley JJ: The use of Vitalium prostheses and implants in the reconstruction of the mandibular arch. Plast Reconstr Surg 8:150, 1951.

407. Genest A: Vitallium jaw replacement. Am J Surg 92:904, 1956.

408. Kleitsch WP: Vitallium reconstruction of a hemi-mandible and temporomandibular joint. Plast Reconstr Surg 7:244, 1951.

409. Sodberg BN, Mulvey IM: Mandibular reconstruction in jaw deformities. Plast Reconstr Surg 2:191, 1947.

410. Mears DC, Rothwell GP: The structure and properties of materials. *In* Mears DC (ed): Materials in Orthopedic Surgery. Baltimore, The Williams and Wilkins Company, 1979, p 29.

411. French HG, Cook SD, Haddad RJ: Correlation of tissue reaction to corrosion in osteosynthetic devices. J Biomed Mater Res 18:817, 1984.

412. Zapfee CA: Chapter 1. *In* Stainless Steels. Cleveland, The American Society of Metals, 1986.

413. Suton EJ, Pollack SR: The biocompatibility of certain stainless steels. *In* Williams DF (ed): Biocompatibility of Clinical Implant Materials. Vol I. Boca Raton, FL, CRC Press, 1987, p 45.

414. Tomashov ND, Chernova GP: Passivity and Protection of Metals Against Corrosion. New York, Plenium Press, 1967.

415. Wallen B, Olson J: Corrosion resistance in aqueous medium. *In* Peckner D, Berustein IM (eds): Handbook of Stainless Steels. New York, McGraw-Hill, 1977, p 89.

416. Cowan RL, Tedmon CS Jr: Intergranular corrosion of iron-nickel-chromium alloys. *In* Fontana MG, Straekle RN (eds): Advances in Corrosion Science Technology. Vol 3. New York, Plenum Press, 1973.

417. Evans UR: The Corrosion and Oxidation of Metals. New York, St. Martin's Press, 1960.

418. Vetter KJ: Electrochemical Kinetics. New York, Academic Press, 1967.

419. Urlig HH: The adsorption theory of passivity and the flade potential. Z Elektrochem 62:626, 1958.

420. Vernon WHJ, Wornwell F, Nurse TJ: A study of the surface film on chromium-nickel (18/8) stainless steel. J Iron Steel Inst London 150:81, 1944.

421. Asami K, Hashimoto K, Shimodaira S: XPS determinations of compositions of alloy surface oxides on mechanically polished iron-chromium alloys. Corros Sci 17:713, 1977.

422. Okamoto G: Passive film of 18:8 stainless steel structure and its function. Corros Sci 13:471, 1973.

423. Rhodin TN: The relation of their films to corrosion. Corrosion, 12:55, 1956.

424. Bowden FP, Williamson JBP, Laing PG: The significance of metallic transfer in orthopedic surgery. J Bone Joint Surg [Br] 37:676, 1955.

425. Colangelo VJ, Greene ND: Corrosion and fracture of type 316 SMO orthopedic implants. J Biomed Mater Res 3:247, 1969.

426. Cahoon JR, Paxton HW: A metallurgical examination of surgical implants which have failed in service. Injury 2:143, 1970.

427. Hughes AN, Jordan BA: Metallurgical observations on some metallic surgical implants which failed in vivo. J Biomed Mater Res 6:33, 1972.

428. Weinstein A, Amstutz H, Pavon G, Franceschini V: Orthopedic implants—a clinical and metallurgical analysis. J Biomed Mater Res Symp 4:297, 1973.

429. Pugh J, Jaffe WL, Jaffe F: Corrosion failure in stainless steel implants. Surg Gynecol Obstet 141:199, 1975.

430. Proctor RPM, Seaton JF: An evaluation of the quality of stainless-steel surgical implants. Injury 8:102, 1975.

431. Hobkirk JA, Rusiniak K: Metallic contamination of bone drilling procedures. J Oral Surg 36:356, 1978.

432. Eriksson Westesson PL: Deterioration of temporary silicone implant in the temporomandibular joint. A clinical and arthroscopic follow-up study. Oral Surg 62:2, 1986.

433. Cahoon JR, Paxton HW: Metallurgical analyses of failed orthopedic implants. J Biomed Mater Res 2:1, 1968.

434. Cahoon JR, Paxton HW: A metallurgical survey of current orthopedic implants. J Biomed Mater Res 4:223, 1970.

435. Hueper WC: Experimental studies in metal cancerigenesis. I. Nickel cancers in rats. Tex Rep Biol Med 10:167, 1952.

436. Schinz HR, Uehlinger E: Metal cancer. A new principle of cancer production. Z Krebsforsch 52:425, 1942.

437. Williams DF: The response of the body environment to implants. *In* Williams DF, Roaf R (eds): Implants in Surgery. London, WB Saunders Company, 1973, p 255.

438. Underwood EJ: Trace Elements in Human and Animal Nutrition. 3rd ed. New York, Academic Press, 1971.

439. Foussereau J, Laugier P: Allergic eczemas from metallic foreign bodies. Trans St John Hosp Dermatol Soc 52:220, 1966.

440. Weinberg ED: Iron and susceptibility to infectious disease. Science 184:952, 1974.

441. Williams DF: The properties and clinical uses of cobalt-chromium alloys. *In* Williams DF (ed): Biocompatibility of Clinical Implants Materials. Vol I. Boca Raton, FL, CRC Press, 1981, p 99.

442. Haynes E: Alloys of cobalt with chromium and other metals. Trans Am Inst Min Metall Pet Eng 44:573, 1913.

443. Prange CH, US Patent 1909 (008, 1933) and 1958 (446, 1934).

444. Schnitman PA, Shulman LB (eds): Dental Implants: Benefit and Risk: Proceedings of a NIA-Harvard Consensus Development Conference. Bethesda, MD, NIH Publication No. 81–1531, 1980.

445. Smith-Petersen MN: Arthroplasty of the hip: A new method. J Bone Joint Surg [Br] 21:269, 1939.

446. Venable CS, Stuck WG: The Internal Fixation of Fractures. Springfield, IL, Charles C Thomas, 1947.

447. Galante JO, Rostoker W, Doyle JM: Failed femoral stems in total hip prostheses. J Bone Joint Surg [Am] 57:230, 1975.

448. Ducheyne P, de Meester P, Aeronoudt E, et al: Fatigue fracture of the femoral component of Charnley and Charnley-Muller type total hip prostheses. J Biomed Mater Res 6:199, 1975.

449. Sury P: Corrosion behaviour of cast and forged implant materials for artificial joints, particularly with respect to compound designs. Corros Sci 17:155, 1977.

450. Sury P, Semlitsch M: Corrosion behavior of cast and forged cobalt-based alloy for double-alloy joint endoprostheses. J Biomed Mater Res 12:723, 1978.

451. Mears DC: The use of dissimilar metals in surgery. J Biomed Mater Res 6:133, 1975.

452. Rostoker W, Pretzel CW, Galante JO: Couple corrosion among alloys for skeletal prosthesis. J Biomed Mater Res 8:407, 1974.

453. Manifold IH, Platts MM, Kennedy A: Cobalt cardiomyopathy in a patient on maintenance haemodialysis. Br Med J 2:1609, 1968.

454. Sullivan J, Parker M, Carson SB: Tissue cobalt content in "beer drinker's" myocardiopathy. J Lab Clin Med 71:893, 1968.

455. Hopkins LL: Distribution in the rat of physiological amounts of injected Cr^{31} (111) with time. Am J Physiol 209:731, 1965.

456. Langard S: *In* Waldron HA (ed): Metals in the Environment. London, Academic Press, 1980.

457. Gross PD, Gold LG: The compatibility of Vitallium and Austanium in completely bur-

ied implants in dogs. Oral Surg 10:769, 1957.

458. Held AJ, Spirgi M: Osteoperiosteal response to various implants in rabbits. Helv Odontol Acta 12:1, 1968.

459. Escalas F, Galante J, Rostoker W, Coogan PS: MP$_{35}$N: A corrosion resistant high strength alloy for orthopaedic surgical implants: Bio-assay results. J Biomed Mater Res 9:303, 1975.

460. Kumar P, Hickl AJ, Asphahani AI, Lawley A: Properties and characteristics of cast, wrought, and powder metallurgy (P/M) processed cobalt-chromium-molybdenum implant materials. *In* Fraker AC, Griffin CD (eds): Corrosion and Degradation of Implant Materials: Second Symposium, ASTM STP 859. Philadelphia, American Society for Testing and Materials, 1985, p 30.

461. Fraker AC, Ruff W: J Metals 22, 1977.

462. Williams DF: Titanium and titanium alloys. *In* Williams DF (ed): Biocompatibility of Clinical Implant Materials. Vol I. Boca Raton, FL, CRC Press, 1981. p 9.

463. Bothe RT, Beaton KE, Davenport HA: Reaction of bone to multiple metallic implants. Surg Gynecol Obstet 71:598, 1940.

464. Leventhal GS: Titanium, a metal for surgery. J Bone Joint Surg [Am] 33:473, 1951.

465. Clarke EGC, Hickmann J: An investigation into the correlation between the electric potential of metals and their behavior in biological fluids. J Bone Joint Surg [Br] 35:467, 1953.

466. Ferguson AB, Akahoshi Y, Laing PG, Hodge ES: Characteristics of trace ions released from embedded implants in the rabbit. J Bone Joint Surg [Am] 44:323, 1962.

467. Meachim G, Williams DF: Change in non-osseous tissue adjacent to titanium implants. Biomed Mater Res 7:555, 1973.

468. Williams DF: Systematic Aspects of Biocompatibility. Boca Raton, FL, CRC Press, 1981.

469. Ferguson AB, Laing PG, Hodge ES: The ionization of metal implants in living tissue. J Bone Joint Surg [Am] 42:77, 1960.

470. Lee ME, Murakami T, Stanczewski B, et al: Etiology of thrombus formation of prosthetic heart valves. J Thorac Cardiovasc Surg 63:809, 1972.

471. Freedus MS, Ziter WD, Doyle PK: Principles of treatment for temporomandibular joint ankylosis. J Oral Surg 33:757, 1975.

472. Hinds EC, Pleasants JE: Reconstruction of the temporomandibular joint. Am J Surg 90:931, 1955.

473. Miller GA, Page HL, Griffith CR: Temporomandibular joint ankylosis: Review of the literature and report of two cases of bilateral involvement. J Oral Surg 33:792, 1975.

474. Rast WC, Waldron AC, Irby WC: Bilateral temporomandibular joint arthroplasty. J Oral Surg 27:871, 1969.

475. Silagi JL, Schow CE: Temporomandibular joint arthroplasty: Review of literature and report of case. J Oral Surg 28:920, 1970.

476. Stratigos GT: Reconstruction of the temporomandibular joint by permanent fixation of Silastic to the temporal bone. Trans Congr Int Assoc Oral Surg 4:284, 1973.

477. Topazian RG: Comparison of gap and interposition arthroplasty in the treatment of temporomandibular joint ankylosis. J Oral Surg 24:405, 1966.

478. Walker RV: Arthroplasty of the ankylosed temporomandibular joint. Trans Cong Int Assoc Oral Surg 4:279, 1973.

479. Nickerson JW, Boering G: Osteoarthritis and internal derangement of the TMJ. Oral and Maxillofacial Surgery Clinics of North America. Disorders of the TMJ—Diagnosis and Arthroscopy 1:27, 1989.

480. Kaban LB, Mulliken JB, Murray JE: Facial fractures in children: 109 fractures in 122 patients. Plast Reconstr Surg 59:15, 1977.

481. Kaban LB: Congenital and acquired growth abnormalities of the temporomandibular joint. *In* Keith DA (ed): Surgery of the Temporomandibular Joint. Boston, Blackwell Science Publications, 1988, p 55.

482. Moss ML, Salentyn L: The capsular matrix. Am J Orthod 56:474, 1969.

483. Rowe NL: Fractures of the jaws in children. J Oral Surg 27:497, 1969.

484. Rowe NL: Ankylosis of the temporomandibular joint. J Coll Surg Edin 27:209, 1982.

485. Wheat PM, Evashus DS, Laskin DM: Effects of temporomandibular joint menistectomy in adult and juvenile primates (abstract). J Dent Res 58:139, 1977.

486. Munro IR, Chen YR, Park BY: Simultaneous total correction of temporomandibular ankylosis and facial asymmetry. Plast Reconst Surg 77:517, 1986.

487. Figueroa AA, Gans BJ, Pruzansky S: Long term follow-up of a mandibular costochondral graft. Oral Surg 58:257, 1986.

488. Kretzschman DP, Marx RE: Autogenous costochondral grafting in the growing child. *In* Irby WB, Shelton DA (eds): Current Advances in Oral and Maxillofacial Surgery. Vol IV. 1983, p 125.

489. Obeid G, Guttenberg SA, Connole PW: Costochondral grafting in condylar replacement and mandibular reconstruction. J Oral Maxillofac Surg 48:177, 1988.

490. Lovasko JH, Laskin DM: Facial growth after condylectomy and alloplastic condylar replacement. J Oral Surg 36:685, 1978.

491. Zide MF, Kent JN: Indications for open reduction of mandibular condyle fractures. J Oral Maxillofac Surg 41:89, 1983.

492. Choung R, Piper MA: Open reduction of condylar fracture of the mandible in conjunction with repair of distal injury: A preliminary report. J Oral Maxillofac Surg 46:257, 1988.

493. Fontenot MG, Kent JN, Anderson RC: Evaluation of articular wear of retrieved glenoid fossa prostheses from the TMJ. Transactions of the 3rd World Biomaterials Congress, Kyoto, Japan, 1988, p 345.

494. Revell PA, Weightman B, Freeman MAR, Vernon-Roberts B: The production and histology of polyethylene wear debris. Arch Orthop Trauma Surg 91:167, 1978.

495. Weightman BO, Paul IL, Rose RM, et al: A comparative study of total hip replacement prostheses. J Biomech 6:299, 1973.

496. Lagrotteria L, Scapino R, Granston AS, et al: Patient with lymphadenopathy following TMJ arthroplasty with Proplast. J Craniomand Pract 4:172, 1986.

497. Dolwick F, Aufdemorte TB: Silicone induced foreign body reaction and lymphadenopathy after TMJ arthroplasty. Oral Surg 59:449, 1985.

498. Kahn A, Stewart C, Teitelbaum S: Contact

mediated bone resorption by human monocytes in vitro. Science 199:988, 1978.

499. Craig R, Shapiro I, Yaari A, McArthur W: Evidence for a role of blood-borne monocytes in osteoclasts. J Dent Res 46:B189, 1977.

500. Fontenot MG, Turner H, Kent JN, Block MS: A comparison of mechanical properties of the temporomandibular joint meniscus and meniscus replacement materials. Trans Soc Biomaterials 8:50, 1985 (11th Annual Meeting of the Society for Biomaterials, San Diego, April 1985).

501. Fontenot MG, Kent JN, Block MS: The compressive creep and stress relaxation of human temporomandibular joint discs and implanted Teflon–Proplast II laminates. *In* Proceedings of the Fourth Southern Biomedical Engineering Conference, Jackson, MS, October 1985, p 160.

502. Fontenot MG, Block MS, Kent JN, Homsy CA: Comparison of mechanical properties of the human TMJ meniscus and Proplast II laminates. *In* Case Reports and Outlines of Scientific Sessions, AAOMS 67th Annual Meeting, Washington, DC, October 1985, p 56.

503. Kent JN, Spagnoli D: Retrospective evaluation of Proplast II–Teflon TMJ disc implants. J Oral Maxillofac Surg 47:92–93, Supp 1, August, 1989.

504. Grote MA, Ryan DE, Komorowski R, et al: Gross anatomy and histology of the temporomandibular joint meniscus in internal derangements (abstract). *In* Proceedings of the Clinical Congress of the American Association of Oral and Maxillofacial Surgeons, 1984, San Diego.

505. 1984 Criteria for TMJ Meniscus Surgery. Chicago, AAOMS, 1984.

506. Dolwick F, Sanders B: TMJ Internal Derangement and Arthrosis. St. Louis, CV Mosby, 1985.

507. Walker RV, Kalamchi S: A surgical technique for management of internal derangement of the temporomandibular joint. J Oral Maxillofac Surg 45:299, 1987.

508. Merrill RG: Historical perspectives and comparisons of TMJ surgery for internal disk derangements and athropathy. J Craniomand Pract 4:74, 1986.

509. Ioannides C, Freihofer HPM: Replacement of the damaged articular disc of the TMJ. J Cranio-Max-Fac Surg 16:273, 1988.

510. McCarty WL: Internal derangement of the temporomandibular joint. *In* Keith DA (ed): Surgery of the Temporomandibular Joint. Blackwell Scientific Publications, Boston, 1989, p 169.

511. Lanz A: Discitis mandibularis. Zentralbl Chir 9:289, 1909.

512. Silver CM, Simon SD, Savastano AA: Meniscus injuries of the temporomandibular joint. J Bone Joint Surg [Am] 38:541, 1956.

513. Silver CM: Long term results of meniscectomy of the temporomandibular joint. J Cranomand Pract 3:47, 1984.

514. Reichenbach E, Grimm G: Indikation und Prognose der Diskusexcision. Fortschr Kiefer Gesichtschir 6:130, 1960.

515. Mayer D: Zur Frage der Diskusentfernung bei der deformierenden Arthropathie des Kiefergelenkes. Deutsche Zahnärtliche Zeitschrtt 19:556, 1964.

516. Dingman RO, Constant E: A fifteen-year experience with temporomandibular joint disorders. Plast Reconstr Surg 44:119, 1969.

517. Agerberg G, Lundberg M: Change in the temporomandibular joint after surgical treatment. Oral Surg 32:865, 1971.

518. Eriksson L: Diagnosis and Surgical Treatment of Internal Derangement of the Temporomandibular Joint. Thesis, Malmö, Sweden, 1985.

519. Brown WA: Internal derangement of the temporomandibular joint: Review of 214 patients following meniscectomy. Can J Surg 23:30, 1980.

520. Boman K: Temporomandibular joint arthrosis and its treatment by expiration of the disc. Acta Chir Scand 95:118, 1947.

521. Sprinz R: Temporo-mandibular meniscectomy in rabbits. J Anat 88:514, 1954.

522. Sprinz R: Further observations on the effect of surgery on the meniscus of the mandibular joint in rabbits. Arch Oral Biol 5:195, 1961.

523. Lekkas K: Unilateral Hyperplasia of the Mandibular Condyle. Thesis, University of Nijmegan, the Netherlands, 1973.

524. Yaillen DM, Shapiro PA, Luscheri ES, Feldman GR: Temporomandibular joint meniscectomy—effects on joint structure and masticatory function in macaca fascicularis. J Maxillofac Surg 7:255, 1979.

525. Ioannides C, Maltha J: Resultaten na meniscectomie. Een dierexperimentele study. (abstract). Dutch Assoc Oral Maxfac Surg, Boekelo 1983.

526. Block MS, Unhold G, Bouvier M: The effect of diet texture on healing following TMJ discectomy in rabbits. J Oral Maxillofac Surg 46:580, 1988.

527. Block MS, Bouvier M: Adaptive remodeling of the rabbit TMJ following discectomy with dietary variations. J Oral Maxillofac Surg, in press.

528. Block MA, Kent JN, Walters PJ, Misiek DJ: Comparison of 5 discectomy treatments in primates. Educational Summaries and Outlines. 71st AAOMS Annual Meeting and Scientific Sessions. J Oral Maxillofac Surg 47[Suppl 1]:76, 1989.

529. Perko M: Indikationen und Kontraindikationen für chirurgische Eingriffe am Kiefergelenk. Schweiz Monatsschr Zahnheilk 83:73, 1973.

530. Rudelt HG: Symptomatik und Behandlungsergebnisse bei Diskusluxationen des Kiefergelenkes. Schweiz Monatsschr Zahnheil 91:566, 1981.

531. Witsenburg B, Freihofer HPM: Replacement of the pathological temporomandibular articular disc using autogeneous cartilage of the external ear. Int J Oral Surg 13:401, 1984.

532. Matukas V, Lachner J: The use of autogenous auricular cartilage for temporomandibular joint discectomy replacement: A preliminary report. J Oral Maxillofac Surg in press.

533. Kent JN, Widner S: Autogenous auricular cartilage grafts. (unpublished data).

534. Tucker MR: Autogenous cartilage as an interpositional material following total meniscectomy of the TMJ (abstract). 69th AAOMS Annual Meeting, Anaheim, CA, September 1987.

535. Golvine SS: Procédé de cloture plastique de l'orbit après l'exenteration. Arch d'Ophthamol 18:679, 1898.

536. McGee M: Temporalis muscle flap for the otologist. Am J Otol 7:409, 1986.

537. Shagets FW, Panje WR, Shore JW: Use of temporalis muscle flaps in complicated defects of the head and face. Arch Otolaryngol Head Neck Surg 112:60, 1986.

538. Renner G, Davis WE, Templer J: Temporalis pericranial muscle flap for reconstruction of the lateral face and head. Laryngoscope 94:1418, 1984.

539. Bowerman J: Reconstruction of the temporomandibular joint for acquired deformity and congenital malformation. Br J Oral Maxillofac Surg 25:149, 1987.

540. Tideman H, Doddridge M: Temporomandibular joint ankylosis. Aust Dent J 32:171, 1987.

541. Habel G, Hensher R: The versatility of the temporalis muscle flap in reconstructive surgery. Br J Oral Maxillofac Surg 24:96, 1986.

542. Blair VP: Operative treatment of ankylosis of the mandible, with a history of the operation and an analysis of 212 cases. Surg Gynecol Obstet 19:436, 1914.

543. Murphy JB: Bony ankylosis of jaw, with interposition of flaps from temporal fascia. Surg Clin JB Murphy 2:659, 1913.

544. Pepper L, Zide MF: Mandibular condyle fracture and dislocation into the middle cranial fossa. Int J Oral Surg 14:278, 1985.

545. Feinberg SE, Larsen PE: The use of a pedicled temporalis muscle–pericranial flap for replacement of the TMJ disc: Preliminary report. J Oral Maxillofac Surg 47:142, 1989.

546. Kent JN: Unpublished data.

547. Al-Kayat A, Bramley P: A modified preauricular approach to the temporomandibular joint and malar arch. Br J Oral Surg 17:91, 1979–1980.

548. Georgiade NG: The surgical correction of temporomandibular joint dysfunction by means of autogenous dermal grafts. Plast Reconstr Surg 30:68, 1982.

549. Topazian R: Comparison of gap and interpositional arthroplasty in the treatment of temporomandibular joint ankylosis. J Oral Surg 24:405, 1961.

550. Popescu V, Vasiliu D: Treatment of temporomandibular ankylosis with particular reference to the interposition of full thickness skin autograft. J Maxillofac Surg 5:3, 1977.

551. Georgiade N, Altany F, Pickell K: Experimental and clinical evaluation of autogenous dermal grafts used in the treatment of TMJ ankylosis. Plast Reconstr Surg 19:32, 1957.

552. Zetz M, Irby W: Repair of the adult temporomandibular joint meniscus with an autogenous dermal graft. J Oral Maxillofac Surg 42:167, 1984.

553. DeChamplain R, Stewart H, Hann J, et al: Histologic fate of dermal grafts following implantation for temporomandibular joint meniscal perforation: A preliminary study. Oral Surg 62:481, 1986.

554. Tucker M, Jacoway J, White R: Autogenous dermal grafts for repair of temporomandibular joint disc perforation. J Oral Maxillofac Surg 44:781, 1986.

555. Eppley et al: 1989 abstract.

556. Meyer RA: The autogenous dermal graft in temporomandibular joint disc surgery. J Oral Maxillofac Surg, 46:948, 1988.

557. Neary JP, Walters PJ: Dermal Grafts following Teflon–Proplast implants. J Oral Maxillofac Surg 47:93, Supp 1, Aug 1989.

558. Lowe O: Über haut Implantation an Stelle der freien faszien Plastik. Med Wochenschr 13:118, 1914.

559. Rehn E: Has kutane and subkutane Bindegewebe als plastisches Material. Med Wochenschr 13:118, 1914.

560. Eitner E: Über Unterpolsterung der Gesichtshaut. Med Klin 16:93, 1920.

561. Uihlein A: Use of the cutis graft in plastic operations. Arch Surg 38:118, 1939.

562. Cannady J: An additional report of some of the uses of cutis graft material in reparative surgery. Am J Surg 67:382, 1945.

563. Joy E, Bonnington G, Langan M: Epithelial inclusion cyst in the temporomandibular joint after a dermal graft. J Oral Maxillofac Surg 45:705, 1987.

564. Peer LA, Paddock R: Histologic studies on the fate of deeply implanted dermal grafts. Observations on sections of implants buried from one week to one year. Arch Surg 34:268, 1937.

565. Thompson N: The subcutaneous dermis graft. Plast Reconstr Surg 26:1, 1960.

566. Gordon S: Surgery of the temporomandibular joint. Am J Surg 95:263, 1958.

567. Imber G, Schwager RG, Gutherie RH, et al: Fibrous capsule formation after subcutaneous implantation of synthetic materials in experimental animals. Plast Reconstr Surg 54:183, 1974.

568. Marzoni FA, Upchurch SE, Lambert CJ: An experimental study of silicone as a soft tissue substitute. Plast Reconstr Surg 24:600, 1959.

569. Hansen WC, Deshazo BW: Silastic reconstruction of temporomandibular joint meniscus. Plast Reconstr Surg 43:388, 1969.

570. Kreutziger KI, Mahan PE: Temporomandibular degenerative joint disease: Diagnostic procedures and comprehensive management. J Oral Surg 40:297, 1975.

571. Alpert B: Silastic tubing for interpositional arthroplasty. J Oral Surg 36:153, 1978.

572. Sanders B, Brady FA, Adams D: Silastic cap temporomandibular joint prostheses. J Oral Surg 35:933, 1977.

573. Bessette RW, Katzberg R, Natiella JR, Rose MJ: Diagnosis and reconstruction of the human temporomandibular joint after trauma or internal derangement. Plast Reconstr Surg 75:192, 1985.

574. Ryan DE: Meniscectomy with Silastic implants. Abstr Clin Congr Am Assoc Oral Maxillofac Surg, San Diego, 1984.

575. Kalamchi S, Walker RV: Silastic implant as a part of temporomandibular joint arthroplasty: Evaluation of its efficacy. Br J Oral Maxillofac Surg 25:227, 1987.

576. Westesson Per-L, Eriksson L, Lindstrom C: Destructive lesion of the mandibular condyle following discectomy with temporary silicone implant. Oral Surg 63:143, 1987.

577. Hall D; Meniscectomy for damaged disk of the temporomandibular joint. South Med J 78:569, 1985.

578. Dolwick MF, Aufdemorte TB: Silicone-induced foreign body reaction and lymphadenopathy after temporomandibular joint

arthroplasty. Oral Surg Oral Med Oral Pathol 59:449, 1985.

579. Gallagher DM, Wolford LM: Comparison of Silastic and Proplast implants in the temporomandibular joint after condylectomy for osteoarthritis. J Oral Maxillofac Surg 40:627, 1982.

580. Homsy CA, Anderson MS: Functional stabilization of prostheses with porous low modulus materials system. *In* Biocompatibility of Implant Materials. Tunbridge Wells, Kent, England, Sector Publishing, 1976, pp 85–92.

581. Dusek JJ, Kent J, Smith P: Proplast-Teflon implants for treatment of TMJ degenerative diseases. Case Reports and Outlines of Selected Scientific Sessions, Annual Meeting of the American Association of Oral and Maxillofacial Surgeons, Chicago, September 1978.

582. Malloy RB, Kent JN, Smith P, Staples A: The treatment of TMJ arthroses with Proplast/Teflon implants. *In* Case Reports and Outlines of Selected Scientific Sessions, Annual Meeting, American Association of Oral and Maxillofacial Surgeons, Washington, DC, September 1981.

583. Vitek Package Insert: Surgical Protocol for Interpositional Implants. Houston, Texas, 1987.

584. Kiersch TA: Proplast Teflon grafts for TMJ surgery. Abstract, VIII International Conference on Oral Surgery, Berlin, West Germany, June 1983.

585. Kiersch TA: The use of Proplast Teflon implants for meniscectomy and disk repair in the temporomandibular joint. 1984 Clinical Congress on Reconstruction with Biomaterials: Current Assessment and Temporomandibular Joint: Surgical Update. Program Outlines and Abstracts, San Diego, January 1984.

586. Merrill RG: A survey of preferred implant after TMJ discectomy. Presented at Western Society of Oral and Maxillofacial Surgeons Annual Meeting, Lake Tahoe, NV, June 1986.

587. Vitek Inc: Survey of TMJ results conducted in January 1986 and mailed to AAOMS membership in April 1986.

588. Calnan J: The use of inert plastic material in reconstructive surgery. Br J Plast Surg 16:1, 1963.

589. Charnley J: Surgery of the hip-joint. Present and future developments. Br Med J 1:821, 1960.

590. Charnley J: Tissue reactions to polytetrafluoroethylene. Lancet 2:1379, 1963.

591. Leidholt JD, Gorman HA: Teflon hip prosthesis in dogs. J Bone Joint Surg [Am] 47:1414, 1965.

592. Heffez L, Mahmood FE, Rosenberg HR, Langer B: CT evaluation of TMJ disc replacement with Proplast Teflon laminate. J Oral Maxillofac Surg 46:657, 1987.

593. Bronstein SL: Retained alloplastic temporomandibular joint disk implants: A retrospective study. Oral Surg 64:135, 1987.

594. Florine BL, Gatto DJ, Wade ML, Waite DE: Tomographic evaluation of temporomandibular joints following discoplasty or placement of polytetrafluoroethylene implants. J Oral Maxillofac Surg 46:183, 1988.

595. Kaplan PA, Ruskin JDZ, Tu HK, et al: Erosive arthritis of the temporomandibular joint caused by Teflon-Proplast implants: Plain film features. AJR 151:337, 1988.

596. Katzberg RW, Laskin DM: Radiographic and clinical significance of temporomandibular joint alloplastic disc implants. AJR 151:736, 1988.

597. Knelland JB, Ryan DE, Carrera G, et al: Failed temporomandibular joint prosthesis: MR imaging. Radiology 165:179, 1987.

598. Schellhas KP, Wilkes CH, El-Deeb M, et al: Permanent Proplast temporomandibular joint implants: MR imaging of destructive complication. AJR 151:731, 1988.

599. Eriksson L, Westesson PL: Deterioration of temporary silicone implant in the temporomandibular joint: A clinical and arthroscopic follow-up study. Oral Surg 62:2, 1986.

600. Moriconi ES, Popowich LD, Guernsey LH: Alloplastic reconstruction of the temporomandibular joint. Dent Clin North Am 30:307, 1986.

601. McBride K: Clinical behavior of synthetic meniscus substitutes (abstract). 68th Annual AAOMS Meeting, New Orleans, September 24–28, 1986.

602. Estabrooks LN, Fairbanks CE, Collett RJ, Miller L: A retrospective evaluation of 301 TMJ Proplast/Teflon implants. Oral Surg (accepted for publication).

603. Timmis D, Aragon S, Van Sickels J, Aufdemorte T: A comparative study of alloplastic materials for TMJ meniscal replacement in rabbits. J Oral Maxillofac Surg 44:541, 1986.

604. James RB: Letter to the Editor. J Oral Maxillofac Surg, 1988.

605. El Deeb M: Silastic and Proplast as a TMJ replacement material in rhesus monkeys (abstract). 69th Annual AAOMS Meeting. Anaheim, CA, September 1987.

606. Rowe NL: Surgery of temporomandibular joint. Proc R Soc Med 65:383, 1972.

607. Hagan W, Anderson J: Rhytidectomy techniques utilized for benign parotid surgery. Laryngoscope 90:711, 1980.

608. Ressner D: Surgical approaches in tumors of the parotid gland: Preservation of the facial nerve and prevention of fistulas. AMA Arch Surg 65:831, 1952.

609. Ozersky D, Baek S, Biller HF: Percutaneous identification of the temporal branch of the facial nerve. Ann Plast Surg 4:276, 1980.

610. Roscic Z: Conservative parotidectomy: A new surgical concept. J Maxillofac Surg 8:234, 1980.

611. Axhausen G: Die operative Freilegung des Kieferglenks. Chiurg 3:713, 1931.

612. Alexander R, James R: Postauricular approach for surgery of the temporomandibular surgery. J Oral Surg 33:346, 1975.

613. Walters P, Geist E: Correction of temporomandibular joint internal derangement by posterior auricular approach. J Oral Maxillofac Surg 41:616, 1983.

614. Winstanly R: Subcondylar osteotomy of mandible in the intraoral approach. Br J Oral Surg 6:134, 1968.

615. Jeter T, Van Sickels J, Nishioka G: Intraoral open reduction with rigid internal fixation of mandibular subcondylar fractures. J Oral Maxillofac Surg 46:1113, 1988.

616. Kent JN, Block MS, Homsy CA, et al: Experience with a polymer glenoid fossa prosthe-

sis for partial or total TMJ reconstruction. J Oral Maxillofac Surg 44:520, 1986.

617. Hinds EC, Pleasants JE: Reconstruction of the temporomandibular joint. Am J Surg 90:931, 1955.

618. Caldwell JB: Surgical management of temporomandibular joint ankylosis in children. Int J Oral Surg 7:354, 1978.

619. Verneuil A: De la création d'une fausse articulation par section on résection partielle de los maxillaire inférieure, comme moyen de remédier à l'ankylose vraie ou fausse de la machoire inférieure. Arch Gen Med V Serie 15:174, 1860.

620. Helferich J: Ein neues Operationserfahren zur Heilung der knochernen Kiefergelenksankylose. Arch F Klin Chir 48:864, 1984.

621. Risdon FE: Ankylosis of the temporomaxillary joint. J Am Dent Assoc 21:1933, 1934.

622. Baer W: Arthroplasty with the aid of animal membrane. Am J Orthod 16:1, 1918.

623. Straith CL, Lewis JR; Ankylosis of the temporomandibular joint. Plast Reconstr Surg 3:464, 1948.

624. Braithwaite F, Hopper F: Ankylosis of the temporomandibular joint. Br J Plast Surg 5:105, 1952.

625. Lindsay JS, Fulcher CL, Sazima HJ, et al: Surgical management of ankylosis of the temporomandibular joint. J Oral Surg 24:264, 1966.

626. Blair VP: The consideration of contour as well as function in operations for organic ankylosis of the lower jaw. Surg Gynecol Obstet 46:167, 1928.

627. Longacre JJ, Gilby RF: The use of autogenous cartilage graft in arthoplasty for true ankylosis of the temporomandibular joint. Plast Reconstr Surg 7:271, 1951.

628. MacIntosh RB, Henny RA: A spectrum of application of autogenous costochondral grafts. J Maxillofac Surg 5:257, 1977.

629. Dingman RD, Grabb WC: Reconstruction of both mandibular condyles with metatarsal bone grafts. Plast Reconstr Surg 31:441, 1964.

630. Ware WH, Taylor RC: Growth center transplantation to replace damaged mandibular condyles. J Am Dent Assoc 73:128, 1966.

631. Snyder CC, Levine GA, Dingman RO: Trial of a sternoclavicular whole joint graft as a substitute for the temporomandibular joint. Plast Reconstr Surg 48:447, 1971.

632. Matukas VJ, Szymela VF, Schmidt JF: Surgical treatment of bony ankylosis in a child using a composite cartilage-bone iliac crest graft. J Oral Surg 38:903, 1980.

633. Sarnat BG, Engle MD: A serial study of mandibular growth after the removal of the condyle in Macaca rhesus monkey. Plast Reconstr Surg 7:364, 1951.

634. Sarnat BG, Muchnic H: Facial skeletal changes after mandibular condylectomy in growing and adult monkeys. Am J Orthod 60:33, 1971.

635. Durkin JF: Secondary cartilage: A misnomer? Am J Orthod 62:15, 1972.

636. Petrovic AG: Mechanisms and regulations of mandibular condylar growth. Acta Morphol Neerl Scand 10:25, 1972.

637. Sorenson DC, Laskin DM: Facial growth after condylectomy or ostectomy in the mandibular ramus. J Oral Surg 33:746, 1975.

638. Moss ML, Salentijn L: The capsular matrix. Am J Orthod 56:474, 1969.

639. Kent JN, James RB: Alloplasts in maxillofacial surgery. Transactions of the 4th Annual Meeting of the Society for Biomaterials and the 10th Annual International Biomaterials Symposium 2:9 San Antonio, TX, April 1978.

640. Christensen RW: Mandibular joint arthrosis corrected by the insertion of a cast-vitallium glenoid fossa prosthesis: A new technique. Oral Surg 17:712, 1964.

641. Hartwell SW Jr, Hall MD: Mandibular condylectomy with silicone rubber replacement. Plast Reconstr Surg 53:440, 1974.

642. Kameros J, Himmelfarb R: Treatment of TMJ ankylosis with methyl methacrylate interpositional arthroplasty. J Oral Surg 33:282, 1975.

643. Kent JN, Carlton DM, Zide MF: Surgical rehabilitation of temporomandibular joint rheumatoid arthropathies. Oral Surg 61:423, 1986.

644. Kent JN, Homsy CA, Hinds EC: Proplast in dental facial reconstruction. J Oral Surg 39:347, 1975.

645. Kent JN, Lavelle WE, Dolon KD: Condylar reconstruction: Treatment-planning. Oral Surg 37:489, 1974.

646. Lewin RW, Wright JA: Silastic ulnar head prosthesis for use in surgery of the temporomandibular joint. J Oral Surg 36:906, 1978.

647. Silver CM, Motamed M, Carlott AE Jr: Arthroplasty of the temporomandibular joint with use of a Vitallium condyle prosthesis: Report of three cases. J Oral Surg 35:909, 1977.

648. Small IA, Brown S, Kobernick SD: Teflon and Silastic for mandibular replacement: Experimental studies and reports of cases. J Oral Surg 22:377, 1964.

649. Cook HP: Teflon implantation in temporomandibular arthroplasty. Oral Surg 33:706, 1972.

650. Struthers AM: Experimental study of polyvinyl sponge as substitute for bone. Plast Reconstr Surg 15:274, 1955.

651. Healy MJ, Sudbay JL, Niebel HH: Use of acrylic implants in one-stage reconstruction of the mandible. Surg Gynecol Obstet 98:395, 1954.

652. Kameros J, Himmelfarb R: Treatment of TMJ ankylosis with methyl methacrylate interpositional arthroplasty. J Oral Surg 33:282, 1975.

653. Kent JN, Block MS: Five-year follow-up of polymer glenoid fossa prosthesis for partial and total TMJ reconstruction. J Oral Maxillofac Surg 46:M15, 1988.

654. Smith AE, Robinson H: A new surgical procedure for the creation of a false temporomandibular joint in cases of ankylosis by means of a non-electrolytic metal. Am J Surg 94:83, 1957.

655. Kiehn CL, DesPrez JP, Converse CF: A new procedure for total temporomandibular joint replacement—case report. Plast Reconstr Surg 53:221, 1974.

656. Hellinger MJ: Bony ankylosis of the temporomandibular joint. Oral Surg 18:293, 1964.

657. Tauras SP, Jordan JE, Keen RR: Temporomandibular joint ankylosis corrected with a gold prosthesis. J Oral Surg 30:767, 1972.

658. Hinds EC, Homsy CA, Kent JN: Use of a biocompatible interface for binding tissues

and prostheses in temporomandibular joint surgery. Oral Surg 38:512, 1974.

659. Kent JN, Misiek DJ: Nine-year report on Proplast coated metallic prostheses for condyle replacement. *In* Saha S (ed): Biomedical Engineering I — Recent Developments. Proceedings of First Southern Biomedical Engineering Conference, Shreveport 1982, p 314.

660. Kent JN, Misiek DJ, Akin RK, et al: Temporomandibular joint condylar prosthesis: A ten year report. J Oral Maxillofac Surg 41:245, 1983.

661. Robinson M: Temporomandibular ankylosis corrected by creating a false stainless steel fossa. J South Calif Dent Assoc 6:186, 1960.

662. Morgan DH: Temporomandibular joint arthrosis corrected and pain, tinnitus, and vertigo. Dent Radiogr Photogr 46:27, 1973.

663. Morgan DH: Surgical correction of temporomandibular joint arthritis. J Oral Surg 33:766, 1975.

664. House LR, Morgan DH, Hall WP: Clinical evaluation of TMJ arthroplasties with insertion of articular eminence prosthesis on ninety patients (an eight-year study). Laryngoscope 87:1182, 1977.

665. Kiehn CL, Des Prez JD, Converse CF: Total prosthetic replacement of temporomandibular joint. Ann Plast Surg 2:5, 1979.

666. Kummoona R: Functional rehabilitation of ankylosed temporomandibular joints. Oral Surg 46:495, 1978.

667. House LR, Morgan HD, Hall WP, Vamvas SJ: Temporomandibular joint surgery: Results of a 14 year joint implant study. Laryngoscope 94:534, 1984.

668. Robinson M: Temporomandibular ankylosis corrected by creating a false Silastic sponge fossa. J South Calif Dent Assoc 36:14, 1968.

669. Robinson M, Arnet G: Cobalt radiation to prevent reankylosis after repeated surgical failures: Report of case. J Oral Surg 35:850, 1977.

670. Seymour RL, Irby WB: Dislocation of the condyle into the middle cranial fossa. J Oral Surg 34:180, 1976.

671. Iannetti G, Martucci E: Fracture of glenoid fossa following mandibular trauma. Oral Surg 49:405, 1980.

672. Howe DJ: Preformed Silastic temporomandibular joint implant. J Oral Surg 37:59, 1979.

672a. Wright KWJ: Friction and wear of materials and joint replacement prostheses. *In* Williams DF (ed): Biocompatibility of Orthopedic Implants. Vol I. 1982, pp 141–195.

673. Payne W, Lyndell W, Frew AL, Staples A: Reconstruction of the temporomandibular joints in a patient with renal osteodystrophy. J Oral Surg 35:394, 1977.

674. Seymour RL, Bray TE, Irby WB: Replacement of condylar process. J Oral Surg 35:405, 1977.

675. Oberg T, Carlsson GE, Fajers CM: The temporomandibular joint. A morphologic study on a human autopsy material. Acta Odont Scand 29:349, 1971.

676. Hansson T, Oberg T, Carlsson GE, Kopp S: Thickness of the soft tissue layers and the articular disc in the temporomandibular joint. Acta Odont Scand 35:77, 1977.

677. Hasson T, Nordstrom B: Thickness of the soft tissue layers and articular disc in temporomandibular joints with deviations in form. Acta Odont Scand 35:281, 1977.

678. Homsy CA: Pseudosynovial fluids based on sodium carboxymethylcellulose. *In* Gabelnick, LH (eds): Rheology of Biological Systems. Springfield, IL Charles C Thomas, 1973, p 278.

679. Hylander WL: The human mandible: Lever or link? Am J Phys Anthropol 43:227, 1975.

680. Smith RJ: Mandibular biomechanics and temporomandibular joint function in primates. Am J Phys Anthropol 49:341, 1978.

680a. Charnley J, Kamangar A: The optimum size of prosthetic heads in relation to wear of plastic sockets in total replacement of the hip. Med Biol Eng 7:31, 1969.

681. McBride KL: Personal communication, 1989.

682. Schellhas KP, Wilkes CH: Temporomandibular joint inflammation: Comparison of MR fast scanning to T_1 and T_2-weighted imaging techniques. AJNR 10:589, 1989, and AJR 152:93, 1989.

683. Schellhas KP, Wilkes CH, Fritts H, et al: MR of osteochondritis dissecans and avascular necrosis of the mandibular condyle. AJNR 10:3, 1989, and AJR 152:551, 1989.

684. Salter RB, Simmons DF, Malcolm BW, et al: The biologic effects of continuous passive motion on full thickness defects in articular cartilage: An experimental investigation in the rabbit. J Bone Joint Surg 62:1232, 1980.

685. Salter RB, Bell RS, Keely FW: The protective effect of continuous passive motion on living cartilage in acute septic arthritis: An experimental investigation in the rabbit. Clin Orthop 158:223, 1981.

686. Salter RB, Simmons DF, Malcolm BW: The biologic effects of continuous passive motion on the healing of full thickness defects in articular cartilage. J Bone Joint Surg 62:1232, 1980.

687. Salter RB, Hamilton HW, Wedge JH, et al: Clinical applications of basic research on continuous passive motion for disorders and injuries of synovial joint: A preliminary report of a feasibility study. J Orthop Res 1:325, 1984.

688. Woo SL, Gelberman RH, Cobb NG, et al: The importance of controlled passive mobilization on flexor tendon healing: A biomechanical study. Acta Orthop Scand 52:615, 1981.

689. O'Driscoll SW, Kumar A, Salter RB: The effect of continuous passive motion on the clearance of a hemarthosis from a synovial joint: An experimental investigation in the rabbit. Clin Orthop 176:305, 1983.

690. O'Driscoll SW, Kumar A, Salter RB: The effect of the volume of effusion, joint position and continuous passive motion on the intraarticular pressure in the rabbit knee. J Rheumatol 10:360, 1983.

691. O'Driscoll SW, Salter RB: The induction of neochondrogenesis in free intra-articular periosteal autografts under the influence of continuous passive motion: An experimental investigation in the rabbit. J Bone Joint Surg [Am] 66:1248, 1984.

692. Fisher RL, Kloter K, Bzdyra B, Cooper JA: Continuous passive motion following total knee replacement. Conn Med 49:498, 1985.

693. O'Driscoll SW, Salter RB: The repair of major osteochondral defects in joint surfaces

by neochondrogenesis with autogenous osteoperiosteal grafts stimulated by continuous passive motion: An experimental investigation in the rabbit. Clin Orthop 208:131, 1986.

694. Van Royen BJ, O'Driscoll SW, Dhert WJA, Salter RB: A comparison of the effects of immobilization and continuous passive motion on surgical wound healing in mature rabbits. Plast Reconstr Surg 78:360, 1986.

695. Shimizu T, Videman T, Shimazaki K, Mooney V: Experimental study on the repair of full thickness articular cartilage defects: Effects of varying periods of continuous passive motion, cage activity, and immobilization. J Orthop Res 5:187, 1987.

696. Mooney V, Stills M; Continuous passive motion with joint fractures and infections. Orthop Clin North Am 18:1, 1987.

697. Coutts L, Toth C, Kaita J: The role of continuous passive motion in the postoperative rehabilitation of the total knee patient. *In* Hungerford D (ed): Total Knee Arthroplasty: A Comprehensive Approach. Baltimore, The Williams and Wilkins Company, 1984, p 126.

698. Goletz TH, Henry JH: Continuous passive motion after total knee arthroplasty. South Med J 79:1116, 1986.

699. Coutts RD, Kaita J, Barr R, et al: The role of continuous passive motion in the postoperative rehabilitation of the total knee patient. Trans Orthop Res Soc 7:195, 1982.

700. Poremba EP, Moffett BC: The effects of continuous passive motion on the TMJ after surgery. Part I. Appliance design and fabrication. Oral Surg 67:490, 1989.

701. Sebastian MH, Moffett BC: The effects of continuous passive motion on the TMJ after surgery. Part II. Appliance improvement, normal subject evaluation, pilot clinical trial. Oral Surg 67:644, 1989.

702. Fontenot MA, Kent JN: Continuous passive motion following total temporomandibular joint replacement. J Oral Maxillofac Surg (Submitted for publication).

703. McBride KL: Personal communication.

704. Kent JN, Block MS: VK-I and II Partial and total TMJ reconstruction devices: Eight-year patient and material evaluation. J Oral Maxillofac Surg, submitted for publication.

705. Rooney TP, Haug RH, Toor AH, Indresano AT: Rapid condylar degeneration after glenoid fossa prosthesis insertion. J Oral Maxillofac Surg 46:240, 1988.

706. Cooney WP III: Total joint arthroplasty: Introduction to the upper extremity. Mayo Clin Proc 54:495, 1979.

707. Schaldach M, Hohmann D (eds): Advances in Artificial Hip and Knee Joint Technology. New York, Springer-Verlag, 1976.

708. Sonneburg I, Sonneburg M: Total condylar prosthesis for alloplastic jaw articulation replacement. J Maxillofac Surg 13:131, 1985.

709. Kent JN, Neary JP, Silvia C, Zide MF: Open reduction of fractured mandibular condyles. Oral Maxillofac Surg Clin North Am 12:69, 1990.

CHAPTER 30

RECONSTRUCTION OF AVULSIVE MAXILLOFACIAL INJURIES

ROBERT E. MARX, D.D.S., and
MARK R. STEVENS, D.D.S.

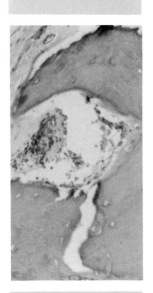

Experience has taught our profession that avulsive injuries to the maxillofacial area include both soft tissue and bone. Most injuries, whether they result from missiles or motor vehicles, also damage tissues at a distance from the avulsive tissue defect and therefore produce intense scarring, with which the reconstructive oral and maxillofacial surgeon must contend. In addition, one often finds foreign bodies in the form of bullet fragments or previous fixation devices, bone sequestra, residual infection foci, and subtle fistulae, which complicate reconstructive efforts (Fig. 30–1). Therefore, the surgeon who approaches maxillofacial reconstruction from trauma-related injuries must plan the reconstruction in a detailed and organized manner. We use five assessments to plan such a reconstruction:

1. Initial general assessment of residual problems
2. Soft tissue needs
3. Hard tissue needs
4. Delayed soft or hard tissue revisional needs
5. Prosthetic rehabilitation

HISTORICAL PERSPECTIVE

Historically, surgeons have gained the most experience with maxillofacial avulsive injuries from the numerous wars that have erupted. However, today, more than at any other time in human history, civilian injuries produce the largest number and most extensive of tissue loss injuries; these civilian injuries have mimicked and become almost indistinguishable from war injuries.

Most authors agree that real reconstruction-replacement of lost tissues began in World War I, and it mostly centered on mandibular reconstruction.[1,2] Ivy reported 123 mandibular bone grafts in 1125 (11 per cent) gunshot wounds by U.S. surgeons in Europe during World War I.[2] Blocker and Stout reported on 1000 mandibular bone grafts accomplished by U.S. surgeons during World War II.[3] The two most striking differences between these two reports 29 years apart were that World War

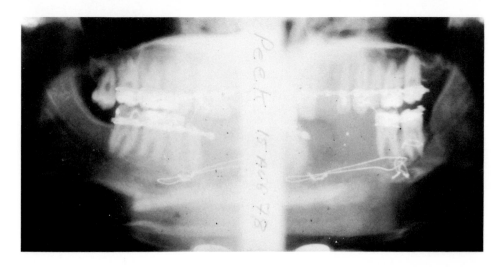

FIGURE 30–1. Residual sequestra of bone and teeth, along with inappropriate wire placements, often complicate reconstructive efforts by producing infection foci, fistula, and mobile segments requiring an initial debridement before definitive reconstruction.

I – related reconstructions were accomplished without antibiotic support and consisted mostly (67 per cent) of local bone periosteal transfers from other areas of the jaw, whereas the World War II experience reflected routine antibiotic use, usually with "sulfa" or the new drug penicillin, and distant block bone transplants from the ilium (81 per cent), ribs (15 per cent), and tibia (2 per cent). Only 1 per cent of these reconstructions used the most common bone graft material today, particulate bone and cancellous marrow, as this concept was first introduced by Mowlem in 1944.[4]

Indeed, Mowlem's introduction of what he called "iliac cancellous bone chips" began the evolution of predictable bone reconstruction of the jaws. His deviation from the accepted standard of that day was significant, but not fully accepted or understood, until the later works of Axhausen,[5] Burwell,[6,7] Boyne,[8,9] and Marx.[10,11] Words from his original article bear repeating:

> In using cancellous chips we are reversing the accepted standard of bone grafting. Instead of splinting the defect with a dense, almost non-cellular transplant which also acts as a bridge for osteogenesis, or as a poor source of new bone, and for neither of these purposes is it histologically suitable, we rely on other methods for fixation and fill the defect with a cellular mass, the survival of which will produce the requisite amount of new bone within a matter of weeks.

The experimental and clinical proof of Mowlem's concept came from those who followed. Axhausen's animal and human studies in 1956 showed that Mowlem's "bone chips" produced an osteogenesis in two phases.[5] The first phase, a cellular phase of proliferation and osteoid production, was followed by a second phase of resorption, but coupled with a replacement-remodeling into a longer lasting mature bone ossicle. Burwell's classic series of animal studies, first published in 1963, identified the source of phase I osteogenesis to be mainly from the endosteal osteoblasts lining the surface of Mowlem's cancellous bone chips.[6,7] He also identified a group of undifferentiated mesenchymal cells within marrow spaces as osteogenic, if stimulated, and referred to them as "littoral cells." [6,7] Boyne, throughout the 1960s and 1970s, brought particulate bone and cancellous marrow grafting to the forefront of mandibular reconstruction.[8] His use of particulate bone and cancellous marrow within metallic trays demonstrated the superior osteogenic capabilities of Mowlem's bone chips and showed that the required splinting of the defect could be managed by tray systems carrying the particulate bone and marrow rather than by splinting with large acellular cortical blocks of bone.[8,9] Marx, in the late 1970s and throughout the 1980s, introduced allogeneic bone trays into popular use as a biocompatible-bioresorbable tray system for particulate bone and cancellous marrow grafts.[10] He demonstrated that allogeneic bone became incorporated into the host tissue bed by vascular and connective tissue ingrowth, rather than being encapsulated, as were the foreign bodies of metallic trays and trays made of other materials. He also showed the second phase of Axhausen's bone regeneration studies to be responsible for the longevity of the bone ossicle through the generation of periosteum and endosteum derived from host tissue cells.[10,11]

The evolution of soft tissue reconstruction has been slower and not fully appreciated until the 1980s. Most soft tissue reconstructions prior to 1980 consisted of local cutaneous facial and cervical flap rotations. Large avulsive defects were reconstructed with techniques borrowed from tumor surgery principles. The deltopectoral flap (Bakamjian flap)[12] and the forehead flap[13] were used most commonly. The deltopectoral flap was used as a single-stage transfer, or was delayed for added length, but was limited to a reconstruction replacing only an epithelium-lined surface (mucosa or skin) and some subcutaneous fat. Most were deficient in bulk and lacked the more useful vascularity of muscle and muscle fascia. Use of such a flap also usually required externalization and tubing, committing the patient to a second surgery to detach its base for replacement back onto the chest, or rotation for further reconstruction of the maxillofacial area. The forehead flap contained a portion of the frontalis muscle but was, for the most part, still a skin–subcutaneous fat transfer. Though its length was severely limited, it was commonly used in reconstructing the mucosal lining of oral defects. Its biggest limitation was the noticeable donor site deformity, leaving the patient was a thin, adynamic forehead appearance after a split-thickness skin graft was placed on the periosteum of the frontal bone.

In 1979, Ariyan introduced the pectoralis major myocutaneous flap as the "flap of the 1980s."[14] Indeed, he was correct, as this flap has become the workhorse of maxillofacial soft tissue reconstruction.[15] Although muscle flaps and even myocutaneous flaps were already in use, to some degree, in breast reconstructions and sternal wound covers, as identified by Mathes, Ariyan's introduction of the pectoralis major myocutaneous flap as a single-stage transfer with a known and predictable axial pattern of vascular flow brought maxillofacial soft tissue reconstruction to a new and higher level. The predictability this flap offered to surgeons has since spawned the development and use of many other myocutaneous reconstructions for the maxillofacial area, such as flaps from the trapezius,[16] latissimus dorsi,[17] sternocleidomastoid,[18,19] and temporalis muscles.[20,21]

ASSESSMENT OF THE PATIENT

In the total scheme of maxillofacial trauma management, the place of reconstruction is that of tertiary care. Patients should be informed that reconstruction is an elective surgery with the primary goals of improving function first and cosmesis second. It should be emphasized to each patient that normalcy and the reconstitution of the same functional range or appearance are never achieved. Reconstructive surgery is a series of compromises in which the procedure of replacing lost tissue with transplanted like or similar tissue — and, at times, implanted devices or appliances — only strives toward these goals. Complete reconstruction is seldom a single surgery, but rather a series of staged surgeries. In our experience, avulsive missile wound injuries require an average of 7.3 surgeries for full reconstruction, and avulsive motor vehicle injuries require an average of 5.7 surgeries. Patients must, therefore, understand and be prepared both physically and emotionally for the many surgeries and for the time required for healing between surgeries.

The planned order of reconstruction is first to replace the avulsed soft tissue mass with special attention to replacing the epithelialized lining of oral mucosa and external skin cover. At the time of such soft tissue reconstruction, scar tissue is excised or released, and residual pathology is eliminated. The second general procedure is to reconstruct bone with special attention to techniques that will provide a lasting and remodeling bone ossicle of sufficient size and in the correct arch form and alignment to the remaining facial bones to provide a stable foundation for dental or maxillofacial prostheses. The third stage is that of tissue revisions. This stage often requires the most surgeries, as scars are revised, soft tissue excesses are debulked and contoured, augmentations of irregularities can be accomplished, and restricting scar bands are further released. The final stage is that of functional dental rehabilitation, and, if required, functional and cosmetic maxillofacial appliances.

The basics of actual patient assessment are as follows:

1. The patient's physiology as related to anesthetic risk is assessed, as one would for any elective surgical procedure. Common to late maxillofacial injuries are airway distortions from scarring, previous tracheostomies, deficient tongue support, and even residual fragments of bone or metal within the airway mucosa (Fig. 30–2). In addition, many will have a limitation of jaw opening because of scarring, which will not improve under anesthesia or paralysis. Therefore, plans for awake, or fiberoptic-assisted intubations are a distinct consideration, as is elective tracheostomy. In our experience, elective tracheostomy is rarely required because of the current level of anesthetic skills and available armamentarium. Only 4 per cent of our patients with post-trauma reconstructions have required tracheostomy, even when the patient presented with a history of previous tracheostomy. The indications for choosing a tracheostomy over intubation vary among cases, and are, therefore, not absolute. We prefer a tracheostomy in the situations when intubation cannot be accomplished or is unsuccessful, when there is tracheal stenosis, when the planned surgery is to place a bulky flap directly into the upper airway, and when the patient preoperatively demonstrates loss of the upper airway in recumbent positions. In the vast majority of cases in which intubation is preferred, plans should be made for delayed extubation 12 to 48 hours after surgery in a controlled environment with the surgical team present and prepared to deal with a loss of upper airway via reintubation, cricothyroidotomy, or tracheostomy. Such loss of upper airway after delayed extubations have been rare events in our experience (0.67 per cent incidence) but are certainly life-threatening events for which one must be prepared.

2. An assessment of the amount of mucosa, skin, and deep anatomic structures that are missing is next. The surgeon should list the suspected missing glandular, muscular, and vascular elements normally present, which, by his or her examination, are not present. One should also estimate the approximate surface size of mucosa and skin that are missing. In addition, one should try to gain a mental picture of the scarring pattern and amount. A knowledge of the type and path of the missile will help in this assessment (Fig. 30–3).

One can often estimate the amount of scar by the distance between the deviated mandible, tongue, commissure, or other known anatomic structures and their normal positions. Each measurement and estimation will be instrumental in planning the type of soft tissue reconstruction, the size of the skin or mucosal surface, the donor tissue most appropriate, and the geometric configuration of the tissue.

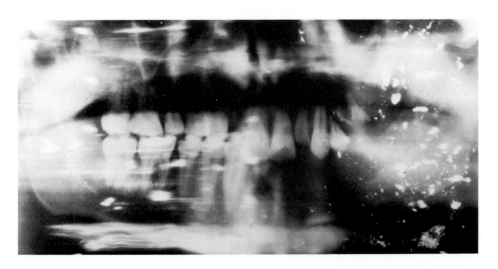

FIGURE 30–2. Residual bullet fragments, as well as bone and tooth fragments and jagged bony edges, must be identified and their influence on reconstructive efforts eliminated.

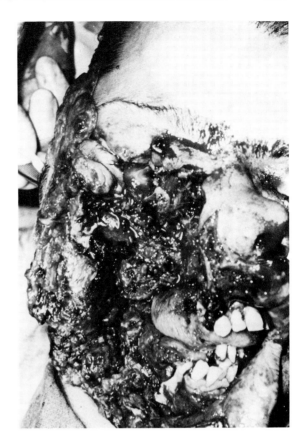

FIGURE 30–3. Photographs of the original injury will permit a better assessment of reconstructive needs. Here, soft tissue lining and cover have been avulsed, as was the bone of the maxilla, mandible, and zygoma, together with separate fractures in each jaw.

3.   The next assessment should be of the residual bone segments. The examiner must be watchful of jagged edges, which may perforate mucosa (Fig. 30–4), of separated islands of implanted bone fragments, of partially regenerated bone from traumatic displacement of periosteum, and of bone segments displaced by muscle pull but now fixed by scarring (see Figs. 30–1 and 30–2). The length of continuity defect is important for bone graft planning, as a useful guideline of 8 to 10 cc of particulate bone and cancellous marrow is ideally required for each 1 cm of continuity defect. Other important questions pertaining to mandibular continuity defects are as follows: Is the condyle present or absent (Fig. 30–5)? Does a hemimandibular defect include the arch curvature anterior to the mental foramen? Does the full arch curvature of the

FIGURE 30–4. Jagged edges of bone, such as these, need to be excised and rounded before bone graft surgery. This film also indicates a bony defect of the symphysis area, which should alert the surgeon to assess the quantity of soft tissue in that area for eventual bone graft placement.

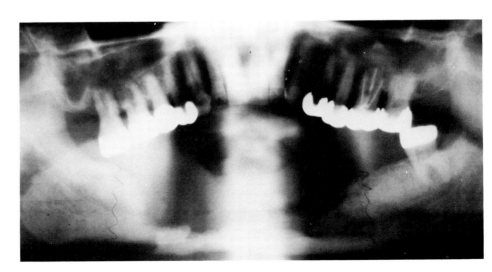

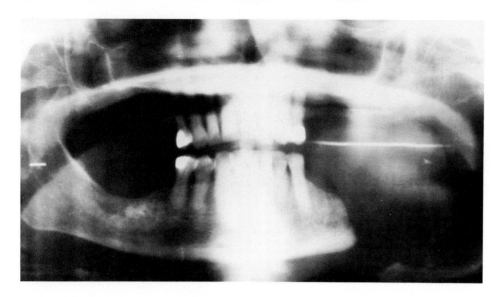

FIGURE 30–5. Radiographs should be assessed carefully for proximal segments. Here no condyle remains, so that a bone graft with an articulating surface must be planned. This film also shows a properly rounded distal bone end and shelf of alveolar crest, which are best suited for development of a graft-to-host union.

symphysis require reconstruction (see Fig. 30–4)? Each area of the mandible requires a different tray shape and size, and the reconstruction of the condyle requires consideration of costochondral grafting, an allogeneic mandibular condyle, or an alloplastic condyle.

4.   The next assessment should be for residual pathology and may be the most important assessment. The most basic reconstructive principle is to advance, rotate, or graft tissue into an infection-free and contamination-free recipient tissue of maximal vascular and cellular content. Post-traumatic wounds often contain residual non-viable tissue or foreign bodies with foci of chronic infection about them. One must meticulously examine for subtle fistulae, areas of granulation tissue, wires, bullet fragments, glass fragments, portions of teeth, and so on (see Figs. 30–1, 30–2, and 30–4). Many tissue beds have clinically seemed healthy, only to harbor such focal areas of microorganisms that have produced a bone graft infection and a lost reconstructive result. Surgically accessible foreign bodies, small, infected foci, jagged bone segments, and scar tissue can usually be excised at the time of soft tissue reconstruction. Since most soft tissue reconstructive procedures use random pattern or axial pattern flaps of excellent vascularity, oral exposures and contaminated tissues do not greatly compromise their success. However, one should not leave excision of residual pathology or the anticipation of oral exposure for the bone reconstructive surgery, as the incidence of graft infection and loss increases to over 35 per cent.

BIOLOGY OF RECONSTRUCTIVE SURGERY

Soft Tissue

The purpose of soft tissue reconstruction, in addition to the quantitative replacement of avulsed soft tissue, is to replace the fibrotic and minimally vascular tissue that results after traumatic wounding with a vascular and cellular tissue not only capable of perfusing transplanted osteogenic cells but also containing a cellular content that can develop into a periosteum. Works by several authors have shown connective tissue cells (fibroblasts) of fascia, dermis, and muscle fascia to be capable of induction-guided differentiation into bone-forming cells that can support bone graft healing, maturation, and remodeling.[5,22,23] Therefore, the desired soft tissue reconstruction should provide a viable tissue bulk, a vascular network, and a population of inducible fibroblast-like cells. To this end, flaps of skin and subcutaneous fat, such as the deltopectoral flap, are less desirable than myocutaneous flaps.

Soft tissue flaps are categorized into two types: random patterns flaps and axial pattern flaps. The random pattern flap depends on a network of small vessels coursing from its base to its tip. Such flaps are limited in thickness and in length. A length-width ratio of 3 : 1 is rarely exceeded in a single-stage transfer. A staged delay can be accomplished to increase the length-width ratio, if necessary. The thickness is usually limited to skin, dermis, and subcutaneous tissue but may include superficial muscles such as the platysma. The networks of the subcutaneous plexus and the dermal plexus, with anastomosis between each, maintain the viability of the flap and its overlying skin territory. Flaps of this type that may be used in maxillofacial reconstructive surgery are skin-platysma rotation flaps, the bipedicled neck flap, the Karapanzic flap,[24,25] and the Abbé-Estlander flap,[26] among others.

Axial pattern flaps are flaps usually of muscle or myocutaneous composites, but they may also consist only of skin and dermis that have known anatomic vascular inflow and outflow coursing along the greatest length of the flap. The axial artery and its corresponding vein make up a closed system of viable tissue. The length is determined only by the length of the axial vessels, which is usually much greater than that of a random pattern flap. Therefore, these types of flaps may be brought from greater distances away from the injured maxillofacial area, such as the chest, back, or neck. The length can be much greater than the width, and the thickness can include muscle, fascia, subcutaneous tissue, dermis, and skin. Flaps of this type that may be used in maxillofacial reconstruction are the pectoralis major myocutaneous flap, the latissimus dorsi myocutaneous flap, the trapezius myocutaneous flap, and the sternocleidomastoid myocutaneous flap, among others. In rare instances, an axial pattern flap may need to be completely detached from its donor site and placed into a maxillofacial recipient site through a microvascular vessel anastomosis to local vessels.[27]

If the vascularity of each type of flap is maintained, the graft has the potential to heal into its recipient area without the shrinkage and contraction seen in free dermis or skin graft procedures. The tissue will also remain supple and retain viable hair follicles, sweat glands, and the coloration of the donor skin. The flaps heal into the recipient tissue bed without changing, but the vessels of the flap anastomose freely with recipient tissue vessels to develop a confluence of their capillary networks.

Hard Tissue (Bone Grafts)

New bone formation occurs through three biologic mechanisms: osteogenesis, osteoconduction, and osteoinduction. Osteogenesis is the production of new bone by proliferation, osteoid production, and mineralization by transplanted osteocompetent cells. It is the main mechanism we as surgeons exploit to graft large bone loss defects. It is the mechanism first discovered by Mowlem and is now advanced to emphasize a greater cellular transplant to achieve predictable bone graft success; it accounts for the greatest amount of bone formed by the graft. Osteoconduction is the production of new bone by the proliferation and migration of local host osteocompetent cells along a conduit. The conduit may be local vessels, epineurium, allogeneic bone, or even certain alloplasts, such as some hydroxyapatite blocks. It accounts for a small amount of the bone derived in bone reconstruction; this bone usually originates from the endosteum of the host bone ends or residual periosteum. Osteoinduction is the formation of bone by connective tissue cells transformed into osteocompetent cells by inductive agents, usually proteins. Since Marshall Urist first published his discovery of bone morphogenetic protein (BMP) in 1965,[28] other inductive agents have been discovered. Most, such as BMP (now shown to be a subset of four similar proteins with differing molecular weights), exist in the noncollagenous organic matrix of mineralized bone, as do others, such as skeletal growth factor and osteogenin.[29,30] Osteoinduction accounts for a small amount of the bone produced by our bone graft systems but may be the important mechanism in inducing the recipient connective tissue fibroblasts about the graft into a periosteum, which accounts, in part, for its longevity.

The sequenced healing of a bone graft consisting of autogenous particulate bone and cancellous marrow is more than simple healing; it is bone regeneration. The amount of bone produced in the graft is dependent on the cellular density of the transplanted cancellous bone. Simmons has stated that the donor site must contain 2000 osteoblasts per milligram of bone as a critical bone transplant density,[31] and Friedenstein has reported that 1×10^6 osteocompetent cells per cubic millimeter are needed within the recipient tissue bed for the formation of new bone.[32] Regardless of actual numbers, the obvious principle is to use cellular cancellous bone, harvest a sufficient quantity of cancellous bone, and compact it into a high cell per unit volume for maximal bone formation. To this end, the ilium remains the preferred donor site because it has been shown to possess four times the osteogenic cellularity of cortical bone (12 per cent to 3 per cent) and twice the osteogenic cellularity (12 per cent to 6 per cent) of other cancellous bone sources.[31] It is also suggested that our rule of thumb (8 to 10 cc of cancellous bone for each 1 cm of defect) be used as a simple yardstick to ensure a sufficient harvest of donor bone.[10,11] The compaction of bone into a higher cellular density per volume by simple syringe compression or hand instrument compression also serves the purpose of increasing graft cellular density in a straightforward manner.

The transplanted cellular bone, mainly the endosteal osteoblasts on the cancellous surface, proliferates and produces new osteoid (Figs. 30–6 and 30–7). The bone produced is a cellular woven type of bone with little structural organization. The cells are in a haphazard arrangement and resemble the cellular bone in a fracture callus (Fig. 30–7). The cancellous bone osteocytes do not survive the transplantation, as they are dependent on their delicate canalicular blood supply and cannot be maintained by nutritional diffusion by virtue of their encasement in mineral matrix. The endosteal osteoblasts and marrow "littoral cells" of Burwell survive owing to their open surface position within the cancellous marrow, thus allowing plasmatic circulation to meet their metabolic and oxygen demands until revascularization. The amount of this first phase of bone is, indeed, dependent on the number of surviving transplanted osteocompetent cells, but also, and most important, it is the maximal bone volume the graft can ever produce. The height and width of the graft obtained at the time of its placement is the maximum it will ever be. The osteocompetent cells will proliferate and produce osteoid within the limits of the cancellous bone volume, but they are not motile cells and will not grow outward to fill a tray not completely filled with cancellous bone.

This first phase of bone will not last very long. Like the fracture callus analogy, it

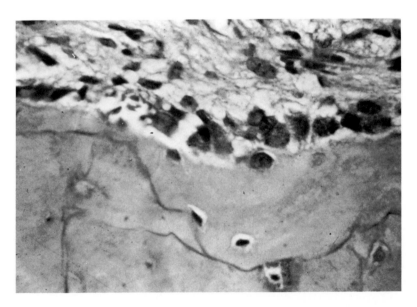

FIGURE 30–6. Endosteal osteoblasts, as seen here, are the cells primarily responsible for osteogenesis within a particulate bone and cancellous marrow graft. These cells are already committed bone-forming cells and, by virtue of their surface position, survive transplantation by existing on nutritional diffusion until a graft vascularity develops. Human graft specimen at time of placement. Original magnification, 16×.

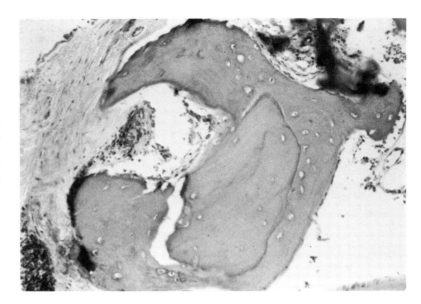

FIGURE 30–7. New osteoid (phase I bone) is produced from the endosteal osteoblasts. The central bone fragment seen here is nonviable. It is, however, surrounded by new osteoid of cellular woven-type bone. Human graft specimen at 4 weeks. Original magnification, 10×.

will undergo an obligatory resorption and replacement. The first phase of bone is resorbed and replaced by a second phase of bone, which is derived from the local cell population of the host and is more structured (Fig. 30–8). This second-phase bone is that responsible for the longevity of the bone ossicle. Internally, the resorption of phase I bone is osteoclast mediated, which means the osteoclasts secrete their coupling factor into the grafted area as they resorb phase I bone. As in all bone resorption, coupling factor stimulates an apposition of new bone into the area of bone resorption as part of the normal physiologic process of all bone remodeling. This coupling factor stimulates host cells to form the new second phase of bone regeneration and establish an endosteal system for long-term bone volume maintenance (Fig. 30–9). Externally, osteoinductive agents from the mineral component of the graft itself or from an allogeneic tray, if one is used, induce the recipient connective tissue cells to form a functional periosteum about the graft (Fig. 30–10). The maturation of the bone ossicle, as well as its volume-maintaining endosteal and periosteal systems, is a second-phase event and will determine the longevity of the graft, as well as the ability of the graft to remodel under appliances and even to osteointegrate dental implants.

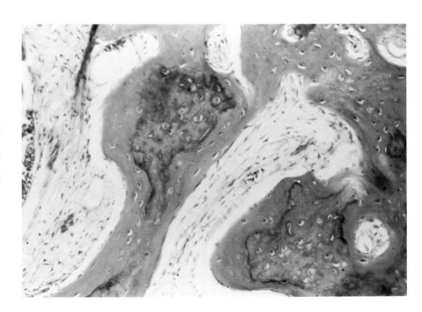

FIGURE 30–8. Centrally positioned phase I bone, which is cellular and haphazard in arrangement, is being replaced by an organized bone derived from host cells, phase II bone. Human graft specimen at 8 weeks. Original magnification, 10×.

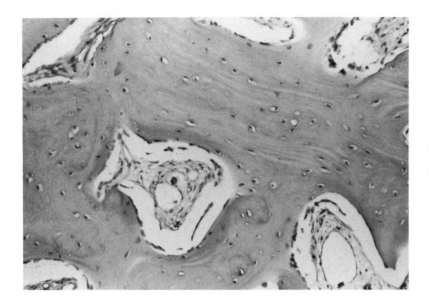

FIGURE 30–9. Mature graft that has developed its own endosteal system of bone maintenance. Human graft specimen at 6 months. Original magnification, 10×.

GOALS OF RECONSTRUCTION (CRITERIA OF SUCCESS)

The surgeon should have a clear and realistic picture of the projected end product of his or her reconstructive efforts. The following are goals toward which reconstruction should strive and may also be used as a measure of a "successful reconstruction":

1. *Restoration of bone continuity.* Particularly as this pertains to the mandible, it achieves two major impacts on the patient. The first is that mandibular continuity restores much of the mechanical stability to the functions of mastication, speech, and deglutition. Even in patients who have lost much of their opening musculature or closing musculature or both, residual musculature, adaptation of accessory muscles, and even the muscles of facial expression provide sufficient and usually very adequate function. The second impact is on the patient's self-image. Restoring jaw continuity even more so than restoring a patient's physical appearance removes much of their self-image of being a "cripple." The feeling of a solid and stable mandible imparts a feeling of control and self-confidence, which often translates into a patient who is more willing to return to an active lifestyle and to the workplace. In addition, bony

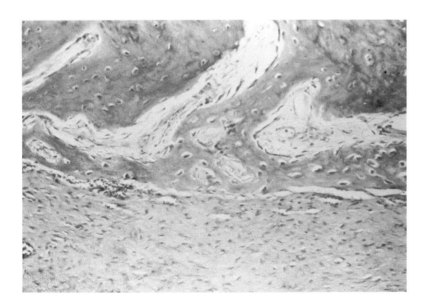

FIGURE 30–10. Mature graft showing a periosteum induced from the connective tissue cells of the recipient bed. Human graft specimen at 1 year. Original magnification, 10×.

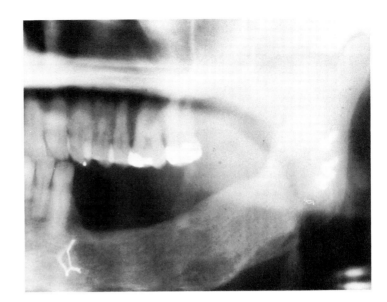

FIGURE 30–11. A film of a graft at 10 years shows the radiographic features of a "successful graft": continuity, alveolar bone height, osseous bulk, and maintenance of bone over time.

continuity of any part of the facial skeleton adds to more normal contours and appearance and thereby assists cosmesis while providing a foundation upon which to accomplish more exacting cosmetic procedures (Fig. 30–11).

2. *Restoration of osseous bulk.* Too often, bone reconstructions that transplant a thin and volume-deficient bone ossicle are published as successes. These have usually resulted from an insufficient harvest of bone graft material (a deficient phase I effect), a resorption of graft with minimal replacement-remodeling from an unimproved scarred and hypovascular tissue bed (a deficient phase II effect), or a microvascular free transfer from a volume-deficient donor site, such as rib, radius, scapula, and so on. Such grafts are prone to fractures, usually do not supply sufficient contour, and can rarely support a prosthetic appliance. Osseous bulk is best achieved through adherence to the biologic principles of bone graft healing. That is, a sufficient quantity of cellular cancellous graft materials should be placed and firmly fixated into a vascular and cellular tissue bed free of contamination (Fig. 30–11).

3. *Restoration of alveolar bone height.* The restoration of alveolar bone height will elevate a mere reconstructive success to a reconstructive-rehabilitative success. A sufficient alveolar bone height is imperative for the retention and stability of conventional prostheses and is necessary for implant systems to osteointegrate effectively. The achievement of good alveolar bone height is accomplished in the dissection to prepare the soft tissue for the graft. The dissection must free all scar within the space of the mandible to a thin, overlying mucosa (1 to 3 mm), without perforation into the oral cavity. Technically, this is achieved by blunt dissection in this area with the instrument spread parallel to the ridge or crestal scar by sharp dissection palpating the maxillary dentition as a guide to tissue thickness, or by dissecting under guidance from another member of the surgical team who has placed a gloved hand within the oral cavity. One should note that any such member of the operating team who violates sterile technique needs to change the complete gown and gloves, not just the contaminated area (Fig. 30–11).

4. *Bone maintenance.* One of the most important aspects of a successful reconstruction is the maintenance of the bone ossicle throughout the lifetime of the patient. Bone grafts that support the second phase of bone regeneration via a cellular and vascular tissue bed or via successful microvascular anastomoses can be expected to stand up to function, and even nonfunction, throughout many years because of their endosteal and periosteal systems. Grafts that fail in the first phase will show either lack of bone formation or resorption of their nonviable mineral matrix in the first 6 months (Fig. 30–12). Grafts that fail in the second phase will show resorption with the 6- to 18-month range (Fig. 30–13). Grafts that maintain or increase their radio-

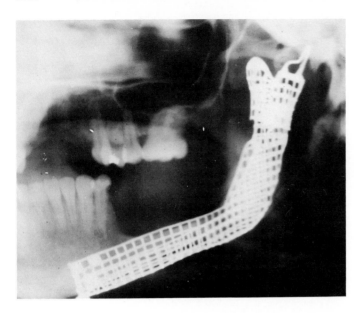

FIGURE 30–12. Lack of bone formation in this crib occurred as a result of devitalization of bone cells via placement into sterile water, a failure of phase I bone formation.

graphic mineral density beyond 18 months almost always maintain their ossicle throughout the patients' lifetime and can, therefore, be considered successful (see Fig. 30–11).

5. *Elimination of soft tissue deficiencies.* Residual soft tissue deficiencies often restrict tongue and lip function, as well as create unseating forces and prevent a seal for prostheses. Such soft tissue deficiencies are eliminated either prior to bone graft tissue flaps or after bone grafting with releasing procedures using split-thickness skin or dermal grafts.

6. *Restoration of facial contours.* The composite of staged soft and hard tissue reconstructions, plus dental and facial prostheses when indicated, should restore facial bone form as well as function. Although cosmetic onlay grafts, contouring procedures, and scar revisions are staged after the basics of soft tissue and bone replacement are done, the best of cosmetic procedures will not provide balanced facial aesthetics if the basics have not been accomplished satisfactorily. Indeed, the

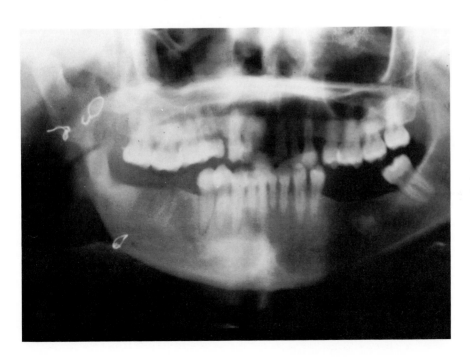

FIGURE 30–13. Late resorption of this graft resulted from a scarred, avascular tissue bed, which was not able to form a periosteum about the graft, a failure of phase II bone formation.

initial soft tissue replacements and bone grafting are of themselves also cosmetic in nature and are a necessary prerequisite for the cosmetic refinements of contour onlays and scar revisions.

SURGICAL APPROACHES—SOFT TISSUE

Dissection of the Tissue Bed

The basic purpose of soft tissue flaps is to replace clinically avulsed tissue bulk and epithelial lining. If the tissue wound is healed, the tissue bed dissection must reopen the assessed initial wound (Fig. 30–14). Scar tissue should be excised wherever possible, and a large defect should be created in tissue that once seemed to be healed. Even the most experienced surgeons continue to be amazed at the size of the defect and the degree of tissue deficiency unmasked and often not fully appreciated in trauma-related defects (Fig. 30–15). The surgeon should not hesitate to communicate a dissection in the neck with an excision of oral mucosa, which creates a through-and-through wound. Skin paddles from myocutaneous flaps can be split not only to replace avulsed soft tissue bulk but also to restore avulsed mucosal or skin epithelium at the same time. If there is the anticipation that a bone graft will be required at a later procedure, a horizontal neck incision should be used and placed in a position to approximate the ideal incisional approach for the bone graft.

As the tissue bed is opened, any residual foreign bodies should be removed and any sharp, bony edges should be excised. The surgeon should not hesitate to expose the residual bone to excise irregular edges and round them in anticipation of bone grafting later. In many instances, a coronoidectomy is accomplished at this time, and the mandible is stabilized by external skeletal pin fixation, internal stabilization plates, or maxillomandibular fixation to maintain the position of the bone segments.

Integral to the development of the recipient tissue bed for a soft tissue flap in many cases is the need to develop a tissue tunnel to bring the flap into the area. The

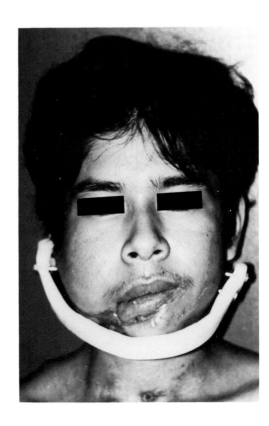

FIGURE 30–14. Typical soft tissue defect of skin and mucosa in addition to bone. It is healed into a contracted tissue mass, which, when released, will unmask a much bigger defect than is often appreciated.

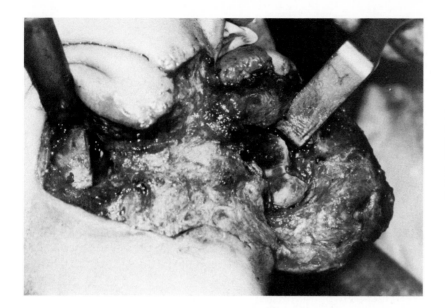

FIGURE 30–15. Soft tissue defect of Figure 30–14 opened to receive a myocutaneous flap. The defect size is seen here to be larger than initially anticipated. Such a complete excision of scar and repositioning of soft tissue are required in soft tissue reconstruction.

pectoralis major chest flap and the latissimus dorsi flap from the back require a subplatysma dissection that extends to the clavicle and communicates with the superficial chest wall. Other flaps from the back, such as trapezius flaps, also require a subplatysma tunnel but, in addition, an extension into the posterior triangle of the neck superficial to the sternocleidomastoid muscle.

In those cases in which an open tissue defect still exists, a soft tissue flap remains possible. However, the tissue bed must have a granulation tissue base that demonstrates fewer than 10^5 organisms per gram of tissue. In open gunshot wounds, *Pseudomonas* and *Proteus* are frequent organisms that must be eradicated. Both organisms are sensitive to several antibiotics, in particular, aminoglycosides. Preflap treatment with antibiotic choices directed by culture and sensitivity studies and wound care consisting of irrigations, debridements, topical antibiotics, and frequent dressing changes is often required to reduce the contamination count to fewer than 10^5 organisms per gram of tissue. In particular, *Pseudomonas* is very sensitive to acidic solutions, so that acetic acid–soaked dressings are of additional value.

The Pectoralis Major Myocutaneous Flap

The pectoralis major myocutaneous flap remains the most useful and common flap employed to replace avulsed soft tissue. The flap, in general, is very predictable; transfers muscle, fat, dermis, and epithelium; involves a straightforward technique; and has low morbidity.

The skin paddle is placed medial and inferior to the nipple of the ipsilateral chest wall over the distal origins of the pectoralis major muscle at the area of the fourth, fifth, and sixth ribs. The size and shape of the skin paddle should be made as to fit best into the recipient site defect. One must, therefore, first develop the recipient site defect before harvesting the tissue flap (Figs. 30–16 and 30–17). If a mucosal epithelial lining is required, as well as overlying skin cover, necessitating a split paddle technique, splitting the skin paddle should be deferred until it is transferred to the recipient site (Fig. 30–18). However, one must anticipate the split and design a widened skin paddle in the area of the anticipated split.

The most straightforward approach to harvest this flap is to begin with a gently curving, oblique chest incision from 4 cm inferior to the lateral one third of the clavicle across the chest to blend into the skin paddle inferior and medial to the nipple (Fig. 30–19). Skin and subcutaneous flaps are next developed to expose the entire pectoralis major muscle, with its muscle fascia remaining on the muscle. The surgeon

FIGURE 30–16. Facial preoperative view shows a severe skin cover and oral mucosal lining deficit with contraction. The lip is scarred down inferiorly, and the tongue is scarred anteriorly to produce lip incompetence and drooling in addition to an obvious deformity.

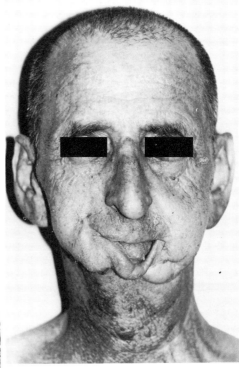

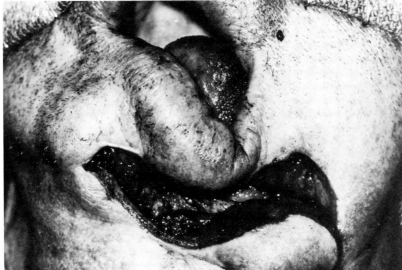

FIGURE 30–17. The recipient site of the patient in Figure 30–16 is developed first. Not until the lip is repositioned and the remaining tissues released can one determine the true size and shape of the skin paddle.

FIGURE 30–18. The patient in Figure 30–16 also required release of oral mucosal scars, unmasking a large mucosal lining deficit. A split skin paddle is required in such deficits.

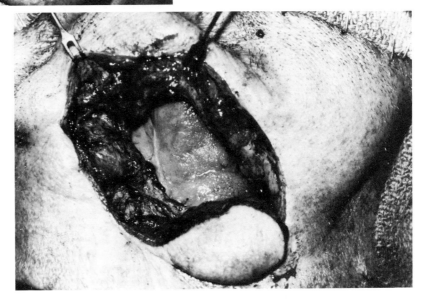

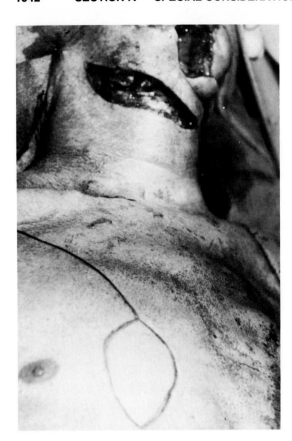

FIGURE 30–19. A widened skin paddle is outlined, anticipating a split. The most straightforward access is achieved by a sloping, oblique incision across the chest and into a skin paddle placed inferior and medial to the nipple.

can take advantage of the relatively avascular plane just superficial to the muscle fascia. As the dissection approaches the skin paddle, one must suture the skin paddle to the underlying muscle fascia to prevent retraction shearing of the delicate perforators arising from, and perpendicular to, the muscle surface, which supply the overlying skin (Fig. 30–20).

The muscle is elevated from its bony origins on the chest, which include the fourth, fifth, sixth, and sometimes seventh ribs, the lateral sternal border, and the clavicle. The muscle is also separated from the rectus fascia as it blends into the fascia at its most inferior extent. The electrocautery unit offers an advantage at this point in that the muscle will pull away from its bony attachment, helping to identify the plane between the muscle's deep surface and the intercostal muscles. Once the dissection elevates the muscle off its bony attachments, an avascular plane between the pectoralis major muscle's deep surface and the pectoralis minor will facilitate the dissection. The main arterial supply and venous drainage are visualized beneath the muscle's deep fascial covering (Fig. 30–21). The main inflow and outflow system is the thoracol-acromial artery and vein. In Ariyan's original description of this flap, and most other modifications, this has been the only vascular network preserved.[14,15] The surgical approach described here also preserves branches from the lateral thoracic artery and vein and from the superior thoracic artery and vein. The preservation of these two additional inflow and outflow systems provides a more assured transfer and allows for a portion of the skin paddle to extend beyond the pectoralis major muscle and, therefore, to be larger and able to reach more distant portions about the maxillofacial area. As the muscle is elevated from the chest wall, the remaining limitation to rotation toward the recipient site is the muscle's insertion on the humerus. This insertion is sharply dissected in its entirety so that the flap's arc of rotation is based on its vasculature as it emerges from the deep surface of the lateral aspect of the clavicle rather than on its insertion about the humerus. A center of rotation here will allow a skin paddle placement anywhere within the upper neck and oral cavity and onto the

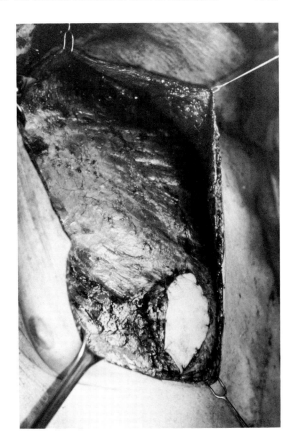

FIGURE 30–20. With skin subcutaneous chest wall flaps developed, the entire pectoralis major muscle is exposed. The skin paddle must be sutured to the muscle fascia, as shown, to prevent shearing of the delicate muscle-to-skin perforating vessels.

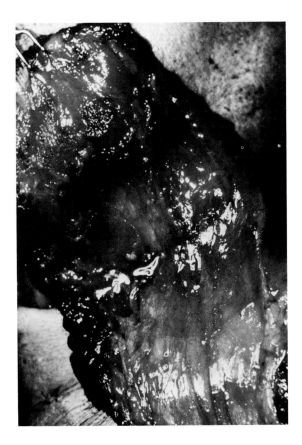

FIGURE 30–21. The main vascular supply of the flap is seen here, in the lower right corner, as a series of three arterial and venous complexes of the thoracoacromial vessels. To the left are branches of the lateral thoracic vessels.

external face as superior as the alar bases anteriorly and the zygomatic arch posteriorly.

The closure of the skin paddle and chest wound is as important as the elevation of the flap itself. If the skin paddle needs to be split to place one portion in the oral cavity and one portion on the external skin surface, it is incised through the full thickness of skin and dermis and into the subcutaneous fat layer to a depth of about 1 cm. The most distal portion of the skin paddle will usually advance into the oral cavity. Its dermis is closed to the oral submucosa, and its skin surface is closed to the mucosal surface. It is well advised to undermine both the skin paddle surface at the dermal level and the mucosal surface at the submucosal level for a distance of 2 to 3 mm for edge eversion. Such an endeavor will reduce invagination of the skin paddle to host-tissue interface, which often gives the skin paddle a "pillow-like" appearance (Figs. 30–22 to 30–24).

The chest is closed in a direct fashion in four layers: the deep subcutaneous layer, a superficial subcutaneous layer, a dermal layer, and a skin surface layer. Suction drains should be placed in both the chest and the neck wounds.

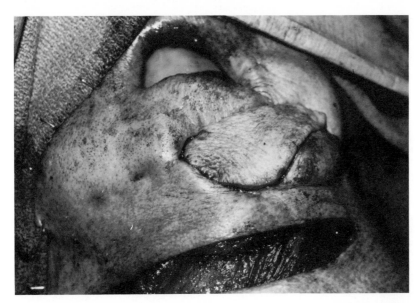

FIGURE 30–22. The muscle has been brought up to the recipient wound through a subplatysmal neck tunnel. The skin paddle here has been split and trimmed to an oral portion and an external chin portion. The muscle can be seen coursing through the neck via the horizontal neck incision, which may be used later to place a bone graft.

FIGURE 30–23. Skin paddle closure should be accomplished in at least two layers. The deep layers are intended to obliterate dead space, and the skin margin is everted as much as possible.

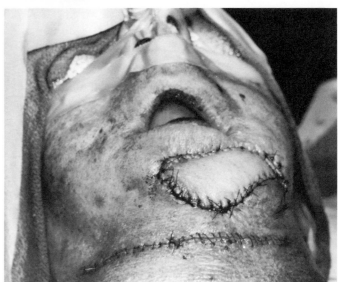

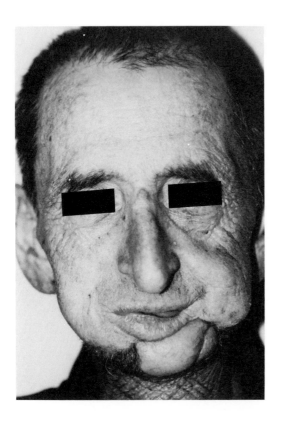

FIGURE 30–24. The healed skin paddles have provided a soft tissue chin and lip support, tongue release, and a quantity of vascular soft tissue into which a bone graft can be placed.

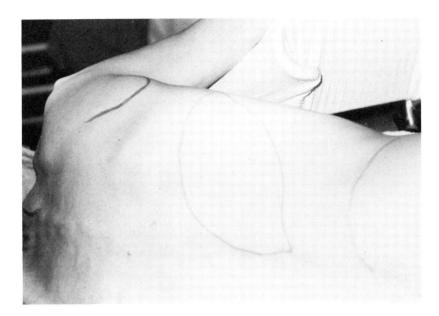

FIGURE 30-25. The latissimus dorsi myocutaneous flap is developed with the patient in a lateral decubitus position. A large skin paddle and broad muscle are obtainable with this flap.

The Latissimus Dorsi Myocutaneous Flap

The latissimus dorsi myocutaneous flap is reserved for the largest of soft tissue needs in the maxillofacial area. This muscle will transfer a broader muscle area and can be anticipated to deliver a larger skin paddle (up to 14 cm × 14 cm) than the pectoralis major myocutaneous flap. The single vascular supply is from the thoracodorsal artery and vein, which arise from the third division of the axillary artery in the axilla proper. Therefore, the flap requires a passage through the axilla to enter the upper lateral chest and lower neck.

The technique is not very different from the elevation of the pectoralis major muscle off the chest. In this case, however, the patient is positioned in a lateral decubitus position after the recipient tissues have been prepared. Another gently curving incision is made across the back from the area of the axilla to a para-midline skin paddle (Fig. 30-25). In a similar fashion to the pectoralis major myocutaneous flap, skin subcutaneous flaps are developed to expose the muscle and its investing fascia. The muscle is separated sharply through its lumbodorsal fascia attachments to

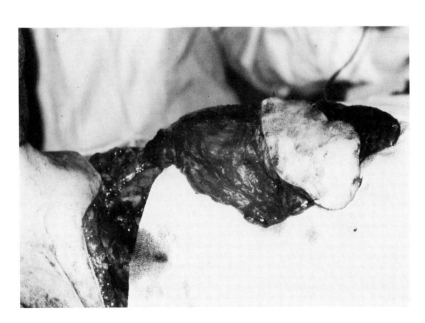

FIGURE 30-26. Skin paddle and muscle are seen here pedicled on the thoracodorsal vessels from the axillary vessels. This complex will be rotated through the axilla and into the neck.

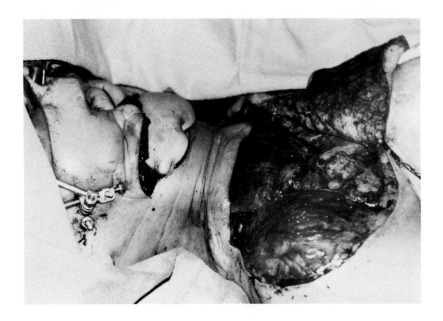

FIGURE 30-27. The latissimus dorsi muscle is seen here tunneled through the neck, and a very large skin paddle is placed bilaterally across the midline.

the posterior ilium and the dorsal spinal processes from T-4 through L-5 (Fig. 30-26). The muscle and its skin paddle are then passed through an axillary tunnel, and the muscle's tendinous insertion onto the humerus is separated for an enhanced rotation and advancement through the subplatysmal neck tunnel. As with the pectoralis major flap, the latissimus dorsi flap requires a wide neck tunnel and, in this case, a wide axillary tunnel (Figs. 30-27 and 30-28). Any restriction within the tunnel can lead to pressures within the tunnel in excess of venous pressure and can therefore limit the flap's outflow, causing congestion, stasis, and possible necrosis.

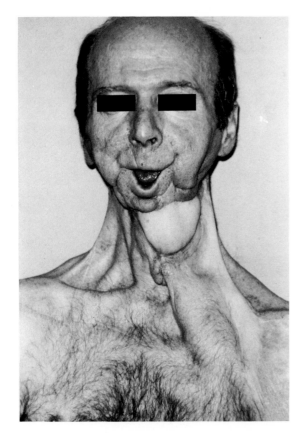

FIGURE 30-28. A latissimus dorsi myocutaneous flap healed into the upper neck area. Note the broad muscle band and large skin paddle, both of which may be further positioned to fill in residual deficiencies if required.

The Trapezius Flap

The trapezius myocutaneous flap is a soft tissue transfer that is employed more often in trauma-related deformities than in cancer-related deformities. The reason is that its vascular base arises from the transverse cervical artery at the root of the neck as part of the thyrocervical trunk. The course of the transverse cervical artery is low in the neck, deep to the sternocleidomastoid muscle at the level of the carotid sheath, and it lies upon the anterior scalene muscle. Its proximity to the carotid sheath near its origin causes it to be sacrificed in most cancer-related neck dissections, but it is often spared in an upper neck or maxillofacial injury (Fig. 30–29).

The course of the transverse cervical artery through the posterior triangle of the neck, supplying the trapezius muscle from its deep surface parallel to the midline of the back, allows for the flap to be based off its anterior-cephalad border. A skin paddle is usually developed between the midline of the back and the medial border of the scapula (Fig. 30–30). The length of the flap is determined by the cephalad-caudad dimension of the muscle, which, in a useful length, extends from about C6 to T9. In the dissection, the muscle with its overlying skin paddle is separated from underlying muscles caudad to cephalad: the upper origins of the latissimus dorsi, the rhomboid major, the rhomboid minor, and the levator scapulae (Figs. 30–31 and 30–32). The

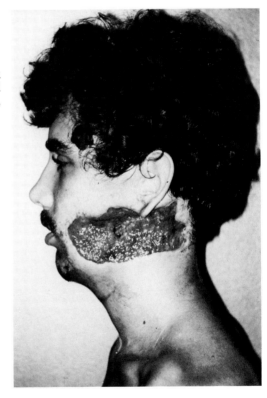

FIGURE 30–29. This type of gunshot wound defect is well suited for a trapezius myocutaneous flap. Injuries to the upper posterior neck and posterior lower facial one third usually spare the thyrocervical vessels, specifically the transverse cervical vessels.

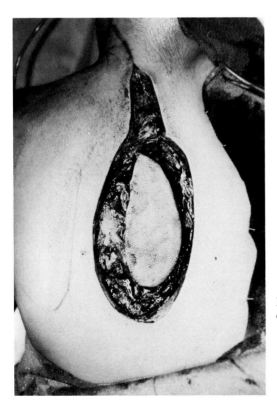

FIGURE 30–30. A skin paddle between the midline and the medial border of the scapula is prepared as part of a trapezius myocutaneous flap.

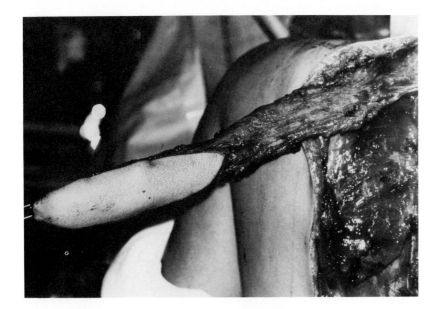

FIGURE 30–31. The trapezius muscle is separated from its deep relations and the midline attachments to the posterior processes of the C6–T9 vertebrae caudad to cephalad.

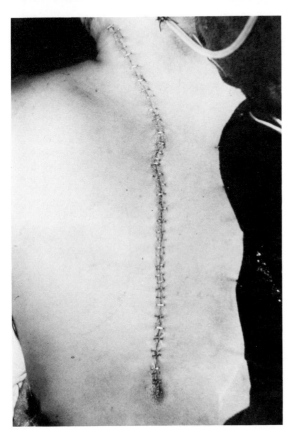

FIGURE 30–32. The donor site defect of a trapezius myocutaneous flap can be closed primarily after tissue undermining.

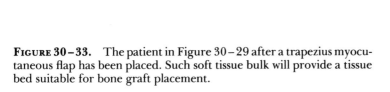

FIGURE 30–33. The patient in Figure 30–29 after a trapezius myocutaneous flap has been placed. Such soft tissue bulk will provide a tissue bed suitable for bone graft placement.

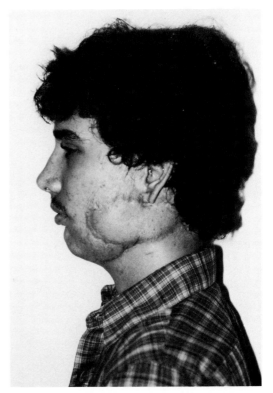

flap is tunneled through the posterior triangle of the neck, superficial to the sterno-cleidomastoid muscle and deep to the posterior edge of the platysma, if present.

The trapezius flap is an excellent choice for soft tissue losses within the posterior triangle of the neck, the area of the angle of the mandible, the preauricular area, and the lateral face and upper neck (Fig. 30–33). The flap's color match with the skin is usually slightly better than that of the pectoralis major myocutaneous flap. The flap has an excellent bulk and will extend to about the commissure as an axial pattern flap. Beyond the commissure, other flaps would be preferred, or the trapezius flap may be detached and reanastomosed as a free vascular transfer.

The Sternocleidomastoid Flap

The superior-based sternocleidomastoid flap can be a very useful locally available myocutaneous flap for defects from the ipsilateral commissure posterior to the angle area. The flap is best used for bulk and skin cover but may also be used for oral lining in the posterior oral cavity (Fig. 30–34). The main axial vessel is the occipital artery, with a branch from the superior thyroid also contributing to the axial flow. Smaller vessels from the inferior thyroid or thyrocervical trunk contribute to the muscle but are sacrificed in flap development and are not important to flap survival. The occipital vessel alone will carry the muscle and its overlying skin to the level of the muscle's bifurcation into sternal and clavicular heads. Longer flaps past this bifurcation, which includes skin in the clavicular and supraclavicular areas, have up to a 50 per cent incidence of distal tip necrosis if based on the occipital artery alone.[18] When such a longer sternocleidomastoid flap is required, the surgeon will need to dissect out and preserve the superior thyroid branch to the muscle. We thus refer to a "short" and a "long" sternocleidomastoid flap[19] (Fig. 30–35).

The dissection begins with incisions directly over the anterior and posterior border of the muscle, thus outlining a skin paddle obliquely oriented in the neck (Fig. 30–36). As with all other myocutaneous flaps, the skin paddle should be sutured

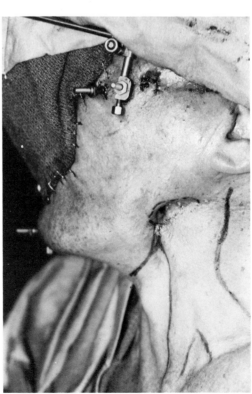

FIGURE 30–34. A residual orocutaneous fistula and soft tissue defect in the angle region such as this is well suited for a superiorly based sterno-cleidomastoid myocutaneous flap.

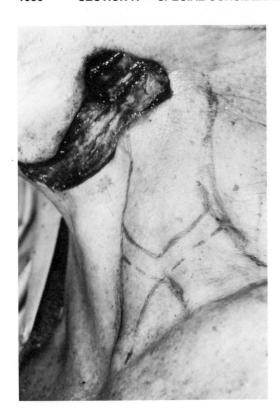

FIGURE 30–35. A "short" sternocleidomastoid flap is outlined here for placement into the prepared soft tissue defect.

down to the muscle. The muscle is separated from its deep tissues, which are the supraclavicular fat pad and the carotid sheath, beginning at the sternal head. The sternal attachment is tendinous, but the clavicular attachment is muscular. If the sternal head is detached and a traction suture is placed, dissection deep to the muscle is facilitated, and the more broadly attached clavicular head is more easily separated.

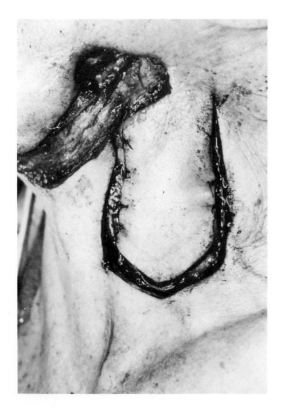

FIGURE 30–36. The sternocleidomastoid myocutaneous flap is developed with either a skin island paddle or a full length of overlying skin. As with all other myocutaneous flaps, the skin paddle must be sutured to the muscle edges.

The muscle fascia on the deep surface of the sternocleidomastoid muscle allows it to separate readily from the carotid sheath. The two most important anatomic structures to be alert for are the superior thyroid branch into the muscle, which enters its deep anterior surface at the carotid sinus level, and the accessory nerve to the muscle itself, as well as to the trapezius, as it exits the muscle's midposterior border at the hyoid level. Contrary to the belief of some surgeons, the accessory nerve does not course deep to the sternocleidomastoid muscle; rather, it courses through it, placing it within the dissection of this flap. The knowledge of its location is important not only in the placement of the sternocleidomastoid flap itself but also for subsequent bone graft placement at a later date. Loss of trapezius function by injury to this nerve will cause a postural shoulder droop, a laterally positioned scapula, and a limited voluntary shoulder elevation.

The flap is rotated into place in what is usually a rotation arc of small degree. The donor site can be closed primarily with an undermining dissection into both the anterior and the posterior triangles of the neck. The flap's main advantages include local availability, good predictability, and the best color match of any flap is used for external skin cover. The limitations of this flap are its size and length. It is useful for only small defects and for those in the upper neck and mandible posterior to the commissure and below the alartragal line (Fig. 30–37).

The Walk-up Flap

The walk-up flap is a recently introduced flap of muscle that uses the unused proximal two thirds of a previously placed myocutaneous flap.[33] Reconstructive surgeons have often found residual soft tissue deficiencies or the need for greater tissue bulk at some time after placement of a myocutaneous flap (Figs. 30–38 and 30–39). Walking up the remainder of the myocutaneous flap can often supply this need and thus avert a second myocutaneous flap.

The principle underlying this flap is the anastomosis of host tissue capillaries with

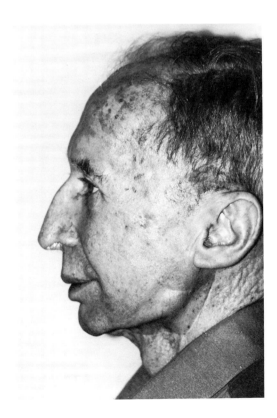

FIGURE 30–37. The healed sternocleidomastoid myocutaneous flap has closed the orocutaneous fistula, has provided soft tissue bulk, and has a very good color match.

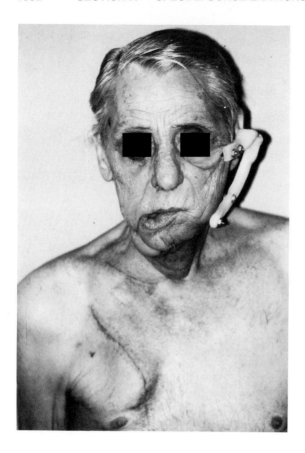

FIGURE 30–38.   A residual soft tissue deficit may persist after a myocutaneous flap. As seen here, a cutaneous and mucosal deficiency remains, causing lip retraction and an insufficient tissue volume into which a bone graft can be placed.

the capillaries of the distal one third of the skin paddle of the original myocutaneous flap. After a myocutaneous flap has been in place for 6 weeks or more, sufficient distal one-third capillary anastomosis with host vessels has occurred to make it possible to transect and ligate the main axial vessels without altering the muscle's viability. Therefore, the proximal two thirds of the original muscle can be detached from its

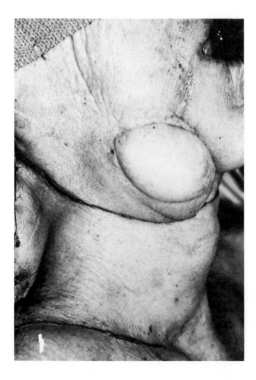

FIGURE 30–39.   A "walk-up" flap of a pectoralis major flap is often approached by using parallel horizontal neck incisions—one in the submandibular region and the other in the clavicular region. The submandibular access will permit development of the recipient tissue, the clavicular access will permit access to the muscle's proximal end, and a subplatysmal tunnel is developed between them.

axial vessels and its tissue bed and can be rotated into another position based on the multitude of small vessels ingrown at its distal one third. The flap is, therefore, changed from an axial pattern flap to a random pattern flap, and the base of the flap is switched to its opposite end.

The biologic concept of walking up a flap is not new. Skin subcutaneous flaps, such as the deltopectoral (Bakamjian flap), and the abdominal flap have historically been tubed and walked up in stages to their desired position in the maxillofacial area.[12,33] However, walking up a muscle is new, since skepticism existed regarding its feasibility because of the inability to tube conveniently an internally placed myocutaneous flap. Since the tubing of an external skin subcutaneous flap places all the perfusion demands on its proximal and distal ends, each responds by increasing its vascular network. The vascular network of the distal end increases over a 6-week period to the point of being capable of maintaining the entire tube if the proximal end is transected. An internally placed myocutaneous flap was originally thought to heal into its recipient tissue bed and develop anastomosing vessels throughout its length; however, it has now been shown that the muscle fascia about the midportion of the muscles used in myocutaneous flaps prevents vascular ingrowth and therefore acts as a tubed flap in and of itself.[33] Since the distal one third of muscles used for myocutaneous flaps is taken from bony attachment areas, there is no fascia about them. This fact further defines the internal tubing principle by allowing reanastomosis to occur at the cut end only and therefore places the greatest perfusion demands on the distal one third.

The most commonly used walk-up flap is one walked up from a previously placed pectoralis major myocutaneous flap. The proximal end is exposed, and its axial vessels are ligated. The remainder of the dissection in the neck frees the muscle from loosely attached tissue throughout its length until the distal one third is reached (Fig. 30–40). At this point, the muscle and subcutaneous tissues of the skin paddle will be more firmly adherent to the tissue bed. If a fluorescein test (1000 mg of sodium fluorescein is given intravenously over 30 seconds, and then the tissue is examined with a Wood light of 5480 Å ultraviolet wavelength in a darkened room) is done, one can see a fill

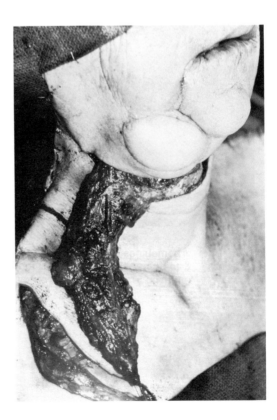

FIGURE 30–40. The pectoralis muscle here has been divided from its proximal axial vessels. It is then dependent on its distal random vessels through its remaining skin paddle area attachments.

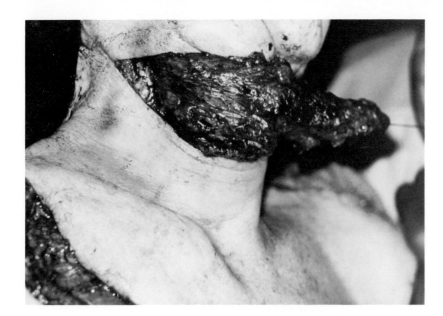

FIGURE 30–41. The "walk-up" flap here is rotated into a position to provide tissue bulk and to obliterate dead space.

of small vessels throughout the muscle, even at its cut original proximal end. The muscle is then rotated into its desired position and sutured into place with many small sutures, which mainly pass through muscle fascia, rather than muscle proper, as sutured muscle will necrose about the suture (Fig. 30–41).

This flap has shown nearly complete viable transfer. It is another very predictable flap the reconstructive surgeon may need to use. It is excellent for adding tissue bulk and contour, as well as for filling in dead space areas. Since the skin overlying it is not in the vascular territory of the muscle, it cannot be used as a strictly defined myocutaneous flap. However, it can be used to increase the epithelialized surface area of skin or mucosa by skin grafting the muscle's surface (Figs. 30–42 and 30–43). Skin and dermal grafts heal readily to the richly vascular muscle surface (Fig. 30–44).

The Cervical Flap

Random-pattern composites of skin and platysma muscle with a variety of designs are, as a group, termed cervical flaps. Such cervical flaps find their best usage in filling

FIGURE 30–42. The viable muscle of a "walk-up" flap may be brought into the oral cavity and skin may be grafted to increase the epithelialized mucosal surface as well as the tissue bulk.

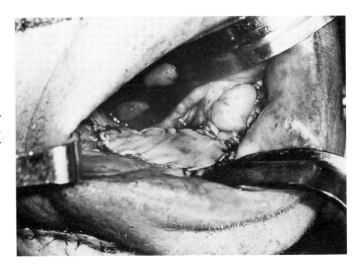

FIGURE 30–43. A split-thickness skin graft can be sutured directly to the muscle surface of a "walk-up" flap. The rich vascularity of the muscle will provide an excellent recipient tissue for a skin graft.

out and covering areas of shallow cutaneous loss and in gaining closure of the "tight neck" at the time of bone graft placement.

The Skin-Platysma Rotation Flap

Most cervical flaps are random-pattern single-pedicled rotation flaps. The base of these flaps may be derived from any point anterior, posterior, superior, or inferior to the defect (Fig. 30–45). The rich anastomotic network of the skin platysma complex allows such a positional choice. The base should be as wide as possible, and the ratio of length to base width should not exceed 3 : 1. The flap is developed with a tip design that geometrically fits into the defect area and is in a position beyond the defect as it relates to the base of the flap (Fig. 30–46). The reason for the added length of the flap is to gain an inverted closure of the flap margin to the defect and to ensure a closure without tension. Although the vascular supply to these flaps is excellent and their thickness is the same as that of adjacent tissue, their contraction vector is greatest in the long axis of the flap. A slightly added length will reduce the tendency for

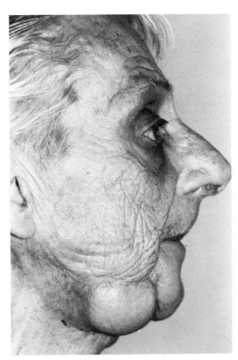

FIGURE 30–44. The additional tissue bulk and lip reposition are apparent after this patient's "walk-up" flap.

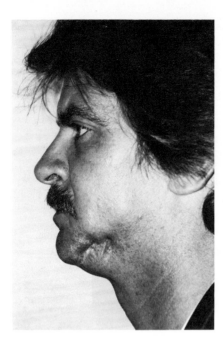

FIGURE 30–45.   Soft tissue deficits of skin and subcutaneous thickness such as this may be corrected by a local cervical rotation flap.

FIGURE 30–46.   In the situation shown in Figure 30–45, a skin-platysma rotation flap of similar thickness may be outlined that will geometrically fit into the tissue defect and provide an incision design that may be used later for bone graft placement.

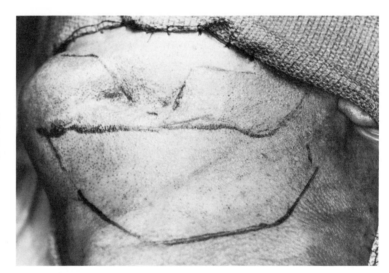

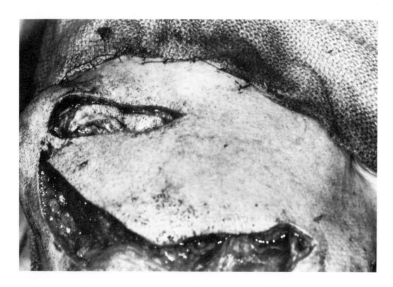

FIGURE 30–47.   Excision of the scar tissue within the defect area should precede the full development and tip design of the local cervical flap.

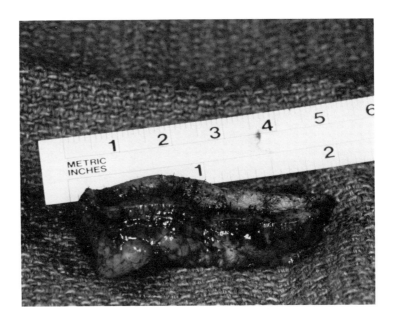

FIGURE 30–48.   The excised scar and its adjacent tissue should be assessed for thickness and identification of anatomic layers. Here the excised edges are skin, dermis, and the full thickness of subcutaneous fat.

dehiscence or a traction-induced, broad scar. Because the flap tip needs to fit into the defect geometrically, as a puzzle piece would, the defect preparation and tissue release should be accomplished before the flap is designed (Fig. 30–47). The flap itself is incised at right angles through the skin and platysma. It is developed and separated off the superficial layer of the deep cervical fascia. Its closure into the defect, as well as the donor site closure, should correspondingly be into the same layers: platysma, subcutaneous fat, dermis, and skin surface (Fig. 30–48). It is advisable to undermine the skin-dermis layer of both the flap and the recipient tissues to assist in an everted closure (Figs. 30–49 to 30–51). If one fails to do so, a sharply indented junction line will occur at the flap–host tissue margin, giving the flap a "pillow effect."

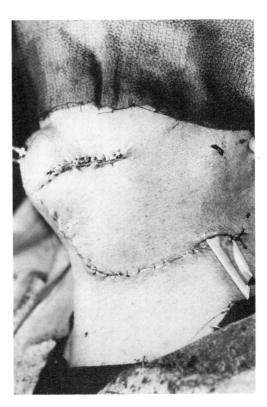

FIGURE 30–49.   Closure of the local cervical flap into the defect with a good geometric fit, creating an evenness of skin thickness in the area.

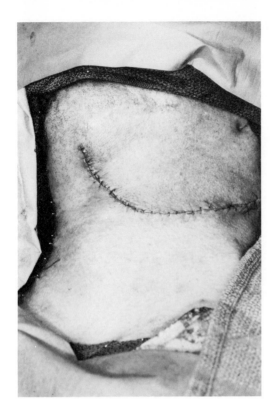

FIGURE 30–50.   The same patient returned for a bone graft 4 months later. The same incision was used to place the bone graft, and the original defect remains corrected, with a minimal scar and a maintenance of tissue thickness.

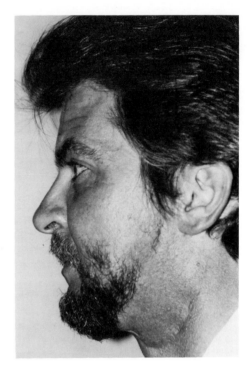

FIGURE 30–51.   The patient's final result shows good facial balance and new hair growth, with the same beard density and color, owing to the use of a local flap with identical color and hair-bearing quality.

The Bipedicled Flap

A special type of cervical flap that is used for some shallow upper neck tissue losses, and more often to gain closure of a "tight neck" during a bone graft placement, is the bipedicled flap. The bipedicled flap is also a skin-platysma complex flap, but one that has continuity with each posterior triangle of the neck. The flap is developed from two parallel incisions in the neck. The upper incision is usually about 3 cm inferior to and parallel to the inferior border of the mandible. The lower incision is at the clavicular level or within the supraclavicular area. Once both incisions are made, the tissue is dissected in the subplatysmal plane to connect each (Fig. 30–52). The flap is then advanced in the superior direction (Fig. 30–53). The clavicular area incision allows a tension-free closure of the "tight neck" in the upper neck area. The tension is, therefore, transferred to the lower neck (clavicular) incision, which may be closed primarily by undermining onto the superficial chest wall or, as is most commonly done, closed by the use of a split-thickness skin graft cover (Figs. 30–54 to 30–56).

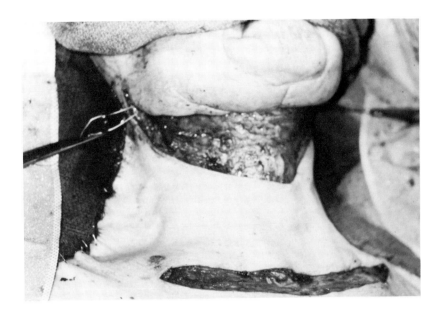

FIGURE 30–52.   The bipedicled neck flap is a skin-platysma composite based on a random vascular pattern from each posterior triangle.

The U-Y Advancement Flap

Another type of cervical flap used almost exclusively in the closure of the "tight neck" during bone graft placement is the **U-Y** closure flap. This is more of a closure technique than a true flap, but it uses the same basic skin-platysma complex of tissues to gain closure. Whereas the bipedicled flap is more useful in the full mandibular bone reconstructions that cross the midline, the **U-Y** closure is employed for the hemimandibular reconstruction closures. One can plan for the option of using a **U-Y** closure approach, if needed, by making a **U**-shaped neck incision for graft bed preparation.

Such an incision approaches to within 1 cm of the mandible, 3 cm from each residual bone end, and slopes lower in the neck to a position 5 cm inferior to the mandible's projected position at the center. During closure, the greatest tension will be at the incision's center point. The tissues are undermined in the neck in the subplatysmal plane to the level of the clavicle. The closure proceeds with the inferior margin closed in an oblique manner, slightly toward the center point of the superior margin. This step creates a vertical leg in the inferior flap at the center of the incision.

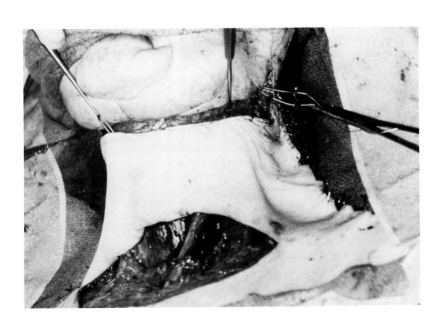

FIGURE 30–53.   The bipedicled flap is advanced superiorly to close a "tight neck" and reduce the tension on the submandibular closure.

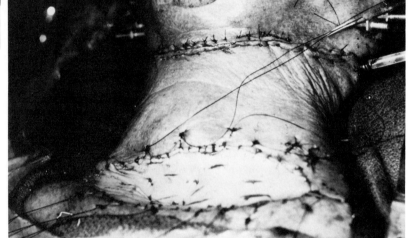

FIGURE 30–54. The bipedicled flap shifts wound tension or the wound to the supraclavicular area.

FIGURE 30–55. A split-thickness skin graft is often used to cover the supraclavicular wound.

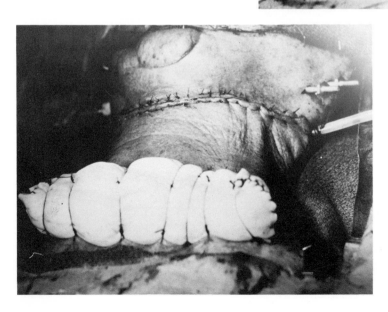

FIGURE 30–56. Split-thickness skin grafts in this area are best adapted to the wound bed with an overlying pressure dressing.

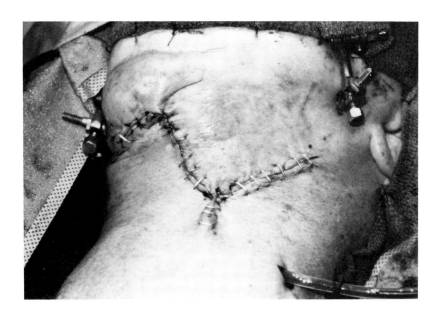

FIGURE 30–57.   A U-Y closure flap is used to close the "tight neck" in a hemimandibular reconstruction.

The vertical leg is closed straight across to create a short-stemmed Y appearance from the original U-shaped incision (Fig. 30–57). Much of the vertical tension within the center of the closure is, therefore, reduced and transferred more evenly throughout the neck.

TECHNIQUE APPROACHES—BONE HARVEST AND TRANSPLANT

Bone Harvest

The essence of successful bone grafting is the viable transplantation of osteocompetent cells. The osteocompetent cells must be in sufficient numbers, and the recipient tissue bed must be sufficiently cellular and vascular, to develop and maintain a self-remodeling bone ossicle.

Numerous articles have described techniques of harvesting bone from ribs, calvaria, anterior ilium, and posterior ilium. Some publications have suggested that calvarial bone is to be preferred because of a claimed resistance to resorption.[34] However, this claim is unproved by any controlled study, and such bone has shown no difference when used as a particulate bone and cancellous marrow graft. However, used as an onlay bone graft, calvarial cortical-cancellous blocks have shown less resorption owing to their more rapid revascularization of a thinner and more cellular cortex.[35]

We have seen no real difference in the osteogenic potential of osteocompetent cells from any of the popular donor sites. The difference in bone ossicle–forming capability seems to reside more in the cellular density and cancellous volume in donor sites than in any perceived advantage related to embryologic derivation, such as "ectomesenchymal bone." Therefore, because of their low cancellous to cortical bone ratio, ribs have historically been a poor bone graft material other than their use as a costochondral graft for joint reconstruction. Calvarial bone harvested between the inner and outer skull tables has a somewhat better cancellous to cortical bone ratio than a rib but usually lacks the volume required of large maxillofacial defects. We therefore reserve calvarial bone for smaller continuity defects (<3 cm) and contour onlay grafts. The ilium, in general, has the greatest concentration of osteocompetent cells and the greatest available volume. The anterior ilium is the preferred donor site for continuity defects of 5 cm or less (i.e., requiring ≤50 cc of cancellous bone). The posterior ilium is the preferred donor site for large bone grafts of greater than 5 cm of continuity defect (i.e., requiring ≥50 cc of cancellous bone).

RIB HARVEST

The best indication for a rib harvest is a costochondral graft intended to restore a rotational type of pseudoarticulation of the temporomandibular joint. In children and adolescents younger than 16, a costochondral graft will exhibit growth via a growth plate–like phenomenon at the bone-cartilage junction. In adults, there is, of course, no growth potential. However, the value of the costochondral graft in an adult remains and resides in its geometric fit into the temporal fossa, its ability to restore the vertical dimension of the ramus, and its ability to form a firm union with the remaining mandible, while not forming a bony ankylosis to the base of the skull. Other graft systems, such as alloplastic trays with alloplastic condyles, allogeneic bone trays of mandible with a hollowed condyle, or an allogeneic ilium segment with a condylar extension, may also be used to reconstruct a functional articulation.

The fifth or sixth rib of either side is preferred. In this harvest, the incision is placed in the inframammary crease, which best hides the scar later (Fig. 30–58). We prefer the right side slightly more than the left, because either side of the rib may be contoured to fit either side of the mandible or facial bones and because postoperative discomfort is less likely to be confused with cardiogenic pain. The inframammary incision usually guides the surgeon to the sixth rib, which is the distalmost rib origin of the pectoralis major muscle. The dissection will, therefore, transect muscle minimally and not affect the future harvest of a pectoralis major myocutaneous flap. The sharp dissection is carried through the full thickness of skin, subcutaneous tissues, and the pectoralis major origins to expose the rib periosteum of what is termed the chest wall cortex (Fig. 30–59). The periosteum should be incised from 1 cm onto the rib cartilage to the full length of rib desired, which is usually to the anterior border of the latissimus dorsi muscle and equates to about 12 cm. The periosteum is reflected carefully from the chest wall cortex around the inferior and superior rib edges to the pleural cortex periosteum. It is advisable to use the common oral and maxillofacial periosteal elevators or molt curettes, rather than the thoracic Doyen rib strippers and elevators (Fig. 30–60). The reason is that ribs have irregularities and bony projections on their pleural cortex, which cause the periosteum and lung pleura to attach tenaciously to each other. The motion of such rib strippers causes them to ride over these small bony projections, catching a small bite of periosteum and pleura in the instrument and thus creating a pleural tear that leads to a pneumothorax. The periosteal reflection of oral and maxillofacial elevators is better able to separate the intact periosteum in these areas. Assistance in reflecting the perichondrium off the cartilage is gained by a releasing incision made at right angles to the midrib incision

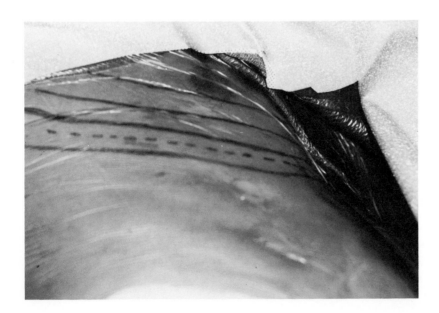

FIGURE 30–58.   Rib harvest incisions are best placed within the inframammary crease in either men or women.

FIGURE 30–59. The dissection to expose the chest wall rib cortex can be guided by placing fingers in the intercostal spaces on each side of the rib and sharply dissecting to the midportion of the rib's cortex.

and carried to each rib edge. This procedure forms a **T** shape in the incision and allows greater access to the rib cartilage area. The rib is separated from the thoracic cage by first cutting through the cartilage with a scalpel blade (Fig. 30–61). This procedure is facilitated by lifting the rib slightly to tense the tissue during transection. Once the rib cartilage is separated, further lifting of the rib will identify any residual periosteal adherence to the pleural cortex. The proximal surface of the rib is cut with a saw or a rib cutter, with the rib lifted once again (Fig. 30–62). The closure is a straightforward layered closure of periosteum, subcutaneous tissues, dermis, and skin surface. A drain is usually not necessary (Fig. 30–63).

Two of the most misunderstood aspects of costochondral grafts are what length of cartilage to include and whether or not to take perichondrium or periosteum as part of the graft. The length of cartilage is not related to the growth of a costochondral graft or to the prevention of bony ankylosis. In a similar fashion, the perichondrium or periosteum does not enhance the growth, survival, or incorporation of a costochondral graft. In a child, the cartilage is easily separated from bone. In an adult, the cartilage is firmly incorporated into the bone. Some have therefore suggested that a perichondrial-periosteal sleeve will reduce the chance of separating the cartilage

FIGURE 30–60. Oral and maxillofacial surgical periosteal elevators are the best instruments to reflect periosteum from a rib without entering the pleural space. They are able to negotiate bone irregularities and pleural-periosteal adhesions without tearing.

FIGURE 30–61. In both adults and children, costochondral grafts require harvest of only a 2- to 3-mm length of cartilage. The cartilage may be separated with a blade.

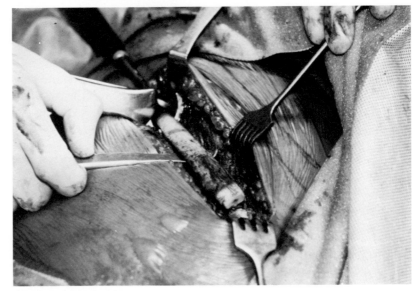

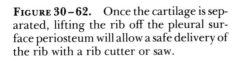

FIGURE 30–62. Once the cartilage is separated, lifting the rib off the pleural surface periosteum will allow a safe delivery of the rib with a rib cutter or saw.

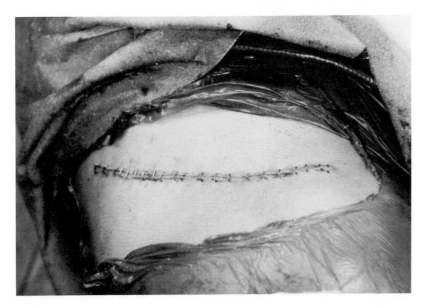

FIGURE 30–63. Closure of the chest is accomplished in anatomic layers. A drain is not usually required.

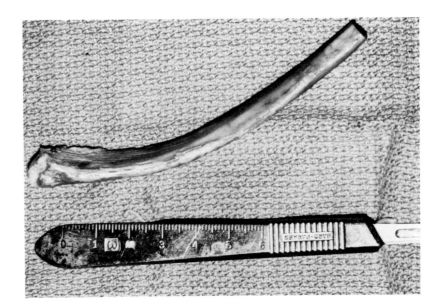

FIGURE 30-64. The rib harvest can extend 10 to 14 cm in length. No periosteum or perichondrium is required, and a 2-ml cap of cartilage is sufficient in all cases and will reduce the probability of cartilage-bone separation in children.

from the bone. Indeed, it does, but it also increases greatly the probability of producing a pneumothorax. The gain when this perichondrial-periosteal sleeve is included must be weighed against the impact of a pneumothorax occurring in a situation in which such a sleeve adds nothing to the graft itself. Another way to reduce the potential of separating the cartilage from the bone is to harvest only a small length of cartilage, 2 to 3 mm. Longer lengths of cartilage not only are unnecessary but also create a long lever arm, which promotes cartilage separation, especially in children. In the adult, even longer cartilage lengths will not separate the cartilage from the bone, but such lengths are superfluous. We therefore recommend a 2- to 3-mm cartilage length without adherent periosteum or periochondrium for both costochondral growth grafts in children and articulation grafts in adults (Fig. 30-64).

CALVARIAL BONE HARVEST

The two biggest advantages of calvarial bone are that one can gain a harvest without risking a functional disturbance of the thorax or an extremity and that one can usually have a completely hidden scar.[35] A transverse incision is made over the parietal bone usually from just behind the helix of one ear to just behind the helix of the opposite ear. The incision is carried down through the five layers of the scalp, with Raney clips added to control hemorrhage as the dissection progresses. Once the skull's outer table is reached, periosteum is reflected for a distance appropriate to the amount of bone required. A bur can be used to create long rectangles or 2 cm × 2 cm grid squares in the outer table. Bone is harvested with a curved osteotome, cleaving the outer table rectangles or grid squares (Fig. 30-65). Once the outer table is removed, along with adherent cancellous bone, the remaining cancellous bone can be curetted from the inner table (Fig. 30-66). Additional cancellous bone may also be curetted from between the two tables both anteriorly and posteriorly if a small curette is used. The closure is another straightforward layered closure. A drain is usually not required if good hemostasis is accomplished prior to closure.

BONE HARVEST FROM THE ANTERIOR ILIUM

There are so many different approaches to harvesting bone from the anterior ilium that a discussion of each is precluded. However, a review of the basic approach to the anterior ilium and its anatomic principles is appropriate.

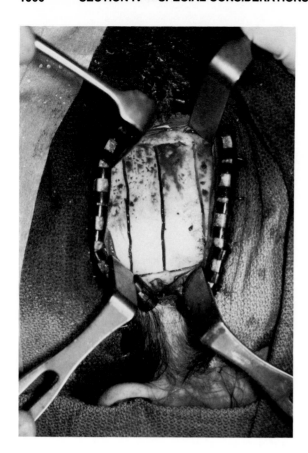

FIGURE 30–66.   Intercortical cancellous bone access gained after removal of outer table in squares.

FIGURE 30–65.   Exposure of the parietal bone of the skull, with grooves placed so that an osteotome can be used to lift the outer table as a graft and also gain access to the intercortical cancellous bone.

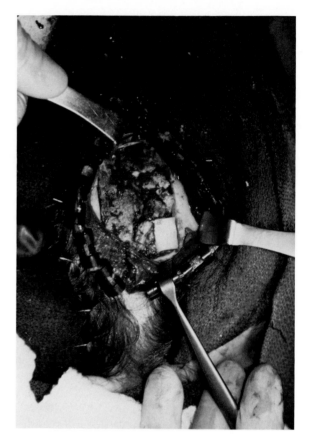

The goal in harvesting bone from the ilium is to obtain as much quality cancellous bone as possible with the least blood loss and with the least effect on the muscles used in walking. The two most important relationships related to blood loss from ilium bone harvest are the position of the patient and the length of time the ilium is open. The two most important anatomic structures related to a temporary or a permanent gait disturbance are the tensor fasciae latae muscle and the psoas major muscle. Since both muscles function in raising the leg at the hip joint, inflammation, injury, or scarring in either of these two muscles will affect normal gait. The lateral approach to the anterior ilium will, therefore, affect gait the most, as the tensor fasciae latae muscle is reflected from the external lip of the anterior ilium. In addition, the tensor fasciae latae muscle is overlaid and adherent to the inelastic tensor fasciae latae sheath, which hampers closing the muscle back to its original insertion level, predisposing to more long-term gait disturbances. Therefore, lateral anterior approaches that do not reflect the tensor fasciae latae muscle insertion, as well as the other lateral cortex muscle attachments, are preferred.

The medial anterior approach affects gait much less, as the large iliacus muscle, which is reflected in this approach, is not a muscle necessary to normal gait. However, a large medial hematoma or excessive trauma during bone harvest that causes psoas muscle inflammation or dysfunction will produce a gait disturbance.

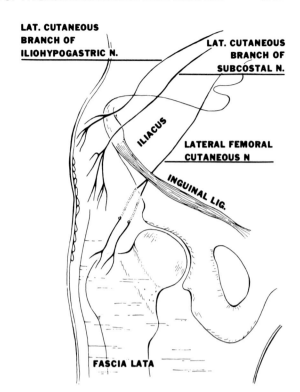

FIGURE 30–67. Relationship of cutaneous nerves to the anterior ilium. Depicted here is a right anterior ilium with relationships seen in about 86 per cent of studied cadaver specimens.

Also germane to the anterior approach to the ilium is the position of sensory nerve trunks. Fortunately, no motor nerves are within the usual surgical fields. The sensory nerve most commonly affected is the lateral branch of the iliohypogastric nerve, which is a dorsal sensory branch of L1. Its course traverses the bony iliac crest in a medial to lateral direction at the tubercle of the ilium, which is in the direct incisional area of the anterior ilium approach because of the cancellous bone available within the tubercle (Fig. 30–67). Injuring this nerve will produce a cutaneous paresthesia or anesthesia over the lateral aspect of the anterior one third of the ilium.

Another nerve that may be affected is the lateral branch of the subcostal nerve, which is a dorsal sensory branch of T12. Its course traverses the bony iliac crest in a medial to lateral direction at the anterior superior spine (Fig. 30–67). Damage to this nerve will produce a cutaneous paresthesia or anesthesia immediately below and slightly lateral to the anterior spine. A third nerve that is rarely affected, but one that has received much attention, is the lateral femoral cutaneous nerve. This nerve is a sensory nerve that separates from the femoral nerve proper and courses through the pelvis upon the medial aspect of the iliacus and upon the lateral aspect of the psoas major (Fig. 30–67). It emerges from the pelvis deep to the inguinal ligament in 86 per cent of people and pierces the tensor fasciae latae laterally to innervate the skin over the lower two thirds of the lateral aspect of the leg.[36] In 12 per cent of people, this nerve courses through the inguinal ligament, which can cause an age-related compression and, therefore, paresthesia called "meralgia paresthetica" (Fig. 30–68). In about 2 per cent of people, this nerve will course over the anterior superior spine and will parallel the lateral branch of the subcostal nerve.[36] This nerve is rarely affected in most anterior ilium harvests because its course is not in the direct path of the surgical approach, except in the 2 per cent of people in whom it courses over the anterior superior iliac spine (Fig. 30–69). However, a medial hematoma can compress the nerve between the iliacus and the psoas major, creating a short-term paresthesia or even an ischemia-related long-term paresthesia.

In consideration of the aforementioned anatomy, the incision should begin 1 cm posterior to the anterior superior spine and should extend to the tubercle of the ilium. It is also advisable to place the skin incision lateral to the bony prominence of the ilium, as incisions directly over the bony prominence will sometimes be irritated by

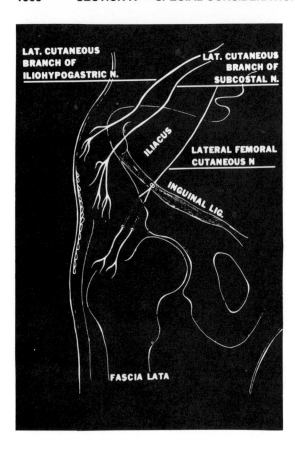

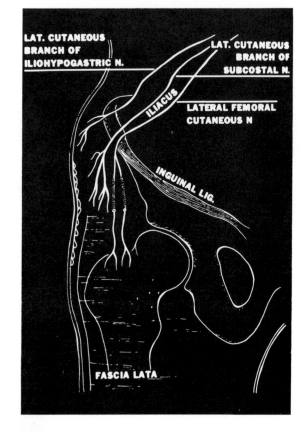

FIGURE 30–68.   Anatomic variation in which the lateral femoral cutaneous nerve courses through the inguinal ligament, observed in 12 per cent of studied cadaver specimens.

FIGURE 30–69.   Anatomic variation in which the lateral femoral cutaneous nerve courses over the edge of the anterior superior iliac spine.

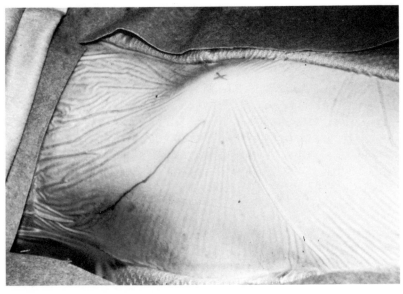

FIGURE 30–70.   The preferred incisional approach to the anterior ilium should be below the crestal height and should end at least 1 cm short of the anterior superior spine.

FIGURE 30–71. An anterior medial approach, seen here, should leave all the periosteum attached to the opposite cortex to avoid avascular necrosis and at least one third of the crest thickness to avoid an irregular hip deformity.

tight-fitting clothes or belts (Fig. 30–70). The incision down to bone need not progress through any muscle. It may be directed medial to the tensor fasciae latae muscle and the gluteus medius and lateral to the iliacus and most of the external abdominal oblique. In the area of the tubercle, fibers of the external abdominal oblique muscle will often extend over the crest and insert into the external lip of the crest with gluteus medius fibers and, therefore, will require some elevation. Once the anterior crest is identified from the tubercle to the anterior superior spine, one may use any of the vast number of osteotomies or ostectomies to harvest bone (Fig. 30–71). However, one should remember that the available cancellous bone in the anterior ilium lies within the upper 2 to 3 cm of the ilium — hence the old term of "iliac crest grafts" — and between the tubercle and the anterior superior spine (Fig. 30–72). Posterior to the tubercle and more than 3 cm inferior to the crest and anterior to the tubercle, little, if

FIGURE 30–72. Cross-sections through the posterior and anterior portions of the ilium. The posterior ilium has a greater reservoir of bone because of a continued thickness between medial and lateral cortices. The anterior ilium's reservoir of cancellous bone is limited to the crestal 2 cm.

any, cancellous bone is available as the medial and lateral cortices draw close together (Fig. 30 – 72). Some of the more common osteotomies used for anterior ilium harvests are, among others, a midcrestal split, or "clam shell"; a medial or lateral pedicled cortical osteotomy, or "trap door"; a crestal pedicled osteotomy, Tschopp approach; or a medial and lateral oblique crestal osteotomy, the Tessier approach.[37] During closure, the surgeon should pay strict attention to reorienting and repositioning muscle attachments in their original positions, if possible. A drain is often required owing to the dead space created by the bone harvest. Small harvests with minimal dead space and good hemorrhage control may not require a drain. Such drains are best placed within the bony cavity, rather than within the soft tissue, as this is where the dead space exists and where postoperative oozing occurs. However, high suction pressures can aspirate bleeding from a closed bony cavity. The vacuum pressures should be via either bulb suction or intermittent low wall suction.

BONE HARVEST FROM THE POSTERIOR ILIUM

The limitation of the anterior ilium approach is the availability of cancellous bone. Most adults will be able to yield only about 50 cc of uncompressed cancellous bone from an anterior ilium harvest. Although slightly more may be obtained, it is done so at a cost of much greater muscle reflection, bone excision, and harvest time, significantly increasing morbidity and blood loss. Therefore, in grafts requiring more than 50 cc of uncompressed cancellous bone, a posterior ilium approach is preferred. In the same person, there is twice as much cancellous bone available in the posterior ilium as in the anterior ilium.[38] The reason is that the thickness of the posterior iliac crest between the medial and lateral cortex continues inferiorly for the full length of the ilium to the sciatic notch. It does not end 2 to 3 cm below the crest, as it does in the anterior ilium (Fig. 30 – 72). For bone graft requirements of 50 cc or greater, the posterior approach has been shown to yield more cancellous bone with much less blood loss, little or no gait disturbance, less pain, and much less morbidity than does an anterior approach.

The key to the reduced blood loss of the posterior ilium approach is the patient's position (Fig. 30 – 73). The position is prone with axillary and upper chest support. A hip support should be placed under the bony pelvis and should not be extended onto the abdomen. This support, together with placing the operating table in a 160-degree reverse flex position, should elevate the buttocks and posterior ilium. Such positioning reduces the venous pressure within the ilium and thus significantly reduces the

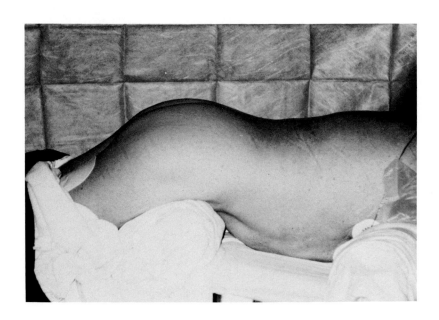

FIGURE 30–73. Patient's positioning for a posterior ilium harvest is prone, with a hip roll placed over the pubic region and two chest rolls placed above the breasts and supporting the axillae; the table is placed in a 160-degree reverse flex position.

oozing type of blood loss during bone harvest. The Wilson frame or lithotomy frames may achieve the same positioning but are not required.

The key to the reduced pain and morbidity of the posterior ilium approach lies in the regional anatomy. The posterior approach is a strictly lateral approach because of the sacroiliac articulation. However, the lateral musculature is mainly the insertion of the gluteus maximus and the posterior portion of the gluteus medius, which are muscles not directly involved in normal gate. Therefore, gait disturbance is minimal. The largest reservoir of cancellous bone lies beneath the gluteus maximus insertion and adjacent to the sacroiliac articulation. There is sufficient bone available there without extending the bone excision or reflecting additional muscle, which makes the harvest time quicker, thus further reducing blood loss and morbidity.

The best incision is a curvilinear incision that comes to parallel the midline 3 cm lateral to the midline over and just lateral to the palpable landmarks of the sacroiliac articulation and the bony projection of the gluteus maximus insertion. This incision avoids the main branches of the superior and middle cluneal nerves while gaining access to the greatest reservoir of cancellous bone (Fig. 30–74). This incision also avoids any muscle dissection except for small branches of the sacroiliac muscle posteriorly, which is not significant. As the incision is deepened through subcutaneous fat, the contour of the crest can be easily identified. It is best to identify the external lip of the posterior ilium and dissect sharply through the lumbodorsal fascia and periosteum to gain access to the bone. In most indications for a posterior ilium approach, a large amount of cancellous bone is required, so a widened access by a lateral cortical plate excision is used. This lateral cortical ostectomy is about 5×5 cm square and encompasses the triangular area of the gluteus maximus insertion. The 5×5 cm square cortical excision is accomplished by first using a saline-cooled saw system to outline the ostectomy through the thickness of the lateral cortex and through the lateral one third of the crest (Fig. 30–75). The cortical cancellous block is then removed by curved osteotomes of about a 1-inch width in sagittal splitlike fashion.

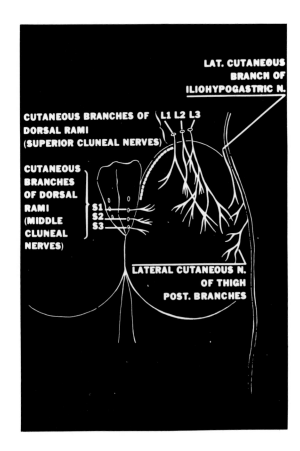

FIGURE 30–74. Posterior ilium regional anatomy. A curvilinear incision gains access to the greatest reservoir of bone, which is adjacent to the sacroiliac articulation and avoids the main branches of the cluneal nerves.

FIGURE 30–75. Removal of a 5-cm × 5-cm lateral cortex is begun with a reciprocating saw and then completed with a curved osteotome.

The cortical cancellous block is particulated after the now exposed cancellous bone is harvested (Fig. 30–76). A 5 × 5 cm cortical-cancellous block particulates into about 20 cc of uncompressed bone. Both the cortical block and the harvested cancellous bone are temporarily stored in a tissue culture medium or in saline (Fig. 30–77).

Once the required cancellous bone is harvested, the bony edges should be smoothed and final hemostasis achieved, with the operator's choice of many available agents, including bone wax, microfibrillar collagen, thrombin, and Gelfoam, among others (Figs. 30–78 and 30–79). Since these harvests are larger than most from other donor sites, a suction drain is advised; it is suggested that the drain exit anterior to the incision so that the patient does not lie on it. When performing closure in this area, the surgeon should also pay close attention to the reapproximation of muscle and fascia, but closure is, nonetheless, very straightforward in this area.

Bone Graft Handling

Since successful bone graft reconstruction depends upon the two fundamental concepts of viable osteocomponent cell transplantation, on the one hand, and their placement into a vascular and cellular tissue bed, on the other hand, maintaining the

FIGURE 30–76. A 5-cm × 5-cm cortical cancellous block is first particulated after the remaining required cancellous bone is harvested. A block this size equates to about 20 ml of uncompressed cancellous bone.

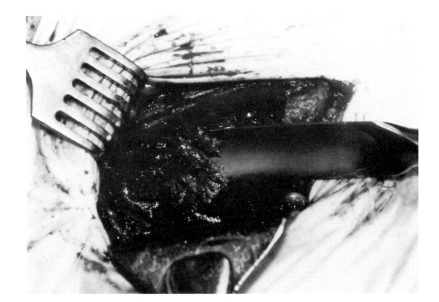

FIGURE 30–77. Cancellous bone is harvested with gauzes first, followed by curettes.

FIGURE 30–78. A "hollowed-out" posterior ilium donor site should have smooth edges, and the contour of the crest should be intact.

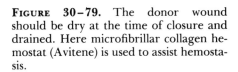

FIGURE 30–79. The donor wound should be dry at the time of closure and drained. Here microfibrillar collagen hemostat (Avitene) is used to assist hemostasis.

viability of cancellous bone in the period between its harvest and its placement is paramount.

The four most important factors affecting graft cell viability, in order, are tonicity of the storage medium, temperature of the storage medium, sterility of bone cell handling, and trauma of bone handling.

STORAGE MEDIA

Distilled water and other such hypotonic solutions are contraindicated as bone cell storage media.[39] Such hypotonic solutions diffuse through cell membranes by a large diffusion gradient to swell the cytoplasm and lead to their death by physical rupture. The contact of graft cells with water usually happens by accident in the following way. Sterile, distilled water is kept on the instrument set to clean instruments and wash handpieces to prevent rusting or "freezing up" of powered instruments. Inadvertent contact with water can and has easily occurred because the solutions (i.e., water and saline and water and tissue culture media) look alike and many operating room personnel feel there is no real difference. However, graft cell contact with water will cause lysis within at least 30 minutes, and probably much sooner.

Graft cells have been observed to be slightly more resistant to hypertonic solutions up to 560 mosm/ml, nevertheless these solutions reduce graft cell numbers and activity.[39] As a matter of maintaining the best probability of cell viability, hypertonic solutions should be avoided. The more hypertonic the solution, the greater the tendency to create a diffusion gradient, drawing free water from the cytoplasm and crenating bone cells.

Keeping bone grafts in blood or a blood-soaked sponge had been an empirically accepted technique for many years. However, several good studies have shown this concept to be physiologically unsound and detrimental to bone cell survival.[31,39] Although blood may superficially seem to be a harmless storage medium and cancellous bone cells normally reside in blood-rich marrow, they do not normally reside within clotted blood, which, indeed, is not a harmless storage medium. Clotted blood contains a host of membrane-toxic intermediates of platelet aggregation and fibrin clot formation, including lysozyme, fibrin split products, fibrinolysins, osteoclast chemotactic factor, and many others. In addition, bone cells placed in a blood-soaked sponge often undergo a degree of drying, which adds to cell death. The fact that graft cells handled in this manner have clinically done reasonably well in the past is related to the hardiness of cancellous bone cells and to the fact that membrane lysis caused by such intermediates is time and temperature dependent. Blood is not a recommended storage medium in current reconstructive surgical practice.

Saline is another storage medium choice and is the most popular one used today. Indeed, saline has been shown to maintain a 93 to 95 per cent rate of viability after 4 hours owing to its isotonicity.[39] However, cellular activity is reduced after saline

FIGURE 30–80.   Harvested cancellous bone should be placed in either saline or a tissue culture medium with a calibrated marked container to assess its correct amount prior to compression.

immersion, and bone cell growth factors are washed out of cells stored in saline.[31] The clinical significance of these findings remains uncertain. To date, clinical results have been excellent with the saline storage medium, but longer storage times may reduce viability.

The most ideal storage medium at present seems to be tissue culture media (Fig. 30–80). These media are commercially available, isotonic, balanced solutions buffered to pH 7.42, and they contain essential organic and inorganic cell nutrients. The ingredients of a sample tissue culture medium (CMRL) are listed in Table 30–1. The advantage of tissue culture media is that they not only maintain absolute cell viability as well as or perhaps slightly better than saline but also maintain cellular activity and seem not to deplete intracellular bone maintenance and growth factors. In studies measuring bone cell turnover, CMRL showed a fivefold increase over saline.[39]

TEMPERATURE

Temperature has been an inadequately studied influence on bone cell survival. However, chilling to the point of physical freezing maintains better bone cell viability. Heating a storage medium is detrimental to survival, owing to direct membrane and intracellular protein coagulation and to the enhancement of toxicity from exogenous agents. The practical difficulty with temperature is its control in the operating room. The theoretical difficulty with temperature is that the optimal temperature for bone cell survival is not known. It is, therefore, recommended that the temperature of the storage media be handled simply by keeping the media refrigerated at 4°C until its use in the operating room; it is then added to the set as bone is harvested and allowed to warm slowly toward room temperature until placement.

STERILITY OF HANDLING

Sterility of technique is an assumed operational imperative in an operating room. Incorporation of just a small inoculum of microorganisms can result in either overt clinical infection or subclinical graft cell death, yielding little bone. Contamination of bone cells, other than by surgical communication with the oral cavity, occurs by mistake, usually by spillage or by contact between the graft material and an unsterile object. If an overt contamination occurs, it is best to discard the graft material and proceed to another harvest. If a lesser contamination occurs, it is inappropriate to autoclave or irradiate the graft material, as that will surely devitalize it. It is also not recommended to treat the graft material with disinfectants or soaps, as they will also significantly reduce viability. It is best to irrigate them thoroughly with the storage medium and then a final time with an antibiotic solution. Although infection or a bacterial effect on the graft may still occur, its probability is reduced.

ROUGH HANDLING

Bone cells seem to be relatively resistant to rough handling by compression or by shearing forces. Neither compaction within a compression testing device or shearing from a bone mill device has been observed to affect cell viability. However, excessive trauma by crushing or particulating into very small pieces has incited inflammation within the tissue bed. As a general principle, trauma during harvesting and placement should be kept to a minimum.

Reconstruction of the Mandible

Reconstruction of the maxillofacial skeleton involves incorporating the principles of bone biology into a technical system of placement supporting that biology. Assuming the tissue bed is as vascular and cellular as one can achieve, and assuming a

TABLE 30–1. CHEMICALLY DEFINED MEDIUM CMRL-1413*

	MG PER 1000 ML	LEVEL IN CMRL-1066†
L-Alanine	30	25
L-Arginine	500‡	70
L-Aspartic acid	10	30
L-Cysteine	179‡	260
L-Cystine	24	20
L-Glutamic acid	10	75
L-Glutamine	292	100
Glycine	17	50
L-Histidine	31‡	20
Hydroxy-L-proline	10	10
L-Isoleucine	52	20
L-Leucine	52	60
L-Lysine	47‡	70
L-Methionine	15	15
L-Phenylalanine	32	25
L-Proline	30	40
L-Serine	12	25
L-Threonine	48	30
L-Tryptophan	10	10
L-Tyrosine	36	40
L-Valine	46	25
Ascorbic acid	50	50
D-Biotin (USP)	1	0.01
Calcium pantothenate	0.5	0.01
Choline chloride	1	0.50
Folic acid (USP)	1	0.01
Inositol (NF)	2	0.05
Cocarboxylase	1	1
Codecarboxylase	1	—
Diphosphopyridine nucleotide	7	7
Flavin adenine dinucleotide	1	1
Glutathione	10	10
Triphosphopyridine nucleotide	1	1
Uridine triphosphate	1	1
Deoxyadenosine	10	10
Deoxycytidine	10	10
Deoxyguanosine	10	10
5-Methyldeoxycytidine	0.1	0.10
Thymidine	10	10
D-Galactose	500	—
D-Glucose	500	1000
Phenol red	20	20
Sodium pyruvate	225	—
NaCl	6800	6800
KCl	400	400
CaCl$_2$	140	200
MgSO$_4$7H$_2$O	240	200
NaH$_2$PO$_4$H$_2$O	50	140
NaHPO$_4$	200	—
NaHCO$_2$	1000	2200

* Registered trademark.
† Thirteen ingredients of CMRL-1066 are not included in CMRL-1415.
‡ Free base.

sufficient quantity of viable cancellous bone cells has been harvested and maintained, the next step is to develop the graft bed and prepare a tray for placement of the graft.

The principles of graft bed preparation are to prepare a tissue bed in the same plane as the avulsed bone, dissect to the submucosa without perforating the oral cavity, and maintain a thickness of external tissue to cover the graft. The matter of crib preparation is one of choice. The ideal crib should become incorporated into the tissue bed, not encapsulated by fibrous tissue. It should also be biocompatible, bioresorbable, and well tolerated in scarred and physically thin tissue. To this end, the preferred crib system is one derived from allogeneic bone. Although a variety of alloplastic cribs are commercially available, with each one touting some superiority related to its mechanical properties, they all, to date, remain as foreign bodies, which are not incorporated into the tissue but, rather, are nonresorbably encapsulated. Nevertheless, successful clinical results may be obtained with alloplastic cribs if sufficient tissue cover is present and the principles of bone regeneration are strictly adhered to. Commercial alloplastic cribs available today are made from such materials as Dacron-coated polyurethane, titanium, stainless steel, and others.

COMPARISON AND CHARACTERISTICS OF ALLOPLASTIC CRIBS

Although biologic encapsulation, nonresorbability, and biologic unadaptability are common to all alloplastic cribs, there exist some technical differences in crib systems. The Dacron-coated polyurethane cribs are radiolucent and therefore do not obscure the postoperative radiographic assessment of graft consolidation. They are also easily cut with scissors for easy contouring and shaping. The material is moderately flexible but is rigid enough to maintain its shape. Its pore size is small, but large enough to allow capillary ingrowth (Fig. 30–81). However, during processing, the Dacron coating will often cover the pores, requiring the surgeon to be observant and reopen the pores with a bur. Titanium is more rigid and, of course, is a metal that obscures complete radiographic visualization of the graft. The material is very biotolerant and is both bendable and able to be trimmed by wire cutters more easily than most other metals. Stainless steel is very rigid. It is difficult to cut or to contour. The stainless steel crib, therefore, should be made in a customized fashion for each patient off a sized model rather than used as an off-the-shelf product (Fig. 30–82). Such cast stainless steel cribs are usually made from wax patterns on dry mandible specimens presized by radiographs or by three-dimensional imaging techniques. In any event, the end product of bone reconstruction that meets the six accepted criteria of success will depend upon the viable cellular density of the graft, the vascularity of the recipient tissue, and the cellularity of the recipient tissue, not on the mechanical or convenience properties of the crib materials.

ALLOGENEIC BONE

The crib preference of these authors is certainly allogeneic bone. As a biologic tissue, it has the advantages of tissue ingrowth and resorbability. The end product is a

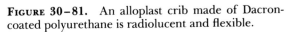
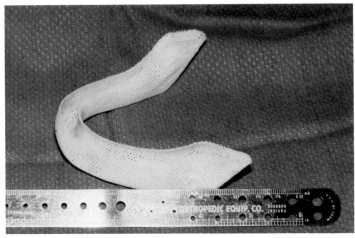

FIGURE 30–81. An alloplast crib made of Dacron-coated polyurethane is radiolucent and flexible.

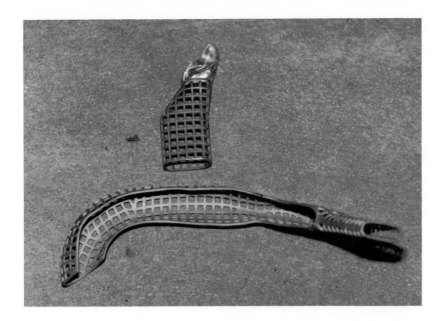

FIGURE 30–82. An alloplast crib made from stainless steel is cast and very rigid. Therefore, it must be sized to the defect as closely as possible in the manufacturing.

crib system that is resorbable, biologically adaptable, and well tolerated in thin tissues and one that does not interfere with later radiographic assessment or secondary vestibuloplasty and scar release surgeries.

Allogeneic bone is nonviable bone. It is used in these cases only as a crib, that is, to maintain a dense consolidation of autogenous cancellous bone in a morphologic shape similar to that of a mandible. Allogeneic bone is harvested from cadaver donors. Some tissue banks harvest the bone under sterile conditions and guarantee the sterility and nontransmissibility of disease by a battery of serologic, microbiologic, and mechanical tests[40] (Fig. 30–83). Other tissue banks harvest bone in a nonsterile fashion and then exogenously sterilize the bone with either 100 Gy of gamma irradiation or with ethylene oxide. Since all mandible specimens are harvested in a transoral and therefore nonsterile manner, each is submitted to exogenous sterilization regardless of the tissue bank of origin. Gamma irradiation will denature bone-inductive proteins, such as BMP and osteogenin, whereas ethylene oxide is reported not to affect inductive agents.[41,42] This factor, however, is not important when an allogeneic

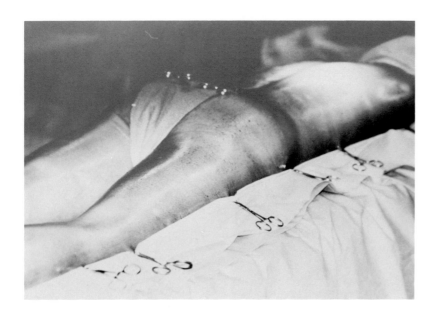

FIGURE 30–83. Tissue harvests from cadaver donor may be accomplished in a sterile fashion, as in an operating room. The tissues are guaranteed sterile by microbiologic testing prior to distribution.

bone is used as a crib. In such usage, the crib need not possess inductive capability, as the autogenous particulate bone and cancellous marrow combination is not only osteogenic but also osteoconductive and osteoinductive.

The most important factor in using allogeneic bone today is the reliability of nontransmission of such diseases as hepatitis, acquired immunodeficiency syndrome (AIDS), Jacob-Creutzfeldt disease, and so on. To date, the tissue bank products available from reputable tissue banks adhering to or exceeding the donor selection and tissue sterility criteria set forth by the South-Eastern Organ Procurement Foundation or the American Association of Tissue Banks have not transmitted a single case of such disease.[43] The isolated and few cases in which disease transmission has been reported have originated from tissue procurement organizations that were not formal tissue banks and were operating outside these regulations. In an elegant study by Buck and Colleagues,[43] the theoretical risk of processing bone from an unrecognized carrier of human immunodeficiency virus (HIV), if currently recommended precautions are taken, was found to be less than 1 in 1 million.

Allogeneic bone most commonly used as a crib for an autogenous particulate bone and cancellous marrow graft is freeze dried, or lyophilized. The freeze-drying process is merely the removal of almost all water from the frozen tissue under a vacuum, so that the solid ice phase goes into the gas vapor phase without decrystallization into a liquid phase, which would disrupt cellular architecture and tissue integrity. The freeze-dried bone is, therefore, indefinitely preserved in a vacuum container with its original morphology intact (Figs. 30–84 and 30–85 A and B). It is guaranteed to be sterile as long as the vacuum is retained in the container, which is checked with spark testing before tissue bank release.

THE PROCEDURE OF BONE RECONSTRUCTION OF THE MANDIBLE

The surgical phase of bone graft surgery is divided into four major subphases: particulate bone and marrow harvest, dissection of the recipient tissue bed, preparation of the allogeneic crib, and placement of the graft. Assumed in this phase is also some sort of mandibular and graft immobilization, which may be accomplished at the beginning of the surgery, such as maxillomandibular fixation via arch bars or external skeletal pins, or even during surgery, as with direct internal fixation via rigid cribs, such as allogeneic ilium and mandible forms or alloplastic cribs.

FIGURE 30–84. Tissue processing at the University of Miami Tissue Bank is accomplished in a sterile fashion at each stage, and the tissue is cultured at each stage. Seen here, tissue specimens are being sealed and cultured prior to shipment.

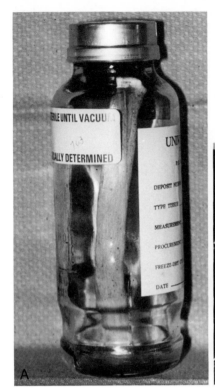
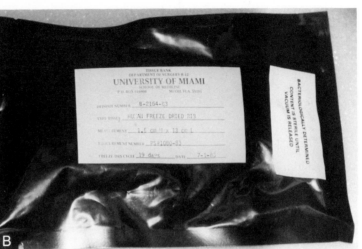

FIGURE 30–85. *A,* A freeze-dried sterile allogeneic rib is seen here with normal morphology vacuum. It is sealed in a Baxter bottle. *B,* Another packaging method is a plastic triple pouch, as seen here. Each specimen is labeled with regard to sterility, specimen type and size, and processing information.

A representative surgery would entail placement of the patient in the preferred fixation after intubation and anesthetic induction in a separate, short procedure. The patient would next be placed in a prone position so that bone from the posterior ilium could be harvested. Since most mandibular reconstructions related to traumatic avulsions produce large continuity defects of more than 5 cm, the posterior ilium approach is preferred. The harvested particulate bone with cancellous marrow is temporarily stored in chilled tissue culture medium as the access incision to the ilium is closed. During this phase of surgery, the allogeneic bone is also being reconstituted in a saline solution and can be initially sized and shaped on a sterile table by another member of the operating team. Once the ilium harvest incision is closed, the patient is returned to the supine position and reprepared and draped for the recipient bed preparation.

Aseptic technique is an imperative in this type of surgery, which amounts to a cellular transplantation of bone cells to a mandibular defect. The scrub and draping of the patient should be accomplished with no less attention to detail than the surgery itself. The tissue should be both scrubbed and painted with a disinfectant soap and solution, respectively.

The prepared field should be very wide. We will usually prepare an area that includes both the posterior and the anterior triangles of the neck, the ear, the preauricular area, the skin and lips below the alar bases, and the entire neck area of intended surgery down to 3 cm below the clavicle. A crushed support towel should be placed in the posterior triangle area, over which another sterile towel is placed and sutured to prevent spillage. In addition, the mouth should be draped out of the field with a separate sterile towel placed at the vermilion-cutaneous junction and sutured into place. An additional barrier of a vinyl drape may also be used. Although difficult to adapt until one becomes practiced at it, the vinyl drape will control the wetting of the drapes during wound irrigations. Such wetting of the drapes acts like a conduit for organisms from the unsterile operating table and its sides to enter the prepared field.

The actual surgical incision should be placed low in the neck and in a gently curved fashion. The low placement in the neck will keep the final position of the incision below the inferior border of the graft. If the incision is placed too high in the neck, it will come to rest over the graft proper as the graft will bring out facial contour and superiorly reposition the incision. This area of greatest graft contour is also the area of greatest wound tension and is most prone to dehiscence. The gently curved shape will blend the incision into neck skinfolds and into the shadow line of the mandible for the least noticeability. In addition, a gently curving scar line is much less obvious to an observer's eye than a straight-line scar, as the old adage of "there is nothing straight in nature" is especially true when applied to skin.

The dissection should proceed through the full thickness of skin and subcutaneous tissues, with the anticipation of encountering intense scarring and distorted anatomy typical of maxillofacial wounds. The surgeon should control small bleeding points directly as the surgery proceeds so as not to obscure visualization or allow multiple small bleedings to add into a larger total blood loss. The dissection should proceed through the platysma and the full thickness of the superficial layer of deep cervical fascia. The dissection should expose and identify, but not progress through, the anterior belly of the digastric and geniohyoid muscles anteriorly and the intermediate tendon, stylohyoid muscle, and posterior belly of the digastric posteriorly. The dissection plane to expose the proximal and distal mandibular segments should be deep to the common facial vein, which is ligated and just superficial to the submandibular gland. This plane will be deep to the path of the facial nerve, provide a sufficiently thick tissue cover for the graft, and avoid communication with the lingual vestibule of the oral cavity.

The proximal and distal bone exposure is accomplished by periosteal incisions over the inferiormost portion of each bone segment. For maximal release of scarred-down periosteum, a 3-cm bone exposure of each end is required. Reflection of host bone end periosteum is made much easier if the bone ends were cut to a straight line and rounded during previous surgeries, which may have been done to stabilize segments, remove foreign bodies, or accomplish soft tissue reconstructions. The host bone ends should also possess a crestal shelf at least 0.5 cm from the nearest tooth, so that tissue reflection does not communicate with the periodontal ligament space or a periodontal pocket with microorganisms. Once each bone end is fully exposed, the tissue bed between each is dissected with the intent of dissecting into the scarred submucosa but avoiding perforation of the oral cavity. As stated earlier, this dissection may be assisted by placing a gloved finger in the mouth to guide the dissection or by assessing the remaining mucosal thickness by palpating it against the maxillary dention or a maxillary denture. We have also found it useful to dissect this area bluntly with a hemostat oriented parallel to the alveolar crest. Since the usual scar pattern develops by a fusion of lingual periosteum and other tissues to their corresponding buccal components, this orientation will tend to open the scar planes without tending to perforate the epithelium of the oral mucosa.

Once the host proximal and distal bone ends are sufficiently exposed and oriented into their correct positions, the crib of choice is contoured and fixated to place. Adaptation of the currently available crib systems is as follows.

Alloplastic Cribs. Whatever the material of the alloplastic crib, it must be adapted to the wound and contoured to overlap the host bone ends on their lateral surface. The surgeon must ensure that all pores remain open and that no sharp edges exist. It is recommended that the height of the buccal and lingual flanges be trimmed down to 1 cm to reduce their presence under the oral mucosa in each respective vestibule.

Fixation of the crib is best accomplished with screws for maximal stability. If a metal crib is used, the screws should be of the same metal type so as not to risk dissimilar metal reactions and potential bone resorption. Crib fixation is best achieved if one uses at least three screws on each host bone segment and if the crib overlaps the host bone for a distance of at least 3 cm (Figs. 30–86 and 30–87).

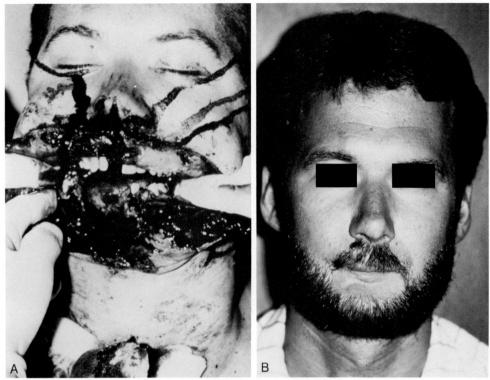

FIGURE 30–86.   *A*, Avulsive gunshot wound to symphysis and body regions of mandible at time of initial management. *B*, Same patient 9 years after bone reconstruction of the mandible.

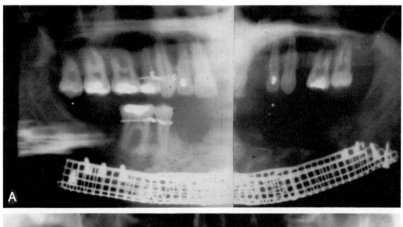

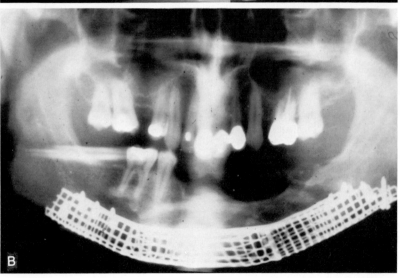

FIGURE 30–87.   *A*, Initial radiograph of bone graft. The crib was fixated with 4 cm of lateral overlap and with four stainless steel screws at each crib-host interface. *B*, Nine-year follow-up radiograph indicates a well-consolidated graft without resorption or loss of alveolar height.

Allogeneic Cribs

Split ribs—mediolateral.   After reconstitution in saline, an allogeneic rib may be split longitudinally with a fine saw or bur into two long cortical strips (Fig. 30–88 *A* and *B*). Once the cancellous bone is removed with a round or pear-shaped bur and the cortex is thinned, each cortical strip should be somewhat bendable. In continuity defects of the mandible that include the body region and curvature of the symphysis, orienting the split rib strips to replace the lingual and buccal cortices of the mandible will naturally define the arch form (Fig. 30–89). The rib strips are fixated with a vertical wire through two vertical holes placed in each host bone end and in each rib end. The lingual cortex replacement rib is sutured to the deep tissue through bur holes placed in the rib strip. The orientation of split rib segments in this manner will serve a similar purpose to that of the dental matrix band and is called the "matrix band concept." That is, the autogenous particulate bone and cancellous marrow combination is "condensed" into the space between the cortical strips, which not only defines the contour and shape of the graft but also will provide a resistance wall needed to achieve a high cellular density of osteocompetent cells by compression. With this orientation, the autogenous particulate bone with cancellous marrow is introduced through the open inferior border area. The height of the final graft will not be determined by the rib height, which is far too small a height to be an acceptable mandibular reconstruction. It will, instead, be determined by the height of the soft tissue dissection. In a similar sense, the inferior border area is not enclosed by a crib, and its form is maintained by the densely compressed autogenous bone (Figs. 30–90 and 30–91 *A* and *B*).

Split ribs—supero inferior.   The split ribs may also be oriented 90 degrees into a superior crest and inferior border replacement orientation. This orientation is indicated for continuity defects that include the body, angle, and/or part of the ramus (Fig. 30–92). Placing rib strips in this orientation will create the curvature of the mandibular angle and posterior ramus very well, as well as the upward curvature of the alveolar crest and ascending ramus (Fig. 30–93). In this orientation, the matrix band concept naturally defines the alveolar height, the angle curvature, and the ramus width. The autogenous particulate bone and cancellous marrow combination

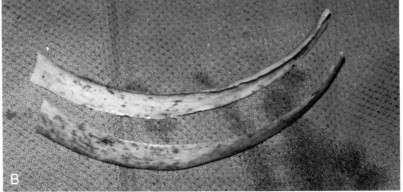

FIGURE 30–88. *A,* Reconstituted allogeneic rib. *B,* Prepared allogeneic rib split longitudinally into two flexible cortical strips.

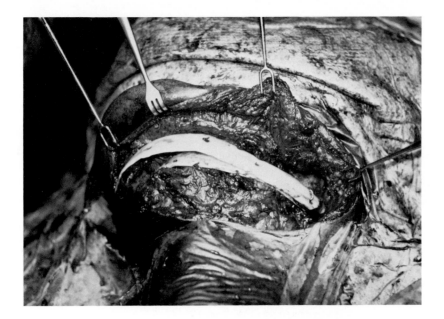

FIGURE 30–89. The two rib strips are placed mediolaterally to achieve the arch form of a mandible and resemble, in principle, a dental matrix band.

is introduced through the open lateral access. The medial limit to the graft is the deep wall of the soft tissue dissection. The rib strips are fixated to the host bone segments by direct wire fixation. The inferior border replacement rib strip will be fixated to the distal bone segment, the inferior border, and the posterior ramus border, with the rib bent to approximate the angle and ramus curvature. The edge of the rib is also sutured to the deep soft tissue through bur holes placed in the rib. This not only will help maintain the rib curvature but also will adapt the deep tissues closely to the rib. The superior crest replacement rib strip is wired to the host bone alveolar crest and to the anterior ramus or condylar neck, incorporating a curvature recapitulating the ascending ramus (Fig. 30–94).

In both approaches, the rib's flexibility and fixation via wiring do not produce sufficient internal rigidity to obviate other fixation. Such patients will require either maxillomandibular fixation or external skeletal pins.

Allogeneic ilium hemimandible forms. An excellent crib for select hemimandibular defects can be fashioned from the ilium. This idea was first suggested by Manchester in 1965 as an autogenous block graft.[44] The "Manchester principle"

FIGURE 30–90. The autogenous particulate bone along with cancellous marrow is placed between the rib cortices. The height of the bone graft will be determined by the soft tissue dissection and the inferior border, by the soft tissue closure about the graft.

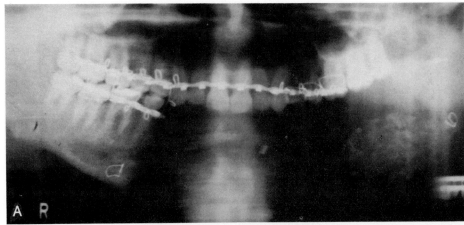

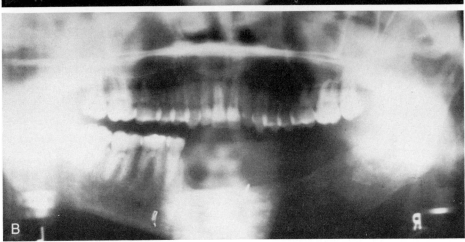

FIGURE 30–91.   *A,* Postoperative radiographs of particulate bone and cancellous marrow grafts will not demonstrate obvious findings for the first 3 to 6 months. *B,* However, such grafts will consolidate and progressively mineralize to result in a dense and well-contoured graft.

identifies a contour similarity between the ipsilateral anterior ilium and the hemimandible (Fig. 30–95). Manchester originally applied this concept to the use of a large autogenous cortical-cancellous graft that produced disappointing results. Gait disturbances and other donor site morbidity, together with graft resorption due to a diminished cellular transplantation of such a block autogenous graft, produced unsatisfactory results, so that the approach became seldom used and nearly forgotten.

FIGURE 30–92.   When there is bony defect of the angle and much of the ramus, such as this, orienting the split-rib segments superoinferiorly is best. Note here the flattened **U**-shaped incision design and the depth of dissection to the level of the submandibular gland and digastric surface.

FIGURE 30–93. Allogeneic split-rib crib in place in a superoinferior orientation, with autogenous particulate bone and cancellous marrow graft placed between segments.

FIGURE 30–94. Four-year follow-up radiograph with consolidated bone, excellent alveolar height, and symmetric contour.

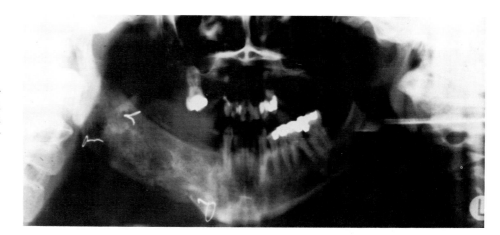

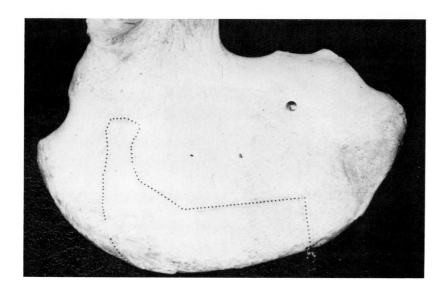

FIGURE 30–95. Contour similarity of ipsilateral anterior ilium to a hemimandible. Here a right hemimandible is drawn on a dry specimen of a right ilium.

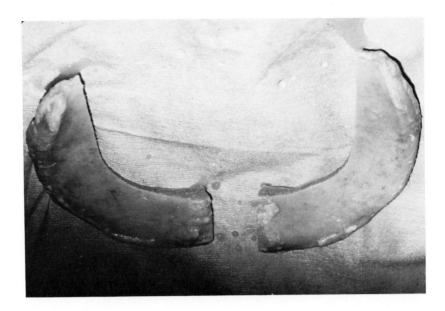

FIGURE 30–96. Hemi-ilium forms for left and right sides cut by tissue banks specifically for hemimandible reconstruction.

However, the "Manchester principle" of the contour similarity between ilium and hemimandible was resurrected by Marx and Kline in 1980 and was shown to be valid when applied to the use of an allogeneic crib.[10] Today it is a commonly used allogeneic crib and also serves as the morphologic basis for the free vascularized bone from the ilium that is based on the deep circumflex iliac artery.

For an allogeneic hemimandibular crib, the tissue bank will cut out a mandibular form, placing the inferior border at the iliac crest, the angle at the tubercle of the ilium, and the ramus just inferior and posterior to the anterior spines (Fig. 30–96). The contour similarity is valid for a continuity defect anywhere from the condyle to the area of the mental foramen (Fig. 30–97). Anterior to the mental foramen, the contour similarity ends as the symphysis curvature begins. The tissue bank specimen is reconstituted and hollowed out (Fig. 30–98 A to C). The lateral cortex of the allogeneic ilium is made to overlap the lateral mandibular cortex of the proximal and distal host bone segments. The allogeneic ilium is then fixated with three bicortical screws in each segment, preferably in a tripod arrangement (Fig. 30–99). In placing such screws, one needs to drill the hole in the allogeneic bone slightly larger than the

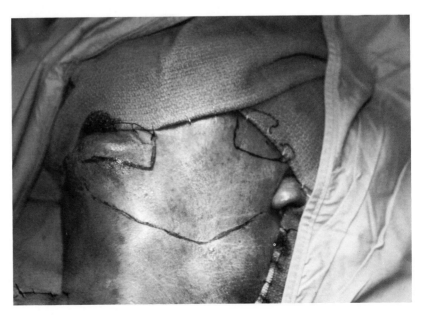

FIGURE 30–97. This type of hemimandibular defect is well suited for a hemimandibular ilium form.

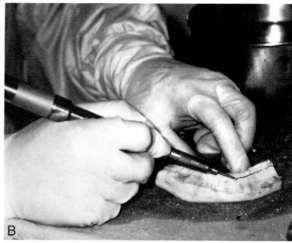

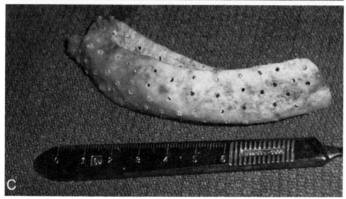

FIGURE 30–98. *A*, Allogeneic hemimandible form for left side prior to hollowing and shaping by the surgeon. *B*, The allogeneic specimen is sized and hollowed on a sterile back table while the recipient site is being dissected. *C*, A completed crib will be hollowed out, have lowered flanges, overlap the host bone ends, and be perforated with revascularization holes.

thread diameter of the screws and the diameter of the hole in the host bone. In this manner, the screw threads will not engage the allogeneic bone but will engage the host bone, drawing them together. The surgeon must also remember that the allogeneic bone crib is not as resistant as a metal plate. Tightening a screw too much may fracture an allogeneic bone crib. Before the crib is fixated into place, the lateral flange should be reduced to no more than 1 cm in height, and the medial flange should be reduced as much as possible while still maintaining support of the autogenous particu-

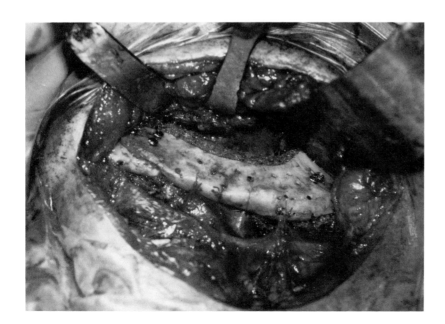

FIGURE 30–99. The hemimandible form may be rigidly fixated with three screws at each end. The soft tissue should also be sutured to the inferior border, as shown here.

Figure 30-100. A 4-year follow-up radiograph shows the contour available with a hemimandible form, as well as a well-consolidated graft. *Note:* At this time, the original allogeneic crib is resorbed.

late bone and marrow graft. Holes are also placed in the inferior border of the crib (crest of the ilium specimen) to suture and adapt the deep soft tissue bed to the crib. The autogenous particulate bone and cancellous marrow graft material is introduced through a lateral access and condensed into the crib. Since this crib system provides rigid internal fixation equal to that provided by an alloplastic crib, maxillomandibular fixation or external skeletal fixation may be eliminated or reduced in time, depending on the final stability of the graft (Fig. 30–100).

Allogeneic mandible cribs. No doubt the ideal morphology for a mandibular reconstruction is that of a mandible itself. However, allogeneic mandibles are one of the least available tissue specimens available from tissue banks today. The reduced availability of mandible specimens comes from state mortician laws and next-of-kin consents limiting donors to those who are intended for cremation. Nevertheless, the demand for mandible specimens in the past decade has generated a tissue bank awareness whereby mandible specimens are now available for almost all cases in which only a mandible will suffice, and the availability is increasing.

Mandible specimens are particularly useful and should be reserved for large continuity defects that cross the midline. Reconstitution time is not critical for allogeneic mandible cribs, as they are hollowed into a crib that is intended to be rigid. In situations in which host bone proximal segments include the rami, the allogeneic mandible crib is hollowed, the condyles are removed, and the medial cortex of the rami is reduced (Fig. 30–101). The allogeneic crib can then overlap its lateral ramus cortex on the lateral aspect of the proximal host segments where it is fixated with screws. In many cases, the anteroposterior length of the allogeneic crib is greater than the soft tissue will permit or greater than the correct alignment to the maxilla. This

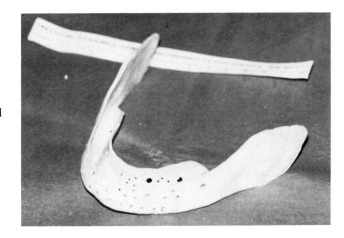

Figure 30-101. Allogeneic mandible crib hollowed and sized to overlap residual host rami on their lateral surface.

anteroposterior length may be adjusted by removing the posterior aspect of the allogeneic crib rami and thereby positioning the crib more posteriorly.

The buccal and lingual flanges should be reduced as much as possible, and bur holes should be placed for maximal revascularization. One should have a slightly higher flange height in the area of the antegonial notch, as this remains the weakest area of the crib. One should also place a series of bur holes at the inferior border, spaced about 1 cm apart, so that the deep tissue bed and musculature may be directly sutured to the bone crib.

Once the crib is fixated into place and the suprahyoid soft tissue is sutured to the inferior border, the autogenous particulate bone and cancellous marrow can be condensed into the crib (Fig. 30–102). One should begin at each host bone area and should be sure that sufficient bone graft material is condensed about each and then advance the condensation out toward the midline. Care should also be taken to condense bone graft material into the hollowed inferior border of the crib.

In situations in which the continuity defect includes one or both of the condyles, the allogeneic mandible can be fashioned into a crib that will also reconstruct this area and the articulation. In these situations, the crib is hollowed in a similar fashion, with the addition of hollowing out the condyle and fashioning a receptacle for the graft material from the ramus. The condyle is hollowed by making openings at the lateral and medial poles. A round bur can then be used to remove the cancellous bone within the condyle area. The ramus is prepared by removing most of the lateral cortex and intercortical cancellous bone from the lateral pole of the condyle to the anterior ramus (Fig. 30–103). One should have a lip of lateral ramus cortex at the posterior border and angle to house the autogenous particulate bone and cancellous marrow. Therefore, the crib in this area will consist mainly of the medial ramus, which is perforated with revascularization holes. The autogenous particulate bone and the cancellous marrow material is condensed against the medial ramus cortex and within the hollowed condyle and condylar neck. The graft material is held in place primarily by its dense compaction and the soft tissue cover (Fig. 30–104). The bone placed in the hollowed condyle of the allogeneic crib consolidates into a morphologically well-rounded pseudoarticulation that is stable throughout the year (Fig. 30–105).

The lateral pterygoid muscle almost never reattaches to a delayed graft placed into the temporal fossa because of its scarring and retraction. In these instances, the patient opens with a rotational motion only and shows a deviation to the surgical side upon wide opening if the opposite side is intact. In cases of immediate reconstructions

FIGURE 30–102. Allogeneic mandible crib in place fixated with three bicortical screws and lagged onto the host rami. The suprahyoid musculature is also sutured to the crib at its inferior border, and the crib is filled with compacted autogenous particulate bone and cancellous marrow.

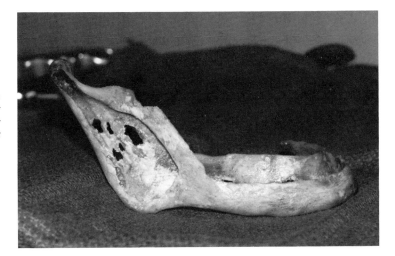

FIGURE 30–103. An allogeneic mandible crib, which must also reconstruct the condyle, is fashioned by hollowing out the condyle through the medial and lateral poles, as well as by removing the cortex of the lateral ramus.

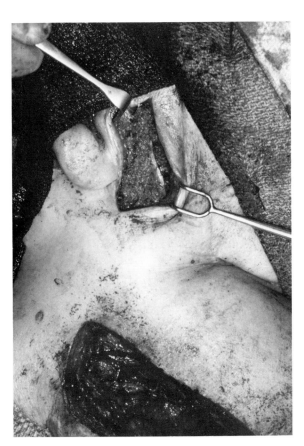

FIGURE 30–104. A preauricular incision may be required to place a crib into the temporal fossa. The autogenous graft material is compacted from this access and is held in place by its compaction and by the soft tissue cover.

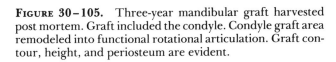

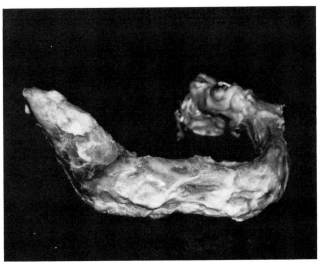

FIGURE 30–105. Three-year mandibular graft harvested post mortem. Graft included the condyle. Condyle graft area remodeled into functional rotational articulation. Graft contour, height, and periosteum are evident.

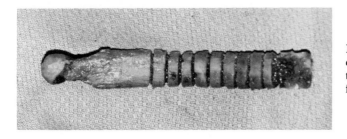

FIGURE 30–106. Autogenous rib prepared for an adult costochondral graft. The costochondral portion is contoured to fit into the temporal fossa, and the inner cortex is scored for bending to a ramus contour.

of tumor defects that include the condyle, the lateral pterygoid can be sutured directly to the graft. In these instances, the return of lateral jaw excursions to the opposite side has been variably realized. The return of such lateral excursions has ranged from 50 per cent to 90 per cent, but the regained ability has never been equal to that of the opposite, unoperated side.

Alternatives to Reconstruct the Condylar Articulation. The goals in reconstruction of the mandible that include the condylar articulation are the same as those for other grafts but must also include the following: (1) an articulation that permits at least rotational opening without pain, (2) a reproducible opening greater than 30 mm, (3) a condylar position that is stable without resorption and without migration, and (4) an articulation that will not ankylose. To this end, there are several modifications of approaches already discussed that will create a functional articulation meeting these criteria.

Costochondral Grafts. Costochondral grafts are a time-honored means of reconstructing a functional articulation. In the adult, a costochondral graft is a nongrowth graft that will morphologically fit into the fossa and achieve a functional rotational articulation (Fig. 30–106). By itself, a costochondral graft is not sufficient in osteogenic cells to reconstruct the full dimensions of the condylar neck or ramus. It is, therefore, recommended that the costochondral graft be supplemented with particulate bone and cancellous marrow, which can be obtained from the remaining portion of the harvested rib, from another rib harvest through the same incision, or from a concomitant ilium harvest. The size of the remaining graft distal to the condyle will determine the amount of particulate bone and cancellous marrow required, and therefore the donor site. Our distinct preference is to place the rib about the posterior ramus border and inferior border rather than on the lateral ramus. If the rib is made to curve about the inferior and posterior borders of the mandible, it will come to lie in the temporal fossa, with its widest dimension mediolaterally, as does the natural condyle with its medial and lateral poles (Fig. 30–107). In this fashion, it provides for a more stable position within the temporal fossa and allows for the autogenous particulate bone and cancellous marrow to be placed against and anterior to it for reconstruction of the ramus and condylar neck.

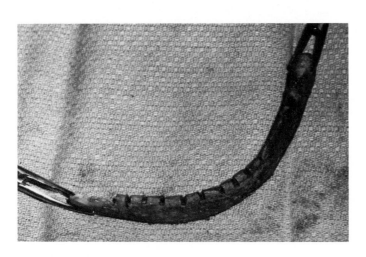

FIGURE 30–107. Scoring the rib will allow it to bend into a posterior ramus and angle contour, with the costochondral end positioned mediolaterally within the fossa. The distal end is reduced to a single cortex for fixation to the inferior border of the host bone.

FIGURE 30–108. Costochondral rib fixated into place, with autogenous particulate bone and cancellous marrow compacted onto it and against host bone.

To facilitate bending the rib, it is scored on its pleural cortex and each rib edge, as was once accomplished for rib graft augmentation of atrophic mandibles (Fig. 30–107). One may also remove some of this cortex just below the cartilage to condense additional bone graft material into this area and remove some of this cortex in the area with which it will overlap the host bone for better fit. The rib is wired to the remaining host bone, and the remainder of the wound is packed with the autogenous particulate bone and cancellous marrow to reconstruct the ramus, angle, and body areas, if required (Figs. 30–108 and 30–109).

Modified Ilium Hemimandible Forms. The Manchester principle–based hemimandibular forms can also be extended into the fossa area. For reconstruction of the condylar articulation, the autogenous bone can be condensed between the cortical plates to reconstruct the ramus. An articulation similar to the hollowed-out allogeneic mandible crib can be achieved by fashioning the crib to extend into the fossa and placing a cap of soft tissue over the crib to serve as the superior limit of the graft (Figs. 30–110 to 30–112). One can use the disc of the joint if it is still present; otherwise, autogenous dermis or periosteum works well, as does allogeneic dura. This system will achieve a stable and functional articulation as well as any of the other systems (Figs. 30–113 and 30–114).

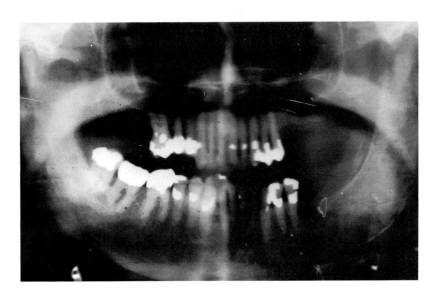

FIGURE 30–109. Three-year follow-up of costochondral graft, with good graft consolidation and ramus contour.

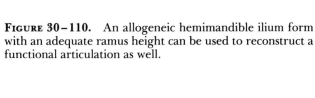

FIGURE 30–110. An allogeneic hemimandible ilium form with an adequate ramus height can be used to reconstruct a functional articulation as well.

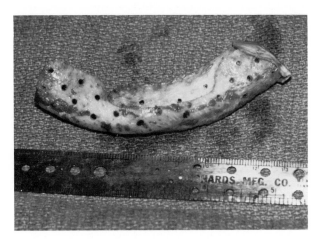

FIGURE 30–111. The crib is, once again, hollowed out to receive the autogenous graft material, and an allogeneic dura cap is sutured to the articulating surface.

FIGURE 30–112. The dura cap keeps the autogenous graft material within the crib, as well as serving as a disclike articulating surface.

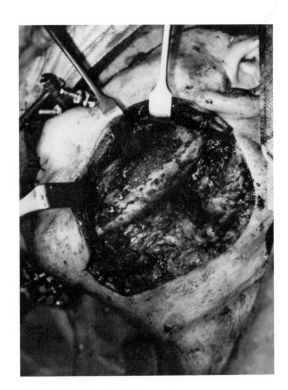

FIGURE 30–113. The crib-and-graft composite is placed into the temporal fossa and fixated to the distal host bone via lateral overlap.

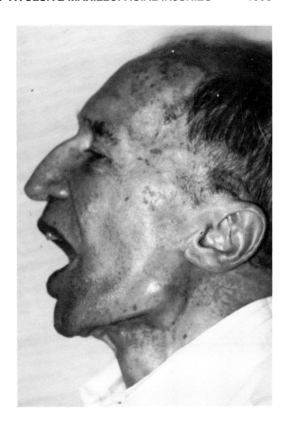

FIGURE 30-114. Such grafts will achieve a stable and functional articulation, as seen here 5 years after placement.

Alloplastic Trays with Alloplastic Condylar Heads. Nearly all alloplastic cribs can be ordered with a condyle. The condyle is usually in continuity with the remainder of the crib but may be attached with a sleeve or screw system to adjust the ramus height. These systems will achieve a functional articulation that is a pseudoarthrosis. However, the stability of these systems is in question, because the alloplastic condyle is in continuity with the rest of the crib, not the bone graft within the crib. Alloplastic condyles have also been known to migrate into the cranial base or become displaced by virtue of eventual loosening of the crib from the host bone. In addition, one must be concerned about soft tissue and bone erosion if an unyielding alloplastic condyle functions against the biologic tissues of the temporal fossa.

THE PROCEDURE OF RECONSTRUCTION OF THE MAXILLA

Surgical reconstruction of the maxilla is less commonly required than that of the mandible. In many instances, facial aesthetics and function, including the replacement of missing teeth, are best served by a maxillofacial prosthesis. Current materials and techniques in maxillofacial prosthetics have provided less of a need for surgeons to bring in distant flaps for soft tissue needs and place bone grafts for avulsed bone. The primary goals of maxillary surgical reconstruction in avulsive wounds have thus become the following:

1. Provide a healthy tissue base for a prosthesis
2. Alter the shape and contour of the maxilla and midface to receive a prosthesis more satisfactorily
3. Provide anchorage via implant fixtures or magnets
4. Replace avulsed soft tissue when a prosthesis is not possible
5. Provide bone grafts or alloplasts for contour when a prosthesis cannot achieve such contour

Provisions of a Healthy Tissue Base. Most tissue bases that are not suitable for a maxillofacial prosthesis are so because of chronic infection foci or hyperplastic

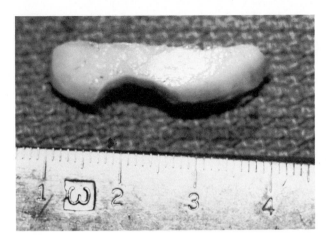

FIGURE 30–115.   Cranial bone graft harvested and contoured to reconstruct the infraorbital rim.

nonkeratinized tissue of sinus or nasal mucosa. Chronic infection is almost always due to the presence of nonviable tissue. Often, simple debridement of residual bone, teeth, or metal fragments will resolve the infection and permit the tissues to heal. Hyperplastic tissue of sinus or nasal mucosa will usually remain hyperplastic, with a boggy consistency and a friable, bleeding quality. This condition results from the drying effect and the difference in resident bacterial flora caused by exposure to the external surface environment. The tissue continually remains inflamed and often desiccates mucus, making a prosthesis difficult to wear comfortably. In such cases, a mucosal excision, often termed a "stripping procedure," and the placement of a split-thickness skin graft will improve the tissue base. A keratinized and fixed tissue without inflammation is a more suitable tissue to interface with a prosthesis.

Alter the Shape and Contour of the Maxilla and Midface to Receive a Prosthesis.   The silicone and rubber flexible materials used today for restoration of facial skin, nasal structures, and ocular prostheses are lightweight enough to be self-retentive without the need for messy and ineffectual adhesives. To this end, small undercuts in tissue contours can serve as the only retentive mechanism required for many prostheses. Flexible prostheses can be compressed during insertion to be placed behind the undercut and then allowed to re-form elastically, so that even a small undercut keeps it in its proper place. The surgeon can often assist in the fitting of such prostheses by onlay grafts of the orbital rims for ocular prostheses or onlay grafts of the nasal piriform rims for nasal prostheses (Fig. 30–115). These situations often

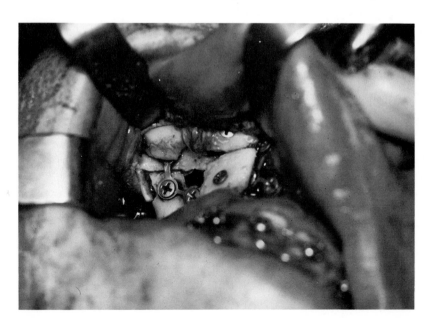

FIGURE 30–116.   Placement of the cranial graft to reconstruct the infraorbital rim and to return the undercut quality provided to the orbital cone by the orbital rims. The graft here is seen fixated above the infraorbital nerve.

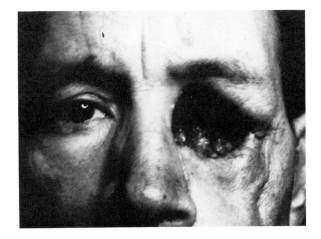

FIGURE 30–117. Exenterated orbital contents with orbital rim undercuts, which will permit a self-retaining prosthesis without the need for adhesives. (Courtesy of Daniel Eaton, BCO.)

FIGURE 30–118. Complete self-retained prosthesis. (Courtesy of Daniel Eaton, BCO.)

lend themselves well to a cranial bone graft (Fig. 30–116). In this instance, it may be the preferred graft material, as the shape of the calvarium's outer table conforms well to the curvatures of the orbital and nasal rims and the quantity of bone is suitably small to gain all that is required from the donor site. In addition, the cortical nature of this type of graft is consistent with the cortical nature of the orbital and nasal rims (Figs. 30–117 and 30–118).

Provide Anchorage via Implant Fixtures or Magnets to Enhance Retention. Osseointegrated implants can often be placed in the remaining maxilla, zygoma, or sphenoid bones to provide a retention focus for a facial restorative prosthesis (Fig. 30–119). Planning of such fixtures requires a precise location of the placement point, which is coordinated with the maxillofacial prosthodontist or facial ocularist to permit maximal usage of the fixture and to ensure that there is sufficient

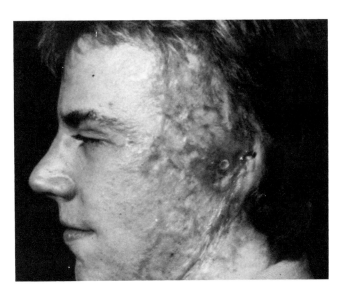

FIGURE 30–119. Avulsed ear from burn injury. Osseointegrated fixtures placed into mastoid bone. (Courtesy of Daniel Eaton, BCO.)

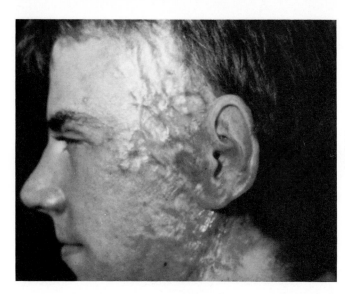

FIGURE 30–120. Ear prosthesis retained through osseointegrated fixtures into mastoid. (Courtesy of Daniel Eaton, BCO.)

bone thickness to accommodate and integrate the fixture (Fig. 30–120). Such planning is assisted best by a computerized tomographic (CT) scan and either stone models of the oral-nasal-antral defect or a facial moulage. The surgical placement of such fixtures is no different in principle or practice than that which is commonly employed in the jaws today. The implant length will usually be very short, as the remaining midfacial bones have limited thickness. The osseointegration time is 6 months.

In areas where the bone thickness is too little to place a fixture or where an osseointegrated fixture is contraindicated for some other reason, a two-piece prosthesis can be placed and samarium-gold magnets used[45] (Fig. 30–121). The first piece is placed into an area of either natural undercuts or surgically created undercuts, which are used as a retentive anchor. The second piece is the prosthesis proper, which gains its retention by magnetic coupling to the retentive anchor piece. The prosthesis proper can, therefore, be removed and cleaned in a straightforward manner without removing the retentive anchor piece. Such magnets have sufficient magnetic fields to provide firm retention for even very heavy or bulky prostheses. These magnets are permanent and completely inert and so will not corrode with time or lose their effectiveness. Their placement is simple. They are placed into each piece of the two-piece prosthesis during processing (Fig. 30–122).

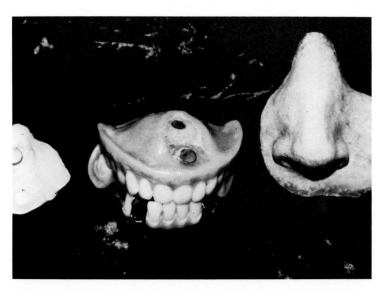

FIGURE 30–121. Maxillary appliance with samarium-gold magnets, which will provide retention for the nasal prosthesis. (Courtesy of Daniel Eaton, BCO.)

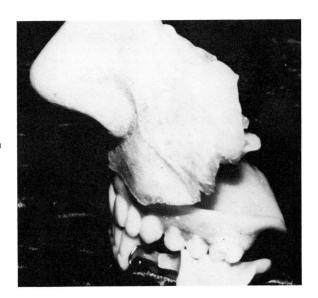

FIGURE 30–122. Magnet-retained nasal complex prosthesis upon maxillary denture. (Courtesy of Daniel Eaton, BCO.)

Replace Avulsed Soft Tissue When a Prosthesis Is Not Possible. Soft tissue reconstruction of the maxillary area is one of the most difficult areas in which to obtain a satisfactory result. Internally, the difficulty arises from the donor site morbidity of flaps required to reconstruct the palatal soft tissues and to close what are often large oral-nasal-antral communications. Although one may use combinations of vomer flaps, tongue flaps, buccal mucosa flaps, buccal fat pad transfers, and so forth, the scarring from these flaps, the effects on function they have, and their less than adequate results in large defects often make these choices unacceptable and are the main reasons why a prosthesis is preferred, if at all possible.

If an internal soft tissue flap is required, the most predictable flap for large defects is the temporal muscle flap.[46] This flap will cover the posterior palatal area and reach to the canine area in almost every case and even to the maxillary incisor area in some cases.[46] It is based on the two deep temporal arteries off the internal maxillary artery. One must therefore be sure the internal maxillary artery was not disrupted during the initial injury and that an external carotid artery ligation was not performed at an earlier surgery. If there is doubt about the integrity of these vessels, an angiogram should be performed.

The flap is developed from two incisions. A temporal or coronal incision is used to detach the muscle's origins from the temporal bone, and a mucosal incision is used over the ascending ramus to expose the coronoid process and provide a conduit through which the muscle can be transposed into the area of the internal defect. The muscle is brought into the defect without attached skin and is sutured to the adjacent soft tissue. The muscle is most often left to epithelialize but can be skin grafted for a quicker epithelial lining. The flap provides a soft tissue seal between the oral and nasal cavities and can be used later as a tissue bed into which a bone graft can be placed.[47]

Externally, reconstruction of the maxillary and midface area is difficult primarily because of tissue bulk and color match and secondarily because of its lack of animation. No distant tissue possesses the same color shading as the midfacial skin. Therefore, every flap is a color mismatch, usually being lighter than surrounding tissue. No distant tissue possesses the variations in tissue thickness that the midfacial skin does. Therefore, every flap has a bulk that is usually too bulky and adynamic to do any more than simply suffice.

When soft tissue is required, local facial or cervical flaps provide the best thickness and color match (Fig. 30–123). Such flaps are random-pattern full-thickness skin-subcutaneous rotation flaps from the preauricular area, postauricular area, or upper neck (Fig. 30–124). The flap is developed superficial to the muscles of facial expression, thereby avoiding injury to the facial nerve, since the nerve courses deep to the muscles and innervates them on their deep surface. Each flap must be planned for

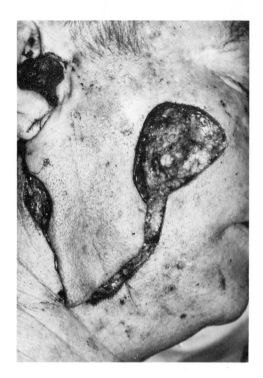

FIGURE 30–123.   Small-to-moderate soft tissue losses of the midface are best reconstructed with local flaps of good color match and tissue consistency.

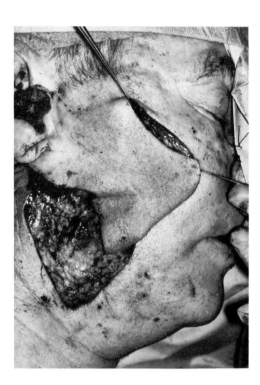

FIGURE 30–124.   Skin subcutaneous composite flaps rotated into the defect area are usually random pattern flaps and, therefore, must have a wide base. Here the flap is enhanced by the transverse facial artery.

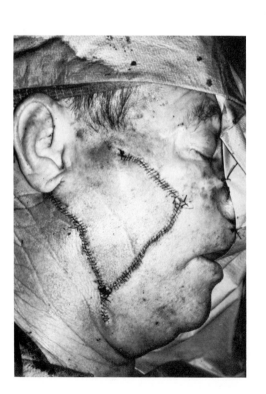

FIGURE 30–125.   Completed local flaps with primary closure, with most of the closure lying within resting skin tension lines.

the individual defect to fit into its unique geometry. However, one should attempt to develop a flap of the same thickness as the defect and to bring the final closure of both the recipient site and the donor site to fall into skinfold lines or the known resting skin tension lines (Fig. 30–125). The development of a local flap requires extensive dissection in the subcutaneous plane, creating a large potential dead space. Absolute hemostasis before closing is a necessity, and small drains and pressure dressings should also be considered to prevent a hematoma, which will lift the flap off the defect area.

Provide Bone Grafts or Alloplasts for Contour When a Prosthesis Cannot Achieve Such Contour. Occasionally, cases will occur that have missing components of the anterior bony maxilla or midface and have a good soft tissue cover, but in which the scar pattern has prevented a prosthesis from providing reasonable contour. Such cases can be reconstructed with bone for a lasting contour. The surgical approach is via a Weber-Fergusson type of incision that does not split the upper lip (Fig. 30–126). The soft tissue incision should begin in the philtrum of the involved side and should be carried around the alar base and lateral nose to the angle area of the eye. It is then extended laterally, in a subciliary fashion, to a distance at the level of the lateral canthus. A tissue plane is developed between the skin-subcutaneous composite superficially and the remaining fibers of the buccinator or buccal submucosa deeply. This dissection is usually complicated by scarring in these tissue planes that has resulted from the original injury. Therefore, in most situations, an arbitrary dissection plane is developed midway between the external skin and the internal buccal mucosa through the scar. If there are remaining portions of the piriform rim, nasal bones, infraorbital rim, or zygoma, they are exposed in the tissue bed for a graft-host interface.

This soft tissue pocket represents a very good tissue bed for a graft despite its degree of scarring and will support a gain in facial contour if a convex graft approximating the maxillary contour is placed within it. Although several alloplastic materials and bone graft sources may be used in this situation, the contour of the ipsilateral anterior ilium is the most similar (Fig. 30–127). One may, therefore, use an autogenous cortical-cancellous block graft supplemented with additional autogenous par-

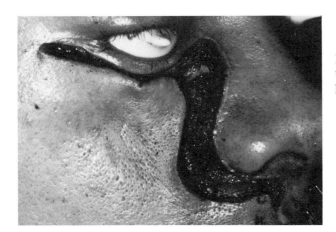

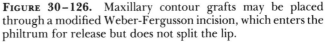

FIGURE 30–126. Maxillary contour grafts may be placed through a modified Weber-Fergusson incision, which enters the philtrum for release but does not split the lip.

FIGURE 30–127. A convex graft for maxillary contour may be obtained from the ipsilateral medial ilium. A cortical cancellous block may be harvested and supplemented with additional cancellous bone.

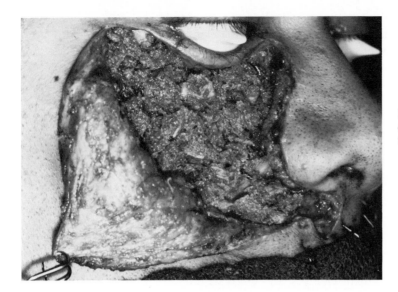

FIGURE 30–128. Particulate bone along with cancellous marrow is stacked upon and against the contour of the medial ilium graft.

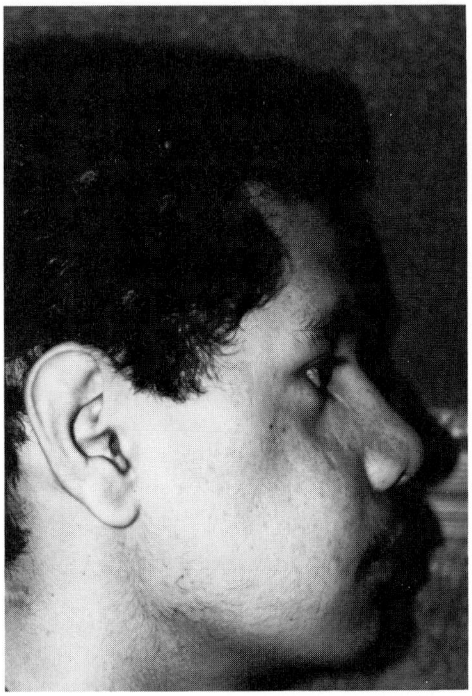

FIGURE 30–129. Contour deficiency of lost hemimaxilla, which could not be improved by a prosthesis.

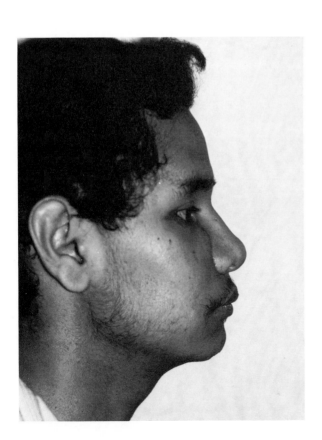

FIGURE 30–130. Contour gained by placement of a graft.

ticulate bone and cancellous marrow or a same-side allogeneic anterior ilium speci-men hollowed into a suitable crib and packed with autogenous particulate bone and cancellous marrow. In each case, the anterior ilium is inverted, so that the iliac crest forms a **J**-shaped alveolar area into which the autogenous bone can be packed and stacked up to achieve an outward contour (Fig. 30–128). If there are remaining adjacent host bones, the medial ilium cortex should be directly wired to each. The end result is a convex anterior medial ilium cortex that forms a tray medially against which an autogenous particulate graft is placed. Wound closure should be accomplished from the lateral canthus area to the medial canthus area and from the philtrum to the medial canthus. In this fashion, the soft tissue skin-subcutaneous cover can be ad-vanced over the additional contour gained by the graft (Figs. 30–129 and 30–130).

PERSPECTIVE

Reconstructive oral and maxillofacial surgery is a rapidly changing and expand-ing field. Within the past decade, there have been many changes, and surely within the upcoming decades, there will be numerous new and promising techniques, mate-rials, and concepts. Some of them will have little scientific data to support them and little real merit, whereas others will truly advance the science and the specialty. It has been the aim of this chapter to present current biologic principles and show how they can be adapted to the uniqueness of each individual's reconstructive needs, rather than give step-by-step guidelines in the style of a handbook. The reader should consider the principles and concepts in this chapter as only guidelines in his or her own treatment planning. Similarly, he or she should look upon the upcoming advances with a critical scientific eye, attempt to separate research from marketing, and look beyond the "how to do it" to see "how it (the new technique) does it."

REFERENCES

1. Kelly, JF: Maxillofacial missile wounds: Evalu-ation of long-term results of rehabilitation and reconstruction. J Oral Surg 31:438, 1973.
2. Ivy RH: Late results of treatment of gunshot fractures of the mandible. JAMA 75:13, 1920.
3. Blocker TG, Stout RA: Mandibular recon-struction, World War II. Plast Reconstr Surg 4:153, 1949.
4. Mowlem R: Cancellous chip bone grafts. Lan-cet 2:746, 1944.
5. Axhausen W: The osteogenic phases of re-generation of bone, a historical and experi-mental study. J Bone Joint Surg 38A:593, 1956.
6. Burwell RG: Studies in the transplantation of bone. VII. The fresh composite of homo-graft-autograft of cancellous bone. J Bone Joint Surg 46B:110, 1964.
7. Burwell RG: The fate of bone grafts. In Re-cent Advances in Orthopaedics. Baltimore, The Williams and Wilkins Company, 1969, pp 116–207.
8. Boyne PJ: Autogenous cancellous bone and marrow transplants. Clin Orthop 73:199, 1970.
9. Boyne PJ, Zarem H: Osseous reconstruction of the resected mandible. Am J Surg 132:49, 1976.
10. Marx RE, Kline SN: Principles and methods of osseous reconstruction. In Murphy BL (ed): International Advances in Surgical Oncology. London, AR Liss, 1983, pp 167–228.
11. Marx RE, Saunders TR: Reconstruction and rehabilitation of cancer patients. In Fonseca, RJ, Davis H (eds): Reconstructive Prepros-thetic Oral and Maxillofacial Surgery. Phila-delphia, WB Saunders Company, 1985, pp 347–428.
12. Krizek TJ, Robinson DM: The Deltopectoral flap for reconstruction of irradiated cancer of the head and neck. Surg Gynecol Obstet 135:87, 1972.
13. Mathog RH, and Smith RO: Temporal artery based forehead flap. Head Neck Surg 1:129, 1978.
14. Ariyan S: The pectoralis major myocutaneous flap. Plast Reconstr Surg 63:73, 1979.
15. Conley JJ, Parke RB: Pectoralis myocutan-eous flap for chin augmentation. Otolaryngol Head Neck Surg 89:1045, 1981.
16. Shapiro MJ: Use of trapezius myocutaneous flaps in the reconstruction of head and neck defects. Arch Otolaryngol 107:333, 1981.
17. Maves MD, Panje WR, Shagets FW: Ex-tended latissimus dorsi myocutaneous flap re-construction of major head and neck cancer defects. Otolaryngol Head Neck Surg 92:551, 1984.
18. Ariyan S: The Sternocleidomastoid myocu-taneous flap. Laryngoscope 90:676, 1980.
19. Marx RE, McDonald DK: The Sternocleido-mastoid muscle as a muscular and myocutan-eous flap. J Oral Maxillofac Surg 42:251, 1985.
20. McGregor IA: The temporal muscle in in-traoral cancer: Its use in repairing the post

excisional defect. Br J Plast Surg 16:318, 1963.

21. Bakamjian VY, Souther SA: Use of temporal muscle flap for reconstruction after orbito-maxillary resection for cancer. Plast Reconstr Surg 56:171, 1975.

22. Gray JC, Phil M, Elves MW: Donor cells contribution to osteogenesis in experimental cancellous bone grafts. Clin Orthop 163:261, 1982.

23. Gray JC, Elves MW: Early osteogenesis in compact bone isografts: A quantitative study of contributions of the different graft cells. Calcif Tissue Int 29:225, 1979.

24. Karapanzic M: Reconstruction of lip defects by local arterial flaps. Plast Surg 93:230, 1974.

25. Jabaley ME, Orcutt TN, Clement RL: Applications of the Karapanzic principle of lip reconstruction following excision of lip cancer. Am J Surg 132:529, 1976.

26. Bowers DG Jr: Double cross-lip flaps for lower lip reconstruction. Plast Reconstr Surg 47:209, 1971.

27. Panje WR: Free flaps vs myocutaneous flaps in head and neck reconstruction. Otolaryngol Clin North Am 15:111, 1982.

28. Urist MR: Bone: Formation by autoinduction. Science 150:893, 1965.

29. Reddi AH: Collagenous bone matrix and gene expression in fibroplasts. *In* Slavkin HC, Greulich RC (eds): Extracellular Matrix Influences on Gene Expression. New York, Academic Press, 1975, pp 619–635.

30. Sampath TK, Muthukumaran N, Reddi AH: Isolation of osteogenin, an extracellular matrix-associated, bone inductive protein by heparin affinity chromatography. Proc Natl Acad Sci USA 84:7109, 1987.

31. Simmons DJ: The care and feeding of grafts: How to pamper bone cells: *In* Holmes RE, Fisher JC (eds): Procedures of Bone Grafting III: Biology and Application for Maxillofacial Indications. San Diego, Plastic Surgery Research Foundation of San Diego, December 1–4, 1988.

32. Friedenstein AJ, Pratetsky-Shapiro II, Petrahova KV: Osteogenesis in transplants of bone marrow cells. J Embryol Exp Morphol 16:381, 1966.

33. Marx RE, Johnson RP: Introducing the Walkup flap. Oral Surg (in press).

34. Kusiak JK, Zins JE, Whitaker LA: The early revascularization of membranous bone. Plast Reconstr Surg 76:510, 1985.

35. Harsha BC, Turvey TA, Powers SK: Use of autogenous cranial bone grafts in maxillofacial surgery: A preliminary report. J Oral Maxillofac Surg 44:11, 1986.

36. Edelson JG, Nathan H: Meralgia paresthetic: An anatomical interpretation. Clin Orthop Rel Res 122:255, 1977.

37. Wolfe SA, Kawamoto HK: Taking the iliac bone graft. J Bone Joint Surg 60A:411, 1978.

38. Marx RE, Morales MJ: Morbidity from bone harvest in major jaw reconstruction. J Oral Maxillofac Surg 48:196, 1988.

39. Marx RE, Snyder R, Kline SN: Cellular survival of human marrow during placement of marrow–cancellous bone grafts. J Oral Surg 37:712, 1979.

40. Malinin TI: University of Miami Tissue Bank: Collection of post mortem tissues for clinical use and laboratory investigation. Transplant Proc 8 [Suppl 1]:53, 1976.

41. Malinin TI, Wu NM, Flores A: Freeze-drying of bone for allotransplantation. *In* Friedlander GE, Mankin HJ, Sell KW (eds): Osteochondral Allografts. Boston, Little, Brown, and Company, 1983, 181.

42. Gardner S: Ethylene oxide, ethylene chlorohydrin and ethylene glycol: Proposed maximum residue limits of exposure. Fed Register 43:27474, 1978.

43. Buck BE, Malinin TI, Brown MD: Bone transplantation and human immunodeficiency virus: An estimated risk of acquired immunodeficiency syndrome (AIDS). Clin Orthop 240:129, 1989.

44. Manchester W: Immediate reconstruction of the mandible and temporomandibular joint. Br J Plast Surg 18:291, 1977.

45. Eaton LD: The prosthetic management and rehabilitation of the orofacial deformity patient. *In* Proceedings of the International Congress on Maxillofacial Prosthetics and Technology, New York. September 6, 1984.

46. Bradley P, Brockbank J: The temporalis muscle flap in oral and maxillofacial reconstruction; a cadaveric, animal, and clinical study. J Maxillofac Surg 9:139, 1981.

47. Demas PN, Sotereanos GC: Transmaxillary temporalis transfer for reconstruction of a large palatal defect: Report of a case. J Oral Maxillofac Surg 47:197, 1989.

MAXILLOFACIAL PROSTHETICS FOR THE TRAUMA PATIENT

BARBARA B. MAXSON, D.D.S., M.S.,
GEORGE A. ZARB, B.CH., D.D.S., M.S., F.R.C.D.(C),
and DENIS C. LEE, B.S., M.C.

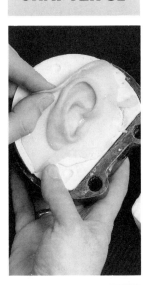

Maxillofacial prosthetics is an old discipline. The rehabilitation of facial form and function with prosthetic devices has been documented as early as 700 BC. The early Etruscans apparently possessed enough vanity and technology to fabricate metal frameworks that included animal teeth for the replacement of human teeth.

It was not until the sixteenth century that Ambrose Paré, a Frenchman, first described the palatal obturator. His prostheses were used for patients with perforated palates. This group included individuals with congenital cleft palates and those with palatal defects that were the sequelae of untreated syphilis.[1]

During the past half century, the development of new materials has been a key factor in creating the discipline of maxillofacial prosthetics with which we are familiar today. The application of ceramic, metal, plastic, and rubber materials to engineering biomechanics both for tissue replacement and as a means of tissue control is a fine example of the possibilities of human ingenuity. Today's materials offer prosthetic replacements that are natural in appearance and possess qualities for restoring a reasonable level of function.

A new era ushered in by the evolution of improved surgical techniques in conjunction with the evolution of biomaterials and engineering science seems to be upon us. The current technology and understanding of tissue biology have paved the way for predictable and reliable dental implantology. Rehabilitation of normal function and optimal comfort have become a reality for many patients who have lost oral and facial tissue because of trauma.

With the ever-expanding level of knowledge, the "team" concept of maxillofacial rehabilitation is increasingly important for the appropriate management of patients. The exchange of ideas and concepts among professionals also creates an environment for stimulating new knowledge. The prospects for the future are both formidable and exciting.

PHASES OF PROSTHETIC REHABILITATION

It is often useful to discuss maxillofacial prosthetic reconstruction in terms of three phases of rehabilitation: the immediate, transitional, and definitive phases.

When trauma has caused minimal tissue destruction, progression from one phase to the next may be rapid, and perhaps one or more of the phases can be eliminated. However, as the severity of the injury increases, the amount of time required to reach definitive reconstruction typically increases.

Final reconstruction may be delayed owing to the extent of the injury and the necessity for multiple surgical interventions. It may also be deferred until there is resolution of the sequelae of traumatic brain injury or psychologic problems or both.

EVALUATION OF NEUROLOGIC, PSYCHOLOGIC, AND SOCIAL STATUS

Knowledge of the trauma patient's neurologic status, psychologic status, and social environment is critical for effective and practical management with prosthetics. The ability of the individual to tolerate the clinical procedures and adjust to a prosthesis is very much dependent upon both mental status and muscle control. The practical necessity for such an appliance depends upon each patient's social situation.

Unfortunately, formal training or experience in the assessment of these factors has been historically lacking in dental education. Therefore, one must often seek the advice of others in planning appropriate prosthetic care for many trauma patients.

Patients with brain injury are often the most difficult to assess. The nursing staff is a good source of information regarding the present status of the patient. The primary physician may be able to predict somewhat the final rehabilitation goals for the patient. Relatives may be helpful, especially if the patient is living in their home. However, parents in particular may have difficulty accepting the changes in their child and may use denial or a variety of other defense mechanisms for coping with their grief. On occasion, they may present a management problem if they have chosen the prosthodontist as a scapegoat.

Psychologic factors may overlie the neurologic status of the brain-injured patient and create some distortion of true functional level. Frustrations related to the dependence imposed by the injury may lead to anger and depression. The resultant behavior may be perceived simply as lack of motivation or lethargy. At the initial appointment, the patient may appear to be unable to cooperate. However, when the patient is teamed with a regular therapist who is familiar with the patient and not so easily manipulated, he or she may be quite capable of compliance. Communication with regular care takers about the behaviors required to accomplish the necessary clinical procedures will facilitate the development of a practical course of treatment. Such communication may also elicit their support in accomplishing the final prosthetic goals. However, it may be unfair to restore patients with complex restorations if these care takers cannot take primary responsibility. The devoted care taker of the present may not be there for the duration.

Facial trauma has its own set of psychologic sequelae. Patients who are left with facial disfigurement after trauma will initially exhibit signs of acute situational stress. Grief is a part of the response to this crisis. The individual must reconcile his or her previous internalized facial image with the present facial appearance.[2] He or she must also cope with the responses of others. The more idealized the internalized image, the more difficult will be the adjustment.[3] It has also been demonstrated that the degree of facial disfigurement does not correlate on a one-to-one basis with the psychologic reaction.[4] If the patient is unable to come to terms with the change, social withdrawal may be a way of coping with unresolved feelings.[5,6]

The psychologic effects of physical attractiveness and the secondary social effects that may result have only very recently been described in the literature. With our democratic natures, we may feel a sense of discomfort when faced with the fact that physical appearance has been found to be an important psychologic variable in all the studies in which it was tested. The "beauty is good" hypothesis suggests that attractive people are perceived to possess many qualities, including intelligence, warmth, and sensitivity. It has also been observed that a person will behave the way that the respondent expects, a situation described as the "self-fulfilling prophecy." The obvious conclusion to be drawn is that facial appearance is an important influence upon how each person is perceived by others and, therefore, upon the kinds of opportunities and experiences that may follow.[7]

Children appear to have more psychosocial problems than adults after facial trauma. There is some evidence that attractive children are given preferential treatment by teachers and parents.[8] Adults, having had a more favorable socialization process and an awareness of social acceptance prior to their injury, may be able to adjust more easily. They may also possess more coping mechanisms than young patients.[9]

A good understanding of the psychologic and social milieu that surrounds each patient can aid the prosthetist or prosthodontist in the development of a course of treatment that will be successful. A closer look at these factors will often reveal the source of treatment failures.

INTRAORAL REHABILITATION

Surgical and Prosthodontic Considerations

When the surgeon suspects that an intraoral prosthesis will be necessary, early conference with the prosthodontist may improve the efficiency of both the surgical and the prosthodontic care. The prosthodontic requirements for reconstruction can be outlined for the surgeon, and surgical limitations can be identified for the prosthodontist. With the present rate of change in state-of-the-art surgical and prosthodontic treatment, the value of this type of communication is obvious.

Some examples of prosthodontic principles that may be important for consideration by the surgeon who manages the patient needing future prosthodontic care deserve mention:

1. Teeth are extremely important to successful intraoral prosthetics. Teeth that are broken down owing to dental caries or traumatic fracture may be critical to prosthodontic success. However, it may be necessary to extract healthy teeth that are situated in a way that will compromise prosthesis stability. Diagnostic casts may be necessary for the restorative dentist to make the appropriate recommendations.[10]

2. When removable intraoral prostheses will be necessary, secondary skin graft vestibuloplasty to recreate residual ridge support, free from the effects of tongue, lip, and cheek movement, is desirable.[10] The use of an immediate surgical stent is mandatory for reliable results (Fig. 31–1A to C). The stent may be removed 10 days postoperatively but should be adapted and worn as a transitional prosthesis until the definitive prosthesis can be completed.

3. An oronasal or oroantral fistula may be small enough to achieve successful surgical closure. However, on occasion the prosthodontist may prefer that it be left open. When a removable maxillary prosthesis will be the definitive reconstruction, the prosthesis will often obturate the defect, and surgical closure is unnecessary. In this instance, preservation of vestibular continuity is a priority over closure of the defect (Fig. 31–2). It is also advisable to avoid the use of soft palate as donor tissue for fistula closure, as secondary scar contracture may subsequently result in mild hypernasality. However, small fistulae (0 to 3 mm in diameter) will complicate impression procedures and are best closed if possible.

4. When the hard palate defect is too large to close surgically, prosthetic obturation will be required. Removal of vomer or nasal conchae may be necessary to create adequate space for the obturator and for patient comfort.[10]

5. When a significant portion of soft palatal tissue is absent, although the posterior border is intact, it may be necessary for effective prosthodontic management to

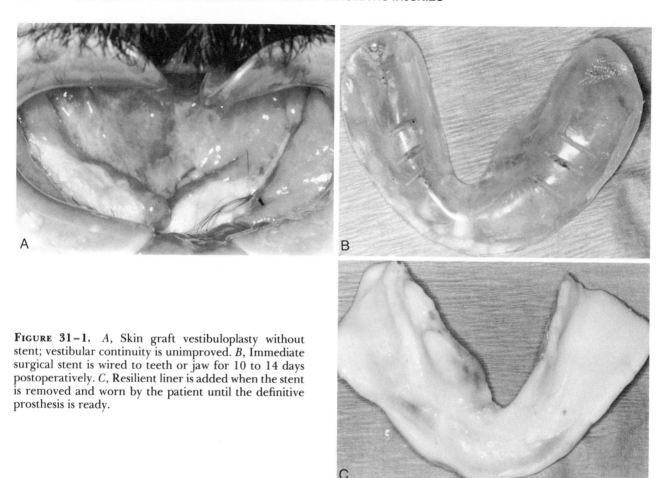

FIGURE 31–1. *A,* Skin graft vestibuloplasty without stent; vestibular continuity is unimproved. *B,* Immediate surgical stent is wired to teeth or jaw for 10 to 14 days postoperatively. *C,* Resilient liner is added when the stent is removed and worn by the patient until the definitive prosthesis is ready.

excise the residual palatal band surgically. Tissue changes from wound contracture may cause the residual soft palate to move forward and down. Extension of the palatal obturator under the band and into the pharynx will encroach upon the posterior tongue and stimulate the gag reflex. In addition, the residual soft palatal band may move enough during normal function that the tissue seal afforded by the obturator bulb is impossible to maintain. Excision of this band of tissue will allow the obturator

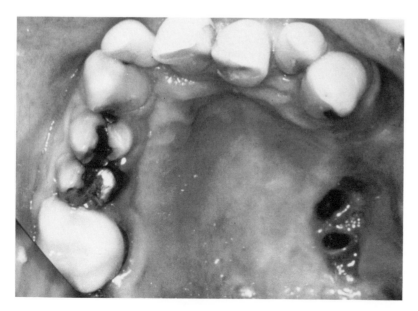

FIGURE 31–2. When a prosthesis will be worn for tooth replacement, efforts to close this defect with a surgical flap may compromise vestibular continuity and prosthetic extension.

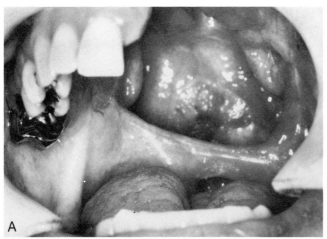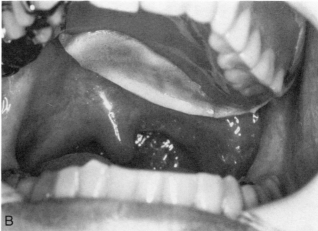

FIGURE 31-3. *A*, The posterior border of this soft palate band has moved forward and toward the tongue as a result of scar contracture. *B*, Attempts at obturation leave the patient with a mild-to-moderate hypernasality.

to extend well above the tongue and into the pharynx, reducing hypernasality and leakage of oral fluids through the nasal cavity. However, this approach may be unadvisable for the edentulous patient, and minor limitations in function may be preferable to loss of the palatal band for obturator retention[11] (Fig. 31-3*A* and *B*).

6. When significant destruction of the mandible necessitates bone grafting, realignment of the remaining teeth may not give the best estimate of an appropriate occlusal vertical dimension. Space between the maxillary tuberosity and retromolar pad is necessary for ideal prosthetic replacement. Surgical stents that observe these landmarks may aid in space maintenance.

7. Lip competence is another important consideration for the patient needing future prosthodontic care. The patient may possess ideal intraoral tissue support for prosthodontic retention and stability. However, without appropriate lip competence, the prosthesis will appear garish, and saliva control will be a continual problem. An overclosed occlusal vertical dimension may be a reasonable solution if lip competence cannot be improved surgically.

Phase I: Immediate Rehabilitation

The immediate phase of reconstruction after trauma most often involves the use of devices for reapproximation and stabilization of normal tissue relationships. This type of appliance provides immobilization and support for hard and soft tissues, which will enable the physiologic process of repair and ensure a more predictable final result.

The surgical splint prosthesis may also be modified to aid in the immediate restoration of certain aspects of function. For example, the surgical splint that is used for stabilization of the fractured maxilla may also obturate a palatal defect to restore normal deglutition and speech.

Phase II: Transitional Rehabilitation

The transitional phase of rehabilitation is most often the phase that is extended in length when the injury is severe or when the patient is not responding to treatment as expected.

The purpose of the interim prosthesis may simply be to improve appearance until healing is complete and definitive restoration can be accomplished. It may temporarily facilitate essential functions, such as speech, oromotor control of food and liquids, or swallowing while the patient is involved in physical therapy or while further surgical reconstruction is under consideration. It may take the form of a functional device to be used by the patient temporarily for maintenance of tissue contours in the face of wound contracture or as an exercise appliance for restoration of functional jaw relationships.

It is also during this phase that the assessment of neurologic potential and resolution of psychologic problems will need to be addressed. The transitional phase can be used to "buy time," which will allow each individual to reach a plateau, both physically and mentally. The way in which the individual responds to treatment during this phase is important information for the restorative dentist when the definitive treatment plan is being formulated.

TRANSITIONAL PROSTHESIS: BASIC DESIGN

The transitional prosthesis should be inexpensive and can be fabricated quickly from a stone model made from a simple irreversible hydrocolloid impression. Acrylic resin is an ideal material, since additions and subtractions are easily accomplished. Wrought-wire clasps adapted to the teeth can be included for retaining the prosthesis.

This type of prosthesis may also be adapted with a resilient liner to be used as a surgical splint in secondary reconstructive surgery, such as vestibuloplasty. The prosthesis with soft reline material can be used as a tissue conditioner prior to definitive impression procedures or simply as a way to maintain the patient's comfort. The major disadvantage of the acrylic resin transitional appliance is its fragility.

TRANSITIONAL RESTORATION OF DENTOALVEOLAR DEFECTS

The most common dentofacial injury is tooth loss. A simple transitional appliance fabricated of acrylic resin and retained by wrought-wire clasps adapted to selected retained teeth can serve as a transitional removable partial denture for tooth replacement. This simple appliance can restore appearance and improve both articulation and mastication. It will also act as a space maintainer until the patient is ready for fixed partial denture reconstruction (Fig. 31–4).

Lengthy physical rehabilitation after spinal cord injury, head injury, or immobili-

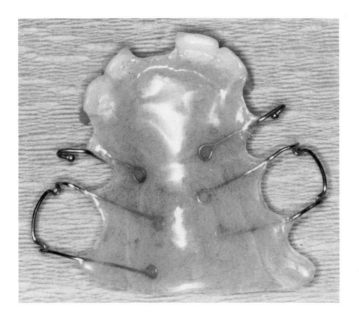

FIGURE 31–4. Basic transitional acrylic resin prosthesis.

zation of fractured limbs may delay definitive oral rehabilitation. Physical therapy is often intensive and tiring, and complex dental restoration may be best delayed until the patient is able to tolerate long dental visits and can be seated comfortably in the dental operatory.

With children, definitive dental restoration must wait until growth and maturation are nearly complete. Multiple transitional prostheses may be necessary in a growing child, especially during the period of mixed dentition.

When the injury is the result of an accident in which litigation to establish fault is involved, a delay in the initiation of definitive dental reconstruction may be advisable.

HARD PALATE DEFECTS

The same basic design can be adapted for transitional obturation of a maxillary hard palate defect. Restoration of oral and nasal integrity with a prosthesis will restore both speech and swallowing to normal functional levels, often without retraining.

When sufficient dentition remains for prosthesis retention and the fistula is fairly small, it is unnecessary to extend the appliance into the defect. In fact, during the transitional phase of rehabilitation, small fistulae typically become smaller as the scar tissue matures. However, extension into the palatal opening may be necessary if the anatomic contours will be used to enhance prosthesis retention or if it is so large that leakage of oral fluids into the nasal cavity is likely.

During the transitional phase, extension into the defect can be accomplished with a resilient soft liner. This measure will facilitate the patient's comfort and allow the tissues to heal, leaving a well-defined scar band. The liner is also easily changed to keep pace with changes in tissue contour, which occur most rapidly during the first 6 months after injury.

SOFT PALATE INSUFFICIENCY

Traumatic injury occurring directly to the soft palate and resulting in palatal insufficiency is uncommon owing to the relatively protected location of the soft palate. When it does occur, surgical flap repair may be the best solution. If adequate tissue is unavailable or surgical reconstruction is not an option, a palatal obturator may be indicated.

With the use of appropriate landmarks, the basic transitional appliance can be adapted for soft palate obturation by an addition that extends into the pharynx. For the adult, palatopharyngeal closure is slightly above the level of the palatal plane at the level of the torus tubarius.[12] Extension of the obturator into the pharynx at this level also prevents encroachment of the prosthesis upon the tongue and subsequent stimulation of the gag reflex.

Since normal palatopharyngeal closure is sphincter-like,[13,14] the prosthesis must accommodate both lateral and posterior pharyngeal wall musculature. The muscular activity of the posterior and lateral pharyngeal walls varies among individuals and may not be symmetric.[15] The position of the soft palate in relation to the pharynx and character of its movement changes with age and the presence of tonsillar tissues.[12] The character of velopharyngeal closure also varies with the physiologic function.[16]

Because velopharyngeal closure is complex and variable,[17,18] it is necessary to develop the contour of the soft palate obturator with a functional technique. The design of the palatal bulb must also be adapted to head posture and swallowing function in addition to speech considerations. A functional impression technique will attempt to accommodate all of the above variables.

Complete separation of the oral and nasal cavities is not necessarily essential for acceptable speech.[19,20] In fact, hyponasal speech can result when the obturator fits too well. Some relief of the functionally adapted obturator may be appropriate. It is important to have the support of a trained listener, such as a speech pathologist, when developing any speech aid prosthesis.

Functional Impression Technique for Palatal Obturation.   To develop an obturator contour that will accommodate functional tissue relationships, the impression material must be able to record the anatomy during function. The material must be soft enough to be molded, but stiff enough to maintain its form.

Most of the rubber impression materials are initially fluid and too difficult to control for this purpose. In addition, when a hard or soft palate fistula is present, materials with high viscosity will flow through the opening and laterally, forming projections like the cap of a mushroom. These projections inevitably tear upon removal of the impression, leaving remnants in the nose that can be aspirated. If the "mushroom cap" has a fairly broad base, it may not tear but may instead cause tissue trauma and pain as the impression is removed.

Putty impression materials can be molded, but to retain their shape they must be used with catalyst and allowed to polymerize. Once polymerized, they are difficult to alter.

A functional impression technique employing impression compound and fluid wax, although no longer used routinely in restorative dentistry, does possess the qualities needed for developing the palatal obturator.[21] Since the materials are heat sensitive, they can be reinserted and readapted indefinitely, which will allow the operator the ability to record multiple functional movements (Fig. 31–5A and B).

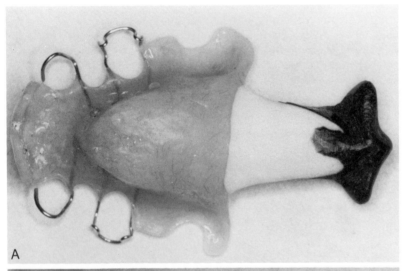

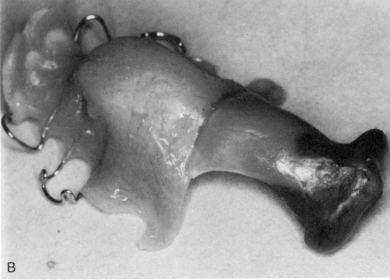

FIGURE 31–5. *A,B,* Dental compound and impression wax technique for the soft palate obturator. (Courtesy of Dr. Thomas J. Bloem.)

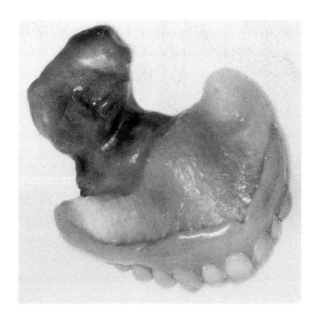

FIGURE 31–6. Soft palate obturator for the edentulous maxilla. (Courtesy of Dr. Thomas J. Bloem.)

The presence of some teeth for retention of the prosthesis is always important but is especially critical for soft palate rehabilitation. The extra weight of the palatal extension and the action of the pharyngeal musculature are additional factors that add to the challenge of prosthesis retention for the edentulous patient (Fig. 31–6).

SOFT PALATE INCOMPETENCE

The finding of hypernasal speech and loss of oral fluids through the nose after trauma is most commonly the result of neurologic deficit associated with brain injury. The hypernasality may persist and is often associated with muscle weakness and incoordination of the musculature involved in articulation.

When the speech pathologist has determined that palatopharyngeal closure is persistently incomplete for purposes of intelligible speech production, referral for a palatal lift prosthesis may be appropriate.

The Transitional Palatal Lift Prosthesis. The palatal lift prosthesis can be tried initially as a transitional appliance to determine the efficacy of a future definitive prosthesis. The patient's acceptance and motivation can be assessed without the financial expenditure associated with the definitive restoration. A realistic estimation of the level of improvement in speech intelligibility that can be accomplished with a prosthesis can also be made with this trial appliance.

At the initial consultation appointment, the evaluation must include the potential for cooperation by the patient, status of the dentition, and condition of the soft palate. The patient must be able to understand the purpose of the prosthesis and his or her role in its use. The early discomfort associated with wearing the appliance and the importance of working with the speech pathologist to achieve an optimal result must be explained to the patient. A description of the impression procedures involved and of the prosthesis itself is also helpful. With children and adolescents, the involvement of a supportive parent can be an important factor.

An examination for dental disease and for assessment of oral hygiene is the next step. With a brain-injured patient, the time from initial injury to speech rehabilitation may be many months. Patients may have been without adequate oral hygiene, and the condition of the dentition may have deteriorated. Some may have had poor dental health prior to their injury. Teeth that are not salvageable should be extracted, and restorable teeth with dental caries should at least receive temporizing treatment. Pulpectomy is also indicated for devitalized teeth that will be retained (Fig. 31–7).

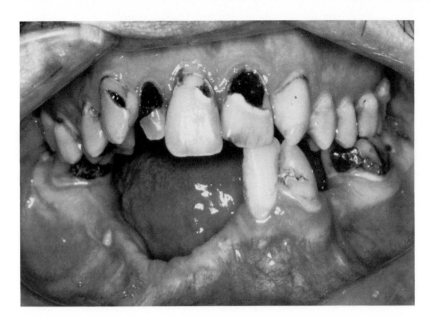

FIGURE 31–7. The management of existing dental disease is the first step in rehabilitating the patient who has suffered head injury.

The preservation of teeth for retention of the palatal lift prosthesis is critical. There must be an adequate number and appropriate positioning of periodontally sound teeth to resist the pressure applied by the palate to dislodge the appliance. A technique for fabrication of a palatal lift appliance for the edentulous maxilla has been described in the literature,[22] but the ability of this restoration to provide soft tissue resistance is greatly reduced without the support of the dentition.

If the oral hygiene is poor, it must be established whether the problem is motivational or related to neuromuscular deficits associated with the injury. Adaptation of oral hygiene devices for the special needs of each patient should be considered. If the patient is unable to do independent mouth care, regular care takers may be trained to assist with oral hygiene. Patients who have the ability to maintain adequate oral hygiene but who lack motivation may be poor candidates for prosthetic therapy.

Assessing the degree of flexibility of the soft palate and sensitivity of the gag reflex can allow a prediction to be made about the amount of difficulty the individual is likely to have adjusting to the prosthesis. Frequently, the patient with neurologic deficit of the soft palate secondary to head injury has a poorly stimulated gag response. This finding usually indicates that the patient will tolerate the palatal extension quite well. Evaluation can be made by placing a tongue blade or similar object lightly against the middle of the hard palate and moving posteriorly until the gag reflex is initiated.

If the decision after examination is to proceed with the transitional palatal lift prosthesis, a maxillary reversible hydrocolloid impression is made. The basic transitional prosthesis design is used with special consideration of the need for extensive clasping. Twenty-gauge wrought-wire Adams clasps on opposing molar and bicuspid teeth, which engage the teeth at the mesial and distal buccal infrabulge, can be adapted to produce a very retentive appliance.[23] Primary teeth, adult teeth with extremely short clinical crowns, or teeth that are tipped palatally may not be suitable for adequate retention. Enamel-bonded composite resin or enameloplasty may be used to improve crown contour for purposes of retention.

The patient is then trained to carry out daily exercises for desensitization of the gag reflex. Desensitization can be accomplished in several weeks with a motivated patient. Tongue blades or plastic spoons make good exercise tools for this purpose. The patient is asked to spend at least four 5-minute sessions per day placing the tongue blade or the convex portion of the spoon progressively farther posteriorly along the soft palate with a light touch. The initial use of a mirror and demonstration of the technique are helpful. If the patient is unable to accomplish the exercises alone, a physical therapist or care taker can be trained to help. The patient is told that the goal of the exercises is to place the tool increasingly farther back along the palate without gagging.

At the initial delivery appointment, the basic prosthesis is first adjusted to fit the patient. If the patient does not find the appliance too uncomfortable, some palatal extension can be initiated at this time. Once the basic prosthesis has been fitted and the clasps have been adjusted, the distance from central incisors to posterior pharyngeal wall can be estimated with a tongue blade used as a ruler.

An autopolymerizing acrylic resin tray material is then added to the prosthesis. The tray material should be formed initially to extend posteriorly along the middle soft palate at the level of the palatal plane. It must be wide enough and thick enough to possess adequate strength. It may then be adjusted with a grinding tool to extend far enough posteriorly so that the appliance can be placed without immediately eliciting the gag response. The patient may look somewhat uncomfortable and may wish initially to keep the mouth open to avoid contact between the prosthesis and the posterior tongue. If the tray needs to be lowered slightly to accommodate a low-drape palate, the resin may be warmed in a bunsen burner and depressed with a wet finger or forceps.

The appropriate distal contour, which may be convex or spoonlike in form, can be formed with dental compound. Customizing the posterior edge of the lift portion in this way should help to prevent irritation, which may be more likely with this arbitrary design. Some extension made laterally at the end of the lift may be well tolerated and may serve to maximize the area of palatal closure.

Conversion of the impression and tray to acrylic resin and incorporation of this portion into the palatomaxillary portion of the prosthesis can be accomplished in the laboratory with autopolymerizing acrylic resin and a pressure pot.

The basic prosthesis plus impression is first invested in irreversible hydrocolloid.[24] The impression portion is cut away, the prosthesis is replaced into the hydrocolloid investment, and autopolymerizing acrylic resin is added to replace the impression and tray portion. It is a good idea to include a wire with retention loops situated lengthwise into the soft palate extension.[25] If the acrylic resin should fracture, the pharyngeal portion will be held by the wire.

The investment is then placed into the pressure pot for curing to minimize the development of porosity in the material. In 5 minutes, the prosthesis is ready to be finished and polished. Further additions to the palatal lift can be accomplished with the same technique at future appointments as the patient adapts to each addition (Fig. 31–8A to F).

For patients with a poor gag reflex and flexible soft palate, nearly the full palatal extension may be added at once. With most individuals, however, serial additions with intervening adaptation periods are necessary to accomplish full extension of the lift.

With each addition, patients are given a schedule for daily wearing of the prosthesis. A typical schedule begins with a 15-minute wearing period four times per day, increasing to 1 hour. Half-hour increments are added with a 2-hour rest between wearing periods until 6 to 8 hours are tolerated at one wearing period. The patient will then wear the appliance daily for at least 1 week before the next addition. Time of wearing should not be increased until the patient is very comfortable with the previous addition.

Many patients find that eating with the prosthesis in place is difficult and may elect to remove it during meals. Although speech may be compromised by velopharyngeal incompetence after head injury, most patients learn to swallow their food without nasal regurgitation.

The head-injured person often has problems with articulation in addition to the hypernasality associated with the incompetent soft palate. The placement of the lift prosthesis will initially compromise articulation, which must be relearned with the prosthesis in place. The speech pathologist can work with the patient during the adaptation stage by assisting with the relearning of articulatory skills and by teaching

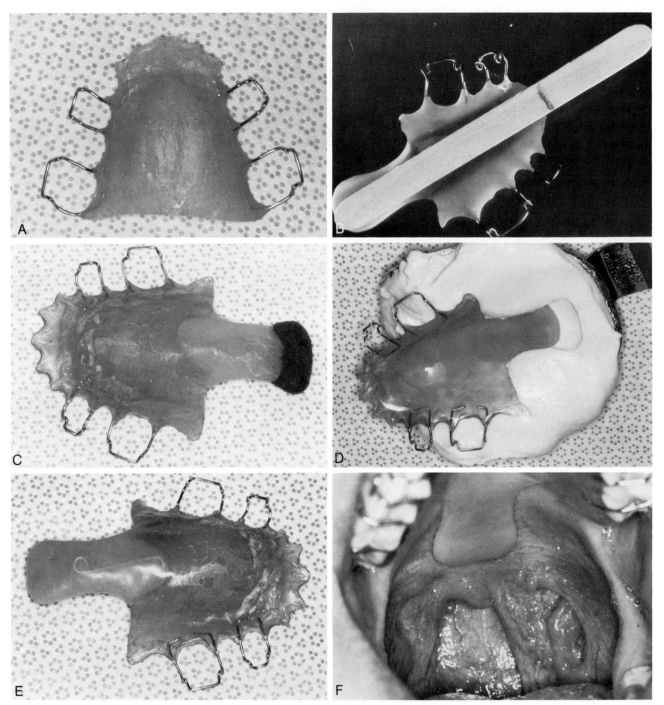

FIGURE 31–8.   Fabrication of a transitional palatal lift prosthesis.   *A,* Opposing Adams clasps can produce adequate retention. *B,* Approximation of palatal extension with a tongue blade. *C,* Extension formed in dental compound. *D,* Irreversible hydrocolloid as an investment for addition to the lift. *E,* Finished prosthesis. *F,* Prosthesis in function. (*B* courtesy of Dr. Thomas J. Bloem.)

exercises to improve muscle strength and coordination. The speech therapist can also monitor progress and give feedback and encouragement. This support is critical to the success of the treatment.

After 6 months, the amount of improvement in intelligibility with the prosthesis in place can be assessed by the speech pathologist and patient, and a decision about the need for a definitive prosthesis can be made. Although some studies have found that increased pharyngeal activity is stimulated by obturator placement in cleft palate patients,[26] others have been unable to repeat this finding.[27] Patients who are neurologically compromised will be the least likely to demonstrate any significant muscle compensation.

THE INTERIM FUNCTIONAL PROSTHESIS

Oral Commissure Prosthesis.   The oral commissure prosthesis is used to prevent microstomia when trauma involving the corners of the mouth or circumoral tissues has occurred. Scar contracture of the tissues that control entrance to the oral cavity may affect the patient's ability to carry out adequate oral hygiene or receive dental treatment. The microstomia may inhibit placement of a removable denture. In young children, it is likely to cause facial disfigurement with restriction of normal dental development.

Burns of the oral commissure.   A more complete discussion of the pathophysiology of burns is presented in Chapter 26.

Burns are the most common injury that require the use of a functional prosthesis for the prevention of microstomia. However, a circumoral stent may offer some benefit in maintaining oral competence in the patient with perioral lacerations that have been primarily closed.

In addition to burns involving the face that are caused by fire, chemicals, or explosion, one may encounter a characteristic electrical burn specific to the oral cavity. This burn is typically caused by biting into a live electrical wire, such as an extension cord. The most common site of injury is the commissure and adjacent lip. This type of wound most often occurs in young children (Fig. 31–9A).

The early lesion is painless because of sensorineural destruction and does not bleed owing to blood vessel coagulation associated with electrical cautery. Careful observation of the patient is necessary in the early phases of wound healing. The central necrotic area of the wound turns to a black eschar and sloughs several weeks after injury, leaving an ulcerated area. The blood vessels are then vulnerable to further injury, and secondary hemorrhage can be a complication in a significant number of patients. Applied pressure is usually adequate to control the bleeding, but electrocautery or ligation of vessels may be required, especially when the labial artery is involved.[28]

Stenting should be accomplished as soon as feasible after debridement. Scar contracture is largely parallel to the horizontal plane, so retraction forces should be placed in this plane also[29] (Fig. 31–9B).

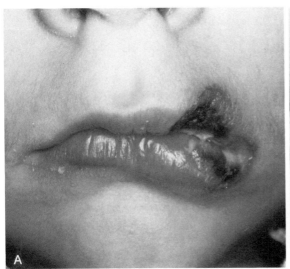 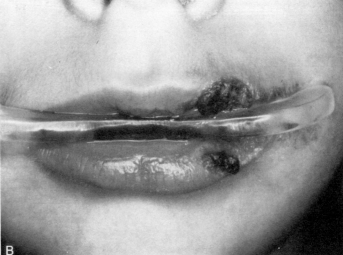

FIGURE 31–9.   Electrical cord burn.   *A,* Presenting lesion. *B,* Oral stent in place. (Courtesy of Dr. Thomas J. Bloem.)

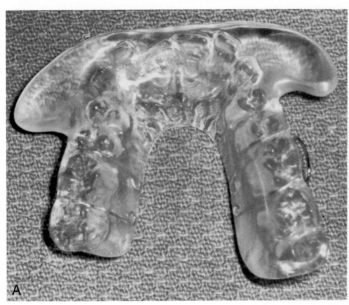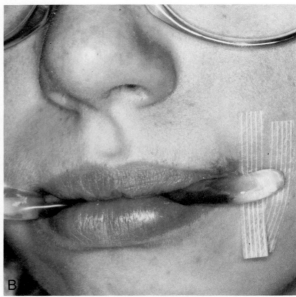

FIGURE 31–10. *A,* A tooth-borne appliance is usually more comfortable when practicable. *B,* A 14-year-old child after dog bite injury involving the commissure.

After the wound has re-epithelialized, it should be monitored for the development of ulceration from the prosthesis. Ideally, one wishes to achieve maximal traction without ulceration. An estimation of the appropriate amount of traction can be made by measuring the distance from the midline to the commissure on the widest smile on the uninvolved side.[28]

General considerations for the circumoral stent.   Intraoral, extraoral, dynamic, and static prostheses have been designed for patients with circumoral trauma. Of necessity all involve an interference with speech, mastication, and appearance. All must be worn continuously for 8 to 12 months. Tooth-borne intraoral appliances are perhaps less cumbersome than the extraoral head gear type (Fig. 31–10*A* and *B*). However, maintaining retention on a long-term basis may be difficult for the patient with primary or mixed dentition. The prosthesis must also be removable to allow for oral hygiene.[28-30]

The patient's compliance is critical to the success of this treatment modality. With a noncompliant patient or when the wound is extensive, several secondary surgical procedures may be necessary. However, the risk of additional scar contracture must be considered in the design of subsequent surgical procedures (Fig. 31–11).

The Trismus Appliance.   Trismus may occur during maxillofacial rehabilitation secondary to temporomandibular joint trauma or scar contracture that may follow an extensive flap reconstruction or primary closure with inadequate local tissue. If left untreated, the patient may complain of eating problems. Without oral access for adequate hygiene and restorative dentistry, the long-term viability of the dentition is at risk. It is therefore important to begin treatment in the immediate postsurgical stage, when primary healing has occurred but before significant scar maturation has developed and the tissues are still pliable.

For patients with teeth, an increasing number of tongue blades taped together can be forced between the dental arches to act as a wedge. Patients have a real numerical gauge of their success with this technique. Multiple exercise sessions each day are appropriate. To apply a constant opening force, a dynamic bite opener can be adapted to the teeth with autopolymerizing acrylic resin. Extraoral elastics that control the amount of force delivered are applied (Fig. 31–12*A* and *B*).

For the edentulous patient, the dynamic bite opener may be adapted with dentures or baseplates. If dentures are used, it may be necessary to remove posterior teeth

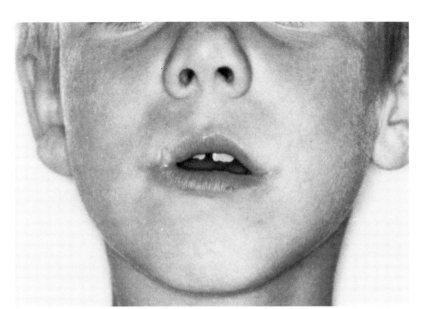

FIGURE 31–11. A noncompliant patient will achieve a less than ideal result.

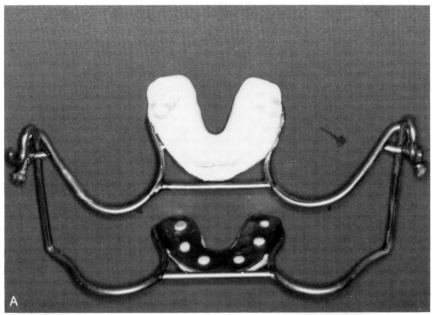

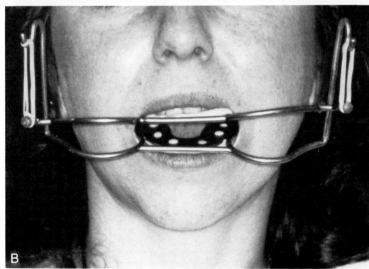

FIGURE 31–12. *A,B,* Dynamic bite opener for trismus.

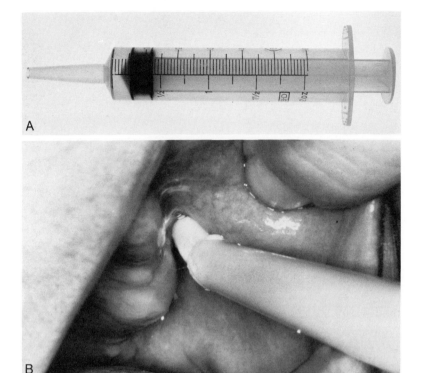

FIGURE 31–13. *A,B,* A 50-ml syringe for delivery of irreversible hydrocolloid impression material.

to gain adequate space.[31] If baseplates are to be fabricated for the edentulous patient, there may be inadequate room for conventional impression trays. Irreversible hydrocolloid may be placed on the convex side of a plastic spoon or wax sheet that has been coated with compatible adhesive. The use of a 50-ml polyvinyl syringe for injection of the impression material into the vestibules and palatal vault prior to introduction of the "tray" may also help to achieve an acceptable record of the edentulous anatomy[32] (Fig. 31–13*A* and *B*).

The patient progressively increases elastic tension with additional twists or increasingly heavier elastic bands. Intermittent resting periods will minimize discomfort. The patient's progress should be checked every few weeks.

When an adequate maximal opening is accomplished, the patient may wish to wear the appliance intermittently for several months to prevent relapse. Patients can be trained to monitor their own stability by measuring the distance at the maximal opening between the maxillary and the mandibular incisor teeth. Continuation of stretching exercises unaided by any tool may be sufficient to prevent relapse. It is likely that maintenance exercise may be necessary for many months after initial treatment to maintain interocclusal space.

Phase III: Definitive Rehabilitation

Treatment planning for definitive prosthetic rehabilitation after maxillofacial injury is appropriate when the patient is both physically and mentally ready to tolerate the lengthy procedures that are often involved. In addition to tissue integrity, tissue form, and functional status, the prosthodontist must also consider the individual needs, expectations, and abilities of patients in determining an appropriate definitive treatment plan. The patient must be able to understand and willingly accept his or her role in successful prosthetic replacement.

Often more than one treatment option may be presented to the patient for consideration. The differences between treatment plans may be related to differences in comfort, function, aesthetics, or any combination of these three prosthetic factors. Costs in terms of time and financial commitment are also necessary considerations. The definitive intraoral prosthesis may be fixed or removable. The degree of difficulty in developing a definitive treatment plan for intraoral reconstruction will usually be in direct relation to the severity of the injury.

In addition to a thorough oral examination and radiographic survey, it will often be necessary to articulate diagnostic models of the dental arches at an appropriate occlusal vertical dimension at centric occlusion. Although these procedures are time consuming, future time can be conserved — and embarrassment averted — by a thorough and carefully considered plan of treatment. Adequacy of interocclusal space, occlusal relationships, and complications created by crown and soft tissue contours are considerations in treatment planning that are often difficult to appreciate by examination alone.

DEFINITIVE RESTORATION OF DENTOALVEOLAR DEFECTS

Restoration of the dentoalveolar defect can be accomplished by either a fixed or removable prosthesis. Although the fixed restoration is preferable for this purpose, when the interdental span is too great or the soft tissue defect too large to produce an adequate cosmetic result, the removable partial denture may be indicated. Time constraints, poor compliance by the patient, or financial limitations may also indicate the removable appliance, even though the fixed restoration is technically possible.

The Tooth-Supported Fixed Partial Denture. The first step in deciding upon the options available for restoration of the dentoalveolar defect is to determine the periodontal status, location in the dental arch, angulation, crown-root ratio, and occlusal relationships of the remaining teeth (Fig. 31–14A to D). Factors for deter-

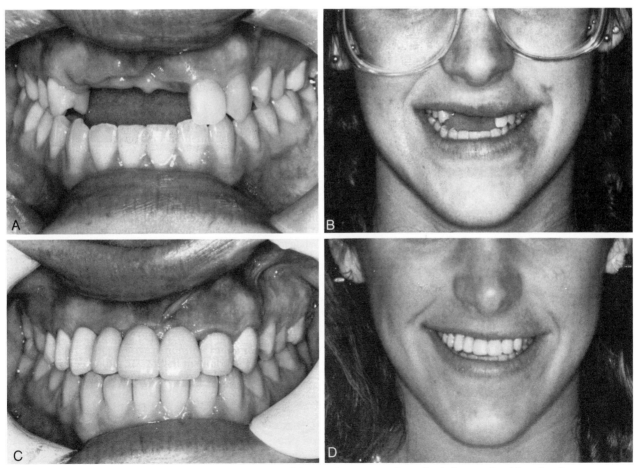

FIGURE 31–14. *A–D,* When ideal conditions exist, restoration of missing teeth with a fixed partial denture can restore function, comfort, and aesthetics.

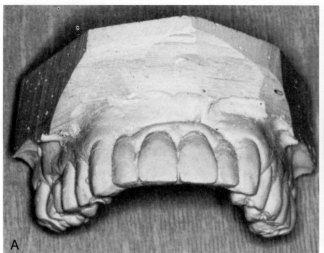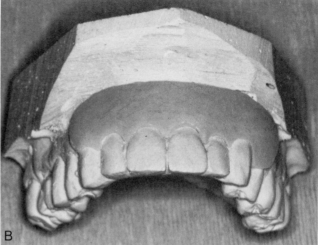

FIGURE 31–15. *A,B,* When the addition of pink porcelain is inadequate for restoration of lip contour, a removable labial flange may provide the extra support.

mining the adequacy of the teeth for support of a fixed partial denture and principles for the development of appropriate retainer and pontic design can be found in an advanced text on crown and bridge prosthodontics. However, special considerations for the patient in the post-trauma period deserve mention.

Sometimes the alveolar defect is so extensive that the replacement teeth will be too long to be aesthetic or the lip contour will be compromised. Addition of pink porcelain to the pontic area that extends beyond the normal cervical area of the replacement teeth into the alveolar defect may be a reasonable solution. Another option may be to fabricate an acrylic resin or silicone removable overlay prosthesis for restoration of gingival and alveolar anatomy (Fig. 31–15*A* and *B*). Surgical management of the defect by particulate bone grafting is still another option prior to prosthetic rehabilitation.

In the restoration of maxillary defects, especially in the anterior dental arch, the effects of the replacement anatomy upon articulation must be considered. Palatal and dental form must be adequately reproduced for the tongue to make the appropriate valving for good articulation. Following tooth preparation, the acrylic resin temporary fixed partial denture can be modified until the patient has acceptable articulation. A stone model of this contour may be sent to the dental laboratory for the technician to use when creating the definitive restoration.

THE REMOVABLE PARTIAL DENTURE

Although the removable partial denture may be a tooth-borne prosthesis for restoration of a simple dentoalveolar defect, it is most often employed when both tooth-bearing and soft tissue–bearing areas will be used for prosthesis support. The alloys in present use for framework construction possess adequate strength and oral biocompatibility to be practical for long-term use. However, neglect or abuse by the patient will significantly shorten the lifespan of any prosthesis.

Basic design principles that are important in conventional removable partial denture construction apply to maxillofacial prosthetics as well. Rigidity, guiding surfaces for framework stability, and harmony of tooth and soft tissue support are important in the production of both a functional and a nondestructive long-term prosthesis. Periodontal considerations, which include retentive and bracing components that deliver forces within physiologic limits, direction of forces parallel to the long axes of the teeth, and a design that is favorable for optimal oral hygiene, are also critical to long-term success.[33] However, some special considerations for partial denture design are often associated with maxillofacial applications.

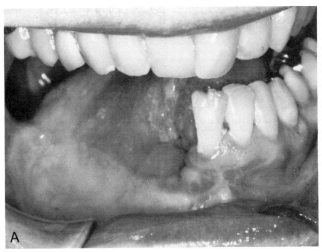 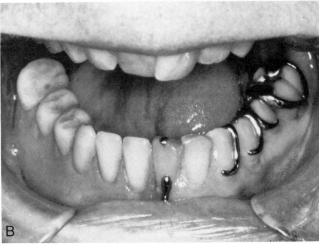

FIGURE 31–16. *A*, Vestibuloplasty may improve soft tissue support for the removable partial denture. *B*, Multiple clasp design can improve retention and help distribute forces among teeth.

Retention and bracing requirements are often far greater for maxillofacial applications than is necessary for the conventional removable partial denture. Poor or insufficient soft tissue base support may dictate the necessity for greater reliance upon the dentition for distribution of forces that may occur during occlusal loading. Surgical procedures such as vestibuloplasty are often needed for improvement of base support (Fig. 31–16A). Functional impression techniques and altered cast impression procedures may be helpful for maximizing hard and soft tissue balance.[34]

Retention that offers purposeful resistance to opposing soft tissue for the palatal lift appliance must be significantly greater than that needed simply to resist the forces of gravity in the conventional maxillary removable partial denture. Combined buccal and lingual retention will increase the amount of force necessary to dislodge the prosthesis, and the use of a lingual plate will also enhance retentive resistance in proportion to tooth span.[35] Clasping of multiple teeth not only increases resistance to removal but also serves to distribute the forces among teeth (Fig. 31–16B).

Linguoversion of retained teeth after injury to the jaws is a common problem associated with removable partial denture framework design. This situation is often found after healing of the mandibular lateral discontinuity defect or the mandibular anterior discontinuity defect. It can also persist after bone grafting of these defects, probably owing to the effects of muscle pull prior to reconstruction. Palatoversion of the maxillary teeth may also occur because of scar contracture when injury to the maxillary bones is extensive and stabilization of the maxilla is by fibrous union. Bilateral buccal and lingual rests with appropriate bracing elements help to direct forces axially[34] (Fig. 31–17).

FIGURE 31–17. Bilateral buccal and lingual occlusal rests will support the distribution of force axially for linguoverted teeth.

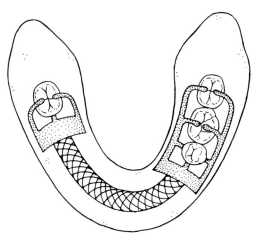

When there is a definitive mandibular discontinuity defect, the direction of occlusal forces is difficult to predict. Jaw closure is no longer in the vertical plane only, muscle-delivered forces are one sided, and location of the fulcrum line is difficult to determine. If there is an abutment on the defect side, it will be out of occlusion as maximal occlusal force is developed on the opposing side. If clasping is to be placed on this abutment, it must be at or above the height of contour or must be flexible enough to prevent development of stresses that exceed physiologic limits.[34]

When remaining teeth are on only one side of the dental arch, the resulting removable partial denture will possess an unusually long lever arm (Fig. 31–18). If both posterior and anterior extensions will be tissue borne, two fulcrum lines will create the potential for leverage in two planes.[34] This situation will contribute to excessive movement of the prosthesis during occlusal function. Rigidity of framework design, adequate bracing, and distribution of forces among teeth and between the tooth and soft tissue support will be important considerations for function and long-term stability of the restoration.

The design for the maxillary prosthesis when an abutment tooth will be in the anterior portion of the dental arch may include a rotational or dual path of insertion to eliminate the need for anterior clasping and to improve aesthetics. Both soft and hard tissue contours must be considered in determining the feasibility of this design for a patient.[36,37]

An occlusal scheme must consider prosthesis stability. If the removable partial denture opposes natural dentition, occlusal contacts should be light in centric occlusion without guiding contacts in lateral or protrusive excursions. Patients will inevitably function on the side with natural tooth contacts. If a complete denture is opposing the removable partial denture, a balanced occlusion will be needed for maintaining denture stability and retention during mastication.

A consistent recall system for patients is necessary for maintenance of the removable partial denture prosthesis. Atrophy of soft tissue support and occlusal wear are two factors that can lead to loss of prosthesis stability. Movement of the unstable prosthesis during function can cause tooth mobility and soft tissue irritation. Because of the compromised soft tissue and the location and number of teeth associated with maxillofacial injury, the potential for damage to the oral structures created by an unstable removable partial denture is significant. Regular examination of periodontal status, occlusal contacts, and prosthesis stability is important for a long-term physiologic and functional result.

The removable partial denture as definitive prosthesis can be adapted to obturate both hard and soft palate defects, as described for the transitional prosthesis.

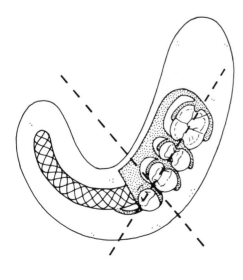

FIGURE 31–18. A long lever arm may lead to excessive movements of the prosthesis during function. Framework design and regular maintenance are important for long-term physiologic harmony between the tissues and the prosthesis.

When healthy teeth are present for prosthodontic support, the removable partial denture will offer adequate retention for restoration of oral function. If the natural tooth contours are unfavorable for framework stability and retention, they may be changed by restoring selected teeth with onlays and crowns. Bonded composite resin techniques may also be used for this purpose.[38] The tooth-supported obturator prosthesis will restore function passively by way of tissue replacement and will restore functional levels of mastication, deglutition, and speech. The tooth-supported removable partial denture with palatal lift extension will serve as a definitive speech aid for the patient with soft palate incompetence.

THE DEFINITIVE COMPLETE DENTURE

When the trauma patient is edentulous and is not a candidate for dental implants, functional prosthetic rehabilitation is greatly compromised. Initially, it is difficult to predict the appropriate anatomic relationships and to stabilize the fractured maxilla or mandible, or both, without the aid of the teeth. After healing, loss of normal edentulous structures may compromise denture retention and stability. Patients with compromised oromotor control or paresthesia of tongue, lip, or cheek will have great difficulty in controlling not only oral secretions but also the complete denture prosthesis.

Vestibuloplasty to maximize the denture-bearing area and a flat plane, balanced occlusal scheme may facilitate denture stability. The cast metal base may be of greater accuracy than the acrylic resin base and may be appropriate for some patients. Denture adhesives may be necessary in some cases owing to the loss of tissue anatomy, alteration in jaw relationships, and neurologic deficits.

When there is a residual hard palate defect, extension into the defect may be tolerated by the patient and can be of some assistance in maxillary denture retention. The functional impression technique described for the transitional soft palate obturator prosthesis is useful for the development of appropriate obturator contour. With this technique, the operator can carefully control the amount of extension into the defect and can more easily achieve the appropriate balance between prosthesis retention and the physiologic limits of the soft tissues. If the extension is large, a hollow bulb or open obturator will eliminate excess weight. Sometimes patients will tolerate a silicone obturator when they will not tolerate methylmethacrylate resin.

Although the challenge that faces the patient who must manage the complete denture prosthesis is formidable, many patients have adapted to the functional deficit and discomfort associated with this type of reconstruction. With the changes in dental epidemiology and technology, future patients will be far less likely to be limited to this type of prosthodontic restoration.

THE DEFINITIVE FUNCTIONAL PROSTHESIS

The development of personal independence is an important goal in the successful rehabilitation of the trauma patient who is left with permanent paralysis after spinal cord injury. Because of the level of innervation, oromotor function is generally left intact.

With some practice and ingenuity, the tongue and associated oral structures may be trained to work a prosthesis like a limb[39] (Fig. 31–19A and B). An appliance can assist the individual in becoming more personally independent and may allow for the development of occupational skills that can lead to financial independence and improved self-esteem[40] (Fig. 31–20A and B).

Creativity in problem solving plus the present range of electronic possibilities can be combined to assist the paraplegic or quadriplegic person in the accomplishment of both simple and complex tasks. The interdisciplinary team can identify and seek solutions for removing the barriers to each individual's independence.

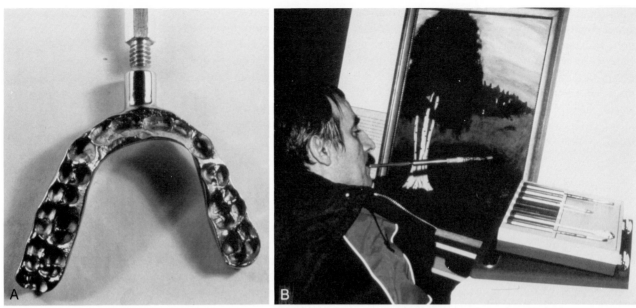

FIGURE 31–19. *A,B,* Orally guided "limb" for the quadriplegic person, which can be adapted for a variety of activities and functions. (Courtesy of Dr. Thomas J. Bloem.)

EXTRAORAL REHABILITATION

The Cranial-Facial Implant

Alloplastic materials have been used in head and neck reconstruction for restoration of cranial and facial defects. These materials can restore tissue contours and produce excellent cosmetic results. For the cranial defect, the implant may also serve a protective function.

If the defect is large, surgical reconstruction may be limited by the amount of donor tissue required. Other considerations that may indicate alloplastic reconstruction rather than autograft procedures include possible resorption and loss of contour of the autograft, avoidance of interruption of the donor site, conservation of operating room time, and ease of obtaining an acceptable cosmetic result.

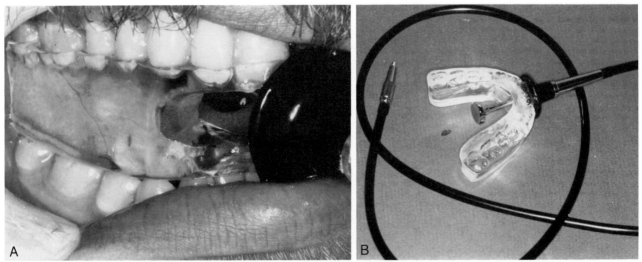

FIGURE 31–20. *A,B,* Paraplegic jeweler used this appliance to control the normally foot-driven handpiece with his tongue, allowing his hands to be free to work the metal.

Alloplastic materials that have been used most often for cranioplasty include metal, acrylic resin, and silicone. Metals have been used less frequently since the evolution of acrylic resins. The disadvantages of metals include high thermal conductivity, which may cause headache or other neurologic symptoms; electrical conductivity, which interferes with interpretation of electroencephalograms; and radiopacity, which interferes with radiographic interpretation. The malleable lightweight metals that are easily adjustable at surgery are subject to deformation and may provide inadequate protection of underlying structures. Metal plates that will have adequate strength must be thin to be of light weight. Often there is a space left between the implant and the base of the defect into which the brain may herniate.[41]

Acrylic resin has been employed for cranioplasty using two distinctly different techniques. Autopolymerizing acrylic resin has been used as a material for direct cranial reconstruction. It is supplied in sterile units and is mixed in the operatory, applied to the defect in the doughy stage during polymerization, molded to the appropriate contour, and allowed to cure. Lubrication of surgical gloves is essential for manipulating the material as it polymerizes.

Although time efficient and inexpensive, there are several significant disadvantages associated with the direct technique.

1. Exposure of the tissues to free monomer is undesirable. However, this can be avoided by placing the material into a polyethylene bag prior to manipulation.[42]

2. Since the polymerization is an exothermic reaction, considerable heat can be generated to underlying structures if the material is not handled extremely carefully.

3. Autopolymerizing acrylic resin is extremely porous and will absorb tissue fluids readily. Over time, this solubility may produce a material that has become soft and spongy.

4. Finally, to comply adequately with occupational health and safety standards, this material should be used with adequate ventilation, which may make it inappropriate for use in the operating room.

Acrylic resin may also be employed for prosthetic replacement of the cranial defect using an indirect method. An impression of the defect can be made with irreversible hydrocolloid that has been reinforced with impression plaster. The impression material may be contained by outlining the area with boxing wax. It is helpful to have an assistant position and stabilize the wax ring. When mixed with additional water, the hydrocolloid may be poured into the wax ring or injected with a large syringe so that it will flow evenly and air pockets will be avoided. Paper clips placed into the hydrocolloid material prior to set will unite the impression material and reinforcing plaster. Consideration of the weight of the plaster reinforcer is important when recording large defects. The defect may be outlined on the skin with an indelible pencil, if necessary, to define the margins. By retracing the outline on the impression, the line may be transferred to the subsequent stone model.[41]

With large cranial defects, the master cast may require alteration so that the implant will fit properly. When pouring the impression for the master model, a ratio of plaster to dental stone may be selected to produce a material that is easily adjusted but stronger than plaster alone. An alternative technique for accomplishing the necessary alteration is to fabricate a negative working cast from the original master model using wax spacers.[43]

A wax pattern inlay can be fabricated to reproduce the appropriate contour. The wax pattern is then flasked. After wax boil-out, the mold is packed with heat-polymerizing methylmethacrylate resin. If the pattern is large, the temperature should be allowed to rise very slowly to avoid porosity. Adequate time should be allotted for curing to allow release of the monomer. After deflasking, the flash is trimmed and holes are drilled through the implant for transport of fluids and ingrowth of fibrous connective tissue.[44] The implant is then ready to be gas sterilized. It should be degassed for 3 days before surgery to avoid tissue irritation.

At surgery, the cranial implant will probably require minor adjustment with a rotary instrument. A well-fitting implant may not require any wires for stabilization.

The surgical procedure for cranioplasty with alloplastic material is brief, and blood loss is negligible.

Modification of the prefabricated acrylic resin implant during the surgical procedure can be accomplished with autopolymerizing acrylic resin to improve the fit.[45] However, this technique carries all the disadvantages of the direct method.

Facial implants can be prepared with the same techniques described for cranioplasty (Fig. 31–21A and B). Chin deformities, malar deficiencies, and frontal bone defects have been frequently selected for alloplastic reconstruction. The most commonly selected materials for cosmetic alloplasty have been methylmethacrylate resin and silicone rubber.

Mentoplasty with alloplastic materials continues to be controversial. Bone resorption beneath chin implants was reported in the late 1960s and early 1970s[46,47] and continues to be noted in the literature.[48] Pressure from the mentalis muscle and damage to the periosteum during the surgical procedure have been implicated as a source for this complication. However, other reports of mentoplasty with similar materials have described long-term success without bone resorption.[49,50]

The risk of infection was reported to be very high for alloplastic reconstruction of frontal defects 40 years ago.[51] Remnants of sinus mucosa may have been responsible for the high infection rate reported. Currently, contraindications to alloplastic implantation of frontal defects include exposed sinus mucosa or communication with nasal or ethmoid mucosa[52] (Fig. 31–22A to D).

A variety of other alloplastic materials for use in craniofacial implantology have been described, including porous polyethylene,[53] Dacron polyurethane,[54] polydimethylsiloxane,[55] polyamide mesh,[56] and a carvable soft silicone elastomer.[57] Given the variety of new materials available and the history of conflicting results with craniofacial alloplasty, controlled clinical studies to determine appropriate applications and long-term success are long overdue.

The ability of the alloplastic implant to provide long-term cosmetic results superior to those achieved with autograft procedures has been responsible for the persistence of these techniques. However, the success of any cosmetic procedure depends upon acceptance by the patient. Functional problems, such as an unnatural feeling over the implanted area, reaction to cold temperatures, mobility, or ability to palpate

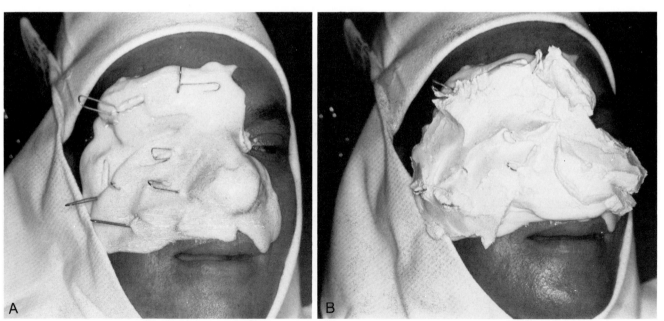

FIGURE 31–21.   *A,B,* Facial moulage technique with irreversible hydrocolloid and impression plaster.

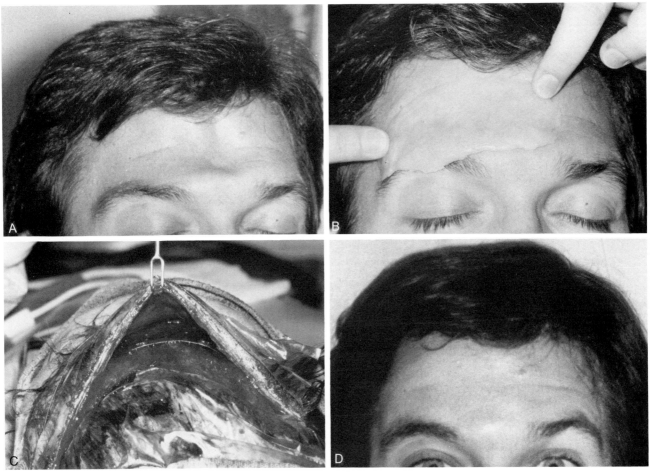

FIGURE 31–22.   Reconstruction of a cranial defect with indirect technique after failure using the direct method.   *A*, Presenting defect. *B*, Wax pattern. *C*, Acrylic resin implant seats into defect with minimal grinding. *D*, Postoperative result.

the prosthesis, may result in an implant that is acceptable aesthetically but unacceptable to the patient.[58]

FACIAL PROSTHESIS

The fabrication of a facial prosthesis is a complex procedure. Its success depends upon many factors. First, the prosthetist as sculptor should have a good education in anatomy and pathology. This knowledge is very important in understanding the effect of the injury upon form and function. The prosthetist must be familiar with the basic features of facial form and the relationship of the muscle and soft tissues to underlying bone structures. The prosthetist as painter must understand the use of color and light to produce an acceptable tissue replacement. The prosthetist as technician must know the characteristics of his or her materials and be skilled in their manipulation.

The Ear Prosthesis

The ear prosthesis is one of the most common prosthetic devices fabricated today. The ear is particularly vulnerable to burns, trauma, carcinoma, and congenital

FIGURE 31–23.   Hair and hats can help camouflage an ear defect.

malformation. Treatment of the ear defect is often very difficult, and many factors must be considered. Surgical reconstruction should be thought about first; however, this may not be a solution for the child until he or she is mature and the ear is fully developed. Parents often wish for immediate surgical reconstruction. Of course, this is not practical, and they must be encouraged to be patient to increase the likelihood of a successful final result. Hair and hats may be used to camouflage the ear defect (Fig. 31–23). Most children under the age of 5 or 6 years are not good candidates for a prosthesis (Fig. 31–24A to F). Most will not possess the patience required for the necessary impression procedures and artwork, nor will they tolerate the nuisance of wearing the appliance. Neither will they have respect for its fragility.

The most important requirement in making a successful ear prosthesis is that both ears appear normal when the viewer is looking straight at the patient. Since there is no way for the observer to inspect two ears closely at the same time, absolute duplication of detail is not as important as the relationship of the two ears viewed as a part of the whole face. If there is a small tag of remaining tissue, it can usually be covered by the prosthesis. If the remaining portion of the ear has normal anatomy, it may be preserved and the prosthesis added to it.

The first step in fabricating the ear prosthesis is the impression procedure. An impression of the unaffected ear and the defect is best made with irreversible hydrocolloid material that is reinforced with fast-setting plaster, as described earlier in this chapter. This measure can be accomplished with the patient reclining on his or her side. In this way, a wax dam may be placed around the area and filled with impression material. When a portion of the ear remains and there is concern that the weight of the material will distort the impression, one may wish to make the impression with the patient sitting in an upright position. However, the impression material must be mixed to the appropriate consistency to control its flow and mixed with hot water so that it sets quickly.

Several points must be considered before making the impression of the ear and lateral head. First, if the whole ear is missing, a line should be drawn with a marker from the corner of the eye to the auditory canal on each side. Second, cotton must be

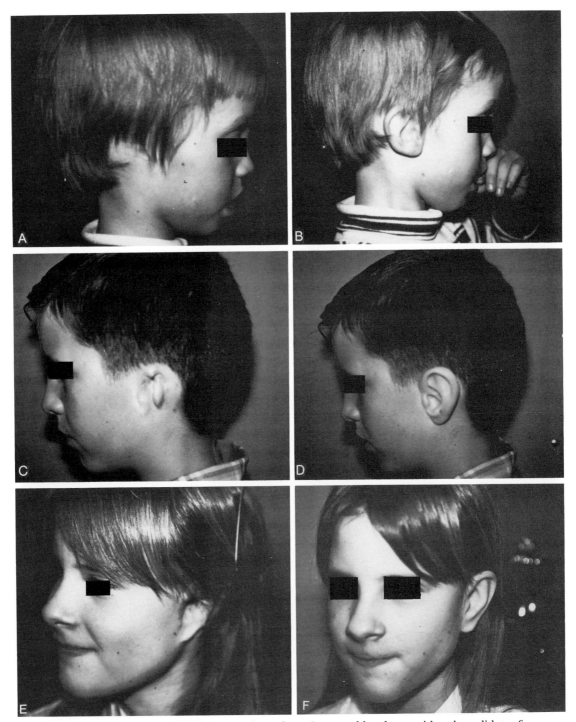

FIGURE 31-24. *A–F,* Children must be at least 5 years old to be considered candidates for facial prosthetics.

placed in the ear canal, and petroleum jelly must be placed on the hair around the area to be duplicated. When the impression is removed, the marker will transfer to the hydrocolloid and may be retraced to ensure transfer to the stone positive. A grid may be used in front of the patient to determine the distance of the ear from the side of the head. This step is important if the area around the auditory meatus is distorted.

The hydrocolloid impression must be poured immediately after removal from the patient to ensure accuracy. An improved stone should be used to create the master

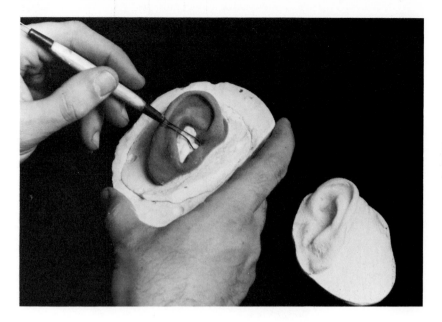

FIGURE 31–25. Sculpting a clay prototype using a mold of the opposing ear as a model.

cast of the defect. This cast will later be incorporated into the final mold that will be used to form the prosthesis.

The prototype for the prosthesis may be formed of clay or wax. Clay prototypes may be done quickly and do not require access to a flame. However, it is important to know the characteristics of the restorative material, which is most often a type of silicone rubber. Some silicone rubbers are very sensitive to the sulfur in most clay and will not cure in a mold made from clay, regardless of how the mold is cleaned. Wax, while more difficult to sculpt, will not present curing problems.

Wax donor ears are available for purchase. Since they may be altered fairly successfully, some sculpting time may be conserved.

Clay, however, is the easiest and quickest to sculpt (Fig. 31–25). When a clay sculpture is made, a "copycat" may be used to check quickly the accuracy of the sculpture (Fig. 31–26A and B). A hard clay may also be removed from the master cast and tried on the patient. White clay can be tinted with colored clay to match the

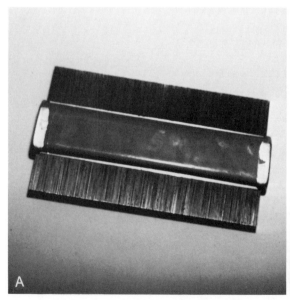
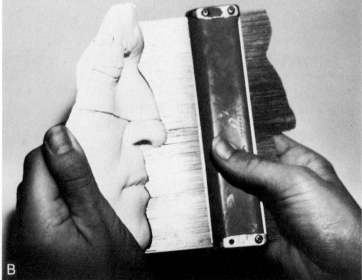

FIGURE 31–26.   *A,B,* A "copycat" may be used to check one's accuracy.

FIGURE 31-27.   A denture flask may be used to support the mold.

patient's skin color. It is easier to make visual comparisons with the normal ear when the color of the clay ear approximates that of the real one. The stone cast of the defect should be reinforced to form the bottom of the mold for the final silicone prosthesis. A denture flask may be used to reinforce the master mold (Fig. 31–27). Metal molds, though very sturdy and reusable virtually indefinitely, require far more effort to fabricate. With today's improved stone, it is possible to make the mold in a denture cup. If the stone is of adequate thickness, added reinforcement will be unnecessary.

For a typical ear prosthesis, a three-piece mold must be used so that the prosthesis may be removed from the mold without tearing and the mold can be left intact for reuse (Fig. 31–28A and B). The pieces must be keyed so that they may be correctly and consistently refitted together. Petroleum jelly or xylene makes a good separator when the separate pieces of the stone mold are poured.

If a patient has a partial ear defect in which the top, bottom, or middle of the ear is missing, there are additional considerations. These remaining portions are often soft and floppy and out of alignment. When making the impression, thick hydrocolloid is placed first behind the remnant to hold it in position. When this hydrocolloid is set, it is covered with more impression material. The impression can be filled with auto-polymerizing acrylic resin, which, if necessary, may be heated and altered after polymerization. The acrylic resin makes a very sturdy mold that does not break as easily as plaster or stone.

There are a wide variety of silicones and separators that may be used for fabricating facial prostheses, and it is up to the prosthetist to choose the appropriate materials. Several medical-grade silicones are available. Typically, the material is supplied as catalyst and base, which, when mixed, is of an initial consistency that it may be poured directly into the mold. The material may require heating or may be room-temperature vulcanizing. It is important to know the properties and handling characteristics of each material. Careful selection of the proper separator and prototype material will ensure a successful final result.

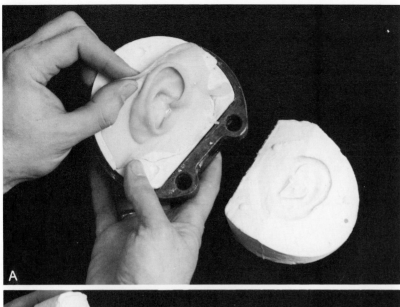

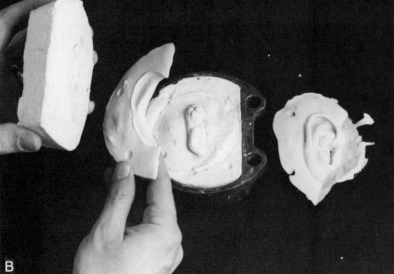

FIGURE 31–28. *A,B,* A three-piece mold must be used for removal of the prosthesis and preservation of the mold.

The first step in the preparation of the silicone is to tint the base material to match the patient's underlying skin color. The translucent silicone must first be made opaque with white pigment, and then appropriate color pigments must be added to produce the desired skin color. The tinted silicone base is mixed with the appropriate amount of catalyst and poured into the mold. After polymerization of the prosthesis and removal from the mold, the ear is trimmed and tried on the patient. Further characterization may then be added to the ear prosthesis. This addition may be applied directly to the surface with a medical-grade silicone adhesive that is tinted with dry earth pigments and thinned to the desired consistency with xylene. This silicone cures quickly in a steam bath. A dulling spray is then brushed onto the prosthesis to remove the shine.

When the prosthesis is ready for delivery to the patient, an adhesive material must be chosen to keep the appliance in place. Epithane adhesive is easily removed from the skin and silicone with the fingers and is quite strong. For very active people, stronger adhesive may be necessary. These stronger adhesives tend to be difficult to remove from the silicone and may require the use of a solvent.

The Nose Prosthesis

The nose prosthesis, although not as common as the ear prosthesis, presents a new set of problems. It is true that many defects involving the nose may be successfully reconstructed with skin grafts or a forehead flap. The prosthesis is often an interim solution until reconstructive surgery can be accomplished. However, the elderly or medically compromised patient who is a poor surgical risk will often settle for a nose prosthesis (Fig. 31–29A and B).

When making an impression of the nasal defect, one must be careful to pack the nasal cavity tightly so that the impression material cannot enter the pharynx and be aspirated. The patient should be in an upright position so that the face, particularly the cheeks, is not distorted.

It is best to make an impression of a large area of the face, including the mouth. It is easier to achieve the correct proportion and alignment of the nose prosthesis when the mouth and eyes are included in the master cast impression.

The patient will usually have a photograph of his or her nose that can be used as a reference. If one is to develop a correct anatomic replica of the original nose, a side view, in addition to the facial view, is essential.

Unless part of the upper lip is missing, it is best to leave the nostrils open to the skin and mucous membrane (Fig. 31–30). This practice allows the patient to blow the nose and wipe it. If there is a flap below the nostril, mucus will seep behind it and loosen the adhesive. There is also a lot of movement in the upper lip, which will loosen the prosthesis.

When the nostrils are to be left open, the prototype is hollowed out, and a two-piece mold is prepared. It is important that the margins of the nasal prosthesis be thin so that they will blend into the face. If the prosthesis must cover a portion of the upper lip, a mustache may be used to camouflage this area. When the lips and chin are involved, the silicone must be extremely soft and flexible to move with the tissues.

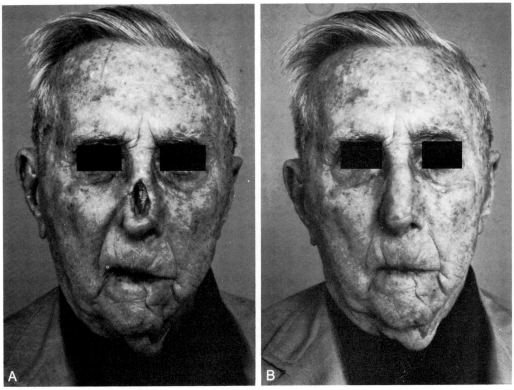

FIGURE 31–29. *A,B,* The elderly patient may wish to avoid surgical reconstruction.

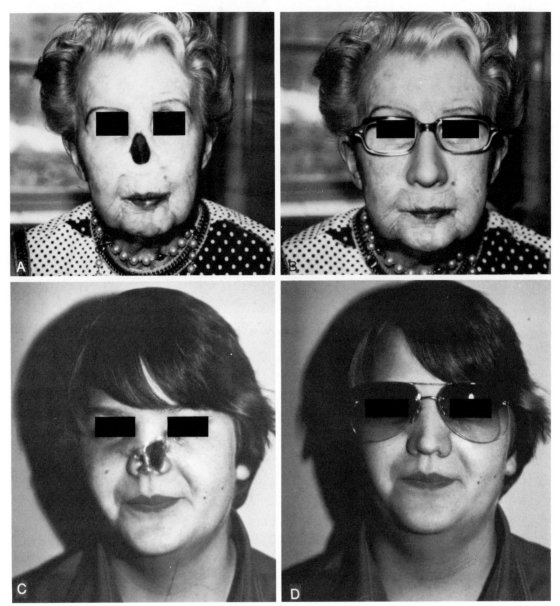

FIGURE 31–30.   *A–D,* When the upper lip is intact, it is best to leave the nostrils open.

The Orbital Prosthesis

Patients with complete exenteration of the orbit are the most difficult and challenging for the prosthetist (Fig. 31–31A). Although the eyelids are missing, there is still muscle around the outer margins of the orbit. When the orbit is filled with impression material, the patient will squint and distort the impression. There is a way to compensate for this problem. After the master cast of the orbit is made, a thin, clear acrylic resin shell is made of the entire area (Fig. 31–31B). If the orbital defect is undercut, the undercut area must be filled in with wax or clay before the acrylic resin shell is made so that it can be removed easily. When the resin shell has cured, it is trimmed and placed on the patient and left there for several minutes. If the patient was squinting when the impression was made, one can see through the acrylic resin shell where there is no contact with skin. The cast may then be altered to compensate for the difference.

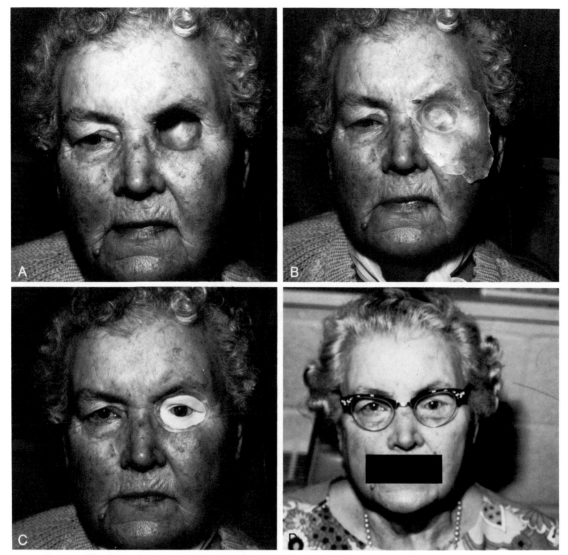

FIGURE 31–31. *A,* Typical orbital defect. *B,* Checking the accuracy of the master cast with a clear acrylic resin shell. *C,* Orientation of the oculus. *D,* The orbital prosthesis.

An ocular prosthesis is then prepared for the patient. Frequently, a stock eye that is suitable may be found (Fig. 31–32). The ocular prosthesis is then placed within the acrylic resin shell as it rests on the patient. With the use of a light source such as a penlight, the oculus is lined up with the normal eye. It is then positioned into place with flesh-colored clay (see Fig. 31–31C). The position of the oculus must be checked for accuracy from the front view, from the side view, and from above the head. The eyelids are then carefully sculpted until the eyes look identical. The plastic shell and clay prototype may be removed from the patient for much of the sculpting.

When the prototype is completed, any acrylic resin showing around the edges of the clay is trimmed. The prototype is then placed back into the patient's cast, and the edges are feathered out onto the stone.

The exposed area of the oculus is covered with a thin film of white silicone adhesive, which is allowed to dry before the top portion of the mold is poured. When the stone has set and the prototype is to be removed from the master cast, the clay should be removed carefully so as not to disturb the film on the oculus. The adhesive will leave a pattern that will allow the oculus to be reglued to the mold with more silicone adhesive before adding the silicone. This adhesive, when cured, will hold the

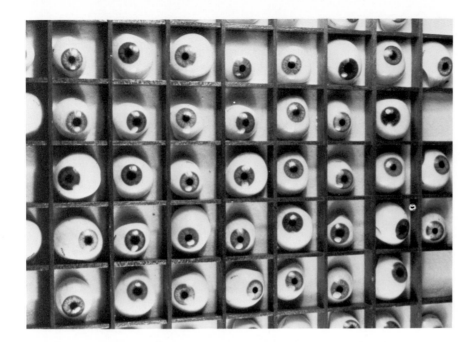

FIGURE 31–32. A stock ocular prosthesis may be incorporated into an orbital prosthesis.

eye in the correct position under a great deal of pressure. The adhesive film is easily removed later from the acrylic resin by buffing. Before adding the silicone portion of the orbital prosthesis, the back of the master cast may be filled with plaster to create a hollow back for the appliance. This practice reduces the weight and increases flexibility, which makes it easier to position on the patient if there is an undercut. After the silicone has been cured, it may be removed from the mold with the oculus in place. The oculus may then be popped out of the silicone portion for polishing while the eyelids are trimmed with fine iris scissors (see Fig. 31–31D).

Fabrication of an Ocular Prosthesis

Before an impression of the defect is made, one should thoroughly examine the external and internal anophthalmic socket, looking for infection and excessive irritation. If any problems are recognized, the patient should be referred back to his or her ophthalmologist.

It is important that an impression tray of the proper size be selected (Fig. 31–33A). It should be tried on the patient and then positioned with the patient in the gaze position (Fig. 31–33B).

This impression tray is attached to a disposable 10-ml syringe. Ophthalmic impression material, which is a medical-grade irreversible hydrocolloid material, is mixed and loaded into the syringe. A tray is placed into the socket with a slight forward pull, and the impression material is injected with a medium steady force (Fig. 31–33C). When the hydrocolloid material begins to overflow, injection stops and the apparatus is held very still until the material is fully cured (2 to 3 minutes). The lids are moved to free any eyelashes and are opened, and the impression is gently removed. The socket is then examined for remnants of impression material, which are removed.

A thick mix of dental stone is placed on a glass slab, and the impression is placed into it. A separator is applied, and the top portion of the mold is poured. The stem should be left exposed (Fig. 31–33D). The stem and impression tray are then removed when the stone is set. The stem should have formed a hole through which the mold can be filled. More separator is applied. The mold is filled with molten wax and allowed to cool (Fig. 31–33E).

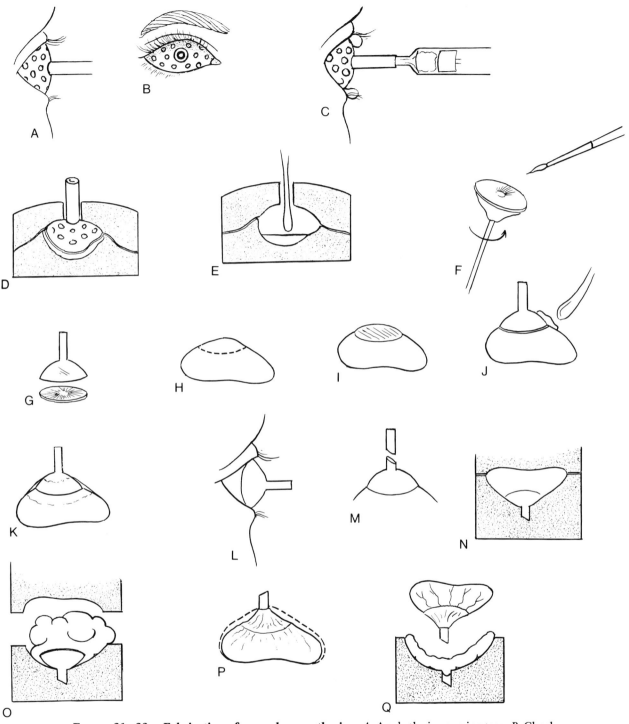

FIGURE 31–33. Fabrication of an ocular prosthesis. *A,* Apply the impression tray. *B,* Check the gaze. *C,* Inject the impression material. *D,* Make a stone mold from impression. *E,* Fill the mold with molten wax. *F,* Paint the iris. *G,* Attach the disc to the corneal button. *H,I,* Shave off the top of the wax prototype. *J,K,* Add the button to the wax prototype. *L,* Verify the position of the iris. *M,* Cut the stem at an angle. *N,* Pour a stone mold. *O,* Pack the white resin into the mold. *P,* Grind away 1 mm of surface. *Q,* Repack the mold with clear acrylic resin and cure.

The next step is the painting of the iris. This may be done in alternative ways. It may be painted on a black disc or on a corneal button that has first been backpainted. Black discs and corneal buttons come in different sizes, although the 11.5-mm size is the most common.

To prepare for painting, the dull side of the disc is attached to a wax "blob" so that the disc may be held without touching the surface where the painting will occur. Oil paints or dry pigments in a poly syrup may be used for painting. Poly syrup is a very thin mixture of clear acrylic resin. Paint mixing should be done on a glass palette with a black back.

Oil paints take several hours to dry but are easier to handle. The disc or button is painted by starting with the pupil and moving outward (Fig. 31–33F). If dry pigments and poly syrup are used, each layer of paint should be coated with clear acrylic resin and dried before adding the next layer. The painting is continued, leaving the inner part near the pupil for last. If the disc is used, the color may be periodically checked by placing a drop of water on it and placing a corneal button over the top of it.

When the disc painting is completed and dry, a small drop of poly syrup is placed on it, and a clean button is placed over it which is allowed to cure under pressure (Fig. 31–33G). When a button is painted, a small, clear acrylic resin shell may be used to cover it and to check the color. The acrylic resin cornea that is placed over the painted area may magnify it. One may need to compensate for this by choosing a slightly smaller disc or button.

Next the wax eye is removed from the mold, trimmed, and smoothed. The top of the wax dome is cut away, and the button is attached with hot wax (Fig. 31–33H to J). The area around the button as well as the entire wax form is smoothed (Fig. 31–33K). This wax form is tried on the patient (Fig. 31–33L). The iris button may be easily moved into position. If there is a stem, it will assist the viewer when the gaze is checked. The stem is then cut off at an angle, which will serve to key it into proper position in the mold (Fig. 31–33M). A small metal flask is used to fabricate the mold from the wax form (Fig. 31–33N). When the stone is set, the wax and button are removed. A separator is then applied. Acrylic resin tinted to the color of the sclera is mixed and allowed to set until it is fibrous. The corneal button and disc are placed in the mold, and the mold is packed with the white resin (Fig. 31–33O). The mold is clamped tightly and placed in a cold pan of water over a heat source. It is brought slowly to a boil and allowed to continue cooking for 1 hour. When the flask is fully cooled, the acrylic resin eye may be removed.

After the flash is trimmed, about 1 mm of acrylic resin is ground away from the surface of the sclera (Fig. 31–33P). It is buffed with pumice until smooth. Veining is added using a fine nylon rag fiber and then is glazed with poly syrup. The sclera is tinted if necessary. The mold is then repacked with clear acrylic resin, and the curing process is repeated (Fig. 31–33Q).

The flask is separated again, and the ocular prosthesis is removed. The flash is trimmed, and the surface is smoothed with a rag wheel and flour of pumice. The smooth surface is then buffed to a high shine. With a 10× loupe, all surfaces are examined for any remaining abrasions or tool marks. Polishing should be repeated until all surfaces have a glistening finish.

Although the facial prosthesis is not a functional substitute, it can provide a good cosmetic appearance for many facial defects. Its use can create an illusion that serves to deter the attention of the casual observer and save the patient much embarrassment.

IMPLANTOLOGY FOR THE TRAUMA PATIENT

It is self-evident that functional compromise and reduction in tissue availability after trauma pose an enormous therapeutic challenge to the prosthodontist. This challenge is met by a profound awareness of two fundamental considerations. The first consideration is that loss of tissue is tantamount to a diverse, but always profound, biologic price that is exacted from potential prosthesis-bearing tissues. This price is reflected in the absence of an attachment mechanism for abutments (loss of periodontal ligament) and the need to place the occlusal load on residual bone. The bone is not longitudinally capable of coping with compressive stresses, as evidenced by studies on residual ridge resorption under removable prostheses. This resorption is probably due to the absence of the osteogenic organizational influence of the periodontal ligament, with a net result that the stresses of function and parafunction induce an ongoing risk of insidious and inevitable reduction in the prosthesis support system. Consequently, the prosthetic support mechanism is in a deficit state. The second consideration is that the biologic price exacted by the traumatic event has to be balanced by the biologic risk inherent in the prosthodontic treatment strategy.[59]

The dental literature indicates that various prosthodontic techniques and designs may modify the environment of the oral cavity, which in turn may lead to an increased risk of dental and gingival disease. In other words, the treatment itself can elicit adverse biologic changes. Ideally, prosthodontic treatment should rely on biomechanical attachment systems that compensate for the deficits as well as minimize the risk of compromising the health of the host tissues even further. Consequently, a major item on the research agenda has been the development of a man-made analogue for tooth roots or dental implants, with all their implied contributions to abutment service and supportive tissue maintenance.

Various objectives have been proposed to justify the routine use of tooth root analogues or dental implants. Quite logically, if these objectives can be met so that routine prescription of implants can be justified in conventional prosthetic treatment planning, the implants can then be prescribed with impunity in the more challenging treatment situations, such as those resulting from trauma.

The following objectives focus on the desirable features of an implant system:

1. Biologic evidence of a predictable and safe attachment mechanism
2. Retrievability
3. Longitudinal evidence of functional performance
4. Versatility of application

P.I. Brånemark and associates have produced compelling evidence from both animal and human research that the dental implant is biologically capable of meeting the above objectives.[60]

1. Evidence for a safe and predictable attachment at the ultrastructural level for commercially pure titanium implants has led to the concept of osseointegration, the process whereby an implanted alloplastic material recurrently demonstrates mechanical and structural interlocking of functional implant and loaded bone. This concept is in striking contrast to the concept of implant retentive efficacy, which is based exclusively on three-dimensional stabilization that is associated with subperiosteal or blade implants.[61]

2. The retrievability of any implant system is of crucial importance. For example, if an implant fails to osseointegrate, it can be easily removed, and the host site will heal with minimal discernible bone loss. After an interval of a few months to allow for bone healing, the bone site can be operated on again, and a new implant can be placed. A very high success rate of "second-time" osseointegration has been observed, which underscores the retrievability of the system.[62]

3. The long-term clinical effectiveness of any therapeutic method reflects the safety of the intervention and its contribution to longitudinal functional restoration. The most scrupulously documented prospective and retrospective data over periods exceeding 5 years have come from Göteborg and other centers where replication studies have been undertaken. A recent multicenter international study endorses the longevity and efficacy of the osseointegration technique, suggesting its reliability in heterogeneous groups of patients with a diversity of systemic health backgrounds.[63]

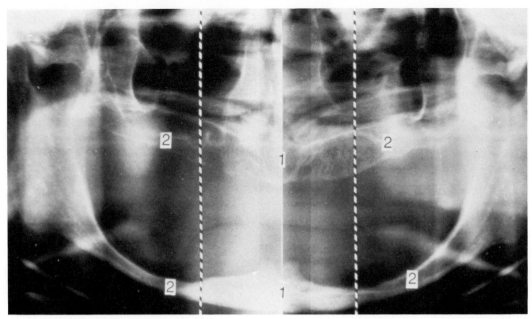

FIGURE 31–34. In the context of documented information underscoring the clinical efficacy of osseointegration, the edentulous arches may be regarded as constituting two zones. Zone 1 is the indicated site for edentulous patients and Class IV partially edentulous patients. Zone 2 is used almost exclusively for Class I, II, and III partially edentulous patients.

4. The initial work by Brånemark was restricted to edentulous patients and was therefore confined to the anterior zones of the jaws (Fig. 31–34). However, the posterior parts of the jaws (zone 2) have been used routinely in the past 5 years with equally good, albeit short-term, results. This finding argues well for diverse applications of, and locations for, osseointegrated implants.

The reliability of osseointegration has had a profound effect on prosthodontic treatment planning. It is possible for the prosthodontist to approach a partially or completely edentulous site or sites without automatically assuming that teeth or ridges or both must be incorporated into abutment or support service. It is, therefore, tempting to envisage a future in which traditional fixed and removable partial dentures and complete dentures will become obsolete, and further research will address the feasibility of such a notion. In the meantime, however, that segment of the population in whom trauma has led to adverse biomechanical sequelae can benefit immeasurably and immediately from the availability of this service.

Prosthodontic Treatment with Osseointegrated Dental Implants

Extensive experience over the past decade with the use of osseointegrated implants in totally and partially edentulous patients endorses their use in such prosthetic designs as fixed full arch or partial arch bridges, overdentures, and single tooth replacements (Fig. 31–35A to E). These experiences have led to our employing osseointegrated abutment support for patients having traumatic injuries associated with the following:

1. Loss of tooth arch continuity
2. Loss of tooth arch continuity and supporting tissues
3. Loss of edentulous supportive tissues

LOSS OF TOOTH ARCH CONTINUITY

The major prosthodontic considerations in patients who have sustained traumatic tooth loss are the integrity of the remaining abutment teeth and the extent of

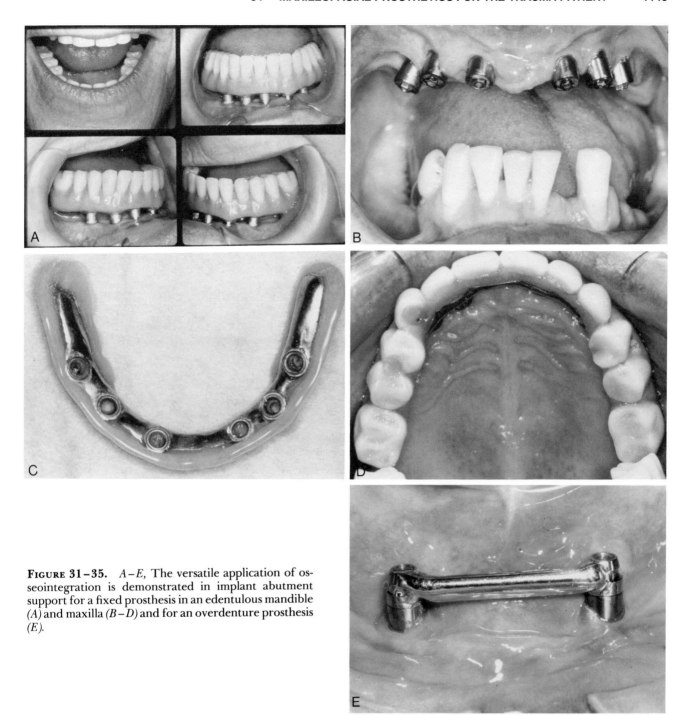

FIGURE 31–35. *A–E,* The versatile application of osseointegration is demonstrated in implant abutment support for a fixed prosthesis in an edentulous mandible *(A)* and maxilla *(B–D)* and for an overdenture prosthesis *(E).*

the resultant edentulous gap. The vast majority of these patients present with variations on the Kennedy-Applegate Class IV or anterior Class III partially edentulous condition. Traditional treatment usually consists of a fixed or acid-etched bridge, depending upon the condition of the adjacent abutment teeth and the length of the edentulous span. Either treatment involves the irreversible preparation of abutment teeth and the attendant risks. However, if residual alveolar ridge dimensions permit, a minimum of two osseointegrated implants can be used to support an electively removable fixed bridge (Figs. 31–36 and 31–37). The dental technology utilized is an abbreviated form of that employed with osseointegrated full arch bridges in edentulous patients. Given the documented long-term success for fixed bridges anchored in this bony site (zone 1, Fig. 31–34), we are tempted to extrapolate that such bridges

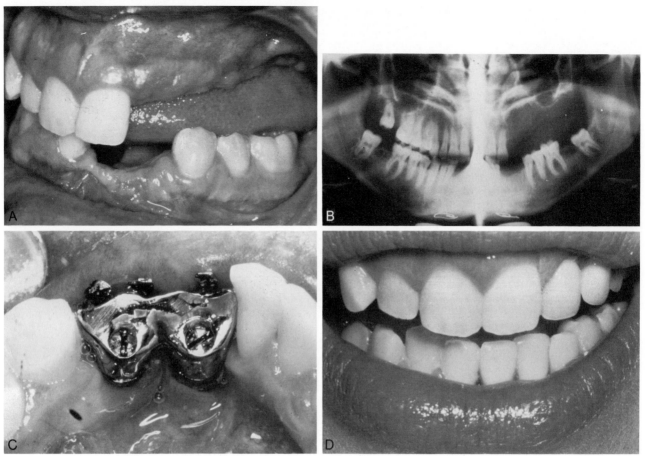

FIGURE 31–36. *A–D,* Case history illustrating the replacement of avulsed anterior mandibular and maxillary teeth.

will demonstrate very favorable longevity. Furthermore, an osseointegrated bridge has all the benefits of fixed and removable prostheses. It is associated with ease of fabrication and the scope for easy servicing without the disadvantages, such as assault on the remaining abutment teeth.

LOSS OF TOOTH ARCH CONTINUITY AND SUPPORTING TISSUES

Unfortunately, tooth loss is frequently accompanied by the even more mutilating loss of supporting alveolar bone. This bone is an integral part of the facial skeleton, and its loss is irrevocable. The partial destruction of the dentition and its supporting tissue underscores even further the importance of attempting to retain the maximal number of tooth abutments by means of endodontic and operative dental procedures. The general principles for working out treatment strategies are determined by the dentist's concern not only with selecting and designing tooth pontics but also with replacing various amounts of related soft tissue areas. Where circumoral activity is minimal (Fig. 31–38), pontics may be designed to compensate for the missing soft tissues. Functional lip movement will not preclude a cosmetically acceptable result, and a certain amount of suprapontic space for easy access for oral hygiene is readily accommodated. Better still, the depleted ridge area can be replaced by an acrylic resin analogue as an integral part of a removable partial denture. When fixed prostheses are not feasible for hygienic, cosmetic, or mechanical reasons, and circumoral movement exposes gingival tissues, the removable partial denture remains an option. The gingival component of the dentogingival prescription can, of course, always be en-

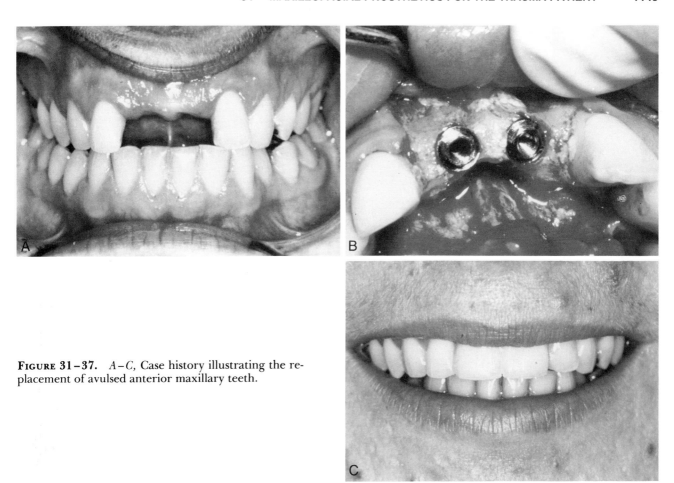

FIGURE 31-37. *A–C,* Case history illustrating the replacement of avulsed anterior maxillary teeth.

larged to allow for enhanced support via a vestibuloplasty procedure (Fig. 31–39). Still, patients are inclined to prefer a fixed prosthesis, irrespective of the extent of morphologic compromise; here again, osseointegrated tooth root analogues promise a bold and innovative solution (see Fig. 31–36 and 31–37). We expect that morpho-

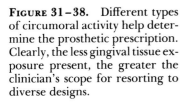

FIGURE 31-38. Different types of circumoral activity help determine the prosthetic prescription. Clearly, the less gingival tissue exposure present, the greater the clinician's scope for resorting to diverse designs.

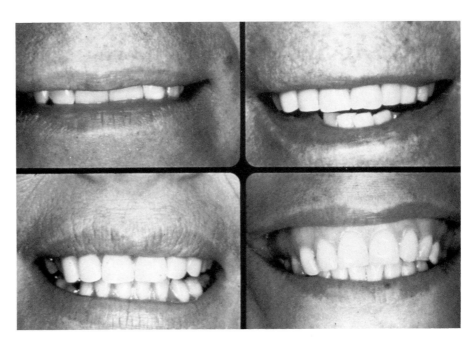

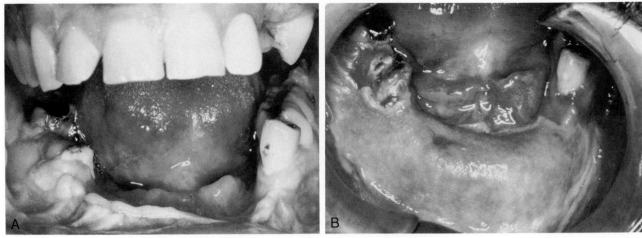

FIGURE 31–39. *A,B,* Advanced residual ridge reduction resulting from a traumatic accident may, to some extent, be compensated for by a vestibuloplasty procedure.

logic situations that are so compromised that they preclude the sort of resolutions just described will eventually be routinely managed with grafting procedures as an integral part of an osseointegration treatment plan.

LOSS OF EDENTULOUS SUPPORTING TISSUES

Trauma to the edentulous patient presents the prosthodontist with a particular challenge, since depleted supporting tissues are now undermined even further. Frequently, a patient's age and health status militate against successful healing of a mandibular fracture site, and the problem of an absent residual ridge is compounded further by a fibrous union and the inevitable mobility in the components of the mandibular body. Meticulous, albeit conventional, clinical procedures will usually alleviate the problems of such patients, although the dentist should devote considerable time to the counseling of patients regarding limitations of the service and to the difficulties encountered by patients in getting accustomed to the prosthesis. When feasible, preprosthetic surgery is prescribed, and our surgical colleagues have proved indispensable in their skillful vestibuloplasty and selective augmentation procedures.

Here again, the concept of osseointegration may prove to be a very useful adjunctive procedure in a couple of ways:

1.   The presence of osseointegrated implants in an extremely resorbed ridge may reduce the risk of further resorption and further vulnerability to trauma. This risk reduction is presumably because of the improved stress concentrations transmitted via the implants. Furthermore, the implants appear to retard the levels of bone loss usually associated with direct complete denture loading of edentulous ridges. This observation has to be tempered by the consideration that extremely resorbed mandibles may be fractured through an implant site. To date, there are only two reports of such fractures in the literature.

2.   When trauma is accompanied by gross tissue loss, implants can be used in two ways. They can be used to create an attachment mechanism exclusively, such as overdenture abutments for the prescribed prosthesis. They can also be used in a grafted site after successful healing of the graft (Fig. 31–40).

ANCHORAGE FOR SOMATOPROSTHESIS

The application of osseointegration to facial bones has afforded improved anchorage for facial somatoprosthesis.[64] Local tissue reaction to an adhesive agent and

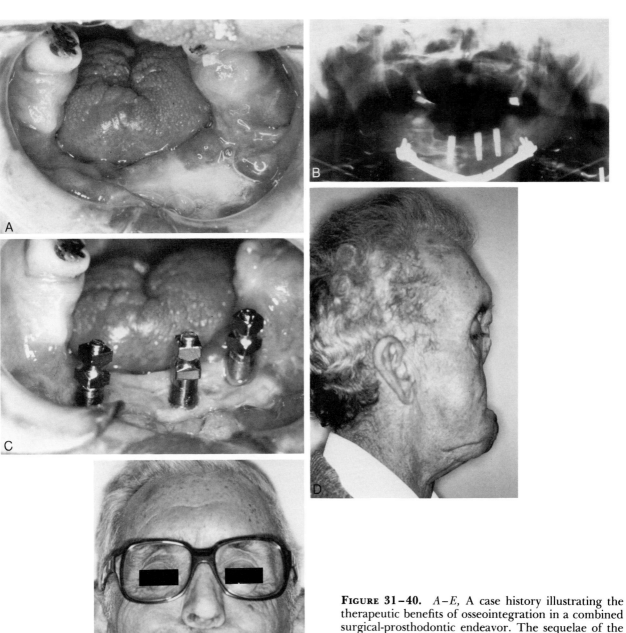

FIGURE 31–40. *A–E,* A case history illustrating the therapeutic benefits of osseointegration in a combined surgical-prosthodontic endeavor. The sequelae of the shotgun injury led to repair of the mandibular discontinuity with subsequent placement of osseointegrated implants for a fixed prosthesis support.

the hygiene problems associated with its application and removal are avoided. A reliable and reproducible positioning of the facial prosthesis that requires little manual dexterity can be accomplished by the patient. It is indeed tempting to suggest that possibilities for the employment of implants in a multiphase context will be limited only by the imagination and ingenuity of the prosthodontist and surgeon responsible for treating the trauma victim.

REFERENCES

1. Bremner MDK: The Story of Dentistry. Brooklyn, Dental Items of Interest Publishing, 1954.
2. Redmond AC, Donner L, Tilghman D: Psychological evaluation of facial change following orthognathic surgery. *In* Lucker G, Ribbens KA, McNamara JA Jr (eds): Psychological Aspects of Facial Form. Ann Arbor, MI, Center for Human Growth and Development, The University of Michigan, 1980.
3. Reiner ML: Rehabilitation of the facially disfigured: A psychological analysis. Ann Dent 36:29, 1972.
4. Munro IR: The psychological effects of surgical treatment of facial deformity. *In* Lucker G, Ribbens KA, McNamara JA Jr (eds): Psychological Aspects of Facial Form. Ann Arbor, MI, Center for Human Growth and Development, The University of Michigan, 1980.
5. MacGregor FC, Abel TM, Bryt A, et al: Facial Deformities and Plastic Surgery—A Psychosocial Study. Springfield, IL, Charles C Thomas, 1953.
6. Molinaro JR: The social fate of children disfigured by burns. Am J Psychiatry 135:979, 1978.
7. Berscheid E: Psychological effects of physical attractiveness. *In* Lucker G, Ribbens KA, McNamara JA Jr (eds): Psychological Aspects of Facial Form. Ann Arbor, MI, Center for Human Growth and Development, The University of Michigan, 1980.
8. Adams GR: Racial membership and physical attractiveness effects on preschool teachers' expectations. Child Study J 8:29, 1978.
9. Murray JE, Swanson LT, Strand RD, Hricko GH: Evaluation of craniofacial surgery in the treatment of facial deformities. Ann Surg 182:240, 1975.
10. Rahn AO, Goldman BM, Parr GR: Prosthodontic principles in surgical planning for maxillary and mandibular resection patients. J Prosthet Dent 42:429, 1979.
11. Curtis TA, Beumer J III: Restoration of acquired hard palate defects: Etiology, disability and rehabilitation. *In* Beumer J III, Curtis TA, Firtell DN (eds): Maxillofacial Rehabilitation: Prosthodontic and Surgical Considerations. St Louis, CV Mosby, 1979.
12. Aram A, Subtelny JD: Velopharyngeal function and cleft palate prosthesis. J Prosthet Dent 9:149, 1959.
13. Skolnick ML, McCall GN, Barnes M: The sphincteric mechanism of velopharyngeal closure. Cleft Palate J 10:286, 1973.
14. Shprintzen RJ, Lencione RM, McCall GN, Skolnick ML: A three-dimensional cinefluoroscopic analysis of velopharyngeal closure during speech and non-speech activities in normals. Cleft Palate J 11:412, 1974.
15. Isshiki N, Honjow I, Morimoto M: Cineradiographic analysis of movement of the lateral pharyngeal wall. Plast Reconstr Surg 40:357, 1969.
16. Shprintzen RJ, McCall GN, Skolnick ML, Lencione RM: Selective movement of the lateral aspects of the pharyngeal walls during velopharyngeal closure for speech, blowing, and whistling in normals. Cleft Palate J 12:51, 1975.
17. Casey DM: Palatopharyngeal anatomy and physiology. J Prosthet Dent 49:371, 1983.
18. Kuehn DP, Folkins JW, Cutting CB: Relationships between muscle activity and velar position. Cleft Palate J 19:25, 1982.
19. Blackfield HM, Miller ER, Owsley JQ, Lawson LI: Comparative evaluation of diagnostic techniques in patients with cleft palate speech. Plast Reconstr Surg 29:153, 1962.
20. Carney PJ, Morris HL: Structural correlates of nasality. Cleft Palate J 8:307, 1971.
21. Desjardins RP, Laney WR: Typical clinical problems and approaches to treatment. *In* Laney WR (ed): Maxillofacial Prosthetics. Littleton, MA, PSG Publishing Company, 1979.
22. Sato Y, Sato M, Yoshida K, Tsuru H: Palatal lift prostheses for edentulous patients. J Prosthet Dent 58:206, 1987.
23. Lang BR: Modification of the palatal lift speech aid. J Prosthet Dent 17:620, 1967.
24. Knapp JG, McDowell GC: Irreversible hydrocolloid used as an investment. J Mich Dent Assoc 63:629, 1981.
25. Gibbons P, Bloomer H: A supportive-type prosthetic speech aid. J Prosthet Dent 8:362, 1958.
26. Rosen MS, Bzoch KR: The prosthetic speech appliance in rehabilitation of patients with cleft palate. J Am Dent Assoc 57:203, 1958.
27. Shelton RL, Lindquist AF, Arndt WB, et al: Effect of speech bulb reduction on movement of the posterior wall of the pharynx and posture of the tongue. Cleft Palate J 8:10, 1971.
28. Reisberg DJ, Fine L, Fattore L, Edmonds DC: Electrical burns of the oral commissure. J Prosthet Dent 49:71, 1983.
29. Gay WD: Prostheses for oral burn patients. J Prosthet Dent 52:564, 1984.
30. Ampil JP, Newell L, Taylor P: A simplified prosthesis for the treatment of burns to the oral cavity. J Prosthet Dent 59:608, 1988.
31. Grisius R, Moore DJ: Miscellaneous prostheses. *In* Beumer J III, Curtis TA, Firtell DN (eds): Maxillofacial Rehabilitation: Prosthodontic and Surgical Considerations. St Louis, CV Mosby, 1979.
32. Knapp JG, McDowell GC: Syringe application of alginate impression material. J Mich Dent Assoc 63:220, 1981.
33. Krol AJ: Removable Partial Denture Design. San Francisco, University of the Pacific School of Dentistry, 1976.
34. Firtell DN, Curtis TA: Removable partial denture design for the mandibular resection patient. J Prosthet Dent 48:437, 1982.
35. Martin JW, King GE: Framework retention for maxillary obturator prostheses. J Prosthet Dent 51:669, 1984.
36. Gay WD, King GE: Applying basic prosthodontic principles in the dentulous maxillectomy patient. J Prosthet Dent 43:433, 1980.
37. Jacobsen TE, Krol AJ: Rotational path removable partial denture design. J Prosthet Dent 48:370, 1982.
38. Taylor TD, Gerrow JD, Brudvik JS: Resin-bonded components for maxillofacial prosthesis construction: A clinical trial. J Prosthet Dent 59:334, 1988.
39. Olsen RA, Prentke EM, Olsen DB: A versatile and easily fabricated mouthstick. J Prosthet Dent 55:247, 1986.

40. Zalkind M, Mitrani Z, Stern N: Mouth-operated devices for handicapped persons. J Prosthet Dent 34:652, 1975.
41. Firtell DN, Beumer J III: Cranial and facial implants. *In* Beumer J III, Curtis TA, Firtell DN (eds): Maxillofacial Rehabilitation: Prosthodontic and Surgical Considerations. St Louis, CV Mosby, 1979.
42. Spence WT: Form fitting cranioplasty. J Neurosurg 11:219, 1954.
43. Aquilino SA, Jordan RD, White JT: Fabrication of an alloplastic implant for the cranial defect. J Prosthet Dent 59:68, 1988.
44. Bessette RW, Cowper T, Natiella J, et al: Histological evaluation of pore size and shape in silicone implants in Rhesus monkeys. Ann Plast Surg 7:447, 1981.
45. Martin JW, Ganz SD, King GE, et al: Cranial implant modification. J Prosthet Dent 52:414, 1984.
46. Robinson M, Shuken R: Bone resorption under plastic chin implants. J Oral Surg 27:116, 1969.
47. Friedland JA, Coccaro PJ, Converse JM: Retrospective cephalometric analysis of mandibular bone absorption under silicone rubber chin implants. Plast Reconstr Surg 57:144, 1976.
48. Peled IJ, Wexler MR, Ticher S, Lax EE: Mandibular resorption from silicone chin implants in children. J Oral Maxillofac Surg 44:346, 1986.
49. Parkes M: Avoiding bone resorption under plastic chin implants. Arch Otolaryngol 98:100, 1973.
50. Mahler D: Chin augmentation — a retrospective study. Ann Plast Surg 8:468, 1982.
51. White JD: Late complications following cranioplasty with alloplastic plates. Ann Surg 128:743, 1948.
52. Schultz RC: Reconstruction of facial deformities with alloplastic material. Ann Plast Surg 7:434, 1981.
53. Shaber EP: Vertical interpositional augmentation genioplasty with porous polyethylene. Int J Oral Maxillofac Surg 16:678, 1987.
54. Stanley RB Jr, Shih T: Reconstruction of large fronto-orbital defects with Dacron polyurethane custom prosthesis and autogenous bone. Laryngoscope 96:604, 1986.
55. Taicher S, Sela M, Lewin-Epstein J, et al: Use of polydimethylsiloxane subdermal implants for correcting facial deformities in Down's syndrome. J Prosthet Dent 52:264, 1984.
56. Beekhuis GJ: Augmentation mentoplasty with polyamide mesh. Update. Arch Otolaryngol 110:364, 1984.
57. Toranto IR: Mentoplasty: A new approach. Plast Reconstr Surg 69:875, 1982.
58. Binder WJ, Kamer FM, Parkes ML: Mentoplasty — a clinical analysis of alloplastic implants. Laryngoscope 91:383, 1981.
59. Zarb GA, Bergman B, Clayton JA, Mackay HF (eds): Prosthodontic Treatment for Partially Edentulous Patients. St Louis, CV Mosby, 1978.
60. Brånemark P-I, Hansson BO, Adell R, et al: Osseointegrated implants in the treatment of the edentulous jaw — experience from a 10-year period (monograph). Stockholm, Almquist and Wiksell, 1977.
61. Albrektsson T, Zarb GA, Worthington P, Eriksson AR: The long-term efficacy of currently used dental implants: A review and proposed criteria of success. Int J Oral Maxillofac Implants 1:11, 1986.
62. Van Steenberghe D, Quirynen M, Calberson L, Demanet M: A prospective evaluation of the fate of 697 consecutive intra-oral fixtures modum Brånemark in the rehabilitation of edentulism. J Head Neck Pathol 6:53, 1987.
63. Albrektsson J: Multi-centre report on osseointegrated oral implants. J Prosthet Dent 60:75, 1988.
64. Parel SM, Brånemark P-I, Tjellstrom A, Gion G: Osseointegration in maxillofacial prosthetics. Part II: Extraoral applications. J Prosthet Dent 55:600, 1986.

CHAPTER 32

INFECTION IN THE PATIENT WITH MAXILLOFACIAL TRAUMA

STUART E. LIEBLICH, D.M.D.,
and RICHARD G. TOPAZIAN, D.D.S.

Infection following a traumatic injury continues to be a major problem despite many advances in the management of the trauma patient. Local infections occurring at the site of injury, such as an osteomyelitis from a jaw fracture, may result in the loss of teeth and bone structure. The individual may survive the initial injury but may be left with significant residual problems, such as a facial deformity or malocclusion and joint dysfunction.

Systemic infections are likely to occur in the traumatized patient through two avenues. First, bacteria may gain direct entry to the host's systemic circulation through the site of injury, intravenous lines, or urinary catheters. Second, invasive manipulations, such as endotracheal intubation, may bypass previously competent host defense mechanisms, causing a pneumonia. Thus, although the maintenance of life is addressed during the initial treatment, early interventions are needed to prevent potentially disastrous infections from occurring. In fact, sepsis is the most frequent cause of death following trauma.[1]

This chapter deals with the causes of infection due to traumatic injuries, suggests those early interceptive methods that are effective at reducing the potential for infection, and describes the treatment of established infections associated with trauma to the maxillofacial structures.

CAUSES OF INFECTION

Local Factors

After sustaining a traumatic injury, the patient has a vastly increased risk of infection. At the local level, the injury may disrupt the skin and mucous membranes, which are the body's initial and perhaps most important defense from bacterial invasion. Intact skin and mucous membranes provide a mechanical barrier to bacterial invasion. Once bacteria have penetrated this barrier through areas of abrasion, laceration, or the avulsion of tissue, the nonspecific and specific host defense mechanisms are needed to control the invasion. If colonization and growth of invading organisms are checked, infection will not develop. This is the usual course of events after an injury involving a break in surface integrity.

It is known that a sufficiently large number of bacteria are needed to produce an infection. Various studies have shown that an initial inoculum must contain at least 10^5 bacteria per gram of tissue for a clinical infection to occur.[2,3] However, in a traumatic injury, far fewer microorganisms may cause infection owing to the presence of devitalized tissues and foreign bodies in the wound.

Normally, surface flora is kept to a minimum by skin appendages that secrete various antimicrobial substances. Sweat gland production of lactic acid, amino acids, uric acids, and ammonia is bacteriostatic.[4] Secretory immunoglobulin A (IgA) in the oral mucosa is also an important component of the host defense mechanism in controlling bacterial colonization or overgrowth on the mucosal surfaces. Thus, a break in the skin or mucosal surface will not, in itself, always provide a large enough inoculum to produce an infection.

Vascularity is also an important local factor in the control of invading organisms. If compromised by vessel trauma, contusion, or edema, the transport of immunologic host defense products to the site of injury is impaired. The decrease in circulation to the tissue provides a more anaerobic environment, which may permit the growth of certain pathogenic organisms that are inhibited by normal tissue oxygen tension. Local compromise in vascularity is sometimes iatrogenically caused by the injection of epinephrine-containing solutions. For example, a subinfective inoculum of *Staphylococcus aureus* will occasionally produce an infection if placed into tissues that have been injected with epinephrine-containing solutions.[5]

Foreign bodies within a wound also permit infection to occur with much lower numbers of organisms. Soil contains infection-potentiating fractions that have been identified. These fractions are highly charged anionic particles that interfere with leukocyte functions and inactive antibiotics.[6] Inoculation with only 100 bacteria per gram of tissue may cause an infection in the presence of soil. Even the placement of a suture will reduce the number of bacteria needed to cause infection by a factor of 10,000.[7] Thus, vigorous debridement and irrigation are necessary components of wound management, along with the use of the lowest number of sutures acceptable.

Nonvital tissue within a wound provides a reservoir and culture medium for invading organisms, allowing proliferation to the extent that a clinical infection will result. Dead space in a closed wound is filled with serous exudate and cellular debris. This area is isolated from the systemic circulation, depriving it of host defense products that enter to phagocytize the bacteria.

Local wound management is, therefore, critical in the prevention of infection. The goal of initial wound therapy is to reduce the number of bacteria to levels that can be readily managed by the host. Debridement of both foreign bodies and devitalized tissues should be accomplished as early as possible. Local anesthetic solutions containing epinephrine should not be used, since they may further compromise the local blood supply, significantly increasing the potential for infection.

Irrigation under pressure is recommended to remove foreign bodies and reduce the local concentration of bacteria. Gross and others[8] showed that wounds contaminated with bacteria and sterilized soil were more likely to be rendered sterile if irrigation was accomplished with jet lavage instead of a bulb syringe. The use of large volumes of irrigation will not be effective unless the pressure equals or exceeds 8 psi. Mechanical irrigation devices are available, but the amount of pressure needed can also be achieved using a 50-ml syringe and a 19-gauge needle. Concerns that the use of high-pressure irrigation in a wound will further inoculate the site by forcing bacteria into the injured tissues are not well founded. Experimental studies have shown that even with high-pressure irrigation bacteria and foreign bodies will not be forced more deeply into the traumatically injured tissues.[9]

The type of solution used for irrigation also is critical. Further devitalization and tissue damage may occur if toxic solutions are used to irrigate wounds. Studies by

Brånemark and colleagues[10] have shown that normal saline solution is the least toxic and best tolerated of the commonly used solutions. Solutions such as hydrogen peroxide cause direct tissue damage and will further devitalize tissue and predispose the wound to infection.

Systemic Factors

Through appropriate wound management, local factors can be controlled and modified by the surgeon to reduce the bacterial load in a wound site. However, it is impossible to sterilize a traumatic wound, and some bacteria will be present in the tissues. The immunocompetence of the host is the factor that usually determines whether or not a clinical infection will occur.

Once an organism has invaded the host through a break in the mechanical barriers, the next line of defense is the blood-transported phagocytic cells, that is, the neutrophils and monocytes. The disruption of the physical barrier provided by the skin and mucosa allows the direct entrance of surface organisms into the deeper tissues. Phagocytosis is necessary to remove the organisms from the tissues.

Phagocytosis involves a coordinated set of actions in order for the microorganisms to be removed. Initially, the circulating polymorphonuclear neutrophils (PMNs) must be brought to the site of the bacterial invasion through the blood stream. When released from the bone marrow, the granulocytes normally have a lifespan of 4 to 8 hours in the blood stream and another 4 to 5 days in the tissues. However, in infected tissues, this span is considerably reduced because as the granulocytes phagocytize and kill the bacteria, they are also destroyed.

Monocytes circulate for a comparable length of time and also function by phagocytizing invading organisms. However, when they leave the circulation, they become established as tissue macrophages and may persist for years in a latent state until recruited by lymphokines secreted by T lymphocytes to phagocytize an organism.

A specific sequence of events is needed to bring neutrophils out of circulation to an extravascular site where organisms are invading. Initially, neutrophils adhere to the capillary endothelial cells through a process known as margination. This process gives the neutrophils a foothold upon entering the extravascular tissues. Margination can be disrupted, for example, by injection of epinephrine or by a traumatic injury, which causes a transitory leukocytosis as the neutrophils are displaced from the endothelial cells back into the circulation.

Once the neutrophils have adhered to the endothelial cells, they can be mobilized to the source of infection by following the chemical gradient of chemotactic factors. Some of the known chemotactic factors include some bacterial toxins, the degenerative products of inflamed tissues, and various reaction products of the complement system and blood clotting systems from the site of injury. The interactions among inflammatory cell exudate, the vascular response to injury, and the release of immunologic mediators are shown in Figure 32–1.

Once the neutrophils are mobilized to the site of the infection, additional reactions are needed for bacterial killing. First, phagocytosis of the organisms must occur. This phagocytosis is enhanced by the local presence of opsonins, which coat the organism, making it more readily phagocytized. Opsonins include the C3b and C5b fragments of the complement system. The phagocytosis of opsonized particles is facilitated in the presence of tuftsin. Tuftsin-releasing enzyme is produced in the spleen and therefore is deficient in splenectomized patients, which increases their risk of infection.[11]

Phagocytosis is also augmented by the presence of the antibody specific to the offending organism. When the antibody fragment attaches to the cell wall of the bacteria, it will activate the complement cascade. As noted, this will improve the host response by the elaboration of chemotactic factors to attract more PMNs and macrophages to the site. Monocytes and neutrophils also have receptors for the Fc fragment of the antibody, which significantly facilitates engulfment of the organism.

INJURY OR INFECTION

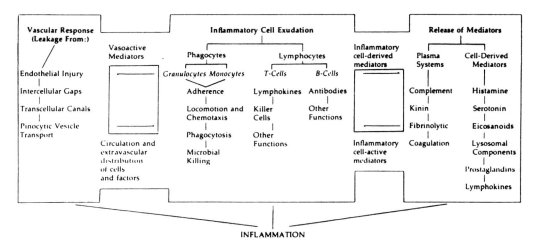

FIGURE 32–1.   The interactions between the vascular response, inflammatory cell exudate, and release of mediators following an injury. (From Maderazo EG: Infections and the host. *In* Topazian RG, Goldberg MH [eds]: Oral and Maxillofacial Infections. Philadelphia, WB Saunders Company, 1987, p 18; with permission.)

As bacterial lysis occurs, released degradation products attract more leukocytes and monocytes to the site of infection. Thus, the host response is augmented and will continue to increase until the infection is cleared.

Once phagocytized, the bacteria are killed through two mechanisms within the neutrophil—the oxygen-dependent and oxygen-independent systems. In the oxygen-dependent system, interactions with reduced nicotinamide adenine dinucleotide phosphate (NADPH) and oxygen create highly reactive and toxic free radicals. This process is also known as the respiratory burst.

The oxygen-independent system involves a lowering of the pH inside a phagocytic vacuole. In the neutrophil, additional bactericidal and bacteriostatic agents are produced, including lysosomes, which digest the bacterial cell wall; lactoferrin, which binds iron; and cationic proteins, which interfere with the metabolism of the organism.

The patient's state of health before trauma and microbial invasion plays a significant role in determining the host defense responses. Certain disease states are known to compromise the four functions of neutrophils discussed previously (adherence, locomotion and chemotaxis, phagocytosis, and microbial killing). For example, a poorly controlled diabetic patient has defects in all of the four functions of neutrophils, despite normal antibody formation and complement activity. The defects in PMN activity can be reversed if adequate amounts of insulin are present and a hyperosmolar state is avoided.

Defects in chemotaxis will be present in patients with inherent deficiencies in complement and in disease states that consume complement, such as systemic lupus erythematosus. In addition, an inhibitor to chemotaxis (chemotactic factor inhibitor, CFI) is found to be present in larger quantities than normal in patients with cirrhosis of the liver, sarcoidosis, and chronic renal disease, thereby increasing the risk of infection after injury.

Patients with certain systemic diseases or deficiencies in the production of the above factors are, as expected, more susceptible to infection. As has been noted, patients who have had a splenectomy are lacking in tuftsin, rendering them especially susceptible to infection by encapsulated organisms such as *Pneumococci,* which resist phagocytosis by the PMNs.

Disorders of phagocytosis and bacterial killing will also increase the chance for infection in these immunocompromised patients. Defects of opsonization can be iatrogenically caused in patients receiving exogenous corticosteroids. The steroid binds to the receptor site on the neutrophil for the antibody fragment of the immuno-globulin, preventing antibody-assisted phagocytosis.

Anergy

After major trauma, a major reduction in immunocompetence may occur. Anergy can often be demonstrated, which shows that a significant loss of the delayed response to infection is attenuated. Severe trauma also causes overactivation of the T cell suppressor population.[12] In addition to these findings, it is known that the stress of trauma increases the output of endogenous epinephrine and corticosteroids. Epinephrine blocks the secretion of insulin, stimulates the release of glucagon, and, along with the steroid, increases gluconeogenesis. This combination of events will lead to an abnormal rise in plasma glucose levels and to a significant increase in the susceptibility to infection. The blood glucose level of the patient in Figure 32–2 was significantly elevated following injury, and the persistent hyperglycemia may have led to immuno-compromise, wound breakdown, and subsequent infection.

MANAGEMENT OF WOUNDS

After the immediate needs for life support are attended to following an injury, the patient's wounds should be treated. Lacerations should be covered with sterile, moist sponges after hemostasis is achieved. Although the emergency room is not always the appropriate place for definitive wound care, since aseptic conditions may be difficult to maintain, the treatment initiated here may prevent infection from occurring and may preserve the maximal amount of tissue.

On the bases of the history of the injury and direct examination, the surgeon should first evaluate the mechanism of injury to distinguish between blunt and sharp injuries. Significantly more force is needed to cause soft tissue injury from blunt trauma as opposed to shear forces, such as glass shards or a knife.[13] The additional absorbed energies from blunt trauma cause a broader area of tissue contusion, ischemia, and necrosis. Thus, the stellate forehead laceration caused by striking a windshield is far more susceptible to infection than is a laceration from a sharp object. The surgeon should consider more aggressive use of debridement and antibiotic prophylaxis in injuries resulting from blunt trauma.

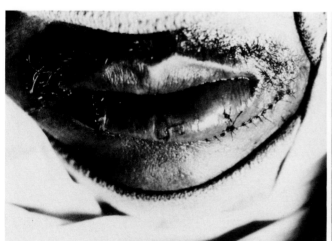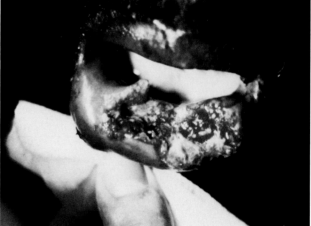

FIGURE 32–2. This patient sustained multiple traumatic injuries, including a laceration of his lower lip, which was primarily closed *(left)*. Breakdown of the wound occurred on the fifth day after the injury *(right)*. The blood glucose level at that time was 380 mg/dl, owing to the systemic response to severe trauma.

In general, the risk of an infection depends upon the following three factors:

1.   The amount and type of microbial contamination of the wound
2.   The condition of the wound at the end of the treatment (the presence of residual necrotic tissue, foreign bodies, and bacterial numbers)
3.   Host susceptibility (Centers for Disease Control [CDC] Guidelines, 1985)[14]

Initial wound management is then directed toward reducing the number of organisms present in the wound. This reduction is done by vigorous cleansing, careful debridement of grossly nonvital tissue, and copious irrigation, under pressure, with normal saline only. Primary wound management needs to be performed with the use of anesthesia to allow thoroughness. Local anesthetics, if used, should be administered by a field block to prevent deep wound inoculation of bacteria, which may occur if injections are made directly into the wound. Solutions without epinephrine should be used to avoid local tissue ischemia.

A decision should be reached early about whether primary closure or delayed closure will be performed. In general, only wounds that are treated early and can be adequately decontaminated should be primarily closed. Facial wounds, because of their rich vascular supply, may be closed primarily after a greater delay than would be acceptable in other areas of the body. The risk of infection of facial wounds is reduced because the preinjury quantity of bacteria in the facial region is usually much less than in other areas, such as the foot, where the numbers and types of bacteria result in a much higher infection rate. Therefore, many authors feel that up to 24 hours following injury is an acceptable period in which to attempt primary closure of facial injuries.[15]

Wounds of the face are usually closed primarily. If adequate debridement, irrigation, and principles of closure are followed, this practice provides the most aesthetically satisfying result. A more detailed coverage of this topic can be found in Chapter 23. In severely contaminated wounds or those in which a significant delay in treatment has occurred, a delayed primary closure technique should be employed. In this technique, the wound is thoroughly debrided, irrigated, and packed open with frequent dressing changes. A "wet to dry" dressing is applied, which involves moistening a sterile gauze in contact with the wound bed and overlaying this with layers of dry gauze. This dressing has a wick effect and draws out serous and any other exudate from the wound. Changing the dressing at least twice a day accomplishes two goals:

1.   It permits observation of the wound bed to determine if an infection is occurring.
2.   The removal of the pack results in debridement of dead cells and exudate that have adhered to the gauze surface.

The wound is repacked at least twice a day and observed for a period of 3 to 5 days. If no signs of infection are present, the wound margins are sharply incised and primarily closed. Wounds treated by delayed primary closure will heal as fast as those closed primarily, as the reparative processes have already been initiated. It has been shown[16] that as long as a clean wound was closed within 4 days following an incision, the wound strength was equivalent at 7 days after wounding whether primary closure or delayed primary closure was used.

Prior to the closure of questionably contaminated wounds, a technique can be used to provide a rapid estimate of the number of bacteria that are present in the wound.[17] This method may then guide the surgeon in determining if a primary or delayed means of closure will be employed. To perform this test, the wound surface is cleansed with isopropyl alcohol to remove surface organisms, and a biopsy specimen is taken from the wound. The specimen is homogenized and diluted 1 : 10 with thioglycolate. With a micropipette, 0.02 ml of the suspension is placed on a glass slide and confined to an area 15 mm in diameter. The slide is oven dried for 15 minutes at 75°C and then Gram stained.

Under high power (97X), the entire slide is examined for the presence of organisms. If any are noted, the wound is considered to contain greater than 10^5 microbes per gram of tissue. As previously discussed, wounds with fewer than this critical number are unlikely to become infected and may be closed primarily. This technique was validated by comparing it with the more time-consuming method of serial dilutions and plating of colonies. The rapid slide technique results correlated with those of the serial method and are available within 1 hour instead of the 24 to 48 hours required for the serial dilution technique.

The method of wound closure will also affect the chance of infection. As previously discussed, each additional suture allows an infection to occur with a smaller number of bacteria. However, to prevent the formation of a residual hematoma, sutures must be placed in sufficient numbers to close all of the dead space. Studies have shown that approximately one third of all wound infections are due to residual hematoma.[18]

Hemostasis should be meticulously achieved, but not at the expense of creating areas of nonvital tissue in the wound. Careful ligation of vessels and appropriate use of electrocautery should be observed. If a hematoma can be predicted because of the exposure of large areas of medullary bone or from the raising of a large flap, drainage of the wound should be established.[19] A closed-system, suction-type drain (e.g., Jackson-Pratt) exiting from a separate stab incision is the least likely to serve as a conduit into the wound for bacterial ingress. Drains should be removed as soon as possible, usually within 48 hours or earlier if drainage has ceased.

Topical hemostatic agents are occasionally needed to arrest bleeding from the cut edges of cancellous bone, from injured organs, and in situations in which the precise source of a continuous ooze cannot be localized. Many formulations are available, including gelatin foam (Gelfoam, Upjohn Company), microfibrillary collagen (Avitene, American Critical Care), and oxidized, regenerated cellulose (Surgicel, Johnson and Johnson). The use of these agents must be tempered by the knowledge that most have been shown to act like foreign bodies, predisposing to infection in situations when a normally subinfective inoculum of bacteria is present. Oxidized, regenerated cellulose is the only hemostatic agent shown to be bactericidal and thus is the preferred agent.[20]

For superficial skin closure, reinforced tape (Steri-strips) has been shown to be superior to a cutaneous suture in terms of preventing infection.[21] If skin sutures are placed, they should be removed in 3 to 5 days to preclude tissue reaction, the formation of stitch abscesses, and permanent scarring.

The surgeon must avoid crushing and damaging the tissues. Devitalized tissues will be caused by grasping the wound margins with tissue forceps. Instead, atraumatic skin hooks should be used and placed from within the wound to elevate the margins for suturing.

PREPARATION OF THE PATIENT FOR SURGERY

Factors influencing infection in the trauma patient who is scheduled for surgery are as follows:

1. The length of the preoperative period of hospitalization
2. The use of razors to shave the operative site
3. The nature of preparation of the operative site

Keeping the preoperative stay short is a factor known to reduce the likelihood of infection by diminishing the period during which colonization with resistant hospital-acquired bacteria may occur. In the traumatized patient, this is accomplished by early operative intervention rather than admitting the patient for a few days prior to surgery. If there will be a delay in scheduling the operation for an open reduction, for example, the patient could be considered for discharge and then readmitted on the day of surgery.

The presence of hair in or around the operative site needs to be considered by the surgeon. It is well documented that preoperative shaving will significantly increase the rate of infection owing to damage to the epidermal barrier and introduction of skin flora into the planned operative site. The preferred method of hair removal is by clipping or depilatory cream. If shaving is necessary, it should be done only at the start of the case.

The physical preparation of the surgical patient is also important in controlling the possibility of an infection. Although antibacterial agents are most often used in surgical preparation, studies have not shown a decrease in the rate of infection compared with that when a simple soap and water scrub is used. This finding is consistent with the fact that it is the mechanical aspect of the surgical "scrub" that reduces the local factors of infection (numbers of bacteria, presence of dirt, and so on) and is of more value than the antibacterial agent. In an open wound, iodophors and chlorhexidine solutions are contraindicated, since they may cause tissue devitalization. A nonionic surfactant (Pluronic F-68) is recommended for cleansing open wounds. This agent will not devitalize tissue and has been shown to be nontoxic even when injected intravenously. Using the surfactant on a sterile sponge, the wound can be thoroughly scrubbed to remove debris and reduce the amount of bacterial flora. Edlich and colleagues recommend using this agent exclusively on traumatic wounds.[13]

PROPHYLACTIC ANTIBIOTICS

The administration of prophylactic antibiotics is often indicated in the injured patient. In the most common classifications of wounds—clean, clean-contaminated, contaminated, and dirty or infected—traumatic wounds fall into the last two categories. Because of this, the risk of infection is much higher in these two types of wounds than in clean operative incisions, and antibiotics prove valuable when administered prophylactically.

To obtain the maximal protective benefit and reduce the rate of infection, prophylactic antibiotics must be administered within 3 hours after the inoculation of bacteria.[22] When the administration of the antibiotic is delayed beyond 3 hours, the bacteria are able to invade and multiply in the wound. The products of hemostasis (e.g., fibrin) further isolate the bacteria from the host defenses, allowing enough bacterial growth to occur and cause an invasive infection.

Thus, the decision of whether to administer prophylactic antibiotics to the trauma patient must be made as soon as the patient presents to the emergency department. The American College of Surgeons recommends the administration of antibiotics to the traumatized patient in those situations listed in Table 32–1.

TABLE 32–1. INDICATIONS FOR THE ADMINISTRATION OF PROPHYLACTIC ANTIBIOTICS TO THE TRAUMA PATIENT

1. When the wound enters a joint space or when it is associated with an open fracture
2. When there is heavy contamination
3. When adequate debridement is not appropriate
4. When debridement is delayed
5. In burns
6. In injuries prone to clostridial infections

From Altheimer WA, Burke JF, Pruitt BA, et al: Manual on Control of Infections in the Surgical Patient. Philadelphia, JB Lippincott, 1984, p 226; with permission.

The seriousness of the consequences of an infection must be considered when determining if an antibiotic should be administered. If the consequence is trivial, such as the occurrence of a dry socket, no antibiotics are needed. However, an infection of a joint or bone from an open fracture may lead to permanent disability and in these situations antibiotics are indicated. They are also indicated with jaw fractures, since teeth and bone may be lost if infection occurs. Maxillofacial wounds communicating with the oral cavity are associated with a higher risk of contamination, since saliva contains 10^{8-9} bacteria per milliliter.[23] These wounds also warrant antibiotic administration.

The surgeon needs to determine the appropriateness of thoroughly debriding and decontaminating the wound. If the injury involves essential structures, such as nerves, glands, or major amounts of facial tissue, the surgeon may be reluctant to debride the area extensively. If nonviable tissue, foreign bodies, and dead space are left behind, the risk of infection is vastly increased despite the use of antibiotics. A delay in debridement and decontamination also permits the wound to fill with serous exudate and cellular debris, and an invasive infection may be initiated.

Other factors that affect the decision of whether or not to use antibiotics may be present. Correlations exist between the length of surgery and the risk of infection. As a general guideline, if the surgery is expected to take more than 4 hours, prophylactic antibiotics should be administered. As noted earlier, certain pre-existing medical conditions that potentiate the risk of infection may be present. Local wound healing and host defenses are often compromised in morbidly obese or malnourished patients, and antibiotics are often given in these situations.[24]

In trauma patients, prophylactic antibiotics should be administered by the intravenous route. Obtaining high serum levels of the antibiotic is mandatory, and additional delays due to absorption from the oral route must be avoided. The intravenous route is also the most predictable method to achieve and maintain blood levels.

The frequency of dosing the antibiotic is related to its half-life ($T\frac{1}{2}$). Repeat doses should be given at an interval of two times the half-life of the drug.[25] A drug such as penicillin has a half-life of 0.5 hour and would be repeated at 60- to 90-minute intervals for prophylaxis.

Once the operative procedure is completed, with the wounds debrided and closed, there is little indication for continuation of antibiotic therapy. However, in cases having the potential for continued salivary leakage, antibiotics are given for a period of 4 to 7 days. An example of such a situation would be an open reduction of a mandibular fracture with a tooth in the line of the fracture. Because of the seriousness of the potential infection (osteomyelitis), antibiotics should be continued until there is soft tissue coverage of any exposed bone, with a minimum of 14 days of therapy.

The choice of antibiotic will be based on the potential type of infection that can occur from the injury. Facial soft tissue wounds are subject to staphylococcal infection, but prospective studies of wounds have not shown a benefit from prophylactic antibiotics.[22] Instead, proper wound care principles (debridement, irrigation, hemostasis, and careful closure) will prevent most infections in this region.

The compromised host is an exception to this guideline. Patients known to have a higher incidence of infections, such as poorly controlled diabetics or asplenic patients, may require antibiotic coverage. Facial lacerations should be treated with vigorous wound care, and a decision should be made about the need for prophylactic antibiotics. The use of a cephalosporin, such as cefazolin, should be considered for facial lacerations, and penicillin should be used only if there is concern for intraoral bacterial contamination. If an antibiotic is used, it needs to be administered immediately upon presentation, since delays reduce its potential effectiveness.

Another group of patients who should have antibiotic coverage are those with prosthetic heart valves, pre-existing organic heart murmurs, and any of the other risk factors for the development of bacterial endocarditis (valvular disease, mitral valve prolapse with insufficiency, and idiopathic hypertrophic subaortic stenosis). Instances of prosthetic valve endocarditis (PVE) have been reported following facial wound infections.[26] Additional complications in the management of such wounds are present, since most of these patients are on anticoagulant therapy.

Recommendations for wound management in patients with prosthetic valves include immediate administration of intravenous antibiotics upon presentation to the emergency department. The regimen used for facial lacerations is cefazolin plus gentamicin.[26] This combination is synergistic against the resistant forms of staphylococci, which are responsible for the majority of cases of PVE. If the patient is allergic to penicillins, vancomycin is used. Wound management should be carried out in the operating room instead of the emergency department even if general anesthesia is not indicated. This practice provides a more aseptic environment and reduces the risk of a hospital-acquired infection. Patients with valvular problems or prostheses may be taking anticoagulants; therefore, meticulous hemostasis is more difficult and requires more attention.

The length of time needed for administration of the antibiotic is determined on the basis of the nature of the wound. Since the wound occurred in the community, it is initially considered contaminated but can be rendered clean by appropriate wound care. In this case, antibiotics would be continued for a maximum of 2 days. If adequate debridement is not possible, a 7- to 10-day course would be indicated.

Patients with prosthetic valves who suffer intraoral wounds, such as a compound mandibular fracture, would be given Regimen B, as described by the American Heart Association. Continued therapy is needed until fracture reduction and stabilization are achieved.

Once the need for antibiotics has been established, administration should follow the guidelines in Table 32–2.

EARLY DETECTION OF INFECTION

After a traumatic injury, careful monitoring of the patient is continually needed to determine if an infection may be occurring. The cardinal signs of rubor, dolor, calor, and tumor may or may not be present. However, early detection of an infection will permit treatment to be more effective than it would be if delayed until a full-blown infection is present.

Local wound changes that indicate a developing infection are redness, increased heat, and localized edema of the wound. The differentiation between cellulitis (which is an early sign of bacterial invasion) and inflammation (which is part of the usual process of wound healing) may be difficult. If the condition is due to the traumatic insult, it will be noted in the first 24 hours following an injury.

If bacteria are responsible for the local tissue damage, the inflammatory response will persist and progress beyond the first 24 hours. Local vasodilatation of capillaries will cause the area to become erythematous and warm. Chemical mediators of inflammation (histamine, bradykinin, serotonin, prostaglandins, and products of the immune system) will collect in the area. Swelling intensifies, and the wound may become indurated as the extravascular fluid clots owing to the presence of fibrinogen and other plasma proteins, which in turn block lymphatic drainage of the injured area.

TABLE 32–2.   GUIDELINES FOR THE ADMINISTRATION OF ANTIBIOTICS TO THE TRAUMA PATIENT

1. Administer immediately on presentation to the emergency room
2. Administer the antibiotics intravenously
3. Dose at two times the half-life of the antibiotic
4. Discontinue the antibiotic at the end of surgery unless persistent contamination is anticipated (e.g., salivary leakage)
5. Choose an antibiotic on the basis of the potential infectious organisms (penicillin for intraoral trauma versus a cephalosporin for contaminated external wounds)

This reaction is the host's attempt to contain or wall off the invading bacteria.

The systemic response to infection and injury will include an immediate leukocytosis, caused by the release of granulocyte-releasing factor from the breakdown of the inflamed tissues. Leukocytes are recruited from the bone marrow and spleen, and marginated intravascular leukocytes are mobilized in response to injury. The stress of the traumatic injury is also known to cause a transient leukocytosis through increased secretion of endogenous corticosteroids and epinephrine.

Inflammation will also cause the release of a colony-stimulating factor that increases the rate of production of leukocytes from the bone marrow. This activity will cause an increase in immature forms (band cells) to be noted in a peripheral blood smear and is more diagnostic of an infectious process than a simple increase in numbers of neutrophils.

The formation of pus at the suspected site of an infection is the result of the continuation of the host response to the invading organisms. As tissue macrophages and neutrophils continue to phagocytize bacteria, they in turn die and lyse. The local blockage of tissue lymphatics causes a cavity to form in the region; this cavity contains a combination of dead white blood cells and necrotic tissue, which is clinically noted as pus. The formation of pus is an irrefutable local sign that an infection is occurring. In the severely anergic patient (anergy may occur even in previously healthy individuals following major trauma), pus may form without the preceding signs of inflammation.[27]

The monitoring of the patient's temperature may also confirm the presence of an infection. Body core temperature is regulated by the hypothalamus and normally fluctuates around a range of 1°F, with the peak temperature occurring at approximately 6:00 PM daily. The diurnal increase in endogenous corticosteroids in the morning usually blunts a fever, so that measurements should be obtained in the late afternoon or early evening, when the corticosteroid levels are the lowest.[1] Rectal temperature recordings should be made, as they reflect body core temperature more accurately.

Fever, a body temperature higher than normal, is usually due to exogenous substances (primarily bacteria and endotoxin) and released endogenous proteins that are known collectively as pyrogens. Pyrogens act on the thermostatic control in the hypothalamus to reset the homeostatic temperature at a higher level, resulting in fever. Endogenous pyrogen is produced from white blood cells, with the major source being neutrophils, monocytes, and eosinophils. Neutrophils are induced to release pyrogen as a result of phagocytosis. This induction is confirmed by the presence of a lag time that occurs between phagocytosis and a rise in temperature.[28] Thus, the neutrophils do not contain pyrogen but are stimulated to form it after contact with exogenous pyrogens.

The differential diagnosis of fever in the trauma patient is often complicated by multisystem injury. An algorithm for guiding the workup of an infection in the trauma patient is presented in Figure 32–3. Clinical inspection of the wound is the most important diagnostic tool in determining if the fever is due to a wound infection. Local signs, such as increasing inflammation, induration, local pain, and edema, often precede frank drainage and pus formation.

Any drainage from a wound site should always be carefully collected for Gram staining and cultures. If local signs warrant, sutures should be removed and the wound opened to permit further evaluation and to allow for drainage. To obtain fluid for cultures, the ideal collection technique is to prepare the skin surface with an antiseptic, allow it to dry, and aspirate the fluid into a sterile syringe. Any air in the syringe is expressed, and the syringe is capped and immediately transported to the laboratory for aerobic and anaerobic cultures. The laboratory should be alerted that anaerobic cultures are being submitted. A Gram stain is also performed at this time to provide immediate evidence of bacterial invasion and some preliminary indication of the type of bacteria present, since the cultures will take at least 24 hours to yield positive results.

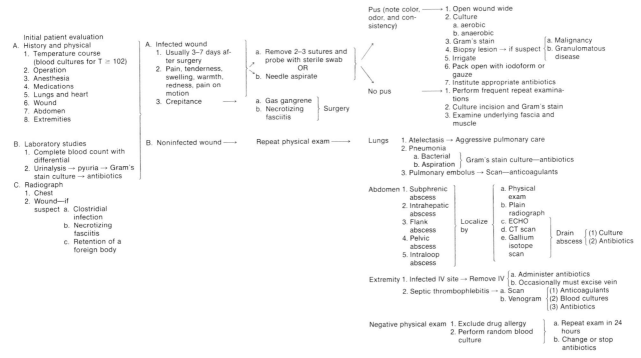

FIGURE 32–3. An algorithm outlining the steps in evaluating the cause of infection in a trauma patient. (From Majeski JA, Alexander JW: Complications of wound infections. *In* Greenfield LJ [ed]: Complications in Surgery and Trauma. Philadelphia, JB Lippincott, 1984, p 30; with permission.)

Other causes for a rise in the patient's temperature must also be considered. The cause of the fever may be differentiated by the time at which it occurs. For example, after an operation, a fever that develops in the initial 24-hour period is often due to atelectasis. Atelectasis is not an established infection; rather, it is the collapse of the small airways that entrap bacteria in the lungs. The alveolar macrophages and recruitment of neutrophils initiate the inflammatory response, pyrogens are produced, and fever ensues. If left untreated, a pneumonia can develop as the bacteria proliferate and invade the collapsed lung segment.

Urinary tract infection should be considered in any patient who has had a Foley catheter placed at some time. Urosepsis in these patients is usually from a hospital-acquired organism, and this necessitates culture and sensitivity testing prior to treatment.

The development of "third-day fever" should alert the surgeon to the possibility of an infection caused by an intravenous catheter. Catheters are responsible for 40 per cent of fevers that develop on the second or third day of hospital admission.[1] As a rule, intravenous sites should be changed every 48 hours. In addition, many hospitals routinely change all lines started in the field or in the emergency room upon admission to the floor. These acutely placed lines are associated with a higher rate of infection.

Finally, the surgeon must be aware of noninfectious causes of fever. The most common is a drug fever, which represents a hypersensitivity reaction. Eosinophils, which are involved in allergic reactions, are stimulated to produce endogenous pyrogens and are often found in increased numbers during a drug fever. An eosinophilia will be noted in the differential white blood cell count in cases of drug fever. Cessation of the offending drug (usually an antibiotic) is indicated, and the temperature will return to normal in 48 to 72 hours.[29]

Patients with maxillofacial trauma often have sustained blunt head injury, which may cause contusion of the hypothalamus. Typically, the loss of temperature regulation in these patients will be noted by periods of hyperthermia and hypothermia.[28]

TREATMENT OF WOUND INFECTION

Once a wound infection is diagnosed, local treatment of the infection will be indicated, and a decision regarding systemic therapy needs to be made. Cellulitis is the most common infection in surgical practice. True cellulitis is an invasive, nonsuppurative infection. The signs of redness, warmth, and pain are due to the inflammatory response elicited by the invading bacteria. Walling off the inflammation is not seen owing to the fibrinolytic agents elaborated by many of the invading organisms, usually beta-hemolytic streptococci.

Cellulitis is managed with antibiotics and warm soaks. Penicillin is the antibiotic of choice for a non–hospital-acquired cellulitis.[30] Early therapy of cellulitis increases the chance that the host response can remove the invading organisms. Incision and drainage are indicated only to relieve pressure and only if ischemia is developing.

Once a localized abscess or collection of pus develops, surgical management of the wound is indicated. The abscess cavity may be surrounded by a cellulitic area, but incision and drainage of the wound are part of the initial management. Surgical drainage provides many important functions in the management of the infection. By establishing drainage, the number of bacteria present in the tissues is significantly decreased. In addition, the local collection of bacterial products, such as endotoxins, is reduced.

The fluids that collect in a wound become less active in supporting host phagocytosis and neutrophil killing. Opsonization is also reduced, and drainage of a wound will improve these vital neutrophil functions.

Finally, drainage of an infection also provides specimens for Gram staining and culture and sensitivity testing. Appropriate antibiotic therapy may be instituted while waiting for the culture results. However, antibiotic administration is not a substitute for surgical management of an infected wound, which should not be delayed.

INFECTIONS CAUSED BY ORAL AND MAXILLOFACIAL TRAUMA

Soft Tissue Lacerations

The large quantities of endogenous organisms contaminating an intraoral tissue injury would apparently predispose many patients to infections. The bacterial count in saliva is quite high (10^{8-9} bacteria per milliliter), with anaerobes outnumbering aerobes by about 5 : 1. In reality, the rate of infection from an intraoral laceration is very low. The well-vascularized tissue may confer an advantage on the host's ability to prevent an infection in the presence of large numbers of bacteria. Complete debridement of devitalized intraoral tissues can be accomplished with less concern for the aesthetic result than would be required for extraoral lacerations.

The routine use of antibiotics for the uncomplicated intraoral wound is probably unnecessary. Instead, thorough debridement, removal of any foreign bodies, irrigation, and careful closure are indicated. If an antibiotic is indicated, penicillin is the drug of choice because of its effectiveness against the oral anaerobes.

Soft tissue lacerations of the face and scalp have also been shown to be relatively resistant to the development of a wound infection. In studies of infections following soft tissue lacerations, the rate of infection of facial lacerations was only 1.3 per cent, compared with 12.5 per cent of lacerations of the feet.[31] This difference in infection rate is most likely due to the lesser number of endogenous bacteria found on the face compared with the feet. It has been shown that all tissues have the same resistance to infection (tongue, fat, muscle, and skin), but an infection uniformly developed in those tissues once a level of more than 10^6 bacteria per gram of tissue was reached.[22]

Again, the decision of whether to use prophylactic antibiotics for lacerations of the face is not a clear-cut one. No study has shown a decrease in the rate of infection if an antibiotic is given. Instead, the clinician needs to be guided by some of the risk factors known to increase the risk of wound infection, as previously discussed.

Thus, in heavily contaminated wounds or in those that are not able to be completely debrided, antibiotics are indicated. An interesting factor may be the length of the wound. Some studies have noted an increase in infection rate based on the number of sutures needed to close the wound. Stellate lacerations with abrasion of the wound edges also have an increased rate of infection compared with simple, linear lacerations.

It must be emphasized that if antibiotics are to be given, they should be administered by a parenteral route immediately upon presentation to the emergency room. There is no benefit to closing a laceration and handing the patient a prescription to be filled at some later time if there is a concern for potential wound sepsis. No prophylactic effect is demonstrated by antibiotics administered 3 hours or more following an injury.[32]

Animal Bites

Lacerations from animal bites are considered heavily contaminated wounds. Immediate treatment of the wound is indicated, with measures directed at reducing the number of organisms present. High-pressure saline irrigation and thorough debridement are the mainstays of treatment.

Dog bites of the face and scalp are much less likely to become infected than those at other sites. Again, studies have failed to demonstrate a significant benefit to the administration of antibiotics for facial wounds caused by animal bites.[33] Instead, of all the variables controlled for, the lack of debridement caused the highest rate of infection.

The microbiology of infections caused by an animal bite will differ from that usually noted in traumatic injuries owing to the different flora of the animal's mouth. A gram-negative rod, *Pasteurella multocida,* is responsible for 30 per cent of infections from dog bites. Its pattern of infection is such that within 24 hours of the injury rapid development of local erythema, pain, and swelling occurs, enabling the diagnosis on the basis of clinical course. If the infection occurs after 24 hours, it is usually caused by *Staphylococcus aureus* or *Streptococcus viridans* and occasionally by *Bacteroides* species and fusobacteria, all of which are common intraoral organisms from a healthy animal.[34]

Asplenic and other immunologically compromised individuals are also susceptible to infection by a group of aerobic, gram-negative bacilli that are found in animals. These organisms are identified by the CDC by alphanumeric names (IIj, EF-4, and DF-2). Infection with these organisms usually manifests with cellulitis, bacteremia, purulent meningitis, and endocarditis. Thus, because of the serious sequelae of this infection, penicillin prophylaxis is indicated after a dog bite in all asplenic and alcoholic patients (including bites by one's own pet).[35] Penicillin is also the drug of choice for the prevention and treatment of *P. multocida* infections; tetracycline and erythromycin may be used in those patients with a known history of an allergic reaction to penicillin.

An additional consideration in the treatment of animal bites is the determination of the need for prophylaxis against rabies. The rabies virus causes an acute encephalomyelitis in those infected, with nearly 100 per cent mortality. Typically, rabies is transmitted through a bite by an infected dog, but cats, horses, cows, skunks, bats, raccoons, and foxes are associated with its transmission. It is unusual to find rabid rodents, lagomorphs (rabbits), birds, or reptiles.

The infection is transmitted from the saliva of an infected animal to the nervous system of the bitten person by spread from the peripheral nerves to the spinal ganglia and into the central nervous system. This migration of the virus occurs rapidly, with viral particles found in the brain within 72 hours.

Bites from animals possibly infected with rabies must be treated aggressively.

Postexposure prophylaxis is given in cases of unprovoked attack from domestic animals (unless the animal is known to be immunized) and in cases of wild animal bites. Initial wound care is important, consisting of thorough irrigation with quaternary ammonium compounds with 70 per cent alcohol, which have been shown to be rabicidal.[36] Rabies immune globulin and active immunization are also given along with prophylaxis against tetanus (see further on).

Human Bites

Many authors feel that human bites are more serious than animal bites and should be treated differently. However, contemporary management that includes debridement, prophylactic antibiotics, and copious irrigation has reduced the infection rate of human bites to the face to around 2.5 per cent.[34] As with animal bites, the anatomic location of the injury plays an important role, with facial injuries having a much lower incidence of infection than extremity wounds.

The aesthetic results of treating a human bite are improved if primary closure can be obtained. A delay in treatment or the failure to surgically debride the wound adequately, however, may lead to wound breakdown and a compromised aesthetic result. Thus, in the attempt to obtain primary closure, extensive surgery may be needed and should probably be undertaken in the operating room.

The high bacterial count of saliva results in an extensive inoculum into the wounded person. Often, the surgeon may elect to treat these wounds by delayed primary closure. In these cases, the wound is packed with moist gauze, which is changed twice a day. The dressing changes remove the fibrinous exudate that collects in the wound and could support bacterial growth. In addition, the twice-a-day dressing changes provide a chance for frequent observation and monitoring for any developing infection. After a 4-day waiting period, primary closure can be done with little risk of infection (Fig. 32–4). This technique of closure is especially indicated if there is a delay in treatment or in the presentation of the patient to the emergency room.

Antibiotics, if indicated, need to be administered immediately upon presentation of the patient. Again, no clinical trial clearly shows an advantage to antibiotics administered for bites to the face. The oral cavity contains predominantly anaerobes sensitive to penicillin, and this is the drug of choice. Antitetanus therapy is unnecessary, since *Clostridium tetani* has never been shown to be present in the mouth.[37]

FACIAL BONE FRACTURES

Because the morbidity of osteomyelitis is so significant, the appropriate management of facial bone fractures is important. Early management is necessary to prevent infection due to the frequency of oral contamination of the fracture site. It is a rare mandibular fracture that is not considered contaminated at the time of presentation. If definitive treatment is to be delayed, temporary intermaxillary fixation is indicated to prevent mechanical pumping of saliva and bacteria into the fracture site. Movement of the fracture also causes rebleeding at the fracture site, which increases the local hematoma and causes a more anaerobic environment. The temporary intermaxillary fixation will also make the patient more comfortable.

Antibiotic Therapy

All jaw fractures involving tooth sockets must be considered compound fractures requiring antibiotic treatment. Peterson[25] states that this should be given in therapeutic doses (as opposed to prophylactic doses) and thus would be continued over 10 to 14 days. Since this decision can be made early, upon examination of the patient, paren-

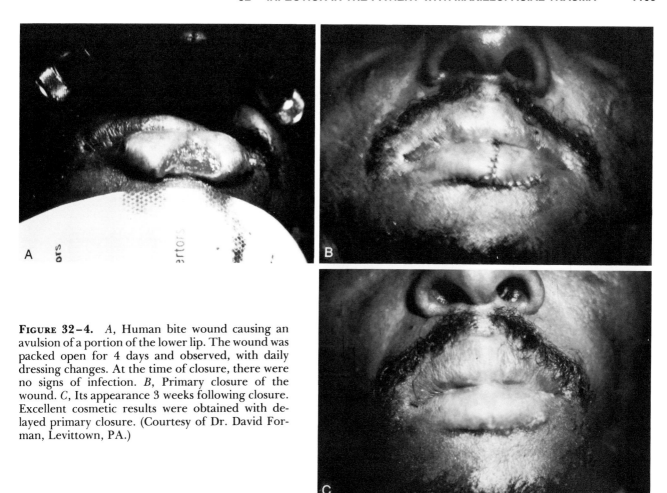

FIGURE 32–4. *A,* Human bite wound causing an avulsion of a portion of the lower lip. The wound was packed open for 4 days and observed, with daily dressing changes. At the time of closure, there were no signs of infection. *B,* Primary closure of the wound. *C,* Its appearance 3 weeks following closure. Excellent cosmetic results were obtained with delayed primary closure. (Courtesy of Dr. David Forman, Levittown, PA.)

teral administration should not be delayed even if definitive treatment of the fracture is deferred. As discussed earlier, delays in the administration of an antibiotic may allow bacteria to become established and isolated from the systemic circulation and to multiply into the critical number needed to cause an infection of the fracture site.

The surgeon's choice of antibiotic will be guided by many factors. These include the following:

1. Identification of the causative agent or the usual organism that may cause an infection if prophylaxis is indicated
2. Use of the least toxic antibiotic
3. The patient's drug history, to avoid known drugs to which the patient has previously reacted adversely
4. Use of a bactericidal drug as opposed to a bacteriostatic one, since the bactericidal drug relies less on the host's resistance, kills the bacteria directly, and works faster
5. The cost of the antibiotic regimen[25]

Management of Teeth Associated with Mandibular Fracture

A significant controversy centers on the management of teeth in the line of fracture and their relationship to causing infection. Studies of complications of mandibular fractures show a higher incidence of infections when teeth are involved in the line of fracture. This finding has led some clinicians to recommend extracting all teeth in the line of fracture. In 1965, Bradley suggested removal of all teeth associated with a fracture.[38] More recently, a retrospective review of 327 mandibular fractures appeared to recommend leaving in place healthy, nonmobile teeth in the line of fracture.[39] Contemporary fracture management supports removing teeth in the line of fracture only if the following conditions exist:

1. The tooth is loose
2. The tooth is grossly carious or periodontally involved
3. More than 50 per cent of the root is exposed in the fracture line
4. Adequate reduction is mechanically blocked by its retention

Retention of healthy, firm teeth may help in the reduction of a fracture as well as preserve the dentition.

Zallen and Curry showed that with the administration of antibiotics the incidence of infections is significantly reduced if teeth are involved with the fracture.[40] Although their study was not controlled, the incidence of infection was 50 per cent without antibiotics and 6 per cent if they were given. In the situation of mandibular fractures that are compounded into the oral cavity (i.e., through the dentoalveolar structures), therapeutic antibiotics should be administered immediately. These fractures are contaminated or even infected at the time of presentation. The antibiotic of choice is penicillin. If the fracture is compounded onto the skin, a penicillinase-resistant penicillin should be added or a semi-synthetic penicillin with a beta-lactamase inhibitor used. Clindamycin is used in patients allergic to the penicillins, or a cephalosporin such as cefazolin can be used, which has been shown to reach high levels in bone. Antibiotic therapy is continued for 10 to 14 days in these cases.

Continued mobility of a fracture causes rebleeding and decreased levels of oxygen tension at the fracture site. These local changes can additionally increase the risk of infection. Bacterial contamination of the fracture site should be reduced upon fixation of the fracture, and some method of temporary fixation should be applied as soon as possible. Open reduction allows debridement of any nonvital tissue and evacuation of a hematoma and permits close alignment of the fracture, thus reducing the dead space. However, open reduction may also result in further devascularization of tissue, especially where small bone fragments in a comminuted fracture have been stripped of the periosteal attachment. Considering these factors, the surgeon should

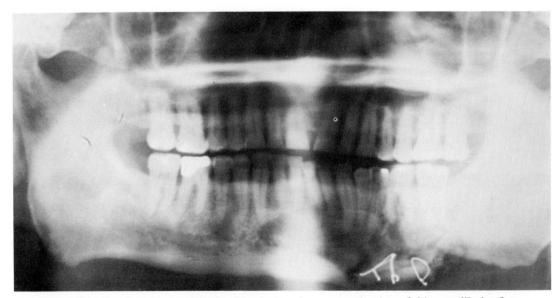

FIGURE 32–5. An osteomyelitis developed after the open reduction of this mandibular fracture. The placement of multiple wires in an area of comminution requires stripping of the periosteum from the small bone fragments and a subsequent devascularization.

exercise good judgment in performing an open reduction when significant communition of the fracture has occurred (Fig. 32–5).

Infections Associated with Fractures

Owing to the compound nature of most fractures of the mandible, the risk of osteomyelitis is significant. Factors associated with an increased incidence of developing an infection after a mandibular fracture are noted in Table 32–3.

Infection of the mandible following a fracture is known as posttraumatic osteomyelitis. After injury and subsequent reduction of the fracture, certain signs and symptoms indicate that an osteomyelitis is developing. The early signs of an acute, suppurative osteomyelitis include the following:

1. Deep, intense pain
2. High, intermittent fever
3. Paresthesia or anesthesia of the mental nerve (arising after the trauma and reduction of the fracture)
4. A clearly defined etiology[41]

At this phase, the infection is spreading through the intramedullary portion of the bone, with little cortical destruction; therefore, radiographs will not show any significant findings. The patient should be administered parenteral antibiotics at this time.

As the osteomyelitis becomes established, a firm cellulitis will develop over the involved portion of the mandible and will lead to intraoral and/or cutaneous sites of drainage. The cellulitis is often firm or "brawny hard" on palpation. Systemic signs are variable but may include a mild leukocytosis with a shift to more immature (band) forms of PMNs, a rise in temperature, and occasionally an increase in the erythrocyte sedimentation rate (ESR).

Although radiographic signs of osteomyelitis are not evident until late in the process or until 50 per cent demineralization has occurred, they may precede the development of frank drainage. Classic radiographic findings of osteomyelitis include a "moth-eaten" appearance of the bone and the development of sequestra, which are islands of devitalized bone. The sequestrum is surrounded by an involucrum (a sheath of new bone), which is separated from it by a radiolucent zone.

The extent of the osteomyelitis will be greater than that noted on routine radiographic examination. To plan the appropriate surgery and ensure adequate treatment, scintigraphy is often a useful adjunctive study. Typically, technetium-99m–labeled phosphate compounds are administered intravenously and become concentrated in areas of increased bone activity. Since this test cannot differentiate between areas of increased formation and areas of resorption of bone, more information regarding the osteomyelitis can be obtained using a subtraction study. This test is performed by rescanning the patient with gallium, which is known to collect in white blood cells. An area that is positive for both technetium and gallium uptake probably represents acute or suppurative osteomyelitis. If the site has an uptake of technetium

TABLE 32–3.   RISK FACTORS FOR OSTEOMYELITIS

1. Ineffective fixation, reduction, and immobilization
2. Delay in treatment ("old" fracture)
3. Delay in administration of antibiotic therapy or inadequate antibiotic therapy
4. More than 50 per cent of a tooth root exposed in a fracture
5. Premature removal of fixation devices
6. Devitalized segments of bone in the fracture site due to excessive stripping of periosteum, overzealous use of transosseous wiring, or overheating of the bone by burs
7. Decreased host resistance or increased susceptibility to infection (e.g., patient is alcoholic, diabetic, and so forth)

but not of gallium, it most likely represents an area of bone repair. Scintigraphy is also useful for monitoring the course of the disease and efficacy of the treatment, and it may also indicate when treatment can be safely stopped.

Once established, a fracture osteomyelitis is treated with a combined surgical and medical approach. Nonvital tissue, foreign bodies, and associated teeth need to be removed. At the surgical procedure, specimens of bone should be meticulously obtained and quickly submitted without secondary contamination for culture and sensitivity testing. This practice must be strictly observed to preserve fastidious anaerobes that may be the causative organism of the osteomyelitis. Debriding infected areas and establishing drainage are important. Continuous irrigation and drainage systems can be placed through a closed wound following appropriate debridement if the infection is extensive or refractory to conventional drainage and irrigation. Antibiotic-containing solutions for irrigation may be of benefit but have not been comprehensively studied for their efficacy. Recent studies of systems that deliver a high concentration of antibiotic locally to a site of osteomyelitis show promise. These systems employ materials that are impregnated with an antibiotic, usually gentamicin, which is then implanted in the infected wound. The benefits of such a system are that high and sustained concentrations of antibiotics are delivered locally, with low systemic levels, thereby reducing the toxic side effects of some agents.

In addition, a means of fixation must be placed to prevent further movement of the fracture segments. This fixation often requires the use of external pins to span the gap created by the removal of the involved bone. Reconstruction of the bony defect is usually not attempted until all signs of infection are gone, usually after a period of at least 2 months. The absence of infection is determined on the basis of no local signs of infection, such as drainage or cellulitis. A bone scan using technetium and gallium subtraction can be used as previously described to corroborate the clinical impression that the infective process has cleared. The secondary reconstruction of continuity defects resulting from an osteomyelitis is discussed in Chapter 30.

This discussion of osteomyelitis is centered on the treatment of this problem in the mandible as opposed to the maxilla and other bones of the facial skeleton. The endochondral bone of the mandible is structurally similar to the long bones of the body, which are more susceptible to osteomyelitis. The intramembranous bone of the maxilla has less medullary tissue and thinner cortical plates, which allow the infection to pass through quickly and into the surrounding tissues and hence not have the opportunity to become as readily established as in the mandible. The blood supply to the maxilla is more extensive, and it is therefore less susceptible to disturbance from infection.

The use of hyperbaric oxygen for osteomyelitis of the mandible has been reported.[42] Its clear benefit over surgical and medical modalities of treatment has not been demonstrated, but it may be of use in cases refractory to more conventional means of therapy.

Midfacial Fractures

Facial bone fractures involving sites in addition to the mandible are usually involved with one or more of the sinuses. The microbiology of an infected sinus differs from that of the oral cavity specifically because of the presence of *Streptococcus pneumoniae* and *Hemophilus influenzae*. However, the healthy sinus has been shown to be a relatively sterile environment,[43] and the choice of prophylactic antibiotics should be based on the most likely source of the potentially infective bacteria.

Le Fort II and III fractures may communicate with the cranial cavity, as evidenced by a cerebrospinal fluid (CSF) leak from the nose or external ear canals (a CSF otorhinorrhea). Antibiotic prophylaxis to prevent the possibility of a meningeal infection is controversial, since studies have not shown a reduction in the incidence of meningitis in patients who have received prophylaxis. In fact, after 5 days of systemic antibiotics, the nasopharynx usually becomes colonized with more resistant organisms,[44] usually acquired in the hospital, making treatment of a meningitis more complicated. Therefore, early reduction of the fractures is indicated, which will usually stop the CSF leak. This reduction is indicated as soon as the patient is neurologically stable.

Nosocomial Infections

The hospitalized, traumatically injured patient is at risk for developing an infection during the period of admission. Nosocomial infections affect a significant number of patients each year, causing delays in discharge, significant morbidity, and increased cost of care.

Traumatized patients are at increased risk of developing a nosocomial infection, since they are a compromised host. The mechanical barrier of the skin and mucous membranes is violated by either injury or interventions such as surgery and intravenous access sites. The host defenses are also reduced owing to some of the systemic effects of the trauma. Of additional concern is the fact that hospital-acquired infections are often from organisms with unusual virulence or resistance to antibiotic therapy.

The diagnosis of a nosocomial infection is similar to that of any other type of infection. The source of the fever in the hospitalized patient may require a full systemic workup, including evaluation of the lungs, wounds, intravenous sites, urine, and blood. Cases of septicemia have been reported to occur because of contaminated intravenous fluids.[45] Thus, the source of the infection may require consideration of many factors.

Owing to the variable resistance patterns of the responsible organisms, antibiotic therapy is withheld until specific cultures and sensitivities are available, if possible. Other therapeutic interventions are important, such as pulmonary physical therapy for suspected atelectasis or pneumonia. Review of the patient's hospital course, including any intravenous sites or catheterizations, may further assist in the investigation. In addition, the bed-ridden, traumatized patient is susceptible to thromboembolism and fat embolism, which may cause fever.

Tetanus

Tetanus is caused by the production of an exotoxin from *Clostridium tetani*, an obligate anaerobe, gram-positive rod. The disease has a fatality rate of about 45 per cent in the United States,[46] but active immunization is successful at preventing the disease.

Since viable spores are present in soil, in house dust, and even on clothing, even minor injuries may cause the disease in unimmunized individuals. The organism is not invasive but gains entry through puncture wounds and lacerations, with the most frequent sites being the hands, feet, and legs.

Upon evaluation of a wound that may be likely to cause tetanus, an immunization history should be obtained. If a full set of three vaccines had been given, and a booster received within the previous 10 years, no further therapy is needed. In cases in which passive immunization is to be given, a single dose of human tetanus immune globulin (TIG) is administered. Subsequently, the patient should complete an active immunization series.

The diagnosis of tetanus is made by clinical signs, since organisms are recovered in only about 30 per cent of cases. The incubation period is 2 to 56 days, with earlier onset associated with a poorer prognosis. The classic signs of trismus (lockjaw), rigidity of the facial musculature (risus sardonicus), and reflex spasms are pathognomonic for the disease. The patient is managed with antiserum (TIG), muscle relaxants, tracheostomy, and antibiotics (penicillin).

CONCLUSION

The acutely injured patient often attracts a great deal of initial attention in the emergency room because of the immediate need for resuscitation. Once the patient's condition is stabilized, the risks of infection should be evaluated and appropriate therapy started. The traumatized patient is severely compromised in the ability to resist even a "normal" bacterial insult. The progression of infection may result in loss of structures, limb, and even life if sepsis occurs. It is, therefore, encumbent upon the treating doctor to be aggressive in wound debridement, bacterial load reduction, and appropriate antibiotic and antitoxin administration, as well as assuming the management of the injuries to maximize the functional and aesthetic result.

REFERENCES

1. Wilson RF: Special problems in the diagnosis and treatment of surgical sepsis. Surg Clin North Am 65:965, 1985.
2. Robson MC, Lea CE, Dalton JB, Heggers JB: Quantitative bacteriology and delayed wound closure. Surg Forum 19:501, 1968.
3. Kass KH: Bacteriuria in the diagnosis of infections of the urinary tract. Arch Intern Med 100:709, 1957.
4. Miller C, Trunkey DD: Infection of sepsis. *In* Flint LM, Fry DE (eds): Surgical Infections. New York, Medical Examiners Publishing Company, 1981, p 8.
5. Miles AA: Nonspecific defense reactions in bacterial infections. Ann NY Acad Sci 66:356, 1956.
6. Haury BB, Rodeheaver GT, Pettry D, et al: Inhibition of nonspecific defenses by soil infection-potentiating factors. Surg Gynecol Obstet 144:19, 1977.
7. Elek SD: Experimental staphylococcal infections in the skin of man. Ann NY Acad Sci 65:85, 1956.
8. Gross A, Bhaskar SN, Cutright DE, et al: The effect of pulsating water jet lavage on experimental contaminated wounds. J Oral Surg 29:187, 1971.
9. Wheeler CB, Rodeheaver GT, Thacker JG, et al: Side-effects of high pressure irrigation. Surg Gynecol Obstet 143:775, 1976.
10. Brånemark PI, Albrektsson B, Lindstrom J, et al: Local effects of wound disinfectants. Acta Chir Scand [Suppl] 357:166, 1966.
11. Fry DE, Polk HC: Host defense in the trauma patient. *In* Richardson JD, Polk HC, Flint LM (eds): Trauma: Clinical Care and Pathophysiology. Chicago, Year Book Medical Publishers, 1987, p 55.
12. Keane R, Munster AM, Birmingham W, et al: Suppressor cell activity after major injury: Indirect and direct functional assays. J Trauma 22:770, 1982.
13. Edlich R, Rodeheaver GT, Thacker JC: Technical factors in the prevention of wound infections. *In* Howard RJ, Simmons RL (eds): Surgical Infectious Diseases. Norwalk, CT, Appleton and Lange, 1987, p 331.
14. Garner JS: CDC Guidelines for prevention of surgical wound infections, 1985. Am J Infect Control 14:71, 1986.
15. Theogaraj SD: Complications of traumatic wounds of the face. *In* Greenfield L (ed): Complications of Surgery and Trauma. Philadelphia, JB Lippincott, 1984, p 10.
16. Shepard GH: The healing of wounds after delayed primary closure. Plast Reconstr Surg 48:358, 1971.
17. Heggers JP, Robson MC, Rostroph JD: A rapid method of performing quantitative wound cultures. Milit Med 134:666, 1969.
18. May J, Chalers JP, Lowenthal J, et al: Factors in the patient contributing to surgical sepsis. Surg Gynecol Obstet 122:28, 1966.
19. Flynn TR, Hoekstra CW, Lawrence FR: The use of drains in oral and maxillofacial surgery: A review and a new approach. J Oral Maxillofac Surg 41:508, 1983.
20. Kuchta N, Dineen P: Effect of absorbable hemostats on intraabdominal sepsis. Infect Surg 2:441, 1983.
21. Mancusi-Ungaro HR, Rappaport NH: Preventing wound infections. Am Family Physician 33:147, 1986.
22. Edlich RF, Kenney JG, Morgan RE, et al: Antimicrobial treatment of minor soft tissue lacerations: A critical review. Emerg Med Clin North Am 4:561, 1986.
23. Becker GD: Identification and management of the patient at high risk for wound infection. Head Neck Surg 8:205, 1986.
24. Conte JE, Jacob L, Polk HC: Antibiotic Prophylaxis in Surgery. Philadelphia, JB Lippincott, 1984, p 17.
25. Peterson LJ: Principles of antibiotic therapy. *In* Topazian RG, Goldberg MH (eds): Oral and Maxillofacial Infections. Philadelphia, WB Saunders Company, 1987, p 136.
26. Colley JL, Nolan SP, Edlich RF: Prosthetic valve endocarditis developing after an infected scalp laceration. J Emerg Med 3:269, 1985.
27. Munster AM: Immunologic response of trauma and burns: An overview. Am J Med 76:142, 1984.
28. Fry DE: Pathophysiology and management of fever. *In* Flint LM, Fry DE (eds): Surgical Infections. New York, Medical Examiners Publishing Company, 1981, p 25.
29. Barrett CR: Common clinical problems in pulmonary disease. *In* Halsted JA, Halsted CH (eds): The Laboratory in Clinical Medicine. Philadelphia, WB Saunders Company, 1981, p 391.
30. Stone HH: Infection. *In* Polk HC, Stone HH, Gardner B (eds): Basic Surgery. 3rd ed. Norwalk, CT, Appleton-Century-Crofts, 1987, p 141.
31. Samson RH, Altman SF: Antibiotic prophylaxis for minor lacerations. NY State J Med 77:1730, 1977.

32. Burke JF: The effective period of preventive antibiotic action in experimental incisions and dermal lesions. Surgery 50:161, 1961.

33. Rosen RA: The use of antibiotics in the initial management of recent dog-bite wounds. Am J Emerg Med 3:19, 1985.

34. Aghababran R, Conte JE: Mammalian bite wounds. Ann Emerg Med 9:79, 1980.

35. Scully RE, Mark EJ, McNeeley B: DF-2 bacteremia after dog bite (Case 29-2986). N Engl J Med 315:241, 1986.

36. Morrison AJ, Wenzel RP: Rabies: A review and current approach for the clinician. South Med J 78:1211, 1985.

37. Earley MJ, Bardsley AF: Human bites: A review. Br J Plast Surg 37:458, 1984.

38. Bradley RL: Treatment of fractured mandible. Am Surg 31:289, 1965.

39. Chuong R, Donoff RB, Guralnick WC: A retrospective analysis of 327 mandibular fractures. J Oral Maxillofac Surg 41:305, 1983.

40. Zallen RD, Curry JF: Study of antibiotic usage in compound mandibular fractures. J Oral Surg 33:431, 1975.

41. Topazian RG: Osteomyelitis of the jaws. In Topazian RG, Goldberg MH (eds): Oral and Maxillofacial Infections. 2nd ed. Philadelphia, WB Saunders Company, 1987, p 208.

42. Knighton DR, Halliday B, Hunt TK: Oxygen as an antibiotic. Arch Surg 121:191, 1986.

43. Cook HE, Haber J: Bacteriology of the maxillary sinus. J Oral Maxillofac Surg 45:1011, 1987.

44. Neely JG, Fine DP, Reynolds AF: The use of prophylactic antibiotics in patients with cerebrospinal fluid otorrhea and rhinorrhea. In Johnson JT (ed): Antibiotic Therapy in Head and Neck Surgery. New York, Marcel Dekker, 1987, p 110.

45. Lieblich SE, Forman D, Berger J, Gold BD: Septicemia secondary to the administration of a contaminated intravenous fluid. J Oral Maxillofac Surg 42:680, 1984.

46. Beaty HN: Tetanus. In Isselbacher KJ, Wintrobe G, Thorn A, et al (eds): Harrison's Principles of Internal Medicine. New York, McGraw-Hill, 1980, p 685.

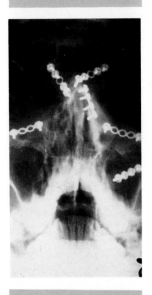

CHAPTER 33

RIGID FIXATION OF FACIAL FRACTURES

JOACHIN PREIN, M.D., D.D.S.,
W. SCHILLI, PROF. DR. MED.,
BEAT HAMMER, M.D., D.D.S.,
J. REUTHER, PROF. DR.,
and STEEN SINDET-PEDERSEN, D.D.S.

STABLE FIXATION OF COMPLEX MIDFACIAL FRACTURES IN ACCORDANCE WITH AO* PRINCIPLES

The majority of injuries to the facial skeleton are the result of traffic accidents. According to most studies, the share of facial injuries caused by sports and work-related accidents and by altercations is below 25 per cent. Most of the facial injuries resulting from automobile accidents are comminuted fractures caused by the usually very severe impact. The incidence of midface fractures has steadily increased in the past few decades. Whereas 30 years ago the ratio of midface fractures to mandibular fractures was 3:1, today it is almost 1:1. The statistical data published are not absolutely representative, since the number of patients treated varies with each hospital.

At the same time, the number of combined injuries has multiplied worldwide.[1-4] Injury to the soft tissue has been seen in up to 50 per cent of all fractures of the face. The most serious of these are damage to the eye caused by thrust against the windshield and frontobasal injuries. In countries in which the use of seat belts in automobiles is mandatory by law, the percentage of such injuries has decreased. However, the number of maxillary fractures has increased.[5-7]

The impact transmitted by a traffic collision is often so severe that the structures in the vicinity of the ensuing midface fractures are also affected. In more than one third of the cases, the neurocranium is involved. The maxilla makes a smooth transition into the neurocranium, so that fractures in these regions should be regarded as one unit.[8,9]

To discuss the diagnosis and treatment of midface fractures, it is necessary to classify them. A classification of midface fractures was first undertaken by René Le Fort in 1901.[10] He was chiefly interested in the most common fracture lines. Wassmund[11] modified this classification in 1927, and Manson,[2] in 1986, broadened the classification to include the frontal bone. None of these schemes took fractures of the zygoma, nose, and orbit into account. Schwenzer and Krüger,[12] therefore, suggested

---

* AO/ASIF (Association for the Study of Internal Fixation)

1172

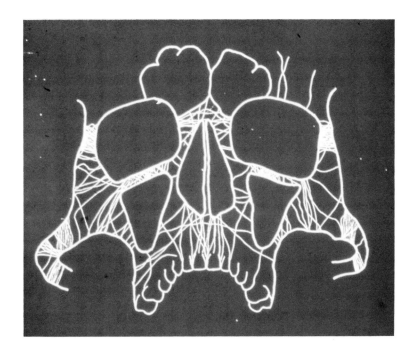

FIGURE 33-1. Fracture lines in midface fractures taken from 100 occipitomental radiographs.

grouping midface fractures into central, centrolateral, and lateral midface fractures. Yarrington[13] proposed a similar classification in 1979. Countless investigations have shown that midface fractures have typical fracture lines in only about every other patient. It has also been observed, however, that there are some areas of the facial anatomy in which fracture lines appear far more often than in others. A drawing of 100 fractures of the midface showed that fracture lines were most often seen in the infraorbital foramen (92 per cent) and in the area of the lateral orbit at the zygomaticofrontal suture (80 per cent) (Fig. 33-1).

The specific injury pattern and displacement result from the type and direction of the impact and from the anatomic conditions. The fragments produced by the fracture are usually displaced from outside to inside. The percentage of lateral fractures is high because we instinctively turn our face at the moment of impact.

The midfacial skeleton is sandwiched between the massive bony neurocranium and the stable mandible. The mandible is supported while kept mobile on the temporomandibular joint. The midfacial skeleton consists of several thin-walled bone compartments. Most of these boxlike cavities are lined with a thin, attached mucous membrane. They have contact with the airways and are therefore contaminated. In the frontobasal region, there is a soft tissue transition to the intracranial space via the fila olfactoria. Mechanically, functional stresses on the midfacial skeleton occur only from chewing. The compressive forces elicited by chewing pressures are transferred from the teeth and the alveolar process of the maxilla to the cranial base via three structural pillars. These vertical supporting pillars include the following:

1. The nasofrontal buttress, which reaches from the canine tooth and extends to the piriform aperture over the anterior lacrimal crest to the medial superior orbital ring

2. The zygomatic buttress, which reaches from the molars to the frontal zygomatic process

3. The pterygoid mandibular pillar, which supports the distal palate at the cranial base

The horizontal support is provided by the alveolar process, with the palate in the lower region and the ring-shaped bone support around the two orbits, which extends laterally into the zygomatic arch and is connected medially through the glabella.

Since the bone is highly resistant to pressure, no strong anatomic structure is

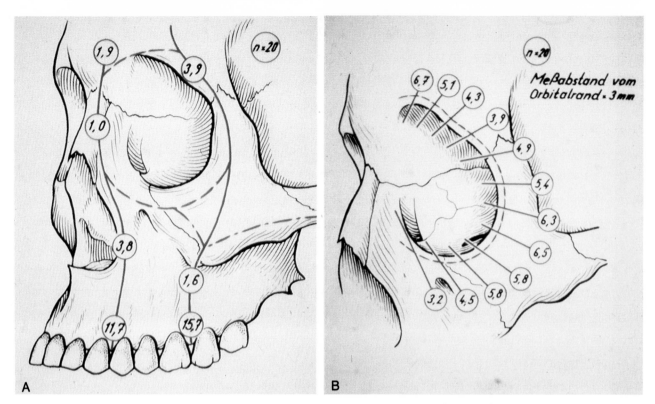

FIGURE 33-2.   *A, B,* Average measured bone thickness on the midfacial skeleton.

necessary to neutralize chewing pressures. Only in the area of the zygomatic arch and the pterygoid process do functional tensile forces act on the midface. For this reason, the greatest bone thicknesses are found in this region. An analysis of bone thickness (Fig. 33–2) shows that in the midface bones of more than 2 mm are to be expected in the area of the pillars, while bones smaller than 1 mm will be found in the rest of the midface, particularly in the canine fossa and in the orbital-ethmoid region.[14,15] Only recently, Manson and colleagues[16] pointed out the importance of these principal buttresses of the maxilla and their relevance for the treatment of midface fractures.

Accurate reconstruction of the facial skeleton after injury is absolutely essential to the proper function of the facial organs. Displacement of as little as 1 mm in the area of the alveolar process can interfere with chewing. Serious problems can result from displacements in the vicinity of the eye. The soft tissue around the eyeball forms a loop on which the eye is suspended. Dislocations at the attachment or deformations of the eyeball lead to movement dysfunctions. The often discussed volumetric alteration caused by a loss of orbital fat is, according to Manson and colleagues,[17] not as important as the deformation of the bony orbit. The medial canthal ligament is important for the fixation of the eyeball. It determines the interpupillary distance, which is specific for each individual and ranges between 32 and 34 mm.

The preservation of the bony contour is a prerequisite for the preservation of the soft tissue contour and, hence, of the face. Defects of the soft tissue are easier to conceal than bone contour defects. This observation makes the facial skeleton one of the most crucial factors for preserving the individual's identity. Losing the shape of one's face as a result of inaccurately reduced bone fragments in the midface is traumatic, as it means a change in one's identity. Even a scarred face retains its identity if the contours have been preserved (Fig. 33–3). Unlike the extremities, where inaccurate bone positioning can be corrected later on, facial bones that heal in the wrong position cannot be satisfactorily reduced, if at all. Additional problems are posed by the thin soft tissue cover, which shrinks and becomes scarred after consolidation. In

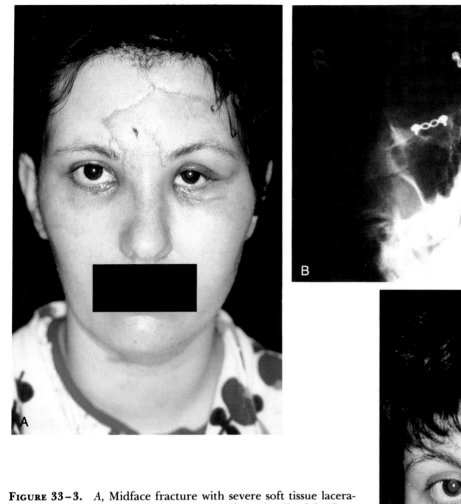

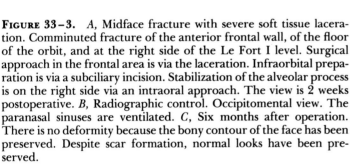

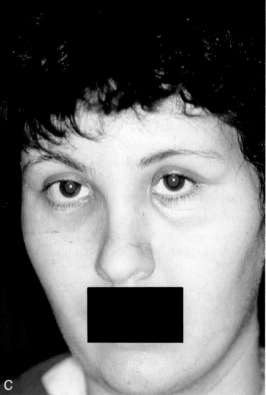

FIGURE 33–3. *A,* Midface fracture with severe soft tissue laceration. Comminuted fracture of the anterior frontal wall, of the floor of the orbit, and at the right side of the Le Fort I level. Surgical approach in the frontal area is via the laceration. Infraorbital preparation is via a subciliary incision. Stabilization of the alveolar process is on the right side via an intraoral approach. The view is 2 weeks postoperative. *B,* Radiographic control. Occipitomental view. The paranasal sinuses are ventilated. *C,* Six months after operation. There is no deformity because the bony contour of the face has been preserved. Despite scar formation, normal looks have been preserved.

assessing the effect of displacement, it must be kept in mind that traumatic displacements of 1 to 2 mm are not rare, while in orthognathic operations, displacements of just a few millimeters are common and effect substantial alterations in the contours of the face.

Diagnosis

The brain is affected in many cases of injury to the facial skeleton; this is indicated by a lowered level of consciousness or by clinical and radiographic signs of skull fracture. Brain injury is present in 20 per cent of patients presenting with one of these symptoms only and in more than 50 per cent of patients with both symptoms.[18,19] In frontobasal injuries, the secretion of a clear, serous liquid along with blood from the nose is sometimes observed, which is a sign of a cerebrospinal fluid fistula. When there is brain involvement, neurosurgical measures must have top priority.

The diagnosis of midface fracture is based on the clinical and radiographic examination. Frequently, clinical examination is able to detect only severe displacement. The presence of soft tissue lacerations cannot be considered a reliable clue to the state of the underlying bony skeleton. The most commonly found fracture lines can be felt around the orbit and on the glabella, as well as on the zygomatic buttress from inside the mouth (see Fig. 33–1). In many cases, hematomas and swelling make it impossible to feel the bone margins and to assess the dislocation. The sensitivity of the outer skin is almost always disturbed, since the fracture lines usually run through the exit foramen of the trigeminal nerve branches.

Displacement of the eyeball caused by displacement in the periorbital region and the ensuing diplopia can be camouflaged by an intraorbital hematoma. A functional disturbance of the eye movement occurs when periocular soft tissue becomes caught in the fracture gaps. This disorder can be detected by means of the forced traction test. Comminution in the area of the orbital funnel in the region of the attachment of the rectus inferior and rectus lateral muscles can lead to Horner's syndrome because of a paralysis of the oculomotor nerve. This paralysis is frequently a sign of a central nervous system injury.

Many patients with fractures in the orbit suffer concomitant injuries to the eyeball (26 per cent).[20] For this reason, every patient with a displaced fracture should be referred to an ophthalmologist. This referral will have no effect on the kind of fracture treatment but, rather, perhaps on the timing, since some severe eye injuries must be treated immediately. An oval or displaced pupil or an intraocular pressure that has dropped below 10 mm Hg calls for immediate intervention by an ophthalmologist.

Displacement of the alveolar process or the entire maxilla interferes with occlusion. The completely luxated mandible is usually movable in its entirety and is displaced dorsocranially. Displacements of the lateral zygoma and zygomatic arch restrict the motion of the mandible.

To diagnose fractures confined to the midface, clinical examination with simple radiographs is sufficient. Radiographs must be taken from at least two projections, and the entire skull must be recognizable in the two projections. The periorbital structures are best identified using the standard occipitomental view at varying angles. The state of the orbital floor can be assessed by means of simple posteroanterior tomography.

For all severe injuries and when there is suspicion of cerebral involvement, computerized tomography (CT) is indispensable. CT has the advantage of being able to assess the underlying brain damage and to identify hematomas and intracranial air as a sign of a frontobasal fracture of the cerebral wall of the sinus cavity. Every brain scan taken for cranial injury should be extended to include the entire midface by means of bone setting. This practice provides valuable information in a relatively short time on the state of the midface skeleton, which is not always visible in the ordinary radiograph. Most displacements in the midface region are frontodorsal, which makes them accessible to axial scans.

For complex situations, especially in the periorbital region, additional semicoronal sections must be carried out. By adjusting window and level settings, not only the bone structures but also the soft tissue can be assessed.

High-resolution imaging has become the expected standard in the case of severe sinufacial and periorbital comminuted fractures. Life-sized three-dimensional images of the facial skeleton can be produced with specially designed computer software. In these images, all fracture lines can be visualized, including the horizontal ones that are so often difficult to depict. This visualization of fracture lines provides a valuable help for drawing up an exact plan of the surgical procedure and the type of bone stabilization. The images can be used to predict whether or not bone grafting will be necessary.[21-23]

Principles of the Surgical Procedure

The surgical goal is to restore the ends of the fracture to their correct anatomic position as accurately as possible. This replacement must be done before the soft tissue injuries are treated. Midface fractures that are not severely displaced consolidate amazingly fast. Pseudoarthrosis is highly unusual. After just 2 weeks, there is usually a tight fibrous connection between the fracture sites, making exact reduction no longer possible. The definitive fracture treatment should therefore be carried out within the first 2 weeks.

In the treatment plan, a distinction has to be made between fractures that are confined to the midface and those that involve the frontobasal region and skull base. These fractures should be regarded as one unit and treated definitively in one surgical session. The exact timing in these cases may have to be determined by the neurosurgical requirements. Severe brain damage or intracranial hematomas sometimes have to be operated on twice.[24] Whenever possible, the method of choice should be the joint operation by neurosurgeon and maxillofacial surgeon. Although the operation takes longer and the danger of contamination seems to be higher, the low risk of postoperative infection is not increased, nor is the incidence of endocranial infection higher. Intensive care treatment is shorter and recovery faster.[25,26]

Reduction is easily achievable in cases of isolated lateral fractures in the midface or central fractures confined to the midface. There are sufficient stable elements of the skeleton along which the reduction can be guided. The lines of these fractures usually pass through thick bone segments, which can be accurately reduced and fixed under visual control.

For fractures that affect the entire face and that are almost always severely comminuted, occlusion is often the only means of controlling the reduction. A concomitant mandibular fracture first must be reconstructed exactly and stabilized by means of osteosynthesis. The maxillary fragment or fragments are then positioned by intermaxillary fixation. This classic conservative treatment is sufficient for closed fractures in which the functional regions, such as the orbit, alveolar process, and nasal cavity, have been preserved.

If the caudal fragment has been pushed in and locked, it cannot be reduced until it has been released. Rowe[27] developed special forceps for this purpose in 1966. The method is adequate if the fracture area is restricted to the maxilla.

When the mandible is displaced and intermaxillary fixation has been performed, the fragment moves whenever the mandible does. Tamponades applied to stop the bleeding become loose, and sutured soft tissue lacerations threaten to open. Therefore, attempts were made to secure the wobbly mandible outside the mouth by enclosing it with splints and fastening it with external bars applied to a plaster head cap. This procedure, however, did not provide adequate stabilization. A major advance was made in 1942, when Adams[28] proposed holding the mandible in place on wires applied to the intact neurocranium. Suspension was done in the frontozygomatic area or around the zygomatic arch, which provides an adequate base for a tamponade, especially Bellocq's tamponade (posterior nasal tamponade). The jaw, however, is pulled dorsally and cranially, which leads to midface shortening and retrusion (Fig. 33–4). Craniofacial suspension combined with intermaxillary fixation has proved to be best suited, as it keeps the mouth from opening, which in turn prevents midface elongation.

To avoid dorsal displacement, Kufner[10] suggested using the area above the glabella for suspension. The wire could be secured through a bur hole in the bone or, even more simply, with a bone screw. These methods are still being employed today, as they are simple and quick. A serious drawback associated with them, however, is the lack of stability. The maxillary fragment can be safeguarded only against caudal

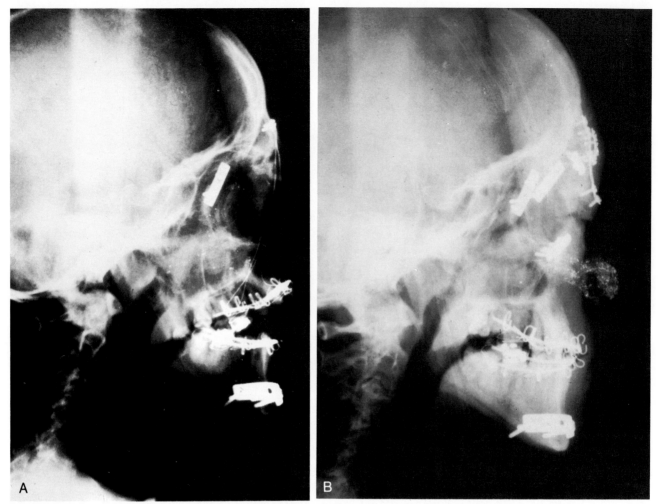

FIGURE 33–4. *A,* Polytraumatized patient. There is fracture of the mandible and the midface, with severe bleeding through the nose. Stabilization of the paramedian fracture of the mandible is accomplished with the eccentric dynamic compression plate (EDCP). The occlusion is reconstructed with intermaxillary fixation. Stabilization of the maxilla is begun with mini-EDCPs on the zygomaticofrontal suture. The bad condition of the patient makes shortening of the operation time necessary. Therefore, posterior tamponade of the nose (a Bellocq's tamponade) and suspension of the movable maxilla by frontomaxillary wires are done. There is release of the intermaxillary fixation to keep a free airway. The radiograph a day afterward shows counterclockwise rotation of the maxilla. The suspending wires are fixed by a screw in the glabella. *B,* Same patient 8 days after completion of the reconstruction of the maxilla and fixation of the fragments in correct position by infraorbital and paranasal plates.

displacement, resulting in the danger that the maxilla will heal too far cranially and dorsally, and the wired area is extremely susceptible to infection. To avoid losing vertical height, rigid fixation from the frontal bone to the alveolus can be accomplished quickly with the aid of a stabilizer instead of wires[29] (Fig. 33–5). But even this is only temporary. In every case, the position of the maxillary fragment must be controlled by lateral radiographic tracing. Unstable maxillary fixation achieved with these methods, despite satisfactory occlusion, can produce considerable facial deformities, such as open bite (see Fig. 33–4). A follow-up of severe Le Fort II and III fractures treated with these methods showed that 49 per cent resulted in a dish face.[30]

Georgiade[31] and others worked on an original idea by Crawford[32] and managed to achieve fairly stable fixation of a maxillary fragment at all three levels. The midface was reduced extraorally and intraorally with fixation elements attached to a halo frame. This method is very involved, and the patient finds it unpleasant. If there is a concomitant fracture of the cervical vertebral column, the same halo frame can be used for extension.

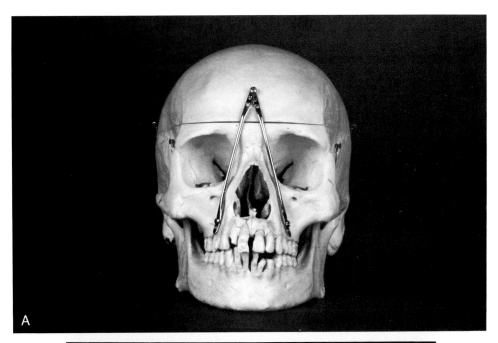

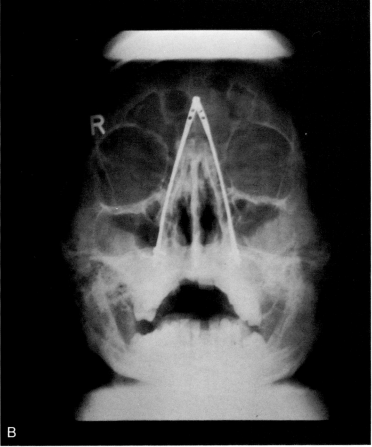

FIGURE 33–5.   *A,* Stabilizer. The stiff, thick wire is flattened with a hole and a sharpened end. It is brought subcutaneously from a vestibular approach paranasally to the glabella. There it is fixed by a screw. The other end is fixed in the alveolar region again by a screw or with an interdental wire ligature. *B,* Clinical example of the use of a stabilizer.

Open reduction in conjunction with subsequent osteosynthesis is the most efficient method, and it is the only feasible method if there are several displaced fragments. Wire ligatures are most often used because they seem to be most suitable for the thin bone structure. The advantages of using wire ligatures are that only a few instruments are required and the procedure is easy to perform. Only very little foreign material is necessary for the osteosynthesis, which is why many surgeons do not even remove the wire.

Nevertheless, the wire ligature does have three disadvantages:

1. It is not functionally stable. The holding power of the osteosynthesis is directly dependent upon the contact area between the appliance and the bone. Since the diameter of the bur hole is greater than that of the wire used, there is little contact between wire and bone (Fig. 33–6).

2. For each wire ligature, when the loop is made, the wire must be led back through the second hole. This process results in considerable denudation and can even lead to displacement of the fragment to be stabilized.

3. Twisting the wire ligature generates uncontrolled pressure. The suture in thin bones often tears; in thick bones, the wire sometimes breaks.

Frequently, severe comminution of the thin bones produces a lack of stability, even after wire sutures have been applied. If the fragment is not fixed at all three levels, it will rotate as a result of forces that occur later on. This fixation at all levels is particularly important in the area of the lateral orbit owing to the pull of the masseter muscle. Secondary displacement in this region can result in malar flattening, enlargement of the orbit with enophthalmos, ocular dystopia, and drooping of the corner of the mouth. Manson and Gruss and their colleagues[26,33] therefore proposed the combination of immediate bone grafting and wire ligatures to improve stability. They used a calvarial graft, which can be easily obtained by using a coronal exposure. A four-point fixation was thereby achieved, and at the same time the bone defects were filled.

Fixation with screws and plates has considerable advantages over wiring, even when the bones are thin. Our studies have shown that sufficient holding power can be

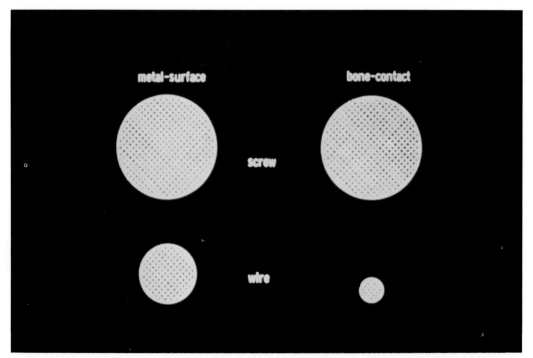

FIGURE 33–6. Comparison of bone contact achieved with wire sutures and with screws.

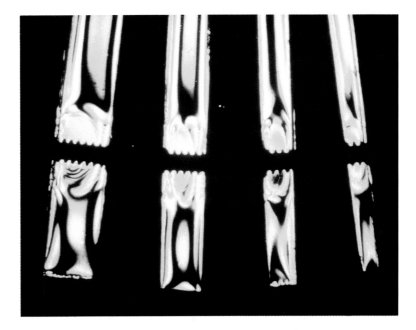

FIGURE 33–7. Photoelastic study: 2-mm screws, tightened, in 5-, 4-, 3-, and 2-mm-thick plastic plates. The colored curve shows that pressure forces can develop even with a thickness of only 2 mm.

attained with a normal osteosynthesis screw with a diameter of 1.5 or 2 mm, even in a bone 2 mm thick (Fig. 33–7). The connection achieved between fragments that are 2 mm thick using a wire that is 0.6 mm thick is five times weaker than the connection achieved with a thin plate and two screws having a diameter of 2 mm. The reason for this difference is that there is more contact area between bone and screw. Thus, given bone that is the same size, much more force can be transferred onto the bone with the osteosynthesis appliance than with the wire (see Fig. 33–6).

Self-tapping screws are used for thin bones, as tapping involves less bone contact.[34] When screws and plates are used, an approach from only one side is necessary.

Because of the thinness of the bone in the midface, the lag screw principle can only seldom be applied (see Fig. 33–14B). Fixation with screws and plates primarily achieves three-dimensional stability. Clinical observations have shown that it is not necessary to replace small unusable or missing bone fragments.[35] This observation has been confirmed by investigations conducted by Paulus and Altermatt.[36] Bone fragments of the facial skeleton fixated with screws and plates, even in the absence of fragment contact, heal in just a few weeks through primary bone reformation, without compression osteosynthesis and without chondral ossification.

Osteosynthesis Material

Since 1972, we have been using the 2-mm screws employed by the AO/ASIF for managing small fragments. These plates were originally designed for veterinary medicine and for hand surgery. They have subsequently been modified for use in craniomaxillofacial surgery (Fig. 33–8). The fragments in the midface only have to be reduced and held in this position. Since this procedure is adaptation osteosynthesis, the plates can be relatively thin. Originally, they were made of stainless steel, like the osteosynthesis appliances used for the extremities. Experience then showed that patients often were not willing to undergo a second operation to have the plates and screws removed. That meant that the material had to be as biocompatible as possible. The AO/ASIF chose pure titanium, which is absolutely biocompatible. No allergic reactions are known. The normal adaptation plates are 0.85 mm thick and are designed to meet the most common requirements. The long, straight plate is the one most frequently used; this is then cut to the length required. It can be contoured at all three levels with a minimum of hole distortion. The plate hole and the screw head are

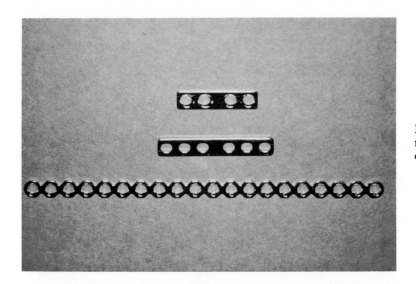

Figure 33–8. Miniplates made of titanium, as recommended by the Association for the Study of Internal Fixation (AO/ASIF).

fitted so that the plate head can be kept as flat as possible. For difficult situations, bendable templates, which facilitate the contouring process, are available.

The AO/ASIF set also contains small compression plates. These are stronger and are also used with the 2-mm screw. They are used for the lateral orbit and the zygomatic arch. Compression osteosynthesis is not necessary to achieve primary bone healing in the midface. At the lateral orbit, the fracture lines often run through the zygomaticofrontal suture. The fracture areas in this region are not clearly delineated because of the collagen fibers. This fact makes it difficult to achieve accurate reduction. The compression hole allows the fragments to approach one another when the screw is tightened. The thicker plate is suitable for this region, as it reliably neutralizes the functional pull of the masseter muscle (Fig. 33–9).

The standard screw we use is 2 mm in diameter. For particularly small fragments, 1.5-mm screws with small plates are available. These smaller screws and plates are compatible with the 2-mm system.

Newly formed bone directly encloses the titanium screws with no layer of connective tissue between (osseointegration). After a time, it may be difficult to remove the screws because not only are greater external forces required but also the screw head must be kept as flat as possible. Thus, if the osteosynthesis material is to be removed later, the combination of steel screws with titanium plates will facilitate removal. With this combination, there is allegedly no corrosion.[37]

Surgical Approach

In the case of maxillary displacement, we first perform intermaxillary fixation with wire ligatures (after the osteosynthesis has been completed, the intermaxillary fixation can be released). If the frontobasal region is involved, this area must then be exposed and cleaned up. Starting from the frontobasal region and proceeding in a caudal direction, the entire midface is reconstructed and fixed, proceeding from the stable to the unstable region. In the area of severely comminuted fractures, the individual incisions should be connected by means of tunneling, so that the covering soft tissue is completely detached from the underlying bone. For isolated fractures confined to single regions, exploration via one single surgical approach is often sufficient. If the skin of the face is lacerated, the surgical approach to the bone is already mapped out. In all other cases, a few classic incisions suffice.

CORONAL INCISION

The coronal incision is placed inside the hairline. The hair does not have to be shaved off the neurocranium. The incision provides a direct view of the entire frontal

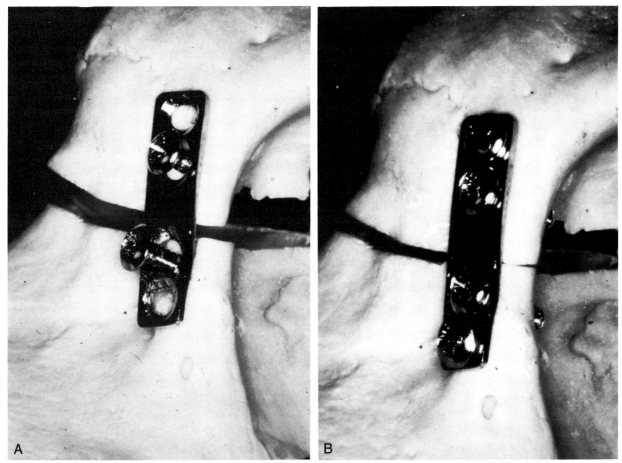

FIGURE 33-9. *A, B,* Effect of the dynamic compression holes of the zygoma plate. The inner holes are drilled eccentrically off the fracture side. By tightening the screws, the screw head glides into the spherically formed plate hole and toward the fracture line. Thus, the two fragments approach. In case of fragment contact, interfragmentary pressure is built up. The outer screws are drilled centrally, that is, neutrally. They work as additional stabilization.

bone, the orbital roof of the glabella, the medial and orbital wall, and the zygomatic arch (see Fig. 33-13).

For supraorbital and periorbital exposure, only dissection is done above the periosteum, and the periosteum is not detached until just before the supraorbital region. Instead of fascia, a part of the periosteum can be used as a free transplant to fill a dural defect.

A semicoronal incision is helpful in unilateral, massive comminuted fractures of the lateral orbit.

SUPRAORBITAL INCISION

The incision runs along the eyebrow or just below it (see Fig. 33-14). It can be enlarged medially and caudally up to the nasolabial fold. The bilateral incisions can be connected via the nasal root (butterfly or spectacles incision) (see Figs. 33-11 to 33-13). The incision provides access to the caudal frontal and frontal sinus, to the roof of the orbit and medial wall, and to the ethmoid region. The practice of stopping the incision over the medial canthal ligament and continuing it below the ligament protects the intact ligament.[38]

Raveh and Vuillemin[8] recommend subcutaneously tunneling the area between the two eyebrows. From this incision next to the roof of the orbit, Raveh explores the ethmoid and the cranial base up to the sella from the caudal side. Raveh refers to this approach, which he also uses for duraplasty, as extracranial-subcranial exposure.

INCISION TO EXPOSE THE ZYGOMATIC BONE AND LATERAL ORBIT

The easiest approach for the zygomaticofrontal suture is the incision in the lateral eyebrow above the lateral edge of the bony orbit (see Fig. 33–17). If the eyebrow is thin, this incision may leave ugly scars, so a horizontal incision in the midline of the upper lid, as for blepharoplasty, is also recommended. This incision provides sufficient view of the lateral orbital region and frequently is the only practical incision for simple zygomatic bone fractures. However, having to extend the incision caudally or laterally may result in scar formation.

APPROACH TO THE INFRAORBITAL REGION AND FLOOR OF THE ORBIT

The direct approach to this region is via the lower orbital rim incision, which is made directly above the infraorbital rim. It must be made into the eyelid skin to prevent the skin from adhering to the rim. The disadvantage of this incision includes the danger of scar formation, lid edema, and ectropion. By using Converse's[39] subciliary incision (Fig. 33–10), one can almost completely avoid such drawbacks.

The orbicularis oculi muscle is detached and folded forward. Increasing experience with blepharoplasty has shown that using the same incision without severing the muscle ("skin only flap") also ensures adequate visualization of the infraorbital rim. Tessier[40] chose the conjunctival approach to avoid scars, which, though seldom, do occur.

Manson and associates[41] suggested combining the infraorbital and lateral approaches. This procedure involves completely detaching the lateral canthal ligament with its periosteal attachments, thus making the entire lateral orbital wall visible (see Fig. 33–19). It is necessary to restabilize the ligament only when the fracture is an older one to prevent deformities or when a coronal incision is used in the patient at the same time.

APPROACH TO THE ZYGOMATIC BUTTRESS AND FRONTOBASAL BUTTRESS

The incision is intraoral and placed in the mucobuccal fold, as for a Caldwell-Luc operation. The mucoperiosteal lobe is dissected up to the infraorbital foramen and upward as far as the zygomatic bone or to the piriform aperture (see Fig. 33–20).

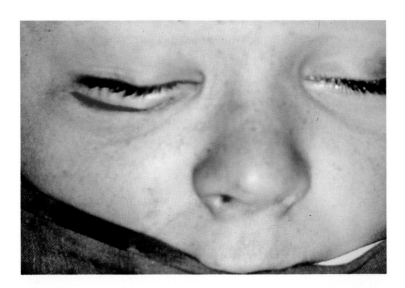

FIGURE 33–10.   Subciliary incision.

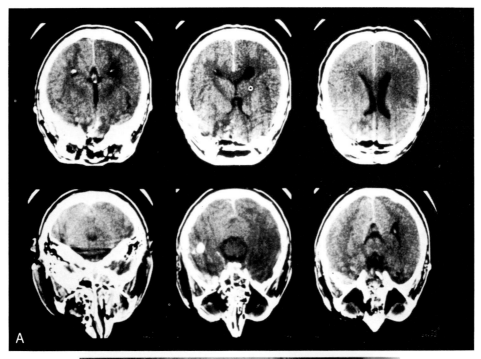

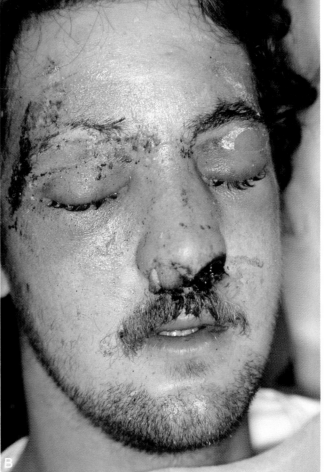

FIGURE 33–11.   *A,* Comminuted central fracture of the midface in the area of the frontal wall of the sinus, of the floor of the orbit, and at the Le Fort I level. *B,* Patient seen 48 hours after accident. Slight skin wounds in the nasal area have been sutured immediately. Nasal tamponade was done to stop bleeding.

Illustration continued on following page.

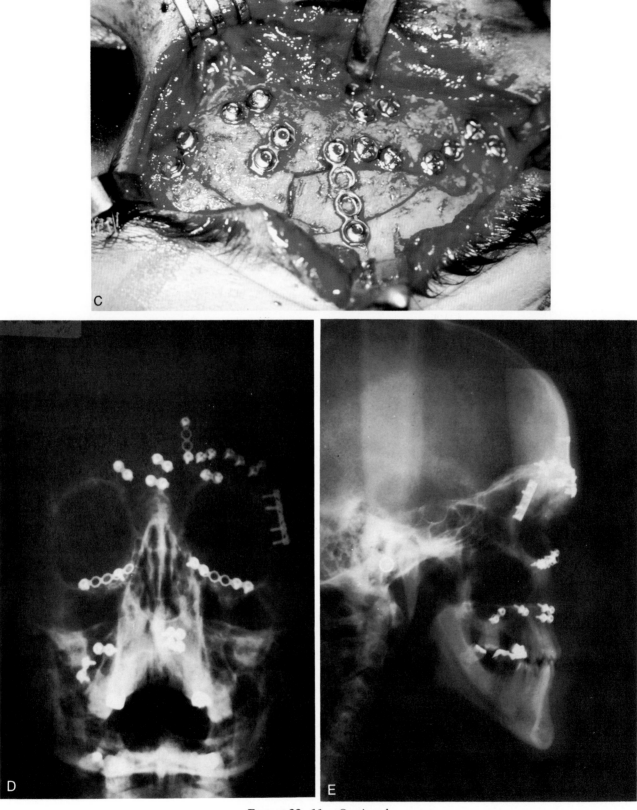

FIGURE 33–11. *Continued*

Legend on opposite page.

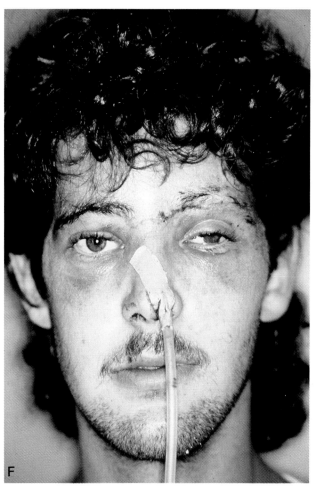

FIGURE 33–11. *Continued. C,* Butterfly incision. After removal of the fragments of the anterior wall, the cerebral wall proves to be intact except for a small area with a small bone fragment and dural laceration. Suturing of the dura and tightening with tissue glue were accomplished. Drainage of the sinus was done with a plastic tube. The anterior sinus wall was reconstructed with small plates. *D,* Occipitomental view. Fixation of the left lateral orbital fracture was done via lengthening of the eyebrow incision. A subciliary incision was used to reconstruct the orbital floor. An intraoral degloving incision was employed for fixation in the area of the zygomatic buttress and the apertura piriformis. *E,* Lateral view. *F,* Ten days after operation. Sinus drainage is by a plastic tube. There is no more swelling.

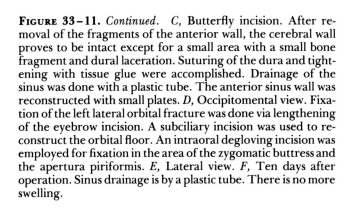

Fractures in the Special Region

FRONTOBASAL FRACTURES

The decision about whether it is necessary to operate transcranially is made by the neurosurgeon. Such an intervention can delay the maxillofacial operation. The frontal bony wall of the frontal sinus, as opposed to the cerebral wall, is frequently crushed. In the case of fractures of the cerebral wall, the torn dura is sutured whenever possible. Dural defects are replaced with a galea periosteal pedicle flap or bridged with free periosteum or free fasciae, which are fastened with tissue glue. If possible, the mucous membrane of the frontal sinus is preserved. Loose bone fragments of the frontal wall are carefully placed aside while the posterior cerebral wall is being treated, after which they are returned to their original position. The frontal wall of the sinus is stably reconstructed by osteosynthesis. Large missing bone fragments are immediately replaced with a calvarial bone graft. We do not see a need for any special drainage if the mucous membrane and the cerebral wall have been preserved. If some of the mucosa and the cerebral bone wall have been lost, the frontal sinus must be drained via a plastic tube for at least 3 weeks. Total loss of the mucosa and cerebral wall requires that the original frontal sinus be filled with a free fat graft to support the duraplasty. Fractures in the frontobasal region are an indication for open reduction (Figs. 33–11 to 33–13).

A plate that lies paranasally and medially with respect to the orbit is usually adequate for fixation of the enophthalmos in the central region. Comminuted fractures of the nose are lifted from an endonasal approach and held with a nose tampon-

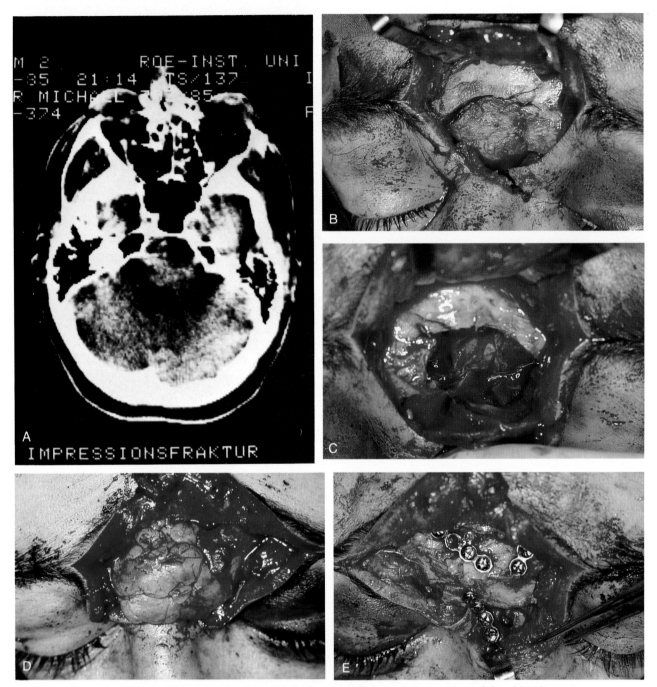

FIGURE 33–12.   *A,* View of the whole frontobasal area. *B,* Laceration of the skin above the glabella. Elongation of the soft tissue wound with a butterfly incision. View of the fractured frontal wall. *C,* After removal of bone fragments of the frontal wall, destruction of the cerebral wall becomes visible. These fragments have to be taken out. The defect is too great; the cerebral wall cannot be reconstructed. *D,* The remaining mucosa of the sinus is removed. The dural fistula is covered with fascia, which is fixed by tissue glue. The whole former frontal sinus cavity is filled with a free fat graft. The fat supports the duraplasty. *E,* Reconstruction of the frontal wall.

Illustration continued on opposite page.

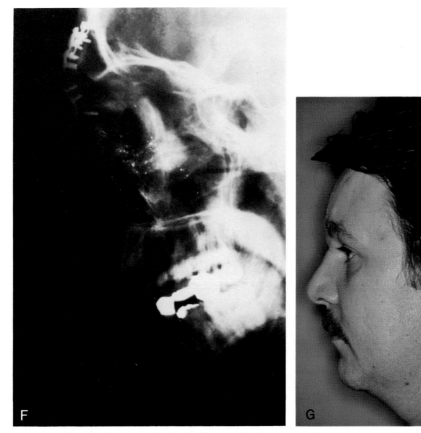

FIGURE 33–12. *Continued.* *F,* Radiograph taken 3 weeks postoperatively. *G,* Clinical view 3 weeks after operation. The profile is reconstructed.

ade. The tampon is placed around a strong tube to allow drainage of the frontal sinus and to keep the nasal airway patent (Fig. 33–14).

Lateral fractures of the superior orbital rim also very often involve the frontal sinus (Fig. 33–14). In this case, the central wall must again be checked by removing loose fragments of the frontal wall. The anterior wall is reconstructed with plates and screws.

FRACTURES IN THE MEDIAL ORBITAL REGION

Depression of the medial orbital wall can lead to enophthalmos. The anatomic contour must be restored. The depressed bone fragment is pushed and reduced in a lateral direction, where it usually remains without fixation. Additional fixation can be achieved by applying lyophilized dura. Bone grafting is necessary for large defects, and a torn canthal fragment must be restored. In most cases, the fragment is torn out with its bony attachment, which then must be fixated in the correct position by osteosynthesis. The torn-out ligament without bony attachment is sutured to bone with nonresorbable suture material.

SIMPLE ZYGOMATIC BONE FRACTURE

A simple zygomatic bone fracture is the most common fracture in the midface and seldom involves skin injury. The massive, tetragonal zygoma with the lateral portion of the orbital floor is broken off and displaced. The classic fracture line runs through the zygomatic arch, through the zygomaticofrontal suture, through the infraorbital foramen, and on the lower zygomatic buttress (see Fig. 33–16). The bone fragment is frequently depressed and locked, so that reduction must be done

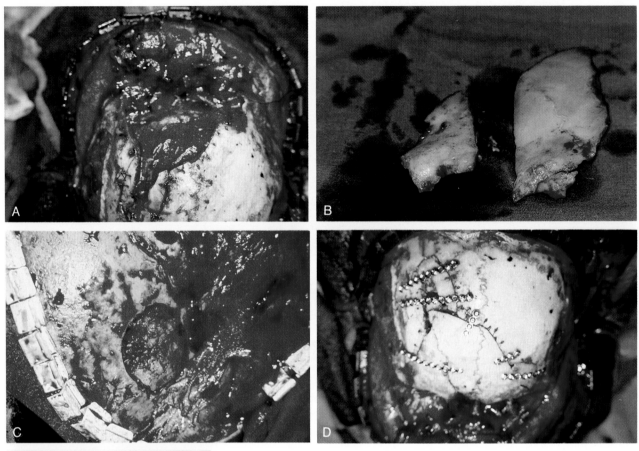

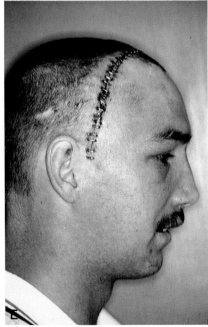

FIGURE 33–13. *A,* Comminuted fracture of the whole frontal plane. Coronal approach. *B,* The fragments of the anterior frontal wall are removed to allow visualization of the posterior wall. They will be replaced and stabilized to reconstruct the anterior wall. *C,* The parietal area can be used as a donor site for a calvarial graft to close the bony defect. *D,* Reconstruction of the frontal plane with plates. *E,* Twelve days after operation. The coronal incision line is visible. To shorten operation time, stable closure was used.

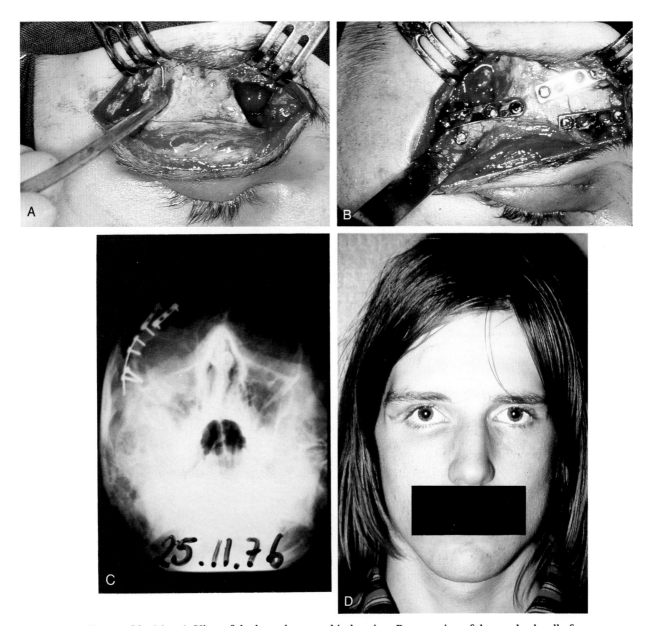

FIGURE 33–14.   *A,* View of the lateral supraorbital region. Preservation of the cerebral wall of the frontal sinus is seen. An eyebrow incision is made. There is a small laceration of the lateral eyelid skin. The mucosa of the floor and dorsal region can be preserved. *B,* Reconstruction of the anterior wall of the sinus with plates and screws. On the right corner, there is fixation of a fragment with a small lag screw. *C,* Radiographic control. *D,* Clinical view seen 4 weeks postoperatively.

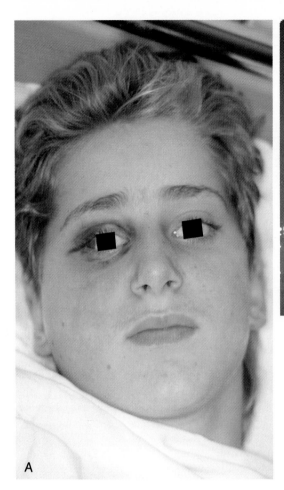

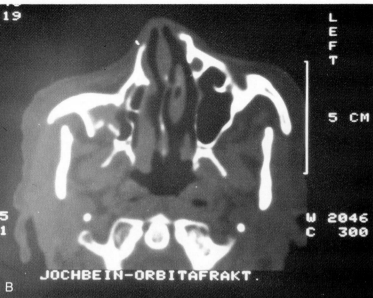

FIGURE 33–15. *A,* Clinical view of a tripod zygoma fracture shows only slight deformity. There is camouflage of the dislocation because of hematoma. *B,* The computerized tomographic (CT) scan shows the severe dislocation in a sagittal-dorsal direction.

outward and upward and requires considerable force. A displacement of the zygoma in the sagittal direction is easy to overlook in simple radiographs (Fig. 33–15). Reduction is performed in the frontal direction either with an elevator via the transtemporal approach along the fasciae of the temporal muscle or more simply with a sharp hook that is inserted over a stab incision below the zygomatic bone (Fig. 33–16). The mobilized and reduced zygomatic body sometimes remains in the normal position, but the pull of the masseter muscle usually causes a rotating displace-

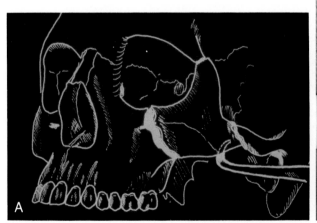

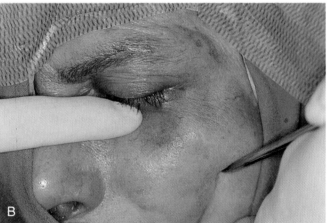

FIGURE 33–16. *A,* Schematic drawing of the reduction of the tripod zygoma fracture with a sharp hook. The hook is inserted by a stab incision through the cheek skin two fingerbreadths to the side and two fingerbreadths below the lateral eyelid angle. *B,* Reduction pull in the frontolateral—in some cases, the frontocranial—direction. The fingertips of the other hand are on the palpable step of the infraorbital rim.

ment. In most cases, exposing the fracture line in the zygomatic frontal region suffices for these fractures (Fig. 33–17).

After the fracture has been exposed, the reduction is controlled by feeling the infraorbital rim and the zygomatic buttress. As there are thick bones in the region of the fracture at the orbital rim, the use of the stronger minicompression plate is indicated. Usually, the reduced fragment must be held in the correct position with a great amount of force during the entire operation. In the case of a one-piece fracture,

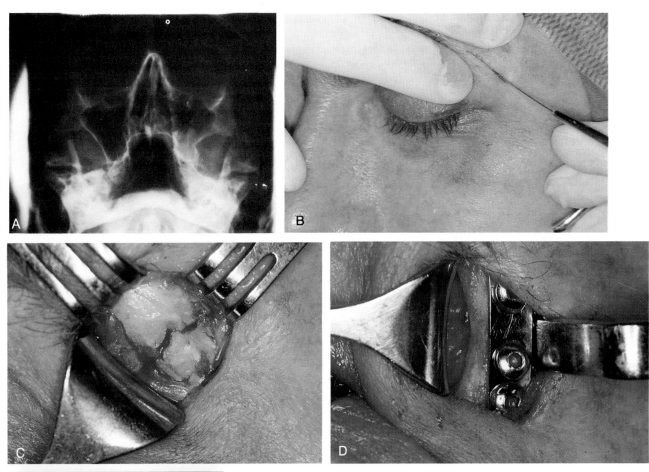

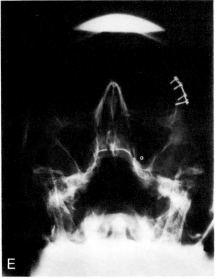

FIGURE 33–17. *A,* Tripod fracture of the left zygoma. Occipitomental view. The fracture line is seen infraorbitally at the zygomatic buttress and at the lateral orbital rim. *B,* Eyebrow incision. It starts 0.5 cm above the lateral canthus and is approximately 4 cm in length. There is sharp dissection to the bone. Subperiosteal preparation is inside the orbit, with freeing of the fracture area with the elevator. By additional pull with the hook, reduction can be completed. *C,* Fracture line with visible dislocation. *D,* AO mini-DCP in situ. Owing to correct reduction, the fracture gap is no longer visible. *E,* Radiographic control 6 months after operation. Pneumatization of the sinus is seen.

the reduced fragment can be stabilized with one single plate, which must be bent carefully.[42] The inside holes are used as dynamic compression holes. The drilled hole is situated eccentrically, away from the fracture. The two inner screws are positioned first, and when they have been tightened, the fractured cheek bone is moved along the bent plate against the frontal bone. Here there is a danger of displacement if the plate has not been sufficiently bent. The reduction is controlled at the infraorbital margin and at the zygomatic buttress. If the fragment turns outward after the screws are tightened, the screws have to be removed and the plate bent more.

Accurate reduction can be given additional stability through the two outer screws, the holes of which are drilled neutrally (centrally). We introduced this method in our department in 1972 and 1 year later were able to compare 30 cases treated in this manner with cases of the same type (single tripod fracture with dorsomedial dislocation) that the same operating team had treated with wire sutures.[43] A comparison showed that 12 per cent of the patients treated with wire sutures had asymmetries, as opposed to 0 per cent of those treated with plates. A permanent disturbance of the

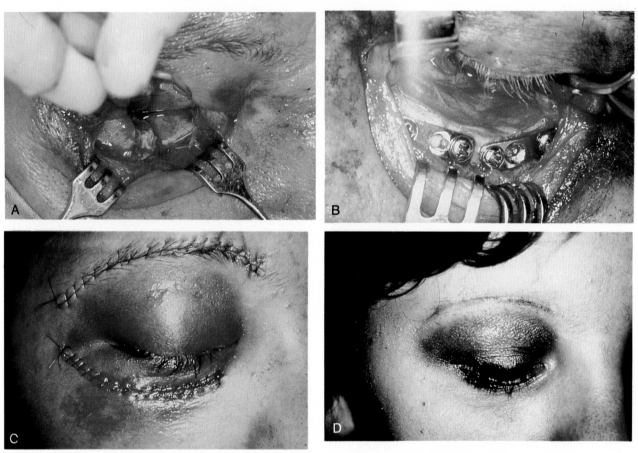

FIGURE 33–18. *A,* View of the infraorbital rim. A subciliary incision is used. After freeing the bony infraorbital rim, subperiosteal preparation of the orbital floor is accomplished. The eyeball is elevated and protected with a small, soft spatula. The incision can be lengthened medially and cranially up to the insertion of the canthal ligament or caudally from the medial corner into the nasolabial fold. The anterior two thirds of the orbital floor can be checked easily. To mobilize a fragment of the orbital rim, it is sometimes necessary to use a fine chisel with rotating movements. *B,* The infraorbital rim is reconstructed and stabilized with plates and screws. Small bony defects are bridged with the plate. If there is a comminuted fracture of the whole orbital ring, the first plate is placed at the zygomaticofrontal suture. The screws of these plates are not completely tightened. During tightening of the screws at the infraorbital rim, the plate placed here must be checked and then finally tightened. The defect of the orbital floor is closed with lyophilized dura. It is placed between periosteum and bone. *C,* The sutured surgical incisions (No. 5–0 nonresorbable suture material). *D,* One year after operation, there are no visible scars.

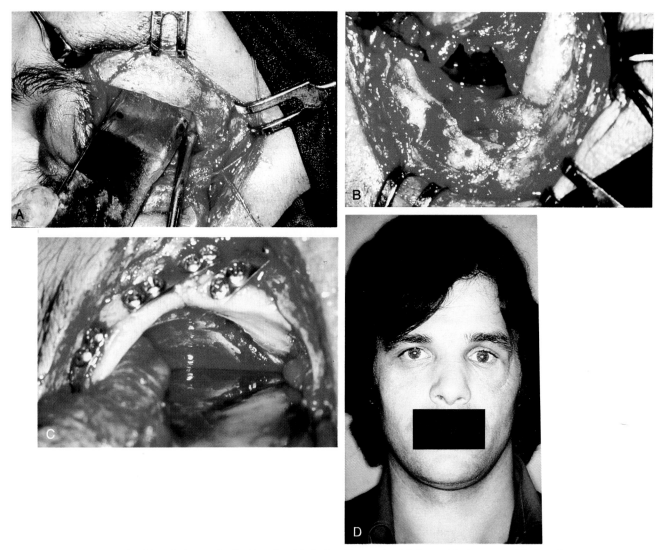

Figure 33–19. *A,* Severely displaced orbital ring fractures, 14 days old. A supraorbital and infraorbital approach is used. *B,* The extreme dislocation and the defect in the orbital floor are visible. *C,* Reconstruction of the bone contour. The defect of the orbital floor is covered with a double-folded lyophilized dura. *D,* Clinical view 6 months after operation. The surgical approach was via the soft tissue laceration.

infraorbital nerve was observed in 24 per cent of the patients treated with wire, compared with 6 per cent of the patients treated with plates. Not one case of diplopia was seen among our 70 patients. Infraorbital exploration was necessary in 50 per cent of the wire-treated patients, as opposed to 0 per cent of the patients treated with plates.

COMMINUTED FRACTURES OF THE ORBITAL FLOOR

The infraorbital region and the floor of the orbit must be revised if the fracture in the infraorbital region is not clearly a simple one, if the reduction is not 100 per cent accurate, or if there are clinical or radiographic signs of invasion into or incarceration of the soft tissue on the orbital floor. The screws on the frontal zygomatic bone are not tightened until the infraorbital rim has been exposed. During inspection of the orbital floor, the incarcerated soft tissue is released. If the infraorbital rim has had to be stabilized, the application of lyophilized dura is sufficient to bridge defects of the orbital floor (Figs. 33–18 and 33–19).

ISOLATED BLOW-OUT FRACTURES

In 1962, McCoy and colleagues[44] pointed out that fractures of the orbital floor always occur by transmission of a force above the surrounding bone. Accordingly, the infraorbital rim is usually involved in isolated blow-out fractures. The rim is stabilized with a small plate, and the orbital floor defect is bridged over with lyophilized dura. We have never felt that a bone graft is indicated to repair the orbital floor defect. The antral tamponade, which used to be applied to support the orbital floor, is unnecessary and only promotes infection.

FRACTURES OF THE ALVEOLAR PROCESS

Fractures over the alveolar process at the Le Fort I level are treated from an intraoral approach. The rigidity of the mini–dynamic compression plates (DCPs) should be taken advantage of in these fractures[45] (ABB). Fitting the fragments right against one another reduces the danger of postoperative displacement, and only one screw per fragment is necessary (Fig. 33–20). The plates in this region must always be removed, as they will interfere with the patient's dentures (Fig. 33–21).

Fractures with larger fragments can be fixated with thin lag screws.[46] In the case of alveolar fractures in which the teeth are loose, the teeth must be secured by means of a dental splint, which is done with strong wire and ligatures. The fixation can be reinforced with self-curing acrylic (a "Schuchardt splint"). In some cases, intermaxillary fixation must be maintained for the dental splinting.

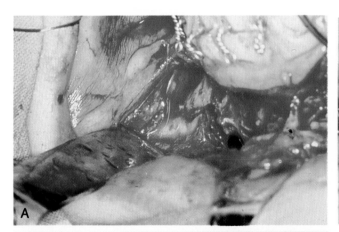
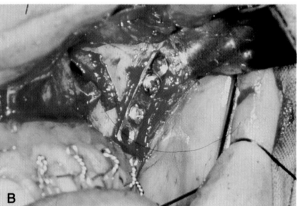
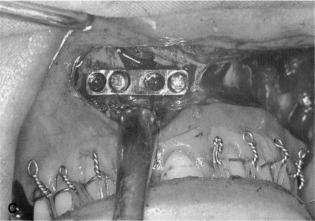

FIGURE 33–20. *A,* Intraoral approach to a comminuted fracture at the Le Fort I level. *B,* Reconstruction of the zygomatic buttress with a zygoma plate. *C,* Fixation of the sagittal split fractures with a zygoma plate below the apertura piriformis.

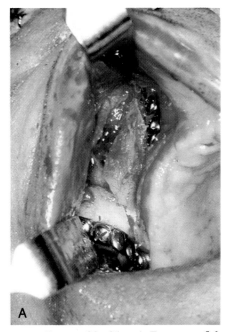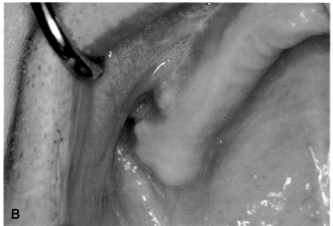

FIGURE 33–21.   *A*, Fracture of the midface. An infraorbital and intraoral approach is used. *B*, View seen 4 months postoperatively. The plate is glimmering through the mucosa. It has to be removed, since it interferes with the denture.

ISOLATED ZYGOMATIC FRACTURES

Isolated zygomatic fractures are very rare. They can usually be reduced by using a sharp hook. If the fragments do not remain in correct position, they can be fixated with a transcutaneous pin, as is used for hand surgery. The best operative approach for an open reduction is the semicoronal incision. With this approach, the arch is best reconstructed with a small plate.

Statistics

Between 1982 and 1985, we treated 456 complex midface fractures according to the foregoing principles. All of the fractures with severe soft tissue lacerations and with displacement were surgically managed with open reduction. A welcome advantage was the minimal and brief postoperative swelling, even after lengthy operations and excessive mobilization of the soft tissue. We administered an antibiotic perioper-

FIGURE 33–22.   Stabilization of a pseudoarthrosis of the maxilla with a split-rib graft, fixed with lag screws.

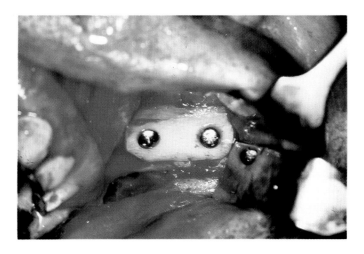

atively as a matter of routine. To reduce swelling, we applied a single dose of corticoid postoperatively.

The only patients not operated on were those whose poor general condition prohibited extensive surgery within the first 3 weeks. This group included patients with mobile fractures of the cervical vertebrae. Some of these patients had to be treated with a combination of surgery and conservative measures because of severe bleeding or to keep the airway patent. Fractures without displacement were treated conservatively. Infection was the most frequent complication and, in most cases, was confined to the soft tissue and could be brought under control with drainage and antibiotic treatment. In only one case (zygomatic buttress) did the plate have to be prematurely removed owing to a purulent osteomyelitis. In one case (a Le Fort II fracture), the entire maxilla was still mobile 1 year after the plate had been removed. It was stabilized once more with split ribs, which were fastened with lag screws (Fig. 33–22).

STABLE FIXATION OF MANDIBULAR FRACTURES IN ACCORDANCE WITH AO PRINCIPLES

JOACHIN PREIN, M.D., D.D.S. and BEAT HAMMER, M.D., D.D.S.

In the past 20 to 25 years, it has become apparent that direct, that is, primary, healing of a fractured bone is possible under conditions of absolute stability.[47,48] This fact brought about intensive development of treatment methods and profound change in the principles of treatment. There is no doubt that the aim of modern fracture treatment is to immobilize a fracture so completely, by means of rigid internal fixation with plates and screws, that primary bone healing without complication is possible despite the maintenance of normal function by the bone concerned. These principles were first applied in surgery of the extremities, and then, from the beginning of the 1970s, the AO principles were gradually introduced into the treatment of mandibular fractures by Spiessl and coworkers.[47,49–51]

For the treatment of fractures of the facial skeleton, there are now two separate sets of AO instruments: one for the lower jaw and one for the upper jaw. For mandibular fractures, almost without exception the thicker (2.0-mm) DCP together with the 2.7-mm cortex screw is used, while for maxillary fractures, miniplates (0.85 mm thick) with 2.0-mm or 1.5-mm screws are used (Fig. 33–23).[52] The absolute objective in the treatment of fractures of the lower and upper jaws is to permit the affected sections of the jaw to bear full functional stress immediately. Recently, it was decided

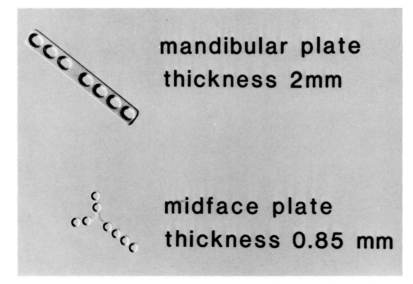

mandibular plate
thickness 2mm

midface plate
thickness 0.85 mm

FIGURE 33–23. In accordance with the different biomechanical situations of the mandible and maxilla, plates of different size are necessary for these areas. They allow either compression osteosynthesis (mandible) or adaptational osteosynthesis (maxilla).

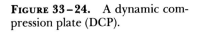 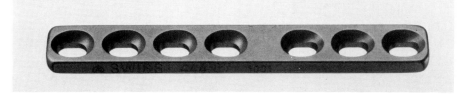

FIGURE 33–24. A dynamic compression plate (DCP).

to manufacture all maxillofacial implants out of titanium so that the plates and screws do not have to be removed.

We regard miniplates as a better form of wire sutures. As only adaptation osteosynthesis can be achieved with these 0.85-mm plates, they cannot stand up well enough to the functional forces that act on the mandible and, therefore, cannot guarantee absolute immobilization of the fracture under full functional stress. Besides the aim of full, immediate, painless stressability under the action of functional forces, absolute immobilization of the fracture under all circumstances must be guaranteed when plates and screws are used, since otherwise the material employed will act as a foreign body and elicit an inflammatory reaction. The experience of the past few years has taught that the most important aim of treatment, precisely in situations in which there is a risk of inflammation (wide-open comminuted fractures), must be absolute immobilization of the fracture ends. This practice is the surest means of preventing an infection or inducing an already present inflammation to regress.

Technique

To guarantee absolutely immobile positioning of the ends of the fractured bone against each other, the fracture is fixed with a special DCP (Fig. 33–24). If these plates are used correctly, the ends of the fracture are pressed together as soon as the eccentrically placed screws are completely tightened (Fig. 33–25). By means of compression, friction is then created and immobilization is guaranteed despite the fluctua-

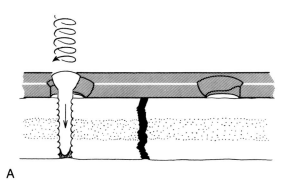
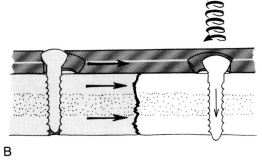

A   B

FIGURE 33–25. Action of the DCP. *A,* Left screw is inserted but not tightened. *B,* Adaptation phase. The right screw is inserted and tightened firmly. During tightening, the head of the screw moves on the gliding plane of the hole in the plate, so that the plate moves in the direction of the single arrow. As soon as the plate meets the head of the screw on the left, the screw draws the fragment in the same direction *(shaded section).* The fracture gap is now apparent only as a line. *C,* Compression phase. The left screw is tightened. Plate is drawn to the left in the direction of the arrows and moves the fragment on the right toward the gap. At the same time, the screw on the left, which is firmly anchored in the fragment, forms a resistance, so that compression of the fragment results. (Courtesy of B. Spiessl.)

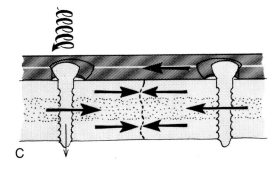

C

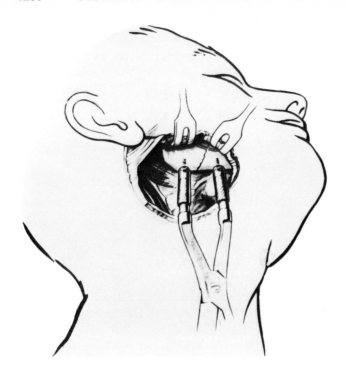

Figure 33–26. Correct use of the repositioning pliers allows repositioning and precompression of the fracture before the plate is put into place.

tions in pressure that occur during function. This immobilization is subject to the condition that the pressure applied in the fixation of the fracture must be higher than the fall in pressure occurring during function.[53,54] The primary requirement for building up the appropriate high-pressure forces is the correct use of the repositioning pliers (Fig. 33–26) and of the DCP with its special oval holes, which function according to the spherical gliding principle.[55]

Experience gained in surgery of the extremities has shown that for biomechanical reasons a pressure plate must always be applied to the side of the bone on which tractional forces act. The traction and pressure sides of the bone are determined on the basis of the muscles that insert into the relevant bone and their tractional effect and also on the basis of the forces arising during function.

If this requirement is imposed on the biomechanical situation obtained in the mandible, it is apparent that in general the cranial side of the mandible is the one on which the tractional forces are observed, while the inferior border of the mandible must usually be regarded as the pressure side under functional conditions (Fig. 33–27). Consequently, osteosynthesis using pressure plates would have to be carried out on the cranial side of the mandible. However, owing to the teeth, which are present in most cases, such a procedure is not feasible. Spiessl,[47,49] therefore, described the special tension band principle for the fixation of mandibular fractures. In accordance with this principle, the tractional forces arising on the cranial side of the mandible are initially neutralized by means of either a tension band applied to the teeth for fractures within the row of teeth or a short DCP acting as a tension band plate for fractures outside the dental arch (Figs. 33–28A and B and 33–29).

Another instrument used for neutralizing the tractional forces on the upper side of the mandible in special situations is the eccentric dynamic compression plate (EDCP).[56,57] These plates are useful in special situations in which the application of either a tension band splint or a plate is not possible. Such situations most commonly occur with partly or completely edentulous mandibles. In patients with full dentition, these plates are applied in preangular fractures, especially in the presence of a fully retained wisdom tooth (Fig. 33–30). If used properly, the EDCP provides for compression not only below the plate but also above, along the fracture line. The outer holes of these four- or six-hole plates are positioned at an angle of 75 degrees (Fig. 33–31).

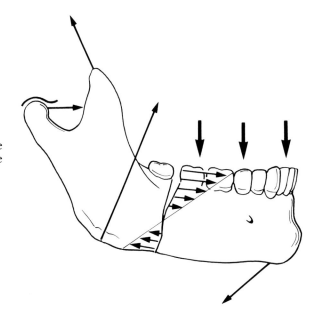

FIGURE 33–27. Traction side *(above)* and pressure side *(below)* are determined by the muscles inserting into the mandible and the forces exerted during function.

It is particularly important to note that in comminuted and defect fractures with considerable bone loss, direct pressure build-up is not possible because it would result in a shortening of the broken section of bone. In these situations, it is necessary to produce absolute stability by means of an appropriately long plate, usually a reconstruction plate. The special advantage of this plate lies in its bendability in all three dimensions, yet it is rigid enough to bridge bony defects, provide sufficient stability, and allow immediate function (Fig. 33–32).

Another possibility of producing interfragmentary pressure is provided by the 2.7-mm cortex screw acting as a lag screw.[58] Lag screws can be used for fracture fixation either alone or in association with a plate. The decision regarding which of the alternatives to choose depends on the course of the fracture, which must be suitably long and oblique to permit the use of at least three lag screws (Fig. 33–33). If

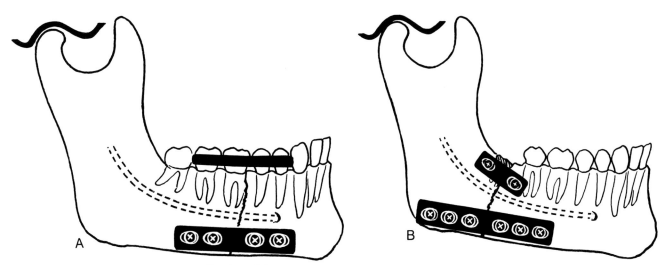

FIGURE 33–28. Application of the tension band principle for fractures within the dental arch *(A)* or for those behind the row of teeth *(B)*. Tension banding is achieved with either a tension band splint or a short, two-hole DCP.

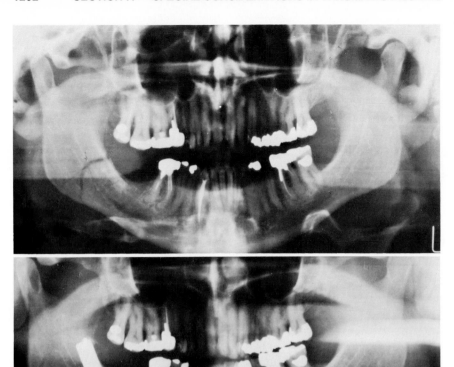

FIGURE 33-29. Stabilization of right preangular fracture with a short, two-hole DCP as a tension band and a four-hole DCP as a stabilization plate.

a lag screw is used in combination with a plate, this screw must be positioned first, and the following screws must be placed in a neutral position within the plate holes.

The 2.7-mm cortex screw used in the mandible is not self-tapping, so the screw hole has to be tapped in advance. The system is bicortical, that is, the screw must take hold of both the inner and the outer cortex (Fig. 33–34).

Appropriate tests with the 2-mm screw, which is used in the midface, have shown that with a bone thickness of about 3 mm or more, prethreaded screws provide a firmer grip than self-tapping screws.[59]

Operative Procedure

The essential precondition for successful osteosynthesis of the mandible with plates is 100 per cent accurate repositioning on the oral side of the fracture. Correct adjustment and fixation of the occlusion must be guaranteed during the entire stage of screw insertion or plate fixation. The maintenance of the correct occlusion during the application of the plate is essential. Disturbances of the occlusion occurring postoperatively are a consequence of failure to ensure correct occlusal positioning during the operation, of an incorrect adjustment of the occlusion, or of careless bending of the plate on the surface of the bone. Since the plates are very rigid and thus ensure absolute stability, they tolerate no negligence in the bending process. Insufficiently bent plates cause distortion of the fracture when the screws are definitively inserted, and this also leads to disturbances of the occlusion.

In most cases, it is simpler to treat the fracture by exposing the mandible from the exterior. In particular, the important precompression of the fracture achieved with

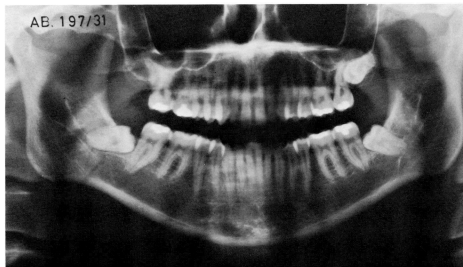

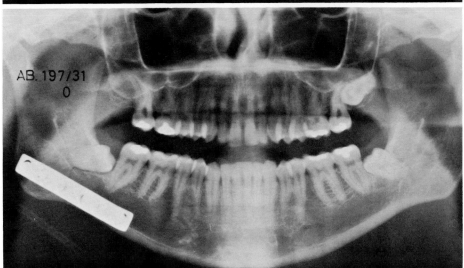

FIGURE 33–30.   Fixation of a preangular fracture with a six-hole EDCP. The fully retained wisdom tooth is not removed and therefore does not allow the application of a short, two-hole DCP acting as a tension band.

repositioning pliers is usually feasible only with external access. With intraoral exposure of the mandible, the repositioning pliers can be applied only for fractures of the chin. As surgeons gain experience, they are increasingly able to treat even fractures of the lateral portions of the mandible via intraoral access. However, the aim of the fracture treatment must be the uncompromising application of the principle of absolute stability, which permits the immediate and total postoperative resumption of function.

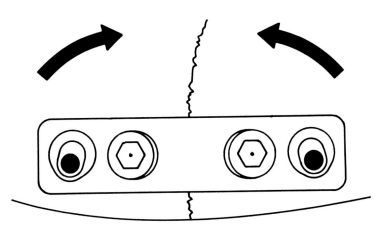

FIGURE 33–31.   EDCP with outer oval holes positioned at a 75-degree angle. If the outer holes are used correctly, the tightening of these screws provides compression along the fracture line above the plate.

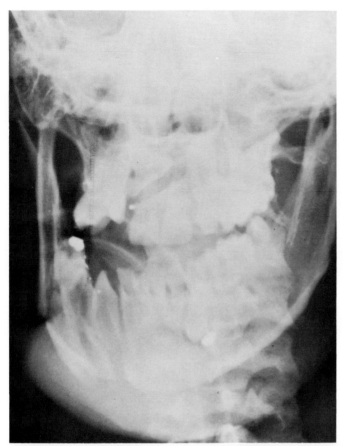

FIGURE 33–32. *Top,* Comminuted fracture of the right horizontal part of the mandible. *Center,* Bridging of the defect with a 16-hole reconstruction plate. Note that there are holes without screws. Screws should be used only where there is solid bone behind. The surgeon should never leave a loose screw inserted. Full arch bars are used in both jaws for intraoperative intermaxillary fixation. *Bottom,* Removal of plate 1 year after the accident.

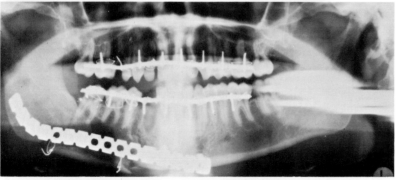

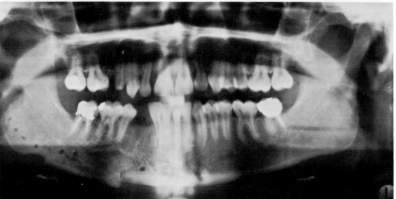

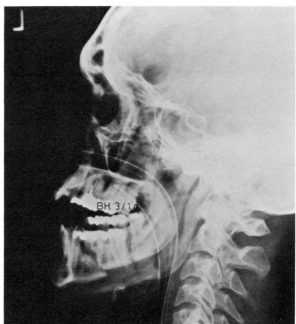

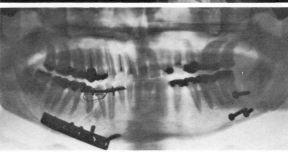

FIGURE 33–33. Bilateral mandibular fracture. *Top,* Fixation with tension band splint and six-hole DCP. *Bottom,* Oblique fracture fixed with three lag screws.

In cases of polytraumas, preoperative radiographs are often inadequate, and, especially for patients in this category, the possibility of obviating any postoperative intermaxillary fixation is important. We know from discussion with course participants during the past few years that when treatment is undertaken via oral access, compromises are made in many cases. The result is instability leading to pseudoarthrosis and inflammation. This unsatisfactory result frequently means that the pathologic phase is prolonged, the patient unfortunately has to have several operations, and costs are inevitably increased. The choice of access depends above all on a correct incision made strictly within a skinfold, so that the best possible result can be achieved from the cosmetic point of view.

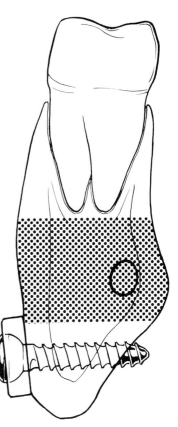

FIGURE 33–34. The screw engages in both cortices.

Finally, we feel that there are absolute and relative indications for the application of rigid internal fixation in maxillofacial fractures. *Absolute* indications are as follows:

1. Wide-open and comminuted fractures
2. Polytraumas, in which facial fractures should be operated upon together with other fractures
3. Mandibular fractures in combination with midface fractures
4. Fractures in edentulous patients
5. Most fractures in combination with condylar or subcondylar fractures

A *relative* indication is a nondisplaced mandibular fracture in the presence of full dentition. These patients with these fractures must be given the choice of either accepting several weeks of intermaxillary fixation or having the fracture rigidly fixed with plates and screws and no intermaxillary fixation. It is our opinion that when possible—that is, when the patient's condition permits, when general anesthesia can be used, and when exposure of the fracture is acceptable—the surgeon must use a method that guarantees undisturbed fracture healing even under the condition of immediate full function.

THE WÜRZBURG TITANIUM MINIPLATE SYSTEM FOR SURGICAL TREATMENT OF MAXILLOFACIAL FRACTURES

The first description of a surgical fracture treatment with plate osteosynthesis probably came from Hansmann (1886).[60] Precise diagnoses could be made by means of the new radiographic technique around the turn of the century, and the new technique of osteosynthesis could be used to an increasing extent with advances in the field of asepsis.[61-64] However, disturbances of healing caused by the materials were frequent, so that these methods of operation were controversial and not generally accepted initially.

The observation that in tuberculous knee joint arthrodesis a more rapid consolidation could be attained with a *"fixateur externe"* by development of pressure[65] led to the development of the modern pressure-plate osteosynthesis. The principle universally applied in engineering—namely, connection of two parts under pressure (as, for example, in almost every screw connection)—was thus adopted. By deformation of materials in the elastic range under the development of pressure, a high stability was attained against bending and, via the surface friction, against rotation. The axial pressure development was implemented for the first time by Danis (1949)[66] in connection with a plate system. The pressure development was attained by means of a clamping bolt. In the subsequent period, others described plate systems in which the axial pressure force arises by the displacement effect of a bone screw with beveled head conus on the edge of a long hole in the plate. The osteosynthesis pressure is established and maintained by deformation of the plate by traction and deformation of the bone by pressure. The principle of the sliding hole was appreciably improved,[69-71] avoiding damage to the material of the plate and the screw head. In the constructions of Mittelmeier[69] and Perren,[71] "pressure sliding holes" were involved and allowed an arrangement of several pressure holes on one side of a plate. In this way, higher pressure values can be attained, as demonstrated by direct measurements on the bone.[72]

Results deriving from general surgery were initially confirmed for oral and maxillofacial surgery by Luhr[70] in experimental investigations. Different plate systems were described for oral and maxillofacial surgery.[70,73,74] These were very rigid plate systems that attained absolute immobilization of the fracture on the basis of the strength of the plate and the axial pressure development.

At about the same time, a completely different concept was developed in France by Michelet[75-78] and later by Champy[79-89] for surgical fracture treatment. These investigators attempted to attain a functionally oriented fracture adaptation and fixation with plate systems that were as small as possible. With these plate systems, it was possible to comply with the stipulations of Pauwels[90] and to apply the plate to the region of the traction side of the bone. For this purpose, Champy and Lodde[83] presented fundamental investigations with photoelasticity methods for treatment of mandibular fractures.

The modern miniplate system can be applied to the mandible via the purely enoral route and to the maxilla from both extraoral and intraoral approaches. The initial reservations with regard to a higher risk of infection for this osteosynthesis could be refuted as being unjustified.[91–102] The simple technique of operation with miniplate osteosynthesis, the surgical access via the oral cavity, which is substantially lower in risk with regard to scar formation and nerve damage than the extraoral approach, dispensing with longer term intermaxillary immobilization, and a lower rate of complications are evidently the reasons why the indication for miniplate osteosynthesis of midface fractures as well as of mandibular fractures has been appreciably extended in recent years. A further decided advantage of the enoral approach is the fact that the osteosynthesis can be applied with continuous checking of occlusion.

Besides a constantly expanding indication in fracture treatment, the miniplate systems developed in the meantime have also been used for surgical correction of dysgnathias in the midface and on the mandible.

Development of the Authors' Own Miniplate System

BIOLOGIC AND MECHANICAL ASPECTS

In close collaboration with the company Oswald Leibinger, we have developed a miniplate system of our own, which also takes into account the experience of Michelet and Champy.[75–89] In the development of this system, we have taken biologic and biomechanical aspects of fracture healing into consideration, such as defined in 1941 by Böhler.[103] Uninterrupted mechanical immobilization of the fracture cleft, adequate blood supply to the fragments, and an intimate contact of the fracture ends play a crucial role in undisturbed fracture healing. With this method, an attempt is made to attain fracture healing that is free of callus if possible, as was observed radiographically for the first time by Lane in 1914[63] and Danis in 1949.[66] This "primary" bone healing was documented histologically in numerous animal experiments and in humans.[71,104–108]

With regard to the rigidity of the osteosynthesis connection, we have taken familiar results of general surgery into consideration. With absolute rigid arthrodesis of a fracture, both the phase of healing and the processes of physiologic remodeling and renewal in the bone, which take place in accordance with the Wolff's transformation principle,[109] are negatively affected. The absolutely rigid immobilization leads to a stress protection resulting in osteoporosis, development of cancellous bone, brittleness, red atrophy, and so forth.[110,111] For this reason, different methods that avoid absolute rigidity of the osteosynthesis connections and take into consideration more biologic, biomechanical factors have also been tested in general surgery.

For the construction of the plate system, it was stipulated that the repositioned fragments be kept securely in position by the osteosynthesis material. In our opinion, the functional loading of the mandible by the differently acting forces and the force movements referred to by Champy and Lodde[80] appear to play a crucial role in establishing the stability of the osteosynthesis material. Wustrow[112] already classified the masticatory forces that act on the mandible and maxilla into a theoretically possible force, the force required physiologically, and the forces that are practically feasible. According to the investigations of Schumacher,[113] theoretically possible forces can be inferred from the cross-sections of the masticatory muscles. From this, roughly 1000 N can be calculated as a theoretically possible force for each side.

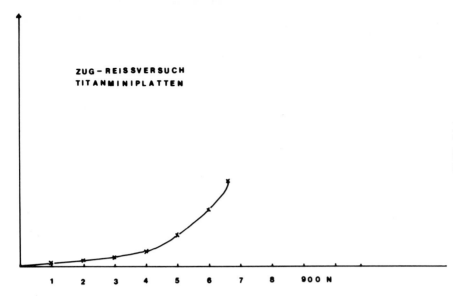

FIGURE 33-35. Tensile strength of Würzburg titanium miniplates in loading on the Universal Test Machine (Zwick) with 20 mm/min elongation.

Uhlig[114] and Kraft[115] found maximal values of 90 N up to 250 N as practically possible forces between antagonistic tooth pairs. Lower forces would also be sufficient to comminute food. In the presence of a fracture, it can be assumed in addition that a protective posture because of pain is present, with even lower values of loading. Schargus[116] established the maximal force in forced opening of the mouth against a resistance as being between 70 N and 100 N. From these values, it can be inferred that for the theoretically possible force an absolutely stable osteosynthesis on the lower jaw is practically impossible, since it is not the stability of the osteosynthesis material that is most significant, but rather the connection between the osteosynthesis plate and the bone via the screw fixation.

As an upper limit for the mechanical loading of the fracture site, we have assumed that about 100 N is sufficient to comminute soft food, so that this force must be eliminated by the osteosynthesis plate. In our stability investigations on our miniplate system, we found a limit of extension at 300 N up to 450 N at the weakest point and tearing at loads over 680 N (Fig. 33–35) in loading on the Universal Test Machine. Besides the absolute level of the masticatory forces, the direction of the masticatory forces is of crucial importance to understand and appraise torsion and bending strain of the mandible.

According to the investigations of Motsch,[117] the mandible is to be regarded as a general lever "with fulcrum in the area of mastication." Owing to the numerous total results of the muscular forces that concentrate the masticatory pressure as economically as possible on the food bolus in a complex cybernetic feedback regulation system,[118] it is not possible to specify a constant, exactly defined point as a fulcrum for the mandible. The masticatory muscles involved always act via a certain force arm, that is, via the horizontal or the ascending mandibular branch of the masticating and the nonmasticating side in accordance with their region of insertion. In the process of mastication, this leads to typical elastic deformations of the mandible, as have been described in photoelasticity experiments.[87,117,119-121] It must be assumed that biting off the essential elastic deformations in the region of the front teeth is based on a bending of the two horizontal branches in a caudal direction. Mainly tensile stress occurs in the alveolar crest region of the horizontal part of the mandible, whereas compressive stresses are developed at the lower edge. In the region between the canine teeth, there are overlapping tensile and compressive loads both in the craniocaudal and in the caudocranial regions. Besides this, torsional forces are also significant.

On the basis of these considerations, Champy has described the treatment of mandibular fractures with monocortically anchored miniplates in the horizontal region of the upper margin of the mandible in the alveolar crest region and has suggested insertion of a second plate on the margin of the mandible in the premolar area beginning over the front area to secure fixation.[88] In the indication for our miniplate system, we take these results into consideration, and they are also confirmed by our clinical experience.

ANATOMIC BASES

With regard to treatment of midface fractures with miniplate osteosynthesis, general agreement does not yet prevail. Champy[85] recommends that miniplate osteosynthesis should be used only in the periorbital region; he regards the infraorbital region and, in particular, the maxilla as not especially favorable locations for plate osteosynthesis. He regards the thin, bony walls of the facial maxillary sinus as being unsuitable for this method. Since a minimal bone thickness must be stipulated for treatment of fractures in the region of the midface, Ewers[14] and Schilly[46] have investigated the bone structures of the periorbital region with regard to their average bone thickness. Average values between 3.2 mm and 6.7 mm have been measured on 20 macerated human periorbital bones. On the basis of photoelastic investigations on Araldite models, they were able to show that a screw with a torque of $0.3 \text{ N} \cdot \text{m}$ can be fixed at this bone thickness.

We have carried out corresponding measurements for the entire facial skeleton with horizontal and sagittal sections on the entire cranial skeleton. In five macerated human skulls, the calotte was initially sawed off horizontally with a bandsaw at the level of the frontal tubera. The occiput was then removed in the frontal plane behind the insertion of the zygomatic arch on the temporal bone. The remaining visceral cranium was sawed through mediosagittally. The right halves of the visceral cranium were sawed up sagittally with a slice thickness of 5 mm. We obtained 8 to 10 sections per preparation, of which the most lateral slice was always a tangential section through the temporal bone. The left halves of the face were cut up horizontally with a layer thickness of 5 mm. We obtained 15 to 18 sections, of which the lowest was a block resection of the alveolar process of the maxilla (Fig. 33–36). The thickness of

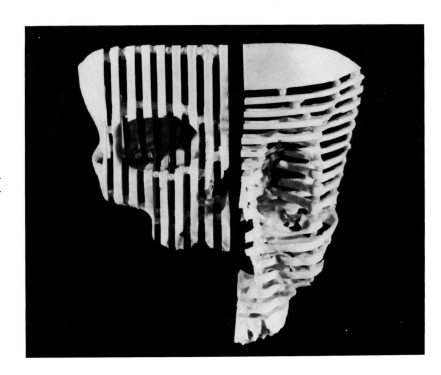

FIGURE 33–36. Reconstructed skull following horizontal and longitudinal sectioning.

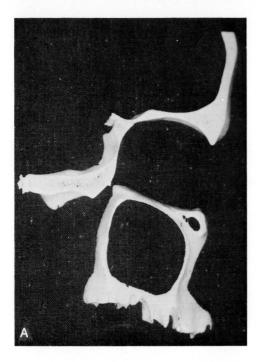

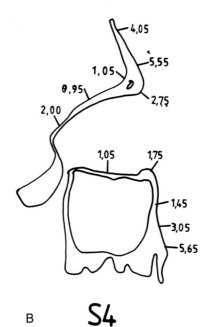

FIGURE 33–37. *A, B,* Measurement of the sectioned skull.

the bone lamella of the visceral cranium was determined at 5-mm intervals on the individual sections with a caliper (Fig. 33–37*A* and *B*). In the entire frontal and temporal region, the thickness of the lamella was about 3 to 4 mm. In the region of the frontal sinuses, there was a thickening of the lamella in the frontal direction up to 7 mm, and in the region of the upper orbital margin in the temporal direction, the thickening was up to 18 mm. On the nasal margin of the orbit, we measured thicknesses between 6 and 7 mm, compared with 5.0 to 5.5 mm in the region of the supraorbital foramen, 4 to 5 mm in the middle region of the upper margin, 4.5 to 5.0 mm in the region of the zygomaticofrontal suture, 5.0 to 6.5 mm on the lateral margin of the orbit, 6 to 8 mm in the region of the zygoma, 2.0 to 3.5 mm in the middle region of the lower margin of the orbit, and 2.5 to 3.5 mm in the nasal region of the lower margin of the orbit. The temporal wall of the orbit in the region of the temporal fossa showed a thickness of 1.0 to 2.5 mm, whereas the nasal and basal orbit wall was only fractions of a millimeter thick because of the immediately adjacent paranasal sinuses. The orbit margin had a thickness that increased from about 1.5 to 3.5 mm from a medial to lateral direction. The nasal bone was found to be between 1.0 and 1.5 mm thick.

The thickness of the anterior wall of the maxillary sinus is subject to major fluctuations. Whereas it is only 1 mm thick in places of the middle region, it may display a thickness of 2.0 to 3.5 mm in the medial and nasal regions. In the region of the infraorbital foramen, the lamella has a thickness of about 3.5 mm. The posterior wall of the maxillary sinus in the region of the infratemporal fossa is also subject to major fluctuations in thickness, but from the top to the bottom, whereas the thickness of the lamella is about 1 to 2 mm at the level of the zygomatic arch, increasing up to 3.5 mm above the alveolar process. The zygomatic arch itself has a thickness of about 3 mm. The alveolar process has a thickness of about 12 mm in the anterior region and a thickness of up to 16 mm in the area of the molars.

The thickness of the lamella in the frontal and temporal regions is relatively constant (3 to 4 mm). Fluctuations in thickness are caused by digital impressions and are found in the margin region of the frontal sinus. In general, the values of our measurements are consistent with those of Ewers.[14] Differences in the values of the lower margin of the orbit are due to the different measurement techniques, since Ewers measured the bone thickness within the facial and orbital cortical bone and we determined the thickness of the bone lamella from the outside to the maxillary sinus. However, these differences are largely negligible.

MECHANICAL INVESTIGATIONS

Besides knowledge of the different bone thicknesses, above all, the stability of miniscrews on thin bone structures plays a crucial role in establishing the indication for an application of miniplates in the region of the midface. The axial force produced by the placement of a screw helps stabilize the plate on the bone. Bone and metal have different stability values.[66] Therefore, the bone should predominate compared with the metal part in the longitudinal section of the screw thread. Because of this fact, the thread pitch cannot be made optionally small.

In the construction of our self-cutting miniscrews, we have attempted to arrive at a certain compromise, although the thread pitch chosen was not so small as to prevent slipping out in the bone. In five maxillary skeletons of freshly slaughtered domestic pigs, we have investigated the maximal torque of our osteosynthesis screws. We have proceeded in such a way that a miniscrew 7 mm long was screwed in with a torque spanner with increasing tightening after predrilling a hole with a diameter of 1.5 mm. In various samples, the maximal cranking torque was found for the different bone thicknesses. Compared with the investigations of Paulus,[122] it was shown that our bone screw possesses adequate stability values in bone from a thickness of 0.75 mm, with corresponding sensitivity (Table 33–1). The fact that an appreciable increase of 2 mm in the torques cannot be observed is attributable to the introduction of two thread turns of our miniscrew in the bone at this bone thickness, so that further thread turns do not give rise to the expectation of an appreciable increase in the torques.

On the basis of these investigations, we can assume that the Würzburg titanium miniplates can be fixed almost anywhere with adequate stability in the midface. Care has to be taken in the reconstruction of structures of the visceral cranium that the plates are applied in the longitudinal direction of the supporting columns of the midface to ensure a maximal force transfer. Since it can be expected that high pulling forces do not act in the region of the skeleton of the maxillary sinus, excessively great demands are also not to be made on the stability of the plates. This observation is confirmed by the investigations of Paulus[122] on plastic models.

OSTEOSYNTHESIS MATERIAL

The choice of the osteosynthesis material was made on the basis of various considerations. First of all, the masticatory forces previously discussed were to be absorbed with sufficient certainty by appropriate miniaturization of the plate system.

TABLE 33-1.   CRANKING TORQUE

Bone Thickness (mm)	2-mm Würzburg Titanium Screw (N·m)	2-mm AO Miniscrew (N·m) (Paulus, 1986)
0.5	0.05	—
0.75	0.15	—
1.0	0.19	0.16
1.5	0.30	0.26
2.0	0.40	0.33
2.5	0.40	0.34
3.0	0.41	0.35
3.5	0.45	0.36
4.0	—	0.37

Further, the material had to display as high a biocompatibility as possible. In addition, it was desirable for the plate material to adapt well to the bone surface without an excessive intrinsic elasticity. After testing various materials, such as implant steels, niobium, tantalum, and titanium, we have decided in favor of titanium.

Several factors supported the choice of titanium. As a pure metal, titanium is exceptionally well tolerated by the tissue, and it is stable to corrosion in the air and in a biologic medium. Titanium is thus especially suitable as a long-term implant. According to current knowledge, it can remain in the body for an unlimited time. Titanium is thus favored at present as a material for dental implants. Conventional implant steel loses its biocompatibility, since hairline fractures arise on the surface at deformation. This situation is the reason for corrosion as well as for metalloses and infections in the implant bed. When titanium comes into contact with oxygen, a dense, stable titanium oxide layer is formed, immediately protecting the titanium from corrosion. This titanium oxide layer is renewed spontaneously (even in a biologic medium) after all deformations. Consequently, the titanium plates remain chemically inert and stable to corrosion. Titanium displays better deformability with appropriate processing compared with implant steels, so that the titanium plates can be adapted very exactly and simply to the bone surface. Owing to the low elasticity module, titanium plates, compared with implant steels, spring back after adaptation to only a very small extent, so that the strain on the bone-screw connection can be kept as small as possible (Table 33–2). Allergic reactions to titanium are not known. Very much lower reflections have been observed from titanium plates than from implant steels in CT and in magnetic resonance imaging (MRI), so that artifacts rarely occur.

Along with the major biologic benefits, which were crucial in the selection of the titanium for our plate system, the physical properties of titanium also influenced our choice. Since different criteria must be fulfilled by screws and plates owing to their mechanical stress and strain both in working and in clinical use, we have employed pure titanium in two different formulations. They hardly differ chemically with regard to their degree of purity, but they possess distinct advantages for clinical application in accordance with their physical index characteristics (Table 33–3).

For screws, a material was chosen with higher hardness and higher elasticity (i.e., lower deformability), with higher tensile strength (i.e., higher load-carrying capacity), and with a lower breaking factor (i.e., lower deformability). The material for plates was chosen in such a way that the elasticity and hardness are lower to attain better deformability. The tensile strength is such that adequate stability is present for the tensile load. However, the elongation at rupture was chosen in such a way that a deformation of the screw holes is largely avoided even though the plate has reasonably good deformability; this is additionally ensured by the individual form. The elasticity module with 108 and 105 kN/mm^2 is half as low as in the corresponding implant steels. This fact means that plastic deformations occur very much earlier, that is, upon exposure to lower forces, than in steel alloys. Thus, lower load-carrying capacity is to be expected for the bone-screw connection, which is finally responsible for the stability of the entire system. On the other hand, the elasticity module of our

TABLE 33-2. MECHANICAL CHARACTERISTICS

	IMPLANT MATERIAL, CHAMPY SYSTEM	TITANIUM (SCREW), WÜRZBURG SYSTEM	TITANIUM (PLATE), WÜRZBURG SYSTEM
Hardness (Brinell number)	120–180	190	143
Elastic limit, 1% (N/mm²)	>235	410	270
Tensile strength (N/mm²)	450–700	540–740	390–540
Elongation at rupture (%)	45	16	22
Transverse deformation (%)	60	16	22

TABLE 33-3. PHYSICAL CHARACTERISTICS

	IMPLANT MATERIAL, CHAMPY SYSTEM	TITANIUM (SCREW), WÜRZBURG SYSTEM	TITANIUM (PLATE), WÜRZBURG SYSTEM
Density (g/cm³)	7.95	4.505	4.505
Specific heat (J/g·°K)	0.50	0.54	0.52
Thermal conductivity (W/m·°K)	15	18	17
Electrical resistance (ohm·mm²/m)	0.75	0.55	0.48
Modulus of elasticity (kN/mm²)	200	108	105

plate system is very much closer to the elasticity of bone, so that negative biologic effects such as those seen in very rigid plate osteosynthesis are not to be expected.

SCREWS

The self-cutting bone screws were constructed on the basis of biophysical considerations and after investigations of stability in biologic experiments (Fig. 33–38). The external diameter is 2 mm, and the screws are available commercially in graduated lengths from 5 to 15 mm. The extremely flat screw head has a single slit and a centering hole to accommodate a screwdriver blade with centering pin. The special design of the screw head increases the load-carrying capacity and facilitates handling. In addition, there is a higher stability to breaking out of the screw wings with exact guidance of the screw by axial application of pressure as well as a secure hold of the screwdriver blade in the screw head. Since only a relatively low tolerance limit is present for the maximal torque or for the cranking torque in the very thin bone structures of the midface, we have made available an additional emergency screw with a diameter of 2.3 mm. This larger screw may be used cautiously when a previous screw is cranked.

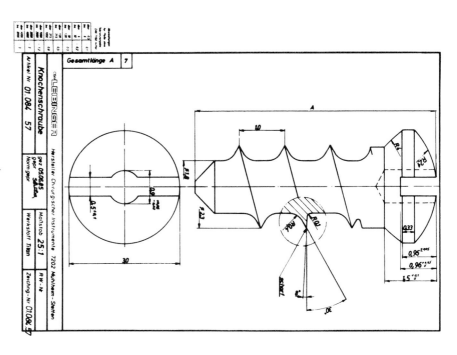

FIGURE 33–38. Design of the Würzburg titanium miniscrew.

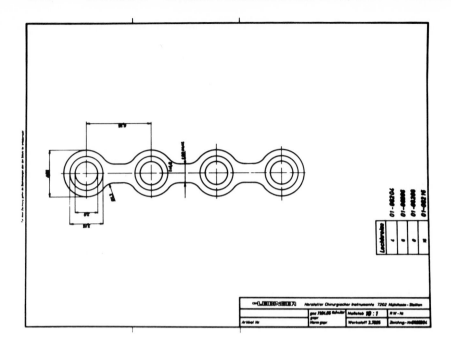

FIGURE 33–39. Computer-calculated basic form of the Würzburg titanium miniplates.

PLATES

The basic form of the Würzburg titanium miniplate system was optimized by computer calculation following experimental investigations and stability studies (Fig. 33–39). The screw hole edge and the thickness of the connecting bridge were chosen in such a way that a deformation of the plate is mainly ensured in the region of the connecting bridge without deformation of the screw edge. The screw hole edge and the screw head are harmonized in such a way that the plate level is exceeded to only a minor extent.

Since the stability of metals is mainly guaranteed by the intactness of their crystal structure, we have attempted to prevent extreme deformations for the different indications by making a large diversity of plates available. The 20 plate variants ensure that the plate may be adapted for the typical indications without appreciable deformation (Fig. 33–40).

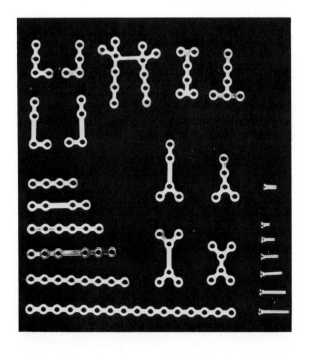

FIGURE 33–40. Typical variations of the Würzburg titanium miniplates and screws.

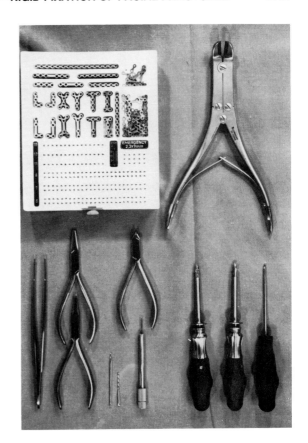

FIGURE 33–41. Set of instruments for the Würzburg titanium miniplate system.

INSTRUMENTS

The concept of the Würzburg titanium miniplate system is based on a user-oriented harmonization of plates, screws, and instruments (Fig. 33–41). For adaptation of the plates, two pointed, flat pliers (Fig. 33–42) and modified three-point bending pliers (Aderer pliers) are provided in the basic equipment. The core of the Aderer pliers is harmonized with the hole distance of the miniplates in such a way that deformation of the plates always occurs only in the region of the connecting bridges (Fig. 33–43).

FIGURE 33–42. Torquing and bending with two pointed, flat pliers.

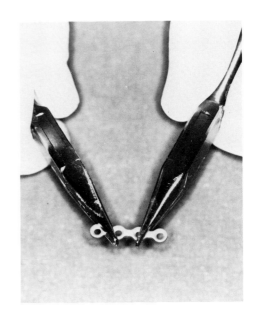

FIGURE 33–43. Modified Aderer three-prong pliers for vertical and horizontal shaping.

The newly developed screwdriver fulfills several functions in one. The collet with socket ensures that the screw can be removed from the Teflon bed, can be transported safely into the area of operation, and can be screwed into the bore hole axially. The centering pin and the centering hole guarantee optimal hold of the screwdriver blade in the screw (Fig. 33–44A). For removal, the collet is put over the screw head and drawn through the socket (Fig. 33–44B). The screw can thus be removed by the instrumentation nurse and given to the surgeon. With an initially closed collet, the screw is first turned axially, the socket is then drawn back, and the screw is finally fixed with an open screw turner blade. With the hand-shaped handle of the screwdriver, a fatigue-free operation of the screwdriver is ensured. The rotatory mechanism, which should be handled only with thumb and index finger, guarantees an adaptation of the screw that is as sensitive as possible.

Clinical Application

In the past 4 years, we have checked the possibilities for using the Würzburg titanium miniplate system in traumatology, in orthopedic surgical operations, and in craniofacial surgery. In particular, this text describes our experience in traumatol-

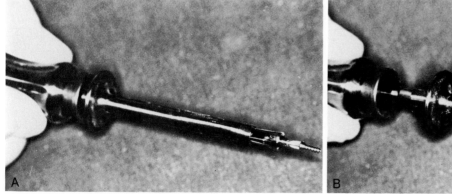

FIGURE 33–44. *A,* Newly developed screwdriver with centering pin guarantees optimal holding of the blade in the screw. *B,* With pushed-down tension sheath, the screw is securely fixed for transportation and screwing.

TABLE 33-4. WÜRZBURG TITANIUM MINIPLATES FOR TREATMENT
OF MIDFACE FRACTURES

	1984	1985	1986	1987	Total
Le Fort I	9	9	5	3	26
Le Fort II	3	9	6	9	27
Le Fort III	15	20	21	16	72
Zygoma	29	32	47	19	127
Total	56	70	79	47	252

ogy. The different indications are based on our experience in treating a total of 252 midface fractures and 315 mandibular fractures (Tables 33–4 and 33–5).

MANDIBULAR FRACTURES

The indication for positioning our miniplate system on the mandible is based in principle on the investigations and results of Champy and Lodde[80-87] (Fig. 33–45). Owing to the plate variations, there are slight differences from the Strasbourg plate system.[123-126] In principle, osteosynthesis with the Würzburg miniplate system is an adaptation osteosynthesis without development of pressure on the fracture cleft.

The use of miniplate osteosynthesis in mandibular fractures is possible, in principle, in all fractures of the mandibular body in the presence of full dentition, partial dentition, or edentulism. The criteria elaborated by Champy and Lodde[80-87] are to be considered with regard to the plate location. In principle, the intraoral approach is used, even if a transbuccal accessory incision is occasionally necessary in the region of the ascending mandibular ramus for insertion of the screws. In multiple fractures of the mandible, it is advisable to carry out splinting to adjust the occlusion. In complicated fractures and poor mucosal conditions, we also recommend additional intermaxillary immobilization until the soft tissue injuries have healed. In agreement with Horch and associates,[125] we treat joint fractures only in special situations.

Fractures in children under 13 years old, in whom the possibility of conservative fracture treatment must always be considered to prevent damage from persistent dental bacteria, are a possible contraindication to the use of miniplate osteosynthesis. In addition, primary osteosynthesis is always to be questioned in pronounced comminuted fractures with soft tissue defects. Further, patients with general diseases that restrict surgical measures are to be excluded from surgical fracture treatment, or, if it does have to be carried out, the advantages and disadvantages are to be considered very carefully.

TECHNIQUE OF OSTEOSYNTHESIS

The technique of using titanium miniplates is demonstrated with a typical fracture location in the region of the mandibular angle (Fig. 33–46A). After fracture repositioning, the miniplate, which has to be fixed with at least two holes in each

TABLE 33-5. WÜRZBURG TITANIUM MINIPLATES FOR TREATMENT
OF MANDIBULAR FRACTURES

	1984	1985	1986	1987	Total
Mandibular body	35	36	62	45	178
Ascending ramus and angular region	26	47	41	23	137
Total	61	83	103	68	315

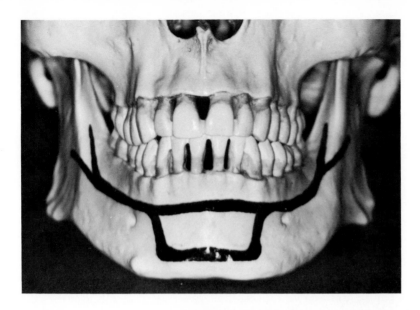

FIGURE 33–45. Anatomic model with ideal osteosynthesis line according to Champy.

fragment, is adapted very meticulously to the bone surface (Fig. 33–46B). The wide selection of plates ensures that unnecessary bending and torsion are avoided. Special care is also to be taken with regard to passive adaptation of the plate to the bone surface. The plate is fixed on the bone surface with a holding instrument, and the first bore hole is predrilled centrally in the plate hole perpendicular to the plate surface with a 1.5-mm spiral bit, and the screw is then screwed in (Fig. 33–46C and D). A length of 5 mm or 7 mm has proved to be an appropriate screw length in mandibular fractures. The remaining screws are inserted in the same way, with special attention to the drilling of the bore holes centrally and perpendicularly with respect to the plate surface (Fig. 33–46E and F). The ideal plate position for various mandibular fractures is shown in Figure 33–45 in accordance with the specifications of Champy.

In the hospital, fracture treatment should be carried out with the patient under general anesthesia, although operations that use local anesthesia are also feasible if appropriate sedation is given. Treatment with the patient under local anesthesia is quite possible above all for fractures in the region of the median and paramedian mandible.

The mucosal incision is carried out as a vestibular incision at the transition from the fixed to mobile mucosa (Fig. 33–47A and B). However, the gingival margin incision has proved especially effective for corresponding periodontal pocket formation. The fracture is exposed in the typical way (Fig. 33–47C and D), and fracture positioning initially is done manually after meticulous removal of hematomas and small bone fragments (Fig. 33–47E). In special cases, temporary adaptation may be carried out by means of a splint dressing or wire accessory ligature in the mandibular angle region. The occlusion should be checked very carefully and safeguarded by intermaxillary immobilization. After careful adaptation of the plate to the bone surface, the bore holes are made as described previously, and the screws are tightened (Fig. 33–47G and H).

In the canine tooth and premolar region, careful dissection of the mental nerve is also to be considered. In this region, we prefer to treat the fracture with two plates: one above and one below the nerve. For this purpose, it is necessary to slit the periosteum around the mental nerve to luxate it without producing tension on the soft tissues of the lip. With this technique, displacement of the nerve from its bony canal seems not to be necessary (Fig. 33–48B). To eliminate torsional forces in the region of the middle of the mandible, Champy recommends two parallel plates. The space between should amount to at least half a centimeter (Fig. 33–48A and C to E). The plate should be first fixed on the lower margin of the mandible to prevent diastasis, which might be induced by the masticatory musculature. According to the

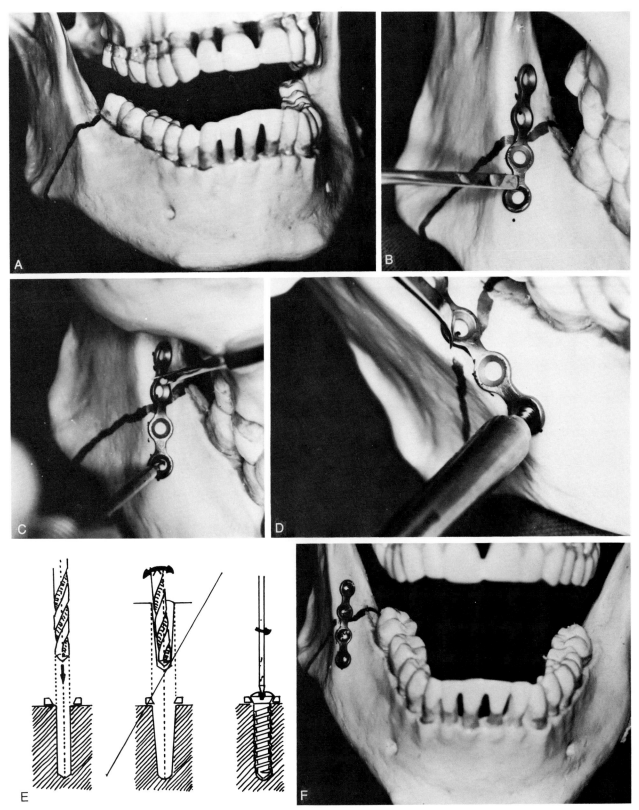

FIGURE 33–46. *A – F,* Technique of osteosynthesis in a fracture model.

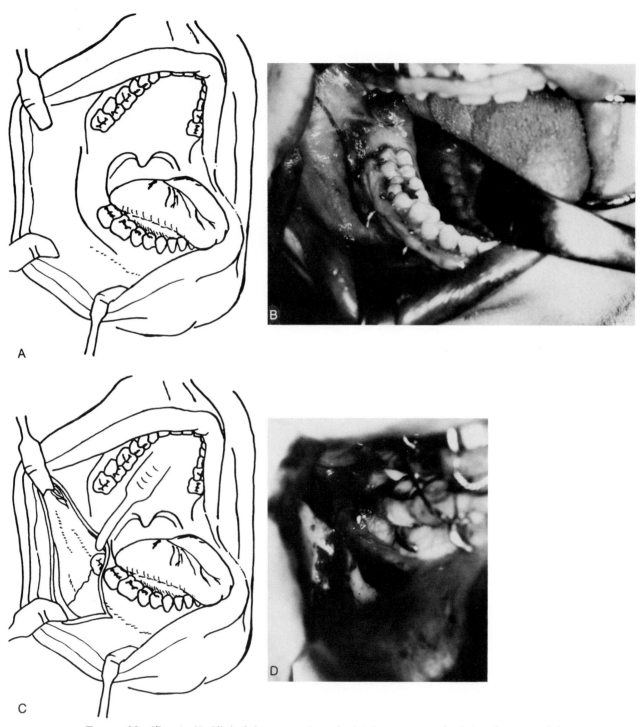

FIGURE 33–47. *A–H,* Clinical demonstration of miniplate osteosynthesis in a fracture of the mandibular angle.

Illustration continued on opposite page.

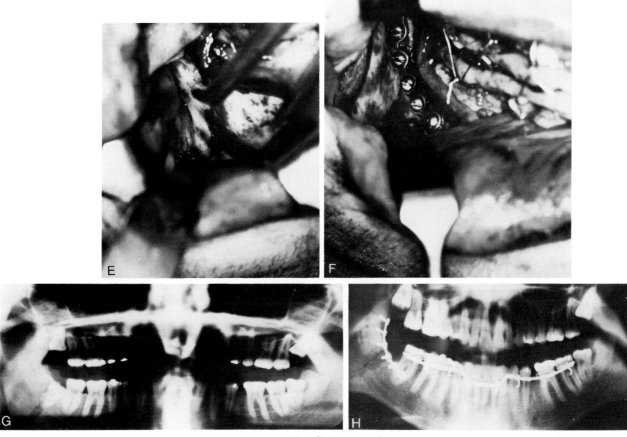

FIGURE 33–47. *Continued*

data of Champy,[79-89] fractures behind the mental foramen are adequately stabilized with one plate (Fig. 33–49*A* to *H*).

Each plate must be fixed with at least two screws in each fragment. If one screw pulls, the emergency screw would be available. If secure fixation fails, a new plate must be used.

In preboring the screw hole, exact attention must be paid to the perpendicular direction of the drill in relation to the plate surface and its central position in the plate hole. Eccentric drilling would result in a conical bone cavity, which is not sufficient for secure fixation of the screw (see Fig. 33–46*D*).

TREATMENT AND AVOIDANCE OF COMPLICATIONS

Analyzing the complications after surgical treatment of fractures with our mini-plate system from the past 4 years, we observed soft tissue infection in 4.1 per cent of cases, abscess of the fracture cleft in 2.74 per cent, and osteomyelitis of the fracture cleft in 2.74 per cent. Altogether, infections could be observed in 9.58 per cent of the patients treated. However, this did not lead to a pseudoarthrosis in the fracture cleft in any case. If these data are compared with the investigations after stable osteosynthesis (there being no difference whether the approach was enoral or extraoral), the values are between 1.25 and 14.1 per cent (with an average value of 6.3 per cent).[92-94,97,99,108,127-130] After purely conservative treatment of the fracture, infections of the fractured cleft are also found in a comparatively large number, averaging 12.9 per cent (range of 4.4 to 19.4 per cent)[131] in follow-up investigations. In analysis of our own cases, it could be observed that the problems of infection decrease with

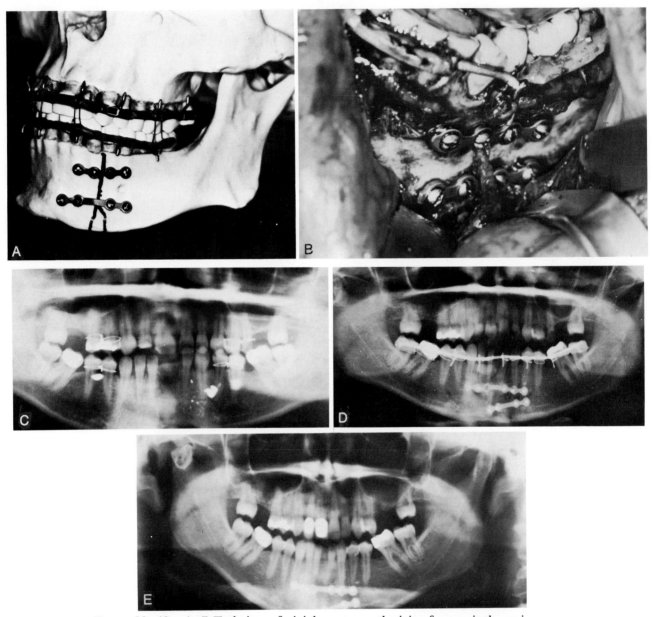

FIGURE 33–48. *A – E,* Technique of miniplate osteosynthesis in a fracture in the canine-premolar region with exposure of the mental nerve.

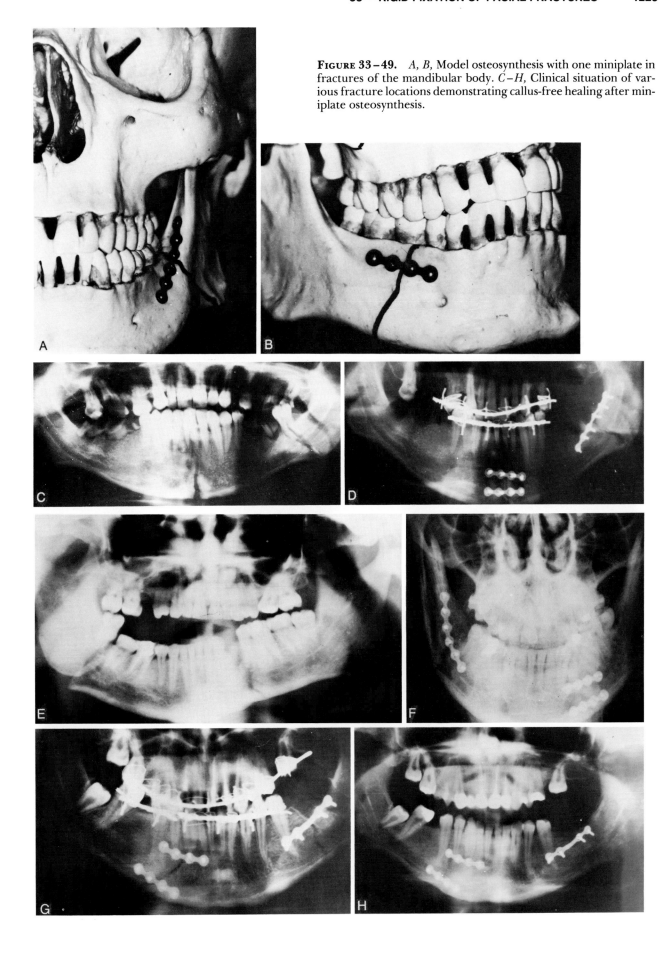

FIGURE 33–49. *A, B,* Model osteosynthesis with one miniplate in fractures of the mandibular body. *C–H,* Clinical situation of various fracture locations demonstrating callus-free healing after miniplate osteosynthesis.

increasing experience in the application of miniplate osteosynthesis. Nevertheless, there remain some cases in which an infection appears to be unavoidable. In uncertain coverage of soft tissues or in extensive soft tissue enoral injuries, we have found it useful to apply intermaxillary fixation until wound healing is complete, in addition to miniplate osteosynthesis. In some patients, this safety measure also appears to be indicated if it is not certain that the patient will not expose the fracture to a maximal masticatory load directly after the operation. In our experience, patients with mandibular fractures often do not have proper insight into the injury, and we have observed patients progress to eating normal food on the second and third days after surgical fracture treatment.

If wound dehiscence occurs, we normally perform an open wound treatment in which lavages with hydrogen peroxide and chlorhexidine are carried out and the bone is covered with a zinc oxide – eugenol tamponade. With this therapy, we have so far always been able to observe complete healing of the soft tissue wounds and an uncomplicated bone healing.

Postoperative complications of soft tissue infection, fracture cleft abscess, or osteomyelitis occurred mainly in patients in whom fracture treatment had to be performed at a later time. In principle, surgical treatment of the fracture proved to be largely free of complications within the first 12 hours after the accident. If treatment of the fracture is not possible in this period for organizational or other reasons, we have found intermaxillary immobilization, in addition to miniplate osteosynthesis, to be especially effective until the soft tissue wound has healed. Perioperative chemoprophylaxis given over 48 hours and exact oral hygiene are of particular advantage. Careful readaptation of the soft tissues — in some cases, in combination with a fibrin tissue adhesive fixation — is especially effective in the postoperative healing situation.

Surgical Treatment of Midface Fractures

For surgical treatment of midface fractures, the specific morphology and biomechanics of the maxilla are of crucial importance. In contrast to the mandible, dislocations of muscular origin in the maxilla are to be expected only on the pterygoid process. In the midface, fracture-dislocations are a manifestation of the intensity and direction of the action of force.

The midface is mainly formed by the maxilla with its processes to the adjacent bones. The thin, bony walls of the mandibles are strengthened by basal arches that form a frame (A Bluntschli [1926] cited by H Rohen [1958]). The course of functionally subdivided trajectories in the region of the jaws was demonstrated by Rohen.[132] The bony structures taking up the pressure of mastication are located on each side in the frontonasal, zygomatic, and sphenoid pillar buttresses.[109,133]

In the treatment of midface fractures, special attention is to be paid to restoring the supporting pillars that take up the masticatory pressure applied by the tooth system (Fig. 33 – 50). The miniplates must be inserted in such a way that they come to rest in the longitudinal direction of these pillars, so that the force transmission is once more ensured. In addition, according to our investigations, a sufficiently thick bone layer in the midface is required, especially in the region of the supporting pillars, to be able to fix the miniscrews with sufficient stability.

Whereas most authors regard the lateral orbit ring as a site for osteosynthesis with miniplates, there are divergent views on the application of miniplates in the remaining pillar buttresses of the midface. In 1978, Champy recommended bilateral plate osteosynthesis for the temporal zygomatic process in Le Fort III fractures.[85,86] However, he advised against using miniplate osteosynthesis for stabilization of Le Fort I fractures. Since stability of the osteosynthesis largely depends on the type of screw and plate as well as on the site of osteosynthesis and the number of osteosyntheses, we believe that we can also recommend our system for adequate stabilization in this region.

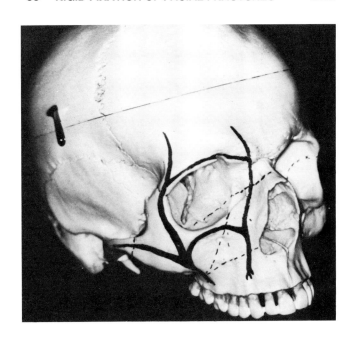

FIGURE 33-50. Anatomic model demonstrating the supporting framework of the maxilla, with the typical fracture lines running rectangular to this system.

CLINICAL APPLICATION

It is recommended in the technical procedure of surgery for miniplate osteosynthesis of midface fractures that splinting should first of all be carried out in a typical way and that the occlusion should be fixed by intermaxillary wiring. Afterward, the individual fracture location should be investigated via appropriate skin incisions and connected together with the appropriate osteosynthesis plates after repositioning of the fragments. At the end of the operation, the intermaxillary wire fixation must be opened again under all circumstances, since the screw fixation in the region of the midface is not sufficiently stable to neutralize the opening forces of the masticatory musculature that act via the mandible.

For surgical fracture treatment in the midface region, different incisions are specified in the literature.[134-136] The approach to the root of the nose, to the walls of the frontal sinuses, and to the rhinobasis is difficult. For a clear exposure of this region, it is mostly necessary to link bilateral Killian incisions with a transverse incision over the glabella.[137] However, the aesthetic result of these approach routes must be designated as exceedingly unsatisfactory.

Tessier first suggested a bicoronal, subperiosteal flap for exposure of the midface region in 1971[138] (Fig. 33-51). In the past 4 years, we have used this route of approach in treating 72 extensive midface fractures of the Le Fort III type. We dispensed with shaving the hair, since the hair can be parted without problems with Nebacetin Ointment after washing twice with a disinfectant solution. After the bitemporal incision, the bleeding can be stopped carefully with appropriate hemostatic clips (in our hospital we use Köllner clips), and the skin galea flap is dissected up to the supraorbital margin. The temporal fascia remains as intact as possible. The periosteal flap can be cut around and used to cover the defect, first in the region of the frontal sinuses or the rhinobasis. After exposure and dissection of the supraorbital nerve, the nose roots, the supraorbital margin, the lateral orbital margin, and the zygomatic bone can be exposed via the bicoronal incision. In cases in which revision of the floor of the orbit appears to be necessary, an infraorbital incision must be applied in addition (Fig. 33-52).

Some authors prefer using the subciliary section or the transconjunctival approach for aesthetic reasons.[40,139,140] In our experience, however, these incisions do not provide a sufficiently clear view, especially when revision of the floor of the orbit or extensive infraorbital reconstruction measures are necessary. Therefore, we

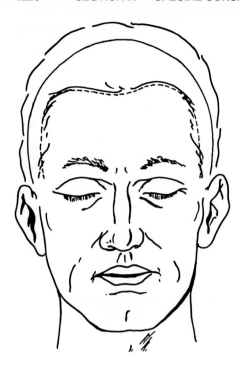

FIGURE 33–51. Skin incisions for exposure of the rhinobasis, the orbit, and the zygoma. Bicoronal incision (———). Hairline incision (– – –).

prefer a modified subciliary incision[141] or an infraorbital incision in the region of the lower lid fold to attain a very clear approach to the floor of the orbit.

In the not very pronounced midface fractures, which also predominate in our patients, the miniplate osteosynthesis can be carried out via the less elaborate approach infraorbitally and at the lateral orbit margin (Fig. 33–52). The intraoral approach has proved to be very effective, at least as an additional measure for Le Fort I fractures or in pronounced comminuted fractures in the region of the facial maxillary sinus wall and the zygoma.

The systematic application of our miniplate system in midface fractures can be demonstrated in schematic drawings of the cranial skeleton. For treatment of the lateral midface fracture, the rule applies that after repositioning with sufficient stabil-

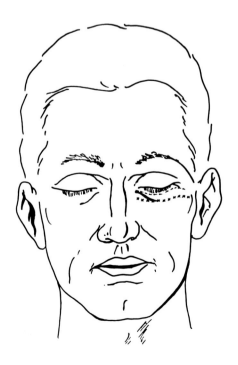

FIGURE 33–52. Skin incisions for exposure of fractures in the area of the zygoma, the orbital floor, and the infraorbital rim. Supraorbital eyebrow incision (———). Subciliary incision (– – –). Infraorbital incision (x x x).

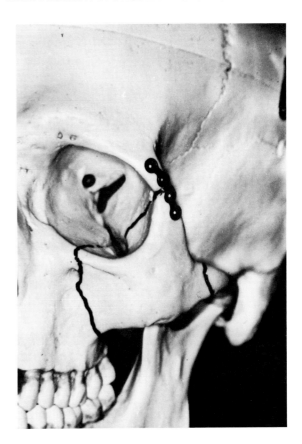

FIGURE 33–53. Anatomic model with miniplate osteosynthesis for stabilization of a zygomatic fracture.

ity, three-point fixation of the impressed zygomatic bone can be obtained with an osteosynthesis plate at the zygomatic suture (Fig. 33–53).

After incision in the region of the eyebrow, the soft tissues are dissected bluntly and sharply, and the periosteum is separated from the bone with the periosteal elevator. After careful inspection of the fracture, the zygomatic bone is repositioned with the zygomatic bone tenaculum, and an anatomic adjustment is carried out after exact adaptation of the miniplate to the bone contour. The plate is fixed in a typical way with two miniscrews at the fractured mobile end of the zygomatic bone and fixed on the zygomatic process of the frontal bone in a typical way (Fig. 33–54*A* to *C*).

Additional fixation on the infraorbital margin with a plate that has been individually adapted in an appropriate manner is to be recommended only in extensive comminuted fractures in the region of the intraorbital ring with involvement of the floor of the orbit (Fig. 33–55*A* and *B*). In those cases, a modified subciliary incision is made in the region of the lower lid fold about 5 mm below the edge of the lid. After this, the orbicularis muscle of the eye is exposed. Under the muscle, the periosteum is incised over the infraorbital margin, and the bone is dissected free (Fig. 33–56). In this way, practically the entire infraorbital margin and the floor of the orbit can be overlooked and appropriately reconstructed, and the bone fragments can be fixed with the miniplates (Fig. 33–57*A* and *B*).

Fractures of the Le Fort type can be stabilized, in principle, in the region of the supporting pillar at the piriform aperture as well as via the zygomaticoalveolar crista (Fig. 33–58).

In the treatment of Le Fort I and II fractures in which the revision of the floor of the orbit or fixation of the nasal skeleton does not appear to be necessary, we prefer the intraoral approach. A vestibular Le Fort I incision is created, and the periosteum is dissected cranially to the infraorbital nerves. After exposure of the fractures, the occlusion is now achieved by means of intermaxillary fixation to enoral splint dressings, and fracture repositioning is subsequently carried out. The supporting pillars of the midface at the piriform aperture as well as the zygomaticoalveolar crista are

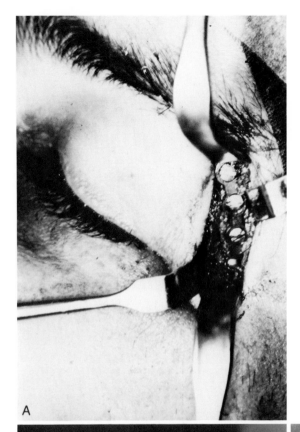

FIGURE 33–54.   *A–C*, Clinical situation for treatment of a zygomatic fracture with one miniplate in the zygomaticofrontal suture.

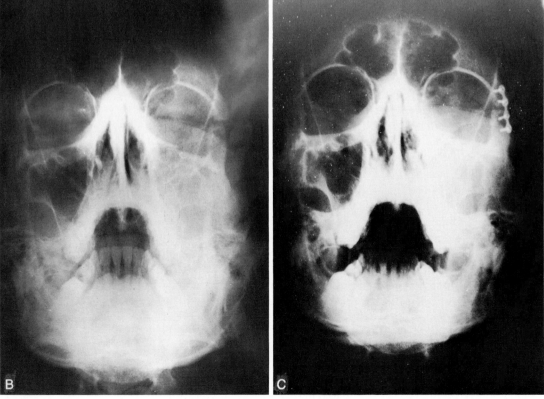

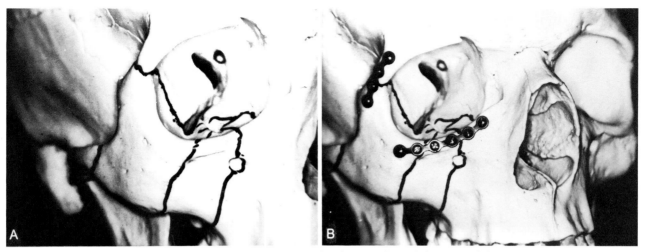

FIGURE 33–55.   A, B, Miniplate osteosynthesis of a complicated fracture of the zygoma and orbital floor.

FIGURE 33–56.   Modified subciliary incision for exposure of the infraorbital rim and floor of the orbit. (Redrawn from Becker R, Austermann KH: Zur Wahl des Zugangsweges bei operative Versorgung von Orbitafrakturen. Fortschr Kiefer Gesichtschir 22:33, 1977.)

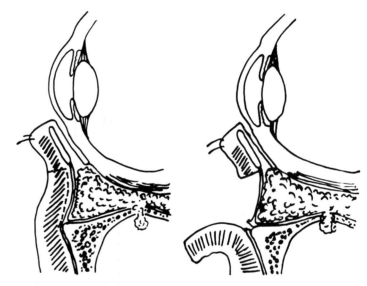

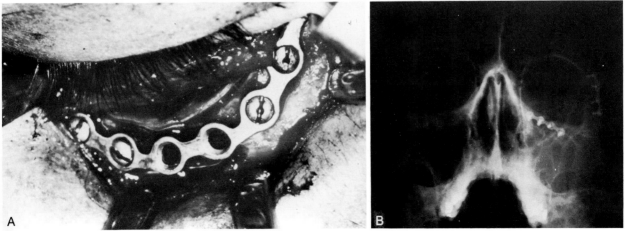

FIGURE 33–57.   A, B, Clinical case of miniplate osteosynthesis in a complicated zygomatic fracture.

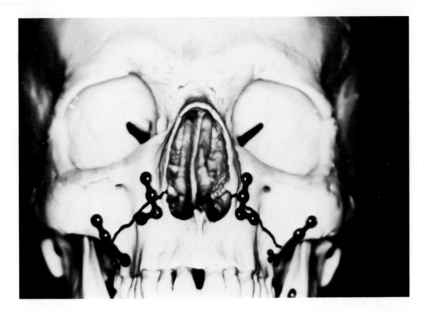

FIGURE 33–58. Anatomic model with miniplate osteosynthesis for Le Fort I fracture.

stabilized after adaptation of the different osteosynthesis plates (we have found the **L** and **Y** as well as the **T** plates to be especially effective). After closure of the mucosa, the intermaxillary fixation is opened again, since the plates fixed on the thin midface bones are not sufficiently secured against the pulling forces of the masticatory musculature.

In Le Fort II fractures, two plates on the infraorbital margin are frequently regarded as sufficient. Depending on the involvement of the nasal skeleton, however,

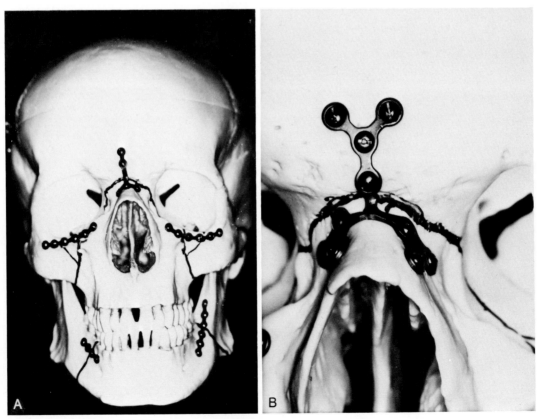

FIGURE 33–59. *A, B,* Anatomic models with miniplate osteosynthesis for a Le Fort II fracture; different miniplates are available for fixation of the root of the nose.

corresponding osteosynthesis in the region of the dorsum of the nose is to be carried out for secure stabilization of the midface fragment (Fig. 33–59A and B). Our variously formed nasal plates are especially suitable for this.

In more extensive midface injuries with frontal impression fractures and rhinobasis fractures, we carried out revision via a bicoronal incision, such as was recommended by Tessier[40,138] (Fig. 33–60A to C). Besides allowing revision of the rhinobasis, the supraorbital and lateral orbit region can be exposed very well. After bone repositioning, the bone fixation can be carried out with individual plates for the nasal bone pyramid or on the lateral orbital margin (Fig. 33–61A and B). In extensive comminuted fractures (Fig. 33–62A), the approach can also be made via an infraorbital incision alone on in combination with an intraoral approach (Fig. 33–62B to D). In cases involving extensive comminuted fractures, additional fixation of the midface by means of craniofacial suspension has also proved to be effective (Fig. 33–63A and B).

On the basis of our own experience during the past 4 years with the treatment of 252 midface fractures with the Würzburg titanium miniplate system, it can be stated that the good experience reported by Michelet, Champy, and many others[46,75–89,102,122,123,136] in the treatment of midface fractures can be absolutely confirmed. The plates can be adapted easily and exactly, enabling fixation of the often very small and thin bone fragments in anatomic position, and intermaxillary fixation can be eliminated.

Owing to the optimal tissue tolerance of the pure metal titanium, removal of the implanted material can be dispensed with in accordance with present knowledge. The exceedingly good tissue tolerance and corrosion resistance will not be changed by deformation (i.e., the alteration of the implant surfaces) in the case of titanium. The

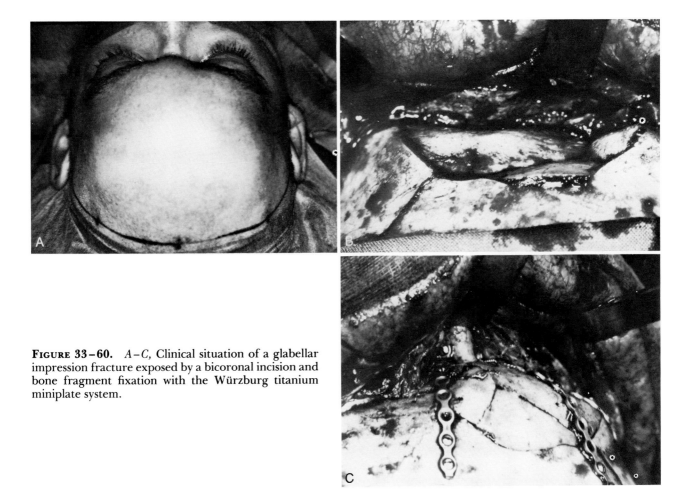

FIGURE 33–60. *A–C,* Clinical situation of a glabellar impression fracture exposed by a bicoronal incision and bone fragment fixation with the Würzburg titanium miniplate system.

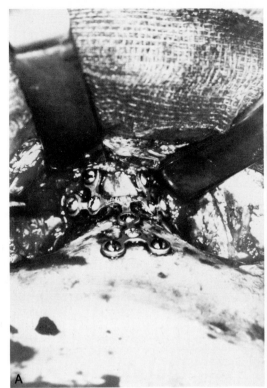

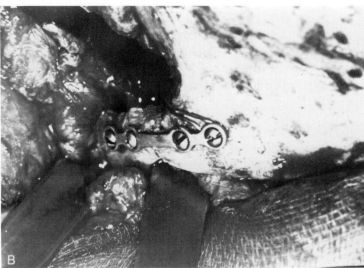

FIGURE 33 – 61.   *A, B,* Exposure of a typical Le Fort III fracture via a bicoronal incision; exact and easy miniplate osteosynthesis is possible on the root of the nose and at the zygomaticofrontal suture.

dense and solid titanium oxide layer is formed once more in the biologic milieu as well as in the air immediately after deformation, so that the titanium plates remain chemically inert and resistant to corrosion. To what extent purely mechanical irritations of the tissue around the implant itself may occasion its removal must be decided in each individual case.

CLINICAL STUDIES OF THE WÜRZBURG TITANIUM MINIPLATE SYSTEM IN MAXILLOFACIAL TRAUMA*

Mandibular Fractures

We are currently undertaking clinical studies of the Würzburg titanium miniplates for treatment of mandibular fractures, and some preliminary results are presented in the following section.[142] The aim of these studies is to investigate whether or not the maxillomandibular fixation period can be reduced or avoided in patients with unilateral or bilateral fractures of the mandible.

UNILATERAL MANDIBULAR FRACTURES

Patients with a unilateral fracture of the angle of the mandible or a fracture anterior to the mental foramen in the presence of a dentition allowing maxillomandibular fixation were included in this study. Patients with other facial fractures or with

* H.P. Phillipsen, Department of Oral Medicine and Diagnostics, Royal Dental College, Aarhus, Denmark, is thanked for preparing the illustrations for this section of Chapter 33.

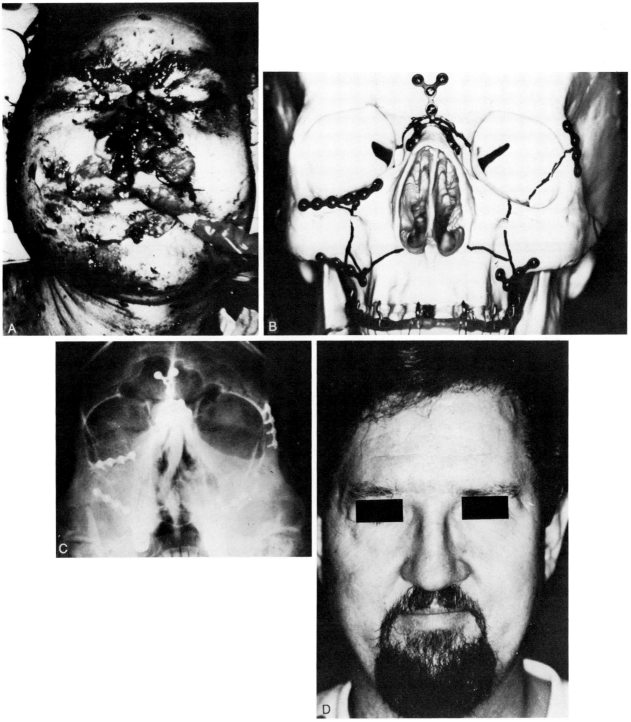

FIGURE 33–62.   *A–D,* Clinical case of a comminuted midface fracture; stabilization with multiple miniplate osteosynthesis on a combined intraoral and extraoral route.

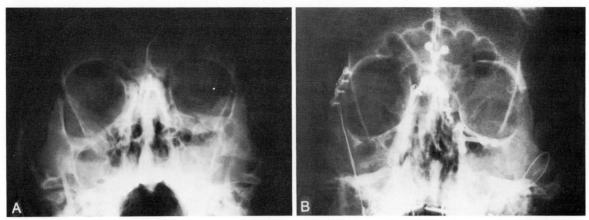

FIGURE 33–63. *A, B,* Preoperative and postoperative radiographs of a comminuted midface fracture; stabilization with multiple miniplate osteosynthesis in combination with craniofacial suspensions.

contraindications to maxillomandibular fixation were not included. On admission of the patients to the hospital, prophylactic antibiotic treatment and chlorhexidine mouthwash were given. All patients underwent surgery while under general anesthesia as soon as possible. During surgery, patients were randomized for either a control group or a test group. The baseline variables of the included patients appear in Table 33–6. All patients were followed for at least 3 months after surgery.

Patients in the control group were treated according to the standard treatment of the department. In patients with fractures of the angle of the mandible, maxillomandibular fixation was applied for 5 weeks, and an upper border wire osteosynthesis was applied (Fig. 33–64). In patients with fractures anterior to the mental foramen, maxillomandibular fixation was applied for 5 weeks, and in addition, a bone plate (stainless steel bone plate, Nichrominox, France) was inserted (Fig. 33–64).

In the test group, maxillomandibular fixation was applied during surgery to reposition the fracture; and in patients with fractures of the angle, one six-hole titanium miniplate was applied from the anterior part of the ramus along the oblique ridge of the mandible (Fig. 33–65), whereas two plates (two four-hole plates or one four- and one six-hole plate) were inserted in fractures anterior to the mental foramen (Fig. 33–66). After osteosynthesis of the fractures, maxillomandibular fixation was released, and the wound was sutured. Elastic maxillomandibular fixation was to be applied if malocclusion developed. Patients were kept on a liquid diet for 10 days and

TABLE 33-6.   BASELINE VARIABLES OF PATIENTS WITH UNILATERAL FRACTURES

VARIABLE	CONTROL GROUP ($n = 17$)	TEST GROUP ($n = 16$)
Sex		
Female	3	2
Male	14	14
Age (yr)		
Median	23	21.5
Range	14–37	17–44
Fracture location		
Anterior to mental foramen	6	6
Angle	11	10

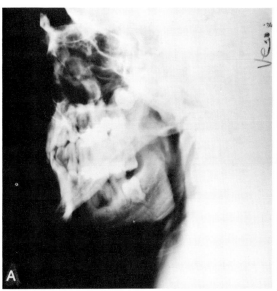

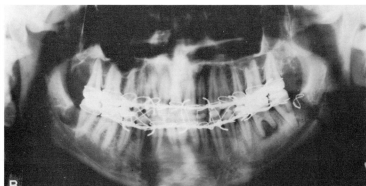

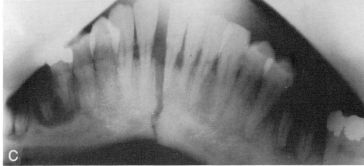

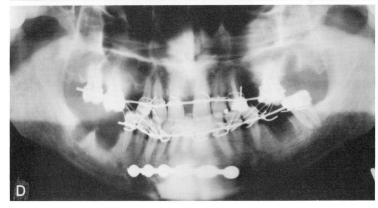

FIGURE 33–64. *A*, The radiograph shows a patient with a fracture of the left angle of the mandible. *B*, The fracture of the angle was treated with maxillomandibular fixation for 5 weeks and a 0.4-mm upper border stainless steel wire osteosynthesis. *C*, The panoramic radiograph shows a patient with fracture of the symphysis of the mandible. *D*, The fracture was treated with maxillomandibular fixation for 5 weeks and a plate osteosynthesis.

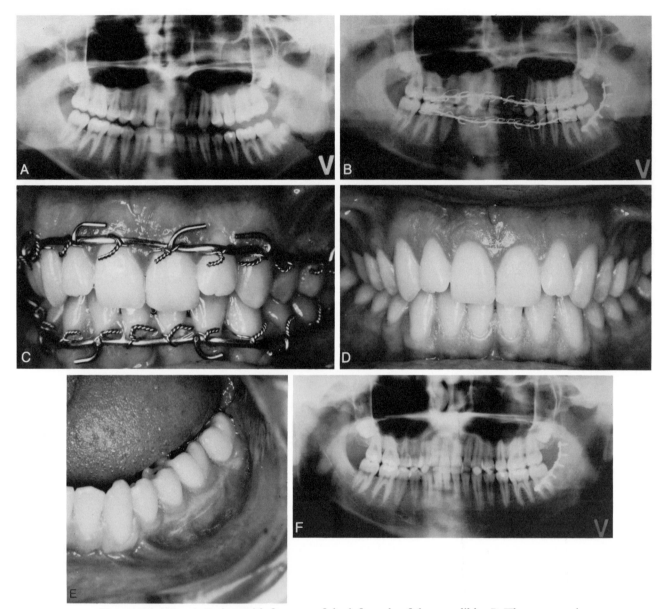

FIGURE 33–65.   *A*, Patient with fracture of the left angle of the mandible. *B*, The panoramic radiograph shows good position of the fracture 2 days after surgery. *C*, The occlusion of the patient 1 week after surgery. *D*, The patient's occlusion 10 months after surgery. *E*, Good healing is seen in the region of the osteosynthesis 10 months postoperatively. *F*, Panoramic radiograph taken 10 months postoperatively shows healing of the bone.

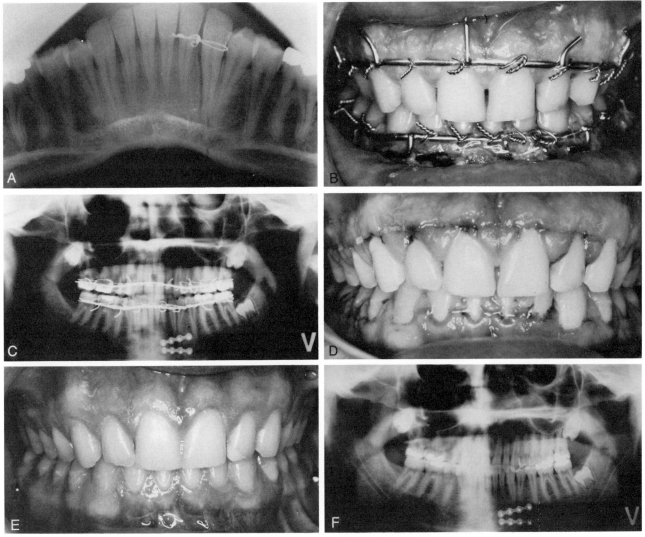

FIGURE 33–66. *A,* The panoramic radiograph shows a fracture of the symphysis of the mandible. *B,* The occlusion of the patient 2 days after surgery. *C,* Panoramic radiograph taken 2 days postoperatively shows good position of the fracture. *D,* The occlusion 5 weeks after surgery is shown; note the contusion of the gingiva caused by the dental arch bars. *E,* The occlusion 5 months after surgery is demonstrated; the gingiva has healed without complications. *F,* Panoramic radiograph taken 5 months postoperatively shows healing of the fracture.

TABLE 33-7. BASELINE VARIABLES OF PATIENTS WITH BILATERAL FRACTURES

VARIABLE	CONTROL GROUP ($n = 16$)	TEST GROUP ($n = 16$)
Sex		
Female	6	4
Male	10	12
Age (yr)		
Median	20	23.5
Range	15–45	19–40
Fracture location		
Anterior to mental foramen	13	16
Angle	19	16

thereafter on a soft diet for 25 days. The arch bars were left in place after surgery so that elastic maxillomandibular fixation could be applied if necessary.

BILATERAL MANDIBULAR FRACTURES

Patients with bilateral fractures of the body of the mandible and a dentition sufficient to allow maxillomandibular fixation were included in the study. All patients were followed for at least 3 months after surgery. The baseline variables are shown in Table 33–7.

A control group of 16 consecutive patients previously treated according to the standard treatment of the department, as described before, were recalled for clinical and radiologic examination (Fig. 33–67). The test group was treated as described previously (Fig. 33–68) and consisted of a group of 16 consecutive patients.

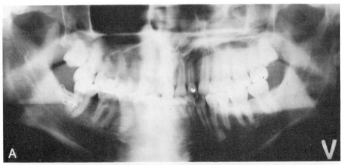
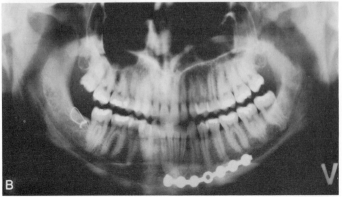

FIGURE 33–67. *A,* Panoramic radiograph shows a patient with bilateral fracture of the angle of the mandible treated with maxillomandibular fixation for 5 weeks and 0.4-mm upper border wire osteosynthesis 2.5 years postoperatively. *B,* Panoramic radiograph shows a patient with bilateral fracture of the mandible, treated with maxillomandibular fixation for 5 weeks, an upper border wire osteosynthesis, and an osteosynthesis plate.

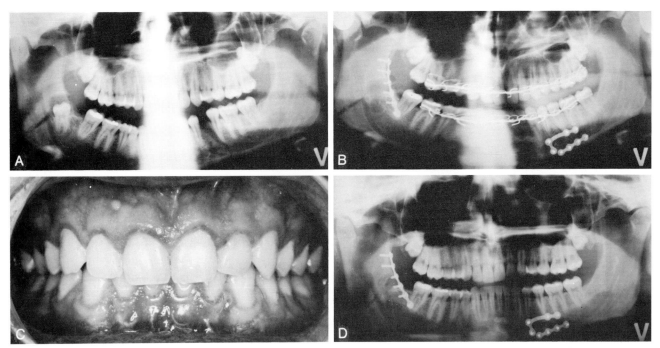

FIGURE 33–68. *A,* Panoramic radiograph shows a patient with fracture of the right angle and left body of the mandible. *B,* The panoramic radiograph shows the position of the fractures 2 days postoperatively. During surgery, it was found that the fracture in the left body was anterior to the mental foramen in the facial cortex; therefore, two bone plates were applied. *C,* The occlusion of the patient 5 months after surgery. *D,* Panoramic radiograph demonstrates healing of the fractures 5 months postoperatively.

RESULTS

The total number of days on which maxillomandibular fixation was applied in the various groups appears in Table 33–8. One patient in the unilateral fracture test group and nine patients in the bilateral fracture test group had minor malocclusions, which could be sufficiently corrected by elastic maxillomandibular fixation applied when the swelling had abated. The period of maxillomandibular fixation varied from 15 minutes to 10 days (median of 3 days). The difference in the total number of days for maxillomandibular fixation between control and test groups was statistically significant in patients with unilateral and bilateral fractures (Table 33–8).

Only minor complications occurred, as appear in Table 33–9. None of the plates were exposed in the patients who experienced partial dehiscence. In the patient who developed infection, antibiotic therapy was continued for 6 weeks after surgery, owing to continued signs of infection. At this time the plate was removed, and it was found that the fracture was stable. The infection abated after removal of the plate. The patient with an unstable osteosynthesis had received a 0.4-mm stainless steel upper border wire, and the proximal fragment was pulled a little upward during the

TABLE 33-8.   TOTAL NUMBER OF DAYS MAXILLOMANDIBULAR FIXATION WAS APPLIED

FRACTURE TYPE	CONTROL GROUP	TEST GROUP
Unilateral	579	5 ($p < 0.01$)
Bilateral	561	30 ($p < 0.01$)

TABLE 33-9.   NUMBER OF PATIENTS EXPERIENCING COMPLICATIONS

	UNILATERAL		BILATERAL	
	Control	*Test*	*Control*	*Test*
Partial dehiscence	—	1	1	—
Infection	—	1	1	—
Unstable osteosynthesis	1	—	—	—
Discomfort from bone plate	1	—	2	—
Malocclusion	—	—	1	—

fixation period; however, no malocclusion developed. In one patient from the bilateral control group, a minor change in occlusion developed during the fixation period and was corrected by occlusal grinding. All fractures except this one healed in a correct position. Three patients who had received stainless steel bone plates complained about "cold" sensations in the region during cold weather.

No adverse reactions to the titanium plates were found in any of the patients, and we have not (by electrometric pulp testing and radiographic examination) found any iatrogenic damage to teeth. A very frequent complaint in the control groups was that of weight loss and tiredness.

In conclusion, the studies have shown that the titanium miniplates allow treatment of unilateral mandibular fractures without maxillomandibular fixation. Bilateral fractures can be treated without maxillomandibular fixation immediately after surgery, and if minor occlusal changes develop, they can be corrected by elastic maxillomandibular fixation applied for a short time. In this way, the patient's comfort is increased, and the risk of complications from anesthesia is reduced when maxillomandibular fixation is avoided in the early postoperative period. Furthermore, patients recover faster when maxillomandibular fixation is not applied, and thus hospitalization time will be reduced.

COMBINED FRACTURES OF THE BODY AND COLLUM OF THE MANDIBLE

In patients with fractures of the collum and body of the mandible, the period of maxillomandibular fixation can be reduced to that necessary for conservative management of the fractured collum, as shown in the clinical example (Fig. 33–69).

Fractures of the Midface

ZYGOMATIC FRACTURES

The indications for the use of miniplates include severely dislocated fractures, with or without intermediary fragments, in which the zygomatic complex remains unstable after repositioning. Contraindications to the use of rigid fixation include severely comminuted or contaminated soft tissues and manifest infection in the region of the osteosynthesis.

Patients are treated while under general anesthesia. If it is uncertain whether osteosynthesis is necessary, the zygomatic complex is first repositioned with a Gillies procedure. In cases in which the zygomatic complex is unstable after repositioning, an incision is made in the lateral parts of the supercilium, and the zygomaticofrontal

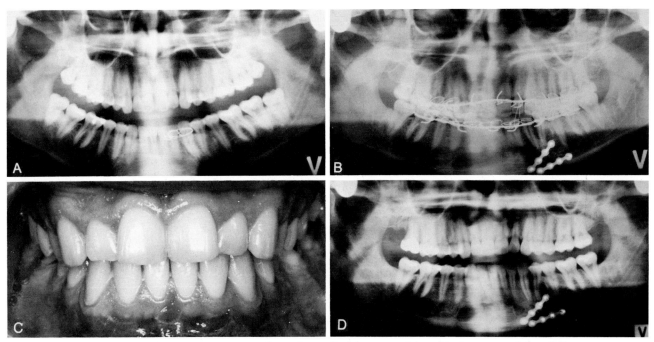

FIGURE 33–69. *A*, The panoramic radiograph shows a patient with fractures of the right collum and the left body of the mandible. *B*, The position of the fractures 2 days after surgery is shown. The patient was treated with elastic maxillomandibular fixation for 1 week and two straight, four-hole miniplates. *C*, The occlusion 5 months after surgery is shown. Note the good healing in the region of the osteosynthesis. *D*, The radiograph demonstrates the healing of the fractures 5 months postoperatively.

suture is exposed. If repositioning has been successfully accomplished, a plate is inserted in this region, and either a straight or a **Y**-shaped plate is used. The latter is preferable when it is a problem to keep the zygomatic complex in a forward position (Fig. 33–70). If there is doubt concerning whether the fracture has been repositioned correctly, if there are intermediary fragments on the infraorbital rim, or if exploration of the orbital floor is indicated, an incision is also made in the lower eyelid along the cleavage lines of the skin, whereafter the region is explored.

When the fractures have been reduced, a plate is first inserted that bridges the zygomaticofrontal suture, and then a plate is installed on the infraorbital rim, as demonstrated in Figure 33–70. Then the orbital floor can be repositioned with a balloon in the maxillary sinus, or in cases of bone loss, a bone graft from the anterior wall of the maxillary sinus of the opposite side can be placed. Screws 5 mm in length are recommended in this region.

We have had good clinical experience with the use of miniplates for treating zygomatic fractures according to the previously described guidelines. The plates have proved to provide good stability, and we have not at the present time experienced any adverse reactions to the osteosynthesis material.

SUPRAORBITAL FRACTURES

In a few cases, we have used miniplates in the supraorbital region to stabilize fractures of the frontal bone in combination with fractures of the zygomatic complex. The access in these cases has been through an incision in the supercilium, respecting the anatomic course of the supraorbital nerve. Screws of a 5-mm length are recommended in this region. A clinical example is demonstrated in Figure 33–71.

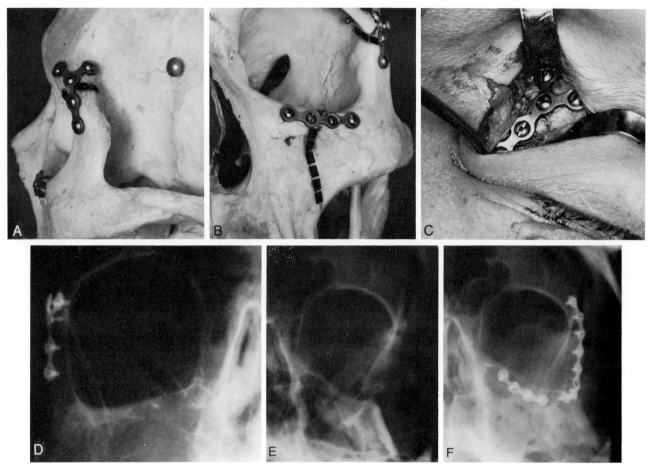

FIGURE 33–70.   *A,* The application of a **Y**-shaped miniplate at the zygomaticofrontal suture is indicated on a model. *B,* A four-hole, straight miniplate applied at the infraorbital rim is indicated on a model. *C,* A **Y**-shaped plate applied at the zygomaticofrontal suture in a patient with fracture of the zygoma is shown. *D,* Radiograph demonstrates the postoperative appearance of the **Y**-shaped plate. *E,* The radiograph demonstrates a patient with a comminuted fracture of the zygoma. *F,* The radiograph demonstrates the reconstructed zygomatic complex.

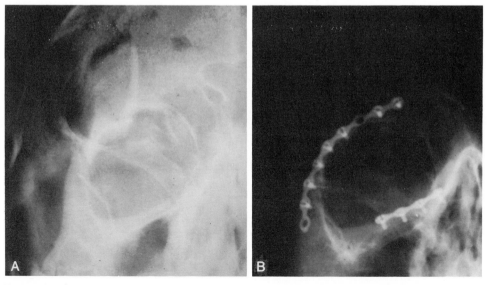

FIGURE 33–71.   *A,* The radiograph demonstrates a patient with fracture of the supraorbital rim and the zygoma. *B,* The fractures have been repositioned and stabilized by miniplates.

MAXILLARY FRACTURES

We have used miniplates in a limited number of patients with maxillary fractures. A case of a unilateral Le Fort I fracture extending from the midline and zygomatic fracture is demonstrated in Figure 33–72. This patient was managed without any suspension wires or maxillomandibular fixation. In conjunction with conventional methods of fixation, the miniplates have also been successfully employed to stabilize fractures at the zygomaticofrontal suture and the infraorbital rim in patients with Le Fort II and Le Fort III fractures. However, it is our experience that plates cannot be used alone in many cases. This restriction is because the anterior walls of the maxilla are usually fractured in a comminuted way, so it is necessary to expose large areas of bone before stable bone is found. Such an exposure of large areas of bone might result in healing problems, and therefore, we have at the present time employed miniplates alone in only a limited number of maxillary fractures.

Other Applications

MAXILLARY OSTEOTOMIES

In Le Fort I osteotomies, the miniplates are stable enough to allow fixation without any postoperative maxillomandibular fixation or suspension wires. When the maxilla has been mobilized, a great deal of attention is paid to removing bone that may interfere with the repositioning of the maxilla. Then the maxilla or the fragments of the maxilla are ligated into a wafer, and maxillomandibular fixation is subsequently applied. This wafer must be made with the mandible in the retruded position, as this is the only position of the condyles that can be reasonably well reproduced while the patient is under general anesthesia. In addition, to prevent luxation or subluxation of the condyles, it is very important that no interference from bone displace the whole maxillomandibular complex when it is repositioned. When a correct position of the maxilla has been achieved, the bone plates are inserted, and if there is any doubt about whether the condyles are in the correct position, this can be checked by removing the maxillomandibular fixation. If, after release of the maxillomandibular fixation, the mandible does not fit directly into the wafer, the miniplates must be removed, and the interferences from bone must be identified and removed. Thereafter, the miniplates can be reinserted. If a minor malocclusion is present after surgery, it has been possible to correct this with elastic maxillomandibular fixation.

In one-piece maxillary osteotomies, four L-shaped plates, one at the infrazygomatic crest and one lateral to the piriform aperture on each side, are usually applied. A case of a two-piece Le Fort I osteotomy with transversal expansion in the midline is demonstrated in Figure 33–73. In this case, four L-shaped plates were applied, and in addition, a straight plate was inserted to stabilize the fragments in the midline, where a mandibular bone graft was placed between the two maxillary fragments.

Conclusion

The Würzburg miniplates represent a tool that is very valuable in maxillofacial traumatology. This tool offers excellent stability and is easily applicable to facial fractures. In mandibular fractures, the miniplates can be readily applied through an intraoral approach, and most mandibular fractures can be treated without maxillomandibular fixation. Thus, operating time, the patient's discomfort, and the risk of anesthesia complications are reduced. Furthermore, a second intervention can be avoided because of the bioinertness of titanium.

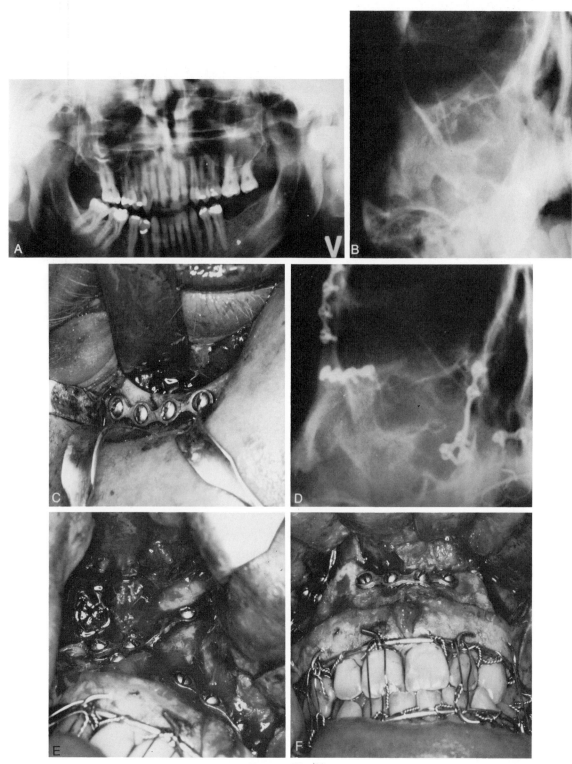

FIGURE 33–72.

Legend on opposite page.

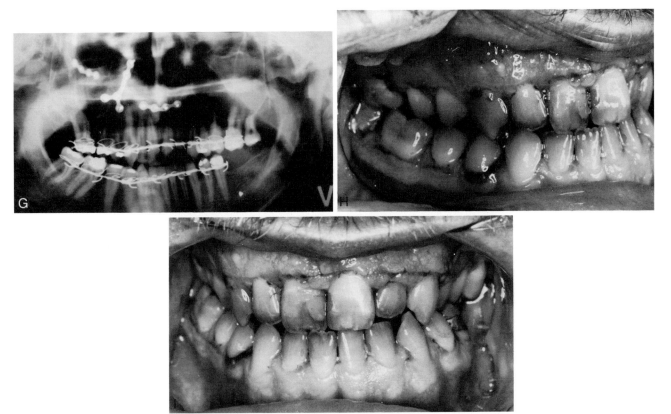

FIGURE 33–72. *A*, Panoramic radiograph of patient with right unilateral Le Fort I fracture of the maxilla; note the "hanging molars" in the right side. *B*, Radiograph shows fracture at the zygomaticofrontal suture and in the lateral parts of the infraorbital rim. *C, D,* Miniplates have been employed to stabilize the zygomatic fracture. *E, F,* Intraoperative view of the two miniplates used to stabilize the fractures; note the incision. Maxillomandibular fixation was applied during surgery to reposition the fractures and was released at the end of surgery. *G*, Panoramic radiograph demonstrates the position of the plates. *H, I,* The occlusion of the patient 4 weeks after surgery.

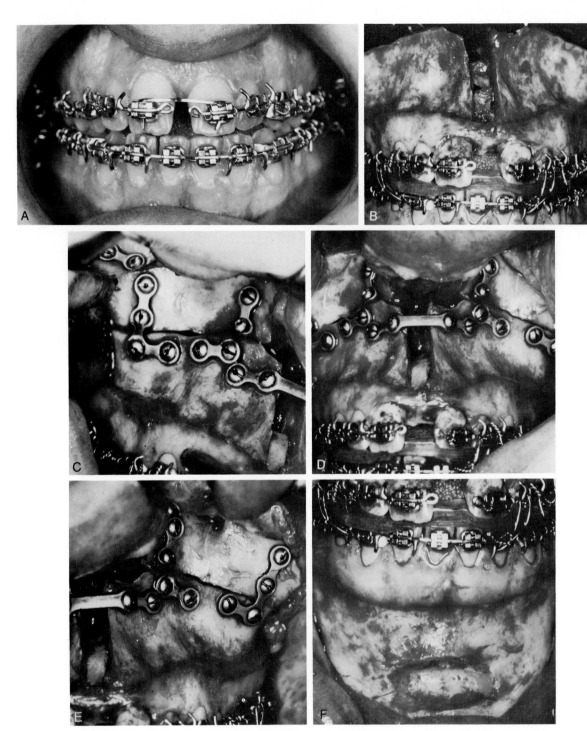

FIGURE 33–73. *A,* Preoperative clinical appearance of a patient prior to Le Fort I osteotomy with transverse expansion and slight advancement. *B,* The maxilla has been mobilized, divided in the midline, and ligated to the mandible with a wafer interposed. A mandibular bone graft was placed in the midline. After maxillomandibular fixation, the entire maxillomandibular block can be brought into contact with the upper parts of the maxilla. *C–E,* Intraoperative view shows the five miniplates applied. Maxillomandibular fixation was released at the end of surgery. *F,* The donor site from which the mandibular bone graft was taken. *G–J,* The clinical and radiologic appearance of the patient 6 months after surgery.

Illustration continued on opposite page.

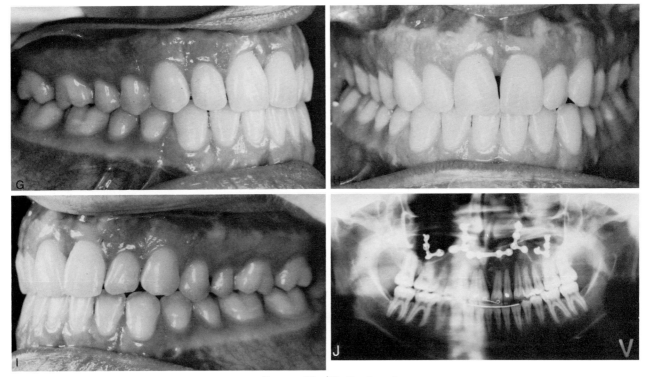

FIGURE 33–73. *Continued*

REFERENCES

1. Blümel J, Pfeifer G: Der Bruchlinienverlauf bei Orbitafrakturen. Fortschr Kiefer Gesichtschir 22:20, 1977.
2. Manson PN: Some thoughts on the classification and treatment of the Le Fort fractures. Ann Plast Surg 17:356, 1986.
3. Meyer H, Reuter E, Schilli W: Ursachen und Verlauf der Frakturen der lateralen Orbita. Fortschr Kiefer Gesichtschir 22:23, 1977.
4. Pfeifer G, Busch W, Rottke B: Verlauf und Auswirkungen des Therapiewandels bei Frakturen des Gesichtsschädels. Fortschr Kiefer Gesichtschir 19:62, 1975.
5. Bramley P: Basic principles of treatment. *In* Rowe NL, Williams JL (eds): Maxillofacial Injuries. Edinburgh, Churchill-Livingstone, 1985, p 43.
6. Mackensen G: Windschutzscheibenverletzungen der Augen. 1. Symposium der Dr. Kurt Steim Stiftung, 1983, p 7.
7. Schilli W: Typische Verletzungsmuster bei Gesichtsschädelverletzungen nach Verkehrsunfällen und ihre Behandlung. 1. Symposium der Dr. Kurt Steim Stiftung, 1983, pp 23–27.
8. Raveh J, Vuillemin T: The surgical one-stage management of combined cranio-maxillofacial and frontobasal fractures. Advantages of the subcranial approach in 374 cases. J Craniomaxillofac Surg 16:160, 1988.
9. Scheunemann H: Zur Erstversorgung von Verletzten im Kiefer- und Gesichtsbereich. Fortschr Kiefer Gesichtschir 19:59, 1975.
10. Kufner J: A method of craniofacial suspension. J Oral Surg 28:260, 1970.
11. Wassmund M: Frakturen und Luxationen des Gesichtsschädels. Berlin, Hermann Meusser, 1927.
12. Schwenzer N, Krüger E: Classification, diagnosis and fundamentals of treatment of midface fractures. *In* Krüger E, Schilli W (eds): Oral and Maxillofacial Traumatology. Chicago, Quintessence Publishing Company, 1986, p 107.
13. Yarrington CT Jr: The initial evaluation in maxillofacial trauma. Otolaryngol Clin North Am 12:293, 1979.
14. Ewers R: Periorbitale Knochenstrukturen und ihre Bedeutung für die Osteosynthese. Fortschr Kiefer Gesichtschir 22:45, 1977.
15. Johns D, Ewans J: Anatomical basis of blowout fracture. J Laryngol 81:1109, 1967.
16. Manson PN, Hoopes JE, Su CT: Structural pillars of the facial skeleton: An approach to the management of Le Fort fractures. Plast Reconstr Surg 54, 1980.
17. Manson PN, Clifford CM, Su CT, et al: Mechanisms of global support and post-traumatic enophthalmos. I. The anatomy of the ligament sling and its relation to intramuscular cone orbital fat. Plast Reconstr Surg 193, 1988.
18. Brocklehurst G, Gooding M, James G: Comprehensive care of patients with head injuries. Br Med J 294:345, 1987.
19. VanHoof RF, Merkx CA, Steckelenburg EC: The different patterns of fractures of the facial skeleton in four European countries. Int J Oral Surg 6:3, 1977.
20. Ionnaides C, Treffers W, Rutten M, Noverrax P: Ocular injuries associated with frac-

tures involving the orbit. J Craniomaxillofac Surg 16:157, 1988.

21. Grivas A, Manson PN, Vannier MW, Rosenbaum A: Post-traumatic orbit evaluation by three-dimensional surface reconstructions. Comput Med Imaging Graph 12:47, 1988.

22. Kassel EE: Traumatic injuries of the paranasal sinuses. Otolaryngol Clin North Am 21:455, 1988.

23. Mayer JS, Wainwright DJ, Yeakly JW, et al: The role of three-dimensional computed tomography in the management of maxillofacial trauma. J Trauma 28:1043, 1988.

24. Joos U, Gilsbach A, Otten J-E: Thirteen years experience with stable osteosynthesis of craniofacial fractures. Presented at Intern Conference of Recent Advances in Neurotraumatology (ICRAN), May 1986, Köln.

25. Götzfried HF, Kunze ST, Laumer R: Endokranielles infektrisiko bei kombinierter neurochirurgisch-kiefer-gesichts-chirurgischer Behandlung des Schädel-gesichtstraumas. Dtsch Z Mund Kiefer Gesichts Chir 8:256, 1984.

26. Manson PN, Crawley WA, Yaremchuk MJ, et al: Midface fractures: Advantages of immediate extended open reduction and bone grafting. Plast Reconstr Surg 76:1, 1985.

27. Rowe NL, Williams JL: Maxillofacial Injuries. Edinburgh, Churchill-Livingstone, 1985.

28. Adams WM: Internal wiring fixation of facial fractures. Surgery 12:523, 1942.

29. Stoll P, Schilli W, Joos U: The stabilization of midface fractures in the vertical dimension. J Maxillofac Surg 11:248, 1983.

30. Stoll P, Joos U, Schilli W: Vermeidung des Dishface bei der Versorgung von Mittelgesichts-frakturen. Fortschr Kiefer Gesichtschir 30:121, 1985.

31. Georgiade NG, Nash T: An external cranial fixation apparatus for severe maxillo-facial injuries. Plast Reconstr Surg 38:142, 1966.

32. Crawford MJ: Appliances and attachments for treatment of upper jaw fractures. US Naval Med Bull 41:1151, 1943.

33. Gruss JS, Mackinnon SE, Kassel EE, Cooper PW: The role of primary bone grafting in complex craniomaxillofacial trauma. Plast Reconstr Surg 75:17, 1985.

34. Bähr W: Erste Ergebnisse biomechanischer Untersuchungen über Osteosyntheschrauben im Mittelgesicht. Dtsch Z Mund Kiefer Gesichts Chir 11:301, 1987.

35. Kellman RM, Schilli W: Plate fixation of fractures of the mid and upper face. Otolaryngol Clin North Am 20:559, 1987.

36. Paulus GW, Altermatt HJ: Knochenbruchheilung am Oberkiefer nach adaptiver Miniplattenosteosynthese. Eine tierexperimentelle Untersuchung. Dtsch Z Mund Kiefer Gesichts Chir 11:46, 1987.

37. Ruedi TH, Perren SM, Pohler O, Riede U: Titan, Stahl und deren Kombination in der Knochenchirurgie. Langenbecks Arch Chir [Suppl Chir Forum] 395, 1975.

38. DeVisscher JGAM, VanderWal KGH: Medical orbital wall fracture with enophthalmos. J Craniomaxillofac Surg 16:55, 1988.

39. Converse JM: Two plastic operations for repair of orbit following severe trauma and extensive comminuted fracture. Arch Ophthalmol 31:323, 1944.

40. Tessier P: The conjunctival approach to the orbital floor and maxilla in congenital malformation and trauma. J Maxillofac Surg 1:3, 1973.

41. Manson PN, Ruas E, Iliff N, Yaemchuk M: Single eyelid incision for exposure of the zygomatic bone and orbital reconstruction. Plast Reconstr Surg 79:120, 1987.

42. Schilli W, Küker J: Behandlung veralteter Jochbeinfrakturen. In Herausgegeben von Hollwich F, Walter C (eds): Plastisch-Chirurgische Massnahmen bei Spätfolgen nach Unfällen. Stuttgart, Georg Thieme Verlag, 1976, p 65.

43. Düker J, Härle F, Olivier D: Drahtnaht oder Miniplatte—Nachuntersuchungen dislozierter Jochbeinfrakturen. Fortschr Kiefer Gesichtschir 22:49, 1977.

44. McCoy FJ, Chandler RA, Magnan CG, et al: An analysis of facial fractures and their complications. Plast Reconstr Surg 29:381, 1962.

45. Schilli W, Niederdelimann H, Härle F: Schrauben und Platten am Mittelgesicht und Orbitaring. Fortschr Kiefer Gesichtschir 22:47, 1977.

46. Schilli W, Niederdelimann H: Internal fixation of zygomatic and midface fractures by means of miniplates and leg screws. In Krüger E, Schilli W (eds): Oral and Maxillofacial Traumatology. Chicago, Quintessence Publishing Company, 1986 and 1977.

47. Spiessl B, Schroll K: Gesichtsschädel. Vol I. In Nigst H (ed): Spezielle Frakturen und Luxationslehre. Stuttgart, Georg Thieme Verlag, 1972.

48. Prein J, Spiessl B, Rahn B, Perren MS: Frakturheilung am Unterkiefer nach operativer Versorgung. Eine tierexperimentelle Studie. Fortschr Kiefer Gesichtschir 19:17, 1975.

49. Spiessl B (ed): New Concepts in Maxillofacial Bone Surgery. Berlin, Springer, 1976.

50. Spiessl B: Internal Fixation of the Mandible. A Manual of AO/ASIF Principles. Berlin, AO/ASIF, 1989.

51. Krüger E, Schilli W (eds): Oral and Maxillofacial Traumatology. Vols I and II. Chicago, Quintessence Publishing Company, 1982 and 1986.

52. Prein J, Hammer B: Stable internal fixation of midfacial fractures. Facial Plast Surg 5:221, 1988.

53. Rahn B: Fundamentals of the healing of fractures of the facial skull. 2. Morphology of fracture healing and its relationship to biomechanics. In Krüger E, Schilli W (eds): Oral and Maxillofacial Traumatology. Vol I. Chicago, Quintessence Publishing Company, 1982, pp 134–144.

54. Prein J, Kellman R: Rigid internal fixation of mandibular fractures—basics of AO technique. Otolaryngol Clin North Am 20:441, 1987.

55. Perren SM, Russenberger M, Steinemann S, et al: A dynamic compression plate in cortical bone healing. Acta Orthop Scand [Suppl] 125, 1969.

56. Schmoker R: The Eccentric Dynamic Compression Plate. An Experimental Study as to Its Contribution to the Functionally Stable Internal Fixation of Fractures of the Lower Jaw. Bern, AO Bulletin, 1976.

57. Niederdellmann H: Fundamentals of healing of fractures of the facial skull. 1. Biome-

chanics. *In* Krüger E, Schilli W (eds): Oral and Maxillofacial Traumatology. Chicago, Quintessence Publishing Company, 1982, pp 125–133.

58. Leonard MS: The use of lag screws in mandibular fractures. Otolaryngol Clin North Am 20:3, 1987.

59. Phillips J, Rahn BA: Comparison of compression and torque measurements of self-taping and pre-taped screws. Plast Reconstr Surg (in press).

60. Hansmann: Eine neue Methode zur Fixierung der Fragmente bei complicierten Frakturen. Verh Dtsch Ges Chir 15:134, 1886.

61. König F: Über die Berechtigung früzeitiger blutiger Eingriffe bei subcutanen Knochenbrüchen. Arch Klin Chir 76:23, 1905.

62. Lambotte A: L'intervention Opératoire dans les Fractures. Paris, Maloine, 1907.

63. Lane WA: The Operative Treatment of Fractures. London, Medical Publishing Company, 1914.

64. Sherman WO: Poor functional results in the treatment of fractures. Trans Sect Orthop Surg AMA 71, 1922.

65. Key JA: Positive pressure in arthrodesis for tuberculosis of the knee joint. South Med J 25:909, 1932.

66. Danis R: Théorie et Pratique de l'Ostéosynthèse. Paris, Masson and Cie, 1949.

67. Bagby GE, Janes JM: The effect of compression on the rate of fracture healing using a special plate. Am J Surg 95:761, 1958.

68. Tamai T, Hoshiko W: A new compression plate for osteosynthesis. Clin Orthop Surg 2:941, 1967.

69. Mittelmeier H: Druckosteosynthese mit Selbstspannenden Platten (Technik und Erfahrungsbericht). Hamburg, Ref Saarl Westpfalz Orthopädentreffen, 1968.

70. Luhr HG: Zur stabilen Osteosynthese bei Unterkieferfrakturen. Dtsch Zahnärztl Z 23:754, 1968.

71. Perren SM, Russenberger J, Steinmann S, et al: A dynamic compression plate. Acta Orthop Scand [Suppl] 125:29, 1969.

72. Hess H: Die Spannungskräfte der Druckplattenosteosynthese. Piezoelektrische Messungen bei verschiedenen Verfahren. Unter besonderer Berücksichtigung selbstspannerder Druckplatten. *In* Otte P, Schlegel KF (eds): Bücherei der Osthopädie. Stuttgart, Enke, 1972.

73. Spiessl B, Schargus G, Schroll K: Die stabile Osteosynthese bei Frakturen des unbezahnten Kiefers. Schweiz Monatsschr Zahnheilk 81:39, 1971.

74. Becker R, Machtens E: Druckplattenosteosynthese zur Frakturbehandlung und bei orthopädisch-chirurgischen Massnahmen am Gesichtsschädel. Osteo-News 19: 1973.

75. Michelet FX, Benoit IP, Festal F, et al: Fixation with blockage of sagittal osteotomy of the ascending branches of the mandible with endobuccal plates in the treatment of anteroposterior malformations. Rev Stomatol 72:531, 1971.

76. Michelet FX, Festal F: Ostéosynthèse par plaques vissée dans les fractures de l'étage moyen. So Rech Odont-Stomat 2:4, 1972.

77. Michelet FX, Deymes J, Dessus B: Osteosynthesis with miniaturized screwed plates in maxillofacial surgery. J Maxillofac Surg 1:79, 1973.

78. Michelet FX, Dessus B, Benvoit JP, Moll A: Les ostéosynthèses mandibulaires sans blocage par plaques stellites miniatures vissées. Rev Stomatol 74:239, 1973.

79. Champy M, Wilk A, Schnebelen JM: Die Behandlung von Mandibularfrakturen mittels Osteosynthese ohne intermaxilläre Ruhigstellung nach der Technik von FX Michelet. Dtsch Zahn Mund Kieferheilk 63:339, 1975.

80. Champy M, Lodde JP: Synthèses mandibulaires. Localisation des synthèses en fonction des contraintes mandibulaires. Rev Stomatol 77:971, 1976.

81. Champy M, Lodde JP, Jaeger JH, Wilk A: Ostéosynthèses mandibulaires selon à technique de Michelet. I. Bases bioméchaniques. Rev Stomatol 77:569, 1976.

82. Champy M, Lodde JP, Jaeger JH, et al: Ostéosynthèses mandibulaires selon la technique de Michelet. II. Présentation d'un nouveau matériel. Résultats. Rev Stomatol 77:577, 1976.

83. Champy M, Lodde JP: Etude des contraintes dans la mandibule fracturée chez l'homme. Mésures théoriques et vérification par jauges extensométriques in situ. Rev Stomatol 78:545, 1977.

84. Champy M, Lodde JP, Grasset D, et al: Ostéosynthèses mandibulaires et compression. Ann Chir Plast 22:165, 1977.

85. Champy M, Lodde JP, Schmitt R, et al: Mandibular osteosynthesis by miniature screwed plates via a buccal approach. J Maxillofac Surg 6:14, 1978.

86. Champy M, Lodde JP, Wilk A, et al: Probleme und Resultate bei der Verwendung von Dehnungsmessstreifen am präparierten Unterkiefer und bei Patienten mit Unterkieferfrakturen. Dtsch Z Mund Kiefer Gesichts Chir 2:41, 1978.

87. Champy M, Lodde JP, Wilk A, Grasset D: Plattenosteosynthesen bei Mittelgesichtsfrakturen und Osteotomien. Dtsch Z Mund Kiefer Gesichts Chir 2:26, 1978.

88. Champy M: Biomechanische Grundlagen der strassburger Miniplattenosteosynthese. Dtsch Zahnärztl Z 38:358, 1983.

89. Champy M, Pape H-D, Gerlach KL, Lodde JP: Mandibular fractures. The Strasbourg miniplate osteosynthesis. *In* Krüger E, Schilli W (eds): Oral and Maxillofacial Traumatology. Vol II. Chicago, Quintessence Publishing Company, 1986, pp 19–43.

90. Pauwels F: Grundriss einer Biomechanik der Frakturheilung. Verh Dtsch Orthop Ges 34:62, 1940.

91. Schroll K: Experimentelle Untersuchungen und klinische Erfahrungen mit der Plattenosteosynthese von enoral bei Frakturen des zahnlosen Unterkiefers. Zahnärztl Welt/Reform 83, 650, 742, 835, 934, 1042, 1974.

92. Höltje W-J, Luhr H-G, Holtfreter M: Untersuchungen über infektionsbedingte Komplikationen nach konservativer und operativer Versorgung von Unterkieferfrakturen. Fortschr Kiefer Gesichtschir 19:122, 1975.

93. Claudi B, Spiessl B: Ergebnisse bei konservativer und operativer Behandlung von Unterkieferfrakturen (ohne Kollumfrakturen). Fortschr Kiefer Gesichtschir 19:73, 1975.

94. Börner K: Klinische Erfahrungen mit der

Druckschienenosteosynthese nach Luhr. Bonn, Med Diss, 1977.

95. Frost D, El-Attar A, Moos K: Evaluation of metacarpal bone plates in the mandibular fracture. Br J Oral Surg 21:214, 1983.

96. Geiger SA, Dumbach J: Post-operative Ergebnisse nach extra- und transoral durchgeführter Kompressionsosteosynthese im Unterkiefer. Dtsch Zahnärztl Z 38:379, 1983.

97. Schettler D, Vogeler E, Bringewald B: Therapiewandel bei Kieferwinkel-frakturen. Dtsch Zahnärztl Z 38:367, 1983.

98. Chuong R, Danoff RB, Guralnick WL: A retrospective analysis of 327 mandibular fractures. J Oral Maxillofac Surg 41:305, 1983.

99. Joos U, Schilli W, Niederdellmann H, Scheibe B: Komplikationen und verzögerte Bruchheilung bei Kieferfrakturen. Dtsch Zahnärztl Z 38:387, 1983.

100. Gerlach KL, Khouri M, Pape H-D, Champy M: Ergebnisse der Miniplattenosteosynthese bei 1,000 Unterkieferfrakturen aus der kölner und strassburger Klinik. Dtsch Zahnärztl Z 38:363, 1983.

101. Weinauer F: Behandlung von Unterkieferfrakturen mit Miniplattenosteosynthesen. Eine Nachuntersuchung von 73 Osteosynthesen in den Jahren 1981–1984. Würzburg, Inaug Diss, 1986.

102. Steinbauer M: Mittelgesichtsfrakturen in den Jahren 1981 bis 1983—ihre Ursachen, Diagnostik und Therapie sowie der Heilungsverlauf. Würzburg, Inaug Diss, 1986.

103. Böhler L: Technik der Knochenbruchbehandlung im Frieden und im Kriege. Vol II. Wien, W Maudrich 49, 1941.

104. Schenk R, Willenegger H: Zum histologischen Bild der sogenannten Primärheilung der Knochenkompakta nach experimentellen Osteotomien am Hund. Experientia 19:593, 1963.

105. Schenk R, Willenegger H: Zur Histologie der primären Knochenheilung. Langenbecks Arch Klin Chir 308:440, 1964.

106. Rhinelander FW, Philips RS, Steel WM, Beer JC: Microangiography in bone healing. J Bone Joint Surg 50A, 1968.

107. Oleruth S, Dankwardt-Lilienström G: Fracture healing in compression osteosynthesis in the dog. J Bone Joint Surg 50B:844, 1968.

108. Luhr HG: Die Kompressionsosteosynthese bei Unterkieferfrakturen. München, Hanser, 1972.

109. Wolff J: Das Gesetz der Transformation der Knochen. Berlin, Hirschwald, 1892.

110. Allgöwer M: Osteosynthese und primäre Knochenheilung. Langenbecks Arch Klin Chir 308:423, 1967.

111. Randzio J: Biomechanische Untersuchungen zur Osteosynthese am Unterkiefer. München, Med Habil Schrift, 1985.

112. Wustrow P: Physikalische Grundlagen der Zahnärztlichen Platte und Brückenprothese. Vol I. Berlin, H Meusser, 1919.

113. Schumacher GH: Funktionelle Morphologie der Kaumuskulatur. Jena, G Fischer, 1961.

114. Uhlig H: Über die Kaukraft. Dtsch Zahnärztl Z 8:30, 1953.

115. Kraft E: Über die Bedeutung der Kaukraft für das Kaugeschehen. Zahnärztl Praxis 13:129, 1962.

116. Schargus G: Experimentelle Untersuchungen über den Halt verschiedener Schienungssysteme. Dtsch Z Mund Kiefer Gesichts Chir 53:378, 1969.

117. Motsch A: Kaufunktion und Kiefergelenkbeanspruchung. Dtsch Zahnärztl Z 23:833, 1968.

118. Graber G: Funktionelle Gebissanalyse. In Schwenzer N (ed): Zahn Mund und Kieferheilkunde. Vol 3. Prothetik und Werkstoffkunde. Stuttgart, Georg Thieme Verlag, 1982.

119. Küppers K: Analyse der Funktionellen Struktur des Menschlichen Unterkiefers. Ergebnisse der Anatomie und Entwicklungsgeschichte, Vol 44, Part 6. Berlin, Springer, 1971.

120. Kessler W: Das spannungsoptische Oberflächenschichtverfahren zur mechanischen Spannungsmessung am menschlichen Unterkiefer unter physiologischer Belastung. München, Med Diss, 1980.

121. Sonnenburg I, Fethke K, Sonnenburg M: Zur Druckbelastung des Kiefergelenkes—eine experimentelle Studie. Anat Anz 155:309, 1984.

122. Paulus GW: Die Knochenbruchheilung am Oberkiefer bei Verwendung von Miniplatten. Erlangen, Med Habil Schrift, 1986.

123. Gerlach KL, Pape H-D: Prinzip und Indikation der Miniplattenosteosynthese. Dtsch Zahnärztl Z 35:346, 1980.

124. Gerlach KL, Pape H-D, Tuncer M: Funktionsanalytische Untersuchungen nach der Miniplattenosteosynthese von Unterkieferfrakturen. Dtsch Z Mund Kiefer Gesichts Chir 6:57, 1982.

125. Horch HH, Gerlach KL, Pape H-D: Indikationen und Grenzen der intraoralen Miniplattenosteosynthese bei Frakturen des aufsteigenden Unterkieferastes. Dtsch Zahnärztl Z 38:447, 1983.

126. Pape H-D, Herzog M, Gerlach KL: Der Wandel der Unterkieferfrakturversorgung von 1950 bis 1980 am Beispiel der kölner Klinik. Dtsch Zahnärztl Z 38:301, 1983.

127. Dunaevskij VA, Solovev MM, Pavlov BL, Magarill ES: Osteosintez pri Perelomach Niznej Celjusti. Leningrad, Medicina, 1973.

128. Härtel J: Komplikationen nach funktionsstabiler Osteosynthese des Unterkiefers. Dtsch Z Mund Kiefer Gesichts Chir 7:52, 1983.

129. Schmitz R, Luhr H-G, Schubert H: Indikation, Technik und klinische Ergebnisse der Kompressionsosteosynthese bei Unterkieferfrakturen. Fortschr Kiefer Gesichtschir 19:74, 1975.

130. Wagner WF, Neal DC, Alpert B: Morbidity associated with extraoral open reduction of mandibular fractures. J Oral Surg 37:97, 1979.

131. Härtel J, Sonnenburg M: Methoden der stabilen Osteosynthese des Unterkiefers (biomechanische, physikalische-technische, histologische und klinische Untersuchungen). Rostock, Med Diss (Prom B), 1977.

132. Rohen JW: Zur Anatomie desprothesenträgers. Dtsch Zahnärztl Z 20:1161, 1958.

133. Pauwels F: Gesammelte Abhandlungen zur Funktionellen Anatomie des Bewegungsapparates. Berlin, Springer, 1965.

134. Bull HG, Ganzer U, Grüntzig J, Schirmer M: Der Schädelbruch. Urban und Schwarzenberg, 1987.

135. Casson PR, Bonanno PC, Converse JM: The midface degloving procedure. Plast Reconstr Surg 53:102, 1974.
136. Chuong R, Kaban LB: Fractures of the zygomatic complex. J Oral Maxillofac Surg 44:283, 1986.
137. Dieckmann J, Hackmann G: Der operative Zugang zur Periorbita bei frontobasalen Frakturen. Fortschr Kiefer Gesichtschir 22:36, 1977.
138. Tessier P: Total osteotomy of the middle third of the face for faciostenoses or for sequelae of Le Fort III fractures. Plast Reconstr Surg 48:533, 1971.
139. Tenzel RR, Miller GR: Orbital blowout fracture repair, conjunctival approach. Am J Ophthalmol 71:1141, 1971.
140. Converse JM, Furmin D, Wood-Smith D: The conjunctival approach in orbital fractures. Plast Reconstr Surg 52:656, 1973.
141. Becker R, Austermann KH: Zur Wahl des Zugangsweges bei operativer Versorgung von Orbitafrakturen. Fortschr Kiefer Gesichtschir 22:33, 1977.
142. Sindet-Pedersen S, Jensen J: Can maxillomandibular fixation be avoided in the treatment of mandibular fractures [abstract]? Annual Meeting of the American Association of Oral and Maxillofacial Surgeons, Boston, 1988.

INDEX

Note: Page numbers in *italics* refer to illustrations; page numbers followed by t refer to tables.